B

THE INFORMED ARGUMENT

A Multidisciplinary
Reader and Guide

THE INFORMED ARGUMENT

A MULTIDISCIPLINARY READER AND GUIDE

FIFTH EDITION

ROBERT K. MILLER
UNIVERSITY OF SAINT THOMAS

THOMSON
™
HEINLE

Australia Canada Mexico Singapore Spain United Kingdom United States

THOMSON
HEINLE

The Informed Argument/Fifth Edition
A Multidisciplinary Reader and Guide
Robert K. Miller

Publisher: Christopher P. Klein
Executive Editor: Michael A. Rosenberg
Acquisitions Editor: John Meyers
Product Manager: Ilse Wolfe West
Developmental Editor: Sarah Heylar Smith
Art Director: Garry Harman
Production Manager: Serena Manning
                    Kathleen Fergusen

For permission to use material from
this text or product contact us:
Tel: 1-800-730-2214
Fax: 1-800-730-2215
Web: www.thomsonrights.com

For more information contact Heinle & Heinle,
25 Thomson Place, Boston, MA 02210 USA, or
you can visit our Internet site at
http://www.heinle.com

ISBN: 0-15-503809-5

Library of Congress Catalog Card Number:
                    97-72225

PREFACE FOR STUDENTS

This book has been designed to help you argue on behalf of your beliefs. Part 1 introduces basic principles of argumentation that you will need to analyze the arguments you read and to compose arguments of your own. Part 2 introduces specific strategies for efficiently and honorably drawing upon the work of other writers so that your arguments will be well informed. The readings gathered in this book provide you with readily available sources upon which to draw when composing a range of writing assignments. There will be times, however, when you discover that you need additional information to clarify or support your thoughts. Part 3, "A Guide to Research," introduces essential strategies for locating what you need on those occasions.

The readings included in *The Informed Argument*, Fifth Edition, are arranged in Parts 4, 5, and 6. In Part 4, "Negotiating Differences," a series of paired essays are brought together as conversations into which you are invited to enter through short exercises emphasizing the ability to restate what others have said and to identify common ground. Part 5, "Sources for Argument," consists of seven sections. In each section several different writers address issues of national concern. Providing you with the opportunity to examine each of these issues from multiple perspectives, the readings gathered in Part 5 form the heart of the book. The range of ideas explored in the book is extended by Part 6, "Some Classic Arguments," fifteen arguments that have influenced the thinking of previous generations. In this part of the book, you will also see how argument can take the form of a dialogue, a poem, a satire, or a letter.

In choosing arguments for you to study, I gave equal consideration to opposing viewpoints. All issues have more than one side. I also included examples of different writing strategies. I did not limit the selections to the most recent works. You will find the date of original publication within the introductory note that comes immediately before each selection. When evaluating sources, recognize that an essay can embody a strong argument or interesting point of view many years after it was written. An old essay can include outdated information, however, so you should consider the date of each source.

If you read carefully, you will find that almost every written argument includes a point that can be questioned. Argument is part of an ongoing process of inquiry; a single argument is unlikely to entirely resolve a complex issue. So don't feel that an argument loses all credibility because you have discovered a flaw in it. Although you should be alert for flaws, especially in reasoning, you should consider the flaw in proportion to the argument as a whole. Some writers undermine their entire argument by contradicting themselves or by making wild charges; others are able to make a strong argument despite one or two weak points. Readers and writers learn from considering diverse points of view and deciding how they inform each other. Argument is not about winning or losing; it is a process devoted to finding solutions to problems. When this process is undertaken honestly, everyone stands to benefit.

This edition contains thirteen essays written by students. They are included to enable you to see how other students have satisfied assignments similar to those you may be asked to undertake. Learn what you can from them, but do not feel they represent perfection. Each of these student writers wrote several drafts, revising extensively before completing the version included in the book. Because revision is a never-ending commitment essential to good writing, these students will probably see things they would like to change now that their essays are in print. I want to thank them for giving me permission to publish their work and remind them to continue writing. I also want to thank the many students who studied the first four editions of this book and helped me to see how it could be improved.

PREFACE FOR INSTRUCTORS

The fifth edition of *The Informed Argument* continues to reflect my belief that learning is best fostered by encouraging students to read, reflect, and write about serious issues. Most of the readings are again arranged into the equivalent of separate casebooks on national issues of the sort that students often want to write about but lack adequate information to do so effectively. Instructors can treat each section either as a self-contained unit or as a springboard to further reading. To facilitate class discussion, every essay has editorial apparatus. This allows for much flexibility. Readings can be assigned in whatever sequence seems appropriate for a particular class. And there is plenty of material, so you can vary the assignments you give to different classes without undertaking an entirely new preparation.

Of the eighty-one selections, fifty are new to this edition. They are drawn from a variety of disciplines to help students master different types of writing and reading. Among the fields represented are biology, business, computer science, economics, education, history, journalism, law, philosophy, political science, psychology, public health, and sociology. In selecting these readings, I was guided by three primary concerns: (1) to give students information for writing arguments of their own, (2) to expose them to diverse points of view, and (3) to illustrate a range of rhetorical strategies. I also chose pieces that require different degrees of experience with reading. Some of the pieces—especially in the early sections—are easily accessible; others are more demanding. My goal was to give students an immediate point of entry into the issues in question and then encourage them to engage with more difficult texts representative of the reading they will be expected to undertake on their own in college and beyond.

The wish to increase diversity within the book led me to include more pieces by women and writers of color and to address issues such as affirmative action and sexual harassment. My wish to encourage open and respectful discussion of how people differ also led me to include a new section focused on the public debate over same-gender marriage—a debate that raises additional questions about the social and political consequences of recognizing differences.

The Informed Argument is designed to satisfy several different educational needs. Part 1 introduces students to the principles they need to understand for reading and writing arguments. I kept the explanations as simple as possible. Examples are provided for each of the concepts discussed, and student essays illustrate both inductive and inductive reasoning as well as the model for reasoning devised by Stephen Toulmin. In addition, two versions of the same student essay illustrate the importance of revision, and another illustrates strategies for definition. Part 1 now also includes an expanded discussion of planning in which the principles of classical arrangement are contrasted with those that inform a Rogerian argument. A discussion of other forms of persuasion, illustrated by a series of advertisements, completes this part of the book.

Part 2, "Working with Sources," discusses the evaluation, annotation, paraphrase, summary, synthesis, and documentation of texts—skills directly related to writing effective arguments but applicable also to many other rhetorical situations. An expanded discussion of plagiarism addresses the serious consequences of dishonesty while recognizing that inexperienced writers sometimes violate academic conventions without being aware of what they are doing. For easy reference, a gray border identifies the pages devoted to documentation. The major documentation styles in use across the curriculum are illustrated—not only those of the Modern Language Association (MLA) and the American Psychological Association (APA), which are discussed in detail (complete with examples of how to cite sources obtained electronically) but also a system of numbered references favored in scientific writing. MLA style is also illustrated by several student essays, most comprehensively by "Crack, Crime, and Kids" which appears, for easy reference, as an appendix. To help students using APA-style documentation, I include the original date of publication within the headnote introducing each of the readings in Parts 4, 5, and 6. Examples of APA and other styles are provided by one or more of the readings included in Part 5.

The book includes almost a hundred suggestions for writing, including several that specifically invite collaboration with other students. Although most writing assignments can be completed by students using the material available to them in *The Informed Argument,* some call for acquiring additional information. Part 3, "A Guide to Research," has been extensively revised to help students find such information efficiently. A new search strategy, emphasizing the use of electronic indexes, takes students through the process of finding articles to locating books and other sources. A new section on the Internet addresses both the benefits and limitations of obtaining data from the World Wide Web. Instructors familiar with earlier versions of *The Informed Argument* will also note that "A Guide for Research" now appears much earlier in the book. By placing it immediately after "Working with Sources," I brought together all parts of the book devoted to introducing principles for discovering ideas and gathering information. The text helps students to see that research can take many forms and, as Richard Larson has argued, "almost any paper is potentially a paper incorporating the fruits of research."

Part 4, "Negotiating Differences," represents significant change in this edition in response to instructors who called for expanding the number of issues addressed in the book. The series of paired arguments in Part 4 are accompanied by an apparatus informed by the principles of Rogerian argument. Rather than following the point/counterpoint model used in forensics, a model that encourages students to focus on who is winning or losing a debate, I presented these pairs as conversations which students are invited to moderate. The skills emphasized in Part 4—listening with respect, paraphrasing accurately, and identifying common ground—will help students when they write arguments of their own and engage in other kinds of problem-solving.

The diversity of material within the book is further extended by Part 6, "Some Classic Arguments." This final group of readings includes such well-known essays as "A Modest Proposal" and "Letter from Birmingham Jail" as well as seldom-anthologized arguments by Charlotte Perkins Gilman, Margaret Sanger, Mahatma Gandhi, and Carl Rogers. However much students benefit from exploring the kind of contemporary issues examined in Parts 4 and 5, they also need to see how current arguments are part of a long and honorable tradition. When reading arguments located in another time and another place, students may be reassured to identify enduring values similar to their own, but they are also likely to encounter values that are startling different from their own—thus gaining another perspective for trying to make sense of the world in which they live.

Instructors new to *The Informed Argument* might note that the book also contains thirteen student essays. Although student essays can be found in many textbooks, seven of the essays have the distinctive feature of responding to sources that are reprinted in the book—making it easier for users to see how other students fulfilled assignments similar to their own. Given the difficulty of arguing effectively and using sources responsibly, students will find these models especially useful.

In completing this edition, I contracted many debts. At the University of St. Thomas, Michael Jordan, Noreen Carrocci, and Ralph Pearson helped arrange a reduced teaching load for me during the semester when I was completing the final manuscript. Dan Gjelten, the acting director of the O'Shaughnessy-Frey Library, gave generously of his time and expertise when I was revising Part 3, "A Guide to Research." Paul Teske was consistently efficient and good humored when helping me with my research, and Molly Meirick gave much appreciated assistance with photocopying. For unfailing encouragement and support, I want to thank Mary Rose O'Reilley and Erika C. Scheurer—colleagues whom I am honored to call my friends.

For helpful advice in planning the Fifth Edition, I want to thank the following: Vicky Anderson, Loyola University of Chicago; J. Robert Baker, Fairmount State College; Valerie Balester, Texas A&M University; Russell Greer, University of Georgia; Shannon Kiser, Shawnee State University; Stephen Larson, Wake Technical Community College; John Orozco, Los Angeles Mission College; William Provost, University of Georgia; and William Scheidley, University of Southern Colorado.

John Meyers, my acquisitions editor at Harcourt Brace, gave sage advice and friendly counsel. Garry Harman designed the cover. Lili Weiner acquired the photographs necessary for clear illustrations. Sarah H. Smith, Denise Netardus, Pam Blackmon, and Nancy M. Land guided the book through a tight production schedule. Maryan Malone, my copyeditor, helped my prose through her careful reading and attention to detail. I especially want to thank Eleanor Garner, who has contributed her expertise to every edition of the book and skillfully negotiated all of the many permissions agreements this edition required. It was my good fortune to have so much valuable assistance.

CONTENTS

Section 2
Immigration: Who Gets to Become an American? 212

Section 3
Same-Gender Marriage: What Is a Family? 254

Section 4
Sexual Harassment: Defining the Boundaries 288

Section 5
Surfing the Web: Who Controls Information?   361

Section 6
Culture and Curriculum: What Should Students Be Taught?   450

THE INFORMED ARGUMENT

A Multidisciplinary
Reader and Guide

PART 1

AN INTRODUCTION TO ARGUMENT

Argument is a means of fulfilling desire. That desire may be for something as abstract as truth or as concrete as an increase in salary. When you ask for an extension on a paper, apply for a job, propose a marriage, or recommend any change that involves someone besides yourself, you are putting yourself in a position that requires effective argumentation. You may also have occasion to argue seriously about political and ethical concerns. Someone you love may be considering an abortion, a large corporation may try to bury its chemical waste on property that adjoins your own, or you may be suddenly deprived of a benefit to which you feel entitled. By learning how to organize your beliefs and support them with information that will make other people take them seriously, you will be mastering one of the most important skills you are likely to learn in college.

Working your arguments out on paper gives you an opportunity to make changes until you are satisfied that your words do what you want them to do. This is an important benefit because constructing effective arguments requires that you think clearly without letting your feelings dominate what you say, and this can be difficult at times. But it can also be tremendously satisfying to succeed in making other people understand what you mean. You may not always convert others to your point of view, but you can earn their respect. This, in a way, is what argument is all about. When you argue for what you believe, you are asking others to believe in you. This means that you must prove to your audience that you are worth listening to. Instead of thinking in terms of "winning" or "losing" an argument, consider argumentation as an intellectual effort designed to solve problems by drawing people together.

1

Bearing this in mind, you should always be careful to treat both your audience and your opponents with respect. Few people are likely to be converted to your view if you treat them as if they are fools or dismiss their beliefs with contempt. Effective argumentation requires an ability to understand differences, for you cannot resolve a conflict you do not understand. When writing an argument, you must demonstrate that you have given consideration to beliefs that are different from your own and have recognized what makes them appealing. However strong your personal convictions may be, you must not let them keep you from learning what others believe. Becoming familiar with diverse points of view will help you to write arguments that address the concerns of people who might otherwise disagree with you. You will be able to develop your own thinking and be more persuasive than writers who seem narrow-minded or overly opinionated.

The readings that form the heart of this book were chosen to make you better informed on a number of important questions so that you can write about them more persuasively. What you read should influence what you think, but, as you read more, remember that controversial subjects are controversial because there is so much that can be said about them—much more than you may have realized at first. You do not need to become an expert on a topic before you can write a thoughtful argument about it, but you do need to be able to support whatever claims you make. If you offer opinions without support, or make a big claim based on little evidence, you are unlikely to be persuasive. Well-educated men and women recognize how little they know in proportion to how much there is to be known. Make sure the conclusions you reach are based on your best efforts toward research and knowledge.

CHOOSING A TOPIC

Almost anything *can* be argued, but not everything *should* be argued. You won't be taken seriously if you seem to argue indiscriminately. Argument should be the result of reflection, not reflex, and argumentation is a skill that should be practiced selectively.

When choosing a topic for a written argument, you should avoid questions that can be easily settled by referring to an authority, such as a dictionary or an encyclopedia. There is no point in arguing about how to spell "separate" or about what city is the capital of Australia: there is only one correct answer. Choose a topic that can inspire a variety of answers, any one of which can be "correct" to some degree. Your challenge is to define and support a position in which you believe even though other people do not yet share your belief.

Almost all intelligent arguments involve *opinions,* but not all opinions lead to good written arguments. There is no reason to argue an opinion with which almost no one would disagree. An essay designed to "prove" that puppies are cute or that vacations can be fun is unlikely to generate much excitement. Don't belabor the obvious. Choose a topic that is likely to inspire at least some controversy, but don't feel that you suddenly need to acquire strange and eccentric opinions.

Be careful to distinguish between opinions that are a matter of taste and those that are a question of judgment. Some people like broccoli, and some people don't. You may be the world's foremost broccoli lover, but no matter how hard you try, you will not convince someone who hates green vegetables to head quickly to the produce department of the nearest supermarket. A gifted stylist, writing in the manner of Charles Lamb or E. B. White, could probably compose an amusing essay on broccoli that would be a delight to read. But it is one thing to describe personal tastes and quite another to insist that others share them. We all have firmly entrenched likes and dislikes. Persuasion in matters of taste is usually beyond the reach of what can be accomplished through the written word—unless you happen to command the resources of an unusually effective advertising agency.

Taste is a matter of personal preference. Whether we prefer green to blue or daffodils to tulips is unlikely to affect anyone but ourselves. Questions of judgment are more substantial than matters of taste because judgment cannot be divorced from logic. Our judgments are determined by our beliefs, behind which are basic principles to which we try to remain consistent. These principles ultimately lead us to decide that some judgments are correct and others are not, so judgment has greater implications than taste. Should a university require freshmen to live in dormitories? Should men and women live together before getting married? Should parents prevent their children from watching television? All these are questions of judgment.

In written argumentation, questions of judgment provide the best subjects. Because they are complex, they offer more avenues to explore. This does not mean that you must cover every aspect of a question in a single essay. Good subjects have many possibilities, and the essays that are written on them will take many different directions. If you try to explore too many directions at once, you might easily get lost—or lose your readers along the way.

When planning your written argument, you may benefit from distinguishing between a *subject* and a *topic:* A topic is part of a subject. For example, "gun control" is a subject from which many different topics can be derived. Possibilities include: state laws affecting handguns, federal laws on the possession of military weapons, the constitutional right to "keep and bear arms," and gun use in criminal activities. Each of these topics could be narrowed further. Someone interested in gun use in criminal activities might focus on the extent to which criminals benefit from easy access to guns or on whether owning a gun serves as a deterrent to crime. Because it is easier to do justice to a well-focused topic than to a broad subject, choosing a topic is one of the most important choices writers need to make.

Some writers successfully define their topics before they begin to write. Others begin to write on one topic and then discover that they are more interested in a different topic, which may or may not be related. Still other writers use specific writing techniques for generating topics. At times, you will be required to write on a topic that has been assigned to you. But whenever you have freedom to choose your own topic, remember that writing may help you to discover what you want to write about. *Freewriting*— writing nonstop for five to ten minutes without worrying about grammar, spelling, style, organization, or repetition—often leads writers to discover that they have more ideas than they had realized. Similarly, *brainstorming*— listing as many aspects about a subject or a topic as come to mind during ten minutes or so—can help to focus an essay and to identify several essential points. In short, you do not need to choose your topic before you can even begin writing, but you should choose and develop a clearly defined topic before you submit an essay for evaluation.

Whether you choose a topic before you begin to write or use writing to discover a topic, ask yourself the following questions:

- Do I know exactly what my topic is?
- Is this topic suitable for the length of the work I am planning to write?
- Do I have an opinion about this topic?
- Would anyone disagree with my opinion?
- Can I hope to persuade others to agree with my opinion?
- Can I support my opinion with evidence?

If you answer yes to all of these questions, you can proceed with confidence.

DEFINING YOUR AUDIENCE

Good writers remember their *audience*—the person or people with whom they are trying to communicate. For example, your audience might consist of a single professor (when no one else will be reading what you write), a group of students (your classmates or members of a writing group), or the citizens of your community (as in a letter to the editor of a newspaper or magazine). All of these are examples of "particular audiences," and you can make certain assumptions about these readers based on your own observations and experience with them.

Instead of writing for a particular audience, some writers prefer to write for a general or universal audience—one in which all readers will have the intelligence and goodwill to listen to a reasonable stranger. When you write for a general audience, a particular audience (such as your professor) may cooperate by reading your work as a member of the larger audience you have invoked. Whatever the size and particularity of the audience you envision, you should maintain the same sense of audience throughout your entire essay.

Defining your audience can help you to choose your topic because a particular audience is likely to find some topics more interesting than others. A clear sense of audience can also help you to shape your style. It would be a mistake, for example, to use complicated technical language when writing for a general audience, and it would be just as foolish to address an audience of experts as if they knew nothing about your topic. You need to avoid confusing people but you must also be careful not to insult their intelligence. Finally, a clear sense of audience will help you to choose the points you want to emphasize in order to be persuasive, and to anticipate the objections that might be raised by readers who disagree with you.

Whether your audience is particular or general, you should assume that intelligent and fair-minded people are usually skeptical about sweeping generalizations and unsupported claims. Unless you are the keynote speaker at a political convention, assigned to rally the members of your party by telling them exactly what they want to hear, there is no reason to expect people to agree with you. If your audience already agrees with you, what's the point of your argument? Whom are you trying to convince? Remember that the immediate purpose of an argument is almost always to reconcile differences. An audience may be entirely neutral, having no opinion at all on the subject that concerns you. But by imagining a skeptical audience, you will be able to anticipate and respond to opposing views, thus building a stronger case.

Before you draft your essay, try listing the reasons why you believe as you do. You may not have the space, in a short essay, to discuss all of the points you have listed. Moreover, you are likely to discover new ideas as you draft and revise—ideas that may prove more important than those with which you began. You can benefit, however, from preliminary planning: Rank your points in order of their importance, and consider the degree to which they would probably impress the audience for whom you are writing. Once you have done this, compose another list: reasons why people might disagree with you. Having explored the opposition's point of view, ask yourself why you have not been persuaded to abandon your own beliefs. What flaw do you see in the reasoning of your opponents? Add to your second list a short response to each of your opponents' arguments.

You are likely to discover that the opposition has at least one good argument, an argument that you cannot answer. This should not be surprising. We may like to flatter ourselves by believing that Truth is on our side. In our weaker moments, we may like to pretend that anyone who disagrees with us is either ignorant or corrupt. But serious and prolonged controversies almost always continue because the opposition has at least one valid concern. Be prepared to concede a point to your opponents when it seems appropriate to do so. You must consider and respond to their views, but your responses do not always have to take the form of rebuttals. When you have no rebuttal and recognize that your opponents' case has some merit, be honest and generous enough to say so.

By making concessions to your opposition, you demonstrate to your audience that you are trying to be fair. Far from weakening your own case, an occasional concession can help bridge the gulf between you and your opponents, making it easier for you to reach a more substantial agreement. It's hard to convince opponents that your views deserve to be taken seriously when you have belligerently insisted that they are completely wrong and you are completely right. Life is seldom so simple. Human nature being what it is, most people will listen more readily to an argument that offers some recognition of their views.

Concessions establish common ground between conflicting parties and diffuse ill feeling that can inhibit persuasion. The number of concessions in an argument will vary, depending on the complexity of the issue, the extent to which people are divided in their opinions, and the writer's ability to reconcile opponents. The length of an argument is also a factor when deciding how many concessions are appropriate. In a short essay, you can usually afford to make only one or two concessions while still advancing your own line of thought. When you are able to write at length, you can concede more.

A good sense of audience will help you decide the nature and number of the concessions you make on any one occasion. Some audiences welcome long arguments; others do not. Some need to hear concessions before they can begin to listen to new ideas; others may be confused if you seem to concede too much. When making concessions, address the most pressing concerns of your audience. Approach your audience as you would when making other writing decisions, such as what tone to use or which examples to employ.

Having a good sense of audience also means illustrating your case with specific examples that your audience can readily understand. It's hard to make people care about abstractions; good writers try to make the abstract concrete. Remember that you might easily lose the attention of your audience, so try to address its most probable concerns.

There is, however, a great difference between responding to the interests of your audience by discussing what it wants to know, and twisting what you say to please an audience with exactly what it wants to hear. The foremost responsibility of any writer is to tell the truth as she or he sees it. What we mean by "truth" often has many dimensions. When limited space forces us to be selective, it is wise to focus on those facets of our topic that will be the most effective with the audience we are attempting to sway. But it is one thing to focus and quite another to mislead. Never write anything for one audience that you would be compelled to deny before another. Hypocrites are seldom persuasive, and no amount of verbal agility can compensate for a loss of confidence in a writer's character.

To better understand the importance of an audience in argumentation, consider the following essay, which was originally published as an editorial in a college newspaper.

TO SKIP OR NOT TO SKIP: A STUDENT DILEMMA

This is college, right? The four-year deal offering growth, maturity, experience, and knowledge? A place to be truly independent?

2   Because sometimes I can't tell. Sometimes this place downright reeks of paternal instincts. Just ask the freshmen and sophomores, who are by class rank alone guaranteed two full years of twenty-four-hour supervision, orchestrated activities, and group showers.

But the forced dorm migration of underclassmen has been bitched about before, to no avail. University policy is, it seems, set in stone. It ranks right up there with ingrown toe nails for sheer evasion and longevity.

4   But there's another university policy that has no merit as a policy and no place in a university. Mandatory Attendance Policy: wherein faculty members attempt the high school hall monitor–college instructor maneuver. It's a difficult trick to justify as professors place the attendance percentage of their choice above a student's proven abilities on graded material.

Profs rationalize out a lot of arguments to support the policy. Participation is a popular one. I had a professor whose methods for lowering grades so irritated me I used to skip on purpose. He said, "Classroom participation is a very important part of this introductory course. Obviously, if you are not present, you cannot be participating."

6   Equally obvious, though not stated by the prof, is the fact that one can be perpetually present but participate as little as one who is absent. So who's the better student—the one who makes a meaningless appearance, or the one who is busy with something else? And who gets the points docked?

The rest of his policy was characteristically vague, mentioning that absences "could" result in a lower grade. Constant ambiguity is the second big problem with formal policies. It's tough for teachers to figure out just how much to let attendance affect grade point. So they doubletalk.

8   According to the UWSP catalog, faculty are to provide "clear explanation" of attendance policy. Right. Based on the language actually used, ninety-five percent of UWSP faculty are functionally incapable of uttering a single binding statement. In an effort to offend no one while retaining all power of action, profs write things like (these are actual policies): "I trust students to make their own judgments and choices about coming, or not coming, to class." But then continues: "Habitual and excessive absence is grounds for failure." What happened to trust? What good are the choices?

Or this: "More than three absences may negatively affect your grade." Then again, they may not. Who knows? And this one: "I consider every one of you in here to be mature adults. However, I reserve the right to alter grades based on attendance."

10   You reserve the right? By virtue of your saying so? Is that like calling the front seat?

Another argument that profs cling to goes something like, "Future employers, by God, aren't going to put up with absenteeism." Well, let's take a reality pill. I think most students can grasp the difference between cutting an occasional class, which they paid for, and cutting at work, when they're the ones on salary. See, college students are capable of bi-level thought control, nowadays. (It's all those computers.)

12   In summary, mandatory attendance should be abolished because:

1. It is irrelevant. Roughly the same number of students will either skip or attend, regardless of what a piece of paper says. If the course is worth anything.

14   2. It is ineffective. It automatically measures neither participation, ability, or gained knowledge. That's what tests are for. Grades are what you end up knowing, not how many times you sat there to figure it out.

3. It is insulting. A college student is capable of determining a personal schedule, one that may or may not always meet with faculty wishes. An institution committed to the fostering of personal growth cannot operate under rules that patron-

ize or minimize the role an adult should claim for himself.

16   4. It is arbitrary. A prof has no right and no ability to factor in an unrealistic measure of performance. A student should be penalized no more than what the natural consequence of an absence is—the missing of one day's direct delivery of material.

5. It abolishes free choice. By the addition of a factor that cannot be fought. We are not at a university to learn conformity. As adults, we reserve the right to choose as we see fit, even if we choose badly.

18   Finally, I would ask the faculty to consider this: We have for some time upheld in this nation the sacred principle of separation of church and state; i.e., You are not God.

Karen Rivedal
Editor

Karen chose a topic that would certainly interest many college students, the audience for whom she saw herself writing. Her thesis is clear: Mandatory class attendance should not be required of college students. And her writing is lively enough to hold the attention of many readers. All this is good.

Unfortunately, Karen's argument has a number of flaws. In paragraph 6, she offers what logicians call "a false dilemma." By asking, "So who's the better student—the one who makes a meaningless appearance, or the one who is busy with something else?" she has ignored at least two other possibilities. Appearance in class is likely to be meaningful to at least some students, and cutting class may be meaningless if the "something else" occupying a student's attention is a waste of time. The comparison in paragraph 10 between reserving the right to lower grades because of poor attendance and "calling the front seat" is confusing. (In conversation after the initial publication of this essay, Karen explained to me that she was making a comparison between professors who "reserve the right to alter grades" and children who call "I got the front seat" when going out in the family car. I then pointed out that this analogy could easily be used against her. The driver *must* sit in the front seat, and surely whoever is teaching a class is analogous to the driver of a car rather than to one of the passengers.) In paragraph 13, Karen claims, "Roughly the same number of students will either skip or attend, regardless of what a piece of paper says," but she offers no evidence to support this claim, which is really no more than guesswork. And because Karen herself admits that many students skip class despite mandatory attendance policies, her claim in paragraph 17 that required attendance "abolishes free choice" does not hold up.

These lapses in logic aside, the major problem with this argument is that Karen misjudged her audience. She forgot that professors, as well as students, read the school newspaper. Students cannot change the policies of their professors, but the professors themselves usually can, so she has overlooked the very audience that she most needs to reach. Moreover, not only has she failed to include professors within her audience, but she has actually insulted them. Someone who is told that she or he is "functionally incapable of uttering a single binding statement" (paragraph 8) is unlikely to feel motivated to change. Only in the very last paragraph of this essay does Karen specifically address the faculty, and this proves to be simply the occasion for a final insult. There may be professors who take themselves too seriously, but are there really that many who believe that they are divine?

It's a shame that it's so easy to poke holes in this argument, because Karen deserves credit for boldly calling attention to policies that may indeed be wrong. Recognizing that her original argument was flawed, but still believing strongly that mandatory class attendance is inappropriate for college students, Karen decided to rewrite her editorial as an essay. Here is her revision:

Absent at What Price?
Karen Rivedal

This *is* college, right? A place to break old ties, solve problems, and make decisions? Higher education is, I thought, the pursuit of knowledge in a way that's a step beyond the paternal hand-holding of high school. It's the act of learning performed in a more dynamic atmosphere, rich with individual freedom, discourse, and debate.

2   Because sometimes I can't tell. Some university traditions cloud the full intent of higher education. Take mandatory attendance policies, wherein faculty members attempt the high school hall monitor–college instructor maneuver. It's a difficult trick to justify as professors place the attendance percentage of their choice above a student's proven abilities on graded material.

This isn't to say that the idea of attendance itself is unsound. Clearly, personal interaction between teacher and students is preferable to textbook teaching alone. It's the mandatory attendance policy, within an academic community committed to the higher education of adults, that worries me.

4   Professors, however, offer several arguments to support the practice. Participation is a popular one. I had a professor whose methods for lowering grades so irritated me that I used to skip out of spite. He said, "Classroom participation is a very important part of

this introductory course. Obviously, if you are not present, you cannot be participating."

Equally obvious, though, is the fact that one can be perpetually present, but participate as little as one who is absent. Participation lacks an adequate definition. There's no way of knowing, on the face of it, if a silent student is necessarily a learning student. Similarly, an instructor has no way of knowing for what purpose or advantage a student may miss a class, and therefore no ability to determine its relative validity.

6   As a learning indicator, then, mandatory attendance policy is flawed. It automatically measures neither participation nor ability. That's what tests are for. A final grade should reflect what a student ends up knowing, rather than the artificial consequences of demerit points.

Some faculty recognize the shortcomings of a no-exceptions mandatory attendance policy and respond with partial policies. Constant ambiguity is characteristic of this approach and troublesome for the student who wants to know just where he or she stands. It's tough for teachers to figure out just how much to let attendance affect grade point. So they doubletalk.

8   This, for example, is taken from an actual policy: "I trust students to make their own judgments and choices about coming, or not coming, to class." It then continues: "Habitual and excessive absence is grounds for failure." What happened to trust? What good are the choices?

Or this: "More than three absences may negatively affect your grade." Then again, they may not. Who knows? And this one: "I consider every one of you in here to be mature adults. However, I reserve the right to alter grades based on attendance."

10   This seems to say, what you can prove you have learned from this class takes a back seat to how much I think you should know based on your attendance. What the teacher says goes—just like in high school.

Professors who set up attendance policies like these believe, with good reason, that they are helping students to learn by ensuring their attendance. But the securing of this end by requirement eliminates an important element of learning. Removing the freedom to make the decision is removing the need to think. An institution committed to the fostering of personal growth cannot operate under rules that patronize or minimize the role an adult should claim for himself.

12   A grading policy that relies on the student's proven abilities certainly takes the guesswork out of grade assigning for teachers. This take-no-prisoners method, however, also demands a high, some say unfairly high, level of personal student maturity. Younger students especially may need, they say, the extra structuring that a policy provides.

But forfeiting an attendance policy doesn't mean that a teacher has to resign his humanity, too. Teachers who care to can still take five minutes to warn an often absent student about the possible consequences, or let the first test score tell the story. As much as dedicated teachers want students to learn, the activity is still a personal one. Students must want to.

14   A "real-world" argument that professors often use goes something like, "Future employers aren't going to put up with absenteeism, so get used to it now." Well, let's take a reality pill. I think most students can differentiate between cutting an occasional class, which they paid for, and missing at work, when they're the ones on salary.

Students who intelligently protest an institution's policies, such as mandatory attendance requirements, are proof-in-action that college is working. These students are thinking, and learning to think and question is the underlying goal of all education. College is more than its rules, more than memorized facts. Rightly, college is knowledge, the testing of limits. To be valid, learning must include choice and the freedom to make mistakes. To rely on mandatory attendance for learning is to subvert the fullest aims of that education.

In revising her essay, Karen has retained both her thesis and her own distinctive voice. Such phrases as "the high school hall monitor–college instructor maneuver," the "take-no-prisoners method," and "let's take a reality pill" are still recognizably her own. But her argument is now more compelling. In addition to eliminating the fallacies that marred her original version, Karen included new material that strengthens her case. Paragraph 3 offers a much needed clarification, reassuring readers that an argument against a mandatory attendance policy is not the same as an argument against attending class. Paragraph 7 begins with a fairly sympathetic reference to professors, and paragraph 11 opens with a clear attempt to anticipate opposition. Paragraph 12 includes another attempt to anticipate opposition, and paragraph 13, with its reference to "dedicated teachers," is much more likely to appeal to the professors in Karen's audience than any statements in the original version did. Finally, the conclusion of this essay is now much improved. It successfully links the question of mandatory attendance policies with the purpose of higher education as defined in the opening paragraph.

Exercise 1

Choose one of the following topics, and list the concerns most likely to be raised by each of the audiences specified for that topic. Although some of these audiences could overlap—a landlord, for example, could be a member of the City Council—imagine separate groups of readers for this assignment.

1. *Topic:* Finding clean, safe, affordable housing
   Audiences: (a) landlords, (b) tenants, (c) City Council
2. *Topic:* Building a large parking garage for a college located in a residential neighborhood
   Audiences: (a) commuting students, (b) neighboring home-owners, (c) the Board of Trustees
3. *Topic:* Closing an unproductive factory
   Audiences: (a) employees, (b) stockholders, (c) owners of nearby businesses
4. *Topic:* Experimenting on animals
   Audiences: (a) people with AIDS, (b) members of the Humane Society, (c) a committee that chooses the research projects that will receive financial grants
5. *Topic:* Restricting car imports
   Audiences: (a) American automobile workers, (b) American drivers, (c) foreign car dealers

DEFINING YOUR TERMS

If you want your arguments to be convincing, they must be understood by your audience. To make sure that your ideas are understandable, you must be careful in your use of words. It is especially important to clarify any terms that are essential to your argument. Unfortunately, many writers of argument fail to define the words they use. It is not unusual, for example, to find writers advocating (or opposing) gun control without defining exactly what they mean by "gun control." Many arguments use words such as "censorship," "society," "legitimate," and "moral" so loosely that it is impossible to decide exactly what the writer means. When this happens, the entire argument can break down.

Don't feel that you need to define every word you use, but be certain to define any important word that your audience might misunderstand. Avoid defining a word by using the same term or another term that is equally complex. For example, if you are opposed to the sale of pornography, you should be prepared to define what you mean by "pornography." It would not be especially helpful to tell your audience that pornography is "printed or visual material that is obscene" because this only raises the question: What is "obscene"? In an important ruling, the U.S. Supreme Court defined "obscene" as material that "the average person, applying community standards, would find . . . as a whole, appeals to the prurient interest," but even if you happened to have this definition at hand, you should ask yourself whether "the average person" understands what "prurient" means—not to mention what the Court may have meant by "community standards." Unless you define your terms carefully, avoiding unnecessarily abstract language, you can end up writing an endless chain of definitions that require further explanation.

The easiest way to define a term is to consult a dictionary. However, some dictionaries are much better than others. For daily use, most writers usually refer to a good desk dictionary such as *The American Heritage Dictionary, The Random House Dictionary,* or *Merriam Webster's Collegiate Dictionary, Tenth Edition.* A good general dictionary of this sort may provide you with an adequate working definition. You may also want to consider consulting the multivolume *Oxford English Dictionary,* which is available in most college libraries and is especially useful in showing how the usage of a word has changed over the years. Your audience might also appreciate the detailed information that specialized dictionaries in various subject areas can provide. Many such dictionaries are likely to be available in your college library. For example, if you are working on a paper in English literature, you might consult *A Concise Dictionary of Literary Terms* or *The Princeton Handbook of Poetic Terms.* For a paper in psychology, you might turn to *The Encyclopedic Dictionary of Psychology,* or, for a paper on a musical topic, *The New Grove's Dictionary of Music and Musicians.* There are also dictionaries for medical, legal, philosophical, and theoretical terms as well as for each of the natural sciences. When using specialized dictionaries, you will often find valuable information, but remember that the definition that appears in your paper should not be more difficult than the word or phrase you originally set out to define.

Instead of relying exclusively on dictionaries, it is often best to define a term or phrase in words of your own. You can choose from among several strategies:

- Give synonyms.
- Compare the term with other words with which it is likely to be confused, and show how your term differs.
- Define a word by showing what it is *not.*
- Provide examples.

Writers frequently use several of these strategies to create a single definition; an entire essay could be devoted to defining one term. Here is an example written by a student:

Homicide
Geoff Rulland

You sit back in your lazy-boy, cold soda In hand, grab the remote control and begin to flip through the channels in search of something interesting to watch. Something on the Channel 9 news catches your ear. You listen intently as the newscaster informs you that a man from a nearby town is being charged with homicide. A lot of people would now sit back and continue the channel scan thinking that the man was a murderer. Would that be a safe assumption?

2   When someone is charged with homicide it doesn't necessarily mean he or she is a murderer. Homicide is classified in court as being "justifiable," "excusable," or "felonious." Murder, which falls into the class of felonious homicide, is "the unlawful killing of a human being with malice aforethought," according to the American Heritage Dictionary. This means that murder is always wrong, but specifying that murder is an "unlawful killing" implies that killing a human being is not always unlawful. A justifiable homicide would be a killing committed intentionally without any evil design or under the circumstance of necessity. For example, when a police officer is trying to catch a dangerous felon, using a gun to wound and possibly kill could be justifiable. An excusable homicide would be the killing of a human being accidentally or in self-defense, such as in the case of a burglar entering your home. Killing him may be the only thing that will save you or your family. Manslaughter is another term often associated with killings that aren't murders. The name gives the impression that someone was brutally slain. Actually it is the accidental killing of one person by another, and it may have been quite mild.

         Black's Law Dictionary defines homicide as "the killing of any human creature or the killing of one human being by the act, procurement, or omission of another." In other words, it's the killing of one person by another in any manner. It doesn't matter if you hit a person accidentally with your car, or if you purposely shot someone, or if you hired a professional killer. Black's then goes on to state the definition as "the act of a human being in taking away the life of another human being." The Webster's New World Dictionary shortens all of that down to "any killing of one human being by another." The key word in this definition is "any." Webster's doesn't say how the killing must be done; it just says that a person is killed.

4   Two words from the Latin language are the main composition of homicide. The first one is homo meaning man and the other is caedere, which ties it to killing, meaning to cut or kill. Homicida, meaning murderer, was the form that was made from those two words which was later changed in Latin to homicidium. After going through the Old French language, the word then made its way into English and into its present form, homicide.

         Homicide is not necessarily a crime. Even though all homicides result in the loss of life, sometimes committing homicide is a person's only choice. Homicide shouldn't be immediately judged as murder or something all-out wrong. The word is "neutral" according to Black's Law Dictionary. It merely states the act of killing and pronounces no judgment on its moral or legal quality.

6   With this in mind, the next time you hear of a homicide on TV you should keep your mind open and neutral. Don't immediately

form the opinion that it was a murder, because a lot of the times you may be wrong. The word merely states that a person was killed, not necessarily murdered.

In defining *homicide,* Geoff uses three of the strategies listed on page 13: He provides examples of homicide; he compares homicide to such terms as *murder* and *manslaughter;* and, by contrasting homicide with murder, he clarifies what homicide is not. In addition to consulting two good desk dictionaries, *The American Heritage Dictionary* and *The Webster's New World Dictionary,* Geoff also took the trouble to consult a legal dictionary. *Black's Law Dictionary* confirmed his sense that homicide is a much broader term than murder, and this became the central idea of his essay. In the fourth paragraph, Geoff reports the origin of the term. Any good dictionary will provide you with some information of this sort, but you must be alert for it. A brief etymology (or derivation) usually appears in italics at either the beginning or the end of dictionary definitions, and this information can often be helpful when you are trying to understand a complex term. In *The Webster's New World Dictionary,* for example, the definition of *homicide* begins:

[M.E.; O Fr.; L.L. *homicidium,* manslaughter, murder < L. *homicida,* murderer < homo. a man + *caedere,* to cut, kill]

Note that the arrows establish the sequence of the word's history. In this case, they are pointing away from Latin (not toward it), indicating the Latin origin. (Arrows pointing to the right would indicate that the earliest term came first, with others appearing in chronological order.) A key to abbreviations used in a dictionary can be found by consulting its table of contents. When you do so, you will probably find that your dictionary contains more information than you had realized.

Before leaving this essay, note that it reveals a good sense of audience. Writing for freshmen in an English class, Geoff recognized that many of his fellow students might find definition to be dry reading. To capture their attention, he begins with an imaginary anecdote addressed, in the second person, directly to readers. Compared with the thousands of essays that have begun "According to *Webster's,* . . . ," this introduction (with which the conclusion is subsequently linked) seems original and likely to encourage further reading. But you should not assume that this strategy would be appropriate for any audience or any writing occasion.

Understanding the meaning of *homicide* could be essential in an argument on capital punishment or gun control. When writing an argument, however, you will usually need to define your terms within a paragraph or two. Even if you cannot employ all the strategies that you might use in an extended definition, remember your various options and decide which will be most effective for your purpose within the space available. (For examples of essays that incorporate definition within arguments, see pages 219–223, 294–299, and 463–469.)

In addition to achieving clarity, definition helps to control an argument by eliminating misunderstandings that can cause an audience to be inappropriately hostile or to jump to a conclusion that is different from your own. By carefully defining your terms, you limit a discussion to what you want to discuss. This increases the likelihood of your gaining a fair hearing for your views.

Exercise 2

Using the strategies listed on page 13, write an essay of definition for one of the following terms:

> affirmative action
> alcoholism
> child abuse
> civil rights
> eating disorder
> family
> feminist
> learning disability
> liberal
> middle class
> progress
> real world
> society
> well-rounded education

PLANNING YOUR ARGUMENT

A good plan grows out of a specific assignment or challenge. Your plan should suit your topic, what you have to say about that topic, and what your audience expects of you. If you have done some preliminary planning—listing reasons why you believe as you do as well as responses to the points most likely to be made by people with differing views—you must now consider a number of questions:

- Where and how should I begin my argument?
- In what order should I arrange the points I want to make?
- How can I most efficiently respond to opposing arguments?
- How should I conclude?

The answers to these questions will vary from one essay to another.

But even if no single plan will work equally well whenever you write, you can benefit from being familiar with some basic principles—for example, classical arrangement, Rogerian argument, and ways of reasoning. For easy reference, these principles are presented here as methods of organization. You should understand, however, that organization cannot be separated from all the other work you do when planning, drafting, and revising an essay. For example, if you are planning to write an argument that follows the principles of classical arrangement, you need to generate ideas that are suitable for this plan—and modify either the plan or the content later, after you have written your first draft. Or, if you begin by generating ideas without considering how you will organize them, you must then decide what kind of organization will be best suited for your ideas and your purpose in communicating them. These steps do not happen in isolation or in a linear progression in which it is impossible to revisit an earlier part of your work. When generating ideas, you might find that a tentative outline for their arrangement is beginning to emerge. Similarly, you might need to generate new ideas after organizing those with which you began, because your plan has helped you to discover a need for more material.

As you study the following plans, you should understand that they are not mutually exclusive. In a classically arranged argument, for example, the statement of background can be done with the kind of nonjudgmental language emphasized in Rogerian argument. Similarly, the summary of opposing views in a Rogerian argument requires the kind of understanding that a writer following a classical arrangement would need to have before engaging in refutation. In both cases, writers need to be well informed and fair-minded. And both classical arrangement and Rogerian argument encourage the use of concessions. The difference between the two is best understood in terms of purpose. Although any argument is designed to be persuasive, the purpose of that persuasion varies from one occasion to another. You might write to persuade other people to accept the legitimacy of your position, even if they continue to hold very different views. You might write to invite other people to change their minds or to undertake a specific action. Or you might write to encourage conflicting parties to accept a compromise. In any case, your plan needs to suit your purpose.

Classical Arrangement

Theories of argument first developed in ancient Greece and Rome, where education emphasized the importance of persuasion. Aristotle defined rhetoric as "the study of all the available means of persuasion," and his ideas—as well as the ideas of many other classical scholars—shaped the approaches to argument that dominated Western thinking for almost two thousand years.

Because these theories developed at a time when most arguments were oral, the great works of classical rhetoric recommended strategies that could be easily understood by listeners. If speakers followed essentially the same plan, listeners were able to follow long, complex arguments because the main components were easily recognizable and the order in which they appeared signaled what was likely to happen next.

Here is the most common plan for organizing an argument along classical lines. The original name of each component in classical rhetoric appears in parentheses.

Introduction *(Exordium)*	The introduction is where you urge your audience to consider the case that you are about to present. This is the time to capture the attention of your readers and introduce your issue.
Statement of Background *(Narratio)*	In the statement of background, you narrate, or tell, the key events in the story behind your case. This is the time to provide information so that your audience will understand the nature of the facts in the case at hand.
Proposition *(Partitio)*	This component divides (or partitions) the part of the argument focused on information from the part focused on reasoning, and it outlines the major points that will follow. You must state the position you are taking, based on the information you have presented, and then indicate the lines the rest of your argument will follow.
Proof *(Confirmatio)*	Adhering carefully to your outline, you now present the heart of your argument: You make (or confirm) your case. You must discuss the reasons why you have taken your position and cite evidence to support each of those reasons.
Refutation *(Refutatio)*	In this key section, you anticipate and refute opposing views. By showing what is wrong with the reasoning of your opponents, you demonstrate that you have studied the issue thoroughly and have reached the only conclusion that is acceptable in this case.
Conclusion *(Peroratio)*	The concluding paragraph(s) should summarize your most important points. In addition, you can make a final appeal to values and feelings that are likely to leave your audience favorably disposed toward your case.

The classical rhetoricians allowed variations on this plan; for example, speakers were encouraged to begin with refutation when an audience was already strongly committed to an opposing point of view. But because the basic plan remains clear and straightforward, it can still help writers organize their thoughts. If you are looking for a way to organize an argument, experiment with classical arrangement and modify it, when necessary, to suit your needs.

The classical arrangement is especially useful when you feel strongly about an issue and must bring an audience around to agreeing with you and undertaking a proposed action. Because classical rhetoric assumes that an audience can be persuaded when presented with solid evidence and a clear explanation of what is wrong with the reasoning of opponents, this plan is most effective when you are writing for reasonable people who share many of your values.

For an example of a classical arranged essay written by a student, see "Regulation of the Internet," by B. J. Nodzon (pages 445–448).

Rogerian Argument

In recent years, many rhetoricians have been influenced by the ideas of Carl Rogers, a psychotherapist who emphasized the importance of communication as a means to resolve conflicts. Rogers believed that most people are so ready "to judge, to evaluate, to approve or disapprove" that they fail to understand what others think. He urged people to "listen with understanding," and recommended a model for communication in which listeners are required to restate what others have said before offering their own views. This restatement should be done fairly and accurately, without either praise or blame; when restatement is done properly, the original speaker should be able to confirm, "Yes, that is what I said."

Although this model may seem simple, Rogers cautioned that it takes courage to listen carefully to views that are contrary to one's own. Moreover, it is especially hard to listen carefully when feelings are strong. The greater the conflict, the greater the chance of misinterpreting what others have said. In a quarrel, for example, people can sometimes talk right over one another, which drives the opposing participants even further apart. If you're interested in what Rogers says about resolving conflicts, you can read his essay "Dealing with Breakdowns in Communication" in Part 6 of this book (pages 647–652).

Scholars are divided about the extent to which Rogers's ideas can be applied to written arguments. Rogers envisioned situations in which individuals were involved in dialogue; a written argument is ultimately a kind of monologue. His commitment to the importance of restating others' ideas (without evaluating them) rests on the assumption that language can be completely neutral—an idea that has been seriously questioned in modern linguistics. And Rogers's emphasis on *learning to listen* may be more helpful to people who are used to speaking than to those who have been silenced in the past. Feminists, for example, have argued that because public discourse has long been dominated by men, women need help in learning how to assert themselves and men need help in learning how to listen.

Nevertheless, writers of argument can benefit from viewing persuasion as a means to resolve conflict and to achieve social cooperation, instead of thinking that the point of an argument is to somehow come out on top by beating down other people's opinions. Planning a Rogerian argument means emphasizing concessions rather than refutation, and placing those concessions early in your essay. Here is one way to organize an argument along Rogerian lines.*

Introduction	State the problem that you hope to resolve. By presenting your issue as a problem in need of a solution, you raise the possibility of positive change. This strategy can interest readers who would not be drawn to an argument that seems devoted to tearing something down.
Summary of Opposing Views	As accurately and neutrally as possible, state the views of people with whom you disagree. By doing so, you show that you are capable of listening without judging and that you have given a fair hearing to people who think differently from you—the people you most need to reach.
Statement of Understanding	Having summarized views different from your own, you now show that you understand that there are situations in which these views are valid. In other words, you are offering a kind of concession. You are not conceding that these views are always right, but you are recognizing that there are conditions under which you would share the views of your opponents.
Statement of Your Position	Having won the attention of both your opponents and those readers who do not have a position on your issue, you have secured a hearing from an audience that is in need of or is open to persuasion. Now that these readers know that you've given fair consideration to views other than your own, they should be prepared to listen fairly to your views.
Statement of Contexts	Similar to the statement of understanding, in which you have described situations where you would be inclined to share the views of your opponents, the statement of contexts describes situations in which you hope your own views would be honored. By showing that your position has merit in a specific context or contexts, you establish that you don't expect everyone to agree with you all the time. The limitations you recognize increase the likelihood

* This plan is adapted from the work of Richard Coe in *Form and Substance*. New York: Wiley, 1981.

	that your opponents will agree with you at least in part.
Statement of Benefits	You conclude your argument by appealing to the self-interest of people who do not already share your views but are beginning to respect them because of your presentation. When you conclude by showing how such readers would benefit from accepting your position, your essay's ending is positive and hopeful.

Although divided into six parts, a Rogerian argument need not be limited to six paragraphs. Depending on the complexity of the issue, the extent to which people are divided about it, and the points you yourself want to argue, any part of a Rogerian argument can be expanded. It is not necessary to devote precisely the same amount of space to each part. For example, there is no reason why you can't devote two paragraphs to your statement of contexts even if you devoted only one to your statement of understanding. You should try to make your case as balanced as possible, however. If you seem to give only superficial consideration to the views of others and then linger at length on your own, you are defeating the purpose of a Rogerian argument.

Rogerian argument is effective in situations where people are deeply divided as the result of different values or perceptions. It is especially useful when you are trying to reconcile conflicting parties and achieve a compromise that will allow these parties to move forward even though some differences remain. Because writing a Rogerian argument makes you a kind of negotiator, this plan may not be suitable when you have strongly held opinions of your own.

For an example of Rogerian argument written by a student, see the essay on same-gender marriage by Dana Simonson (Part 5, pages 284–286).

Exercise 3

Experiment with Rogerian strategies by forming a small group that includes people who hold different views on a specific issue. Each person should speak for two or three minutes. Each new speaker should begin by restating the views of the preceding speaker, without evaluating them, and then ask, "Is that accurate?" After the first speaker, all other speakers must paraphrase the previous speaker; they can deliver their own views only when they have been told by the preceding speaker that they have accurately paraphrased what they heard. When the last speaker has spoken, the first speaker should restate that person's views. After everyone has spoken, each group member should draft a paragraph that describes what has happened in the group and evaluates how successfully the speakers have managed to restate others' views without judging them.

Using Logic

The planning of an argument is also shaped by the kind of reasoning a writer employs. The two types of logic emphasized in classical rhetoric are *inductive reasoning* and *deductive reasoning*. In addition to recognizing induction and deduction, contemporary rhetoric also employs less formal models.

Reasoning Inductively When we use *induction*, we are drawing a conclusion based on specific evidence. Our argument rests on a foundation of details that we have accumulated for its support. This is the type of reasoning that we use most frequently in daily life. In the morning, we look at the sky outside our window, check the outdoor temperature, and perhaps listen to a weather forecast before dressing to face the day. If the sun is shining, the temperature is high, and the forecast is favorable, we would be making a reasonable conclusion if we decided to dress lightly and leave our umbrellas at home. We haven't *proved* that the day will be warm and pleasant, we have only *concluded* that it will be. This is all we can usually do in an inductive argument—arrive at a conclusion that seems likely to be true. Ultimate and positive proof is usually beyond reach, and writers who recognize this and proceed accordingly will usually arrive at conclusions that are both moderate and thoughtful. Such writers recognize the possibility that an unanticipated factor can undermine even the best of arguments. A lovely morning can yield to a miserable afternoon, and we may be drenched in a downpour as we hurry home on a day that began so pleasantly.

Inductive reasoning is especially important in scientific experimentation. A research scientist may have a theory that she hopes to prove. But to work toward proving this theory, hundreds, thousands, and even tens of thousands of experiments may have to be conducted to eliminate variables and gather enough data to justify a generally applicable conclusion. Well-researched scientific conclusions sometimes reach a point where they seem uncontestable. For many years, Congress has required the manufacturers of cigarettes to put on every package a warning that smoking can be harmful to the smokers' health. Since then, additional research has supported the conclusion that smoking can indeed be dangerous, especially to the lungs and the heart. The statement "smoking can be harmful to your health" now seems to have entered the realm of established fact. But biologists, chemists, physicists, and physicians are usually aware that the history of science, and the history of medicine in particular, is an argumentative history full of debate. Methods and beliefs established over many generations can be overthrown by a new discovery. Within a few years, that "new discovery" can also come under challenge. So the serious researcher goes back to the lab and keeps on working—ever mindful that truth is hard to find.

Induction is also essential in law enforcement. Police officers are supposed to have evidence against someone before making an arrest. Consider, for example, the way a detective works. A good detective does not arrive at the scene of a crime already certain about what happened. If the crime seems to be part of a pattern, the detective may already have a suspicion about who is responsible. But a good investigator will want to make a careful study of every piece of evidence that can be gathered. A room may be dusted for fingerprints, a murder victim photographed as found, and if the body is lying on the floor, a chalk outline may be drawn around it for future study. Every item within the room will be cataloged. Neighbors, relatives, employers, or employees will be questioned. The best detective is usually the detective with the best eye for detail and the greatest determination to keep searching for the details that will be strong enough to bring a case to court. Similarly, a first-rate detective will also be honest enough never to overlook a fact that does not fit in with the rest of the evidence. The significance of every loose end must be examined to avoid the possibility of an unfair arrest and prosecution.

In making an inductive argument, you will reach a point at which you decide that you have offered enough evidence to support the thesis of your essay. When you are writing a college paper, you will probably decide that you have reached this point sooner than a scientist or a detective might. But whether you are writing a short essay or conducting an investigation, the process is essentially the same. When you stop citing evidence and move on to your conclusion, you have made what is known as an *inductive leap.* In an inductive essay, you must always offer interpretation or analysis of the evidence you have introduced; there will always be at least a slight gap between your evidence and your conclusion. It is over this gap that the writer must leap; the trick is to do it agilely. Good writers know that their evidence must be in proportion to their conclusion: The bolder the conclusion, the more evidence is needed to back it up. Remember the old adage about "jumping to conclusions," and realize that you'll need the momentum of a running start to make more than a moderate leap at any one time.

If you listen closely to the conversations of people around you, the chances are good that you'll hear examples of faulty inductive reasoning. When someone says, "I don't like Chinese food," and reveals, under questioning, that his only experience with Chinese food has been a frozen Chinese dinner, we cannot take the opinion seriously. A sweeping conclusion has been drawn from flimsy evidence. People who claim to know "all about" complex subjects often reveal that they actually know very little. Only a sexist claims to know all about men and women, and only a racist is foolish enough to generalize about the various racial groups that make up our society. Good writers are careful not to overgeneralize.

When you begin an inductive essay, you might cite a particular observation that strikes you as especially important. You might even begin with a short anecdote. A well-structured inductive essay would then gradually expand as the evidence accumulates, so that the conclusion is supported by numerous details. Here is an example of an inductive essay written by a student:

In Defense of Hunting
David Wagner

I killed my first buck when I was fourteen. I'd gone deer hunting with my father and two of my uncles. I was cold and wet and anxious to get home, but I knew what I had to do when I sighted the eight-point buck. Taking careful aim, I fired at his chest, killing him quickly with a single shot.

2   I don't want to romanticize this experience, turning it into a noble rite of passage. I did feel that I had proved myself somehow. It was important for me to win my father's respect, and I welcomed the admiration I saw in his eyes. But I've been hunting regularly for many years now, and earning the approval of others no longer seems very important to me. I'd prefer to emphasize the facts about hunting, facts that must be acknowledged even by people who are opposed to hunting.

It is a fact that hunters help to keep the deer population in balance with the environment. Since so many of their natural predators have almost died out in this state, the deer population could quickly grow much larger than the land can support. Without hunting, thousands of deer would die slowly of starvation in the leafless winter woods. This may sound like a self-serving argument (like the words of a parent who beats a child and insists, "This hurts me more than it does you; I'm only doing it for your own good"). But it is a fact that cannot be denied.

4   It is also a fact that hunters provide a valuable source of revenue for the state. The registration and licensing fees we pay are used by the Department of Natural Resources to reforest barren land, preserve wetlands, and protect endangered species. Also there are many counties in this state that depend upon the money that hunters spend on food, gas, and lodging. "Tourism" is our third largest industry, and all of this money isn't being spent at luxurious lakeside resorts. Opponents of hunting should realize that hunting is the most active in some of our poorest, rural counties—and realize what hunting means to the people who live in these areas.

It is also a fact that there are hundreds of men and women for whom hunting is an economic necessity and not a sport. Properly preserved, the meat that comes from a deer can help a family survive a long winter. There probably are hunters who think of hunting as a recreation. But all the hunters I know—and I know at least twenty—dress their own deer and use every pound of the venison they salt, smoke, or freeze. There may be a lot of people who don't have to worry about spending $3.00 a pound for steak, but I'm not one of them. My family needs the meat we earn by hunting.

6   I have to admit that there are hunters who act irresponsibly by trespassing where they are not wanted and, much worse, by

abandoning animals that they have wounded. But there are many different kinds of irresponsibility. Look around and you will see many irresponsible drivers, but we don't respond to them by banning driving altogether. An irresponsible minority is no reason to attack a responsible majority.

I've listened to many arguments against hunting, and it seems to me that what really bothers most of the people who are opposed to hunting is the idea that hunters <u>enjoy</u> killing. I can't speak for all hunters, but I can speak for myself and the many hunters I personally know. I myself have never found pleasure in killing a deer. I think that deer are beautiful and incredibly graceful, especially when in movement. I don't "enjoy" putting an end to a beautiful animal's life. If I find any pleasure in the act of hunting, it comes from the knowledge that I am trying to be at least partially self-sufficient. I don't expect other people to do all my dirty work for me, and give me my meat neatly butchered and conveniently wrapped in plastic. I take responsibility for what I eat.

8   Lumping all hunters together as insensitive beer-drinking thugs is an example of the mindless stereotyping that logic should teach us to avoid. The men and women who hunt are no worse than anyone else. And more often than not, the hunting we do is both honorable and important.

David has drawn on his own experience to make an articulate defense of hunting. He begins with an anecdote that helps to establish that he knows something about the subject he has chosen to write about. The first sentence in the second paragraph helps to deflect any skepticism his audience may feel at this early stage in his argument, and the last sentence in this paragraph serves as a transition into the facts that will be emphasized in the next three paragraphs. In paragraph 3, David introduces the evidence that should most impress his audience, if we assume that his audience is unhappy about the idea of killing animals. In paragraphs 4 and 5, he defends hunting on economic grounds. He offers a concession in paragraph 5 ("There probably are hunters who think of hunting as a recreation") and another concession in paragraph 6 ("I have to admit that there are hunters who act irresponsibly"). But after each of these concessions he manages to return smoothly to his own thesis. In paragraph 7, he anticipates an argument frequently made by people who oppose hunting and offers a counterargument that puts his opponents on the defensive. The concluding paragraph may be a little anticlimactic, but within the limitations of a short essay, David has made a strong argument.

Reasoning Deductively Sometimes it is best to rest an argument on a fundamental truth, value, or right rather than on specific pieces of evidence. You should try to be specific within the course of such an essay, giving examples to support your case. But in deductive reasoning, evidence is of secondary importance. Your first concern is to define a commonly accepted value or belief that will prepare the way for the argument you want to make.

The Declaration of Independence, written by Thomas Jefferson (pages 601–604), is a classic example of deductive reasoning. Although Jefferson cited numerous grievances, he rested his argument on the belief that "all men are created equal" and that they have "certain unalienable Rights," which King George III had violated. This was a revolutionary idea in the eighteenth century, and even today there are many people who question it. But if we accept the idea that "all men are created equal" and have an inherent right to "Life, Liberty, and the pursuit of Happiness," then certain conclusions follow.

The right, value, or belief from which we wish to deduce our argument is called our *premise*. Perhaps you have already had the experience, in the middle of an argument, of someone's saying to you, "What's your premise?" If you are inexperienced in argumentation, a question of this sort may embarrass you and cause your argument to break down—which is probably what your opponent had hoped. But whether it is recognized or not, a premise is almost always lurking somewhere in the back of our minds. Deduction is most effective when we think about values we have automatically assumed, and then deliberately build our arguments on them.

A good premise satisfies two requirements:

- It is general enough that your audience is likely to accept it, thus establishing a common ground between you and the audience you hope to persuade.
- It is specific enough to prepare the way for the argument that will follow.

It usually takes much careful thought to frame a good premise. Relatively few people have carefully articulated values always in mind. We often know what we want—or what our conclusion is going to be—but it takes time to articulate the fundamental beliefs that we have automatically assumed. This is really what a premise amounts to: the underlying assumption that must be agreed on before the argument can begin to move along.

Because it is difficult to formulate an effective premise, it is often useful to work backward when you are outlining a deductive argument. If you know the conclusion you expect to reach, write it down, and number it as statement 3. Now ask yourself why you believe statement 3. This should prompt a number of reasons; group them together as statement 2. Now that you can look both at your conclusion and at the immediate reasons that seem to justify it, ask yourself whether you've left anything out—something basic that you skipped over, assuming that everyone would agree with that already. When you can think back successfully to what this assumption is, knowing that it will vary from argument to argument, you have your premise, at least in rough draft form.

This process may be difficult to grasp in the abstract, so consider an outline for a sample argument. Suppose that the forests in your state are slowly dying because of the pollution known as acid rain—one of the effects of burning fossil fuel, especially coal. Coal is being burned by numerous industries not only in your own state, but in neighboring states as well. You hadn't even realized that there was a problem with acid rain until last summer, when fishing was prohibited in your favorite lake. You are very upset about this and declare, "Something ought to be done!" But as you begin to think about the problem, you recognize that you'll have to overcome at least two obstacles in deciding what that "something" should be. Only two years ago, you participated in a demonstration against nuclear power, and you'd also hate to see the United States become more dependent on foreign oil. So if you attack the process of burning coal for energy, you'll have to be prepared to recommend an acceptable alternative. The other question you must answer is: Who's responsible for a problem that seems to be springing from many places in many states? Moreover, if you decide to argue for a radical reduction in coal consumption, you'll have to be prepared to anticipate the opposition: "What's this going to do to the coal miners?" someone might well ask. "Will you destroy the livelihood of some of the hardest working men and women in America?"

You realize that you have still another problem. Your assignment is for a thousand-word deductive argument, and it's due the day after tomorrow. You feel strongly about the problem of acid rain, but you are not an energy expert and there is a limit to how much you can discuss in a short essay. Your primary concern is with the effects of acid rain, which you've witnessed with your own eyes. And although you don't know much about industrial chemistry, you do know that acid rain is caused principally by public utilities' burning coal that has a high percentage of sulfur in it. Recognizing that you lack the expertise to make a full-scale attack on coal consumption, you decide that you can at least argue on behalf of using low-sulfur coal. In doing so, you will be able to reassure your audience that you want to keep coal miners at work, you recognize the needs of industry, and you do not expect the entire country to go solar by the end of the semester.

Taking out a sheet of paper, you begin to write down your outline in reverse:

3. Public utilities should not burn coal that is high in sulfur content.
2. Burning high-sulfur coal causes acid rain, and acid rain is killing American forests, endangering wildlife, and spoiling local fishing.

Before going any further, you realize that all of your reasons for opposing acid rain cannot be taken with equal degrees of seriousness. As much as you like to fish, recreation does not seem to be in the same league with your more general concern for forests and wildlife. You know that you want to describe the condition of your favorite lake at some point in your essay, because it gave you some firsthand experience with the problem and some vivid descriptive details. But you decide that if you make too much of fishing, you risk sounding as if you care only about your own pleasure.

You now ask yourself what lies behind the "should" in your statement 3. How strong is it? Did you say "should" when you meant "must"? Thinking it over, you realize that you did mean "must," but now you must decide who or what is going to make that "must" happen. You decide that you can't trust industry to make this change on its own because you are asking it to spend money that may reduce profits. You know that, as an individual, you don't have the power to bring about the change you believe is necessary, but you also know that individuals become powerful when they band together as a group. In terms of power, the most important group is probably the government we have elected to represent us. (Be careful with a term like "government" and avoid such statements as "The government ought to do something about this." Not only is the "something" vague, but we don't know what kind of government you want to take charge.) Most of us are subject to government on at least three levels: municipal, state, and federal. You decide to argue for *federal* legislation, because acid rain is being generated in several different states—and then is carried by air currents to still others.

You should now be ready to formulate your premise. Your conclusion is going to demand federal regulation, so, at the very beginning of your argument, you need to establish the principle that supports this conclusion. You realize that the federal government cannot solve all problems; you therefore must define the nature of the government's responsibility so that it will be clear that you are appealing legitimately to the right authority. Legally, the federal government has broad powers to regulate interstate commerce, and this may be a useful fact in your argument because most of the industries burning coal ship or receive goods across state lines. More specifically, ever since the creation of Yellowstone National Park in 1872, the U.S. government has undertaken a growing responsibility for protecting the environment. Acid rain is clearly an environmental issue, so you would not be demanding anything new, in terms of governmental responsibilities, if you appealed to the type of thinking that led to the creation of a national park system in 1916 and the Environmental Protection Agency in 1970.

You know, however, that there are many people who distrust big government, and you do not want to alienate anyone by appealing to Washington too early in the essay. A premise can be a single sentence, a full paragraph, or more—depending on the length and complexity of the argument. The function of a premise is to establish a widely accepted value that even your opponents should be able to share. You would probably be wise, therefore, to open this particular argument with a fairly general statement—something like: "We all have a joint responsibility to protect the environment in which we live and preserve the balance of nature on which our lives ultimately depend." As a thesis statement, this obviously needs to be developed in the paragraph that follows. In the second paragraph, you might cite some popular examples of joint action to preserve the environment, pointing out, for example, that most people are relieved to see a forest fire brought under control or an oil slick cleaned up before it engulfs a long stretch of coastline. Once you have cited examples of this sort, you could then remind your audience of the role of state and federal government in coping with such emergencies, and emphasize that many problems are too large for states to handle. By this stage in your essay, you should be able to narrow your focus to acid rain, secure in the knowledge that you have laid the foundation for a logical argument. *If* the U.S. government has a responsibility to help protect the environment, and *if* acid rain is a serious threat to the environment of several states, then it follows logically that the federal government should act to bring this problem under control. A brief outline of your argument would look something like this:

1. The federal government has the responsibility to protect the quality of American air, water, soil, and so on—what is commonly called "the environment."
2. Acid rain, which is caused principally by burning high-sulfur coal, is slowly killing American forests, endangering wildlife, and polluting lakes, rivers, and streams.
3. Therefore, the federal government should restrict the use of high-sulfur coal.

Once again, this is only an *outline*. An essay that makes this argument—explaining the problem in detail, anticipating the opposition, and providing meaningful concessions before reaching a clear and firm conclusion—would amount to several pages.

By outlining your argument in this way, you have followed the pattern of what is called a *syllogism*, a three-part argument in which the conclusion rests on two premises, the first of which is called the *major premise* because it is the point from which the writer begins to work toward a specific conclusion. Here is a simple example of a syllogism:

MAJOR PREMISE: All people have hearts.
MINOR PREMISE: John is a person.
CONCLUSION: Therefore, John has a heart.

If the major and minor premises are both true, then the conclusion reached should be true. Note that the minor premise and the major premise share a term in common (in the example, people/person). In a written argument, the "minor premise" would usually involve a specific case that relates to the more general statement with which the essay began.

A syllogism such as the one just cited may seem very simple. And it can be simple—if you're thinking clearly. On the other hand, it's even easier to write a syllogism (or an essay) that breaks down because of faulty reasoning. Consider the following example:

MAJOR PREMISE: All women like to cook.
MINOR PREMISE: Elizabeth is a woman.
CONCLUSION: Therefore, Elizabeth likes to cook.

Technically, the *form* here is valid. The two premises have a term in common, and if we accept both the major and minor premises, then we will have to accept the conclusion. But someone who thinks along these lines may be in for a surprise, especially if he has married Elizabeth confidently expecting her to cook his favorite dishes every night just as his mother used to do. Elizabeth may *hate* to cook, preferring to go out bowling at night or read the latest issue of the *Journal of Organic Chemistry*. A syllogism may be valid in terms of its organization, but it can also be *untrue* because it rests on a premise that can be easily disputed. Always remember that your major premise should inspire widespread agreement. Someone who launches an argument with the generalization that "all women like to cook," is likely to lose many readers before making it to the second sentence. Some generalizations make sense and some do not. Don't make the mistake of confusing generally accepted truths with privately held opinions. You may argue effectively on behalf of your opinions, but you cannot expect your audience to accept an easily debatable opinion as the foundation for an argument on behalf of yet another opinion. You may have many important things to say, but nobody is going to read them if alienated by your major premise.

You should also realize that, in many arguments, a premise may be implied but not stated. You might overhear a conversation like this:

"I hear you and Elizabeth are getting married."
"Yes, that's true."
"Well, now that you've got a woman to cook for you, maybe you could invite me over for dinner sometime."
"Why do you think that Elizabeth will be doing the cooking?"
"Because she is a woman."

The first speaker has made a number of possible assumptions. He or she may believe that all women like to cook, or perhaps that all women are required to cook whether they like it or not. If the second speaker had the patience to continue this conversation, he would probably be able to discover the first speaker's premise. A syllogism that consists of only two parts is called an *enthymeme*. The part of the syllogism that has been omitted is usually the major premise, although it is occasionally the conclusion. Enthymemes usually result when a speaker or writer decides that it is unnecessary to state a point because it is obvious. What is obvious to someone trying to convince us with an enthymeme is not necessarily obvious to those of us who are trying to understand it. Although an enthymeme might reflect sound reasoning, the unstated part of the syllogism may reveal a flaw in the argument. When you encounter an enthymeme in your reading, you will often benefit from trying to reconstruct it as a full syllogism. Ask yourself what the writer has assumed, and then ask yourself whether you agree with that assumption. One sign of a faulty deductive argument is that a questionable point has been assumed to be universally true, and you may need to discover this point before you can decide that the argument is either invalid or untrue.

Deductive reasoning, which begins with a generalization and works to a conclusion that follows from that generalization, can be thought of as the opposite of *inductive reasoning*, which begins with specific observations and ends with a conclusion that goes beyond any of the observations that led up to it. So that you can see what a deductive essay might look like, here is a short essay written by a student:

Preparation for Real Life
Kerstin LaPorte

In order for all children to reach their fullest potential as adults, it is imperative that they be prepared for careers that will help them be productive members of society. Through the school system, taxpayers are responsible for providing the educational opportunities for the development of minds, so that when these students become adults, they too will be able to take their turn for supporting the education of a future generation. But many property owners have grown increasingly angry over the continual raises in their taxes, and this hostility is being expressed toward the school system that these overtaxed people have to support.

2   Cuts in spending are made, but these cuts are not reflected in the sports department. The costs of maintaining sports programs are immense. The money that is taken out of the average annual school budget for the equipment for training players, providing uniforms, and paying coaches is more than most taxpayers realize. I too am a taxpayer whose taxes go up each year. It is my view that this money would be better spent on more up-to-date textbooks, lab equipment in the science department that is not outdated, the newest computer technology, adequate tools and machinery for the wood and metal shops, and libraries that are stocked with the necessary books and magazines to complement all academic subjects. These investments will help a much larger percentage of the school population and develop skills in accord with public needs.

It would be a terrible loss to many people who gain a great deal of satisfaction out of participating in sports activities if these activities were to be completely phased out. Therefore I advocate that sports programs for adolescents be community-sponsored. Clubs, sponsored by participating members, local merchants, and private individuals, combined with fund-raising, would provide all the sports activities that have no place in an academic field.

4   Proponents of school-sponsored sports would argue that the children of lower-income families would not be able to participate in a community club due to any costs this would incur. I firmly believe that if a student from a poor family has a special talent, clubs would probably vie for his or her membership, helping him or her with any financial deficiencies. Once the potential for a finely tuned athlete is seen, one who can help win the game or competition for the club, funding will be available for his or her recruitment.

The importance of physical fitness is not to be understated. Students need to be physically active in order to maintain mental and physical stamina. Therefore, a scaled-down physical education department must remain within the schools. If done for at least 30 minutes 3–5 times a week, aerobic exercise such as running, walking, and Jazzercize raises the heart rate sufficiently to promote physical fitness. It is not necessary to build pools, tennis courts, football stadiums, baseball parks, and basketball courts. Neither have I ever been able to justify the purchasing of cross-country skis, archery, weight lifting, and gymnastic equipment with academic funding. The maintenance of all the sport grounds and equipment involved, plus the replacement of broken or outdated equipment, is also an added annual expense to the community.

6   Just as students who have similar interests form clubs, which meet outside of school hours, students interested in further physical fitness can organize biking, skiing, or running clubs. This would involve the use of their own equipment, occur on their own time, and fill the void left if sports training is taken out of the school curriculum.

If there were to be a major change in the approach to our sports programs, the existing buildings, equipment, and outdoor facilities in and around the schools must not be wasted. The clubs could lease those premises, and any member would be eligible to utilize the facilities during club hours. This would include student members, who could go and work out during their free hours if they wanted. In this manner, the costs would not detract from the academic necessities, and the facilities already built would not go to waste.

8   Opponents to my proposal might ask: What about funding for such extracurricular activities as band, art, drama, and choir? There too, a very basic introduction to these fields is reasonable, just as scaled-down physical education would suffice. If a child shows promise of being a gifted musician, artist, actor, or singer, he or she can go on to obtain private instruction.

What about some of the academic subjects that seem unrelated to the job market, such as history, sociology, and psychology? Successful interaction between people depends on some knowledge of human nature, and these subjects are only on an introductory basis. As far as history goes, I would be scared to death to have a generation of voters go to the polls with no knowledge of the workings of government, ours or anyone else's, and, unaware of the mistakes of the past, try to make wise decisions for the future.

10   As a future teacher, I have been reminded over and over again that it is imperative that I be a good role model for my students. Coaches of competitive sports are role models also. They promote healthy lifestyles by discouraging students from smoking and drinking. They do the best they can to make their students' experiences enjoyable by providing proper motivation and support. This need not end with the removal of the sports programs from the school. These same people can either stay in the teaching field in another capacity or work for the community clubs.

     Yes, it is true that active daily training builds a particular responsibility and perseverance that will be needed in "real life." However, this "daily training" can be accomplished within the academic field also, and will serve to engender the school spirit that pro sports people feel is necessary in the educational environment. Forensics, math competitions, essay contests, and history debates all contribute to build public speaking ability, alleviate math anxiety, and promote an increased ability for self-expression in writing, which will aid students' ability to synthesize and analyze information and formulate informed opinions.

12   Extensive sports training through the school system prepares a very small percentage of the school population for a successful future, as very few individuals are lucky enough to go on to pro careers. Let's take the money that goes for sports and use it to support an up-to-date, academic education that will prepare all children for real life.

This essay has many strengths. The topic was well chosen, not only because many people are interested in school sports, but also because Kerstin's view of sports is likely to inspire controversy—hence the need for her argument. As already noted, good writers do not belabor the obvious. Writing this essay for an audience of students (with whom she shared an earlier draft for peer review), Kerstin realized that many of her classmates believed in the importance of school sports and that their convictions on this issue could keep them from listening to what she had to say. She therefore adopted a deductive strategy in order to establish some common ground with her opponents before arguing that school systems should not fund sports. Her opening paragraph establishes the premise on which her argument is based: The function of education is to help children "reach their fullest potential as adults" and prepare them to become "productive members of society." Her minor premise appears in paragraph 12: "Extensive sports training through the school system prepares a very small percentage of the school population for a successful future. . . . " If we accept both the major and minor premises, then we should be prepared to accept the conclusion: "Let's take the money that goes for sports and use it to support an up-to-date, academic education that will prepare all children for real life."

As you can see from this example, deduction allows a writer the chance to prepare the way for a controversial argument by strategically opening with a key point that draws an audience closer, without immediately revealing what exactly is afoot. With a genuinely controversial opinion, one must face the risk of being shouted down—especially when addressing a potentially hostile audience. Like Rogerian argument (pages 19–21), deductive reasoning increases the chance of gaining a fair hearing.

A writer who uses deduction should still remember to address those concerns most likely to be raised by opponents. In "Preparation for Real Life," Kerstin begins paragraphs 4, 8, and 9 by anticipating opposition and then responding to it. She also makes a number of important concessions. In her third paragraph, she concedes, "It would be a terrible loss to many people who gain a great deal of satisfaction out of participating in sports activities if these activities were to be completely phased out." The fifth paragraph begins by recognizing, "The importance of physical fitness is not to be understated." Paragraph 11 also begins with a concession: "Yes, it is true that active daily training builds a particular responsibility and perseverance that will be needed in 'real life.'" And, in paragraph 10, Kerstin admits that coaches can be good role models. These are all concessions that should appeal to men and women who value sports. But Kerstin does not simply let these concessions sit on the page. In each case, she immediately goes on to show how the concession does not undermine her own argument. Whatever your own views on this topic may be, you should realize that concessions need not weaken an argument. On the contrary, they can strengthen an argument by making it more complex.

The moment at which writers choose to anticipate opposition will usually vary; it depends on the topic, how much the author knows about it, and how easily he or she can deal with the principal counterarguments that others might raise. But whether one is writing an inductive or deductive argument, it is usually advisable to recognize and respond to opposition fairly early in the essay. You will need at least one or two paragraphs to introduce your topic, but by the time you are about one-third of the way into your essay, you may find it useful to defuse the opposition before it grows any stronger. If you wait until the very end of your essay to acknowledge that there are points of view different from your own, your audience may have already put your essay aside, dismissing it as "one-sided" or "narrow-minded." (Classical arrangement, discussed on pages 17–19, provides an alternative strategy in which counterarguments are discussed near the end of the essay. This strategy assumes that readers are familiar with the plan being used and understand that opposing views will be considered before the writer concludes.) Also, it is usually a good idea to put the opposition's point of view at the beginning of a paragraph. By doing so, you can devote the rest of that paragraph to your response. It's not enough to recognize the opposition and include some of its arguments in your essay. You must try to show your audience what to make of the counterarguments you have acknowledged. If you study the organization of "Preparation for Real Life," you will see that Kerstin begins paragraphs 3, 4, 5, 8, and 11 with sentences that acknowledge other sides to the question of public funding for school sports. But she was able to end each of these paragraphs with her own argument still moving clearly forward.

One final note: Although it is usually best to establish your premise before your conclusion, writing an essay is not the same as writing a syllogism. In "Preparation for Real Life," the minor premise does not appear until the last paragraph. It could just as easily have appeared earlier (and actually did so in a preliminary draft). Writers benefit from flexibility and the ability to make choices, depending on what they want to say. When you read or write deductive arguments, you will find that relatively few of these arguments proceed according to a fixed formula that determines exactly what must happen in any given paragraph.

Exercise 4

Draft a list of five widely accepted values or principles. Express each as a statement that would enjoy general support. Then identify at least two specific conclusions that could be drawn from each of them if they were used as premises for deductive arguments.

Reasoning by Using the Toulmin Model   Although both inductive reasoning and deductive reasoning suggest useful strategies for writers of argument, they also have their limitations. Many writers prefer not to be bound by a predetermined method of organization and regard the syllogism, in particular, as unnecessarily rigid. To make their case, some writers choose to combine inductive and deductive reasoning within a single essay—and other writers can make convincing arguments without the formal use of either induction or deduction.

In an important book first published in 1958, a British philosopher named Stephen Toulmin demonstrated that the standard forms of logic needed to be reconsidered because they did not adequately explain all logical arguments. Emphasizing that logic is concerned with probability more often than certainty, he provided a new vocabulary for the analysis of argument. In Toulmin's model, every argument consists of these elements:

CLAIM: The equivalent of the conclusion or whatever it is a writer or speaker wants to try to prove.

DATA: The information or evidence a writer or speaker offers in support of the claim.

WARRANT: A general statement that establishes a trustworthy relationship between the data and the claim.

Within any argument, the claim and the data will be explicit. The warrant may also be explicit, but it is often merely implied—especially when the arguer believes that the audience will readily agree to it.

To better understand these terms, let us consider an example adapted from one of Toulmin's:

CLAIM: Raymond is an American citizen.
DATA: Raymond was born in Puerto Rico.
WARRANT: Anyone born in Puerto Rico is an American citizen.

These three statements may remind you of the three elements in a deductive argument. If arranged as a syllogism, they might look like this:

MAJOR PREMISE: Anyone born in Puerto Rico is an American citizen.
MINOR PREMISE: Raymond was born in Puerto Rico.
CONCLUSION: Raymond is an American citizen.

The advantage of Toulmin's model becomes apparent when we realize that there is a possibility that Raymond was prematurely born to French parents who were only vacationing in Puerto Rico, and he is now serving in the French army. Or perhaps he was an American citizen but became a naturalized citizen of another country after defecting with important U.S. Navy documents. Because the formal logic of a syllogism is designed to lead to a conclusion that is *necessarily* true, Toulmin argued that it is ill-suited for working to a conclusion that is *probably* true. Believing that the importance of the syllogism was overemphasized in the study of logic, Toulmin argued that there was a need for a "working logic" that would be easier to apply in the rhetorical situations in which people most often find themselves. He designed his own model so that it can easily incorporate *qualifiers* such as "probably," "presumably," and "generally." Here is a revision of the first example:

CLAIM: Raymond is probably an American citizen.
DATA: Raymond was born in Puerto Rico.
WARRANT: Anyone born in Puerto Rico is entitled to American citizenship.

Both the claim and the warrant have now been modified. Toulmin's model does not dictate any specific pattern in which these elements must be arranged, and this is a great advantage for writers. The claim may come at the beginning of an essay, or it could just as easily come after a discussion of both the data and the warrant. Similarly, the warrant may precede the data or it may follow it—or, as already noted, the warrant may be implied rather than explicitly stated at any point in the essay.

If you write essays of your own using the Toulmin model, you may find yourself making different types of claims. In one essay, you might make a claim that can be supported entirely by facts. For example, if you wanted to argue that the stock market should be subject to greater regulation, you could define the extent of current regulation, report on the laws governing overseas markets, and cite specific abuses such as scandals involving insider trading. In another essay, however, you might make a claim that is easier to support with a mixture of facts, expert opinion, and appeals to the values of your audience. If, for example, you wanted to argue against abortion, your data might consist of facts (such as the number of abortions performed within a particular clinic in 1997), testimony on which it is possible to have a difference of opinion (such as the point at which human life begins), and an appeal to moral values that you believe your audience should share with you. In short, you will cite different types of data depending on the nature of the claim you want to argue.

The nature of the warrant will also differ from one argument to another. It may be a matter of law (such as the Jones Act of 1917, which guarantees U.S. citizenship to the citizens of Puerto Rico), an assumption that one's data have come from a reliable source (such as documents published by the Securities and Exchange Commission), or a generally accepted value (such as the sanctity of human life). But whatever your warrant, you should be prepared to back it up if called on to do so. No matter how strongly you may believe in your claim, or how compelling your data may be, your argument will not be convincing if your warrant cannot be substantiated.

The Toulmin model for argumentation does not require that you abandon everything you've learned about inductive and deductive reasoning. These different systems of logic complement one another and combine to form a varied menu from which you can choose whatever seems best for a particular occasion. Unless your instructor specifies that an assignment must incorporate a particular type of reasoning, you will often be able to choose the type of logic you wish to employ, just as you might make any number of other writing decisions. And having choices is ultimately a luxury, not a burden.

For an example of a student essay that reflects the Toulmin model for reasoning, consider the following argument on the importance of studying history:

History Is for People Who Think
Ron Tackett

Can a person consider himself a thinking, creative, responsible citizen and not care about history? Can an institution that proposes to foster such attributes do so without including history in its curriculum? Many college students would answer such a question with an immediate, "Yes!" But those who are quick to answer do so without reflecting on what history truly is and how and why it is important.

2   History is boring, complain many students. Unfortunately, a lot of people pick up a bad taste of history from the primary and secondary schools. Too many lower-level history courses (and college level, too) are just glorified Trivial Pursuit: rife with rote memorization of dates and events deemed important by the teacher and textbooks, coupled with monotone lectures that could induce comas in hyperactive children. Instead of simply making students memorize when Pearl Harbor was attacked by the Japanese, teachers should concentrate on instilling an understanding of why the Japanese felt they had no alternative but to attack the United States. History is a discipline of understanding, not memorization.

Another common complaint is that history is unimportant. But even the most fanatic antihistory students, if they were honest, would have to admit that history is important at least within the narrow confines of their own disciplines of study. Why be an artist if you are merely going to repeat the past (and probably not as expertly, since you would have to spend your time formulating theories and rules already known and recorded in Art's history)? Why write The Great Gatsby or compose Revolution again? How could anyone hope to be a mathematician, or a scientist, without knowing the field's history? Even a genius needs a base from which to build. History helps provide that base.

4   History is also important in being a politically aware citizen. Knowing that we entered World War I on the side of the Allies in part because Woodrow Wilson was a great Anglophile, as some historians charge, is not vital to day-to-day life. But it is important to know that the economic reparations imposed on Germany after the war set the stage for the rise of Hitler and World War II and that that war ended with a Russian domination of Eastern Europe that led to the Cold War, during which political philosophies were formulated that still affect American foreign and domestic policies. This type of history enables citizens to form an intelligent worldview and possibly help our nation avoid past mistakes. Of course, this illustration is simplified, but the point is as valid as when Santayana said that without history, we are "condemned to repeat it." This does not mean that history will repeat itself exactly, but that certain patterns recur in history, and if we understand the patterns of what has gone before, perhaps we can avoid making the mistakes our ancestors made.

A person can live a long life, get a job, and raise a family without having any historical knowledge. But citizens who possess a strong knowledge of history are better prepared to contribute intelligently to their jobs and their society. Thus, knowing which Third World nations have a history of defaulting on loans can help a bank executive save his or her institution and its customers a great deal of grief by avoiding, or seeking exceptional safeguards on, such loans. And knowing the history of U.S. involvement in Central and South America, from naval incidents with Chile in the 1890s to trying to overthrow the Sandanistas in Nicaragua in the 1980s, can help Americans understand why many people and nations are concerned about U.S. policies in the region. More importantly, Americans cannot intelligently determine what those policies should be without a knowledge of history.

6   Now, if history is important enough to be required in college, how many credits are enough and what sort of history should be taught? American, European, Eastern, Latin American, or yet another? First, a course in American history must be required. Students can little appreciate the history of others, without first knowing their own. Second, since we more and more realize that we are members of a "global community," at least one world history course should be mandated. Though there is no magic number of credits that will ensure the student's becoming a thinking, creative member of society, history can help fulfill the collegiate purpose of fashioning men and women with the potential for wisdom and the ability to critically appraise political, economic, and moral issues. Thus, history should be a required part of the college curriculum.

In arguing on behalf of history, Ron shows that he is well aware that many students would like to avoid history courses. Paragraphs 2 and 3 are devoted to anticipating and responding to opposition. Although Ron concedes that history can be boring if it is badly taught, and makes an additional concession at the beginning of paragraph 5, he still insists that all college students should be required to take at least two history courses. The *claim* of this essay is "history should be a required part of the college curriculum." The *warrant* behind this claim is a value that is likely to be widely accepted: A college education should help people to think critically and become responsible members of society. This warrant underlies the entire argument, but it can be found specifically in the last paragraph where Ron refers to "the collegiate purpose of fashioning men and women with the potential for wisdom and the ability to critically appraise political, economic, and moral issues" immediately before making his claim.

Submitting *data* to support this claim presented the writer with a challenge: It would be difficult to obtain statistics or other factual evidence to prove that the claim fulfills the warrant. A reader might agree with the warrant and still doubt whether requiring college students to study history would give them the ability to think critically about political and moral issues. Ron chose to support his claim by defining history as "a discipline of understanding, not memorization" and providing several examples of historical events that are worth understanding: the Japanese attack on Pearl Harbor, the consequences of World War I, and the nature of U.S. involvement in Central and

South America. Additional support for the claim is provided by appeals to other values, which Ron has assumed his audience to possess. Paragraph 3 includes an appeal to self-interest: Knowing the history of your own field can save you from wasting time. This same strategy is employed in paragraph 5, where Ron suggests that knowledge of history can lead to better job performance. All of the examples found within the essay are clearly related to the values that the argument has invoked, and, within the limitations of a short essay, Ron has done a good job of supporting his claim.

AVOIDING LOGICAL FALLACIES

An apparently logical argument may reveal serious flaws if we take the trouble to examine it closely. Mistakes in reasoning are called logical *fallacies*. This term comes from the Latin word for deceit, and there is some form of deception behind most of these lapses in logic. It is easy to deceive ourselves into believing that we are making a strong argument when we have actually lost our way somehow, and many fallacies are unintentional. But others are used deliberately by writers or speakers for whom "winning" an argument is more important than searching for truth. Here is a list of common fallacies that you should be careful to avoid in your own arguments and remain alert to in the arguments of others.

Appealing to Pity

Writers are often justified in appealing to the pity of their readers when the need to inspire this emotion is closely related to whatever they are arguing for, and when the entire argument does not rest on this appeal alone. For example, someone who is attempting to convince you to donate one of your kidneys for a medical transplant would probably assure you that you could live with only one kidney and that there is a serious need for the kidney you are being asked to donate. In addition to making these crucial points, the arguer might move you to pity by describing what will otherwise happen to the person who needs the transplant.

When the appeal to pity stands alone, even in charitable appeals where its use is fundamental, the result is often questionable. Imagine a large billboard advertisement for the American Red Cross. It features a close-up photograph of a distraught (but nevertheless good-looking) man, beneath which, in large letters, runs this caption: PLEASE, MY LITTLE GIRL NEEDS BLOOD. Although we may already believe in the importance of donating blood, we should question the implications of this ad. Can we donate blood and ask that it be reserved for the exclusive use of little girls? Is the life of a little girl more valuable than the life of a little boy? Are the lives of children more valuable than the lives of adults? Few people would donate blood unless they sympathized with those who need transfusions, and it may be unrealistic to expect logic in advertising. But consider how weak an argument becomes when the appeal to pity has little to do with the issue in question.

Someone who has seldom attended class and failed all his examinations but then tries to argue, "I deserve to pass this course because I've had a lot of problems at home," is making a fallacious appeal to pity. The "argument" asks the instructor to overlook relevant evidence and make a decision favorable to the arguer because the instructor has been moved to feel sorry for him. You should be skeptical of any appeal to pity that is irrelevant to the conclusion or that seems designed to distract attention from the other factors you should be considering.

Appealing to Prejudice

Writers of argument benefit from appealing to the values of their readers. Such appeals become fallacious, however, when framed in inflammatory language or when offered as a crowd-pleasing device to distract attention from whether the case at hand is reasonable and well informed. A newspaper that creates a patriotic frenzy through exaggerated reports of enemy "atrocities" is appealing to the prejudicies of its readers and is making chances for reasonable discussion less likely. Racist, sexist, classist, and homophobic language can also be used to incite a crowd—something responsible writers should take pains to avoid doing. Appeals to prejudice can also take more subtle forms. Politicians may remind you that they were born and raised in "this great state" and that they love their children and admire their spouses—all of which are factors believed to appeal to the average man and woman but which nevertheless are unlikely to affect performance in office. When candidates linger on what wonderful family life they enjoy, it may be time to ask a question about the economy.

Appealing to Tradition

Although we can learn from the past and often benefit from honoring tradition, we can seldom make decisions based on tradition alone. Appealing to tradition is fallacious when tradition becomes the only reason for justifying a position. "We cannot let women join our club because we've never let women join in the past" is the equivalent of arguing: "We shouldn't buy computers for our schools, because we didn't have computers in the past." The world changes, and new opportunities emerge. What we have done in the past is not necessarily appropriate for the future. If you believe that a traditional practice can guide us in the future, you need to show why this is the case. Do not settle for claiming: "This is the way it always has been, so this is the way it always has to be."

Arguing by Analogy

An analogy is a comparison that works on more than one level, and it is possible to use analogy effectively when reasoning inductively. You must first be sure that the things you are comparing have several characteristics in common and that these similarities are relevant to the conclusion you intend to draw. If you observe that isolation produces depression in chimpanzees, you could argue that isolation can cause a similar problem for human beings. The strength of this argument would depend on the degree to which chimps are analogous to humans, so you would need to proceed with care and demonstrate that there are important similarities between the two species. When arguing from analogy, it is important to remember that you are speculating. As is the case with any type of inductive reasoning, you can reach a conclusion that is likely to be true but not guaranteed to be true. It is always possible that you have overlooked a significant factor that will cause the analogy to break down.

Unfortunately, analogies are often misused. An argument from analogy that reaches a firm conclusion is likely to be fallacious, and it is certain to be fallacious if the analogy itself is inappropriate. If a congressional candidate asks us to vote for him because of his outstanding record as a football player, he might be able to claim that politics, like football, involves teamwork. But because a successful politician needs many skills and will probably never need to run across a field or knock someone down, it would be foolish to vote on the basis of this questionable analogy. The differences between football and politics outweigh the similarities, and it would be fallacious to pretend otherwise.

Attacking the Character of Opponents

If you make personal attacks on opponents while ignoring what they have to say, or distracting attention from it, you are using what is often called an *ad hominem* argument (Latin for "to the man"). Although an audience often considers the character of a writer or speaker in deciding whether it can trust what he or she has to say, most of us realize that good people can make bad arguments, and even a crook can sometimes tell the truth. It is always better to give a thoughtful response to an opponent's arguments than to ignore those arguments and indulge in personal attacks.

Attributing False Causes

If you assume an event is the result of something that merely occurred before it, you have committed the fallacy of false causation. Assumptions of this sort are sometimes called post hoc reasoning, from the Latin phrase *post hoc, ergo propter hoc*, which means "after this, therefore because of this." Superstitious people offer many examples of this type of fallacious thinking. They might tell you, "Everything was doing fine until the lunar eclipse last month; *that's* why the economy is in trouble." Or personal misfortune may be traced back to spilling salt, stepping on a sidewalk crack, or walking under a ladder.

This fallacy is often found in the arguments of writers who are determined to prove the existence of various conspiracies. They often seem to amass an impressive amount of "evidence"—but their evidence is frequently questionable. Or, to take a comparatively simple example, someone might be suspected of murder simply because of being seen near the victim's house a day or two before the crime occurred. This suspicion may lead to the discovery of evidence, but it could just as easily lead to the false arrest of the meter reader from the electric company. Being observed near the scene of a crime proves nothing by itself. A prosecuting attorney who would be foolish enough to base a case on such a flimsy piece of evidence would be guilty of *post hoc, ergo propter hoc* reasoning. Logic should always recognize the distinction between *causes* and what may simply be *coincidences*. Sequence is not a cause because every event is preceded by an infinite number of other events, all of which cannot be held responsible for whatever happens today.

This fallacy can be found in more subtle forms in essays on abstract social problems. Writers who blame contemporary problems on such instant explanations as "the rise of television" or "the popularity of computers" are no more convincing than the parent who argues that all the difficulties of family life can be traced to the rise of rock and roll. It is impossible to understand the present without understanding the past. But don't isolate at random any one event in the past, and then try to argue that it explains everything. And be careful not to accidentally imply a cause-and-effect relationship where you did not intend to do so.

Attributing Guilt by Association

This fallacy is frequently apparent in politics, especially toward the end of a close campaign. A candidate who happens to be religious, for example, may be maneuvered by opponents into the false position of being held accountable for the actions of all the men and women who hold to that particular faith. Nothing specific has been *argued*, but a negative association has been either created or suggested through hints and innuendos.

Begging the Question

In the fallacy of begging the question, a writer begins with a premise that is acceptable only to anyone who will agree with the conclusion that is subsequently reached—a conclusion often very similar to the premise itself. Thus, the argument goes around in a circle. For instance, someone might begin an essay by claiming, "Required courses like freshman English are a waste of time," and end with the conclusion that "Freshman English should not be a required course." It might indeed be arguable that freshman English should not be required, but the author who begins with the premise that freshman English is a waste of time has assumed what the argument should be devoted to proving. Because it is much easier to *claim* that something is true than to *prove* it is true, you may be tempted to beg the question you set out to answer. This temptation should always be avoided.

Equivocating

Someone who equivocates uses vague or ambiguous language to mislead an audience. In argumentation, equivocation often takes the form of using one word in several different senses, without acknowledging the change in meaning. It is especially easy to equivocate when using abstract language. Watch out in particular for the abuse of such terms as "right," "society," "freedom," "law," "justice," and "real." When you use words like these, make sure your meaning is clear. And make doubly sure your meaning doesn't shift when you use the term again.

Ignoring the Question

When someone says, "I'm glad you asked that question!" and then promptly begins to talk about something else, she or he is guilty of ignoring the question. Politicians are famous for exploiting this technique when they don't want to be pinned down on a subject. Students (and teachers) sometimes use it too, when asked a question that they want to avoid. Ignoring the question is also likely to occur when friends or lovers have a fight. In the midst of a quarrel, we may hear remarks like, "What about you!" or "Never mind the budget! I'm sick of worrying about money! We need to talk about what's happening to our relationship!"

Jumping to Conclusions

This fallacy is so common that it has become a cliché. It means that the conclusion in question has not been supported by an adequate amount of evidence. Because one green apple is sour, it does not follow that all green apples are sour. Failing one test does not mean that you will necessarily fail the next. An instructor who seems disorganized the first day of class may eventually prove to be the best teacher you ever had. You should always try to have more than one example to support an argument. Be skeptical of arguments that seem heavy on opinion but weak on evidence.

Opposing a Straw Man

Because it is easier to demolish a man of straw than to address a live opponent fairly, arguers are sometimes tempted to pretend that they are responding to the views of their opponents when they are only setting up a type of artificial opposition which they can easily refute. The most common form of this fallacy is to exaggerate the views of others or to respond only to an extreme view that does not adequately represent the arguments of one's opponents. If you argue against abolishing Social Security, you should not think that you have defended that program from all its critics. By responding only to an extreme position, you would be doing nothing to resolve specific concerns about how Social Security is financed and administered.

Presenting a False Dilemma

A false dilemma is a fallacy in which a speaker or writer poses a choice between two alternatives while overlooking other possibilities and implying that other possibilities do not exist. If a college freshman receives low grades at the end of the first semester and then claims, "What's wrong with low grades? Is cheating any better?" he or she is pretending that there is no other possibility—for example, that of earning higher grades by studying harder, a possibility that is recognized by most students and teachers.

Reasoning That Does Not Follow

Although almost any faulty argument is likely to have gaps in reasoning, this fallacy—sometimes called the *non sequitur* (Latin for "it does not follow")— describes a conclusion that does not follow logically from the explanation given for it.

Gaps of this sort can often be found within specific sentences. The most common type of non sequitur is a complex sentence in which the subordinate clause does not clearly relate to the main clause, especially where causation is involved. An example of this type of non sequitur would be: "Because the wind was blowing so fiercely, I passed the quiz in calculus." This is a non sequitur because passing calculus should not be dependent on the weather. A cause-and-effect relationship has been claimed but not explained. It may be that the wind forced you to stay indoors, which led you to spend more time studying than you usually do, and this in turn led you to pass your quiz. But someone reading the sentence as written could not be expected to know this. A non sequitur may also take the form of a compound sentence: "Mr. Blandshaw is young, and so he should be a good teacher." Mr. Blandshaw may indeed be a good teacher, but not just because he is young. On the contrary, young Mr. Blandshaw may be inexperienced, anxious, and humorless. He may also give unrealistically large assignments because he lacks a clear sense of how much work most students can handle.

Non sequiturs sometimes form the basis for an entire argument: "William Henderson will make a good governor because he is a friend of working people. He is a friend of working people because he has created hundreds of jobs through his contracting business." Before allowing this argument to go any further, you should realize that you've been asked to swallow two non sequiturs. Being a good governor involves more than being "a friend of working people." And there is no reason to assume that Henderson is "a friend of working people" just because he is an employer. He may have acquired his wealth by taking advantage of the men and women who work for him.

Sliding Down a Slippery Slope

According to this fallacy, one step will inevitably lead to an undesirable second step. An example would be claiming that legalized abortion will lead to euthanasia or that censoring pornography will lead to the end of freedom of the press. Although it is important to consider the probable effects of any step that is being debated, it is fallacious to claim that people will necessarily tumble downhill as the result of any one step. There is always the possibility that we'll be able to keep our feet firmly on the ground even though we've moved them from where they used to be.

Exercise 5

Read a series of editorials and letters in a newspaper of your own choice. Look for examples of logical fallacies. Bring your favorite example to class and explain what is wrong in the reasoning.

UNDERSTANDING OTHER FORMS OF PERSUASION

Of the various forms of persuasive writing, logical argument is the most honorable. Although logic can be abused, its object is truth rather than manipulation. Whether we are writing a logical argument or simply trying to understand one, we have to be actively involved with ideas. That means we have to *think*. We may be influenced by what we know of the writer's credibility and by whether she or he has touched our hearts within the argument as a whole. But behind any logical argument is the assumption that reasonable people should agree with its outcome—not so much because it is gracefully written (although it may be that), but because it has brought us closer to knowing truth.

There are other types of writing that rely on an indirect appeal to the mind, exploiting what is known about the psychological makeup of an audience or its most probable fears and desires. Successful advertising is *persuasive* in that it encourages us to buy one product or another, but it is not necessarily logical. Few people have the money, time, or inclination to sample every product available for consumption. When we buy a particular mouthwash, toothpaste, soap, or soft drink—and even when we make purchases as large as a car—we may simply choose the cheapest product available. But bargain hunting aside, we are frequently led to purchase brands that advertising has taught us to associate with health, wealth, and happiness. A prominent greeting card company insists that we send their cards if we really and truly care about someone. A soft drink company assures us that we will be young and have fun if we drink its best-known brand. One popular cigarette is associated with the masculinity of mounted cowboys, and another implies a dubious link with the women's movement. Almost no one really believes this sort of thing when forced to stop and think about it. But we often act without thinking, and this is one of the reasons why advertising has been able to grow into a billion-dollar industry. Through the clever use of language and visual images, advertisers can lead people into a variety of illogical and possibly ruinous acts.

This, then, is the principal distinction between argument and other types of persuasion: Argument seeks to clarify thought; persuasion often seeks to obscure it. Argument relies on evidence or widely accepted truths and does not necessarily dictate any particular course of action. Persuasion, on the other hand, can work altogether independent of the facts as we know them (such as how much money we can afford to spend before the end of the month), and it is almost always designed to inspire action—whether it is buying a new kind of deodorant or voting for the candidate with the nicest teeth. Persuasion can thus be a form of domination. It can be used to make people agree with the will of the persuader, regardless of whether the persuader is "right" or simply selling his or her services by the hour.

Argument may include an appeal to our emotions; persuasion is likely to emphasize such appeals. A persuasive writer or speaker knows how to evoke feelings ranging from love, loyalty, and patriotism to anger, envy, and xenophobia. An audience may be deeply moved even when nothing substantial has been said. With a quickened pulse or tearful eyes, we may find ourselves convinced that we've read or heard something wonderfully profound. A few days later, we may realize that we've been inhaling the intoxicating fumes of a heavily scented gasbag, rather than digesting genuine "food for thought."

Analyzing Advertisements

Although persuasion is by no means limited to advertising, advertisements represent a form of persuasion that we regularly encounter in our daily lives. Recognizing that people are often bored by ads because there are so many of them, advertisers must be doubly persuasive: Before they can persuade us to buy a particular product or engage a specific service, advertisers must begin by persuading us to pay attention to the ad. Because advertisements cannot be taken for granted, advertising agencies have attracted some highly talented people, and a successful advertising campaign usually involves much planning. Different advertisements employ different strategies, and if you think about the ads you encounter, you will find that they often include more than one message. Consider the examples on pages 48 through 59.

At first glance, the advertisement for Evian® Natural Spring Water (Figure 1) seems directed exclusively at pregnant women. The use of the second person, as in "If you plan to breast feed, experts say you should drink up to *30% more water* every day," seems to exclude anyone who is *not* planning to breast feed: a large market sector that includes women who are unable to have children, as well as many other women, and all men.

But although the written text seems to target only a small percentage of potential buyers of imported spring water, the ad as a whole is designed to persuade a much larger group. By associating their product with motherhood, the advertisers have made an appeal to feeling. According to an old adage, mothers are as American as apple pie, so by associating a European

FIGURE 1

product with motherhood, the advertisers are appealing to a widely held American value. Respect for mothers is not uniquely American, however. Mother figures are revered in many different cultures, so the ad has the potential to reach a very large market. Although it is directly addressed to pregnant women, it is subconsciously directed at anyone who values motherhood. The opening line, "Mommy, can I have a drink of water?" invites readers to assume the role of children. If we are turning to our mothers for a drink of water, and good mothers are drinking Evian Natural Spring Water, then readers can hope that they will get Evian water from their mothers. If our "mommies" are no longer around to quench our thirst, then we will have to do the next best thing: Head to the store for a bottle of the water good enough for mothers to give their children. To put this ad's message simply: "Mothers are good. Evian water is good for mothers. If you are a good mother, you should buy some. If you are a good child, you should also buy some."

On closer examination, we can see that the persuasive appeal of this ad involves a number of other elements. Consider the positive connotations of such italicized words as *eating, maintain, lubricate, process, cleanse,* and *life.* The woman is wearing a white dress, emphasizing the purity that apparently comes with drinking the product in question. She is thoroughly at ease, reclining, a book in hand. What could be more peaceful? The image suggests the comfort that comes with wealth. After all, for every pregnant woman who can lounge in the French Alps, there are many hundreds who are working for a living. Thus, in addition to being the drink of mothers, Evian water becomes the drink of wealth and privilege. If you cannot afford a new BMW but want the illusion that you too live in a world like this, you can at least start buying what is being marketed as the right water for those who are healthy, wealthy, and cool.

Like the ad for Evian water, the ad for Saturn automobiles (Figure 2) also involves linking the product with a positive image. In this case, the association is with physicians. But rather than settling for a relatively simple message such as "Product X is the preferred brand of nine out of ten doctors," the Saturn ad conveys a message that is more complex. The doctors in question are all young and unconventional—so unconventional that they have apparently driven some distance from a hospital for an outdoor lunch without even removing their stethoscopes. Their youth and attire emphasize that these doctors are different from the stereotypical image of physicians as highly paid professionals who take themselves seriously. As such, these four doctors— perfectly balanced in terms of gender, and representing four different cultures—are perfect clients for "A Different Kind of Company. A Different Kind of Car."

Although both their clothing and the accompanying text emphasize that Jim, Ed, Janet, and Beth are all doctors, they are also presented as good-natured and unthreatening. Three are eating simple lunches from brown paper bags, and the fourth has a plaid lunch box reminiscent of elementary school. Moreover, it is surely no accident that two of the doctors are eating

Drs. Junkins, Kwiatkowski, Cuervo, and Huang haven't been doctors long enough to know they're supposed to drive one of those overpriced luxury imports.

When Ed, Janet, Beth, and Jim emerged, successfully, from medical school, they felt the gratification of having achieved a lifelong goal, while also confronting a hard reality common to most young doctors—a ton of student loan debt. (You could buy five Saturns with what a new M.D. typically owes.)

In Ed's case, that hard reality also included his 10-year-old car—nobody could tell him how much time it had left. Since a *Say ahh! Our hunch is that at least 9 out of 10 doctors would really love how easy Saturns are to take care of. (But don't quote us on that. Ask your doctor.)* pediatric resident's life is ruled by a beeper (and because you can't tell a sick kid that the tow truck was late), Ed bit the bullet and went looking for a new car.

While he was making the rounds of the car dealerships in town, Ed discovered Saturn. Where, along with the simple, painless way one shops at our showrooms, he liked the rather healthy range of standard features offered and (especially) the fact that the price of a Saturn did not put him into a state of shock.

Since then, mostly on his referral, many of Ed's colleagues have been filling the hospital parking lot with new Saturns. (Apparently, the people who pay most attention to a doctor's advice are other doctors.)

The Saturn SL1

A Different Kind *of* Company. A Different Kind *of* Car.

The Doctors are pictured with a 1995 Saturn SL1. M.S.R.P. for the 1994 Saturn SL1 is $10,850, including retailer prep and optional passenger-side mirror. Tax, license, transportation, and other options are extra. If you'd like to know more about Saturn, and our new sedans, coupes, and wagons, please call us any time at 1-800-522-5000. © 1993 Saturn Corporation.

FIGURE 2

Jim, Ed, Janet, and Beth (left to right) bought their Saturns at Saturn of Owings Mills and Saturn of Glen Burnie.

FIGURE 2 *(Continued)*

fruit and the background is dominated by a large tree. These images combine to suggest that Saturn is a car for intelligent, nice, young professionals who value diversity, health, and fresh air.

The written text (in which we are quickly put on a first-name basis with strangers) reinforces the message that these unknown people—whose expertise has nothing whatsoever to do with cars—are typical of the good people who know what it's like to be in debt, drive an old car, and need reliable transportation. The informal, almost gossipy text emphasizes Ed's search for a car rather than specific features of the car on display. We read briefly about a "rather healthy range of standard features," but the details of the car are presumably less important than relating to the attractive people who are pictured as representative owners. Note that the car itself is obscured by the doctors in the photograph, and product information about the car is relegated to small print at the bottom of the left-hand page. Once again, a product is being sold because of the associations advertisers establish with it—not because of its specific qualities.

Exercise 6

Six other advertisements are reproduced on pages 54–59. Choose one and write an essay of approximately five hundred words explaining how the ad attempts to be persuasive.

Recognizing Flaws in Persuasion

Just as some advertisements are more appealing than others, so are some ads more questionable than others. Many ads are relatively straightforward, but others may approach dishonesty. When analyzing persuasion, wherever you encounter it and in whatever form, you should be alert not only for the various types of fallacious reasoning discussed earlier, but also for the following flaws.

Bogus Claims A claim can be considered bogus, or false, whenever persuaders promise more than they can prove or deliver. If a Chicago restaurant offers "fresh country peas" in the middle of January, you might want to ask where these peas were freshly picked. And if a large commercial bakery advertises "homemade pies," try asking whose home they were made in. You'll probably get some strange looks, because many people don't pay close attention to language. But good writers become good writers in part because they have eyes that see and ears that hear.

If a toothpaste promises to give your mouth "sex appeal," you'd still better be careful about whom you try to kiss. A claim of this sort is fairly crude, and therefore easily recognizable. But bogus claims can take many forms, some more subtle than others. A television advertisement for a new laxative may star a woman in a white coat, with a stethoscope around her neck. The advertisement implies—without necessarily saying so—that the product in question is endorsed by physicians. Ads of this sort are also likely to speak vaguely of "recent studies," or better yet, "recent *clinical* studies," which are declared to have proved a product's value. The product may indeed have value; on the other hand, it may be indistinguishable from its competition except in price and packaging. You might like it when you try it. But well-educated people should always be a little skeptical about promises from strangers.

When writing an essay, it is easy to fall into the habit of making bogus claims when reaching for generalizations to support your point of view. Imitating the style of the advertisements with which they are familiar, careless writers sometimes refer to those ever-popular "recent studies" that conveniently seem to support whatever is being argued. Such phrases as "Recent studies have shown" enable writers to avoid identifying who did the research. A recent study may provide the evidence to prove a point, but a good writer should be prepared to cite it, especially when the claim is surprising. It is one thing to write "Recent studies have shown that nutrition plays an important role in maintaining good health"—a generalization that enjoys wide acceptance. It would be something else altogether to toss off a claim like "Recent studies have shown that Americans have the most nutritious diet in the world." A specific claim requires specific support—not just a vague reference to an unidentified study. We cannot evaluate a recent study if we do not know how it was undertaken and where the results were published.

Writers who like to refer to "recent studies" are also fond of alluding to unspecified statistics, as in "Statistics have shown . . ." or "According to statistics . . . ." Statistics can be of great value, but they can also be misleading. Ask yourself whether a statistic raises any unanswered questions, and note whether the source has been revealed. Similarly, turn a critical eye on claims like "It is a well known fact that . . ." or "Everybody knows that . . . ." If the fact *is* well known, why is the writer boring us with what we already know? If the fact is *not* well known, as is usually the case when lines of this sort are thrown about, then the writer had better explain how he or she knows it.

In short, if you want to avoid bogus claims, never claim anything that would leave you speechless if you were called on to explain or defend what you have written.

Loaded Terms   Good writers have good diction; they know a lot of words and, just as important, they know how to use them accurately. They know that most words have positive or negative *connotations*—associations with the word that go beyond its standard definition or *denotation*. "Placid," "tranquil," or "serene" might all be used to describe someone who is "calm," but each word creates a slightly different impression. Experienced writers are likely to pause before choosing the adjective that best suits their subject.

A term becomes *loaded* when it is asked to carry more emotional weight than its context can legitimately support. A loaded term is a word or

FIGURE 3

With all the milk I drink, my name might as well be Calcium Ripken, Jr. Really, I'm a huge milk fan. Besides being loaded with calcium, there's nothing like it when it's ice cold. Which is why I drink the recommended 3 glasses a day. And as you'd probably guess, I'm not one to miss a day.

MILK

Where's *your* mustache?™

CAL RIPKEN, JR. © 1998 NATIONAL FLUID MILK PROCESSOR PROMOTION BOARD

FIGURE 4

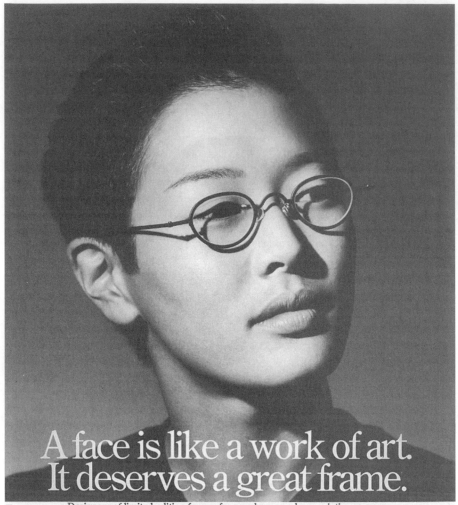

FIGURE 5

FIGURE 6

FIGURE 7

To Trena Brown, whose family has a history of breast cancer, our

search for a cure has a special urgency.

Drug companies are currently testing 73 medicines for

cancer in women,

including 52 for

breast cancer.

Progress like

this from pharma-

ceutical company

research provides

the best hope for conquering diseases like cancer, and

dramatically reducing health costs.

Call or write to learn more about our research on new

medicines for cancer and other diseases.

America's Pharmaceutical Research Companies

Pharmaceutical Manufacturers Association, 1100 15th St., NW, Box N, Wash., DC 20005. 1-800-538-2692.

FIGURE 8

phrase that goes beyond connotation into the unconvincing world of the heavy handed and narrow minded. To put it simply, it is *slanted* or *biased*.

Loaded terms may appeal to the zealous, but they mislead the unwary and offend the critically minded. For example, when an aspiring journalist denounces the Clinton "regime" in the school newspaper, he is taking what many men and women would consider a cheap shot—regardless of their own politics. "Regime" is a loaded term because it is most frequently used to describe military dictatorships. Even someone who is politically opposed to Bill Clinton should be clearheaded enough to speak of the Clinton *Administration,* which is the term best suited for a political discussion of the U.S Presidency.

Like "regime," many words have such strong connotations that they can become loaded terms very easily. In the United States, for example, terms such as "socialist," "feminist," "family," and "natural" all inspire responses that can affect how an audience responds to the context in which these words appear. Moreover, an unloaded term can become loaded within a specific context. To manipulate reader response, a writer may introduce unnecessary adjectives. A political correspondent might write "Margaret Ong, the wealthy candidate from Park Ridge, spoke today at Jefferson High School." The candidate's income has nothing to do with the news event being reported, so "wealthy" is a loaded term. It's an extra word that serves only one function: to divide the candidate from the newspaper's audience, very few of whom are wealthy. It would not be surprising if some readers began to turn against this candidate, regardless of her platform, simply because they had been led to associate her with a background that is alien to their own.

Do not make the mistake of assuming that loaded terms occur only in political discourse. They can be found almost anywhere, if you take the trouble to read critically and intelligently. You may even find some in your textbooks.

Misrepresentation   Misrepresentation can take many forms. Someone may come right out and lie to you, telling you something you know—or subsequently discover—to be untrue. In the course of writing a paper, someone may invent statistics or alter research data that point to an unwelcome conclusion. And then there is *plagiarism*—taking someone else's words or ideas without acknowledgment and passing them off as your own. (For a discussion of plagiarism, see pages 72–74.)

There are always going to be people who find it easy to lie, and there isn't much we can do about this except to keep our eyes open, read well, and choose our friends with care. But we ourselves can be careful to act honorably and to follow the guidelines for working with sources that appear in Part 2 of this book. There is, however, a common misrepresentation that must be understood as part of our introduction to the principles of argument and persuasion: Dishonest writers will often misrepresent by twisting what their opponents have said.

The most common way in which writers misrepresent opposing arguments is through oversimplification. The ability to summarize what others have said or written is a skill that cannot be taken for granted, and we will turn to it shortly. There is always the possibility that someone may misrepresent an opponent accidentally—having failed to understand what has been said or having confused it in reporting it. But it is also possible to misreport others *deliberately*. A complex argument can be reduced to ridicule in a slogan, or an important element of such an argument could be entirely overlooked, creating a false impression.

Have the courage to ask for evidence whenever someone makes a questionable claim. When you find it necessary to quote someone, make sure you do so not only correctly but also *fairly*. The concept of "quoting out of context" is so familiar that the phrase has become a cliché. But clichés sometimes embody fundamental truths, and here is one of them: quotations should be more than accurate; they should also reflect the overall nature of the quoted source. When you select a passage that truly represents the thesis of another's work, you can use it in good conscience—as long as you remember to put it in quotation marks and reveal to your readers where you got it. If you fasten onto a minor detail and quote a line that could be misunderstood if lifted away from the sentences that originally surrounded it, then you are guilty of misrepresentation.

Bogus claims, loaded terms, and misrepresentation are almost always to be found in that extreme form of persuasion known as *propaganda*. Strictly defined, propaganda means only the systematic use of words and images to propagate (or spread) ideas, but the abuse of propaganda within the past century has made the word widely associated with dishonesty. (For an extended definition of this term, see "The Purpose of Propaganda," by Adolf Hitler, pages 633–640.) Because the techniques of persuasion are easy to abuse, you should use them with great care. If you are trying to move an audience to action, you may find it useful to appeal to the heart as well as to the head, but you should try to avoid appealing to the heart alone. When appealing to the mind, it is always more honorable to address an audience as intelligent and thoughtful adults than to subtly exploit their subconscious hopes and fears.

An essay or speech that works primarily by inspiring an emotional response is most likely to succeed only when an audience can be called on for immediate action. If a senator can inspire colleagues moments before a critically important vote, or an evangelist can move a congregation to generosity just as the collection plate is about to be passed, then the results of such persuasion may be significant. But opportunities of this sort are rare for most writers. Almost everything we write can be put aside and reconsidered at another time. Irrespective of the ethical importance of arguing what is true and not just what is convenient, there is also a very practical reason for trying to argue logically: The arguments that carry the greatest weight are usually the arguments that are capable of holding up under analysis. They make *more* sense as we think about them, not less. Whereas persuasion relies on impulse, argument depends on conviction. Our impulses may determine what we do this afternoon, but our convictions shape the rest of our lives. If you make a genuinely logical argument, you may make some people angry with you, but you will not be accused of dishonesty. When you abandon logic for other persuasive techniques, make sure that you are simply making a change in writing strategy. Never write anything that you don't believe. This does not mean that there's anything wrong with writing fiction or satire. But it does mean that good writers shouldn't tell lies.

PART 2

WORKING WITH SOURCES

READING CRITICALLY

Although reading can be a pleasure, and many people find it relaxing to read material that provides a temporary escape from daily concerns, serious reading requires an active response on your part. When reading in college, or in whatever profession you are preparing for, you need to think about what you read. To make sure that you have mastered the content of what you have read, you must be able to identify key points—such as an author's thesis—and any points that you find difficult to understand. But beyond working to understand the material before you, you should also be prepared to *evaluate* it. As students, you will sometimes be confronted with more information than you can digest with ease. You will also find that different writers will tell you different things. When this happens, inexperienced readers sometimes become confused or discouraged. Being able to recognize what material deserves the closest reading, and what sources are the most reliable, is essential to coping successfully with the many academic demands made on your time. By reading critically, and reading often, you can acquire skills that will help you in almost any college course.

As you read the material collected in this book, you will find that some articles are easier to read than others. It would be a mistake to assume that the easiest material is necessarily the most reliable. On the other hand, it would also be wrong to assume that long, difficult articles are reliable simply because they are long and difficult. Whether you are preparing to write an argument of your own or simply trying to become better informed on an issue that has more than one side, you can benefit from practicing specific strategies for critical reading.

Previewing

Even before you begin to read, there are a few steps that you can take to help you benefit from the reading you are about to undertake. A quick preview, or survey, of a written text should give you an idea of how long it will take to read, what the reading will probably reveal, and how useful the reading is likely to be. When you glance through a newspaper, identifying stories that you want to read and others that you merely want to skim over, you are practicing a simple type of preview—one that is often guided primarily by your level of interest in various issues. But when previewing reading material in college, it is usually wise to ask yourself some questions that go beyond whether you happen to find a topic appealing.

How Long Is This Work?   By checking the length of a work before you begin to read, you can estimate how much reading time the material will demand, based on the speed and ease with which you normally read. The length may also be a clue in determining how useful a text may be. Although quantity is no sure guide to quality, a long work may contain more information than a short work. When reading an article in an anthology or in a magazine, you can quickly flip ahead to see where it ends. And when doing research (discussed in Part 3 of this book), you can usually learn the length of a work before you even hold it in your hand. This information is included in periodical indexes, book catalogs, and many Web sites. (See the illustrations on pages 100, 103, and 110.)

What Can I Learn from the Title?   Although some titles may be too general to communicate what you can expect when you read the works in question, a title often reveals an author's focus. An article called "Drugs and the Modern Athlete" will differ in focus from one called "Drug Testing and Corporate Responsibility." Moreover, a title can often indicate the author's point of view. Examples within this book include "In Defense of Hunting," "A Proposal to Abolish Grading," "A Case for Gay Marriage," "The Value of the Canon," and "The Purpose of Propaganda."

Do I Know Anything about the Author?   Recognizing the names of established authorities in your field becomes easier as you do more reading, but many written sources offer information that can help you estimate an author's credibility when that author is unfamiliar to you. A magazine article may identify the author at the beginning or the end of the piece, or on a separate page (often called "Notes on Contributors" and listed in the table of contents). A biographical sketch of the author can usually be found on a book jacket, and a list of his or her other published works may appear at either the front or the back of the book. Anthologies often include introductory headnotes describing the various writers whose work has been selected. In *The Informed Argument,* most headnotes indicate the authors' credentials for writing on the topic at hand. An author may have already published other works on the same subject. On the other hand, some authors choose to write about topics that are not directly related to their field of expertise. Suppose, for example, that you are about to read an argument on nuclear energy. By noting whether the article was written by a utility executive or an environmental activist, you can prepare yourself for the sort of argument you are most likely to encounter. If the article is written by a famous authority on child care, you might ask yourself whether that author will be a credible authority on nuclear power plants. Remember, however, that experts can make mistakes, and that important arguments can be written by someone new to the field. The best way to appraise any author's credibility is to read that person's work, noting how much evidence is provided to support the claims and how fairly the author seems to treat other people.

What Do I Know about the Publisher?   An important work can be published by an obscure publisher, and a small magazine may be the first to publish an author destined to win a Pulitzer prize. The reputation of a publisher is not an automatic guide to the reliability of a source, but there are a few factors that can help you determine whether a source is likely to be worthwhile. University presses tend to expect a high degree of scholarship, and academic journals usually publish articles only after they have been examined by two or three other experts in that field. When you read an article in a popular magazine, the nature of that magazine may suggest what it is likely to publish. For example, an article on hunting in *Field & Stream* is almost certain to be very different from one on hunting in *Vegetarian Times*. If you read widely in periodicals, you will eventually find that some magazines and newspapers consistently reflect political positions that might be characterized as either "liberal" or "conservative." When you make a discovery of this sort, you can often make a pretty good guess about what kind of stand will be taken on issues discussed in one of these periodicals. This guess can prepare you to note any bias within the articles. Once again, remember that you are only making a preliminary estimate when previewing. The best way to judge a work is to read it carefully.

Is There Anything Else I Can Discover by Skimming through the Material?
A quick examination of the text can identify a number of other features that can help you orient yourself to what you are about to read. Consider the length of the average paragraph; long paragraphs may indicate a densely written text that you will need to read slowly. Are there any special features, such as tables, figures, or illustrations that will give you visual aids? Are there any subtitles? If so, they may provide you with a rough outline of the work in question and indicate points where you may be able to take a break if necessary. Quickly reading the first sentence in every paragraph may also give you a sense of the work's outline. In some cases, a writer may actually provide you with a summary. Articles from scholarly journals are often preceded by an *abstract* (or summary) that can help you understand the article and estimate the extent to which it is likely to be of use to you.

(See the examples on pages 321–22 and 480.) Articles without abstracts may include a brief summary within the text itself; check the first few and last few paragraphs, the two locations where writers most often summarize their views. Finally, be sure to note whether the work includes a reference list. Scanning a bibliography—noting both how current the research seems and how extensive it is—can help you appraise a writer's scholarship and alert you to other sources that you may want to read on your own.

Annotating

Marking a text with notes, or *annotating* it, can be a great help when you are trying to understand your reading. Annotation can also help you to discover points that you might want to question when you evaluate this work. One of the advantages of owning a book—or having your own photocopy of an excerpt from a book or magazine—is that you can mark it as heavily as you wish without violating the rights of others. When you are annotating a text that is important to you, you will usually benefit from reading that text more than once and adding new annotations with each reading.

Equipped with a yellow felt-tipped pen, some students like to "highlight" the passages that seem most important to them. If this technique has worked well for you, there is no reason why you should feel compelled to abandon it. But it has two disadvantages. One is that highlighting cannot be erased. Some students find themselves with yellow-coated pages because they were initially unable to distinguish between main points and supporting details—and were later unable to remove unnecessary highlighting when they came to understand the text better. A second problem is that highlighting pens usually make broad marks ill-suited for writing. If you read with a pen like this in hand, you will need to reach for another pen or pencil whenever you want to add comments in the margin.

When reading, especially when reading a text for the first time, you might benefit from an alternative to highlighting. Try using a pen or pencil and simply marking in the margin a small check (✓) when a line seems important, an exclamation point (*!*) when you find surprising information or an unusually bold claim, and a question mark (*?*) when you have trouble understanding a particular passage or find yourself disagreeing with what it says. This simple form of annotation can be done very easily, and if you use a pencil, you will be able to erase any marks that you later find distracting.

When you are able to spend more time with a text, and want to be sure that you understand not only its content but also its strengths and weaknesses, then additional annotations are in order. Use the margins to define new words and identify unfamiliar allusions. Write comments that will remind you of what is discussed in various paragraphs. Jot down questions that you may subsequently raise in class or explore in a paper. By making cross references (like *cf.* ¶ *3* beside a later paragraph), you can remind yourself of how various components of the work fit together and also identify apparent contradictions within the work. Finally, whenever you are moved

1776 | When in the Course of human events, it becomes nec-

such as Americans

essary for one people to dissolve the political bands which have connected them with another, and to as-

such as English

Why should nations have "equal station" when some are more powerful than others?

sume among the powers of the earth, the separate and equal station to which the Laws of Nature and of Na-ture's God entitle them, a decent respect to the opin-ions of mankind requires that they should declare the causes which impel them to the separation.

Is "Nature's God" different from "God"?

We hold these truths to be self-evident, that all men are created equal, that they are endowed by their Creator with certain unalienable Rights, that among these are Life, Liberty and the pursuit of Happiness.

Why "self-evident"?

Couldn't he prove them?

Does this include women ???

That to secure these rights, Governments are insti-tuted among Men, deriving their just powers from the consent of the governed. That whenever any Form of Government becomes destructive of these ends it is the Right of the People to alter or to abolish it, and to institute new Government, laying its foundation on

Permanent, "not to be separated"

If the rights to life & liberty are "unalienable" how come we have capital punishment and prisons?

So the Civil War was ok?

such principles and organizing its powers in such form, as to them shall seem most likely to effect their Safety and Happiness. Prudence, indeed, will dictate that Governments long established should not be changed for light and transient causes; and accordingly all experience has shewn, that mankind are more dis-posed to suffer, while evils are sufferable, than to right themselves by abolishing the forms to which they are accustomed. But when a long train of abuses and

Wrongful seizure

usurpations, pursuing invariably the same Object evinces a design to reduce them under absolute Despotism, it is their right, it is their duty, to throw off such Government, and to provide new Guards for their future security. Such has been the patient suffer-ance of these Colonies; and such is now the necessity

What's the difference between a "right" and a "duty"?

which constrains them to alter their former Systems of Government. The history of the present King of Great Britain is a history of repeated injuries and usurpa-tions, all having in direct object the establishment of an absolute Tyranny over these States. To prove this,

George III (ruled from 1760 to 1820)

impartial let Facts be submitted to a candid world.

Why is the capitalization so weird?

FIGURE 1

to a strong response—whether you are agreeing or disagreeing with what you have read—write that thought down before you lose it. An annotation of this sort can be useful when you are reviewing material before an exam, and it may very well be the seed from which a paper will later grow.

To give you an example of annotation, on page 67 is an annotated excerpt from The Declaration of Independence. (The full text, unannotated, appears in Part 6, pages 601–604.) As you examine it, remember that readers annotate a text in different ways. Some annotations are more thorough and reflective than others, but there are no "correct" responses against which your own annotations must be measured. You may notice different aspects of a text each time you reread it, so your annotations are likely to accumulate in layers. Annotations have been reproduced here in both printing and script, to suggest how they accumulated during more than one reading.

Summarizing

Summarizing a work is one of the best ways to demonstrate that you have understood it. On many occasions, you will be required to summarize what others have said or written—or even what you yourself have said or written. This skill is especially important in argumentation. You will have to be able to summarize the main arguments of your opponents if you want to write a convincing argument of your own. And researched papers will become ridiculously long, obscure, and unwieldy if you lack the ability to summarize your reading.

There is no clear rule to determine what passages are more significant than others. Every piece of writing must be judged on its own merits, and this means that you must consider every paragraph individually. The first sentence of a paragraph may be important if it introduces a new idea. Unfortunately for writers of summaries (but fortunately for readers, who would be easily bored if every paragraph followed the same mechanical pattern), the first sentence may simply be a transitional sentence, linking the new paragraph with whatever has preceded it. The *topic sentence* (also called the *thesis sentence*) is the single most important sentence in most paragraphs—the exceptions are very short paragraphs that serve only as transitions. (Transitional paragraphs do not advance a new idea; they simply link together longer paragraphs devoted to ideas that are related, but not closely enough so that the paragraphs can flow smoothly together.) It is important to remember that the topic sentence can occur anywhere in a paragraph.

As you read the material you want to summarize, limit yourself to marking no more than one or two sentences per paragraph. You should identify the topic sentence, and you may want to mark a line that contains an important supporting detail. At this point, you may choose to copy all the material you have noted onto a separate sheet of paper. But do not think that this means you have completed a summary. What you have are the notes for a summary: a collection of short quotations that are unlikely to flow smoothly together. A good summary should always be easy to read. After you take your notes, you must shape them into a clear, concise piece of writing.

As a writer of summary, be prepared to *paraphrase*—to restate in your own words something you've read or heard. There are many different reasons for paraphrasing, and you've probably been practicing this skill since you were a child. We frequently paraphrase the words of others to soften unpleasant truths. Sometimes we may even be tempted to restate a relatively mild statement more harshly, to make trouble for someone we don't like. But in writing summary, we should paraphrase only to make complex ideas more easily understandable. A paraphrase can be as long as the original material; under some circumstances, it may even be longer. So don't confuse paraphrase with summary. Paraphrasing is simply one of the skills that we call on when we must write a coherent summary.

Reading over the quotations you have compiled, look for lines that seem longer than they have to be and ideas that seem unnecessarily complicated. Lines of this sort are likely subjects for paraphrase. As you restate these ideas more simply, you may also be able to include details that appeared elsewhere in the paragraph and seem too important to leave out. You should not have to restate everything that someone else has written, although there's nothing necessarily wrong in doing so. A summary can include direct quotation, so long as the quotations are relatively short and have a clarity that you yourself cannot surpass.

The next step is to reread your paraphrasing and any quotations that you have included. Look for gaps between sentences, where the writing seems awkward or choppy. Eliminate all repetition, and subordinate any ideas that do not need to stand alone as separate sentences. Rearrange any sentences that would flow better in a different sequence, and add transitional phrases wherever they can help smooth the way from one idea to the next. After you have made certain that your sentences follow in a clear and easily readable sequence and have corrected any errors in grammar, spelling, or syntax, you should have an adequate summary of the material you set out to cover. You would be wise to read over what you have written at least one more time, making sure that the content accurately reflects the nature of whatever is being summarized. Be absolutely sure that any direct quotations are placed within quotation marks.

Writing summary requires good editorial judgment. A writer of summary has to be able to distinguish what is essential from what is not. If the material being summarized has a particular bias, then a good summary should indicate that the bias is part of the work in question. *But writers should not interject their own opinions into a summary of someone else's work.* The tone of a summary should be neutral. You may choose to summarize someone's work so that you can criticize it later, but do not confuse summary with criticism. When summarizing, you are taking the role of helping other writers to speak for themselves. Don't let your own ideas get in the way.

Good summaries vary in length, depending on the length and complexity of the original material and on how much time or space is available for summarizing it. It's unusual, however, to need more than 500 words to summarize most material, and you may be required to summarize an entire book in less than half that length. When summary is being used as a preliminary to some other type of work—such as argument or analysis—it is especially important to be concise. For example, if you are summarizing an argument before offering a counterargument of your own, you may be limited to a single paragraph. The general rule to follow is: Try to do justice to whatever you are summarizing in as few words as possible, and make sure that you have a legitimate reason for writing any summary that goes on for more than a page or two.

Experienced writers know that summary is a skill worth practicing. If you find summary difficult, remind yourself that it combines two skills of fundamental and inescapable importance: reading and writing. Well-educated men and women must be proficient in both. Summarizing tests not only your ability to write simply and clearly, but also your ability to comprehend what you read. The selections in Parts 4 and 5 of this book will provide you with many opportunities for summarizing. For an example of summary see the essay by Sara Jenkins at the end of the section on gun control (pages 210–211).

Synthesizing

Synthesis is closely related to summary, and it demands many of the same skills. The principal difference is that while summary involves identifying the major points of a single work or passage, synthesis requires identifying related material in two or more works and tying them smoothly together. Synthesis is often an extension of summary because writers may need to summarize various sources before they can relate these sources to one another. Synthesis does not necessarily require you to cover *all* the major points of the individual sources. You may go through an entire article or book and identify only one point that relates to another work you have read. And the relationships involved in your synthesis may be of various kinds. For example, two different authors may have made the same claim, or one might provide specific information that supports a generalization made by the other. On the other hand, one author might provide information that makes another author's generalization seem inadequate or even wrong.

When reading material that you may need to synthesize, ask yourself: "How does this material relate to whatever else I have already read on this topic?" If you are unable to answer this question, consider a few more specific questions: Does the second of two works offer support for the first or does it reflect an entirely different thesis? If the two sources share a similar position, do they arrive at a similar conclusion by entirely different means or do they overlap at any points? Would it be easier to compare the two works or to contrast them? This process of identifying similarities and differences is essentially what synthesis is all about.

When you have determined the points that link your various sources to one another, you are ready to write a synthesis. To see how a synthesis can be organized, let us consider an example. Suppose you have read four articles on the subject of AIDS, written, respectively, by a scientist, a clergyman, a gay activist, and a government official. You were struck by how differently these four writers responded to the AIDS epidemic. Although they all agreed that AIDS is a serious problem, each writer advanced a different proposal for fighting the disease. Your synthesis would probably begin with an introductory paragraph that includes a clear thesis statement, for example: "Although there is widespread agreement that AIDS is a serious problem, there is no consensus about how this problem can be solved." Each of the next four paragraphs could then be devoted to a brief summary of one of the different points of view. A final paragraph might emphasize the relationship that exists among the several sources, either by reviewing the major points of disagreement among them or by emphasizing one or two points about which everyone agreed. Your outline for this type of synthesis would be:

PARAGRAPH ONE:	Introduction
PARAGRAPH TWO:	Summary of first writer (scientist)
PARAGRAPH THREE:	Summary of second writer (clergyman)
PARAGRAPH FOUR:	Summary of third writer (gay activist)
PARAGRAPH FIVE:	Summary of fourth writer (government official)
PARAGRAPH SIX:	Conclusion

Any good outline allows for some flexibility. Depending on the material and what you want to say, your synthesis might have fewer than or more than six paragraphs. For example, if two of your sources were especially long and complex, there is no reason why you couldn't devote two paragraphs to each of them, even though you were able to summarize your other two sources within single paragraphs.

An alternative method for organizing a synthesis involves linking two or more writers within paragraphs that focus on specific issues or points. This type of organization is especially useful when you have detected a number of similarities that you want to emphasize. Suppose that you have read six essays about abortion. Three writers favored legalized abortion, for much the same reasons; three writers opposing abortion offered arguments that they shared in common. Your assignment is to identify the arguments most used by people who favor legalized abortion and those most used by people who oppose it. Your outline for synthesizing this material might be organized like this:

PARAGRAPH ONE:	Introduction
PARAGRAPH TWO:	One argument in favor of abortion that was made by different writers
PARAGRAPH THREE:	A second argument in favor of abortion that was made by different writers

PARAGRAPH FOUR: One argument against abortion that was made by different writers

PARAGRAPH FIVE: A second argument against abortion that was made by different writers

PARAGRAPH SIX: Conclusion

Suppose, during the course of your reading, you identified several other arguments both for and against legalized abortion. You have decided not to include them within your synthesis, however, because each point came up only within a single work, and your assignment was to identify the most used arguments on this subject. If you feel uneasy about ignoring these additional points, you can easily remind your audience, in either your introduction or your conclusion, that other arguments exist and you are focusing only on those most frequently put forward.

For an example of a synthesis written by a student, see the essay by Jessica Cozzens, in Part 5, at the end of the section on sexual harassment (pages 357–360).

AVOIDING PLAGIARISM

To plagiarize (from *plagiarius,* the Latin word for "kidnapper") is to steal—to be guilty of what the Modern Language Association calls "intellectual theft." Plagiarism is also a form of cheating, an activity that sometimes prompts the cliché that "Cheaters are only cheating themselves." There is some truth to this idea; someone who plagiarizes a paper is losing out on an opportunity for learning, in addition to running a serious risk. The risks are considerable. In the workplace, intellectual theft (of an essay, a song, or a proposal) can lead to lawsuits and heavy financial penalties. In a college or university, students who commit intellectual theft face penalties ranging from a failing grade on a paper to expulsion from the school. They are not the only ones who are hurt, however. In addition to hurting themselves, plagiarists injure the people they steal from; the professors who take the time to read and respond to the work of writers who are not their own students; classmates, whose grades may suffer from comparison if a clever plagiarism goes undetected; and the social fabric of the academic community, which becomes torn when values such as honesty and mutual respect are no longer cherished.

The grossest form of plagiarism involves submitting someone else's paper as your own. Services that sell papers advertise on many college campuses, and obliging friends or roommates can sometimes be persuaded to hand over one of their own papers for resubmission. In cyberspace, the World Wide Web provides ample opportunities for downloading a paper written by someone else. Many schools have home pages that include model student essays, and if you look long enough you may well find something that seems likely to fulfill an assignment you don't want to write. The electronically sophisticated can also piece a paper together by lifting paragraphs from a number of sources on the Internet and typing in commands that will paste these blocks together. No one engages in such overt plagiarism accidentally. There is usually an explanation for this kind of cheating, but an explanation is not an excuse. If ever tempted to submit someone else's work as your own, be guided by this simple rule: *Don't do it.*

On the other hand, it is also possible to plagiarize without meaning to do so. Learning how to work with sources takes instruction, time, and practice. Some students come to college inadequately prepared; their high school teachers may not have noticed when the students' papers were more or less copied out of encyclopedias or other sources. If this happens often enough, the ill-prepared student might be genuinely confused about what it means to be an honest writer. Research on plagiarism also shows that different cultures have different understandings of who "owns" ideas. Students who come to American colleges from cultures in which language and ideas are considered common property might think they are doing only what is expected of them when they patch together the unattributed words of other people.

Whatever the reason, students sometimes plagiarize by drawing too heavily on their sources. They may forget to put quotation marks around lines that they have taken word for word from another source, or they may think they don't need to quote if they have changed a few words. Such students need to learn that it is important to give credit to the *ideas* of others, as well as to their *words*. If you take most of the information another writer has provided and repeat it in essentially the same pattern, you are only a half-step away from copying the material, even if you have changed the exact wording.

Here is an example:

Original Source

Hawthorne's political ordeal, the death of his mother—and whatever guilt he may have harbored on either score—afforded him an understanding of the secret psychological springs of guilt. *The Scarlet Letter* is the book of a changed man. Its deeper insights have nothing to do with orthodox morality or religion—or the universal or allegorical applications of a moral. The greatness of the book is related to its sometimes fitful characterizations of human nature and the author's almost uncanny intuitions: his realization of the bond between psychological malaise and physical illness, the nearly perfect, if sinister, outlining of the psychological techniques Chillingsworth deployed against his victim.

Plagiarism

Nathaniel Hawthorne understood the psychological sources of guilt. His experience in politics and the death of his mother brought him deep insights that don't have anything to do with formal religion or morality. The greatness of *The Scarlet Letter* comes from its characters and the author's brilliant intuitions: Hawthorne's perception of the link between psychological and physical illness and his almost perfect description of the way Roger Chillingsworth persecuted his victim.

This student has simplified the original material, changing some of its wording. But he is clearly guilty of plagiarism. Pretending to offer his own analysis of *The Scarlet Letter,* he owes all of his ideas to another writer who is unacknowledged. Even the organization of the passage has been followed. This "paraphrase" would still be considered a plagiarism even if it ended with a reference to the original source (p. 307 of *Nathaniel Hawthorne in His Times,* by James R. Mellow). A reference or footnote would not reveal the full extent to which this student is indebted to his source.

Here is an acceptable version:

Paraphrase

As James R. Mellow has argued in *Nathaniel Hawthorne in His Times, The Scarlet Letter* reveals a profound understanding of guilt. It is a great novel because of its insight into human nature—not because of some moral about adultery. The most interesting character is probably Roger Chillingsworth because of the way he was able to make Rev. Dimmesdale suffer (307).

This student has not only made a greater effort to paraphrase the original material, but he has also introduced it with a reference to the original writer. The introductory reference to Mellow, coupled with the subsequent page reference, "brackets" the passage—showing us that Mellow deserves the credit for the ideas in between the two references. Additional bibliographical information about this source is provided by the list of works cited at the end of the paper. Turning to the student's bibliography, we find:

Mellow, James. *Nathaniel Hawthorne in His Times.* Boston: Houghton, 1980.

One final caution: It is possible to subconsciously remember a piece of someone else's phrasing and inadvertently repeat it. You would be guilty of plagiarism if the words in question embody a critically important idea or reflect a distinctive style or turn of phrase. When you revise your draft, look for such unintended quotations; if you use them, show who deserves the credit for them, and *remember to put quoted material within quotation marks.*

For practice in paraphrasing and quoting, see the exercises in Part 4 (pages 127, 131, 136, 144, 157, and 171).

DOCUMENTING YOUR SOURCES

"Documenting your sources" means revealing the source of any information you report. You must provide documentation for:

- Any direct quotation.
- Any idea that has come from someone else's work.
- Any fact or statistic that is not widely known.

The traditional way to document a source is to footnote it. Strictly speaking, a "footnote" appears at the foot of the page, and an "endnote" appears at the end of the paper. But "footnote" has become a generic term covering both forms. Most writers prefer to keep their notes on a separate page because doing so is easier than providing space for them at the bottom of each page. The precise form of such notes varies, depending on the style manual being followed. Here is how a documentary footnote would look according to the style guidelines of the Modern Language Association (MLA):

A. *Bibliographic Form*

> Katz, Jonathan. <u>The Invention of Heterosexuality</u>. New York:
> Plume, 1996.

B. *Note Form*

> [1] Jonathan Katz, <u>The Invention of Heterosexuality</u> (New York: Plume, 1996) 37.

The indentation is reversed, the author's name is not inverted, and the publishing data are included within parentheses. Also, the author is separated from the title by a comma rather than a period. A subsequent reference to the same work would follow a shortened form:

> [5] Katz 183.

If more than one work by this same author is cited, then a shortened form of the title would also be included:

> [7] Katz, <u>Heterosexuality</u> 175.

Documentary footnotes require what most authorities now regard as unnecessary repetition, because the author's full name and the publishing data are already included in the bibliography. Many readers object to being obliged to turn frequently to another page if they want to check the notes. Some writers still use notes for documentation purposes. But most important style guides now urge writers to provide their documentation parenthetically within the work itself, reserving numbered notes for additional explanation or discussion that is important but cannot be included within the actual text without a loss of focus. Notes used for providing additional information are called *content notes*. The essays in Part 5 by Anita Hill (pages 301–316), Stephanie Riger (321–338), and Robert Goldman (410–444) include content notes.

The form of your documentation will vary, depending on the subject of your paper and the requirements of your instructor. Students in the humanities are usually asked to follow the form of the Modern Language Association (MLA) or the recommendations in *The Chicago Manual of Style*. Students in the social sciences are often expected to follow the format of the American Psychological Association (APA). Students in the natural sciences are usually required to use either a parenthetical system resembling that of the APA or a system that involves numbering their sources. Make sure that you understand the requirements of your instructor, and remember that you can consult a specific manual in your field if you run into problems. Here is a list of manuals that can be found in many college libraries:

American Chemical Society. *The ACS Style Guide: A Manual for Authors and Editors.* Washington: Amer. Chemical Soc., 1986.

American Institute of Physics. *AIP Style Manual.* 4th ed. New York: Amer. Inst. of Physics, 1990.

American Mathematical Society. *A Manual for Authors of Mathematical Papers.* Rev. ed. Providence: Amer. Mathematical Soc., 1990.

American Psychological Association. *Publication Manual of the American Psychological Association.* 4th ed. Washington: Amer. Psychological Assn., 1994.

The Chicago Manual of Style. 14th ed. Chicago: U of Chicago, 1993.

Council of Biology Editors. *Scientific Style and Format: The CBE Style Manual for Authors, Editors, and Publishers.* 6th ed. New York: Cambridge UP, 1994.

Gibaldi, Joseph. *MLA Handbook for Writers of Research Papers.* 4th ed. New York: Modern Language Assn., 1995.

Harvard Law Review Assn. *The Bluebook: A Uniform System of Citation.* 15th ed. Cambridge: Harvard Law Review Assn., 1991.

A detailed discussion of all of these styles is beyond the range of this chapter, but the following pages provide model entries for the most frequently used styles.

Parenthetical Documentation: The MLA Author/Work Style

Since 1984, the Modern Language Association has recommended that parenthetical documentation take the place of endnote or footnote citations. In MLA form, the author's name is followed by a page reference. It is not necessary to repeat within the parentheses information that is already provided within the text. If you are used to using footnotes for documentation, this format may seem a little strange at first, but it has the great merit of being easy to use and easy to understand. (Remember that additional information on these sources will be provided in a separate bibliography.)

A. A Work by a Single Author

> Henry James often identified wickedness with sexual duplicity (Kazin 227).

or

> Alfred Kazin has argued that Henry James identified wickedness with sexual duplicity (227).

There is no punctuation between the author's name and the page reference when both are cited parenthetically. Note also that the abbreviation "p." or "pp." is not used before the page reference.

B. A Work with More Than One Author

> Cleanth Brooks and Robert Penn Warren have argued that "indirection is an essential part of the method of poetry" (573).

or

> Although this sonnet may seem obscure, its meaning becomes clearer when we realize "indirection is an essential part of the method of poetry" (Brooks and Warren 573).

Note that when a sentence ends with a quotation, the parenthetical reference comes before the final punctuation mark. Note also that the ampersand (&) is not used in MLA style. When referring to a work by more than three authors, you should follow the guidelines for bibliographic entries and list only the first author's name followed by "et al." (Latin for *et alii*, "and others").

> These works "derive from a profound disillusionment with modern life" (Baym et al. 910).

C. A Work with a Corporate Author

When a corporate author has a long name, you should include it within the text rather than within parentheses. For example:

> The Council on Environmental Quality has reported that there is growing evidence of ground water contamination throughout the United States (81).

rather than

> There is growing evidence of ground water contamination throughout the United States (Council on Environmental Quality 81).

Although both of these forms are technically correct, the first is preferred because it is easier to read. Long parenthetical references intrude unnecessarily, interrupting the flow of ideas.

D. A Work with More Than One Volume

When you wish to cite a specific part of a multivolume work, include the volume number between the author and the page reference:

> As Jacques Barzun has argued, "The only hope of true culture is to make classifications broad and criticism particular" (2: 340).

Note that the volume number is given an arabic numeral, and a space separates the colon and the page reference. The abbreviation "vol." is not used unless you wish to cite the entire volume: (Barzun, vol. 2).

E. More Than One Work by the Same Author

If you cite more than one work by the same author, you need to make your references distinct. You can do so by putting a comma after the author's name and then adding a shortened form of the title: (Hardy, *Mayor* 179). But your paper will be easier to read if you include either the author or the title directly in the text:

> Twain's late work reflects a low opinion of human nature. But when Satan complains that all men are cowards (<u>Stranger</u> 184), he is only echoing Col. Sherburn's speech in <u>Huckleberry Finn</u> (123-24).

F. A Quotation within a Cited Work

If you want to use a quotation that you have discovered in another book, your reference must show that you acquired this material secondhand and that you have not consulted the original source. Use the abbreviation "qtd. in" (for "quoted in") to make the distinction between the author of the passage being quoted and the author of the work in which you found this passage:

> In 1835, Thomas Macaulay declared the British to be "the acknowledged leaders of the human race" (qtd. in Davis 231).

G. A Quotation of Poetry

Identify line numbers when you quote poetry, but do not use the abbreviations "l." or "ll." These abbreviations can easily be confused with numbers. Write "line" or "lines" in your first citation of poetry; subsequent citations should include only the line numbers. Quotations of three lines or less should be included directly into the text of your paper. Separate the lines with a slash (/), leaving space both before and after the slash:

> Yeats returned to this theme in "The Second Coming": "The best lack all conviction, while the worst / Are full of passionate intensity" (7-8).

Each line of longer quotations should begin on a new line, indented one inch (or ten spaces) from the margin.

Parenthetical Documentation: The APA Author/Year Style

The American Psychological Association (APA) requires that in-text documentation identify the author of the work being referred to and the year in which the work was published. This information should be provided parenthetically; it is not necessary to repeat any information that has already been provided directly in the sentence.

A. One Work by a Single Author

> It has been argued that fathers can play an important role in the treatment of eating disorders (Byrne, 1987).

or

> Byrne (1987) argued that fathers can play an important role in the treatment of eating disorders.

or

> In 1987, Katherine Byrne argued that fathers can play an important role in the treatment of eating disorders.

If the reference is to a specific chapter or page, that information should also be included. For example:

> (Byrne, 1987, p. 93)
> (Byrne, 1987, chap. 6)

Note that the abbreviations for page and chapter emphasize the distinction between the year of publication and the part of the work being referred to.

B. A Work with Two or More Authors

If a work has two authors, you should mention the names of both authors every time a reference is made to their work:

> A recent study of industry (Cole & Walker, 1997) argued that . . . .

or

> More recently, Cole and Walker (1997) have argued that . . . .

Note that the ampersand (&) is used only within parentheses.

Scientific papers often have multiple authors because of the amount of research involved. In the first reference to a work with three to five authors, you should identify each of the authors:

> Hodges, McKnew, Cytryn, Stern, and Kline (1982) have shown . . . .

Subsequent references to the same work should use an abbreviated form:

> This method was also used in an earlier study (Hodges et al., 1982).

If a work has six authors (or more), this abbreviated form should be used even for the first reference. If confusion is possible because you must refer to more than one work by the first author, list as many coauthors as necessary to distinguish between the two works.

C. A Work with a Corporate Author

When a work has a corporate author, your first reference should include the full name of the corporation, committee, agency, or institution involved. For example:

> (United States Fish and Wildlife Service [USFWS], 1997)

Subsequent references to the same source can be abbreviated:

> (USFWS, 1997)

D. A Reference to More Than One Work

When the same citation refers to two or more sources, the works should be listed alphabetically according to the first author's name and separated with semicolons:

> (Pepler & Rubin, 1982; Schlesinger, 1996; Young, 1994)

If you are referring to more than one work by the same author(s), list the works in the order in which they were published.

> The validity of this type of testing is now well established (Collins, 1988, 1994).

If you refer to more than one work by the same author published in the same year, distinguish individual works by identifying them as "a," "b," "c," etc.:

> These findings have been questioned by Scheiber (1997a, 1997b).

Organizing a Bibliography

Documenting your sources parenthetically or with notes allows you to reveal exactly which parts of your paper are supported by or owed to the works you have consulted. A bibliography, which is a list of the sources consulted, is also essential so that readers can evaluate your research and possibly draw on your sources for work of their own.

Works Cited in MLA Style

In an MLA-style bibliography, the works cited are arranged in alphabetical order determined by the author's last name. MLA style requires that the author's first name be given. Every important word in the titles of books, articles, and journals is capitalized. The titles of books, journals, and newspapers are all underlined (italicized). The titles of articles, stories, and poems appear within quotation marks. Second and subsequent lines are indented one-half inch (or leave five spaces blank). Here are some examples:

A. A Book with One Author

Mukherjee, Bharati. The Holder of the World. New York: Knopf, 1993.

Although it is important to give the author's full name, the book's full title, and the place of publication, you should use a shortened form of the publisher's name (Alfred A. Knopf, in this case).

B. A Book with Two or Three Authors

Gilbert, Sandra M., and Susan Gubar. The Madwoman in the Attic: The Woman Writer and the Nineteenth-Century Literary Imagination. New Haven: Yale UP, 1979.

Note that the subtitle is included, set off from the main title by a colon. The second author's name is not inverted, and abbreviations are used for "University Press" to provide a shortened form of the publisher's name. For books with three authors, put commas after the names of the first two authors; separate the second two authors with a comma followed by "and."

C. An Edited Book

Baldick, Chris, ed. Oxford Book of Gothic Tales New York: Oxford UP, 1992.

D. A Book with More Than Three Authors or Editors

Black, Laurel, et al., eds. New Directions in Portfolio Assessment: Practice, Critical Theory, and Large-Scale Scoring. Portsmouth: Boynton, 1994.

Give the name of the first author or editor only, and add the abbreviation "et al."

E. Edition after the First

Champion, Larry S. The Essential Shakespeare: An Annotated Bibliography of Major Modern Studies. 2nd ed. New York: Hall, 1993.

F. A Work in an Anthology

O'Brien, Patricia. "Michael Foucault's History of Culture." The New Cultural History. Ed. Lynn Hunt. Berkeley: U of California P, 1989. 25-46.

Note that a period comes after the title of the selection but before the second quotation marks. A period is also used to separate the date of publication from the pages between which the selection can be found. No abbreviation is used before the page reference.

G. A Translated Book

Eco, Umberto. The Aesthetics of Thomas Aquinas. Trans. Hugh Bredin. Cambridge: Harvard UP, 1988.

H. A Work in More Than One Volume

Leckie, Robert. The Wars of America. 2 vols. New York: Harper, 1992.

I. An Introduction, Preface, Foreword, or Afterword

Dove, Rita. Foreword. Jonah's Gourd Vine. By Zora Neale Hurston. New York: Harper, 1990. vii-xv.

J. An Article in an Encyclopedia

Hunt, Roberta M. "Child Welfare." The Encyclopedia Americana. 1993 ed.

For citing material from well-known encyclopedias, give the author's name first, then the article title. If material is arranged alphabetically within the source, which is usually the case, there is no need to include volume and page numbers. You should give the full title of the encyclopedia, the edition if it is stated, and the year of publication (e.g., 11th ed. 1996). When no edition number is stated, identify the edition by the year of publication (e.g., 1996 ed.). If the author of the article is identified only by initials, look elsewhere within the encyclopedia for a list identifying the names these initials stand for. If the article is unsigned, give the title first. (Note: This same form can be used for other reference books, such as dictionaries and the various editions of *Who's Who*.) For an example of how to cite an electronic encyclopedia, see T below.

K. A Government Publication

United States. Federal Bureau of Investigation. Handbook of Forensic Science. Washington: GPO, 1994.

For many government publications, the author is unknown. When this is the case, the agency that issued the publication should be listed as the author. State the name of the government (e.g., "United States," "Florida," "United Nations") followed by a period. Then give the name of the agency that issued the work, using abbreviations only if you can do so clearly (e.g., "Bureau of the Census," "National Institute on Drug Abuse," "Dept. of Labor") followed by a period. The underlined title of the work comes next, followed by another period. Then give the place of publication, publisher, and date. Most federal publications are printed in Washington by the Government Printing Office (GPO), but you should be alert for exceptions. (Note: Treat pamphlets just as you would a book.)

L. A Journal Article with One Author

Swann, Karen. "The Sublime and the Vulgar." <u>College English</u> 52 (1990): 7-20.

The volume number comes after the journal title without any intervening punctuation. The year of publication is included within parentheses after the volume number. A colon separates the year of publication and the page reference. Leave one space after the volume number and one space after the colon.

M. A Journal Article Paginated Anew in Each Issue

Williams, Jeffrey. "The Life of the Mind and the Academic Situation." <u>College Literature</u> 23.3 (1996): 128-146.

In this case, the issue number is included immediately after the volume number, and the two are separated by a period without any intervening space.

N. An Article from a Magazine Published Monthly

Renfrew, Colin. "World Linguistic Diversity." <u>Scientific American</u> Jan. 1994: 116-123.

Instead of citing the volume number, give the month and year of the issue. Abbreviate the month when it has more than four letters. (May, June, and July are spelled out.) For an example of how to cite an article from a magazine published monthly which was obtained through a computer database, see **R**.

O. An Article from a Magazine Issued Weekly

Wilkinson, Alec. "The Confession." <u>New Yorker</u> 4 Oct. 1993: 162-171.

The form is the same as for an article in a magazine that is issued monthly, but you add the day immediately before the month. Note that a hyphen between page numbers indicates consecutive pages. When an article is printed on nonconsecutive pages—beginning on page 34, for example, and continuing on page 78—give only the first page number and a plus sign: 34+.

P. An Article from a Daily Newspaper

Reich, Howard. "Limited Ambition." <u>Chicago Tribune</u> 9 Feb. 1997, final ed., sec. 7: 13.

If more than one edition is available on the date in question, specify the edition immediately after the date. If the city of publication is not part of the newspaper's name, identify the city in brackets after the newspaper title. Because newspapers often consist of separate sections, you should cite the section number if each section has separate pagination. If a newspaper consists of only one section, or if the pagination is continuous from one section to the next, then you do not need to include the section number. If separately paginated sections are identified by letters, omit the section reference (sec.) but include the letter of the section with the page number (e.g., 7B or D19). If the article is unsigned, begin the citation with the title of the article; alphabetize the article under its title, passing over small words like "a" and "the." For an example of how to cite a newspaper article accessed through a computer service, see V.

Q. An Editorial

> Wicker, Tom. "The Key to Unity." Editorial. <u>New York Times</u> 30 Jan. 1991, natl. ed.: A15.

Editorials are identified as such between the title of the article and the title of the newspaper or magazine.

R. Printed Material Accessed from a Periodically Published Database

> Holtzman, Henry. "Team Management: Its Time Has Come . . . Again." <u>Managing Office Technology</u> Feb. 1994: 8. <u>ABI/Inform</u>. CD-ROM. UMI Proquest. Oct. 1994.

Include the same information you would provide for a magazine or journal article: author (if known), article title, journal title, date of print publication, and page reference. Then cite the database you used, the medium through which you accessed it (e.g., a CD-ROM, a diskette) and the vendor that made this medium available. Conclude with the date of electronic publication.

S. Nonprinted Material Accessed from a Periodically Published Database

> African Development Bank. "1995 AFDB Indicative Learning Program." 19 Sept. 1995. <u>National Trade Data Bank</u>. CD-ROM. U.S. Commercial Service. Mar. 1996.

Give the author's name (a corporate author in this case), the title of the material in quotation marks, the date it was prepared (if given), the title of the database, publication medium, vendor, and the date it was published electronically. Underline the title of the database.

T. A Non-Periodical Publication on CD-ROM

> Hogan, Robert. "Abbey Theater." <u>The Academic American Encyclopedia (1995 Grolier Multimedia Encyclopedia)</u>. CD-ROM. Danbury: Grolier, 1995.

If no author is identified, begin with the work's title; if no author or title is available, begin with the title of the product consulted.

U. A Publication on Diskette

> Gradecki, Joe. <u>The Virtual Reality Construction Kit</u>. Diskette. New York: Wiley, 1994.

Follow the same pattern you would for a book, but add a medium description after the work's title.

V. A Printed Publication Accessed through a Computer Service

> Rothstein, Richard. "Labor Market, Not Schools, Will Aid Latino Education Woes." <u>Los Angeles Times</u>. 21 July 1996, home ed.: m2. <u>Times Mirror</u>. On-line. Nexis. 10 Oct. 1996.

Follow the same pattern you would for the print equivalent (in this case, a newspaper article), then add the underlined title of the database, the publication medium, the name of the computer service, and the date you accessed it.

W. Material from an Electronic Journal or Newsletter Obtained through a Computer Network

> Brent, Doug and Joe Amato. "The Brent–Amato Exchange." <u>EJournal</u>. 1.2-1 (Oct. 1991): n. pag. Online. Internet. 31 Oct. 1994. Available FTP: http://rachel.albany.edu/~ejournal/v/n2-1.html.

Add the electronic address for your source at the end of the entry if required to do so by your instructor or if you think this information would be useful for readers.

X. An Electronic Text Obtained through a Computer Network

> Shakespeare, William. <u>A MidSummer Night's Dream</u>. <u>Annotated Hypertext Edition</u>. Ed. J.B. Siedlecki. Online. Internet. 31 Oct. 1996. Available FTP: http://quarles.unbc.edu/midsummer/info.html.

If the text has been edited, include the editor's name immediately after the title of the text.

Y. An Interview

> Nelson, Veronica. Personal interview. 16 Aug. 1997.

If you interview someone, alphabetize the interview under the name of the person interviewed.

References in APA Style

In APA style, the reference list is arranged alphabetically, the order being determined by the author's last name. The date of publication is emphasized by placing it within parentheses immediately after the author's name.

Authors submitting articles for publication are expected to indent the first line of each reference five spaces (leave five spaces blank). Additional lines are placed flush with the left margin in this case. However, the APA *Publication Manual* (4th ed.) distinguishes between papers submitted for publication and papers submitted for a college course. When papers are submitted for a college course, APA recommends a hanging indent style (similar to MLA indention), which is what is shown in the following illustrations. Ask your instructor which format is preferred at your school.

A. Book with One Author

> Sullivan, A. (1995). <u>Virtually normal</u>. New York: Knopf.

Note that the author's first name is indicated only by an initial. Capital letters are used only for the first word of the title and the first word of the subtitle if there is one. (But when a proper name appears within a title, it retains the capitalization it would normally receive, for example: *A history of ideas in Brazil.*) The name of the publisher, Alfred A. Knopf, is given in shortened form. A period comes after the parentheses surrounding the date of publication, and also after the title and the publisher.

B. Book with Two or More Authors

> Youcha, C., & Seixas, J. (1989). <u>Drugs, alcohol, and your children: How to keep your family substance-free</u>. New York: Crown.

An ampersand is used to separate the names of two authors. When there are three or more authors, separate their names with commas and put an ampersand immediately before the last author's name.

C. Edited Book

> Preston, J. (Ed.). (1992). <u>A member of the family: Gay men write about their families</u>. New York: Dutton.

The abbreviation for editor is "Ed."; it should be included within parentheses between the name of the editor and the date of publication. The abbreviation for editors is "Eds." Give the names of all editors, no matter how many there are.

D. Article or Chapter in an Edited Book

> Howard, A. (1992). Work and family crossroads spanning careers. In S. Zedeck (Ed.), <u>Work, families, and organizations</u> (pp. 70-137). San Francisco: Jossey.

Do not invert the editor's name when it is not in the author's position. Do not put the title of the article or chapter in quotation marks. Use a comma to separate the editor from the title of the edited book. The pages between which the material can be found appear within parentheses immediately after the book title. Use "p." for page and "pp." for pages.

E. Translated Book

> Calasso, R. (1993). <u>The marriage of Cadmus and Harmony</u> (T. Parks, Trans.). New York: Random. (Original work published 1988)

Within parentheses immediately after the book title, give the translator's name followed by a comma and the abbreviation "Trans." If the original work was published earlier, include this information at the end.

F. Revised Edition of a Book

> Hopkins, B. R. (1993). <u>A legal guide to starting and managing a nonprofit organization</u> (2nd ed.). New York: Wiley.

The edition is identified immediately after the title. Note that edition is abbreviated "ed." and should not be confused with "Ed." for editor.

G. Book with a Corporate Author

> American Red Cross. (1993). <u>Standard first aid</u>. St. Louis: Mosby.

H. Multivolume Work

> Jones, E. (1953-57). <u>The life and work of Sigmund Freud</u> (Vol. 2). New York: Basic.

The volume number is included within parentheses immediately after the title. When a multivolume book is published over a number of years, list the years between which it was published.

I. Journal Article with One Author

> Butler, A. C. (1996). The effect of welfare benefit levels on poverty among single-parent families. <u>Social Problems, 43,</u> 94-115.

Do not use quotation marks around the article title. Capitalize all important words in the journal title and underline. Put a comma after the journal title and then give the volume and page numbers. Abbreviations are not used for "volume" and "page." To distinguish between the numbers, underline the volume number and put a comma between it and the page numbers.

J. Journal Article with More than One Author

> Nugent, J. K., Lester, B. M., Greene, S. M., Wieczorek-Deering, D., & O'Mahoney, P. (1996). The effects of maternal alcohol consumption and cigarette smoking during pregnancy on acoustic cry analysis. <u>Child Development, 67,</u> 1806-1815.

K. Journal Article Paginated Anew in Each Issue

> Major, B. (1993). Gender, entitlement, and the distribution of family labor. Journal of Social Issues, 49(3), 141-159.

When each issue of a journal begins with page 1, you need to include the issue number in parentheses immediately after the underlined volume number.

L. Article from a Magazine Issued Monthly

> Baker, K. (1997, February). Searching the window of nature's soul. Smithsonian, pp. 94-104.

Within parentheses immediately after the author, include the month of issue after the year of publication. Use "p." or "pp." in front of the page number(s). Do not include the volume number. Follow the same form for an article in a weekly magazine issued on a specific day, but add the day after the month:

> Hazen, R. M. (1991, February 25). Why my kids hate science. Newsweek, p. 7.

M. Article from a Newspaper

> Bishop, J. E. (1996, November 13). Heart disease may actually be rising. Wall Street Journal, p. B6.

Place the exact date of issue within parentheses immediately after the author. After the newspaper title, specify the page number(s).

N. Government Document

> National Institute of Alcohol Abuse and Alcoholism. (1980). Facts about alcohol and alcoholism (DHHS Publication No. ADM 80-31). Washington, DC: U.S. Government Printing Office.

List the agency that produced the document as the author if no author is identified. Within parentheses immediately after the document title, give the publication number (assigned to the document by the government); it can usually be found on or near the title page and should not be confused with the call number that a library may have assigned to the document.

O. Anonymous Work

> A breath of fresh air. (1991, April 29). Time, p. 49.

Alphabetize the work under the first important word in the title, and follow the form for the type of publication in question (in this case, a magazine published weekly). Use a short version of the title, in quotation marks, for the parenthetical citation in the text: ("Breath," 1991).

P. An Online Journal Article

> Fletcher, G. J. (1996, November). Assessing error in social judgment: Commenting on Koehler on base rate [9 paragraphs]. Psychology [online], 5 (10). Available E-mail: psyc212@csc.canterbury.ac.nz or http://cogsci.ecs .soten.ac.uk/cgi-bin/newpsy?5.10

Include the publication medium within brackets immediately after the journal title. A bracketed description of the article's length is optional. Because a period at the end of the citation could be mistaken as part of the electronic address, the APA recommends omitting the final period.

Q. An Online Abstract

> Dickenson, A. H. (1996, November 12). Plasticity: Implications for opioid and other pharmacological interventions in specific pain states. BBS Special Issue: Controversies in Neuroscience v: Persistent Pain: Neuronal Mechanics and Clinical Implications. [On-line]. Available FTP: http://www.cogsci .soton.ac.uk/bbs/archive/bbs.neur5.dickenson.html

In article titles, capitalize only the first letter of the first word in the title (and subtitle when there is one) and any word that would be capitalized when not part of a title. In journal titles, however, capitalize all key words.

R. An Abstract on CD-ROM

> Gowan, M. E., & Zimmerman, R. A. (1996). Impact of ethnicity, gender, and previous experience on juror judgments in sexual harassment cases. [CD-ROM]. Journal of Applied Social Psychology, 26, Abstract from: SilverPlatter File: PsychLIT Item: 83-29094

Include the item number at the end of the entry.

Numbered Systems

In a numbered system, the bibliography may be arranged in alphabetical order (determined by the authors' last names) or in the order in which the works are cited within the paper itself. Once this sequence is established, the items are assigned numbers in consecutive order beginning with 1, and these numbers are used as citations within the paper. There are many variations on the particular form of the bibliographical entries; authors of scientific papers should adopt the style recommended by the journal for which they are writing. But here are examples of two frequently used forms:

A. Biology

1. Avila, V L. Biology: A Human Endeavor. Chula Vista; Bookmark, 1992. 899 p.
2. Batistatou, A, Green, L. 1993. Internucleosomal DNA cleavage and neurona; cell survival death. The Journal of Cell Biology. 22: 523-532.

Note that neither book nor journal titles are underlined. Quotation marks are not used for article titles. The names of multiple authors are separated with a comma rather than an ampersand. The year of publication appears in different positions, depending upon the nature of the work.

B. Chemistry

(1) Rea, W. J. <u>Chemical Sensitivity</u>; Lewis: New York, 1992.
(2) Cargill, R. W. <u>Chem. Soc. Rev.</u> **1993**, 22, pp. 135-141.

Note that book publishers' names appear before the city of publication. Journal titles are abbreviated, and article titles are not included. Boldface the year of publication for journal articles. Lines after the first are not indented.

Although the precise form of the bibliography will vary from discipline to discipline, certain features remain constant when a numbered system is used:

- Whenever the same source is cited, the same number is cited.
- Numbers appear on the same line as the text, and they are usually either underlined or italicized to distinguish them from other numbers in the text.

With these two points in mind, you should not confuse a numbered system of references with the use of numbered footnotes. When footnotes are used, numbers appear in consecutive order and each number is used only once. When a numbered system of references is used, the same number appears whenever the source assigned that number is cited within the text, and the numbers will not necessarily be consecutive.

C. A Numbered Reference

There are approximately 125,000 children at risk of developing Huntington's disease (4).

or

There are approximately 125,000 children at risk of developing Huntington's disease.[4]

or

There are approximately 125,000 children at risk of developing Huntington's disease (<u>4</u>, p. 22).

For an example of a numbered system in use, consult an issue of *Science,* a journal that can be found in most libraries, or see the paper by Amy Karlen in Part 5 (pages 576–579).

A CHECKLIST FOR DOCUMENTATION

Whether you document your sources by using footnotes or one of the recommended systems for parenthetical references, you should honor the following principles:

1. Remember to document any direct quotation, any idea that has come from someone else's work, and any fact or statistic that is not widely known.
2. Be sure to enclose all quotations in quotation marks.
3. Make sure that paraphrases are in your own words but still accurately reflect the content of the original material.
4. Remember that every source cited in a reference should have a corresponding entry in the bibliography.
5. Be consistent. Don't shift from the author/year system to the author/work system in the middle of your paper.
6. Try to vary the introductions you use for quotations and paraphrases, and make sure that the material in question has been incorporated smoothly into your text. Read your first draft aloud to be better able to judge its readability.
7. When you mention authorities by name, try to identify who they are so that your audience can evaluate the source. (For example, "According to Ira Glasser, Executive Director of the American Civil Liberties Union, recent congressional legislation violates. . . . ") Do not insult the intelligence of your audience by identifying well-known figures.
8. If in doubt about whether to document a source, you would probably be wise to go ahead and document it. But be careful not to overdocument your paper. A paper that is composed of one reference after another usually lacks synthesis and interpretation.

PART 3

A GUIDE TO RESEARCH

Writing effective arguments requires being able to locate and draw on information that will help you develop and support your ideas. When a topic involves an issue with which you have personal experience, you might need only to search your own mind for the information you need to write persuasively. But writers often discover that they must look beyond themselves to gather the necessary information—they must engage in *research*.

If you associate research with long papers due at the end of a semester, you may be losing sight of the many other occasions when you search for information. Any time you seek to gather information before making a decision, you are practicing a kind of research. If, for example, you are trying to decide whether to buy a particular car, you might interview people who already own the same model, read magazine articles about the car, and take a showroom vehicle out for a test drive to experience its performance. In other words, you interview people with expertise on your topic, you conduct a periodical search, and you undertake trial testing. Academic research requires all of these activities—and more—although the degree to which you need to pursue a specific research activity is likely to vary as you move from one project to another. Academic research also requires that you honor specific conventions by using sources responsibly and documenting where your information comes from. (See pages 74–90.) Nevertheless, the prospect of doing research shouldn't be frightening. Most people do research to some extent throughout their lives—and not just for long, formal papers. The key to successful research is simple: Be prepared to look in different places until you find what you need.

Scholars traditionally distinguish between primary and secondary research. *Primary research* requires firsthand experimentation or analysis. This is the sort of research done in scientific laboratories and in archives that house original manuscripts. If you interview someone, design and distribute a survey, conduct experiments, or analyze data that have not been previously published, you are also conducting primary research. Some of the "Suggestions for Writing" that appear later in this book invite you to undertake this kind of work.

You will also have many occasions for practicing *secondary research,* which means investigating what other people have already published on a given subject. College students are usually expected to be proficient at secondary research. To do this activity efficiently, you must know how to develop a search strategy. Different projects will require different strategies. The strategy outlined in this part of the book assumes that you will be writing arguments using material from *The Informed Argument* and will supplement this material with additional data. As your research needs change from one assignment to another, you will probably use different indexes and online services. But the illustrations from the following search will provide you with sufficient information to proceed efficiently when you decide to move beyond the articles gathered in Parts 4–6 of this book.

GETTING STARTED

One of the first goals of any researcher is to decide where to focus. The more specific your search, the greater your chance for efficiently locating the material you need and then writing a well-supported paper. When you know what you are looking for, you can gauge what you need to read and what you can probably afford to pass over—a great advantage when confronted by the staggering amount of information that a good college library, or the Internet, makes available to researchers.

Do not think that you must have a clear focus before you begin your search, however. An excellent topic might emerge if you scan how information on your subject area has been classified by professional catalogers. Periodical indexes (pages 95–103) usually divide large subjects into specific components, online databases allow you to combine different terms, and search engines for navigating the Internet will alert you to diverse topics within your subject area. By using key words and checking different sources, you can discover what topics have generated the most recent interest. You can judge, at this point, which topics would be the easiest to research and which would be the most manageable. If you are overwhelmed by the number of citations in your research area, you probably need to narrow your topic. On the other hand, if you have difficulty finding material, you may need to broaden your search.

Another way to get started is to discuss your subject with other people. Talking over the possibilities with your instructor may help you to discover a topic that suits both your own interests and the requirements for the paper in question. Conversation with students and friends may be fruitful as well. A class discussion devoted to one of the arguments in this book may leave you intrigued by a topic that you had not previously considered. Electronic discussion groups, which can be accessed through the Internet, provide a further opportunity for exploring issues with other people. Talking, like writing, is a way of learning. When you have the chance, don't hesitate to bounce ideas around with people you trust. (For additional information on choosing a topic, see pages 2–4 and the writing assignments that appear at the end of each section in Part 5.)

AVOIDING SELECTIVE RESEARCH

Although you may have a tentative thesis in mind when you begin your search, do not formulate your final thesis until your research is complete. Your search strategy should be designed to answer a question that you have posed to yourself, such as: "What can be done to reduce drug-related crime?" This is very different from starting your research with your thesis predetermined. A student who is convinced that the way to reduce drug-related crime is to legalize drugs may be tempted to take notes only from sources that advocate this position—rejecting as irrelevant any source that discusses problems with this approach. Research, in this case, is not leading to greater knowledge or understanding. On the contrary, it is being used to reinforce personal beliefs that may border on prejudice.

We have seen that "anticipating the opposition" (pages 5–6, 16–21) is important even in short arguments. It is no less important in a researched paper. Almost any topic worth investigating will yield facts and ideas that could support different conclusions. The readings assembled in this book demonstrate that it is possible to take significantly different positions on gun control, immigration law, and same-gender marriage—among other issues. As you may have already observed, some of the most opinionated people are also the most ignorant. Well-educated people, because they have been exposed to different points of view during their education, are usually aware that most problems are complex. Good students remember this when they are doing research. They allow their reading to influence their thought; they do not let their thoughts restrict their reading. Your own research may ultimately support a belief that you already hold, but it could just as easily lead you to realize that you were misinformed. When taking notes, remember the question that you have posed for yourself. Do not waste time recording information that is not relevant to that particular question. But you should not overlook material that directly concerns your question just because you don't agree with what the material says. If you have a good reason to reject the conclusion of someone else's work, your paper will be stronger if you recognize that this disagreement exists and then demonstrate why you favor one position over another—or show how different positions can be reconciled.

SEARCHING FOR MAGAZINE AND JOURNAL ARTICLES

Magazines, bulletins, and scholarly journals are all called *periodicals* because they are published on a regular schedule—once a week or once a month, in the case of a magazine, or four times a year, in the case of a scholarly journal. Although researchers can seldom afford to rely exclusively on periodicals for information, the indexes and abstracting services that enable them to locate relevant periodical articles are essential in most searches. Periodicals often include the most current information about a research area, and they can alert you to other important sources through book reviews as well as through the citations that support individual articles.

The best known of these indexes is the *Readers' Guide to Periodical Literature,* which is now available online through OLLC *FirstSearch* (a service which provides access to over 40 electronic indexes, all searches using the same commands), in addition to being published in the green volumes that have been familiar to library users for several decades. The *Readers' Guide* covers over 250 magazines; material is indexed by subject and by author. Because it indexes popular mass-circulation periodicals, it will lead you to articles that are relatively short and accessible. *InfoTrac,* another computerized index for periodicals in general circulation, offers a similar advantage.

Most college libraries have a variety of other indexes that will point you toward more substantial material, and you should be prepared to move beyond the *Readers' Guide* in any serious search. Almost every academic field has its own index available in regularly printed volumes, and most electronic versions of these indexes are now including *abstracts* (short summaries of the articles indexed). Among the specialized indexes most often used are the following:

Applied Science and Technology Index	*Index to Legal Periodicals*
Art Index	*Index Medicus* (for medicine)
Biological and Agricultural Index	*Music Index*
Business Periodicals Index	*Philosopher's Index*
Education Index	*Science Citation Index*
Humanities Index	*Social Sciences Index*

Anyone doing research in literature should also be familiar with the *MLA International Bibliography* (for books and articles written about English, American, and foreign-language literature) and the *Essay and General Literature Index* (for essays and articles that have appeared in books rather than in journals).

If you have difficulty finding material, or if you are in difficulty because you have found too much, you can broaden or narrow an online search by using *Boolean operators*—words that instruct a database to narrow a search or to broaden it. Suppose that you are researching the relationship between drug use and violent crime. Searching for *drugs* alone would gather an unwieldy amount of material, including articles on new prescriptions for arthritis and other information that is irrelevant to your topic. If you enter *drugs and crime* as your subject, you will be alerted only to articles that mention both drugs and crime. This is still a big subject, so if you are conducting a search along these lines, you could enter additional search terms, such as *gender*, which would narrow the search to articles discussing the role of gender in drug use and crime. Adding *women*, or *youth*, on the other hand, would identify articles mentioning both drugs and crime and either women or youth. By playing with terms this way, and discovering how much material is available on any given combination, you can find a specific topic for a researched paper within a larger subject area.

The advantage of consulting the *Readers' Guide* online is readily apparent from the accompanying illustrations. After instructing the computer to search for the subject (su) *drugs and crime*, the person conducting this online search in 1996 discovered 674 articles, compared to one article on the subject in the printed volume for May 1996. (See Figures 1 and 2.) To discover additional articles through printed volumes would require consulting other volumes and following up on a range of cross-references (see Figure 3). A computer can do that task within seconds.

A disadvantage of using the *Readers' Guide* is also readily apparent: Few college professors are likely to be impressed by the credibility of research drawn from *People, Time,* or *U.S. News & World Report.* If you have access to the *Readers' Guide* through *FirstSearch*, you should also have access to *Periodical Abstracts*, which covers approximately 1,500 journals, giving you access to the kind of material you would locate through the *Readers' Guide* as well as much more scholarly work.

```
+ * * * * * * * * * * * * * List of Records * * * * * * * * * * * * * * * +
DATABASE: ReadGuideAbs                    LIMITED TO:
SEARCH: su·drugs and crime FOUND 674 Records
   NO.___SOURCE_____TITLE_____YEAR
    1     People Wkly      Death on the border.                    1996
    2     Time             What Dole must say.                     1996
    3     U S News World R Popgun politics.                        1996
    4     N Y Times (Late  Drugs, guns and just don't do it.       1996
    5     N Y Times (Late  Drugs, guns and vigilante justice in So 1996
    6     Public Interest  Legalization madness.                   1996
    7     N Y Times (Late  Dole campaign says it has hardly begun  1996
    8     N Y Times (Late  Campaigning on portents of doom and boo 1996

HINTS: More records type . . . F.    View a record . . type record number.
       Decrease number of records . . . . type L (to limit) or A (to 'and').
       Do a new search . . . . . . . . . . . . . . . . type S or SEARCH.

ACTIONS: Help  Search  And  Limit  Print  Email  Database  Forward

RECORD NUMBER (or Action):
```

FIGURE 1
Citations from *Readers' Guide Abstracts,* an online service covering the years 1983–1996 in this case

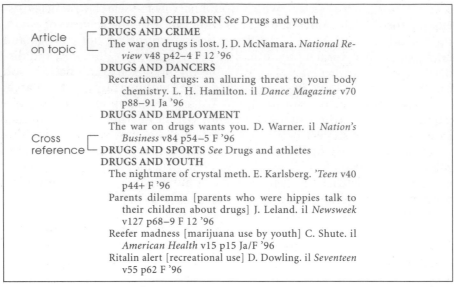

FIGURE 2
Excerpt from a bound volume of *Readers' Guide*

FIGURE 3
Cross-reference from a bound volume of *Readers' Guide*

Although there is some overlapping from one index to another, each index covers different periodicals. The records you find in one will usually vary from the records you find in another. This is worth remembering, for two reasons:

1. You should not get easily discouraged when searching for periodical literature. If you cannot locate any material in the past few

years of one index, try another index that sounds as if it might include records on your subject.

2. Many subjects of general interest will be found in more than one index. If you consult more than one index, you are increasing the likelihood of being exposed to different points of view.

Of the various specialized indexes that can lead you exclusively to material in professional journals, the *Social Sciences Index* is especially useful for locating information on drug use and crime, for it indexes literature in sociology, psychology, and political science. Like the *Readers' Guide,* it can be consulted in bound volumes or online, with the online service providing abstracts as well as citations. Figure 4 reproduces the content of a screen providing instructions for using *Social Science Abstracts* on OLLC *FirstSearch.* Figure 5 shows the first eight citations located when searching for articles on the relationship between drug use and crime. Figure 6 shows a sample abstract from this search. Note that a scholarly publication like the *Journal of Criminal Law and Criminology* would not be indexed by the *Readers' Guide* and that a journal like this is likely to provide more credible data than an issue of *People.* Note also that the journal article identified in Figure 6 is twenty-six pages long, a length unlikely to be possible in a general-circulation magazine.

Figure 7 shows an early screen for OLLC *FirstSearch,* the online service used to discover the material from the *Social Science Abstracts* cited on page 100. Access to the *Social Science Abstracts* was obtained by entering number 13 from this screen. Access to the *Readers' Guide* was obtained by entering number 7. If you continued to research through this online service, you would find additional material on drugs and crime by selecting "News &

```
* * * * * * * * * * * * * * * * * Search * * * * * * * * * * * * * * * * * * *
DATABASE: SocSciAbs

  ┌─SEARCH────────DESCRIPTION──────────────────────────────EXAMPLES──────────┐
  │ Subject       Type the label SU: and a word(s).        su:fashion        │
  │               (Subjects, abstracts and titles)         su:decision making│
  │ Author        Type the label AU: and the author        au:huether        │
  │               name or any part of the name.            au:milton yinger  │
  │ Title         Type the label TI: and the title         ti:psychology     │
  │               or any word(s) in the title.             ti:academic freedom│
  └──────────────────────────────────────────────────────────────────────────┘

HINTS:   Other ways to search . . . . . . type H <database name> LABELS.
         Include plural (s and es) or possessive . . . type + at end of word.
         Return to List of Records screen . . . . . . just press Enter.

ACTIONS: Help  Limit  Database  Wordlist  Reset

SEARCH WORD(S) (or Action): su:drugs and crime
```

FIGURE 4

Instructions for using *Social Science Abstracts*

```
+ * * * * * * * * * * * * * List of Records * * * * * * * * * * * * * * * * +
DATABASE: SocSciAbs                      LIMITED TO:
SEARCH: su:drugs and crime FOUND 200 Records
_____NO.___SOURCE_____TITLE_____YEAR
       1    Br J Criminol    In search of the high life: drugs, crim  1996
       2    Far East Econ Re Dying for attention: lacking parents' c  1996
       3    Br J Criminol    Young adult offenders, alcohol and crim  1996
       4    Economist        Innocence lost.                          1996
       5    J Crim Justice   Recidivism among boot camp graduates: a  1996
       6    J Res Crime Deli Gender, power, and alternative living a   1996
       7    Acta Sociol      Drugs, crime, and other deviant adaptat  1995
       8    Crime Deling     Drug policy and community context: the   1996

HINTS: More records type . . . F.    View a record . . type record number.
       Decrease number of records . . . . type L (to limit) or A (to 'and').
       Do a new search . . . . . . . . . . . . . . type S or SEARCH.

ACTIONS: Help  Search  And  Limit  Print  Email  Database  Forward

RECORD NUMBER (or Action):
```

FIGURE 5

The first of two hundred records discovered when searching *Social Science Abstracts*

```
* * * * * * * * * * * * * * * Full Record Display * * * * * * * * * * * * * *
DATABASE: SocSciAbs                      LIMITED TO:
SEARCH: su:drugs and crime

 Record 15 of 200___ YOUR LIBRARY (MNT) MAY OWN THIS ITEM___( PAGE 1 OF 3)

       AUTHOR: Blumstein, Alfred.
        TITLE: Youth violence, guns, and the illicit-drug industry.
       SOURCE: The Journal of Criminal Law & Criminology v. 86 (Fall '95)
               p. 10-36
     ABSTRACTS: Part of a special issue on firearms and violence in the U.S.
               The writer investigates several empirical aspects of
               changing crime patterns in recent years and identifies the
               nature of these changing patterns. Three major changes
               between 1985 and 1992 are that homicide rates by youths aged
               18 and under, the number of homicides committed by juveniles
               with guns, and the drug arrest rates of nonwhite juveniles
               have all more than doubled. The growth in youth homicide is
               attributed to the recruitment of youths into illicit drug
               markets. The illegal nature of these markets means that
               young people are likely to carry arms for self-protection.
               This initiates an escalating process: the more arms in the
               community, the greater the incentive for people to arm
               themselves.
   STANDARD NO: 0091-4169
          DATE: 1995

HINTS:   Another page . type F or B.    Another record . type record number.
         See which libraries may own this item . . . . . . . . type LIB.
         Return to Record List . . . . . . . . . . . . . just press Enter.

ACTIONS: Help  Search  Print  Email  Order  LIBraries  Forward  Back

RECORD NUMBER (or Action):
```

FIGURE 6

Sample abstract from *Social Science Abstracts*

```
* * * * * * * * * * * * * Topic Area Selection * * * * * * * * * * * * * * *

____NO.____TOPIC AREA_____NO.____TOPIC AREA_____
    1     Arts & Humanities        ·  8    General Science
    2     Business & Economics        9    Life Sciences
    3     Conferences & Proceedings   10   Medicine & Health
    4     Consumer Affairs & People   11   News & Current Events
    5     Education                   12   Public Affairs & Law
    6     Engineering & Technology    13   Social Sciences
    7     General & Reference         14   All Databases

HINTS:   Select a topic area . . . . . . . . . . . type topic area number.
         Get help . . . . . . . . . . . . . . . . . . . . . . . type H.
         Get News . . . . . . . . . . . . . . . . . . . . type H NEWS.
         See hours of operation . . . . . . . . . . . . . . type H HOURS.

ACTIONS: Help  Database  Reset

AREA NUMBER (or Action):
```

FIGURE 7
An introductory screen for *FirstSearch*

Current Events" or "Public Affairs & Law." You might also discover material through "Business & Economics" (both crime and drug abuse affect the economy) and "Conferences & Proceedings" (law enforcement officers, attorneys, and scholars are likely to give presentations on drugs and crime).

SEARCHING FOR NEWSPAPER ARTICLES

You can access many newspaper articles by using the "News & Current Events" option provided by *FirstSearch* (see Figure 7). As shown in Figure 1, the *Readers' Guide* will also lead you to some newspaper articles. For a serious electronic search of newspaper articles on a research topic involving a public policy issue, use Lexis-Nexis, a powerful database that searches for news articles and legal documents worldwide—often locating material only a day or two after its publication—and may provide wire service dispatches that have not yet made their way into the papers. Figure 8 shows one of the first screens that comes up in a search using Lexis-Nexis. You can narrow or expand your search by limiting yourself to the last two years or going back further, focusing on a particular region, or choosing to search a particular kind of text such as newsletters or newspapers. By entering MAJPAP (for major papers), and then "drugs crime and youth," the person conducting this search discovered thirty-three stories. ("Drugs and crime" alone yielded over 1,000 stories, which required narrowing the search further by focusing on "youth" in addition to "drugs and crime.") You can choose whether to view citations only, citations with summaries, and—when you find something that seems especially promising—full text, which you might then be able to print out, depending on the nature of the service your library provides. Figure 9 shows the first five citations identified during this 1996

```
MAJPAP

Please ENTER, separated by commas, the NAMES of the files you want to
search. You may select as many files as you want, including files that do
not appear below, but you must enter them all at one time. To see a
description of a file, ENTER its page (PG) number.
          FILES - PAGE 1 of 89 (NEXT PAGE for additional files)

NAME    PG DESCRIP          NAME    PG DESCRIP        NAME    PG DESCRIP

                    T H E   N E W S   L I B R A R Y
--Full-Text Group Files--  --Full-Text By Type--   --Full Text by Region--
CURNWS  1 Last 2 years      MAGS    3 Magazines          --Papers & Wires--
ARCNWS  1 Beyond 2 years    MAJPAP  3 Major Papers  NON-US 1 English Non-US
ALLNWS  1 All News Files    NWLTRS  3 Newsletters   US     1 US News
                            PAPERS  3 Newspapers         --US Sources--
                            SCRIPT  3 Transcripts   MWEST  3 Midwest
--Group File Exclusions--   WIRES   3 Wires         NEAST  3 Northeast
ALLABS  4 All Abstracts     -----Hot Files-----     SEAST  3 Southeast
NONENG  1 Non-English News  HOTTOP  2 Hot Topics*   WEST   3 West
TXTNWS  1 Textline News*    OJCIV   2 OJ Civil*        ------Assists------
TODAY   1 Today's News*                             GUIDE  2 Descriptions*
                                                    LNTHS  2 L-N Index Ths*
Files marked * may not be combined.
```

FIGURE 8
An introductory screen for Lexis-Nexis. Reprinted with the permission of
LEXIS-NEXIS, a division of Reed Elsevier Inc. LEXIS and NEXIS are registered
trademarks of Reed Elsevier Properties Inc.

```
                    LEVEL 1 - 33 STORIES

1.   Los Angeles Times, November 3, 1996, Sunday, Ventura County Edition,
Page 1 1477 words, CITIES SEEK TO STEM TIDE OF TEEN CRIME, DRUG ABUSE;
GOVERNMENT: LOCAL EFFORTS TO DEVELOP YOUTH MASTER PLANS ARE AIMED AT
REDUCING THE GROWING VIOLENCE AMONG CHILDREN OF BABY BOOMERS., MACK REED,
TIMES STAFF WRITER

2.   The Jerusalem Post, October 3, 1996, Thursday, NEWS; Pg. 3, 534
words, Drug crimes on rise among youth, Itim

3.   The Tampa Tribune, July 3, 1996, Wednesday, FLORIDA EDITION, Pg. 2,
194 words, Camp focuses on drugs and youth crime, A Tribune staff report,
FORT MEADE

4.   The Baltimore Sun, April 10, 1996, Wednesday, HOWARD EDITION, Pg. 3B,
741 words, 'Posse' created as detour on youths' road of life; Church
outreach program hopes to steer children away from drugs, crime, Alisa
Samuels, SUN STAFF

5.   Los Angeles Times, February 7, 1996, Wednesday, Home Edition, Part A;
Page 8; National Desk, 858 words, PARENTS AT CENTER OF TALE OF HORRIFIC
CHILD ABUSE; CRIME: THEY ARE IN CHICAGO JAIL, ACCUSED OF MOLESTATION,
INJECTING CHILDREN WITH DRUGS AND FEEDING THEM RATS. CHARGES BASED ON
YOUTHS' ACCOUNTS., By JUDY PASTERNAK, TIMES STAFF WRITER, CHICAGO
```

FIGURE 9
Citations from Lexis/Nexis. Reprinted with the permission of LEXIS-NEXIS, a
division of Reed Elsevier Inc. LEXIS and NEXIS are registered trademarks of
Reed Elsevier Properties Inc.

```
                    LEVEL 1 - 1 OF 33 STORIES

                 Copyright 1996 Times Mirror Company
                        Los Angeles Times

           November 3, 1996, Sunday, Ventura County Edition

  SECTION: Metro; Part B; Page 1; No Desk

  LENGTH: 1477 words

  HEADLINE: CITIES SEEK TO STEM TIDE OF TEEN CRIME, DRUG ABUSE;
  GOVERNMENT: LOCAL EFFORTS TO DEVELOP YOUTH MASTER PLANS ARE AIMED AT
  REDUCING THE GROWING VIOLENCE AMONG CHILDREN OF BABY BOOMERS.

  BYLINE: MACK REED, TIMES STAFF WRITER

   BODY:

     Born during a brainstorm two years ago, a method for combating the rise
  of violence and drug use among teens is growing ever more popular with
  governments in Ventura County: the youth master plan.

     Such plans are meant to knit together schools, police, businesses,
  social service agencies and families in a safety net so tight that only
```

FIGURE 10
The beginning of a full text article found online

search; Figure 10 reproduces the beginning of the full text of one of the citations retrieved online. (Note: Not all libraries have access to Lexis-Nexis, while some which do charge for this service.)

Your college or community library may also provide you with the equipment to search online for articles in a local paper. If you are unable to search for newspapers online, look for printed volumes of the *New York Times Index,* which has been published annually since 1913 and is updated frequently throughout the current year.

USING ABSTRACTING SERVICES

Although many electronic indexing services such as *Readers' Guide Abstracts* and *Social Science Abstracts* are now offering summaries of current articles along with the citations a search identifies, they do not consistently provide abstracts for all of the material they index. There are other services that specialize in abstracts. Important abstracting services in printed volumes include:

Abstracts in Anthropology	*Historical Abstracts*
Academic Abstracts	*Physics Abstracts*
Biological Abstracts	*Psychological Abstracts*
Chemical Abstracts	*Sociological Abstracts*

These abstracts are organized in different ways, and you may need to consult one volume for the index and another volume for the matching abstracts. When using bound volumes, consult the instructions that can be found within them. Nowadays, however, there is no reason to consult printed volumes of abstracts unless you do not have access to electronic databases. Almost all college libraries provide access to at least a few electronic databases. Hundreds of databases are published, however, with new ones becoming available almost daily. Ask your reference librarian if there are electronic resources in your library that are appropriate to your research.

Although it does not cover precisely the same sources as *Psychological Abstracts*, the *PsycLIT* database provides much easier access to comparable scholarship in the field. Figure 11 shows an abstract located by searching *PsycLIT* for material on "drugs and crime." Other databases provide a similar service for research in other disciplines.

Abstracts offer a great advantage over bibliographical citations, because it can be hard to tell from a title whether an article will be useful. The summary provided by an abstracting service can help you to decide whether you want to read the entire article. A good rule to follow with abstracts is that if you can't understand the summary, you probably won't understand the article. Another point to remember is that many abstracting services are international in their coverage. Just because an article summary is written in English does not mean that this is the language of the article itself; be alert for notations such as *(Chin), (Germ),* or *(Span),* which indicate when an article is published in another language. Finally, remember that good researchers never pretend to have read an entire article when they have read only an abstract of it. Use abstracts as a tool for locating material to read, not as a substitute for a full-length reading.

USING THE INTERNET

First developed by the U.S. military, the Internet is an electronic "network of networks" linking millions of computers through telecommunication lines. This network allows the quick exchange of information between connected computers on a worldwide scale. The kind of information that can be found on the Internet is very diverse, but includes library catalogs, government documents and data, and material published by commercial organizations, special interest groups, and even individuals who wish to make contact with others who share their concerns.

In the 1990s, the most common way to search the vast amount of information on the Internet is to use the World Wide Web, a graphical interface that makes it possible to navigate the Internet by "pointing and clicking." If you are new to the Internet, check to see whether your library or academic computing office provides introductory workshops. Your college or community bookstore may also carry one of several guides to using the Internet that have been published in recent years.

```
SilverPlatter 3.11      PsycLIT Journal Articles 1/90-12/96
No.    Records    Request
1:      12413     DRUGS
2:       1918     CRIME
3:        112     DRUGS and CRIME
4:      12413     DRUGS
5:       1918     CRIME
6:         30     (DRUGS and CRIME) in TI
                                                              1 of 1
                                              Marked in Search: #6
TI  DOCUMENT TITLE: Sweeping out drugs and crime: Residents' views of the
Chicago Housing Authority's Public Housing Drug Elimination Program.
AU  AUTHOR(S): Popkin,-Susan-J.; Olson,-Lynn-M.; Lurigio,-Arthur-J.;
Gwiasda,-Victoria-E.; et-al
IN  INSTITUTIONAL AFFILIATION OF FIRST AUTHOR: Abt Assoc, Bethesda, MD, US
JN  JOURNAL NAME: Crime-and-Delinquency; 1995 Jan Vol 41(1) 73-99
IS  ISSN: 00111287
LA  LANGUAGE: English
PY  PUBLICATION YEAR: 1995
AB  ABSTRACT: Surveyed residents' perceptions of the effects of the
Chicago Housing Authority's Public Housing Drug Elimination Program
(PHDEP) on drugs and crime in 2 housing developments chosen for their
preexisting differences in crime rates and population stability. 262
residents (aged 16 yrs or older) were surveyed, and 39 residents were
interviewed. Overall, respondents in the better organized development
reported more favorable perceptions of PHDEP's impact. (PsycLIT Database
Copyright 1995 American Psychological Assn, all rights reserved)
KP  KEY PHRASE: Chicago Housing Authority Public Housing Drug Elimination
Program; drugs & crime; 16 yr old & older residents of housing
developments
DE  DESCRIPTORS: CRIME-PREVENTION; HOUSING-; DRUGS-; ADOLESCENCE-;
ADULTHOOD-
CC  CLASSIFICATION CODE(S): 4270; 42
PO  POPULATION: Human
AG  COMPOSITE AGE GROUP: Adolescent; Adult
UD  UPDATE CODE: 9507
AN  PSYC ABS. VOL. AND ABS. NO.: 82-27532
JC  JOURNAL CODE: 1194
```

FIGURE 11

A sample abstract obtained through PsycLIT after narrowing a search to articles that mention both drugs and crime in their titles

Because the Internet provides access to apparently unlimited information, some users have discovered that the same technology that makes searching so efficient, in one sense, can make it time-consuming in another. You may find yourself scrolling through an endless series of documents and losing sight of your main objective while pursuing an elusive loose end.

You must also be aware of a key difference between material published on the Internet and material published in print. Writers who publish in print receive professional editorial support. Editors decide what material is worth printing and then assist writers when preparing work for publication. The Internet operates without editors, however. Anyone with a little knowledge of

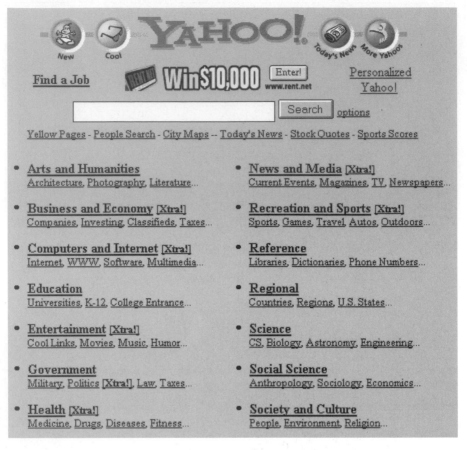

FIGURE 12
An introductory screen for searching the World Wide Web (Text and art-
work copyright 1996 by YAHOO!, INC. All rights reserved. YAHOO! and the
YAHOO! logo are trademarks of YAHOO!, INC.)

computers can publish whatever comes to mind. In a sense, the Internet is
wonderfully democratic, and many people have enjoyed activities such as
creating a Web site for their cat and connecting with other cat fanciers. On
the other hand, the Internet also carries hate speech, crank editorials, and
hard-core pornography. (See pages 361–448 for information on recent attempts to regulate the Internet.) When searching the Internet, you must
carefully evaluate the material you locate—and recognize that this material
can range from first-rate scholarship to utter trash.

Still, the Internet is a wonderful resource for anyone prepared to navigate it. The challenge is how to find your way through the huge amount of
material floating around you in cyberspace. Computer experts have developed systems called *search engines* that work as indexing services for the
World Wide Web. Those most commonly used today are *Yahoo!, Alta Vista,*

New drug plan targets youth, crime

President to outline policy goals

April 29, 1996
Web posted at: 10:45 a.m. EDT

President Clinton arrived Monday in Coral Gables, Florida, where, in a speech at a high school, he is expected to outline a new five-part national drug control strategy.

Sources say the speech, aimed at restoring the Clinton administration's leadership in the war on drugs, will emphasize boosting drug education and reducing illegal drug use among young people. The growing use of methamphetamines is to get special attention.

Clinton left for Miami Monday morning

Other goals will include cutting drug-related crime; increasing funds for treatment of drug abusers and other steps to cut the health and welfare costs of drugs; tightening up on the flow of drugs on land, at sea and in the air; and cutting off the source of drugs, both internally and internationally.

"Our challenge right now is young people and crime," retired Gen. Barry McCaffrey, White House drug policy chief, said Sunday on NBC's "Meet the Press." "Those are the two places where it seems to me we've got to get moving."

McCaffrey, who assumed his post several weeks ago amid charges that the administration's drug policy was a failure, said that while the number of Americans using illegal drugs dropped from 22 million people 15 years ago to 11 million today, and that cocaine use is down 30 percent in the past three years, there has been a sharp rise this decade in young people smoking marijuana.

McCaffrey said the administration will continue to support drug courts, which give first-time abusers a right to stay in school or jobs and get treatment rather than serve a prison sentence. Drug courts, he said, cost $1,000 per person rather than the $15,000 it costs to keep a drug abuser locked up for a year.

McCaffrey

FIGURE 13
A CNN web page discovered through YAHOO! (Text and artwork copyright 1996 by YAHOO!, INC. All rights reserved. YAHOO! and the YAHOO! logo are trademarks of YAHOO!, INC.)

Infoseek, and *Lycos*. Once you learn how to use one of these systems, you can easily learn how to adapt to the others. No search engine provides a complete, error-free index to electronic documents, so serious research often demands using more than one system—just as you would use more than one periodical index when looking for information.

Search engines require you to identify your research topic by typing key words into an entry box, as you would when conducting a periodical search or searching a library catalog by subject area. After you have entered your search terms, you will be given a list of Web sites that match your request. Each of these sites can, in turn, lead you to others—the kind of help you also experience when you consult the bibliography of a book or periodical article. The principal difference in searching on the Internet is the speed with which you can move from one site to another. Do not expect instant access to anything you want to view, however. Long documents, and documents from heavily visited sites, can sometimes take several minutes to download.

Like other electronic resources, search engines provide help screens with instructions on the best ways to search. These instructions change as the technology changes, and it is wise to review them whenever you are in doubt about how to proceed. Figure 12 shows the introductory screen for *Yahoo!,* one of the most widely used search engines in the 1990s. Figure 13 shows a Web page located when using *Yahoo!* to search for information on the relationship between drug use and crime.

Remember that the Internet is constantly changing. In 1996, it was estimated that a new Web page was appearing every 15 seconds. New search systems are being developed almost monthly. Because the Internet accesses so much information, some researchers make the mistake of thinking anything they need to find must be available electronically. When you retrieve documents from the Internet, do so with caution. Because you are visiting a world without editors, the documents you retrieve may include errors. And because not every scholar chooses to make completed work available electronically, you can miss important material if you try to do all your research on the Internet.

LOOKING FOR BOOKS

Now that computers make it possible to consult indexes outside of libraries, print out the full text of periodical articles, and spend hours at a time exploring the World Wide Web, it can be tempting to avoid looking for *books* on a subject. Books remain essential to scholarship, however. Although the books you locate in your library may vary in quality, books often represent the final and most prestigious result of someone else's research. It is common, for example, for a scholar to publish several journal articles in the process of writing a book. Much of the best information you can find appears somewhere in a book, and you should never assume that your research subject is so new, or so specialized, that your library will not have books on it. A topic that seems new to you may not necessarily be new to others.

Unlike many other resources, books can accompany you wherever you go. They don't need to be plugged in, and they can be read as easily in bed as at a desk. But no matter how informative or enjoyable books may be, they still take time to read. With this in mind, some researchers look for books at the beginning of their search. Others turn to books after they have investigated the periodical literature to focus their interests and identify the most influential works in their field. Whenever you choose to look for books on your topic, be sure that you do so well before your paper is due. A book full of important information will be of little help if you haven't left yourself time to read it.

Using the Main Catalog

Although some libraries still use catalogs consisting of alphabetically arranged cards in multiple drawers, most college libraries now provide computer access to their collection of books. If you have a computer with a modem, you might be able to search your library's collection from the convenience of your own home or office. By using a computer terminal in the library, however, you can easily get help if you run into difficulties. In an age when many people feel overwhelmed by the mass of information that is available on most subjects, professional librarians can often come to the rescue.

Computerized catalogs enable users to search for books by author, title, or subject. Most of these catalogs also permit a search for material via a call number or a "key word"—a word likely to appear somewhere in the title or description. In addition to providing all of the information about a book that could be obtained from a card catalog, computerized catalogs are usually designed to report whether the book is currently available. Computerized catalogs help make research efficient by providing instant access to information that might otherwise be recorded in the different drawers of a card catalog. If you have access to a computerized catalog but are unfamiliar with how to use it, you should be able to find user information posted near the computers. The program will provide instructions on the screen once you begin.

If you are limited to a card catalog, do not be discouraged. Until fairly recently, card catalogs were the standard means through which scholars did their research. But you should be prepared to look in more than one place. Card catalogs usually include two or three cards for every book the library owns. This allows you to locate books in a variety of ways, depending on how much you know. You may be looking for books by a particular author, so find your library's *author cards*. You may know the title of a book but not who wrote it, so find your library's *title cards*. These two kinds of card are often filed in the same set of drawers and called an *author/title catalog*. In addition, you may be able to look for books on your subject through a separate *subject catalog*. When you are unable to find material under the heading you have consulted, you should explore alternative headings. Books on the Civil War, for example, might be listed under "War Between the States." You might find a cross-reference directing you to the appropriate heading, or you may need to draw on your own ingenuity. If you are sure that the library must have books on your subject and you are simply unable to find the correct subject heading, ask a librarian for help.

Figures 14 and 15 show how a catalog card compares to an entry on a computer screen. The two entries are very similar despite some minor differences in format. As you do research, you should expect to find variations on these examples. Author cards, title cards, and subject cards will each have slightly different headings so that they can be filed in different places. And the precise format of a computerized entry depends on the program employed by the library you are using.

There is no foolproof method for determining the quality or usefulness of a book from a catalog entry. The best way to judge a book is always to read it. But a catalog listing can reveal some useful clues if you know how

```
03 DEC 96   UNIVERSITY OF ST. THOMAS—O'SHAUGHNESSY-FREY LIBRARY    12:57 pm
                           Public Access Catalog
Call Number  ST. THOMAS                                Status: checked In
             HV5825 .C88 1993
     AUTHOR  Currie, Elliott.
      TITLE  Reckoning : drugs, the cities, and the American future / Elliott
             Currie.
    EDITION  1st ed.
  PUBLISHER  New York : Hill and Wang, 1993.
    DESCRIPT  vi, 405 p. ; 24 cm.
      NOTES  Includes bibliographical references and index.

                                         ----More on Next Screen----
  Press <Enter> to see next screen :
SO=Start Over, B=Back, RW=Related Works, R=Request, C=Copy status
SB=Save Bib, <Enter>=Next Screen, SBLIST=Saved Bib List
ALT-F10  HELP | VT-100 | FDX | 9600 N81 | LOG CLOSED | PRT OFF | CR | CR
```

FIGURE 14
An entry from a computer catalog

to find them. Consider, for example, the date of publication. There is no reason to assume that new books are always better than old books, but unless you are researching a historical or literary topic, you should be careful not to rely heavily on material that may be out of date. Consider also the length of the book. A book with 300 pages is likely to provide more information than a book half that size. A book with a bibliography may help you to find more material. Finally, you might also consider the reputation of the publisher. Any conclusion that you draw at this point should be tentative. But some books are better than others, and it is your responsibility as a

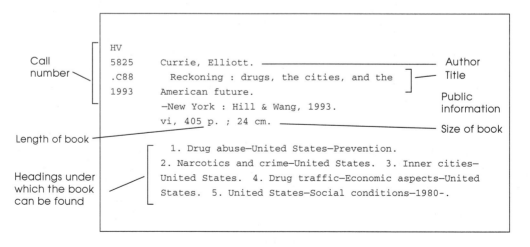

FIGURE 15
An author card from a card catalog

researcher to evaluate the material that you use. (For additional information on evaluating sources, see pages 64–66.) If you are fortunate enough to find several books on your subject, select the books that seem the best.

Understanding Classification Systems

Most American libraries use one of two systems for classifying the books in their collections: the Dewey Decimal system or the Library of Congress system. If you understand these systems, you can save valuable time in the library by knowing where to look for material when you are already working in the stacks.

The Dewey Decimal system classifies books numerically:

000–099	General Works
100–199	Philosophy
200–299	Religion
300–399	Social Sciences
400–499	Language
500–599	Natural Sciences
600–699	Technology
700–799	Fine Arts
800–899	Literature
900–999	History and Geography

These major divisions are subdivided into units of ten to identify specializations within each general field. For example, within the 800–899 category for literature, American literature is found between 810 and 819, English literature between 820 and 829, German literature between 830 and 839—and so forth. Specific numbers narrow these areas further: 811 represents American poetry, for example, and 812 is for American drama. Additional numbers after a decimal point enable catalogers to classify books more precisely: 812.54 would indicate an American play written since 1945. To distinguish individual books from others that are similar, an additional number is usually placed beneath the Dewey number.

Most libraries that use the Dewey Decimal system combine it with one of three systems for providing what is called an "author mark." These systems (referred to as Cutter two-figure, Cutter three-figure, and Cutter-Sanborn) all work according to the same principle. Librarians consult a reference table that provides a numerical representation for the first four to six letters of every conceivable last name. The first letter of the author's last name is placed immediately before this number, and the first letter of the first significant word in the title is placed after the number. Here is a complete call number for *Cat on a Hot Tin Roof,* by the American playwright Tennessee Williams:

812.54
W675c

Although the Dewey Decimal system remains the most widely used system for the classification of books in American libraries, many university libraries prefer to use the Library of Congress system, which uses selected letters of the alphabet to distinguish twenty-one major categories as opposed to the Dewey Decimal system's ten:

A   General Works
B   Philosophy, Psychology, and Religion
C   General History
D   Foreign History
E-F   American History (North and South)
G   Geography and Anthropology
H   Social Sciences
J   Political Science
K   Law
L   Education
M   Music
N   Fine Arts
P   Language and Literature
Q   Science
R   Medicine
S   Agriculture
T   Technology
U   Military Science
V   Naval Science
Z   Bibliography and Library Science

USING OTHER LIBRARY RESOURCES

Because of the great amount of material being published, most libraries are now using devices that allow for material to be stored in less space than would be required by its original form. When looking for books or articles, you may need to use some type of *microform:* printed material that has been reduced in size through microphotography. Libraries that use microform provide users with special devices that magnify the material in question—whether it is available on microfilm or microfiche—a flat sheet of microfilm.

Even when space is not an issue, most libraries can afford to purchase only a fraction of the material that is published each year. Although a good college library should give you all the sources you need for most papers, you may occasionally find it necessary to look beyond the library where you normally do your research. If you live in or near a city, several other libraries may be available. If this is not the case, remember that most libraries also provide an interlibrary loan service, which will allow you to request a book or journal article that your own library does not possess. When a library offers interlibrary loan, you will be asked to provide bibliographical information about the material you are requesting. Librarians will then do the work of locating and securing a copy of the book or article for you. You should ask for material only if you are reasonably certain that it would be useful for you, and that an equivalent resource is not already available in your own library. You should also recognize that obtaining a source through interlibrary loan can take two weeks or longer, so it will be of no use if you defer your research until a few days before your paper is due.

CONDUCTING INTERVIEWS AND SURVEYS

For some topics, you may want to conduct original research through interviews or surveys.

Although *interviews* are usually inappropriate for papers in the natural sciences, they can be useful in most other fields. If you are writing a paper on drug use and crime, for example, you might interview someone working in law enforcement, such as a police officer or a public defender. You might also interview teenagers who have used drugs, or residents in a neighborhood plagued by drug-related crime. Remember that you can learn useful information from many different kinds of people. Interviews do not have to be limited to celebrities or nationally recognized authorities. If you have the opportunity to interview a respected authority on your subject, you should take advantage of it. But many citizens in your own community have their own stories to tell.

Remember also that interviews need to be planned ahead, and you should prepare a list of questions before you go. As a general rule, it is better to compose questions that will take several sentences to answer rather than questions that might be answered with a single word. But don't feel compelled to adhere rigidly to the questions you prepare in advance. A good interviewer knows how to ask a follow-up question that is inspired by a provocative response to an earlier question. Do not get so caught up in the interview, however, that you forget to take careful notes. (If you want to use a tape recorder, courtesy demands that you ask permission to do so when you arrange for the interview.) Because you will need to include the interview in your bibliography, record the date of the interview and the full name and credentials or position of the person you interviewed.

When you ask the same questions of a number of different people, you are conducting a *survey*. When a survey is long, complex, and administered to a large sample group, researchers seeking to analyze the data they have gathered will benefit from having a working knowledge of statistics. But, for many undergraduate research projects, a relatively simple survey can produce interesting and useful data. The first step is to compose a list of relevant questions. Then decide whether you want to administer the survey orally or distribute it in a written form. Each question should be designed to elicit a clear answer that is directly related to the purpose of the survey. You must then decide how many people you will need to interview to have a credible sample of the population that concerns you; for example, if you want to survey college freshmen at your school, you should find out how many freshmen are registered and how many freshmen responses would be necessary for your audience to be persuaded that your results are representative. One advantage of an oral survey is that you are immediately aware of your response rate; with a written survey, weeks can pass before you discover that an insufficient number of people responded to your request for information. On the other hand, written surveys give you clear records to work from. A good rule to follow when conducting a written survey is to distribute at least twice as many copies as you really need to have returned to you.

Another factor to consider is whether it would be useful to analyze your results in terms of such differences as gender, race, age, income, or religion. If so, you must design a questionnaire that will provide you with this information. Be aware, however, that many potential respondents may have legitimate concerns about protecting their privacy. Ask for no more information than you need, and ask respectfully for that information. Give respondents the option of refusing to answer any question that makes them uncomfortable, and honor any promises you make about how you will use the data you gather.

COMPILING A PRELIMINARY BIBLIOGRAPHY

As you begin locating sources of possible value for your paper, you should be careful to record certain essential information about the books and articles you have discovered. You will need this information in order to compile a preliminary bibliography. For books, record the full title, the full name of the author or authors, the city of publication, the publisher, and the date of publication. If you are using a particular part of a book, be sure to record the pages in question. And if you are using an article or a story included in an anthology edited by someone other than the author of the material you are using, make the distinction between the author and title of the selection and the editor and title of the volume. When you have located articles in periodicals, record the author(s) of the article, the title of the article, the title of the journal in which it was published, the volume number, the issue number (if there is one), the date of the issue, and the pages between which the article can be found. (For examples of bibliographic form, see pages 80–90.)

One way to compile a preliminary bibliography is to use a set of 3 × 5 index cards, recording each source on a separate card. This involves a little more trouble than jotting references down on whatever paper you have at hand, but it will be to your ultimate advantage. As your research progresses, you can easily eliminate any sources that you were unable to obtain—or any that you have rejected as inappropriate. This method will make it easier to arrange your sources in the order required for your formal bibliography at the end of your finished paper. Some researchers prefer to use a computer notebook; others work directly from computer printouts of sources located during their search. Whatever method you use, be sure to keep accurate records. No one enjoys discovering a failure to record an important reference—especially if this discovery comes after the paper is written and shortly before it must be handed in.

Figure 16 shows a sample bibliography of sources discovered from the search illustrated earlier, on the relationship between drug use and

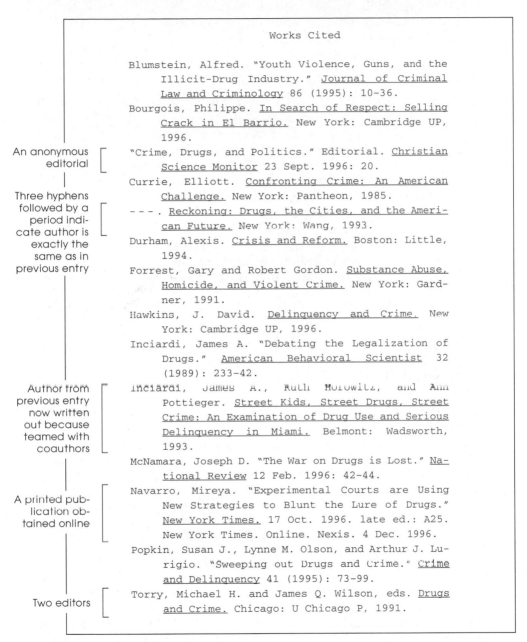

Works Cited

Blumstein, Alfred. "Youth Violence, Guns, and the Illicit-Drug Industry." Journal of Criminal Law and Criminology 86 (1995): 10-36.

Bourgois, Philippe. In Search of Respect: Selling Crack in El Barrio. New York: Cambridge UP, 1996.

An anonymous editorial — "Crime, Drugs, and Politics." Editorial. Christian Science Monitor 23 Sept. 1996: 20.

Currie, Elliott. Confronting Crime: An American Challenge. New York: Pantheon, 1985.

Three hyphens followed by a period indicate author is exactly the same as in previous entry — - - - . Reckoning: Drugs, the Cities, and the American Future. New York: Wang, 1993.

Durham, Alexis. Crisis and Reform. Boston: Little, 1994.

Forrest, Gary and Robert Gordon. Substance Abuse, Homicide, and Violent Crime. New York: Gardner, 1991.

Hawkins, J. David. Delinquency and Crime. New York: Cambridge UP, 1996.

Inciardi, James A. "Debating the Legalization of Drugs." American Behavioral Scientist 32 (1989): 233-42.

Author from previous entry now written out because teamed with coauthors — Inciardi, James A., Ruth Horowitz, and Ann Pottieger. Street Kids, Street Drugs, Street Crime: An Examination of Drug Use and Serious Delinquency in Miami. Belmont: Wadsworth, 1993.

McNamara, Joseph D. "The War on Drugs is Lost." National Review 12 Feb. 1996: 42-44.

A printed publication obtained online — Navarro, Mireya. "Experimental Courts are Using New Strategies to Blunt the Lure of Drugs." New York Times. 17 Oct. 1996. late ed.: A25. New York Times. Online. Nexis. 4 Dec. 1996.

Popkin, Susan J., Lynne M. Olson, and Arthur J. Lurigio. "Sweeping out Drugs and Crime." Crime and Delinquency 41 (1995): 73-99.

Two editors — Torry, Michael H. and James Q. Wilson, eds. Drugs and Crime. Chicago: U Chicago P, 1991.

FIGURE 16
An MLA-style bibliography

crime. It is titled and arranged according to the conventions recommended by the Modern Language Association introduced in Part 2, "Working with Sources." Note the significance of the title, "Works Cited." A bibliography for a researched paper should consist only of works that are actually cited.

If you would like to see the paper that came out of this search, see the Appendix (pages 682–690). For additional information on MLA-style documentation, see pages 76–78 and 81–85.

TAKING NOTES

Note taking is essential to research. Unfortunately, few researchers can tell in advance exactly what material they will want to include in their final paper. Especially during the early stages of your research, you may record information that will seem unnecessary when you have become more expert on your topic and have a clear thesis. So you will probably have to discard some of your notes when you are ready to write your paper.

By using a note card system, you allow for flexibility when you are ready to move from research to composition. The odds are against discovering material in the exact order in which you will want to use it. By spreading out your note cards on a desk or table, you can study how they best fit together. You can arrange and rearrange the cards until you have them in a meaningful sequence. This system only works, however, when you have the

---

Prison as Deterrent

(Currie 161)

"But prison may not only fail to deter; it may make matters worse. The overuse of incarceration may strengthen the links between street and prison and help to cement users' and dealer's identity as members of an oppositional drug culture, while simultaneously shutting them off from the prospect of successfully participating in the economy outside the prison."

FIGURE 17
Sample note card

self-restraint to limit yourself to recording one fact, one idea, or one quotation on each card, as shown in Figure 17. Many of your cards will have a lot of empty space that you may be tempted to fill. Don't. As soon as you decide to put two ideas on the same card, you have made an editorial decision that you may later regret. The cost of a set of note cards is minimal compared to the amount of time you must invest in research and writing.

Sorting your note cards is also one of the easiest ways to determine whether you have enough material to write a good paper. If your notes fall into a half-dozen different categories, your research might lack focus. In this case, do some more research, concentrating on the category that interests you the most. If, on the other hand, your notes fall into a clear pattern, you may be ready to start writing. The point at which you move from research into writing will depend not only on your notes but also on the length of the paper you have in mind: Long papers usually involve more research than short papers. If you classify your notes every few days during the process of doing your research, you will be in a position to judge when you have taken as many notes as you need.

ORGANIZING A RESEARCHED PAPER

If you have used a note card system, you may be able to dispense with an outline and compose your first draft by working directly from your notes—assuming that you have sorted them carefully and arranged them into an easily understandable sequence. At some point, however, most writers find it useful to outline the ideas they plan to cover. Anyone who lacks experience in writing long papers is especially likely to benefit from taking the trouble to prepare an outline. Depending on your writing process, you can outline before attempting to write or after you have completed a first draft.

The patterns discussed in Part 1 for classical arrangement and Rogerian argument (pages 17–21) can be adopted for researched papers of almost any length. Another possibility is to employ a standard formal outline:

    I. Major idea
        A. Supporting idea
            1. Minor idea
                a. Supporting detail
                b. Supporting detail
            2. Minor idea
        B. Supporting idea
    II. Major idea

And so forth. Subdivisions only make sense when there are at least two categories—otherwise there would be no need to subdivide. Roman numeral I usually implies the existence of Roman numeral II, and supporting idea A implies the existence of supporting idea B. Formal outlines are usually parallel, with each part in balance with the others.

Your outline may consist of complete sentences or simply a list of topics, but you should follow consistently whichever system you choose. The extent to which you benefit from an outline is usually determined by the amount of effort you devote to preparing it. The more developed your outline, the more likely you are to have thought your essay through and considered how it can be best organized. Your outline may show you that you have much to say about one part of your paper and little about another. This could result in a lopsided paper when the parts are supposed to be of equal importance. In this case, your outline may lead you to do some additional research to obtain more information for the part of the paper that looks as if it is going to be weak. Or you may decide to rethink your essay and draft another outline, narrowing your paper to the discussion of the part that had most interested you. Either of these decisions would make it easier for you to write a well-organized paper by reducing the risk of introducing ideas you could not pursue.

Many writers prefer to work with less formal outlines. Two widely used alternatives to a formal outline are *listing* and *mapping*. When organizing a paper by listing, writers simply make a list of the various points they want to make without worrying about Roman numerals or indention. They then number the points on the list in the order they plan to discuss them. When mapping, writers create circles or blocks on a page, starting with their main idea. A different idea is noted in each circle or block, and then lines are drawn to connect ideas that are related. There is no single method that works equally well for all writers. Unless you are specifically instructed to complete a certain type of outline, practice whatever kind of outlining works best for you.

You should remember that an outline is not an end in itself; it is only a device to help you write a good paper. You can rewrite an outline much more easily than you can rewrite a paper, so do not think of an outline as some sort of fixed contract that you must honor at all cost. Be prepared to rework any outline that does not help you to write better.

WRITING A RESEARCHED PAPER

When planning a researched paper, you should allow ample time for drafting and revising. Ideas often evolve during the writing process. Even if you have extensive notes, you may discover that you lack information to support a claim that occurred to you when you sat down to write. You would then need to do some more research or modify your claim. The first draft may also include paragraphs that do not relate to the focus of your paper, and these will need to be removed once you realize that they do not fit. Cutting and adding are normal in the writing process, so do not be discouraged if you need to make changes.

One of the challenges involved in writing a researched paper is the need to integrate source material into a work that remains distinctively your own. Many papers suffer because they include too many long quotations or because quotations (be they long or short) seem arbitrarily placed. Make sure that any quotations in your paper fit smoothly within the essay as a whole: Provide transitions that link quotations to whatever has come before them. As a general rule, anything worth quoting at length requires some discussion. After you have quoted someone, you should usually include some analysis or commentary that will make the significance of the quotation clear. Let your readers know how you would like them to respond to the material that you are citing. Identify what you agree with and what you question.

To help keep your paper your own, try to avoid using long quotations. Quote only what you need most, and edit long quotations whenever possible. Use the ellipsis (. . .) to indicate that you have omitted a word or phrase within a sentence, leaving a space before and after each period. (Add a fourth period with no space before it when the ellipsis follows a completed sentence.) When editing quotations in this way, make sure that they remain clear and grammatical. If the addition of an extra word or two would help make the quotation more easily understandable, you can make an editorial interpolation by enclosing the inserted material within square brackets [ ]. If your keyboard does not have brackets, you can draw them in by hand.

Remember also that sources do not need to be quoted in order to be cited. As noted in Part 2 (pages 68–70), paraphrasing and summarizing are important writing skills. When revising your paper, use these skills whenever possible. They can help you to avoid writing a paper that sounds like nothing more than one quotation after another, or using quotations that are so heavily edited that readers start wondering about what you have cut out. When you put another writer's ideas into your own words (being careful, of course, to provide proper documentation), you are demonstrating that you have control over your material. And by doing so, you can often make your paper more readable.

Above all else, remember that you are a writer as well as an investigator. Although research is essential to the process of writing a researched paper, there is more to the researched paper than research alone. Almost all researched papers require that you have a thesis about your topic, and that thesis should be distinctively your own. Unless specifically instructed otherwise, you should think of papers that use information drawn from sources as *arguments—arguments* that are informed and supported by evidence you have discovered through research.

PREPARING YOUR FINAL DRAFT

After investing considerable time in researching, drafting, and revising your paper, be sure to allow sufficient time for editing your final draft. If you rush this stage of the process, the work you submit for evaluation may not adequately reflect the investment of time you gave to the project as a whole. Unless instructed otherwise, you should be guided by the rules in the following checklist.

A CHECKLIST FOR MANUSCRIPT FORM

1. Papers should be typed or word-processed. Use nonerasable 8½ by 11-inch white paper. Type on one side of each page only. Double-space all lines, leaving a margin of one inch on all sides. If word-processing, use a printer that will produce well-defined letters.

2. In the upper left corner of page 1, or on a separate title page, include the following information: your name, your instructor's name, the course and section number, and the date the essay is submitted. (For an example, see p. 682.)

3. Number each page in the upper right corner, ½-inch from the top. If using MLA-style documentation, type your last name immediately before the page number. If using APA-style documentation, type a shortened version of the title (one or two words) before the number.

4. Make sure that you consistently follow a documentation style that is acceptable to your instructor, and give credit to all of your sources.

5. Any quotation of more than four lines in an MLA-style paper, or more than forty words in an APA-style paper, should be set off from the rest of the text. Begin a new line, indenting one inch (or ten spaces) to form the left margin of the quotation. The indention means that you are quoting, so additional quotation marks are unnecessary in this case (except for quotations within the quotation).

6. Proofread your paper carefully. Typographical errors or careless mistakes in spelling or grammar can cause your audience to lose confidence in you. If your instructor allows ink corrections, make them as neatly as you can. Redo any page that has numerous or lengthy corrections.

7. If you have word-processed your paper, be sure to separate pages that have been printed on a continuous sheet. Whether your work is word-processed or typed, use a paper clip to bind the pages together.

PART 4

NEGOTIATING DIFFERENCES

The readings collected in this Part provide an introduction to complex questions about which differing views are held. Although you may choose to write an argument of your own on one of these topics at some point, "Negotiating Differences" is designed to give you practice in paraphrasing and summarizing material that you have read carefully. If you already have an opinion on any of the topics discussed in this Part, or if you find yourself forming an opinion as you read the selections, you must not let your own views interfere with your ability to understand what other writers have to say. As Carl Rogers argues in "Dealing with Breakdowns in Communication" (pages 647–652), "the major barrier to mutual interpersonal communication is our very natural tendency to judge, to evaluate, to approve or disapprove, the statement of the other person, or the other group."

Because this tendency is so natural and most of us do it so routinely, it would be easy to slip into evaluating the arguments paired in this part of the book. In some pairings, you might decide that two writers of equal ability have been evenly matched; in others, you might observe that one writer is more persuasive than the other. For the time being, however, resist the temptation to decide who "won" an argument. The arguments selected represent different voices in a national conversation—not evenly matched opponents in a rhetorical wrestling match. In the long run, some voices earn more respect because they are articulate, fair-minded, and well informed—hence the importance of developing your own skills in argumentation. The challenge for the moment, however, is for you to develop your skills as a careful listener, regardless of whether you approve or disapprove of a particular voice or the views expressed. This skill is worth practicing

121

because life is not a debate. When two speakers square off against each other in a debate, or on a television talk show, you might well expect them to be evenly matched. In real-life situations, however, argumentation often involves conflicts among people who have achieved different degrees of education and power. People in some cultures may be accustomed to letting the strongest factions prevail, but in a democracy we should be willing to let many voices be heard. Listening respectfully to diverse voices does not mean that you have to agree with them; it means only that you need to pay attention and avoid letting your own opinions interfere with your ability to take in what other people are saying. For anyone interested in argument as a kind of problem solving, the ability to listen is essential—whether the speaker is articulate or inarticulate, reasonable or inflammatory.

When you compose arguments of your own, you will eventually need to evaluate the ideas of others and the data you discover, for critical thinking demands this kind of careful judgment. The assignments in Parts 5 and 6 will provide you with many occasions for evaluating the arguments of other writers and responding to them. You must be careful, however, not to evaluate prematurely. If your sympathy or antipathy for a writer's position—or any feelings you might have about the writer in question—keeps you from paying close attention to the content being presented, you can easily end up misunderstanding the writer's views and fostering further misunderstanding when you write arguments of your own. Effective argumentation requires that you cultivate the ability to suspend your own opinions and listen with empathy to what other people think. The purpose of argumentation, after all, is to persuade an audience to respect your position and possibly to change its own stance. You cannot realistically expect to persuade people who feel that you have ignored or misunderstood what they believe.

Understanding the ideas of others is only the first important step. You must then demonstrate in your writing that you have achieved this understanding—by accurately quoting key passages and by paraphrasing and summarizing what you have read. Paraphrasing is especially useful because when you put another person's words into words of your own that accurately and fairly restate what has been said or written, you show that you have fully understood them. When you quote, on the other hand, readers may wonder whether you have understood what you are quoting. With this in mind, you should always be prepared to comment on anything you quote, rather than letting quotations speak for themselves. As a general rule, the longer the quotation, the more you need to say about it.

The skills emphasized in "Negotiating Differences" should be practiced regularly—they are not just isolated warm-ups undertaken prior to an exercise in argumentation. But the ability to quote, paraphrase, and summarize accurately is so important that it deserves extra practice, especially if you are sincerely interested in resolving conflicts instead of simply trying to impose your own views on others. At stake here are not only skills that are useful in themselves but also an approach to argument that emphasizes resolving conflicts by giving fair attention to the views of those involved in the conflicts. This model for argumentation calls for bringing people together rather than beating opponents in a debate. As you read the following essays, focus on understanding what each writer is saying and on identifying common ground where the opposing parties can meet.

RESPONSES TO PUBLIC EDUCATION

Although the quality of public education varies from one school district to another—and often among schools in the same district—many Americans are beginning to believe that good schools are rare. Reports of overcrowded classrooms, outdated facilities, drug use, and violent behavior can be found in newspapers across the country. In addition, many parents have grown increasingly concerned by the curriculum offered their children, raising questions about textbooks that teach evolution, courses devoted to sex education, and libraries that contain books challenging traditional values. Still other parents worry that the curriculum is being watered down and that standards for academic achievement are being lowered.

What then is the future of public education? Can we recommit ourselves as a nation to the belief that every child is entitled to a free public education that ensures literacy and civic responsibility? Or do we decide that public schools as we have known them are ill-suited to the needs of a new century?

The answers to these questions are as varied as the population in our schools. The following two essays focus on one of many recent proposals for improving American education: giving parents vouchers that can be used for their children's education at either private or public schools. Both essays were originally published in Education Week *during the summer of 1996. Jerome J. Hanus teaches government at American University in Washington, DC. Peter W. Cookson Jr. is director of the Center for Educational Outreach and Innovation at Columbia University, New York.*

JEROME J. HANUS

THE CASE FOR SCHOOL VOUCHERS

It is the public school's moral culture and not merely a concern with academic quality that underlies the controversy over government subsidization of nonpublic schools. If public schools became first-rate academically, there would still be a demand for private schools. It is the desire to offer one's child a vision of a moral life that may be at variance with that of the culture dominant in the local public school that drives a parent to seek alternative schools, especially nonpublic ones. Today, close to 15 percent of parents with school-age children have voted with their feet (and money) to educate their children in schools where they find the culture more amenable to their moral values. Unless we understand this point we will never comprehend why not providing financial assistance to dissenting parents is a massive social injustice. To correct this injustice, we must confront the arguments that are raised against school choice.

2   The first argument is that aid to sectarian schools would violate the establishment-of-religion clause of the First Amendment. However, many legal experts believe that there are sufficient U.S. Supreme Court precedents to sustain a comprehensive school-choice plan so long as the destination of the money is specified by the parent and not the school. As long as the tuition voucher becomes the parent's, it is no business of the state to which of several accredited schools the voucher goes. The cases usually invoked as precedents are: *Everson v. Board of Education* (sustained state reimbursement to parochial-school parents for bus transportation); *Mueller v. Allen* (upheld the use of state-income-tax deductions for tuition and other expenses); and *Zobrest v. Catalina Hills* (upheld a publicly paid sign-language interpreter for pupils in a Catholic school). This line of reasoning would also ensure that additional government regulations would not be imposed on the private schools. Just as food stamps (a form of voucher) do not require additional regulations on grocery stores, so school vouchers would not carry with them the regulations that have made public schools much less effective than they could be.

Second, an argument of the teachers' unions is that voucher legislation will lead to the bankruptcy of public schools. However, at most, the value of the voucher would only be the average cost per public school child. If the child does not attend a public school then, of course, the public school would not and should not receive that money. Instead, the money would follow the child and the public schools would be no worse off. Since private school parents already pay school taxes, the only difference would be that they are now participating in the distribution of their tax monies.

4   A third argument is that nonpublic schools will do so well in meeting the desires of parents for a sound academic and moral education that there will be a mass migration from public to private schools. However, since critics also like to say that private schools really don't do a better job than the public schools, such a migration should not occur. These critics cannot have it both ways: Either public schools are doing well or they aren't. If the latter, then they should fail or else meet the competition. In the latter case, which is the more likely, American education as a whole cannot help but benefit.

We should note that over 20 foreign nations have subsidized sectarian education for many years and have not experienced the dire effects anticipated by American teachers' unions. Readers of *Education Week* are familiar with most of the above arguments. What they may not be aware of, however, is that expanding the private school sector will immediately benefit teachers. More teachers will be required because the new schools created will be smaller and more collegial. Parents will appreciate that teachers are now responsible for both academics and the character formation of their children and that they are teaching in that particular school because they agree with its moral culture.

6   Social justice requires that all parents, rich and poor, be able to direct the education of their children according to the dictates of their consciences and not according to those of school bureaucracies. It is time for school vouchers. ❖

PETER W. COOKSON, JR.

THERE'S NO ESCAPE CLAUSE IN THE SOCIAL CONTRACT

The deregulation of the public school system through the widespread use of school vouchers would lead to an elementary and secondary school system that is fragmented, inefficient, and inherently unequal. Surveys show that Americans want a public school system that is safe, productive, just, and rooted in the community. There are very few Americans that want to give public funds to private schools, or to corporate-sponsored educational-management organizations, known on the stock market as "EMOs." Public dollars belong in public schools that are democratically controlled, accountable to the public, and open to all children. Vouchers are a "back to the future" educational-reform strategy more suited to the age of Dickens than to the information age.

2   The use of vouchers to deregulate public education is poor public policy because:

• Education is a political right and not a property right. Libertarians who argue for school vouchers generally treat education as though it were a personal or property right that belongs solely to the individual, to be discharged as he or she wishes. In effect, libertarians argue for a separation between school and community. This perspective is a deep misreading of human development and the necessity of communal living. Liberty is not a wall that separates individuals from the community, but a bridge that makes social cooperation possible. Education is a political right guaranteed by the 14th Amendment, which recognizes that the community has positive obligations to all citizens, including children.

• Educational markets do not work the way their advocates imagine. Drawing on Adam Smith's* invisible-hand imagery, market advocates create the impression that markets operate in a self-correcting manner, yet the United States has the widest gap between the rich and the poor of any

---

* Adam Smith (1723–1790), a Scottish economist, advocated a policy called *laissez-faire* through which wealth is created by labor with little government regulation.

industrialized nation—and that gap is getting wider. Markets are power structures and, as such, are a fundamentally inappropriate way to create institutions that care for the young. A school system that assumed the characteristics of the real marketplace would inevitably cast aside the academically weak, the disadvantaged, and the handicapped as unprofitable—very likely under the label of "unteachable." Blaming the victim would be further institutionalized, where the bottom line was the ledger, not the learner.

• The use of public funds to support religious organizations is unconstitutional. For more than a decade religious organizations have been attempting to secure more public dollars for their schools. In a civil society, individuals are free to pursue their own visions of paradise, but the public is not obliged to pay for these visions. The use of public funding to support religious schools would produce an uncivil society, the very thing the framers of the Constitution intelligently worked to avoid.

• There is no known relationship between deregulation and student achievement. In thinking about practical policies to improve American schools, vouchers must rank among the lowest in terms of expected effectiveness for generating greater student achievement. Compared with preschool programs, compensatory education, preparation for work, and the better preparation of teachers, the policy of school deregulation seems a very long shot, indeed. Voucher advocates produce studies that they claim prove private schools are better than public schools. This evidence is scanty at best and far too weak to support the reorganization of American public education. Questionable data are not a sound basis for good public policy.

• The use of vouchers will resegregate and restratify society. Evidence from other countries indicates that unregulated school choice leads to increased social stratification. Computer simulations that test the effect of vouchers on access to education indicate that voucher plans would not equalize educational opportunity across income groups. Voucher schemes could make an already unjust school system even more unjust.

• Voucher schemes are bureaucratic nightmares waiting to be born. The distribution of vouchers could not occur without state regulation and without great expense.

Schools belong to the communities in which they are located; they are the symbols of a neighborhood's pride and the aspirations of people who know each other through work, community service, or mere proximity. The last thing we need is a disruption of a delicate social fiber that is already stretched thin. Voucher advocates suggest to us a stark utopia of rational choosers, cleverly manipulating the educational marketplace. I suggest that what is desperately needed is a recommitment to communities, their schools, and the children they serve through a reinvigoration of those public institutions that were established to level an unequal playing field, to promote a feeling of civic participation, and to ensure that equality of opportunity remains the bedrock of modern democracy. ❖

SUGGESTION FOR WRITING

Reread both "The Case for School Vouchers" and "There's No Escape Clause in the Social Contract." Try not to evaluate these essays by judging who makes the stronger case. Concentrate simply on understanding their content. Then imagine that you are either Hanus (responding to Cookson's essay) or Cookson (responding to Hanus's essay) and write a letter to the other writer. The purpose of your letter is to establish a friendly dialogue with a colleague with whom you share a common interest. Demonstrate that you understand the other's views by devoting most of your letter to paraphrasing his argument.

RESPONSES TO GRADING

Is grading the best way to assess how well people are learning and performing? Although a grade, be it an A or a C–, seems to offer a clear message, how is the grade determined and how are people affected by this method of assessment? Do students perform better when they know they will be graded on an assignment than when they know there will be no grade? Are teachers giving artificially high grades to please students and minimize complaints? Would both students and teachers find schoolwork more liberating if they didn't have to worry about whether a specific essay exam will earn a B– or a B? Or do we need such distinctions to make students competitive in a demanding world?

However happy or unhappy you may be with your own GPA, consider both the advantages and disadvantages of grading as you read the following two essays. John Leo is a columnist for U.S. News & World Report, *which published "A for Effort" in 1993. Paul Goodman (1911–1972) was an influential college professor in the 1960s. "A Proposal to Abolish Grading" is from his book* Compulsory Miseducation *(1964).*

JOHN LEO

A FOR EFFORT

What is the hardest mark to get at many American colleges?

2   Answer: C. Like the California condor, it is a seriously endangered species. It may need massive outside help to survive. Otherwise, it could easily go the way of marks like D, E and F, all believed to be extinct.

Harvard instructor William Cole put it this way in an article in the *Chronicle of Higher Education:* A generation or two ago, students who mentally dropped out of classes settled for "a gentleman's C." Now, he says, perfunctory students get "a gentleperson's B," and "a gentleperson's A–" is not out of the question, especially in the humanities. An English tutor told

Harvard Magazine, "In our department, people rarely receive a grade lower than B–. Even B– is kind of beneath mediocre."

4   As college tuition has climbed, grade inflation has risen right along with it, perhaps muting complaints about what it all costs. At Harvard in 1992, 91 percent of undergraduate grades were B– or higher. Stanford is top-heavy with A's and B's too; only about 6 percent of all grades are C's. At Princeton, A's rose from 33 percent of all grades to 40 percent in four years.

Because of grade inflation, outstanding students and average students are often bunched at the top. "In some departments, A stands for average," Harvard senior Dianne Reeder said at a panel discussion on inflated grades last spring. "Since so many of us have A– averages, our grades are meaningless."

6   The avalanche of A's is producing a similar avalanche of students graduating with honors. *Harvard Magazine* cites an unidentified dean of admissions at a top-six law school saying his office ignores magna cum laude and cum laude honors from Harvard because so many applicants have them. In 1993, 83.6 percent of Harvard seniors graduated with honors.

Vanishing breed. This is a national problem. Outside of economics, science and engineering, collegians are getting such good marks these days that it seems average students are disappearing from the campus, all replaced by outstanding achievers. It's reminiscent of Garrison Keillor's fictional Lake Wobegon, where "all the children are above average."

8   What is going on here? Market forces surely play a role. Colleges are competing for a pool of students who expect and sometimes demand high marks. "Students complain in ways they didn't before," says Martin Meyerson, former president of the University of Pennsylvania. "Teachers find it easier to avoid the hassle and just give higher grades." And good marks sustain enrollments in academic departments, a sign of success for professors.

Many people think grade inflation started with the generous marks professors gave to mediocre students in the '60s to keep them out of the draft during the Vietnam War. Fallout from the '60s is involved; during the campus upheavals, radicals attacked grading as a display of institutional power over the young. And, in general, the post-'60s makeover of campuses has been crucial.

10   "Relativism is the key word today," says Cole. "There's a general conception in the literary–academic world that holding things to high standards—like logic, argument, having an interesting thesis—is patriarchal, Eurocentric and conservative. If you say, 'This paper is no good because you don't support your argument,' that's almost like being racist and sexist."

The current campus climate makes professors reluctant to challenge grade inflation. Harvard Prof. Harvey Mansfield said during the panel discussion on grading that "professors have lost faith in the value of reason and hence lost faith in the value of their status. Their inability to give grades that reflect the standards of their profession is a sign of a serious loss of morale." Boston University Prof. Edwin Delattre says, "If everything is subjective and arbitrary, and you try to apply standards, you run afoul of the prevailing ethos of the time."

12   Still, whatever the failings of the academy, inflated grades don't start there. The same virus has afflicted high schools for at least two decades. Since 1972, when the College Board began keeping tabs, the percentage of college-bound seniors reporting high marks in school has almost tripled. In 1972, 28.4 percent of those taking the test said they had A or B averages in high school. By 1993, it was 83 percent. This happened while SAT scores were falling from a mean combined score of 937 to the current 902.

For whatever reasons (and the feel-good self-esteem movement is surely one), marks have broken free of performance and become more and more unreal. They are designed to please, not to measure or to guide students about strengths and weaknesses.

14   Give A's and B's for average effort and the whole system becomes a game of "Let's Pretend." Parents are pleased and don't keep the pressure on. Students tend to relax and expect high rewards for low output. What happens when they join the real world where A and B rewards are rarely given for C and D work? ❖

PAUL GOODMAN

A PROPOSAL TO ABOLISH GRADING

Let half a dozen of the prestigious Universities—Chicago, Stanford, the Ivy League—abolish grading, and use testing only and entirely for pedagogic purposes as teachers see fit.

2   Anyone who knows the frantic temper of the present schools will understand the transvaluation of values that would be effected by this modest innovation. For most of the students, the competitive grade has come to be the essence. The naive teacher points to the beauty of the subject and the ingenuity of the research; the shrewd student asks if he is responsible for that on the final exam.

Let me at once dispose of an objection whose unanimity is quite fascinating. I think that the great majority of professors agree that grading hinders teaching and creates a bad spirit, going as far as cheating and plagiarizing. I have before me the collection of essays, *Examining in Harvard College,* and this is the consensus. It is uniformly asserted, however, that the grading is inevitable; for how else will the graduate schools, the foundations, the corporations *know* whom to accept, reward, hire? How will the talent scouts know whom to tap?

4   By testing the applicants, of course, according to the specific task-requirements of the inducting institution, just as applicants for the Civil Service or for licenses in medicine, law, and architecture are tested. Why should Harvard professors do the testing *for* corporations and graduate schools?

The objection is ludicrous. Dean Whitla, of the Harvard Office of Tests, points out that the scholastic-aptitude and achievement tests used for *admission* to Harvard are a super-excellent index for all-around Harvard performance, better than high-school grades or particular Harvard course-grades. Presumably, these college-entrance tests are tailored for what Harvard and similar institutions want. By the same logic, would not an employer do far better to apply his own job-aptitude test rather than to rely on the vagaries of Harvard section-men? Indeed, I doubt that many employers bother to look at such grades; they are more likely to be interested merely in the fact of a Harvard diploma, whatever that connotes to them. The grades have most of their weight with the graduate schools—here, as elsewhere, the system runs mainly for its own sake.

6   It is really necessary to remind our academics of the ancient history of Examination. In the medieval university, the whole point of the grueling trial of the candidate was whether or not to accept him as a peer. His disputation and lecture for the Master's was just that, a masterpiece to enter the guild. It was not to make comparative evaluations. It was not to weed out and select for an extramural licensor or employer. It was certainly not to pit one young fellow against another in an ugly competition. My philosophic impression is that the medievals thought they knew what a good job of work was and that we are competitive because we do not know. But the more status is achieved by largely irrelevant competitive evaluation, the less will we ever know.

(Of course, our American examinations never did have this purely guild orientation, just as our faculties have rarely had absolute autonomy; the examining was to satisfy Overseers, Elders, distant Regents—and they as paternal superiors have always doted on giving grades, rather than accepting peers. But I submit that this set-up itself makes it impossible for the student to *become* a master, to *have* grown up, and to commence on his own. He will always be making A or B for some overseer. And in the present atmosphere, he will always be climbing on his friend's neck.)

8   Perhaps the chief objectors to abolishing grading would be the students and their parents. The parents should be simply disregarded; their anxiety has done enough damage already. For the students, it seems to me that a primary duty of the university is to deprive them of their props, their dependence on extrinsic valuation and motivation, and to force them to confront the difficult enterprise itself and finally lose themselves in it.

A miserable effect of grading is to nullify the various uses of testing. Testing, for both student and teacher, is a means of structuring, and also of finding out what is blank or wrong and what has been assimilated and can be taken for granted. Review—including high-pressure review—is a means of bringing together the fragments, so that there are flashes of synoptic insight.

10   There are several good reasons for testing, and kinds of test. But if the aim is to discover weakness, what is the point of down-grading and punishing it, and thereby inviting the student to conceal his weakness, by faking and bulling, if not cheating? The natural conclusion of synthesis is the insight itself, not a grade for having had it. For the important purpose of placement, if one can establish in the student the belief that one is testing

not to grade and make invidious comparisons but for his own advantage, the student should normally seek his own level, where he is challenged and yet capable, rather than trying to get by. If the student dares to accept himself as he is, a teacher's grade is a crude instrument compared with a student's self-awareness. But it is rare in our universities that students are encouraged to notice objectively their vast confusion. Unlike Socrates,* our teachers rely on power-drives rather than shame and ingenuous idealism.

Many students are lazy, so teachers try to goad or threaten them by grading. In the long run this must do more harm than good. Laziness is a character-defense. It may be a way of avoiding learning, in order to protect the conceit that one is already perfect (deeper, the despair that one *never* can be). It may be a way of avoiding just the risk of failing and being down-graded. Sometimes it is a way of politely saying, "I won't." But since it is the authoritarian grown-up demands that have created such attitudes in the first place, why repeat the trauma? There comes a time when we must treat people as adult, laziness and all. It is one thing courageously to fire a do-nothing out of your class; it is quite another thing to evaluate him with a lordly F.

12   Most important of all, it is often obvious that balking in doing the work, especially among bright young people who get to great universities, means exactly what it says: The work does not suit me, not this subject, or not at this time, or not in this school, or not in school altogether. The student might not be bookish; he might be school-tired; perhaps his development ought now to take another direction. Yet unfortunately, if such a student is intelligent and is not sure of himself, he *can* be bullied into passing, and this obscures everything. My hunch is that I am describing a common situation. What a grim waste of young life and teacherly effort! Such a student will retain nothing of what he has "passed" in. Sometimes he must get mononucleosis to tell his story and be believed.

And ironically, the converse is also probably commonly true. A student flunks and is mechanically weeded out, who is really ready and eager to learn in a scholastic setting, but he has not quite caught on. A good teacher can recognize the situation, but the computer wreaks its will.   ❖

SUGGESTION FOR WRITING

Write a three-page transcript in which you join John Leo and Paul Goodman in a discussion about the harmful effects of grading. You are not required to take a stand on grading or to advocate a specific position, but you can include relevant information from your own experience with grades. When you write dialogue for Leo and Goodman, make sure the words you attribute to them reflect the positions they took in their essays.

---

* Socrates (469–399 BC), an important Greek philosopher, emphasized the importance of self knowledge. The acquisition of such knowledge could be facilitated by dialogue between a teacher and a student, now called the Socratic method. For an example, see pages 581–587.

RESPONSES TO CLONING

In February 1997, a team of Scottish scientists led by Ian Wilmut and Keith Campell announced that they had successfully cloned an adult sheep the preceding summer. Because this was the first time an adult mammal had been successfully cloned, the creation of this sheep—named "Dolly" after Dolly Parton—made front page news around the world and prompted extensive discussion.

Some commentators considered how cloning might preserve endangered species, enable the creation of human organs for transplant surgery, and eventually lead to cloning human beings. Others raised questions about the ethics of such work. The two short arguments that follow appeared within the first three days of this debate. Daniel Kevles is the director of the Program in Science, Ethics and Public Policy at the California Institute of Technology; his argument first appeared as an editorial in the New York Times. *Ellen Goodman is a nationally syndicated columnist who writes for the* Boston Globe.

Daniel J. Kevles

STUDY CLONING, DON'T BAN IT

In "Songs of Innocence," William Blake asked, "Little Lamb, who made thee?" The answer for Dolly the sheep is Dr. Ian Wilmut and his colleagues at the Roslin Institute near Edinburgh. Dolly, as the world now knows, is a clone, a duplicate of one genetic parent. Her birth marks a milestone in our ability to engineer animals for food and medicine. It also signals that humans can, in principle, be cloned, too. That prospect troubles many people, but they ought not be too concerned about it at the moment.

2   Dolly has provoked widespread ethical foreboding. The Church of Scotland suggested that cloning animals runs contrary to God's biodiversity. Dr. Wilmut himself said that cloning humans would be "ethically unacceptable." Carl Feldbaum, president of the Biotechnology Industry Organization, urged that human cloning be prohibited in the United States. (President Clinton asked a Federal bioethics commission for a speedy review of the implications of mammalian cloning.)

The outcry over Dolly calls to mind the great biologist J.B.S. Haldane's "Daedalus," a slim book of reproductive utopianism published in 1924. Haldane held that Daedalus of Greek mythology was the first biological inventor (the first genetic engineer, we would say) because he was connected with the procreation of the Minotaur through the coupling of Pasiphaë and the Cretan bull. Daedalus escaped punishment from the gods for his hubris. Haldane noted, but he suffered "the agelong reprobation of a humanity to whom biological inventions are abhorrent."

4   If Daedalus did not offend the gods of his day, many people have in-
dicted biotechnologists for affronting God in ours. Yet Haldane, for one,
knew that although biological innovations are often initially seen as perver-
sions, over time, they become accepted as "a ritual supported by unques-
tioned beliefs and prejudices." As technologies improve, people recognize
them as advantageous. Society, through its legislatures and courts, figures
out how to resolve the problems they posed at the outset.

      In this way, artificial insemination of humans, considered tantamount
to adultery before World War II, has become widely accepted. So have reproductive methods like in vitro fertilization and surrogate motherhood.
People abort fetuses with genetic disorders, administer growth hormones to
smallish children and use insulin made by bacteria injected with a human
gene.

6   Scientists have long speculated about manipulating genes to produce
new Einsteins, Heifetzes, and Hemingways. Now impresarios can dream of
cloning Kareem Abdul Jabar and raising their own Dream Team.

      The fantasies are endless, but they are just fantasies. People are the
products not only of their genes but of their environments. Today an Einstein clone might grow up to be Steven Spielberg. Anyway, no one knows
what genes contribute to the qualities we most admire and value, whether
virtuosity of the pan, the pitch or the piccolo.

FIGURE 1
"Dolly"

8   Still, Dolly heralds wondrous innovations with huge economic implications (that Dr. Wilmut held back the news of Dolly's birth until he could register a patent has been reported without comment). Someday an infertile couple might choose to have a child by cloning one or the other partner. A cancer victim might use his DNA to clone spare body parts—liver, pancreas, lungs, kidneys, bone marrow.

     For now, cloning should rightly be confined to animals. But as the technology evolves to invite human experimentation, it would be better to watch and regulate rather than prohibit. Outlaw the exploration of human cloning and it will surely go offshore, only to turn into bootleg science that will find its way back to our borders simply because people want it.

10   As with so many previous advances in biology, today's affront to the gods may be tomorrow's highly regarded—and highly demanded—agent of self-gratification or health. ❖

Ellen Goodman

HELLO DOLLY

I'm glad they started with sheep. Individuality was never the ewes' strong point. Sheep don't march to the bleat of a different drummer. Aside from the occasional black sheep, they're a pretty uniform and docile flock.

2   What are they bred for anyway? Lamb chops? Wool? Nursery rhymes? You might call them sheepish if you weren't trying desperately by now to block this metaphor.

     Nevertheless, what a great public din followed the announcement that Dr. Ian Wilmut had a little lamb. The Scottish embryologist created the first clone of an adult mammal. He named her Dolly and then proceeded to make five more carbon copies, although we don't yet know what they were named. (Molly, Polly, Lolly, Holly and, surely, Folly?)

4   The bulletin about Dolly and the five Xeroxes—is this beginning to sound like a rock group?—received the same public whine of outrage that follows other great scientific surprises that blindside us with anxiety.

     "But you said . . . that we wouldn't be cloning big mammals for eons." "You said that 'Jurassic Park' was sci-fi and 'Multiplicity' was silly-fi." And now you are saying "Hello, Dolly."

6   Of course, many scientists still insist we won't be able to clone people any day soon. But the man who owns the patent for this little procedure acknowledges that "there is no reason in principle why you couldn't do it." He just adds quickly, "All of us would find that offensive."

     Offensive? Call that Scottish understatement. Creepy is a better word, not to mention ethically appalling. For openers, Wilmut had to use 300 embryos to get his Dolly. He had a number of deformed offspring who died along the way.

8   Beyond that, it doesn't take Hollywood to imagine all sorts of ghoulish new scenarios. Cloning organ donors? Ensuring "spares" for family heirs? Buying genetic immortality?

Today bioethicists may describe self-cloning as the most narcissistic act imaginable. But before Dolly, there was some pretty strong competition for that title. Remember Robert Klark Graham, who died just last week? He was the fellow who set up the so-called Nobel sperm bank in California. As many as 213 children were born with sperm from those little narcissus bulbs.

10   There's also a growing private market in reproductive biology. Americans are saving thousands of extra embryos in freezers. They're selling eggs and renting wombs. They're leaving sperm behind when they go to war. And that's not counting the cryogenics customers.

If I can find any good news in the Valley of the Dollys, maybe the cloning controversy will help us get a grip on the current argument about nature vs. nurture.

12   Of late, it seems that our fascination with the biological basis of everything has led to a belief that DNA is destiny. In a perverse way, Dolly may force us to remember that people are not just conceived; we are raised. We are the products of our environments as well as our genes.

Despite all the master race fantasies, cloning would be a rather inefficient and dicey operation. Clones are essentially identical—though delayed—twins. Same DNA, different people.

14   Imagine if we'd cloned Albert Einstein, everyone's favorite genius. In late 20th century America, however, Al the Second might stay home with the kids so his Mileva could finally get her PhD. Or, everything being relative, he might find modern physics dull.

Imagine cloning Tiger Woods. Since you cannot also clone his entire upbringing, the Tiger Cub might take all of his golf potential and become a second-rate flutist.

16   As for the narcissist raising his or her real inner child? This you-clone won't have your parents, your fourth-grade teacher or the thousands of accidental experiences that made you who you are. What you might get, as a clone-parent, is an adolescent rebellion of mythic proportions.

The point is that we can clone biological potential but not real people. At 7 months, Dolly is all done. At 7 months, we've just begun.

18   One of the things that may or may not be built into the human DNA, but distinguishes us, is a unique sense of self. It's this very understanding that sends out warning bells at the very possibility of a Xeroxed "me." It's the quite proper instinct that now demands a universal No! Humans are not for cloning.

Science leads, but we don't have to follow. At a time when geneticists look at us as programmed bits of DNA, this flock is a reminder that we are, after all, the shepherds, not the sheep. ❖

SUGGESTION FOR WRITING

Reread these two articles. When you are confident that you understand their content, consider what the authors' tone reveals about their personalities. Based on how the authors sound in their essays, write a description of David Kevles and a description of Ellen Goodman. Support your conclusions with specific lines from their work. If you were asked to moderate a disagreement between these two people, how would you get them to listen to you?

RESPONSES TO PHYSICIAN-ASSISTED SUICIDE

The debate over euthanasia took on new urgency in the 1990s as a Michigan-based physician, Dr. Jack Kevorkian, gained national notoriety for helping patients end their lives, and courts began ruling that citizens have a right to physician-assisted suicide—the active participation of a doctor in response to a patient's wish to die. A procedure along these lines is significantly different from deciding to remove life support systems from a patient who does not want extraordinary measures taken to prolong vital functions, such as respiration, when there is no hope of recovery or even of a return to consciousness. At issue is the difference between allowing someone to die a natural death through nonintervention, and facilitating a premature death through lethal injection or by other means.

Although other countries are struggling with these same choices, the discussion of physician-assisted suicide in the United States involves more than medical ethics and the rights of patients to make decisions regarding their treatment—important though these concerns are. As you will see in the following essays, the debate also involves fundamental questions about individual liberty and the extent to which it can be restricted by the state. Ernest Van Den Haag is a psychoanalyst who has published widely on political and ethical concerns. His essay, "Make Mine Hemlock," was first published in 1995 by the National Review. *Stephen L. Carter is the William Nelson Cromwell Professor of Law at Yale University. "Rush to a Lethal Judgment" was first published in 1996 in the* New York Times Magazine.

ERNEST VAN DEN HAAG

MAKE MINE HEMLOCK

Before Christianity, governments were unconcerned with suicide, which was thought expedient in some circumstances and required by honor in others. However, with the coming of Christianity suicide became a sin, a violation of God's commandments. As unrepentant sinners, suicides were denied burial in consecrated ground and expected to end in Hell. Life was thought to be a gift from God, Who ordained its beginning and end. We possessed the life created by Him, but He owned it. Our possession could not license us to destroy what did not belong to us.

2   As the grip of Christianity weakened, this part of religion was secularized, as were many others. Suicide became a transgression against nature, not God, usually explained by mental derangement. Absent derangement, suicide was considered a crime against society, thought to own individuals more or less as God had been thought to before. Only in our time has it come to be believed that individuals collectively own society, rather than vice versa. They also are thought to own themselves. Without God (or slavery) no one else really could. Owners can dispose of what they own as they see fit. We thus each become entitled to control our life, including its duration, to the extent nature permits, provided that this control does not harm others in ways proscribed by law.

Very few people are inclined to commit suicide. But this hardly seems a good reason to prevent it, although sometimes it is asserted or implied that the unpopularity of suicide argues for its immorality and for preventing it. Yet, those who do not wish, or do not feel they have the moral right to, end their life can easily refrain. It is not clear on what grounds a government, or anyone else, could be entitled to prevent a competent person from controlling the duration of his or her life.

4   Although the foregoing view seems irrefutable, not everyone accepts it. It is contrary to tradition, wherefore many obstacles remain in the way of people who try to shorten their life. These obstacles can be nearly insurmountable for those who most wish to do so because of a disabling disease. They may be forced to go on living against their will. Even some healthy persons find the obstacles quite forbidding. They may have to jump out of windows, or use drugs which are difficult to obtain and of the specific effects of which they are not fully informed. Physicians and other experts, who do know the proper combination and quantities of drugs needed, usually refuse help, either because of moral objections or in fear of legal liabilities. They impose their own socially supported moral beliefs on patients who do not share them, but cannot act unaided. Dr. Jack Kevorkian is a rare and courageous exception.

To be sure, compassionate physicians may feel that terminal patients in extreme pain should be helped to end such pain. They may discreetly prescribe anesthetics which end suffering by ending life. There have been no successful prosecutions for this quasi-legal practice, although some unsuccessful ones have been brought and physicians who prescribe painkillers in the required quantities assume some risk. Physicians also may withhold life-prolonging treatment at the directions of patients or of legal guardians. Patients do have a legal right to refuse any treatment—though the extent of that right is not well defined. However, merely withholding treatment still may lead to an unnecessarily prolonged, stressful, and perhaps painful way of dying.

6   Even physicians such as Dr. Kevorkian, willing to take major legal risks, have helped only patients who were incurable and, in most cases, had

reached a terminal stage. This takes the decision on whether to end life out of the hands of a mentally competent patient and places it into the hands of a physician, who must decide that the patient is terminal enough, or has suffered enough, before helping him to die. He may also refuse to help at all.

Giving physicians (or any other persons) the authority to veto a patient's decision seems unwarranted. Physicians are trained in how to treat diseases so as to prolong life. They are not experts on whether or not to prolong it. There is no training for making such a decision. Indeed, physicians are taught *(primum non laedere)* always to prolong life. No respect is instilled for the patient's wishes, if he prefers to shorten his life. Yet, whether and when to end a person's life is a moral, not a medical, decision, for the patient to make, not the doctor. The physician's task is to inform the patient of his prognosis, perhaps to advise him, and, above all, to help him carry out his decision.

8   Imagine a 20-year-old patient hospitalized for a condition which, although incurable, is neither terminal nor acutely painful. In the patient's rational, carefully considered view his condition denies him the pleasures of life. He wants to die, but needs assistance. Since he is neither terminal nor suffering unbearable pain, most physicians would be unwilling to help and would run a major legal risk if they did. Again, imagine a 90-year-old who feels that life is of no further interest to him, although he is neither terminal nor in pain. He too will find it hard to persuade a physician to help him die if he cannot do so by himself.

For good or bad reasons, people commit suicide every day. Since many would-be suicides act on impulses which may turn out to be temporary, forcing a moderate delay seems in their interest and legitimate—but is not to be confused with preclusion. Imagine now a healthy young man who, perhaps influenced by Arthur Schopenhauer's philosophy,* has decided to commit suicide. Before he has a chance to kill himself, a traffic accident leaves him paralyzed and hospitalized, incurable but not terminal. He now has additional reasons to end his life but is less able, perhaps altogether unable, to do so unless aided. Although we do not make it easy, we cannot prevent an able person from ending his life anytime he wants to. But we can prevent a disabled person from doing the same. Thus we add to the disability nature or accident has inflicted.

10   This seems odd because our compassionate society usually goes out of its way to help the disabled overcome whatever handicaps are in the way of their desires. Employers are legally compelled to hire disabled persons, schools to make special arrangements to teach them. Public buildings and transportation are made accessible to the wheelchair-bound. Yet, when it comes to suicide, we refuse to allow any assistance to the disabled. We exploit their disability to prevent them from doing what able-bodied persons can do. On all other occasions we try to compensate for the

---

* A German philosopher, Arthur Schopenhauer (1788–1860) saw life as a constant conflict resulting in frustration and pain.

disadvantages nature inflicts on some. Yet when assistance is essential to enable the disabled to commit suicide, we threaten to prosecute anyone who helps them.

Despite the receding influence of religious ideas and our official unwillingness to impose them, and despite the precariousness of the notion that society has a compelling interest in preventing suicide, we continue to treat life as a social duty that individuals, however disabled, should not be helped to shirk. It is not clear to whom the duty to live could be owed. Once the government no longer legally recognizes God as the authority to which duties are owed, nature cannot have prescriptive authority to force unwilling persons to live, since such authority would have to come from God. Only society is left as the source of this alleged duty. But society cannot be shown to have a compelling interest in forcing persons to live against their will. Moreover, such an interest would hardly justify the cruelty involved. To be sure, the great majority has an instinctive wish to live. But why should we enforce the gratification of this wish on those who, for whatever reason, decide not to gratify it?

A Right to Die?

12   Since, from a secular viewpoint, the moral right to die can hardly be less fundamental than the moral right to live, our non-recognition of the former must flow from unacknowledged residual theological notions which we have officially renounced imposing on non-believers. Dimly realizing as much, most persons opposed to assistance in suicide tend to avoid moral arguments in favor of prudential arguments. These are of two kinds. The first questions the mental competence of individuals who want to hasten their death. The second questions the disinterestedness of persons willing to help them. We must also deal with questions about ending the life of persons who are in a terminal phase of disease, but not mentally competent to make decisions, and of persons in a permanent coma. These are particularly sticky questions, since ending the life of these two classes of patients would be homicide, justifiable or not, rather than suicide, since, by definition, the patients do not make the decision themselves.

How can we assess the mental competence of a physically disabled person who decides on suicide? The task is daunting but not impossible. First of all, prejudicial notions must be discarded. A patient who wants his life ended need not be mentally sick, clinically depressed, or temporarily deranged. The idea that he must be mentally sick merely justifies a conclusion foreordained by circular reasoning. Having discarded prejudicial notions, psychiatrists, using their customary methods, can ascertain whether the patient knows who and where he is, and whether his mental processes are realistic and logical to the normal degree. A conversation about what led to his decision is apposite as well. Reasonable opponents of suicide, religious or not, may be invited to participate where feasible. (The whole process could be videotaped if the patient's competence is controversial.) Beyond the judgment of the psychiatrist, based on these data, nothing is needed. The patient's decision should be accepted.

14   Intellectual competence is to be investigated, not what is sometimes referred to as emotional health. "Emotional health" is not a clinical concept, but a moral concept quite amorphous and subject to fashion. It allows the imposition of moral views on a patient who may be diagnosed as emotionally ill if he does not share them.

How can we make sure that no one will be pressed to end his or her life by self-interested relatives, friends, enemies, or caretakers? What about undue influence? Safeguards have long been developed to make sure that a patient's decisions about his last will are uncontaminated. These safeguards can be used as well to ensure that his decision about assisted suicide is independent. Where there are problems with the medical prognosis on which the patient's decision may depend, these must be dealt with by means of second or third opinions.

16   As for the terminal patient who is incompetent or unconscious, if he has provided instructions while competent, they should be followed. If he has not, the decision of relatives and legal guardians must be followed, unless there is evidence to make them suspect. If the situation is cloudy (or if the patient has no relatives) the hospital could name someone, preferably a physician familiar with the patient's syndrome, but practicing elsewhere, to make the decision. If his prognosis and decision agree with those of the treating physician there is no problem. If not, the two physicians will have to ask a third physician willing to decide within 36 hours. Decisions should be independent of the views of hospital administrators and allow ending life when there is no chance of regaining consciousness.

Sometimes an analogy between assisted suicide and abortion is suggested. Indeed, opponents of one usually oppose the other as well; in both cases the opposition may ultimately rest on traditional religious ideas even if the opponents are not religious. But the analogy is misleading. Abortion destroys a fetus with the consent of the mother and usually reflects her interests. The fetus does not make the decision and cannot be consulted. Conceivably the fetus could have an interest in survival. If allowed to develop, the fetus may be expected to desire and enjoy life. In contrast, assisted suicide shortens the life of a patient who has decided himself that prolongation does not serve his interests. Surely, the normal fetus could not be assumed to have an interest in self destruction. The suicidal patient does. (Conflicts about abortion usually are about alleged fetal *v.* alleged maternal rights, with some denying fetal rights. But no one would deny that suicide patients are persons who have rights.)

18   Most arguments about assisted suicide can be dealt with in a reasonable, if not perfect, way. However, the "slippery slope" argument,* though influential, is hard to deal with rationally. It suggests that, once we allow doctors to shorten the life of patients who request it, doctors could and

---

* For a description of slippery slope arguments, see pp. 45–46.

would wantonly kill burdensome patients who do not want to die. This suggestion is not justified. The specter of Nazi practices is usually raised to make it credible. But Nazi practices were imposed on physicians and hospitals by political directives which did not evolve from any prior authority given physicians to assist in suicide. There was no "slippery slope." Nor can it be found elsewhere in medical practice. Physicians often prescribe drugs which, in doses greater than prescribed, would kill the patient. No one fears that the actual doses prescribed will lead to the use of lethal doses. No one objects to such prescriptions in fear of a "slippery slope." The "slippery slope" idea seems fortunately to be an unrealistic nightmare. Authorizing physicians to assist in shortening the life of patients who request this assistance no more implies authority to shorten the life of patients who want to prolong it, than authority for surgery to remove the gall bladder implies authority to remove the patient's heart. ❖

STEPHEN L. CARTER

RUSH TO A LETHAL JUDGMENT

Many years ago, a psychiatrist who was treating someone I loved asked me to remember that she had the right to kill herself if she wanted to. Sometimes, he said softly, the decision to commit suicide is the decision of a rational mind, a reasonable if tragic answer to the question of whether life is worth continuing.

2   When he said "right," he did not, of course, mean constitutional right; he meant moral right, a part of human dignity. As long as her mind was sound, she had the right as an autonomous individual to decide whether to continue living. Her responsibilities to her loved ones and her community might have carried weight in the moral calculus, but the final decision had to be hers alone.

Although I saw the logic of his position then and see it now, the law has traditionally offered a rather different understanding. Suicide was a felony under England's common-law regime, and was illegal everywhere in the United States into this century. Some cynics have identified the age-old prohibition on suicide as a matter of royal selfishness—at common law, if you committed a felony, your worldly goods went to the crown—but the better answer is that the laws reflected a strong belief that the lives of individuals belonged not to themselves alone but to the communities in which they lived and to the God who gave them breath.

4   Nowadays, we have a broader notion of individual autonomy. Our laws increasingly reflect the belief that our lives do belong to us alone. Some anti-suicide statutes are still on the books, but today the societal distaste for suicide is registered through the civil, not the criminal, law: people who try suicide but do not succeed may be involuntarily hospitalized to determine

whether they are continuing threats to themselves. So although we certainly try to prevent suicide, we no longer punish it.

There is one exception: most jurisdictions continue to treat the person who directly assists someone else's suicide as a felon. That is the basis, for example, of Michigan's prosecutions of the notorious "suicide doctor," Jack Kevorkian, who, as of this writing, has been involved in more than 30 suicides. Many a family harbors its secret story of indirect assistance—leaving the bottle of sleeping pills within reach of the dying relative, for example—but the reason for the secrecy in part has been the traditional view that assistance of any kind is at least immoral and often illegal.

6   In recent months, however, two Federal appellate courts have held that terminally ill patients have a constitutional right to seek the assistance of physicians in ending their lives. With the entire dispute plainly on its way to the Supreme Court anyway, opponents and supporters of what has come to be called the "right to die" are even now battling their way through the implications. The moral questions raised by assisted suicide are weighty, but our ability as a society to deal with them has been seriously weakened by the judicial rush to enshrine one side's moral answer in the framework of constitutional rights.

The two cases presented the same basic question, but the courts dealt with it in very different ways. In March, the Court of Appeals for the Ninth Circuit, based in San Francisco, decided the case of *Compassion in Dying v. State of Washington,* resting the right to assisted suicide for the terminally ill on the due process clause of the 14th Amendment, the same provision in which the courts have located the abortion right. The right to choose how to end one's own life, the court explained, was a direct descendant of the right to choose whether to bear a child, and, as with abortion, the state must have a very strong reason before it may interfere.

8   Then, less than a month later, the Second Circuit struck down New York's assisted-suicide ban in the case of *Quill v. Vacco.* The Second Circuit rejected the due process argument, pointing out that the United States Supreme Court has limited that approach to cases in which the state is interfering with a fundamental liberty "deeply rooted in this Nation's history and tradition," like the freedom to marry or procreate. The right to obtain assistance in suicide, the court sensibly concluded, does not fit this definition. But the *Quill* court found a rationale of its own: the right to assisted suicide is supported, said the judges, by another part of the 14th Amendment—the equal protection clause. Why? Because New York allows mentally competent terminally ill patients on life support to direct the removal of the supporting apparatus, even when the removal will hasten or directly cause their deaths, but prohibits those who do not need life support from obtaining drugs to hasten or directly cause their deaths. So the state is discriminating, in the court's terms, by allowing some of the terminally ill, but not others, to die quickly.

The logic of *Quill,* although more attractive than that of *Compassion in Dying,* seems terribly forced, not least because the state allows many other distinctions among the terminally ill—for example, wealthier patients often have access to experimental drugs and therapies that others do not. These distinctions may not always seem sensible or fair but they hardly rise to the level of constitutional concern.

10   And there is a larger analytical problem with both decisions. If the right to choose suicide with the help of a physician is of constitutional dimension, it is difficult to discern how it can be limited to those who are terminally ill. Terminal illness is not a legal category—it is a medical category, and one that even doctors sometimes have trouble defining. Some of us who teach constitutional law—the old-fashioned types, I suppose—still tell our students that constitutional rights arise by virtue of citizenship, not circumstance. This implies that each of us (each who is a competent adult, at least) possesses an identical set of rights. So if there is indeed a constitutional right to suicide, assisted or not, it must attach to all citizens.

    If the right to pursue assistance in suicide attaches to all citizens, then the Constitution is at present being violated by all the state laws permitting the involuntary hospitalization of individuals who try suicide. Instead of locking them up, we should be asking them if they would like assistance in their task. In fact, the Second Circuit has matters precisely backward: if everybody except the terminally ill were allowed to seek the assistance of physicians in suicide, the equal protection claim might have merit. If, on the other hand, the terminally ill are allowed to seek suicide, the court's concern for equality might suggest that everybody should be allowed to do it, lest the state discriminate between two groups who want to die, those who desire to commit suicide because they are terminally ill and those who desire to commit suicide because they are dreadfully unhappy.

12   Except in emergencies, a court decision is the worst way to resolve a moral dilemma. Constitutional rights, as they mature, have a nagging habit of bursting from the analytical confinements in which they are spawned. When the Supreme Court struck down organized classroom prayer in 1962, nobody other than a few opponents of the rulings, dismissed as cranks, envisioned a future in which courts would order traditional religious language and symbols stripped from official buildings and state seals. And did the justices who voted to legalize abortion in 1973 really imagine that two decades later, the United States would be home to 1.5 million abortions a year?

    In the case of the right to assisted suicide, the risks are many. For example, it is far from obvious that the right can be limited to adults. The abortion right isn't. The Supreme Court has ruled that pregnant minors must be allowed to demonstrate to a judge that they are mature enough to make up their own minds about abortion. It does not take much of a stretch to imagine a judge concluding that a young person mature enough to decide that a child should not come into the world is also mature enough to decide that her (or his) own life is not worth living.

14   And there are other, more ominous difficulties. Some worried medical ethicists have predicted that a right to assisted suicide might lead exhausted

families to encourage terminally ill relatives to kill themselves. Moreover, women are more likely than men to try suicide, but men succeed much more often than women. With the help of health care workers, women, too, might begin to succeed at a high rate. Is this form of gender equality what we are looking for?

But the biggest problem with the idea of a constitutional right to assisted suicide is that the courts (if the decisions stand) are preempting a moral debate that is, for most Americans, just beginning. To criticize the constitutional foundation for the recent decisions is not at all to suggest that the policy questions are easy ones. There are strong, thoughtful voices—and plausible moral arguments—on both sides of the assisted-suicide debate, as there are in the larger euthanasia debate. The questions are vital ones: Do our mortal lives belong to us alone or do they belong to the communities or families in which we are embedded? Will this new right give the dying a greater sense of control over their circumstances, or will it weaken our respect for life?

16   These are, as I said, weighty questions, and the policy arguments on either side are the stuff of which public political and moral debates are made. And a thoughtful, well-reasoned debate over assisted suicide is precisely what we as a nation need; we do not need judicial intervention to put a decisive end to a conversation that we as a people have scarcely begun. Because the arguments on both sides carry such strong moral plausibility— and because the claim of constitutional right is anything but compelling— the questions should be answered through popular debate and perhaps legislation, not through legal briefs and litigation. In an ideal world, the Supreme Court would swiftly overturn *Quill* and *Compassion in Dying,* allowing the rest of us the space and time for the moral reflection that the issue demands. ❖

Suggestion for Writing

Drawing on both Van Den Haag and Carter, summarize the arguments that have been made in favor of physician-assisted suicide; then summarize the arguments that have been made against it. Do not let your own opinion affect your ability to summarize the views of others fairly.

RESPONSES TO AFFIRMATIVE ACTION

The civil rights movement of the 1960s dramatized the extent to which racism had kept black Americans from enjoying the same opportunities that are offered to whites. Important though it was to end segregation and extend voting rights to citizens who had been deprived of these rights, the struggle for social justice could not end there. Economic opportunity had to be fostered as well, and affirmative action began in the 1970s as a means for achieving this goal. According to the thinking of the times, it was not enough for government and business to open doors that had been previously closed to African Americans and other minorities. Steps needed to be taken to make sure that minorities understood these doors were open and they were welcome to pass through them. Simply put, "affirmative action" means making an active effort to help members of historically oppressed groups gain admission to American universities and entrance into a diverse range of jobs previously reserved for white males.

A generation has come of age since then, and affirmative action is now associated in many minds with quotas and racial preferences. Voters in California made headlines in 1996 when they approved an initiative ending affirmative action as a factor for admission to the University of California. Similar initiatives soon followed, and affirmative action as understood during the final years of the twentieth century seems unlikely to remain the same in the twenty-first century. How then should we respond to the inequality that continues to trouble our country? The following essays offer alternative models for efforts to achieve social justice. Constance Horner was a guest scholar in the Brookings Governmental Scholars program when she first published "Reclaiming the Vision" in 1995. "Reaffirming Our Actions" is excerpted from Michael Tomasky's 1996 book, Left for Dead: The Life, Death, and Possible Resurrection of Progressive Politics in America.

CONSTANCE HORNER

RECLAIMING THE VISION:
What Should We Do after Affirmative Action?

The powerful moral vision that generated America's civil rights movement is on the brink of disintegration. Unless that vision—of a racially integrated society aspiring to equal justice and equal opportunity for black Americans—is reclaimed, the United States will, on the cusp of a new millennium, fail at a crucial political task it has assigned itself since the Civil War. It will also diminish its signal historical standing as creator of exemplary solutions to the deepest dilemmas of civic life.

2   That is why the current debate over affirmative action matters greatly. How America deals with the challenges posed by this issue and how we explain what we are doing will define our strongest commitments and ideals for our time, just as our words and deeds over the 45 years of the Cold War defined our commitment to political and economic liberty in that time. For there can be no mistaking that civic harmony among racial and ethnic groups is among the most salient global challenges of the next half-century.

With the irony that colors so much of human affairs, the 30-year series of public policy and judicial decisions we know as affirmative action has come to threaten the vision of a just and integrated society that gave birth to it. Yet in the minds of many black Americans, affirmative action is identified with a national commitment to their advancement.

4   There is little question that affirmative action will be modified, phased out, or even, under a cascade of Supreme Court decisions, state initiatives, and federal legislative action, abruptly terminated. Therefore it is vital to understand the full range of reasons for its rejection. Black Americans should not come to believe that the decision against it constitutes a rejection of the vision that brought it into being, and the country needs an understanding of the elements that would comprise an effective replacement for it.

What Next?

A democratic polity can change the means by which it achieves its ends, provided that it operates in good faith and gives those most vulnerable to democratic decisions, the minority, reason to believe in the majority's good faith. Examining the sources of discontent with affirmative action policies and practices will help not only to design sound replacement policies, but also to create and sustain an expectation of good faith in the deliberations about what to do next.

6   One of the dilemmas confronting people in public life critical of affirmative action has been the concern that calling it into question would be viewed by black Americans as, at best, indifference to their historic plight or, at worst, a contributor to resurgent racism. Some proponents of affirmative action have, over several decades, taken advantage of this concern to enforce a politically correct silence that has precluded the incremental correction of a public policy gone awry that is preservative of peaceful democratic change. Indeed, some of the explosive force of the current critique results from the unleashed resentment over this intimidation.

    Supporters of affirmative action have put forth various economic, political, and psychological explanations for the burgeoning opposition to it. Opposition results, they say, from a generalized hostility ("white male rage") stemming from low wage growth and job loss, exacerbated by partisan Republicans inflaming a "wedge" issue for the next election, or from the flaring up of a permanent or "institutional" racism that can never be fully suppressed, only contained through political *force majeure.**

8   At root these arguments are premised on an expectation of bad faith and a presumption of economic determinism. As such they deny the strength and persistence in American culture of the premises on which the civil rights movement was based and flourished—a sense of fairness, a belief in racial integration, and a presumption that a civically activist polity will voluntarily (if slowly) make positive social change. Therefore, whatever their truth, these

---

* *Force majeure* is French for an unexpected event that disrupts the way society normally operates.

explanations are questionable and limited guides to constructing a sustainable next generation of efforts to increase equality of opportunity.

Moreover, they fail as full explanations for why the broad national revulsion toward the practices of affirmative action (including that felt by women and, to a lesser extent, blacks, its intended beneficiaries) is being expressed at this time and with such force.

10   Polls defining affirmative action as racial preferences show overwhelming white rejection (in the neighborhood of 75 percent) and an almost equal split for and against among blacks (46 percent for, 52 percent against in an April *Washington Post*-ABC national poll). An entirely separate set of polls taken in the same time frame suggests that an additional or different—and far more benign and hopeful—interpretation of the antipathy to affirmative action is available than the angry class- and race-based explanations advanced to date.

Antipathy toward "Big Government"

Almost 70 percent responding to one national poll indicated a belief that "the federal government controls too much of our daily lives." Another poll had two-thirds of Americans choosing "big government" as the country's gravest peril. In the light of these data and much more confirming their findings, it is hard to escape the observation that antipathy to big government and to affirmative action have emerged together as two of the most powerful political sentiments achieving national expression at this time. Although simultaneity does not demonstrate connection, it is at least suggestive of it.

12   The 30-year growth of affirmative action's regime of federal statute, regulation, judicial decision, and administrative practice, burgeoning well beyond its straightforward original purposes of nondiscrimination and equality of opportunity, not outcomes, has not occurred in a vacuum. It has developed simultaneously with and as part of the federal government's regulatory curtailment of private, discretionary, and voluntary action in many areas of American life—a curtailment compounded by federal support for social programs embodying and projecting values most Americans reject. The huge Republican [Congressional] victory in November likely reflected a rejection on both counts—a rejection of the degree of regulatory intrusion and a rejection of some of the values embodied in social welfare programs. It is very likely that rejection of affirmative action has been greatly intensified by its association with both, as well as by its provenance in the Democratic party—the "mommy party" for the "nanny state." If this is so, Americans may be viewing affirmative action as a regulatory structure to be dismantled more than a moral vision to be fulfilled. The moral vision was of a nondiscriminatory, integrated society; the regulatory structure, intending to integrate, now separates. The moral vision was democratically and openly implemented through legislation to affirm a commitment to equal

opportunity and equal justice before the law; the regulatory structures are developed by fiat-oriented bureaucracies and by judges disdainful of the context of competing values and of the enormous vitality and variety of a culture bursting the bonds of regulatory structures and reverting to earlier, more clearly defined values in many areas.

OMB Directive 15

To see these conflicts in play, one need only look at what is happening to a little-known but powerful directive governing the federal government's collection of racial statistics. Promulgated in 1977, Office of Management and Budget Directive 15, "Race and Ethnic Standards for Federal Statistics and Administrative Reporting," governs the categories the Bureau of the Census may use in assessing the country's racial composition. The racial statistics developed through its categories serve as the basis for enforcement of voting and other civil rights by the Department of Justice, the Equal Employment Opportunity Commission, and the civil rights offices of other federal agencies. Billions of dollars of federal spending are targeted for women and racial and ethnic minorities on the basis of these statistics. (Even Small Business Administration set-aside programs directed to "socially and economically disadvantaged" individuals and institutions are *de facto** allocated largely by race and ethnicity because administrative practice and law "presume" that certain racial and ethnic groups are "disadvantaged.") Allocation of not inconsiderable political power, through the drawing of congressional district lines, is based on their collection. Determinations of "adverse impact" in private-sector hiring practices rest on a racial count of an area's labor pool, and lawsuits may follow.

14   Virtually every arena of activity is affected by these categories. According to a Congressional Research Service report, "targeted funding, in various forms, and minority or disadvantaged set-asides or preferences have been included in major authorization or appropriation measures of agriculture, communications, defense, education, public works, transportation, foreign relations, energy and water development, banking, scientific research and space exploration, and other purposes." The distribution of a great deal of public and private money and a considerable amount of political power relies on the racial and ethnic numbers produced under Directive 15.

Currently, people being counted by the census under the categories of OMB Directive 15 are asked to identify themselves racially as white, black, Asian-Pacific Islander, American Indian-Alaskan native, or "other." If "other" is selected, the census taker is expected to "reclassify" that person into one of the four groups on the basis of appearance. (People are also asked an "ethnic" question as to whether they are Hispanic.) These tidy boxes constructed by the federal government bear, as is obvious, very little relationship to the

---

* *de facto* is Latin for "actually" or "in reality."

racial and ethnic variety of the country. The OMB, as a result, is agonizing over whether to add a new category, "multiracial." So far it has been unable to do so (except in limited testing). Ironically, and much to the point of the country's discontent with government's affirmative action structures, the use of racial categorization is imposing a powerful set of incentives for those receiving benefits to remain distinctly within their categories.

16   Thus a governmental structure whose original intent was to overturn a regime of segregation has been transformed into an apparatus supporting its return. Policies growing out of a national commitment to racial integration and designed to facilitate integration instead entitle and empower on the basis of separation. To do so, moreover, these policies must deny the reality of an increasingly racially mixed society. Indeed, the government's difficulty in changing OMB Directive 15 must call into question the degree of confidence the public may repose in its commitment to the ideal of racial integration. It surely must at least raise a suspicion that a tolerance (if not a preference) for separatism has infiltrated and is delegitimizing a significant underpinning of affirmative action.

Counterproductive Racial Pigeonholes

Meanwhile, American social vitality defines and discredits the official racial demarcations. In spite of the stresses and strains of historic antagonisms, racial and ethnic groups continue to integrate, even in the most intimate realms of marriage and family. Although the last state anti-miscegenation laws were struck down as recently as 1967, according to the latest census data more than 4 percent of blacks, and 6 percent of black men, are married to nonblacks. Ten percent of black men aged 25–34 have entered interracial marriages, mostly with white women. Thirty percent of Hispanics are married to non-Hispanics. Transracial adoption, strongly discouraged by most state and municipal governments, has nonetheless continued to grow. A provision in the Republican "Contract with America" denies federal funds to agencies that discriminate on the basis of race in child placement. The U.S. Department of Health and Human Services, long an opponent of transracial adoption, has recently, and grudgingly, yielded to public anger over adoptable black children languishing in foster care and issued guidelines that no longer actively discourage such adoptions.

18   Rita Simon, an academic sociologist who studied transracial adoption for several decades, was quoted in *USA Today* as believing that "Where we come down on transracial adoption should tell us what we really think about integration and separation." She reports polling data indicating that 70 percent of black and whites support such adoption. Syndicated columnist Ellen Goodman writes of children like multiracial golf star Tiger Woods, who is of black, Thai, Chinese, and American Indian origins, as affording America a racial "demilitarized zone" and a bridge among the races.

But interracial marriage and transracial adoption are small indicators of the extent to which government's racial and ethnic categories fail to comport with reality, compared with the consequences of the great wave of immigration since those categories were devised. Immigration now accounts for 37 percent of national population growth. More than one million legal and illegal immigrants enter the United States every year—in absolute numbers an historic peak—with the number of countries sending immigrants rising from 21 in 1970 to 27 in 1980 to 41 in 1990. More than 150 languages are spoken in the United States, and Americans claim almost 300 racial and ethnic groups. There is even an intellectual attack on the existence of race as a scientifically reliable concept among geneticists and physical anthropologists. Stanford genetics professor Luigi Cavalli-Sforza believes that classifying by race is a "futile exercise." In a February 13 *Newsweek* poll, one-third of American blacks said that blacks should not be considered a single race.

20   It would be naive to view these trends as suggesting that the country has, only 30 years after the end of legally sanctioned racial segregation, reached the point where there is no further need for the interventions of government to forestall or punish continuing acts of racial discrimination and to help expand opportunity for advancement. But it is also naive to ignore the belief of opponents of affirmative action that the federal government has far exceeded the bounds of common sense in the structures it has devised to ensure equal opportunity and that indeed many of those structures, like OMB Directive 15, now impede racial integration and advancement by their overreach and by their disconnection from a changing social reality.

Betraying the Vision of an Integrated Society

The static regulatory vision of racial America is empirically outmoded. It is also antithetical to the long-term interests of blacks. Drawing voting district lines on the basis of race and other mechanisms such as those proposed by Lani Guinier, for example, furthers separation by race on so crucial an act of citizenship as voting; it trades a short-term electoral reward for the creation of the idea of permanent, irreducible, separate interests based on race, hardly a vision of an integrated society. Maintaining important permanent structures based on race posits permanent separation and therefore economically, politically, and intellectually counterproductive isolation.

22   It is simply not possible to reduce the salience of race by enhancing its salience. The widespread application of lower standards for academic admissions, for example, has drawn ill-prepared students in over their heads and created, by this artificially contrived mismatch of student and school, the impression of black intellectual inferiority, a reactivation of the racial stereotype most dangerous to black advancement. These admission policies have allowed white-governed institutions to "feel better about themselves" at the expense of the full development of black intellectual potential. They have produced a college dropout rate for blacks of almost two-thirds. They have led to the spectacle of a university president, however unintentionally,

questioning the "genetic, hereditary" capacities of black students. They have led to speculation by the chair of the U.S. Commission on Civil Rights in congressional testimony that if tests determined college admissions and entry-level jobs, "Asians and Jewish Americans would hold the best jobs everywhere and populate almost entirely the best colleges and universities." Similar policies have led municipal police and fire departments to hire, in the 1980s, underqualified recruits who were not able to achieve promotion in the '90s, thereby creating for blacks the appearance of racist promotion policies and for whites the appearance of black incapacity. When public and private institutions have denied or obscured the practices of these admissions and hiring policies, from a concern that the beneficiaries would be embarrassed or a fear that the policies would fail of public support in the sunshine, they have created a cynical distrust about their fairness or good sense that has contributed mightily to the strength of the opposition to affirmative action.

A New Beginning

Now, uphill, good faith must be reclaimed. It would be a tragic failure of American civic genius, and a great cruelty, not to take this opportunity to think the issue of equality of opportunity anew. Along with other 30- to 50-year-old structures of government, affirmative action is crumbling under the pressure of change. But if the regulatory structure on which affirmative action relies is, at best, counterproductive to the accomplishment of the purposes in forming the civil rights movement and the antidiscrimination legislation that grew out of it, what then is to be done?

24   New approaches should align minority interests with ascendant and longstanding American values, so they will be both powerful and sustainable. What might such approaches look like?

First, public policy should promote racial integration, not only at work and at school, but also in the home. Anything weaker will allow separatists and racists, white and black, the wedge they need to indulge the fantasy of a more "comfortable" life, which is socially, if not legally, separate. The moral vision that galvanized national support for the civil rights movement was not "separate but equal."

26   Second, intentional racial discrimination of the sort the Civil Rights Act of 1964 had in mind should be powerfully stigmatized and punished. The law is a teaching instrument. The moral fuzziness of affirmative action has confused this teaching and undercut it.

Third, where intellectual attainment is probably the basis for decisions, as in some but not all entry-level hiring, promotions, and academic admissions, standards should be applied nonracially with no *de facto* "race norming." That implies the probability of some near-term decline in numbers of blacks in exchange for strengthened confidence in those who, in time, achieve in equal numbers. At the same time, there must be a revitalized commitment to dramatic improvement in the quality of education.

Since, for the foreseeable future, almost all students will be in the public education system, its reform must be the focus of attention. There is general agreement on much of what needs to be done. Schools should run year-round. Teachers should be hired competitively and paid accordingly. Black mayors and city councils should stop using schools as jobs programs and be willing to hire the best teachers nationally, regardless of race. Curricula should be basic, tough, challenging, and fad-free. Parents with vouchers might accomplish these and other goals.

28   For 20 years, public agencies have devoted extraordinary resources to assembling racially representative workforces. The next generation of policies should be clearly non-racial and announced as such. Practical ways to bring race-based hiring to an end should be developed and implemented in ways that assure continuing public confidence in public process.

Fourth, federal regulation—fiat—to assure outcomes, should generally be replaced by greater room for discretion to offer opportunity. That will transform resentful but minimal "compliance" that is taken out of the hides of "beneficiaries" in other ways, into voluntary moral acts of good citizenship and common sense. It's not naive—it's human nature. People resent losing the opportunity to do the right thing freely.

30   Fifth, tortured attempts to substitute additional economic for racial entitlements should be dropped; as thinly disguised generic redistributionist policies, they are entirely contrary to the thinking of the times, administratively nightmarish, and therefore not at all likely to work.

Sixth, the bourgeois practices that help poor people improve their circumstances—study, work, saving, marriage, child-bearing, in that order—should be preached, not dismissed or ridiculed as they have been since the 1960s, and rewarded in the design of public policies.

However Long It Takes

32 Finally, American leaders in every sector and of all races should make the same kind of commitment to racial integration they made after World War II to fighting and winning the Cold War. Affirmative action arose from an impatience that the consequences of several hundred years of slavery and discrimination could not be overcome quickly. For many, those consequences have been largely overcome. For many others, they have not. How long the effort takes is less important than that it be headed in the right direction.

New directions, embodied in values and practices that have worked for America before, may help solve the problems of race in ways that can be sustained. If sustained, they will provide a model for other societies facing worse divisions and internal conflict. ❖

Michael Tomasky

REAFFIRMING OUR ACTIONS

In the late nineties, just as the welfare laws are going to be rewritten and the immigration laws reworked, so too is affirmative action going to be changed. How quickly and how sharply the right can dismantle affirmative action will depend on a number of things: the success of the vote on California's programs this November, certainly; the level of support from the interests that finance national politics; and the lack of public support for affirmative action. And, as with welfare and immigration, the left faces this basic choice: We can either dig in our heels and argue for the status quo, even though every indication is that the status quo will not hold, or we can try to find ways to redefine affirmative action on terms acceptable both to us and to a majority of Americans, instead of trotting out rhetoric that has simply been dragged out of the cupboard too many times.

2   A sad example of this presented itself in the summer of 1995, when the Board of Regents of the University of California system voted to end affirmative action. Looking for an issue to bolster his failed presidential candidacy, Governor Pete Wilson was pushing this action, and since most of the regents had been appointed by Wilson and previous Republican governors, the measure's chance of passage was pretty strong from the start. But the president of the university system was opposed to the change, as were several regents, other political leaders and of course a vocal contingent of students.

Out to Sacramento flew Jesse Jackson. Jackson asked permission to speak, and requested more than the fifteen minutes usually allotted to guest speakers. Permission was granted, and Jackson launched into a forty-five-minute diatribe in which he invoked Orval Faubus and George Wallace and warned the board, If you do this, we'll shut down your campuses and clog your streets. Meanwhile, his presentation did not demonstrate that he knew the first thing about minority enrollment levels at various U.C. schools. Jackson's speech, one witness told me, changed the dynamic of the debate—and not, from a pro-affirmative action point of view, for the better.

4   The truth is that affirmative action today is an ambiguous enterprise, both practically and morally. In practice, affirmative action has contributed to more racial mixing, and it is partially responsible for the more integrated society we now live in, although no one can be sure how much so. Also, the question of whether it helps those who need help least, or at any rate leaves behind those who most need help (two slightly different things), has not been satisfactorily settled. But it's on moral terms that affirmative action's authority has most dissipated. Affirmative action was well grounded and morally necessary as reparations policy for aggrieved black Americans; but somewhere over the years, it changed from reparations policy to diversity policy, including not only blacks but women, Latinos, any and all minority

groups, even some groups with little realistic claim of historical discrimination. A diversity policy of this sort—particularly one maintained not by popular opinion but by court orders and executive mandates—became harder to justify as either equitable or as a true reflection of the historical circumstances each of the groups faced. And in an era when everyone has faced declining wages and less job security, it was inevitable that the current challenges to it would arise.

It is undeniably the case that affirmative action, even as it has helped integrate the country, has been divisive and lacks popular support. For example, in a *Washington Post* survey for March 1995, 75 percent of those polled said they oppose preferences on the basis of past discrimination. That included 81 percent of whites and *46 percent* of blacks. Other surveys have issued similar findings, which suggest that black Americans, rather than reflexively supporting this policy, have given the issue deep thought—and that civil rights groups toeing the status quo line on affirmative action are rather badly out of touch with nearly half the constituency they claim to represent. As with the cross-racial support for Proposition 187, this cannot be because all these people are yahoo racists and sexists. Instead, they act in accordance with a sense of fairness and morality.

6   The best moral claim that can be made for affirmative action is as reparations policy, and it's a strong one. To put a slightly different spin on an old argument, consider the literal cash cost to black America of slavery and Jim Crow and official and unofficial segregation: the job changes and wages lost, the entrepreneurial openings denied, the education denied, the medical care denied, the housing denied, the property left to rot or burn by white owners, the bank loans never given, the jobs proffered always, until very recently, at the bottom of the wage structure. Each of these affected millions of people from, say, the founding of the Republic (we could go back further, of course) until, for all reasonable purposes and for all but a slim few, the 1970s when affirmative action really kicked in. What are those losses worth, to put it in terms easily comprehensible to the lawyer, businessperson and insurance adjustor, in cash? Untold billions. In this respect, white society has only just begun paying black people back.

White society *does* owe black society big-time, and reparations are morally necessary. But today, affirmative action is not a reparations policy; it's a diversity policy. It became a diversity policy throughout the course of the seventies as it was expanded from a program for the uplift of black Americans into a program designed to serve more and more underrepresented groups brought within its ambit. So affirmative action now includes people in several other categories; what about them? White women face discrimination in this country, but is it anywhere near on a par with what blacks have faced? I've no doubt that Latinos are subjected to difficulties here, but America did not enslave them for 250 years (and they did come here by choice). Aleuts certainly face hardships, but does white America owe Aleuts what it owes blacks? It clearly does not. I wouldn't say that women, Latinos, Aleuts and the rest deserve no preferential treatment whatever, just that their claim on white America's conscience is not remotely the same as blacks'. An affirmative action practiced similarly for all these groups has a far less certain moral claim to make than one that seeks to atone explicitly for the peculiarly horrid history of white treatment of blacks.

8   I do not suggest an affirmative action limited to black Americans only. Such a program would probably have even less chance than the current one does of surviving politically, since giving women, Latinos and all the others a stake in the program expands its constituency and brings it that much more support. Besides, diversity is a good thing. But where do its demands logically stop, and why? If affirmative action covers, say, the daughter of a wealthy Cuban-American building contractor, why should it not cover, say, the son of a poor white coal miner from eastern Kentucky? Would that young man—and Appalachian mining families can with justification call themselves a disadvantaged group—not "diversify" Harvard? The distinctions become more and more nebulous, more and more hair-splitting and more and more obsessed with ranking Americans' disadvantage based solely on their ethnicity and gender. Usually, it's true, a white male has certain built-in advantages; but only usually. What about the unusual ones who, as jobs go south and wealth becomes even more concentrated, are growing in number?

The left hasn't dealt squarely with such questions. The simple demand that affirmative action be expanded to include newly discovered outgroups, proceeding from the simple assumption that all white males, regardless of their station, constitute one large in-group, just can't hold. It's not practically the case, and it's not morally right. The attempt to pull the price of past discrimination out of the hides of people who were not responsible for it is an ambiguous undertaking. And issues have a way of connecting themselves to one another: For example, a policy of affirmative action for diversity's sake cannot long coexist with a policy of open immigration, as political scientist Jim Chapin has observed. Why should a woman from Argentina or a man from Antigua, both fresh on these shores, be beneficiaries of affirmative action? Public opinion—and not just white public opinion—will never support that, and it should not be expected to.

10   The University of California regents, in rescinding racial preferences, passed a resolution that continues to emphasize "commitment to diversity" as a U.C. goal. Will black and Latino enrollment remain at current levels? No; everyone concedes they'll go down, although by how much is debated. But black and Latino enrollment levels in the U.C. university system aren't that high now—about 5 percent and 15 percent, respectively. It's obvious that the real problem is not that admittance policies aren't liberal enough racially but that black and Latino children face inferior and badly funded public education.

Attacking lack of access to capital and public education imbalances requires a program more radical than affirmative action, as does attacking the vast inequities and difficulties that millions of working people face. But we can be sure that affirmative action supporters like the Clintons and most other Democrats would never undertake such a program, because doing so would require taking on the real culprits of working-class people's problems, and the Clintons, like the Democratic Party as a whole, are too dependent on the largesse of those culprits' political action committees. Of course, the left can't cashier affirmative action on the right's terms, of which the California initiative is a prime example. Proposals like that must be fought. But what the left must do in the long run is produce an answer that (1) lays out a real and unifying program and (2) speaks in plain language to the mass of voters and convinces them of the value of our arguments. I hardly need to point out, given public opinion on the issue today, that the failure to do so will almost surely result in affirmative action being cashiered on the right's terms.

12   The most hopeful suggestions for what can exist post-affirmative action have come from some on the left but also, and in the main, from thinkers like William Julius Wilson, who are, whether fairly or not, more often called liberal or moderate. These categories, we can be sure, will prevent many who regard themselves as the last true representatives of the real left from entertaining the first thought of considering their proposals. But Wilson's well-known call for universal remedy programs that would address black poverty but also help working-class and poor whites (which he's been making since the late seventies) has to be heeded. He points out, rightly, that "only with multiracial support could programs of social and economic reform get approved in Congress." I would suggest not that class become the sole criterion for affirmative action programs but that it be included as part of a formula that continues to rely to some extent on race, gender and ethnicity. The point is that care must be taken so that black concerns are not relegated to some kind of secondary status but that black concerns and white concerns are made one and the same, with just the sort of class-tinged fillip that one would hope would be appealing to leftists.

Former New York City schools Chancellor Ramon Cortines introduced a plan that serves as an example of a way to proceed. It may shock outsiders to learn that despite general trends, New York City is still home to a few of the finest public high schools in the country—Peter Stuyvesant in lower Manhattan and the Bronx High School of Science are best known. Students who attend these schools are virtually assured that life's various doors will swing wide open to them. Of course, admission to these schools is highly competitive, and enrollment has been almost exclusively white and Asian. Before Mayor Rudolph Giuliani bullied him out of town, Cortines put into place an academy for promising low-income pre-teens to prepare them for the rigors of these high schools. The goal, of course, is to raise minority enrollment, which the program will if it's well run. But it is not an explicitly race-based program—15 percent of the children in the first class were white—and does not seek to raise minority enrollment through the courts or the imposition of quotas. Compare this with the mess—legal, practical, ethical—San Francisco has on its hands in trying to run its high school admissions programs, which are based firmly on quotas and have created deep interracial tension. Of course, when the time actually comes that a few white students are displaced from Bronx Science in favor of graduates of Cortines's academy, there will be some complaints, but those can be more easily isolated because no one will be able to say that, on merit, the minority kids don't deserve to be there.

14   This is the sort of program the left needs to propose. It is specific, it values diligence and perspicacity as well as disadvantage, its goal is one with which few people would disagree, and it achieves the goal by means of a plan that is rooted in fairness and opportunity. Per-pupil funding in public education, and the very fundamental question of how public education is financed—mostly through property taxes, which is why wealthy suburbs can spend more than $10,000 per child and some poorer areas, both urban and rural, perhaps $3,000—is another issue the left should press. Again, a program to address this blatantly unfair system would not be race-based per se—the poor white child in eastern Kentucky benefiting as much as the black child in Roxbury—but would certainly help lift minority children and give them a better chance. Programs like these, guided by principles like these, have the potential to pull together a mighty coalition.

Such programs, and an attempt to put together such a coalition, require from the left some degree of faith in the mass of people to be fair and make reasonable moral judgments. They also require faith in democracy's resilience and absorptive powers. Having faced far more venom and violence than any civil rights leaders face today, Martin Luther King Jr. and his contemporaries never lost that faith. They were not naïve about the depth of racism or the intractability of the ruling elites, and they never brushed aside or downplayed racism; but they believed that most people, confronted with hard evidence and compelling moral arguments, could overcome racism and think and act in a better way. The left has no such faith right now, which is why people have no faith in us.   ❖

SUGGESTION FOR WRITING

Write a report, addressed to Constance Horner and Michael Tomasky, in which you summarize what you learned from their essays. Identify the points on which they seem to agree.

RESPONSES TO PUBLIC FUNDING FOR THE ARTS

In past centuries, artists, sculptors, poets, and composers often had to rely on patrons' material support in order to have the freedom to create. Wealthy individuals often undertook this responsibility—sometimes because they truly cared for art, sometimes because they wanted the prestige of being associated with it. During the Middle Ages and the Renaissance, the Church was also a major patron of art in Western Europe. But who pays for art today? A successful rock star can make millions of dollars on a single tour, but a young composer writing a new symphony may be struggling to pay the over-due rent.

Inspired by the way a number of other nations were providing public funding to foster the creation and performance of art, Congress created the National Endowment for the Arts (NEA) in 1965. Since then, the NEA has provided important support both to individuals and to institutions such as dance companies and museums. It has also supported projects that have generated much controversy. When the NEA was created, the United States considered itself the richest country in the world. Now we worry about the size of the national debt. What will be the future of the NEA in this era of tight money? Should Congress continue to fund it, or should the government get out of the business of art?

Margaret Spillane, who teaches writing at Yale, first published "Is the NEA for Everyone?" in a 1995 issue of The Progressive. *Gene Edward Veith, Dean of the School of Arts and Sciences at Concordia University-Wisconsin, first published "The Velvet Prison and the Closed Academy" in a 1995 issue of* Society.

MARGARET SPILLANE

IS THE NEA FOR EVERYONE?

Several weeks ago, the great American Social Realist painter Jack Levine turned eighty years old. He was born in a working-poor neighborhood of Boston, the eighth child of an immigrant shoemaker. Yet by the time he was in his mid-teens, he could already draw like a Renaissance master. That's because from the age of nine, Levine's talent was given both space and structure in an after-school art program at a Boston settlement house. Whenever he felt like it, he could stroll over to the Museum of Fine Arts and study the techniques of the Old Masters up close. Later, a Harvard University scholar and artist heard about young Levine's great promise, and he provided the teenager with further education in the materials, discipline, and history of drawing and painting.

2   Coming from difficult economic circumstances, Levine might have been forced in spite of his splendid training to abandon his fledgling art career and take a job to help his family. But in the Depression, the Works Progress Administration was treating art-making as an occupation, and was providing artists with the opportunity to earn a modest living putting in regular working hours in the studio. Levine became one of America's most articulate and unsparing social painters, in the tradition of Daumier, Goya, and Hogarth.*

* Honoré Daumier (1808–1879), Francisco José de Goya y Lucientes (1746–1828), and William Hogarth (1697–1764) all created art that uses satire as a means for achieving social justice.

So what does this story have to do with the current gleeful climate of art-bashing, as right-wingers in Congress try to wipe out the National Endowment for the Arts, which Newt Gingrich has sneeringly labeled "a plaything of pork"? Simply this: art can't flourish just by betting on the sheer force of individual talent to prevail. To survive, art requires both fostering at critical moments, and a community awake to the benefit of having people producing art in its midst.

4   The kill-the-NEA movement claims that the Endowment hands out checks to artists who are the enemies of mainstream America, that it is sucking cash right out of the pockets of decent, small-town folks, and using it as welfare checks for fancy artists in the urban fleshpots who spit on all that decent Americans value.

However, 95 percent of the Endowment's budget goes not to individuals but to institutions—and not just big-city orchestras and museums, but arts projects in rural community centers, town halls, regional festivals, and other social and civic institutions. The argument that corporate funding should replace federal funding can't stand up in regions of the country where there is no corporate presence to solicit. Perhaps the Chicago Symphony and the Santa Fe Opera could eventually cover the loss of Endowment funds by even more exhaustive campaigns among big businesspeople, but that strategy won't work for the Yup'ik Dance Festival in Mountain Village, Alaska, or the Folklife Project in Eunice, Louisiana.

6   It is these under-served areas that are likely to suffer most if NEA money is slashed from the federal budget.

Gingrich should look around his home state of Georgia to see the sorts of projects the NEA's helped underwrite. In the town of Pineview (population 450), a mural is under way that depicts the community as it looked fifty years ago. A similar community-history mural is in the works in Hawkinsville. Colquitt has produced *Swamp Gravy,* a stage play built entirely from oral histories and traditional tales gathered in the region. NEA money has also supported part of Atlanta's annual Black Arts Festival, which provides a breathtaking range of African American music, visual art, traditional crafts, theater, and music.

8   As I write this, I'm listening to *Meeting in the Air,* a double-CD collection of sacred music from the Cherokee, black, and white populations who live at the place where Georgia, Tennessee, and North Carolina come together. I feel lifted off my chair by the splendid wave of voices, which I surely would never have heard if NEA funding hadn't made it possible to find these exceptional—but geographically isolated—talents, and to permit the John C. Campbell Folk School in Brasstown, North Carolina, to record them. While the singing groups are treasures in their own communities, their gifts are now available to the ears of a wider world. In that corner of the Appalachians, there are no corporate donors to fund such projects, because there are no corporations.

Preserving traditional arts is a hard sell to corporations, since the potential for large-scale reflected glory is simply not there. Why would Philip

Morris want to fund an elderly shape-note singer's recording session when it can throw cash at big-audience, high-profile events like the Brooklyn Academy of Music's annual Next Wave Festival and see its name splashed across all of BAM's stationery and newspaper ads?

10   As for Newt's charge that NEA grants constitute funding for "avant-garde people who are explicitly not accepted by most of the taxpayers who are coerced into paying for it," it should be pointed out that the father of bluegrass, Bill Monroe, has been honored as an NEA National Heritage Fellow as has the blues guitarist and singer John Lee Hooker and B.B. King and Earl Scruggs. You still want to talk elitism, Newt?

In terms of helping to balance the government's books, even total elimination of the NEA will have almost no effect at all, since, according to the National Arts Alliance, cultural funding is a mere two ten-thousandths of 1 percent of the federal government's budget. That comes to 64 cents per person per year, far below the arts-funding level of any of our major allies.

12   That tiny bit of federal cash, however, multiplies like loaves and fishes. According to the Alliance, every dollar awarded by the NEA attracts $11 more from state and local arts agencies, foundations, corporations, and other public entities. Nationally, the not-for-profit arts generate $37 billion in economic activity, and sustain 1.3 million jobs. Some data suggest that cutting federal funding will likely hurt local economies, since the presence of arts institutions has been shown to spur urban renewal and attract new businesses. Not-for-profit arts organizations are hardly sinkholes for federal cash. Indeed, they create $37 billion in economic activity, support 1.3 million jobs, and return $3.4 million in income-tax revenue to the federal treasury.

Pushing these facts forward has become one of the two principal activities of arts fundraisers, who have been forced to frame their concerns in corporate language. The fundraisers' other task is to stress the educational component in whatever project they're supporting. Paul Goldberger, in a recent *New York Times* article, wondered if art's terrifying power wouldn't be undercut by such insistence that it be "useful."

14   Oddly enough, this idea of a purposeful art poses no problem for some of the most risk-taking arts organizations, such as Houston's DiverseWorks. When performance artist Rhodessa Jones comes to DiverseWorks in February, she'll also be working with girls detained at the juvenile-probation department. As one of the professionals participating in the Architecture Resource Center's Urban Design Lab in the New Haven public schools, Sam Gardner feels no need to apologize for the program's usefulness. Says Gardner: "We're not talking about 'art for art's sake,' but art for community's sake—alive, tied to the real world."

Urban individuals and agencies receiving Endowment money are hardly spending their grants in blissful isolation from the masses. Jazz composer and pianist Harold Danko just received an Endowment grant that will pay for publicity and musicians' fees for a series of concerts of his compositions this spring in New York City. A music professional for twenty-five years, Danko sees his concert series as a way of putting jazz back out in public. "People used to learn jazz by going to hear each other play, not by going to conservatories," he says.

16   Ensuring such public access to the arts is one of the most critical battles in the NEA war. "You want to see elitism?" asks Samuel Sachs II, director of the Detroit Institute of Art. "Try cutting out funding to museums. The price of admission will shoot up past $20, and then nobody but the rich will be able to afford to look at paintings."

Down the road is the Detroit Symphony, which remains accessible not only to subscription ticket holders from Grosse Pointe, but also to the residents of inner-city Detroit. Some of the schools in Detroit's strapped public system would have no music component to their curriculum if it weren't for the participation of Detroit Symphony musicians, who put in classroom hours and provide on-site introductions to the classical repertory for students at Orchestra Hall. Gifted students—along with other community members—are eligible to become members of the Civic Orchestra, which under the aegis of the Detroit Symphony provides tuition-free instruction and an opportunity for regular public performance.

18   Ensuring that citizens, through a government agency, are able to participate in the fostering of the artists in our midst is not a matter of political party. After all, it was that original elite-basher, Richard M. Nixon, who gushed about the National Endowment for the Arts when he was President. "We should seek to encourage and develop individual artistic talent and new concepts in arts, just as we do in science and technology," Nixon said. "I will support that institution as the instrumentality of the federal government to nourish talent and contribute to the support of our museums, of the performing arts, and a flourishing of all the arts."

If it was safe enough for Nixon, it ought to be safe enough for Newt.

20 Jack Levine, in his ninth decade, is still painting every day, just as he always has. The stamina that has permitted him to paint his unsparing social commentaries is formidable to contemplate. But the professional means of fighting that good fight might never have been possible without community and government support in the formative moments of his career.

Levine has withstood the onslaught of five decades of art fads. His work has not always been the most appreciated, and certainly not the most remunerated. But it endures. Building endurance in those gifted members of our communities who take the difficult and uncertain path of making art should be a matter of national priority. The NEA was founded to do just that. ❖

Gene Edward Veith

THE VELVET PRISON AND THE CLOSED ACADEMY

Much of the criticism of the National Endowment for the Arts (NEA) comes from those who are outraged by some of its controversial grants. Citizens irate over their tax dollars going to support Joel-Peter Witkin's photographs of corpse desecration and Ron Athey's blood-sport performance art are demanding that federal funding for the arts be stopped. On the other side are advocates for the arts, who stress the importance of the arts, even controversial work, to the national culture.

2   There is, however, another dimension to the debate that deserves to be considered: Does state funding, in fact, cause the arts to flourish? Supporters of the NEA assume that it does, but what is the net effect of the NEA on the aesthetic life of the nation? Also missing in the debate is a historical perspective: Have state subsidies for the arts generally supported works of excellence or of mediocrity? Is their legacy one of artistic freedom or artistic control?

To answer these questions and to form a larger perspective on the NEA controversy, it will be helpful to consider three case histories of state support for the arts: the system of total subsidy for the arts as developed by the former Soviet Union, the more benign state sponsorship of the arts as practiced in France during the nineteenth century, and the grants-making system currently in place in the United States. Once these three models of state patronage and their effect on the arts have been surveyed, we will return to the question of how best to fund the arts in a free, democratic society.

4   In the former Soviet Union and its socialist satellites, the arts were totally subsidized by the state. Artists were fully supported, with generous stipends, dependable exhibitions, and a high social status. Except for the threat of censorship, the Soviet system would seem to have been an artists' paradise. "Artists, as a group, are today distinguished representatives of the organized intelligentsia," wrote Miklós Haraszti, a poet and author of a book entitled *The Velvet Prison,* a study of the arts under Communism:

> We are the blessed ones, the true elite: it is our privilege (and duty, of course) to shape the general taste, to represent the nation, and to determine the uses of tradition. If our I.D. card registers us as "artist" or "writer," every policeman will salute us, even if we are young or shabbily dressed. Today society tenders its respect in exchange for our loyalty. No artist, however mediocre his talent, is forgotten. No work goes unrewarded.

Haraszti wrote his book before the fall of the Communist system in the Soviet bloc and Eastern Europe, and he was arrested for his dissident opinions. He shows that state control of the arts was not accomplished so

much by overt censorship as by the state's financial generosity. "The bureaucrats did not aim to silence artists; their only tyranny was generating
massive financial support and an insatiable demand for more art."

6   Haraszti shows that artists at first eagerly embraced socialism, and he
explains why artists tend to be attracted to left-wing ideologies. The artistic
pose of social rebellion and contempt for the bourgeoisie tends to make left-
wing ideologies inherently fashionable. Furthermore, socialism seems to
give to art and to artists a higher status than capitalism does. Whereas under
capitalism art is reduced to the status of a commodity, under socialism art is
part of the cultural superstructure. Under capitalism, artists are oppressed
workers; under socialism they are makers of culture. The artists of Eastern
Europe did their part to overthrow bourgeois capitalism; once socialism was
in place, however, artists learned that their new-found status had a price.

Haraszti documents how artists under Communism were co-opted by
the state. Artists were given economic security, a guaranteed audience, and
social prestige. In exchange for this massive financial support, artists simply
had to adhere to Marxist ideology. It is true that the state would occasionally resort to overt censorship and the arrest of artists who were not politically correct, but although the history of Soviet art includes stories of heroic
dissidents, most artists complied voluntarily. In fact, the bureaucracies that
controlled the arts were staffed not by philistines or KGB agents, but by
other artists. For the most part, artists policed themselves, following the
party line so as not to jeopardize their privileges and their funding.

8   "To be sure, the cocoon spun around the artist, first as a kind of frame
and later as a casting mold, could interfere with artistic development," Haraszti writes. "Security certainly provides a different basis for artistic development than does the risk concomitant with a free-market economy. A new
starting line was drawn, ensuring that, instead of competition, the impartial
love of the state would govern careers." As a result, artists found themselves
confined in a "velvet prison" in which they could live a pleasant life in exchange for their freedom.

Artistic freedom under capitalism, according to Haraszti, comes from
the diversity of the marketplace. If one group rejects an artist's work, he can
appeal to other individuals and groups, or create just for himself. Under socialism, there is only one patron—the state—which thus exercises complete
control.

10   As for the society as a whole, Haraszti writes, "art remained a gift and
message of the state." The result was a "directed culture," organized from
above. Normally, a society's art expresses its people's deepest values, reflecting their complexity and creativity. Art imposed from above is inevitably
one-dimensional.

According to the tenets of socialist realism, art that displayed individualism or pursued beauty for its own sake reflected capitalistic, bourgeois
values. Instead, artists were expected to depict class stereotypes and socialist
propaganda. Originality and aesthetic excellence were suspect. Even when
the socialist stylistic requirements were relaxed, the quality of art scarcely

improved. The moral compromise necessary for artists' professional success vitiated their work—having exchanged their personal integrity for economic security, artists' attempts at originality, honesty, and expressiveness were rendered unintentionally ironic. Only the dissident artists, working at great risk in defiance of the state, produced art that was alive and authentic.

12   The directed culture of socialism gave lavish support to the arts, but the art it produced was arid and academic, politically correct, but aesthetically superficial. Total state subsidy for the arts led not only to conformity, censorship, and oppression; it led to artistic mediocrity.

The French Academy

Defenders of the NEA's more controversial grants point out that artistic innovations often encounter intense opposition. The Impressionists, for example, initially provoked great hostility and near riots. State funding of unpopular work is necessary, they say, in order to promote artistic change. The example of the Impressionists is indeed instructive, but it suggests rather the opposite conclusion. Impressionism was opposed not so much by the public but by the state patronage system and the artists who were subsidized by the state.

14   The French monarchy patronized art systematically after Louis XIV founded the Royal Academy for Painting and Sculpture in 1667. After a brief hiatus during the Revolution, the Napoleonic emperors resumed the institution of an academy to cultivate the national art. The Academy of Fine Arts was made up of the most respected artists of the day. Unlike in the Soviet Union, the government was not concerned with political censorship, but with giving positive support for the arts. Nevertheless, the result was another "directed culture," which tended to exclude artistic innovators and to entrench artistic mediocrity.

By the middle of the nineteenth century, according to John Russell Taylor in his *Impressionist Dreams,*

> art in France had settled into a rut. For any would-be artist, progress toward official recognition involved submission to the art establishment, which ordained that you could not do this before you had done that, that you had to have attended the right school (the École des Beaux-Arts) or have been the pupil of one of the right painters. Above all, you had to have the approval of the ultimate authority, the Academy of Fine Arts, and exhibit at the academy's biennial Salon before anyone would take you seriously and buy your work.

16   The Impressionists and other *avant garde* artists were excluded from the academy's exhibitions, which favored the neoclassicism of Ingres and that of his less-talented imitators. The excluded artists rebelled not just against the favored academic style but against the very institutions of state patronage. Shut out from state patronage, they appealed to the free market.

Patricia Mainardi, in her book *Art and Politics of the Second Empire,* has documented the decline of the official arts establishment as state patronage gave way to the rise of the middle class and the triumph of free market economics. In the seventeenth century, the academy went so far as to forbid its members from exhibiting their works publicly. "The very idea of exhibition," observes Mainardi, "was tainted with the commercialism that Academicians were trying to escape." After a while, works were exhibited—culminating in the great showcases of French culture known as the "Universal Expositions" of 1855 and 1857—but purists of the academy were appalled at the prospect of charging admission to see works of art. "If in conservative quarters exhibitions still preserved a taint of commercialism, the whiff of a bazaar, how much worse to add to that the idea of theatre—the 'show' with paid admission."

18   At issue, of course, was not only the alleged purity of the arts but major issues of class and politics. The aristocratic power structure scorned the "bourgeoisie," not merely for their allegedly vulgar taste but because they represented democracy and capitalism and the end of feudal privilege and elitism. Radicals such as Émile Zola* railed at both the political and artistic despotism that loomed behind the nineteenth-century "culture wars": "As far as Government is concerned, there are only two possible routes: the most absolute despotism or the most complete liberty. . . . I mean by despotism the most absolute autocratic reign of the Académie des beaux-arts."

Artists began bypassing the official channels of state patronage and became entrepreneurs on the model of other successful capitalists—charging admission, putting on "shows," forming art dealerships, and selling to the public. In the 1870s the Impressionists defied the academy by putting on exhibitions of their own. Finally, Mainardi writes, "the bourgeoisie had replaced the Academy as the arbiter of taste." In 1881, the government abandoned the academy, removing the final obstacle to the flowering of twentieth-century art.

20   The artists' conventional scorn for "bourgeois values" and their fear of their work being reduced to a "capitalistic commodity" are associated with socialism and the left-wing *avant garde*. This association, however, originated in the arch-conservatism of the feudal upper class and its elitist patronage of the arts. Historically, it was the bourgeoisie with their free markets who liberated the arts. State patronage, on the other hand—whether of the Right or the Left—has always tended to inhibit the arts.

The Academy of Grants Makers

The United States today has no all-encompassing arts bureaucracy on the scale of that of the Soviet Union or nineteenth-century France. American artists are not, as yet, wholly dependent on the state, and thus they retain a measure of independence. Nevertheless, the structure of arts funding in the United States is creating an arts establishment different only in degree from

---

* A French novelist and journalist, Émile Zola (1840–1902) exposed injustice and advocated social reform.

the Soviet Artists' Union and the French Academy of Fine Arts. The result is another kind of directed culture that interferes with the free development of the arts.

22   The National Endowment for the Arts was created in 1965, one of Lyndon Johnson's federal programs that would help constitute the "Great Society." The theory behind all of the Great Society programs was that the central government should increase its power and its responsibilities in order to address national problems. These could then be solved by applying federal funds and establishing bureaucracies of experts. The federal government would direct the economy in order to eliminate poverty. The federal government would likewise apply its dollars and its expertise to improve the artistic climate of the nation.

As a government publication of the Great Society era proudly points out, "The National Endowment for the Arts is the first Federal agency in the history of the United States given a specific mandate to encourage the development and growth of the arts throughout the Nation." Those who argue for the necessity of state patronage to the artistic vitality of the nation might wonder how American art developed and grew before 1965. In fact, the major movements and innovations in American art—from abstract expressionism to styles that seem most radically contemporary, such as pop art—all had their origins before 1965 and the establishment of the NEA. One is hard pressed to think of any significant artistic developments since.

24   Unlike the Soviet arts bureaucracy, the National Endowment for the Arts has sought to avoid even the very appearance of political control of the arts. According to its mission statement, "it must not, under any circumstances, impose a single esthetic standard or attempt to direct artistic content." While this prohibition prevents overt political control of the arts, it puts those who administer the funds in a very difficult position. Without applying an aesthetic standard or judging the artistic content of works of art, how can the agency decide what art to fund and what art to reject? Although the mission statement also calls for the NEA to "foster the excellence, diversity and vitality of the arts in the United States," how can it determine excellence without reference to an aesthetic standard or artistic content?

The solution to this intractable dilemma was to remove government representatives from the grants-awarding process altogether. The necessary artistic judgments would be made instead by a panel of independent experts. Under the peer-review system, grant decisions are made by panels of artists, critics, and other insiders of the art world. The NEA's methodology of peer review has seemed so fair and so reasonable—particularly in light of our society's widespread artistic illiteracy—that it has been adopted by state councils, private foundations, corporations, and even private buyers.

26   The arts in America have thus become highly dependent upon grants. Whether these are federal grants or private grants, from tax dollars or corporate profits, they tend to be awarded on the same basis and by the same panels of experts. As a result, artists no longer have to create works that

appeal to the public. They have to create works that appeal to the grants makers.

This class of certified experts—the academics, critics, and artists who make up the peer review panels—constitutes a de facto Artists' Union, a de facto academy. The relatively small amount of funding from the federal government—$171 million per year—is multiplied in its effect when state governments, corporations, and even private buyers follow the same procedures and defer to the same peer-review panels.

28   The process of peer review insulates art from the culture. Artists create for each other, rather than for an audience. Since decisions for funding are made by critics and other artists, the art world has become self-contained. Cut off from the society as a whole and indifferent to ordinary citizens, contemporary art is becoming increasingly irrelevant to the culture as a whole.

Historically, patrons have supported art that they like, so that there is a genuine connection and relationship between the artist and the audience. Under the current system of art funding, those who pay for the art farm out the task of selection to professionals. Thus, patrons are often alienated from the works they have paid for. Taxpayers complain about NEA-funded art that violates their values; corporations fund art that mocks corporations; public spaces are filled with art that nobody likes. As long as art is funded from the top down, it has no reason to appeal to anyone except the grants makers.

30   It may seem better to have artists distribute the funding than politicians or philistines, but artists were in charge of both the French Academy of Fine Arts and the Soviet Artists' Unions. Simply having artists distributing the money does not prevent the stultifying effects of a culture directed from above. It must be remembered that artistic revolutions are inevitably reactions against other artists, as new styles compete against the established styles. Established artists will thus tend to oppose artists who represent a different aesthetic. Giving artists control over the funding of other artists is a formula for stylistic stagnation and aesthetic mediocrity.

Today, post-Marxism, performance art, and the aesthetics of shock are in vogue among the arts establishment. These movements are beloved by peer review panels, but they outrage laypeople and are also singularly unfruitful aesthetically. Post-Marxism substitutes race, gender, and sexual preference for Marx's emphasis on social class. Post-Marxists interpret society in terms of the oppression of women, blacks, gays, and—now—animals. Artistically, post-Marxism manifests itself in confrontational, in-your-face political propaganda, which is becoming increasingly similar to the strident, cartoon stereotypes of socialist realism.

32   Performance art takes as its maxim the notion that art can be defined as anything done by an artist. Instead of painting a picture or making a sculpture, performance artists dispense with the work of art altogether and simply display themselves. Under the aesthetics of shock, the very notion of beauty is derided as a "bourgeois" concept, with its connotations of order,

idealism, and desire to please. Instead, many critics are saying, the purpose of art is to assault the sensibilities, to open up people's minds by shocking them into new levels of awareness.

Thus, the homoerotic photographs of Robert Mapplethorpe, the pornographic self-displays of Annie Sprinkle, the sadomasochistic bloodletting performed by Ron Athey, the exhibits of artists' bowel movements at the Whitney Museum, and other examples of controversial art are well within the canons favored by the contemporary art world. Such art outrages the public, as it was intended to, but it is by no means outrageous to the art world. What the public thinks is radical art represents nothing more than the status quo.

34   Few would argue that the arts today are flourishing in terms of quality or creativity. Ironically, in their zeal to favor art on the "cutting edge," the NEA and its parallel grants-making institutions have managed to do what cultural conservatives have always failed to do: They have destroyed the *avant garde*—not by censorship but by turning it into the establishment.

In art schools and in garret studios, young artists are complaining about the pressure to be not only politically correct but also artistically correct so that they can get exhibited and get grants. Many police themselves and try to find ways of fitting in to the "directed culture" dictated from on high rather than experimenting with perhaps more promising aesthetic theories.

36   The current system of arts patronage is bad for society, and it is bad for art. Because of the wall between artists and the general public, the public has become cut off from serious art, abandoned to the vulgarity and tastelessness of pop culture. Artists, in turn, are cut off from ordinary human life, which has always inspired the most profound art. Instead, they indulge themselves with inside jokes, esoteric experimentation, and voguish political statements, childishly trying to shock the American public instead of enriching their lives. Artists and the public have in common only a mutual contempt.

Ironically, postmodern critical theory is making some of the same complaints, though it tends to ignore the connection to the way art is funded. Postmodern theorists are decrying the elitism of the arts. They are advocating audience-centered aesthetic theories and urging serious artists to stop denigrating popular culture. They are calling for greater diversity and pluralism in the arts.

38   Postmodern theorists, however, assume that elitism can be eliminated by appropriating images from the pop culture and by becoming politically engaged. They seek to involve the audience not by pleasing them but by interactive technology and by making them feel uncomfortable. Their idea of diversity is ideologically conforming art that has been produced by artists of various genders, races, and sexual preferences. The postmodernists—subsidized as they are by the grants-making establishment—remain elitist, artist-centered, and ideologically predictable. What is needed instead is a

diversity of styles and ideas, expressed in art that the rest of the culture actually enjoys and finds meaningful.

Like the French Academy of Fine Arts and the Soviet Artists' Unions, the American experiment in governmental patronage has resulted in a directed culture, which dooms art to aesthetic mediocrity and cultural irrelevance. It is no accident that those contemporary art forms that are currently most innovative and alive—architecture, literature, film, music—are those that are least supported by the state.

Art and the Free Market

40 The opposite of censorship is "the marketplace of ideas," in which various points of view can compete with each other and individuals are free to accept or reject them. In a free artistic marketplace, undisturbed by state intervention or professional party lines, art would emerge that would appeal to different audiences. The NEA currently invokes a pluralism of race, gender, and sexual preference, but in its patronage of contemporary art permits little aesthetic or ideological diversity. The free market would create a genuine artistic pluralism. There could still be leftist, gay, and feminist art, addressing those communities and interest groups, but there could also be conservative, classical, and religious art (types now generally excluded from the canon of acceptable and grant-worthy art). The free market would give the arts a diversity of styles, a pluralism of ideas.

Artists instinctively draw back from such capitalist notions, afraid of turning their work into just another economic commodity. Their preference for socialist solutions, however, leads only to artistic slavery, as Miklós Haraszti has shown from his own bitter experience. Historically, free markets, free societies, and artistic freedom have always gone together and mutually enforced each other.

42 Advocates for the arts of the high culture worry that the masses will never respond to serious works of art. The crowd that watches the Home Shopping Network and buys Elvis paintings on black velvet will never have a taste for more challenging aesthetic experience. State funding, it is argued, is necessary to keep the high culture alive, in face of the onslaught of the mass culture.

This argument, though reminiscent of the aristocratic disdain for the vulgar masses that characterized the French academy, deserves consideration. First, it could be argued that much of the contemporary art currently being subsidized by the state is closer to the Elvis painting than to the Impressionists. The current arts establishment is not particularly friendly to the aesthetic standards traditionally upheld by the high culture. In fact, works that do appeal to the classical absolutes—the true, the good, and the beautiful—tend not to get the grants.

44 Second, the notion that the public will never accept good art is exaggerated and goes against history. It was the common people who crowded

in to see Shakespeare's plays, while the university-educated elite scorned them for not following the unities of Greek drama. The first important movement in American art, the Hudson River school,* was largely funded by ordinary Americans who not only paid admission to see the new paintings but bought lottery tickets to try to win one—a funding method that was considered unspeakably vulgar by those who felt American artists should imitate the Europeans but that fit perfectly with the cultural dynamism of the New World democracy. That today's pop culture is so shallow and that the public is so poorly educated in the arts may in large part be due to their abandonment by serious artists, an abandonment made possible by the current system of arts patronage.

The government could even participate in the free market of the arts. It could support the arts not by constructing a federal bureaucracy but by purchasing works of art. Just as the government has a legitimate nonregulatory impact on a free economy by spending money for national defense and other public goods, the government can spend money on art. If the people and their elected representatives are so inclined, a democratic government can erect monuments, decorate its buildings, subsidize orchestras, and fund art museums (although such projects are properly the function of local rather than federal governments). The key is that the government receive something tangible for its investment.

46   In one of the many anomalies of the current approach to arts patronage, the NEA and similar grants makers pay for works of art but then leave them in the hands of the grant writers. This kind of patronage—which is often spent on ephemeral "performance" or "conceptual" art—does not increase the nation's treasury of art, much less commission works of power and significance. While it avoids the commodification of art, in line with both socialist and aristocratic theory, it downplays the status of the artistic work as an object of meaning and value.

During the Depression, when the government felt it necessary to help artists along with other displaced workers, it did not give them unrestricted grants. Rather, it paid them to paint murals in post offices. The result was genuine public art. In small towns across America, the local Works Progress Administration (WPA) post office is likely to have a mural in a Thomas Hart Benton† style, representing the community's history and culture. These murals were not capitulations to the mass taste but genuine works of art, accessible rather than esoteric and designed to enrich the lives of ordinary people rather than to amuse the theoreticians of the art world.

48   Governments of the past often spent great sums on the arts, but they always got something for their money. Even the Pharaoh and Louis XIV were more like private patrons than governmental agencies. They bought art they liked. Richard Goldthwaite has shown that the explosion of art in the Renaissance was made possible not by indiscriminate government

---

* For an example of a painting from this movement, see p. 543.
† Thomas Hart Benton (1889–1975) is best known for the dramatic murals of American life he painted in the 1930s and '40s.

largesse, much less by closed artistic sects, but by nouveau-riche merchants, status-conscious nobility, and the newly emerging middle class—in short, by an awakened private sector whose demand for artistic excellence fueled the Renaissance. This is the best model for supporting the arts in a free society.

For art to thrive, there must be a dynamic relationship between artists, their audiences, and the culture as a whole. Efforts to direct the arts from above, whether by force or by generosity, whether cynical or well-intentioned, inevitably interfere with the artistic process and disrupt the mutually beneficial relationship between art and culture. Despite the insecurity and risk that it entails for artists, freedom, in the long run, is good for the arts. ❖

SUGGESTION FOR WRITING

Reread both of these essays, paying particular attention to how Spillane and Veith view government. Then write a summary of what Spillane expects from government, followed by a summary of what Veith expects. When you are sure the summaries you have written accurately reflect the views of each of these writers, write a summary of your own position.

PART 5

SOURCES FOR ARGUMENT

SECTION 1

GUN CONTROL: TRIGGERING A NATIONAL CONTROVERSY

ELIZABETH J. SWASEY

NRA WOMAN'S VOICE

Although the debate over gun control often seems dominated by men, women have a vital concern in the outcome of this debate. The following essay was first published in a 1993 issue of *The American Rifleman,* which is published by the National Rifle Association—a powerful lobby against gun control. As you read it, consider whether Swasey speaks *for* women or whether she is directing her argument *to persuade* an audience of women.

One of America's most powerful politicians said on the May 2 edition of "Meet the Press:" " '. . . to prevent you from getting weapons you need to defend yourself' is a very difficult case to make morally."

2   It sure is.

Just ask Suzanna Gratia.

4   It was Suzanna's desire to obey Texas law that caused her to experience hell on earth and made her an instant orphan. On Oct. 16, 1991, Suzanna dutifully left her handgun in the trunk of her car while she joined her parents for lunch at Luby's cafeteria in Killeen, Tex. Minutes later, a madman entered and slaughtered 22 people—including Suzanna's parents. Today, Suzanna will tell you how, lying face-down on the floor, she reached for her purse . . . for a gun to stop the killing, a gun that wasn't there—thanks to Texas' law against concealed carry.

But that powerful politician wasn't talking about Suzanna. He was talking about the Muslims in Bosnia–Herzegovina.

6   If this politician supports the right of citizens in a country half a world away to defend themselves, surely he supports the right of American women like Suzanna to do the same, right? Wrong.

This politician is Vice President Al Gore who, as a U.S. senator, voted against the instant criminal background check while voting for a ban on certain semi-automatics.

8   No one doubts that following the breakup of Yugoslavia, the horror has been unspeakable—including horrors perpetrated against women. The January 4 cover of *Newsweek* featured "A Pattern of Rape, War Crimes in Bosnia." The cover story said 30,000–50,000 Muslim women have been raped in Bosnia. But twice that number of women—106,593 to be exact—were raped in America in 1991 alone.

The fact is, there's a war going on in America, too. Every day, Americans face an enemy that is very real: criminals. In his State of the Union address, President Clinton railed against "violent crime which terrorizes our people and which tears our communities apart."

10   The war in America is the war against crime. Unfortunately, the good guys aren't taking any prisoners.

We didn't even take Mark Steven Hughes. After bludgeoning 10-month-old James Pompa to death, Mark Steven Hughes pled guilty to "injury to a child" in Texas and received a 10-year sentence. With "good time" jail credit, Hughes became eligible for parole six months before he was even sentenced.

12   Why aren't we taking any prisoners? Simple. Politicians prevent us from doing so by voting against building more prison space. They say "it's too expensive."

But according to National Institute of Justice, it's actually 17 times cheaper to keep criminals in jail: keeping a criminal in jail for one year costs some $25,000, whereas releasing him early results in an average of 187–287 crimes a year committed by that one criminal, at a cost to society of $430,000. This figure doesn't include the cost of human suffering.

14   There is a war going on. And until we start taking prisoners to local jails and state and federal prisons and keeping them there—citizens like Suzanna will likely come face-to-face with criminals like Mark Steven Hughes.

What happens then? In states without concealed carry laws, the answer depends on where the attack takes place.

16   Most state legislators support the citizen's right to use a firearm to defend him or herself at home, yet some oppose concealed carry legislation. This makes sense only if you believe the right of self-defense depends on where the victim is attacked: if inside the home then self-defense applies, if outside then it does not.

      Why shouldn't our right to defend ourselves in the manner we choose extend into places outside the home, where women are even more vulnerable? Those opposing concealed carry answer "because it poses a threat to public safety." But like the argument about building prisons, this too fails in the face of facts.

18   Florida enacted a concealed carry law in 1987. Before the law, Florida's homicide rate was 11.7 per 100,000. By 1991, it dropped 20% to 9.4 per 100,000. This compares with a 14% increase in the national average over the same period. (All figures: FBI Uniform Crime Reports.)

      Clearly, allowing law-abiding citizens to carry concealed firearms poses no threat to public safety. VP Gore must know this; like Florida, his home state of Tennessee allows licensed citizens to carry concealed firearms.

20   And right now, honest citizens in Missouri, North Carolina and Texas are asking their state legislatures for the ability to defend themselves against violent criminal attack regardless of where that attack takes place. They're calling for passage of concealed carry laws in their states.

      We can only hope our elected officials, both on the federal and state level, apply the same standard to honest citizens on American soil as they do to Muslims in Bosnia.

22   After all, there's a war going on in America, too. ❖

Questions for Meaning

1. Why does Swasey believe that American citizens should be allowed to carry concealed weapons?
2. How does Swasey support her claim that, in the war against crime, "the good guys aren't taking any prisoners"?
3. Why do legislators who believe in the right to self-defense nevertheless object to citizens' carrying concealed weapons?
4. Vocabulary: perpetrated (8), bludgeoning (11), vulnerable (17).

Questions about Strategy

1. Swasey does not immediately identify the politician she quotes in her opening paragraph. What does she gain by temporarily withholding this information?
2. Consider the brevity of paragraphs 2 and 3, each of which consists of a single sentence. How does this paragraphing influence the way you read these sentences?
3. How effective is the analogy Swasey makes between violence in Bosnia–Herzegovina and violence in the United States? Could an

opponent use this analogy to argue against laws permitting citizens to carry concealed weapons?

4. Is the information provided about Mark Steven Hughes relevant to Swasey's argument? Why is it included?

RUTH ROSEN

DOMESTIC DISARMAMENT: A WOMEN'S ISSUE?

Although women are being encouraged to buy guns for their own protection, they are also being urged to lead the fight for stricter gun control. A feminist scholar who writes regularly about contemporary issues, Ruth Rosen is the author of *The Lost Sisterhood: Prostitution in America* (1982) and editor of *The Mamie Papers* (1972). As she explains in the following article, she was drawn into the debate over gun control by Betty Friedan. (An argument by Friedan, the first president of the National Organization for Women, can be found in Part 6, pp. 673–676.) When reading Rosen's argument, which was first published in 1993, note how she links guns with concerns traditionally associated with women.

I've never considered packing a gun. Not after two young women were recently mugged on a sunny Saturday afternoon two blocks from my home. Not after a drive-by shooting occurred less than a mile from my neighborhood. Not after a crazed former client entered a San Francisco law office across the Bay, pulled out a satchel of assault weapons, and turned a high-rise office building into a killing field.

2   But if the gun industry has its way, it would sell me and every adult American woman a small, pearl-studded handgun to match her wardrobe. "The well dressed woman of the nineties will be armed," declares one gun advertisement targeted at fashion-conscious middle-class women. Along with a pink-handled semi-automatic "lady's gun," women are urged to purchase such "fashion accessories" as thigh holsters or modified handbags in which to pack a handgun. Also promoted is a midriff holster—beige with lace trim—that conceals a gun between a woman's breasts.

About four years ago, gun manufacturers realized that they had run out of male customers. Women, however, had barely been tapped. Like the tobacco industry in the 1960s, which tried to convince us that truly emancipated women smoked long, thin cigarettes, the gun industry has launched a new and sinister marketing campaign aimed at American women.

4   The Second Amendment Foundation, a nonprofit organization that fights gun control, recently started publishing a new magazine called *Women and Guns*. Some gun ads promise equal access to the wonderful

world of guns. In 1990, *American Firearms Industry*, a trade journal, informed retailers that "One of the quickest ways to boost firearms sales is to inform the public that you are offering women the same fun shooting opportunities as the men."

Most often the ads play upon women's fears of random violence and rape. They know that empty parking lots and darkened streets frighten us. They know that neither our bedrooms nor our offices feel safe. They know we fear rape more than burglary. So they target suburban women, exploit deep-seated racism, and promise protection from "them," code word for inner-city marauders.

6   The advertising campaign has even penetrated mainstream women's magazines such as *Ladies' Home Journal*. One ad shows a mother gently putting a child to bed. The text ominously warns women, "Self protection is more than your right—it's your responsibility." In ads for the tiny Derringer and "pen" guns, the weapon has been transferred from a man's to a woman's hand. A recent Smith & Wesson brochure displays an old handgun reconfigured by "ergonomic research" to fit a woman's hand. It is called the Lady Smith Revolver and is displayed alongside a rosebud and fur coat.

To most progressives and feminists, gun control has always felt like a lost cause: the National Rifle Association (NRA) seemed invincible and anyway, wasn't violence merely the symptom of deeper economic inequities and social injustices?

8   In the wake of growing gun violence, however, women from different sides of the tracks have begun to identify gun violence as a women's issue. In housing projects across the nation, local women have organized their communities against gun violence. At the same time, Adelle Simmons of the John D. and Catherine T. MacArthur Foundation and Marjorie Craig Benton, a longtime political activist in Chicago, contacted Betty Friedan with an idea whose time they felt had come: identifying gun control as a major women's issue of the 1990s.

I must confess that when Friedan invited me to a national conference on gun violence as a women's issue, I felt enormous skepticism. Don't we women have enough of a political agenda without adding gun control? Moreover, I don't believe that women are inherently more peaceful than men; we just haven't been given the opportunity to demonstrate how many atrocities we might commit.

10   Curious, I nevertheless trudged reluctantly to the conference, held in South Central Los Angeles one week after the second verdict in the Rodney King case was announced.* After three days of listening to feminists, public health officials, gun-control advocates, police officials, and, most

---

* Rodney King was severely beaten by Los Angeles police in 1991. This beating was captured on videotape, and many Americans who saw this tape were outraged when the police officers in question were acquitted of all but one charge in 1992. A second trial in 1993 found two of the officers guilty of violating King's civil rights. Before this verdict was announced, authorities in Los Angeles feared an outbreak of violence.

impressively, grass-roots activists from impoverished and devastated housing projects, I returned home a convert.

This is the story of that intellectual conversation.

12   The first reason that women should confront gun violence is that we are being targeted by an industry that wants us to join the vigilante crowd. Buying a gun, however, is an "individual solution," which only helps the gun industry turn women's fears into profits. The real feminist solution to our fears, Friedan insists, is for women to organize and fight for "domestic disarmament." "Women have secured many rights," the feminist leader observes, "but now they must fight for the fundamental right to be free from fear."

The second reason gun control is a women's issue is that no one else is as well organized—or seems to care enough—to protect our families and communities from random gun violence. After losing several relatives to gun violence, Eleanor Montano founded Mothers and Men Against Gangs, a grass-roots group in Los Angeles that enforces street curfews, intercedes with violent gang members, and imposes a neighborhood curfew. Montano is a tough, articulate woman who commands grudging respect from kids on the street. To her, the struggle against gun violence is a "women's issue" by default; in poor neighborhoods too many men are dead or in prison. "It's up to women," she says. "The mothers of the children who are daily killed by drive-by shootings have to banish guns." She and others rein in gang members by assigning them graffiti removal and other improvement projects. She personally takes kids loaded on drugs to Narcotics Anonymous and has even started a tattoo-removal program. During the past year, drive-by shootings have plunged 49 percent in her area.

14   In projects all over the country, such women have already organized against gun violence. These women, unsung heroines of local grass-roots organizations, receive relatively little publicity but are responsible for maintaining whatever safety zones exist in their communities. Through long nights, they walk the streets, arms folded across their chests, trying to convince gang members to turn in their weapons and handing over kids who break curfew to the police.

These are not the women buying guns. It is largely middle-class women, assured by the gun industry that they can purchase protection, who must be persuaded of their folly. Few of them know, for example, that buying a gun offers a false sense of security. According to research published in the *New England Journal of Medicine,* a handgun in the home is forty-three times more likely to kill a member of the family or an acquaintance than an intruder. Los Angeles Police Chief Willie Williams worries about the thousands of guns purchased just before the second trial of the four officers accused of beating Rodney King. "My biggest fear: Those guns are under pillows and they are on night stands. The people who bought them are not going to complete their training and those guns are headed for tragedy."

16   And it is the young who suffer the most when they find those half-hidden guns. The statistics quickly numb the mind. Every day fourteen

children in the United States are killed by guns. For teenage boys, gunshot deaths outnumber all natural causes combined. More than 135,000 students now carry handguns to school every day; some schools have had to install metal detectors and build high concrete walls just to protect their students from stray gunfire. On a recent weekend, twenty youths were shot in North Richmond, a poor community slightly north of Berkeley, California. Just another drive-by shooting; didn't even make the evening news. When blacks kill blacks, it doesn't make the front page. When a disgruntled white man kills lawyers in a fancy high-rise building, the media rush in and broadcast the news across the nation.

Gun violence is so pandemic that the Centers for Disease Control have identified it as the nation's number one public health problem. More than two million weapons are churned out by gun manufacturers every year. Add that to the estimated two hundred million firearms already in private hands and it's no wonder that more and more people die in front of a gun barrel. Every twenty-four hours handgun-wielding assailants rape thirty-three women, rob 575 people and assault 1,116 people. Every year, more than 24,000 Americans are killed—whether by homicide, suicide, or accident—with handguns.

18   More Americans recognize that rather than protecting us from potential tyranny—as our forefathers imagined—guns now threaten the very survival of the nation's citizens and communities. A new consensus is shaping up. According to a recent Louis Harris poll, American public opinion is rapidly swinging in favor of more stringent gun control measures. Nine out of ten Americans support the Brady Bill,* a relatively weak proposal that would require a five-day waiting period before a handgun may be purchased. Four out of five U.S. citizens surveyed believe that the easy availability of guns has contributed to an atmosphere of violence that endangers children. For the first time, a majority of Americans (52%) expressed their support for a ban on all handguns. This is a dramatic change from the past. And there is a gender gap among those polled: 61 percent of women but only 41 percent of men favored such a ban (with exceptions granted only by a court).

The time is ripe for challenging the once invincible NRA. According to recent reports, the leadership of the NRA appears to be drifting away from its membership. Committed to absolutist positions, the leadership won't even support the Brady Bill. In contrast, the membership wants to keep its hunting rifles and shotguns, but is horrified by the growing number of military weapons in the hands of urban criminals and gangs. Despite stiff opposition, four states—Connecticut, New Jersey, California, and Hawaii—have been able to ban the sale of assault weapons. In Minnesota, gun owners have become liable for negligently stored firearms. Virginia narrowly passed a bill limiting the purchase of handguns to one per month,

---

* The Brady Bill requires a waiting period and record search for the legal purchase of a handgun; it became law in 1993.

a defeat for the NRA. It's seemingly a ludicrous restriction, but it limits the sale of guns to other parts of the country.

20   There are plenty of good reasons, therefore, why everyone—not only women—should use their organizational skills and lobbying power to push for stricter federal legislation, including bans on all handguns. But it is women, from grassroots neighborhood groups to the PTA to NOW, who are the best organized constituency in American civil society. As Eleanor Roosevelt used to say when a problem seemed intractable, "Let the women do it."

Betty Friedan is convinced that her political Geiger counter is as accurate as it was when she wrote *The Feminine Mystique* or founded NOW. Now is the time, Friedan argues, for women's organizations to resist the campaign to sell women guns and join women in the poorest communities who have been fighting to save their communities. "Thirty years ago, when the women's movement began," she says, "we wanted to start with the most elementary issues for women. But we have enough empowerment now to move on to broader issues."

22   Those who propose a women's campaign to ban all guns have in their mind models of women's power to challenge established authority. They remind skeptics—like myself—of the women and mothers in Chile and Argentina who launched effective campaigns against the military by picketing and plastering neighborhoods with posters of their "disappeared" children. Or they point to Mothers Against Drunk Driving, which arguably became *the* primary force behind the successful effort to change the nation's drunk-driving laws. Or they point to the women's peace encampments of the early 1980s, which publicized the lunacy of stockpiling cruise missiles in Europe.

These are persuasive arguments, even to women like myself, who have preferred to argue our causes as citizens, rather than claim moral superiority as women or mothers. Dr. Garen Wintemute, a professor of community and international public health at U.C. Davis Medical School who has tracked the gun industry's campaign to sell guns to women, says, "The possibility that excited me the most is that gun control might become another area in this century where women act as our national conscience."

24   I confess to a certain aversion to act as men's national conscience, but I see his point. And I am reluctantly seduced by his current fantasy: "Think of the power of women protesting around the Smith and Wesson building." Yes. Imagine thousands of women in the Connecticut River Valley and in Southern California—where most of our guns are manufactured—attracting media attention to the products that threaten the safety and health of those we love. Like the Madres in Argentina, perhaps women would carry pictures of the children who have died from drive-by shootings, or from playing with carelessly hidden loaded guns.

Growing numbers of women activists, public health officials, and gun control organizations are now poised to force "domestic arms control" onto the political agenda. Finding the right language is important to this campaign. Rather than using the umbrella term "gun control," which only plays into the rhetoric of the NRA, women are addressing gun violence as an issue of safety and public health. "Guns destroy families. Let's destroy guns," is one of the popular slogans of this incipient movement. Rather than pushing for regulation, both feminist and grass-roots activists, who cross class lines in this struggle, are asserting freedom from fear as a basic human right.

26   Many tactics are being bandied about. Some suggest that weapons should be identified as hazardous materials that endanger public health. Others advocate educating the public about the cost of gun violence. (Each gunshot wound costs about $13,000 in health care, 80 percent of which is paid by the public.) Some U.S. senators are sponsoring legislation that would ban the manufacture, sale, and possession of semi-automatic assault weapons. Others want to ban private ownership of all guns, arguing that a civilized society should not allow its citizens to be tyrannized by the constant fear of death.

What might progressives and feminists do? For starters, we can begin to place domestic disarmament on the political agenda. During the 1970s and 1980s we excavated and publicized all kinds of hidden injuries, including marital and date rape, sexual harassment, and wife battering. Gun violence is not such a hidden problem. Domestic disarmament, moreover, crosses class and race lines; it has already mobilized women from diverse backgrounds. Progressive legislators should take the issue of domestic disarmament before the Armed Services Committee as a national security problem. Lawyers might bring liability test cases against gun manufacturers. Media critics can expose the fallacies of NRA ads. They should also try to convince the print and television media to name the gun manufacturer in every story they publish on gun violence. Organizers can gather women and children to picket gun manufacturing sites. The possibilities are endless.

28   The goal is domestic disarmament. Although progressives and feminists must confront the social and economic inequities that give rise to hopelessness and rage, we must also ban the weapons people use to kill each other.

And to those women seduced by the NRA's ads, we should say, don't pack a gun, ladies: picket a gun manufacturer instead. Guns are killing us, not protecting us. The best way to protect our families and communities is to boycott the gun industry and ravage their profits.   ❖

Questions for Meaning

1. According to Rosen, why have gun manufacturers begun to target women?
2. Why are women buying guns? What kind of women are most likely to respond to advertisements such as those described in paragraphs 2 and 6?
3. Why does Rosen believe that the NRA is no longer invincible? What evidence does she provide to support this claim?

4. Does Rosen have reason to believe that women can successfully work for social justice?
5. Vocabulary: marauders (5), reconfigured (6), ergonomic (6), wake (8), intractable (20), aversion (24), incipient (25).

Questions about Strategy

1. Although she favors gun control, Rosen opens her argument with examples of violence that could inspire other women to purchase guns. How do these examples ultimately work to her advantage?
2. How does Rosen go about identifying gun control as a women's issue? How successful, in your opinion, is this strategy?
3. Paragraphs 9 and 24 open with confessions. What effect do these confessions have on Rosen's credibility?
4. Where does Rosen link her concern about violence with concerns about racism? What assumption is she making about her audience?

James D. Wright

IN THE HEAT OF THE MOMENT

James D. Wright is a nationally recognized authority on gun control and other social issues. Favrot Professor of Human Relations at Tulane University, he is the author of *Under the Gun: Weapons, Crime, and Violence in America* (1983); *Address Unknown: The Homeless in America* (1989); and, coauthor of *In the Line of Fire: Youths, Guns, and Violence in Urban America* (1995). He first published the following article in a 1990 issue of *Reason,* a journal that promotes libertarian views.

Bob and Jim are good drinking buddies. After a night at their favorite bar, they head back to Jim's trailer for some whiskey. Jim begins praising his new girlfriend. Bob questions her fidelity and claims that he has slept with her. Seized by uncontrollable rage, Jim grabs a loaded .44 from the kitchen drawer and ends the conversation with a bang.

2   This is the sort of scenario that most people probably imagine when they hear that the majority of murders involve individuals who knew each other before the crime. Based on this impression, gun-control advocates argue that most homicides do not involve murderous intent. Rather, they are committed in the heat of the moment, in disputes or altercations among loved ones or close associates that escalate into rage—disputes that turn fatal not so much because anyone intended to kill but because, in that lamentable fit of anger, a gun was at hand. And if that is really how most murders happen, it follows that if fewer guns were "at hand," fewer murders would be committed.

But the data on relationships between homicide victims and their killers tell a different story. The conclusion in favor of gun control simply does not follow from the evidence.

4   FBI figures for 1987 and 1988 reveal that murders by strangers—for example, in the course of a robbery—are rare. They account for only about one in eight homicides (12.6 percent). But this does not imply that the remaining seven in every eight homicides involve loved ones slaying one another. After all, very few people love everyone they meet. Just how close is the relationship between victim and killer in the typical murder?

In many cases—nearly a third of the total—the authorities simply cannot determine the relationship. Next to "unknown," the largest relationship category is "acquaintance," accounting for approximately one additional third of the murders. You might think that "acquaintance" refers to fairly close associates, but the FBI tallies neighbors, friends, boyfriends, girlfriends, and all types of relatives in their own separate categories. If there were any degree of intimacy or closeness between acquaintances, the FBI would almost certainly classify the homicide under another heading. In this context, "acquaintance" means only that the victim and killer had some idea of each other's identities before the murder.

6   All categories of relatives combined account for about one in six murders (15.9 percent on average). About half of these are slayings of spouses by spouses. Friends and neighbors add an average of 9.8 percent to the annual homicide total. Altogether, then, relatives, friends, and neighbors commit only about a quarter (25.7 percent) of murders. So it's not true that "most" murders involve persons who share some degree of intimacy or closeness. Most murders—some three-quarters of them—are committed by casual acquaintances (30.2 percent), perfect strangers (12.8 percent), or persons unknown (31.2 percent).

Gun-control advocates, however, can easily convey the opposite impression of these data. By simply omitting the unknown relationships from the calculation and including casual acquaintances within the category of intimates, they can make it seem as if every murder other than those committed by perfect strangers involves intimates. But given what the category of acquaintance specifically omits, this would be an irresponsible misrepresentation.

8   That most murder victims know their killers prior to the crime is scarcely a surprise. That people know one another is not in itself evidence that they like one another. Ordinarily, the only people a murderer would have good reasons to kill would be people he or she knows. Indeed, slayings in the course of some other felony are the only obvious exception; random killings are understandably quite rare. So contrary to the common assumption, some degree of prior acquaintance between victim and offender definitely does not rule out murderous intent.

Cases of family members slaying one another figure prominently in the gun-control debate but represent fewer than one-sixth of all murders.

Studies of family homicide have shown that most of these families (about 85 percent of them) have had previous domestic quarrels serious enough to bring police to the residence; in nearly half the cases, the police had been called to the residence five or more times before the killing occurred. Indeed, most of the families in which such homicides occur have histories of abuse and violence going back years or even decades. These slayings are generally not isolated outbursts of rage between normally placid and loving couples. They are, instead, the culminating episodes in long, violent, abusive family relations.

10 At least some family homicides probably do result from the stereotypical "moment of rage." Others result from a thoroughly willful intention to kill. Knowing only that victim and killer are related by blood or marriage does not in itself tell us which explanation is correct for a given homicide.

Consider the bizarre case of Theron and Leila Morris, a Florida couple recently accused of killing their son, Christopher. Police say the Morrises were plotting with their son to murder his ex-wife for her insurance money. Then the conspirators learned that the ex-wife's insurance policy had lapsed, so there was nothing to be gained in killing her. Evidently annoyed by this turn of events, the Morrises then allegedly plotted between themselves to kill Christopher, in order to collect on *his* insurance policy, which was still in force and worth twice what his ex-wife's policy was worth. The Associated Press reported that the parents were also angry with Morris because he had "sold them bogus cocaine for $1,000 that they had intended to resell."

12 Morris's killing will appear in the FBI's 1990 Uniform Crime Report tabulation as a family homicide; having been slain by his own parents, he will be included in the category "son." What, then, will we know about the circumstances of his death, given that he was the child of his killers? Nothing at all.

How many murders are committed in a moment of rage, brought to fruition largely because a gun was available, and how many result from an unambiguous intention to kill? The fact is, nobody knows the answer to this question. An adequate answer would require getting inside the heads of murderers as they contemplate and commit their crimes.

14 Clearly, though, the assumption that heat-of-the-moment murders far outnumber willful murders cannot be justified by evidence on prior victim–offender relationships. Such information does not support conclusions about homicidal motives or about the number of slayings that might be prevented if fewer guns were available. ❖

Questions for Meaning

1. According to Wright, why do advocates of gun control believe that reducing the number of guns in circulation would reduce the number of murders committed?

2. Why does Wright believe that gun control is unlikely to reduce the murder rate?
3. According to the categories used by the FBI, what does it mean to be the "acquaintance" of a murder victim?
4. Vocabulary: fidelity (1), altercations (2), placid (9), tabulation (12), fruition (13).

Questions about Strategy

1. Wright begins his argument with a fictional example that does not represent what his research has revealed. What is the advantage of this strategy?
2. Where does Wright show that he is aware of arguments supporting gun control? Does he make any concessions?
3. Wright devotes two paragraphs to the story of Theron, Leila, and Christopher Morris. What is this example meant to establish?

JOSH SUGARMANN

THE NRA IS RIGHT

Most of the debate over gun control has focused on whether there's a need to restrict handgun ownership. In the following essay, first published in 1987, Josh Sugarmann argues on behalf of banning handguns altogether. A freelance writer living in New York, Sugarmann was communications director of the National Coalition to Ban Handguns, from 1984 to 1986. His book *The National Rifle Association: Money, Firepower, and Fear* was published in 1992.

One tenet of the National Rifle Association's faith has always been that handgun controls do little to stop criminals from obtaining handguns. For once, the NRA is right and America's leading handgun control organization is wrong. Criminals don't buy handguns in gun stores. That's why they're criminals. But it isn't criminals who are killing most of the 20,000 to 22,000 people who die from handguns each year. We are.

2   This is an ugly truth for a country that thinks of handgun violence as a "crime" issue and believes that it's somehow possible to separate "good" handguns (those in our hands for self-defense) from "bad" handguns (those in the hands of criminals).

Contrary to popular perception, the most prevalent form of handgun death in America isn't murder but suicide. An additional 1,000 fatalities are accidents. And of the 9,000 handgun deaths classified as murders, most are not caused by predatory strangers. Handgun violence is usually the result of people being angry, drunk, careless, or depressed—who just happen to have a handgun around. In all, fewer than 10 percent of handgun deaths are felony-related.

4   Though handgun availability is not a crime issue, it does represent a major public health threat. Handguns are the number one weapon for both murder and suicide and are second only to auto accidents as the leading cause of death due to injury. Of course there are other ways of committing suicide or crimes of passion. But no means is more lethal, effective, or handy. That's why the NRA is ultimately wrong. As several public health organizations have noted, the best way to curb a public health problem is through prevention—in this case, the banning of all handguns from civilian hands.

The Enemy Is Us

For most who attempt suicide, the will to die lasts only briefly. Only one out of every ten people attempting suicide is going to kill himself no matter what. The success or failure of an attempt depends primarily on the lethality of the means. Pills, razor blades, and gas aren't guaranteed killers, and they take time. Handguns, however, lend themselves well to spontaneity. Consider that although women try to kill themselves four times as often as men, men succeed three to four times as often. For one reason: women use pills or less lethal means; men use handguns. This balance is shifting, however, as more women own or have access to handguns. Between 1970 and 1978 the suicide rate for young women rose 50 percent, primarily due to increased use of handguns.

6   Of course, there is no way to lock society's cupboard and prevent every distraught soul from injuring him or herself. Still, there are ways we can promote public safety without becoming a nation of nannies. England, for instance, curbed suicide by replacing its most common means of committing suicide—coal stove gas—with less toxic natural gas. Fifteen years after the switch, studies found that suicide rates had dropped and remained low, even though the number of suicide *attempts* had increased. "High suicide rates seem to occur where highly lethal suicidal methods are not only available but also where they are culturally acceptable," writes Dr. Robert Markush of the University of Alabama, who has studied the use of handguns in suicide.

Most murders aren't crime-related, but are the result of arguments between friends and among families. In 1985, 59 percent of all murders were committed by people known to the victim. Only 15 percent were committed by strangers, and only 18 percent were the result of felonious activity. As the FBI admits every year in its *Uniform Crime Reports,* "murder is a societal problem over which law enforcement has little or no control." The FBI doesn't publish separate statistics on who's killing whom with handguns, but it is assumed that what is true of all murders is true of handgun murders.

Controlling the Vector

8   Recognizing that eliminating a disease requires prevention, not treatment, health professionals have been in the forefront of those calling for a national ban on handguns. In 1981, the Surgeon General's Select Panel for the Promotion of Child Health traced the "epidemic of deaths and injuries among children and youth" to handguns, and called for "nothing short of a total ban." It is estimated that on average, one child dies from handgun wounds each day. Between 1961 and 1981, according to the American Association of Suicidology, the suicide rate for 15- to 24-year-olds increased 150 percent. The report linked the rise in murders and suicides among the young to the increased use of firearms—primarily handguns. In a 1985 report, the Surgeon General's Workshop on Violence and Public Health recommended "a complete and universal ban on the sale, manufacture, importation, and possession of handguns (except for authorized police and military personnel)."

Not surprisingly, the American Public Health Association, the American Association of Suicidology, and the American Psychiatric Association, are three of the 31 national organizations that are members of the National Coalition to Ban Handguns (NCBH).

10   Comparing the relationship between handguns and violence to mosquitos and malaria, Stephen P. Teret, co-director of the Johns Hopkins Injury Prevention Center, says, "As public health professionals, if we are faced with a disease that is carried by some type of vehicle/vector like a mosquito, our initial response would be to control the vector. There's no reason why if the vehicle/vector is a handgun, we should not be interested in controlling the handgun."

The NRA refers to handgun suicides, accidental killings, and murders by acquaintances as "the price of freedom." It believes that handguns right enough wrongs, stop enough crimes, and kill enough criminals to justify these deaths. But even the NRA has admitted that there is no "adequate measure that more lives are saved by arms in good hands than are lost by arms in evil hands." Again, the NRA is right.

12   A 1985 NCBH study found that a handgun is 118 times more likely to be used in a suicide, murder, or fatal accident than to kill a criminal. Between 1981 and 1983, nearly 69,000 Americans lost their lives to handguns. During that same period there were only 583 justifiable homicides reported to the FBI, in which someone used a handgun to kill a stranger—a burglar, rapist, or other criminal. In 1982, 19 states reported to the FBI that not once did a private citizen use a handgun to kill a criminal. Five states reported that more than 130 citizens were murdered with handguns for each time a handgun was justifiably used to kill a criminal. In no state did the number of self-defense homicides approach the murder toll. Last year, a study published in the *New England Journal of Medicine* analyzing gun use in the home over a six-year period in the Seattle, Washington area, found that for every time a firearm was used to kill an intruder in self-defense, 198 lives

ended in murders, suicides, or accidents. Handguns were used in more than 70 percent of those deaths.

Although handguns are rarely used to kill criminals, an obvious question remains: How often are they used merely to wound or scare away intruders? No reliable statistics are available, but most police officials agree that in a criminal confrontation on the street, the handgun-toting civilian is far more likely to be killed or lose his handgun to a criminal than successfully use the weapon in self-defense. "Beyond any doubt, thousands more lives are lost every year because of the proliferation of handguns than are saved," says Joseph McNamara, chief of police of San Jose, who has also been police chief in Kansas City, a beat cop in Harlem, and is the author of a book on defense against violent crime. Moreover, most burglaries occur when homes are vacant, so the handgun in the drawer is no deterrent. (It would also probably be the first item stolen.)

14   Faced with facts like these, anti-control advocates often turn to the argument of last resort: the Second Amendment. But the historic, 1981 Morton Grove, Illinois, ban on handgun sale and possession exploded that rationale. In 1983, the U.S. Supreme Court let stand a lower court ruling that stated, "Because the possession of handguns is not part of the right to keep and bear arms, [the Morton Grove ordinance] does not violate the Second Amendment."

Criminal Equivocation

Unfortunately, powerful as the NRA is, it has received additional help from the leading handgun control group. Handgun Control Inc. (HCI) has helped the handgun lobby by setting up the perfect strawman for the NRA to shoot down. "Keep handguns out of the wrong hands," HCI says. "By making it more difficult for criminals, drug addicts, etc., to get handguns, we can reduce handgun violence," it promises. Like those in the NRA, HCI chairman Nelson T. "Pete" Shields "firmly believe(s) in the right of law-abiding citizens to possess handguns . . . for legitimate purposes."

16   In its attempt to paint handgun violence solely as a crime issue, HCI goes so far as to sometimes ignore the weapon's non-crime death tally. In its most recent poster comparing the handgun murder toll in the U.S. with that of nations with strict handgun laws, HCI states: "In 1983, handguns killed 35 people in Japan, 8 in Great Britain, 27 in Switzerland, 6 in Canada, 7 in Sweden, 10 in Australia, and 9,014 in the United States." Handguns *killed* a lot more than that in the United States. About 13,000 suicides and accidents more.

HCI endorses a ban only on short-barrelled handguns (the preferred weapon of criminals). It advocates mandatory safety training, a waiting period during which a background check can be run on a purchaser, and a license to carry a handgun, with mandatory sentencing for violators. It also endorses mandatory sentencing for the use of a handgun in a crime.

According to HCI communications director Barbara Lautman, together these measures would "attack pretty much the heart of the problem."

18   HCI appears to have arrived at its crime focus by taking polls. In his 1981 book, *Guns Don't Die—People Do*, Shields points out that the majority of Americans don't favor a ban on handguns. "What they do want, however, is a set of strict laws to control the easy access to handguns by the criminal and the violence prone—*as long as those controls don't jeopardize the perceived right of law-abiding citizens to buy and own handguns for self defense* [italics his]." Shields admits "this is not based on any naive hope that criminals will obey such laws. Rather, it is based on the willingness of the rest of us to be responsible and accountable citizens, and the knowledge that to the degree we are, we make it more difficult for the criminal to get a handgun." This wasn't always HCI's stand. Founded in 1974 as the National Council to Control Handguns, HCI originally called a ban on private handgun possession the "most effective" solution to reducing violent crime rapidly and was at one time a member of NCBH. Michael Beard, president of NCBH, maintains the HCI's focus on crime "started with a public relations concern. Some people in the movement felt Americans were worried about crime, and that was one way to approach the problem. That's the problem when you use public opinion polls to tell you what your position's going to be. And I think a lot of the handgun control movement has looked at whatever's hot at the time and tried to latch onto that, rather than sticking to the basic message that there is a relationship between the availability of handguns and the handgun violence in our society. . . . Ultimately, nothing short of taking the product off the market is really going to have an effect on the problem."

HCI's cops and robbers emphasis has been endlessly frustrating to many in the anti-handgun movement. HCI would offer handgun control as a solution to crime, and the NRA would effectively rebut their arguments with the commonsensical observation that criminals are not likely to obey such laws. I can't help but think that HCI's refusal to abandon the crime argument has harmed the longterm progress of the movement.

Saturated Dresser Drawers

20   In a nation with 40 million handguns—where anyone who wants one can get one—it's time to face a chilling fact. We're way past the point where registration, licensing, safety training, waiting periods, or mandatory sentencing are going to have much effect. Each of these measures may save some lives or help catch a few criminals, but none—by itself or taken together—will stop the vast majority of handgun suicides or murders. A "controlled" handgun kills just as effectively as an "uncontrolled" one.

Most control recommendations merely perpetuate the myth that with proper care a handgun can be as safe as any other. Nothing could be further from the truth. A handgun is not a blender.

22   Those advocating a step-by-step process insist that a ban would be too radical and therefore unacceptable to Congress and the public. A hardcore 40 percent of the American public has always endorsed banning handguns. Many will also undoubtedly argue that any control measure—no matter how ill-conceived or ineffective—would be a good first step. But after more than a decade, the other foot hasn't followed.

In other areas of firearms control there has been increasing recognition that bans are the most effective solution. The only two federal measures passed since the Gun Control Act of 1968 have been bans. In each case, the reasoning was simple: the harm done by these objects outweighed any possible benefit they brought to society. In 1986, Congress banned certain types of armor-piercing "cop-killer" bullets. There was also a silver lining to last year's NRA–McClure–Volkmer handgun "decontrol" bill, which weakened the already lax Gun Control Act of 1968, making it legal, for instance, for people to transport unloaded "not readily accessible" handguns interstate. A last-minute amendment added by pro-control forces banned the future production and sale of machine guns for civilian use.

24   Unfortunately, no law has addressed the major public health problem. Few suicides, accidental killings, or acquaintance murders are the result of cop-killer bullets or machine guns.

Outlawing handguns would in no way be a panacea. Even if handgun production stopped tomorrow, millions would remain in the dresser drawers of America's bedrooms—and many of them would probably stay there. Contrary to NRA fantasies, black-booted fascists would not be kicking down doors searching for handguns. Moreover, the absolute last segment of society to be affected by any measure would be criminals. The black market that has fed off the legal sale of handguns would continue for a long while. But by ending new handgun production, the availability of illegal handguns can only decrease.

26   Of course, someone who truly wants to kill himself can find another way. A handgun ban would not affect millions of rifles and shotguns. But experience shows that no weapon provides the combination of lethality and convenience that a handgun does. Handguns represent only 30 percent of all guns out there but are responsible for 90 percent of firearms misuse. Most people who commit suicide with a firearm use a handgun. At minimum, a handgun ban would prevent the escalation of killings in segments of society that have not yet been saturated by handgun manufacturers. Further increases in suicides among women, for instance, might be curtailed.

But the final solution lies in changing the way handguns and handgun violence are viewed by society. Public health campaigns have changed the way Americans look at cigarette smoking and drunk driving and can do the same for handguns.

28   For the past 12 years, many in the handgun control movement have confined their debate to what the public supposedly wants and expects to hear—not to reality. The handgun must be seen for what it is, not what we'd like it to be.   ❖

Questions for Meaning

1. Why does Sugarmann believe that banning handguns would reduce the number of deaths that occur each year in the United States?
2. What causes of handgun violence are identified by Sugarmann?
3. What does Sugarmann mean by "strawman" in paragraph 15?
4. How does Sugarmann's position differ from the policy of Handgun Control Inc.?
5. Why is it that men kill themselves more often than women do even though women attempt suicide more frequently?
6. Vocabulary: tenet (1), prevalent (3), predatory (3), nannies (6), rationale (14), fascists (25), curtailed (26).

Questions about Strategy

1. Consider the title of this essay. Why do you think Sugarmann chose it?
2. Does Sugarmann make any concessions to opponents of gun control?
3. Why does Sugarmann link gun control with public health campaigns?
4. Sugarmann devotes five paragraphs to attacking an organization that is working to control handguns, an organization with which he might have forged an alliance. Was this wise? Did he have any choice?

ROGER KOOPMAN

SECOND DEFENSE

After graduating from the University of Idaho in 1973, Roger Koopman served as a congressional press secretary and administrative assistant before becoming a public relations specialist for the National Rifle Association's Institute for Legislative Action. He left the NRA in 1980 to pursue a business career in western Montana. A regular political columnist for the *Bozeman Daily Chronicle,* he has published articles in many national magazines. "Second Defense" was first published in 1990 by *Outdoor Life.*

Last year was a rough one for the right to keep and bear arms. Fueled by the school-yard tragedy in Stockton, California,* the Second Amendment's organized enemies have made great strides. Yet the erosion of our rights cannot be blamed on mere circumstance; the fault rests squarely in the laps of gun owners themselves, who for years have been employing every possible argument to defend their constitutional rights except the constitutional one.

---

* In January, 1989, a man with an automatic rifle sprayed bullets into the school-yard of an elementary school in Stockton, killing five students and wounding twenty-nine others as well as a teacher before killing himself.

2   In reality, we couldn't have played into the gun controllers' hands more if they had written the script! Consider, for example, our response to the current hysteria over so-called "assault rifles." We have argued, ad nauseam, that people should be "allowed the right" to own these firearms (whatever they are) because of the "legitimate uses" (whatever that means) for such guns, uses that include hunting, target practice, collecting, competitive shooting and self-defense. The predictable result? Whenever gun owners seem to be outnumbered by non-gun owners in a particular area, the legislatures and city councils have gone right ahead and banned these guns anyway, regardless of whether there are "legitimate uses" for them or not.

       That's politics, and the process is, to say the least, a two-edged sword that groups such as the National Rifle Association have lived by—and, at times, died by. Certainly no one would suggest that the battles the NRA fights shouldn't be fought. But the Constitution of the United States transcends politics, and its wisdom and truth are not dependent upon the nightly opinion polls on CNN News. The Constitution's Second Amendment does not speak in terms of "legitimate" and "illegitimate" uses for privately owned firearms. Rather, it proclaims, in simple and emphatic words, that a "free State" is secure only if the people's right to "keep and bear Arms" remains inviolate.

4   The gun control issue, then, is never a question of what the government "allows" us to own. The Constitution states that government has *no authority* over the firearms ownership of the people. The people, not the government, possess an absolute right in the area of gun ownership. If you or I want to own an AR-15 or any other gun, it is none of the government's business *why* we want it, and certainly none of its business to presume that we may be up to no good. In a free society, the salient question is *never* whether the government can trust the people, but always whether the people can trust their government. The history of the Second Amendment makes this point ever so clear. You could spend a lifetime studying the writings of the Founding Fathers and would never find among any of them the kinds of sentiments expressed by our 20th century gun controllers—sentiments that reflect a profound distrust for a free people. You would not find a single person among all of the founders of our nation who was worried about firearms in the hands of the citizenry. The very idea is preposterous.

       What you *will* find is that there was a very widespread concern over firearms in the hands of the government, especially in the form of a federal "standing army." As great scholars of human history, our forefathers knew full well the threat to liberty posed by governments that developed a monopoly of force over the people. Thus, they authored the Second Amendment, guaranteeing that an armed citizenry (spoken of as the "militia") would always hold sway over the central government and would be a constant check against governmental excesses.

6   As with so many constitutional principles in this century, the essence of the Second Amendment has been turned upside down by an anti-gun establishment that reveres big government and distrusts the people. Make no mistake about it. What these folks stand for is a total reversal of our

constitutional system, where rights and powers become vested *not* in the people, but in the government. They promote an alien, Old World mentality that turns the citizenry against itself by convincing us that we should "trust" the government and distrust our neighbor. Understood in this way, the issue becomes a lot larger than our opportunity to shoot a deer or plink a can. The issue is not guns; the issue is freedom, and it involves not just gun owners, but everyone—especially our children.

It's vitally important that we not allow the gun control lobby and its friends in the national media to paint us into a corner and narrowly define our position as "pro-gun." We are "pro-constitution" and "pro-freedom." And for goodness' sake, let's not fall into the trap of debating among ourselves what types of guns are "needed" and what guns can be outlawed; what gun-related freedoms are "necessary" and what ones we can afford to lose. Freedom is indivisible. Once we accept the notion that government has the right to deny *any* of our firearms rights, we have thrown in the towel and torn apart our Constitution.

8   If we are going to start winning these battles and regaining ground already lost, we must start framing the so-called "gun issues" in constitutional terms, and show how *every* citizen has a stake in the outcome. Even in states such as Montana, where I reside, the gun control lobby can carry the day by dividing and conquering the general populace with convincing, if thoroughly unconstitutional arguments. I am reminded of a proposal in the last legislative session that would have returned to Montana citizens at least a measure of their *rights* to carry firearms in a concealed fashion—something that the law enforcement community has always enjoyed the undisputed "right" to do. Following a heavy lobbying effort against the bill by some (not all) of these law enforcement people, legislators who should have known better were convinced to vote the measure down. Yet by doing so, they were essentially saying that law enforcement personnel (an arm of local and state government) possess firearms rights that the citizenry at large could be denied. The problem, of course, was that few, if any, of the legislators were made to look at the issue in constitutional terms.

In recent years, the battle lines on gun control have gradually shifted. Defenders of the Second Amendment are now fighting not only the Liberal Left, but an increasing number of persons claiming to speak for the law enforcement community—our traditional ally! This is cause for real concern, not only strategically, but philosophically. Should current trends toward the polarization of law enforcement with the armed citizen continue, it raises an ominous specter: Are we moving toward a society that will be dominated by law and order "professionals" who reign supreme over a disarmed and once free people?

10   The advice of Larry Pratt, executive director of Gun Owners of America, is well worth repeating. Pratt warns that it is the natural tendency of government to concentrate power by "reserving for itself the monopoly of fire power." He also believes that sport shooting is a pleasant derivative of underlying constitutional principles, but it is not the reason the Founders

wrote the Second Amendment. It was their deep concern over the power of government, with its standing military, that made them seek to guarantee for all time the right of every citizen to be armed.

The issue, indeed, is freedom. You will not find a single government in the world today that would be able to enslave its people *if* those people enjoyed the unrestricted right to private gun ownership. It couldn't be done. China, on the other hand, tells us a very different story. It is not so much that an armed citizenry could have fought off the tanks in Tianamen Square* as it is that an armed citizenry would have seen to it that the tanks were never there in the first place. The point is no less valid for this place we call America—the land of the free. ❖

Questions for Meaning

1. Would Koopman accept any government restraints on the ownership of guns?
2. According to Koopman, why was the Second Amendment written into the Constitution?
3. In paragraph 7, Koopman claims "Freedom is indivisible." What does he mean by this?
4. Why did Koopman favor legislation in Montana that would have made it legal for citizens to carry concealed weapons?
5. Vocabulary: ad nauseam (2), transcends (3), salient (4), vested (6), polarization (9).

Questions about Strategy

1. Koopman begins his argument by claiming that opponents of gun control have ignored the constitutional argument that the Second Amendment protects the right to "keep and bear Arms." Is this claim convincing?
2. Consider how Koopman quotes the Second Amendment in paragraph 3. Why doesn't he quote the entire Amendment?
3. How fairly does Koopman characterize advocates of gun control?
4. Why does Koopman emphasize children at the end of paragraph 6? What is he implying here?
5. Koopman claims that opponents of gun control should describe themselves as "pro-constitution" or "pro-freedom" rather than "pro-gun." What is the difference? Has attention to language of this sort helped to shape the debate over any other public issues?

---

* A public space in the heart of Beijing that was the site of a large political protest which was violently suppressed by the Chinese government in 1989.

DANIEL D. POLSBY

SECOND READING
Treating the Second Amendment as Normal Constitutional Law

Daniel D. Polsby is Kirkland & Ellis Professor of Law at Northwestern University. He has also taught at Cornell University, the University of Michigan, and the University of Southern California. In this essay, first published in 1996, he argues that courts need to clarify the meaning of the Second Amendment. As you read, note how Polsby's interpretation of this amendment is shaped by his knowledge of its context: the first ten amendments to the Constitution, collectively known as the Bill of Rights.

It has not been long since the Second Amendment moldered in the torpid backwaters of constitutional law studies. Swollen with materials pertaining to the Equal Protection Clause and the First Amendment, the leading law school casebooks of the 1960s, '70s, and '80s had little or nothing to say about the right of the people to keep and bear arms. Indeed, most such books had not so much as an index entry on the subject. In the entire 20th century the Supreme Court has not decided a single case concerning the states' power to regulate firearms, and in the past generation's political debates about gun control legislation, the Second Amendment has played a marginal and, one must say, somewhat abject role. It has been waved talismanically by the (usually) losing side (consisting of firearms enthusiasts), who sense an "abridgment" of their "rights" in any firearms regulation, and scoffed at by the winning side (anti-gun advocacy groups and their allies in government), who argue that by its very terms, the Second Amendment guarantees only the rights of states to have well-regulated militias, and not the right of individuals to have firearms. There is, then (say the winners), no constitutional reason for society to put up with high rates of suicide, accidents, and lethal criminal violence caused by the too-easy availability of guns, especially when those problems can be curtailed by making firearms harder and harder to come by, if not downright impossible for private citizens to obtain legally.

2   Hunters, target-shooters, and gun collectors have always been great devotees of the Second Amendment, and until quite recently by far the majority of writing on the subject was to be found in magazines dealing with outdoor recreation, hunting and fishing, or firearms hobbies. This writing often contains interesting anecdotes about people using guns to defend themselves from animals or criminals, and one sometimes finds references to or quotations from the thought of the illustrious men of the Founders' generation, especially Madison and Jefferson. Generally speaking, though, it must be said that even among enthusiasts who think about the Second

Amendment quite a lot, there has been little appreciation for the intricate and nuanced way in which constitutional analysis is practiced, and has to be practiced, by judges and lawyers.

For the legal profession, constitutional text, history, precedent, and matters of expediency are all important, and no one provision of the Constitution is to be seized upon without due recognition of its context in the Constitution as a whole, and for the strands of doctrine that the Supreme Court has elaborated over the years to translate the words of the document into the actions of the government. The "freedom of speech and the press" that journalists habitually ascribe to the Founding Fathers is more aptly attributed to Supreme Court Justices Oliver Wendell Holmes Jr. and Louis D. Brandeis, whose opinions in a series of cases in the 1910s and '20s gave a modern form to the question of how "the freedom of speech" differs from "speech" *simpliciter* and what the limits of that freedom might be. Similarly, one might well say that the First Amendment's freedom of religion, such as it is, was for all practical purposes invented in the 1940s by Justices William O. Douglas, Robert Jackson, and Hugo Black and in the 1950s and '60s by Justice William Brennan.

4   This is a game in which the Second Amendment has never really played. It's true that there was little occasion for litigation prior to the late 1960s, because until then governments at every level did little to regulate firearms. Yet even in the years since the federal Gun Control Act of 1968, when gun restrictions of various kinds began to proliferate, courts and scholars were quite content to allow politics to take its course without reflecting on what the Constitution might have to say about the role of private firearms in American life. The fact that the Second Amendment found no champion among policy-making elites surely tells more about the social psychology of the class from which lawyers and social scientists are drawn than it does about the Constitution's text and structure. The modern American legal profession especially has been thoroughly acculturated to Max Weber's* conception of the modern state as the monopolist of all legitimate force—a principle in undeniable tension with the private keeping of arms for self-defense.

But the Second Amendment's era of marginality may well be ending. In the law journals if not yet in media of mass circulation, the Second Amendment has captured the attention of scholars, including some of the most eminent and respectable in the field, who find, somewhat to their own surprise as they reflect upon the matter for the first time, that the private right to keep and bear arms is very much in character with the Bill of Rights as a whole and with the thinking of the Framers of the Constitution.

6   Despite its renaissance in the law reviews, however, it must be said that in practice the Second Amendment has not yet acquired full membership in

---

* The German sociologist, Max Weber (1864–1920) emphasized how societies are shaped by specific values and leaders.

the league of serious constitutional rights. Plaintiffs who go to court to overturn firearms restrictions usually prefer not to base their cases on Second Amendment arguments. An example is the litigation testing the validity of the 1993 Brady Law. The (eventually unsuccessful) challenge to this law was not based on the Second Amendment at all, but on the 10th Amendment claim that the federal government should not be allowed to oblige state officials to do (more or less costly) background checks on handgun buyers. The lawyers who bring these cases appreciate (as their fiery clients usually do not) that lower courts at least are unlikely to dispute the right of legislatures at any level of government strictly to regulate most varieties of firearms, up to and including prohibiting their sale and ownership altogether. Partly this response is simply routine deference to legislative prerogatives. Courts generally endeavor to uphold legislative decisions rather than undermine them. But in this instance judicial deference is more than routine, because, as Duke law professor William Van Alstyne has written, Supreme Court cases interpreting the Second Amendment are, for all practical purposes, missing in action. There simply is no modern jurisprudence that explains to judges the meaning of "the right to keep and bear arms" and the scope of their authority to decide that a given piece of legislation constitutes an infringement of that right. If ever there was a situation designed to play on the inherent timidity of lower-court judges, this is it.

A single example will suffice to show how decisive the virtual absence of interpretative precedents can be. In 1981 the trustees of a tiny bedroom suburb of Chicago enacted an ordinance forbidding the private possession of handguns within the village limits. The law was immediately challenged in federal district court on a Second Amendment theory (among other grounds). In due course the U.S. Court of Appeals for the Seventh Circuit received the case, known as *Quillici v. Village of Morton Grove,* and upheld the law, finding that there was no authentic Second Amendment issue raised by the case. It cited as authority the most recent Supreme Court pronouncement on the subject, *Presser v. Illinois,* decided in 1886, many years before the "incorporation" doctrine was conceived. In the 19th century it was conventionally said that the Bill of Rights constrained only national and not state government. A few years before *Presser,* for example, the Supreme Court clearly held (in *United States v. Cruikshank*) that neither the Second Amendment *nor the First* creates any individual rights that a state government need respect. The Court, of course, has long since repudiated this principle; beginning in the 1930s, it applied ("incorporated") one provision of the Bill of Rights after another to limit the authority of the states. But it has never done so with respect to the Second Amendment, leaving an opening for *Quillici*-type decisions.

8   Second Amendment enthusiasts are understandably eager to see this anomaly corrected. Nevertheless, there is reason not to jump at every perceived legislative affront with a new lawsuit. The procedural posture of a case—especially a novel case—can matter enormously to its outcome. To maximize one's chance of winning, it is important to align one's case with

legislation rather than against it. Congress has power under Section 5 of the 14th Amendment to define and protect substantive due process rights from state encroachment. Suppose Congress enacted that the right to bear arms is an individual right that (along with the rest of the Bill of Rights) is "incorporated," so as to be fully applicable against the states, and suppose the gun control law of some states—say, New York—infringed upon that right. In the resulting litigation, the always-tilted playing field would for a change favor the Second Amendment. Instead of remaining in the Supreme Court's dead-letter office, the Second Amendment would move to the status of normal constitutional law.

Normal constitutional argument begins with text. The first question to consider, then, is: What does the Constitution say about the right to keep and bear arms? There seem to be two main theories of what sense is conveyed by the language of the Second Amendment. The theory that is most often encountered by the intelligent lay public reads the words to say something like: "In order to make themselves secure, states have a right to have a well regulated militia, and Congress may not restrict state regulation of militia members' weapons." This is approximately the interpretation favored by most major newspapers' editorial writers, by gun control groups, and by a broad swath of conventional public opinion, running the partisan gamut from left (e.g., Rep. Charles Schumer of New York) to right (e.g., President Nixon) and most political shades in between.

10   But in places where close attention is paid to what words actually say, the states'-rights reading of the Second Amendment has attracted surprisingly little support. After all, the Second Amendment does not say, "A well regulated militia, being necessary to the security of a free state, shall not be infringed." Nor do the words of the amendment assert that "the right of the people to keep and bear arms" is conditional upon membership in some sort of organized soldiery like the National Guard. Indeed, if there is conditional language in the Second Amendment at all, evidently the contingency runs the other way: "Because the people have a right to keep and bear arms, states will be assured of the well regulated militias that are necessary for their security." Some version of this reading is supported by almost all of the constitutional historians and lawyers who have published research on the subject. Indeed, this view is so dominant in the academy that Garry Wills, the lone dissenter among historians on the proper reading of "the right of the people to keep and bear arms," has dubbed it the Standard Model of the Second Amendment.

Are these textual arguments dispositive? In some (increasingly rare) instances, lawyers are prepared simply to read what the Constitution says and end the conversation at that point. For example, if some question arose about the eligibility of a person who had not "attained to the age of thirty-five years" to serve as president, most lawyers would probably be content simply to follow the command of Article II, Section 1 rather than attempt to penetrate to the deeper meaning the clause must surely have.

12   But a number of scholars, including some friendly to a broad reading of the Second Amendment like Van Alstyne and University of Texas law professor Sanford Levinson, agree that the Second Amendment is so obscurely drafted as almost to invite confusion and misunderstanding. Where text is inadequate standing alone, one needs historical tools to explain what the provision's language actually meant. And even lawyers who, like me, do not find the draftmanship all that confusing recognize that arguments, especially arguments about "the right of the people to keep and bear arms" that have become politically incorrect as the 20th century draws to a close, will acquire extra cogency by pointing out that the Founding Fathers of our country are at one's side. Whether or not the meaning of the text seems clear, it is always helpful to adduce evidence of how the drafters of the Bill of Rights would have understood a particular provision's language.

Unhappily, in many cases, including some of the most vexing, such evidence is unavailable. We can only extrapolate and conjecture about how the Founders would have understood the First Amendment's "freedom of the press" to apply to the Playboy Channel, or how the "search and seizure" language of the Fourth Amendment would have been thought to bear on overheard cellular telephone calls. But no ambiguity at all surrounds the attitude of the constitutional generation concerning "the right of the people to keep and bear arms." To put the matter bluntly, the Founders of the United States were what we would nowadays call gun nuts. "One loves to possess arms," Thomas Jefferson wrote to President Washington (whose own gun collection, Don Kates notes, contained more than 50 specimens). And to his teenage nephew, the author of the Declaration of Independence had this to say: "A strong body makes the mind strong. As to the species of exercises, I advise the gun. While this gives a moderate exercise to the body, it gives boldness, enterprise and independence to the mind. Games played with the ball, and others of that nature, are too violent for the body and stamp no character on the mind. Let your gun therefore be the constant companion of your walks."

14   Addressing Virginia's constitutional ratification convention with characteristic exorbitance, Anti-Federalist icon Patrick Henry declared that "the great object is that every man be armed. . . . Everyone who is able may have a gun." And James Madison, author of the Bill of Rights, recognized "the advantage of being armed, which the Americans possess over the people of almost every other nation," whose tyrannical governments are "afraid to trust the people with arms."

There are at least scores of contemporaneous expressions of similar import. But if one is trying to fathom whether or not the Second Amendment recognizes an individual right, perhaps the most significant fragment of history is this: The idea that the Second Amendment guarantees a collective but not an individual right originated in the 20th century with gun control groups and politicians. The theory was simply unknown at the time of the Constitution's drafting and for more than a century thereafter. (There were antigun ideologues in 18th-century America, but these were the Quakers, who rejected the use of arms by anyone, individuals and communities alike.) The "collective rights" theory seems to have flowered in the 1960s or '70s as a prop in national political debates about gun control laws. The most famous and widely cited argument for this position appeared in *Parade* magazine in 1990, ostensibly authored by former Chief Justice Warren E. Burger, a judge not famous then or now as a consitutional authority and whose 30-year judicial career had in any case included not a single Second Amendment decision.

16   Akhil Amar of Yale Law School has famously argued that the Bill of Rights can and should be read as a coherent document, rather than as a grab bag of snippets and special pleadings. Taken as a whole, Amar argues, the Bill of Rights is a sort of constitution that embodies a consistent theory, not only about the moral personality of human beings but also about the state and especially its lawless tendencies under the stress and strain of political conflict. In connection with the Second Amendment, this approach has special attractions, because the basic interpretative questions concerning the Second Amendment—what is the "right" and when is it "abridged"?—do not have any specifically "Second Amendment" answers. But if the Bill of Rights is taken as a congruous and interconnected whole, it might be possible to begin the analysis by piggybacking on the fairly deep jurisprudence of constitutional rights that has developed in connection with other amendments.

To begin with, as Amar and others have pointed out, keeping and bearing arms is not the only "right of the people" mentioned in the Bill of Rights. The First Amendment forbids Congress to abridge the "right of the people" peaceably to assemble; the Fourth Amendment forbids violation of the "right of the people" to be secure in their persons, houses, papers, and effects against unreasonable searches and seizures. The right to keep and bear arms, then, should probably be understood as cognate in some way to those rights—surely in the sense that it is possessed by individuals as those other rights are, and also in the sense that, like those other rights, the right to keep and bear arms is in some way fundamental to the preservation of republican citizenship.

18   It is beyond all rational doubt that this understanding reflects the view of the Founders. They took from Locke the principle that people have a right to defend themselves, with arms if necessary, and from both Hobbes and Locke*—to say nothing of their own experience with the Crown—the principle that central governments have a tendency, which requires systematic mitigation, to become overmighty with those subject to their power. The purpose of an armed population was to guarantee that the central government could *not* possess a monopoly of violence (no wonder modern-day

---

* The English philosophers Thomas Hobbes (1588–1679) and John Locke (1632–1704) offered significantly different models of the social contract between individual citizens and their government. Having a negative view of human nature, Hobbes defended the absolute authority of the state. Believing that people are fundamentally good, Locke emphasized that individuals have inalienable rights and may need to break with a government that overly restricts freedom.

liberals find the Second Amendment so hateful) and to assure that citizens would have the wherewithal to defend themselves and their communities against tyrants and wrongdoers.

It remains to be answered when it might be said that this right has been abridged. One of the by-products of the political polarization concerning the Second Amendment is that all sides seemingly agree that this is a question that need never be seriously addressed. True-believing gunnies think of any form of taxation or regulation of firearms should be regarded as "abridgement," no interpretation necessary. True-believing gun controllers, by embracing the "collective rights" theory of the Second Amendment, hardly need to reach the question of "abridgement," because their interpretation denies the legal standing of any individual or organization—anyone who is not a "state"—to raise the question. What is needed is some principled way to locate sane middle ground that gives routine scope to state police powers yet respects and defers to the constitutional norm involved in keeping and bearing arms.

20   There are several ways one could get a handle on this problem. First, the language of the Second Amendment itself invites one to differentiate between arms that can be kept and borne (i.e., carried) and other arms. This is not the sort of difference that could support a regulatory or legislative distinction, like the "assault weapons" provisions in the 1994 Omnibus Crime Act, between functionally equivalent firearms based on such cosmetic attributes as possession of a pistol grip, flash suppressor, or bayonet lug. But it would make sense of a distinction between rifles, shotguns, and pistols on the one hand and hydrogen bombs on the other. So as a first cut at the problem, one might say that infringement in the constitutional sense does not occur when a statute or regulation imposes burdens on possession of weapons other than those that militiamen might be expected to bring ("bear") into the field with them when summoned from their homes.

It might also make sense to allow legislatures to recognize that in certain circumstances firearms constitute a special danger. One thinks in particular of saloons: Perhaps guns and alcohol do not mix, just as (according to the laws of many states and communities) naked dancers and alcohol don't mix. This sort of limitation on the bearing of arms does not readily emerge from constitutional history or text. It would be defended simply on prudential grounds, the thought being that it is implausible that the right to keep and bear arms would be the only constitutional right not subject to some kind of rule of reason. Though philosophical firearms enthusiasts—like journalists, pornographers, and other single-issue partisans—tend to understand the term *right* quite absolutely, anyone interested in preserving a system of political and civil rights that impinge and abut on one another will have to take a more refined view of the matter.

22   We allow the state to regulate the time, place, and manner of speech, or acts (like burning one's draft card) that are heavily laden with speech-like (that is, communicative) content—but we allow this regulation only subject

to an all-important qualification. It must not discriminate on the basis of a communication's content, and it must be no more expansive than necessary to accomplish its purpose. Regulating the speech of Democrats more restrictively than that of Republicans, or allowing anti-abortion posters in a certain public place while forbidding abortion-rights posters, would not be regulation that was neutral in its attitude toward a constitutionally protected value. It would be censorship—a pretextual act inherently hostile toward that value. Even formally neutral regulation could disclose such hostility if it exceeded what was necessary to accomplish a proper purpose. For example, if a municipality banned all public speech whatsoever to preserve public peace and quiet (in itself a perfectly licit end), courts would say this action, though formally "neutral," was too broad to be sustained.

The Second Amendment should be seen as analogous. There would be no "abridgement" if regulation were aimed at the time, place, and manner in which firearms are used. The community has a legitimate interest in seeing to it that arms are not kept or borne negligently. It might well be permissible to pursue this interest by insisting that those who keep and bear arms receive adequate education, on the firing range and in the classroom, to assure the responsible exercise of this right. Such a law would not be invalid unless it appeared that it was being utilized pretextually—like the extravagant "literacy tests" that Jim Crow* voting registrars in the South used to impose on black voters—to subvert or disparage that constitutional right. Any government burden on "the right of the people to keep and bear arms" must have an important purpose and must be justified *in spite of,* and not *because of,* its tendency to discourage the keeping and bearing of arms.

24   Firearms regulations should be subject to the heightened scrutiny that courts reserve for impositions on other fundamental rights, which means that serious and skeptical consideration will be given to the claim that regulation is necessary, that the means chosen correspond to that claim of need, that the state interest is a very important one, and that the regulations are no more extensive than they have to be to address that interest. As with any civil right, the burden of persuasion should remain with the proponent of legislation that restricts or burdens the right to keep and bear arms, rather than, as with ordinary legislation, on the opponent. But a public policy of simply discouraging people from owning or using firearms is not, in and of itself, a constitutionally permissible objective, any more than discouraging people from religious observance would be permissible to some future, oh-so-progressive government that considered religion as hopelessly déclassé as progressives nowadays consider the right to keep and bear arms. Thus the Los Angeles Police Department has behaved unconstitutionally by refusing, over a period of many years, to exercise its statutory discretion to issue carry permits, because the department didn't think it a good idea for people

---

* Jim Crow was a black character in minstrel shows popular in the nineteenth century. His name became synonymous with legislation passed after the Civil War in an attempt to keep African-Americans from enjoying their full rights as citizens.

(other than police officers) to carry guns around. And any statute or regulation that burdens the right to keep and bear arms on the ground that guns are a public health hazard should enjoy the same frosty reception in court that would be given to a statute or regulation that burdened the free exercise of religion as a mental health hazard.

The constitutional norms involved in the Second Amendment, unlike those elsewhere in the Bill of Rights, are undeniably controversial. No one scorns the freedom of religion or the freedom of the press; but the propositions that government should not have a monopoly of the means of violence and that "the people" should be entitled (if not obliged) to defend with arms their persons and communities—these are much against the grain of (and, as Sanford Levinson wrote, very much an embarrassment to) the cosseted intelligentsia of 1990s America. It is especially easy to empathize with the policy intuitions of this elite if one is a member of it. But our instincts about firearms are wrong. We upper-middle-class opinion leaders misunderstand the world; we abide in safety behind a ring of steel. Police officers and security guards keep and bear our arms for us, so that we do not remember how constantly we need them. The values and assumptions that gave rise to the Second Amendment come from a world different from the one we inhabit, a world full of irrational hatreds, mortal dangers, and armed enemies. It represents a serious failure of imagination not to recognize how temporary remissions from this dangerous world have been, and not to learn from the Bill of Rights what its drafters had to teach.   ❖

Questions for Meaning

1. What different factors shape the way we should interpret the Constitution?
2. How does Polsby paraphrase the Second Amendment?
3. How does its context, within the Bill of Rights, help clarify the meaning of the Second Amendment?
4. To what extent are responses to the Second Amendment influenced by cultural changes? What cultural norms prevailed in the lives of the men who drafted the Bill of Rights? What makes these norms seem questionable today?
5. According to this argument, does government have any legitimate authority to limit the "right of the people to keep and bear Arms"?
6. Vocabulary: marginal (1), talismanically (1), nuanced (2), acculturated (4), prerogatives (6), jurisprudence (6), anomaly (8), contingency (10), dispositive (11), extrapolate (13), exorbitance (14), déclassé (24), cosseted (25).

Questions about Strategy

1. Polsby makes numerous references to social class. What role do these references have within his argument?

2. Why does Polsby quote Thomas Jefferson and Patrick Henry? Do these quotations help his argument?
3. How fairly does Polsby treat people with whom he disagrees?
4. Consider the analogy drawn in paragraph 24 between owning a gun and practicing a religion. On what grounds is Polsby able to make this analogy? Do you find it persuasive?

William R. Tonso

WHITE MAN'S LAW

A professor of sociology at the University of Evansville, William R. Tonso is the author of *Gun and Society: Existential Roots of the American Attachment to Firearms* (1982) and *The Gun Culture and Its Enemies* (1989). Drawing on the work of a number of other scholars, he argues that the demand for gun control is the result of prejudice against minorities and the poor. This essay, first published in 1985, provides an example of his views.

Chances are that you've never heard of General Laney. He hasn't had a brilliant military career, at least as far as I know. In fact, I'm not certain that he's even served in the military. General, you see, isn't Laney's rank. General is Laney's first name. General Laney does, however, have a claim to fame, unrecognized though it may be.

2 Detroit resident General Laney is the founder and prime mover behind a little-publicized organization known as the National Black Sportsman's Association, often referred to as "the black gun lobby." Laney pulls no punches when asked his opinion of gun control: "Gun control is really race control. People who embrace gun control are really racists in nature. All gun laws have been enacted to control certain classes of people, mainly black people, but the same laws used to control blacks are being used to disarm white people as well."

Laney is not the first to make this observation. Indeed, allied with sportsmen in vocal opposition to gun controls in the 1960s were the militant Black Panthers. Panther Minister of Information Eldridge Cleaver noted in 1968: "Some very interesting laws are being passed. They don't name me; they don't say, take the guns away from the niggers. They say that people will no longer be allowed to have (guns). They don't pass these rules and these regulations specifically for black people, they have to pass them in a way that will take in everybody."

4 Some white liberals have said essentially the same thing. Investigative reporter Robert Sherrill, himself no lover of guns, concluded in his book *The Saturday Night Special* that the object of the Gun Control Act of 1968 was black control rather than race control. According to Sherrill, Congress

was so panicked by the ghetto riots of 1967 and 1968 that it passed the act to "shut off weapons access to blacks, and since they (Congress) probably associated cheap guns with ghetto blacks and thought cheapness was peculiarly the characteristic of imported military surplus and the mail-order traffic, they decided to cut off these sources while leaving over-the-counter purchases open to the affluent." Congressional motivation may have been more complex than Sherrill suggests, but keeping blacks from acquiring guns was certainly a large part of that motivation. . . .

There is little doubt that the earliest gun controls in the United States were blatantly racist and elitist in their intent. San Francisco civil-liberties attorney Don B. Kates, Jr., an opponent of gun prohibitions with impeccable liberal credentials (he has been a clerk for radical lawyer William Kunstler, a civil-rights activist in the South, and an Office of Economic Opportunity lawyer), describes early gun control efforts in his book *Restricting Handguns: The Liberal Skeptics Speak Out.* As Kates documents, prohibitions against the sale of cheap handguns originated in the post-Civil War South. Small pistols selling for as little as 50 or 60 cents became available in the 1870s and '80s, and since they could be afforded by recently emancipated blacks and poor whites (whom agrarian agitators of the time were encouraging to ally for economic and political purposes), these guns constituted a significant threat to a southern establishment interested in maintaining the traditional class structure.

6   Consequently, Kates notes, in 1870 Tennessee banned "selling all but 'the Army and Navy model' handgun, i.e., the most expensive one, which was beyond the means of most blacks and laboring people." In 1881, Arkansas enacted an almost identical ban on the sale of cheap revolvers, while in 1902, South Carolina banned the sale of handguns to all but "sheriffs and their special deputies—i.e., company goons and the KKK." In 1893 and 1907, respectively, Alabama and Texas attempted to put handguns out of the reach of blacks and poor whites through "extremely heavy business and/or transactional taxes" on the sale of such weapons. In the other Deep South states, slavery-era bans on arms possession by blacks continued to be enforced by hook or by crook.

The cheap revolvers of the late 19th and early 20th centuries were referred to as "Suicide Specials," the "Saturday Night Special" label not becoming widespread until reformers and politicians took up the gun control cause during the 1960s. The source of this recent concern about cheap revolvers, as their new label suggests, has much in common with the concerns of the gun-law initiators of the post-Civil War South. As B. Bruce-Briggs has written in the *Public Interest,* "It is difficult to escape the conclusion that the 'Saturday Night Special' is emphasized because it is cheap and is being sold to a particular class of people. . . . "

8   Those who argue that the concern about cheap handguns is justified because these guns are used in most crimes should take note of *Under the Gun: Weapons, Crime, and Violence in America,* by sociologists James D. Wright, Peter H. Rossi, and Kathleen Daly. The authors, who undertook an

exhaustive, federally funded, critical review of gun issue research, found *no conclusive proof that cheap handguns are used in crime more often than expensive handguns.* (Interestingly, the makers of quality arms, trying to stifle competition, have sometimes supported bans on cheap handguns and on the importation of cheap military surplus weapons. Kates observes that the Gun Control Act of 1968, which banned mail-order gun sales and the importation of military surplus firearms, "was something domestic manufacturers had been impotently urging for decades.") But the evidence leads to one conclusion that cheap handguns are considered threatening primarily because minorities and poor whites can afford them.

Attempts to regulate the possession of firearms began in the northern states during the early part of the 20th century, and although these regulations had a different focus from those that had been concocted in the South, they were no less racist and elitist in effect or intent. Rather than trying to keep handguns out of the price range that blacks and the poor could afford, New York's trend-setting Sullivan Law, enacted in 1911, required a police permit for legal possession of a handgun. This law made it possible for the police to screen applicants for permits to possess handguns, and while such a requirement may seem reasonable, it can be and has been abused.

10 Members of groups not in favor with the political establishment or the police are automatically suspect and can easily be denied permits. For instance, when the Sullivan Law was enacted, southern and eastern European immigrants were considered racially inferior and religiously and ideologically suspect. (Many were Catholics or Jews, and a disproportionate number were anarchists or socialists.) Professor L. Kennett, coauthor of the authoritative history *The Gun in America,* has noted that the measure was designed to "strike hardest at the foreign-born element," particularly Italians. Southern and eastern European immigrants found it almost impossible to obtain gun permits.

Over the years, application of the Sullivan Law has become increasingly elitist as the police seldom grant handgun permits to any but the wealthy or the politically influential. A beautiful example of this hypocritical elitism is the fact that while the *New York Times* often editorializes against the private possession of handguns, the publisher of that newspaper, Arthur Ochs Sulzberger, has a hard-to-get permit to own and carry a handgun. Another such permit is held by the husband of Dr. Joyce Brothers, the pop psychologist who has claimed that firearms ownership is indicative of male sexual inadequacy.

12 Gun-control efforts through the centuries have been propelled by racist and elitist sentiments. Even though European aristocrats were members of a weapons-loving warrior caste, they did their best to keep the gun from becoming a weapon of war. It was certainly all right to kill with civilized weapons such as the sword, the battle ax, or the lance; these were weapons that the armored knights were trained to use and which gave them a tremendous advantage over commoners who didn't have the knights' training or possess their expensive weapons and armor. But guns, by virtue

of being able to pierce armor, democratized warfare and made common soldiers more than a match for the armored and aristocratic knights, thereby threatening the existence of the feudal aristocracy.

As early as 1541, England enacted a law that limited legal possession of handguns and crossbows (weapons that were considered criminally dangerous) to those with incomes exceeding 100 pounds a year, though long-gun possession wasn't restricted—except for Catholics, a potentially rebellious minority after the English Reformation. Catholics couldn't legally keep militia-like weapons in their homes, as other Englishmen were encouraged to do, but they could legally possess defensive weapons—except, as Bill of Rights authority Joyce Lee Malcolm has noted in her essay "The Right to Keep and Bear Arms: The Common Law Tradition," during times "of extreme religious tension."

14   According to Malcolm, when William and Mary* came to the English throne, they were presented with a list of rights, one of which was aimed at staving off any future attempt at arms confiscation—"all Protestant citizens had a right to keep arms for their defence." England then remained free of restrictive gun legislation until 1920 when, even though the crime rate was very low, concern about the rebellious Irish and various political radicals ushered in today's draconian gun laws. (Colin Greenwood, former superintendent of the West Yorkshire Metropolitan Police, has discovered in his research at Cambridge University that the English gun crime rate is significantly *higher* now than it was before that nation's strict gun laws were enacted.)

Alas, the European aristocracy wasn't able to control gun use, and at least in part, the spread of effective firearms helped to bring down aristocracy and feudalism. By contrast, in 17th-century Japan the ruling Tokugawa Shogunate was able to establish a rigidly stratified society that deemphasized the development of guns and restricted arms possession to a warrior aristocracy, the *samurai*. When Commodore Perry[†] "reopened" Japan to the rest of the world in the middle of the 19th century, few Japanese were familiar with guns (the sword was the most honored weapon of the samurai) and the most common guns were primitive matchlocks similar to those introduced to Japan by the Portuguese in the middle of the 16th century. As post-Perry Japan modernized and acquired a modern military, it also quickly developed modern weaponry. But a citizenry without a gun-owning tradition was easily kept in place in a collectivist society where individuals were more susceptible to formal and informal social controls than are westerners.

16   The preceding are just samples of the political uses to which gun controls have been put throughout the world. Nazi Germany, the Soviet Union, and South Africa are modern examples of repressive governments that

---

* William III (1650–1702) and his wife Mary I, the protestant daughter of James II, came to power in 1689 after a period of civil unrest.

† Matthew Calbraith Perry (1784–1858), an American Naval officer, negotiated an 1854 treaty that permitted American ships to use two Japanese ports.

use gun control as a means of social control. Raymond G. Kessler, a lawyer-sociologist who has provided some of the most sociologically sophisticated insights into the gun control issue, suggests in a *Law and Policy Quarterly* article that attempts to regulate the civilian possession of firearms have five political functions. They "(1) increase citizen reliance on government and tolerance of increased police powers and abuse; (2) help prevent opposition to government; (3) facilitate repressive action by government and its allies; (4) lessen the pressure for major or radical reform; and (5) can be selectively enforced against those perceived to be a threat to government."

Of course, while many gun control proponents might acknowledge that such measures have been used in the ways Kessler lists, they would deny that the controls that they support are either racist or elitist, since they would apply to everybody and are aimed at reducing violence for everybody. Yet the controls that they advocate are in fact racist and classist in *effect,* and only the naive or the dishonest can deny their elitist *intent.*

18 Kessler has also written that while liberals are likely to sympathize with the poor and minorities responsible for much of this nation's violent crime, when they are victimized themselves, "or when they hear of an especially heinous crime, liberals, like most people, feel anger and hostility toward the offender. The discomfort of having incompatible feelings can be alleviated by transferring the anger away from the offender to an inanimate object—the weapon."

A perfect example of this transference is provided by Pete Shields, the chairman of the lobbying group Handgun Control Inc., whose son was tragically murdered with a handgun by one of San Francisco's Zebra killers—blacks who were killing whites at random in the early 1970s. This killing was carried out by a black man who was after whites—his own skin color and that of his victim were important to the killer—but in his grief, the white liberal father couldn't blame the criminal for this racist crime. So the gun was the culprit. The upshot is that we now have Handgun Control Inc., with its emphasis on the *weapon* used to commit a crime rather than the criminal. Yet blacks and minorities, who would be prevented from defending themselves, are likely to be harmed most by legislation proposed by Handgun Control Inc., the National Coalition to Ban Handguns, and other proponents of strict handgun controls.

20 Since the illegal possession of a handgun (or of any gun) is a crime that doesn't produce a victim and is unlikely to be reported to the police, handgun permit requirements or outright handgun prohibitions aren't easily enforced. And as civil liberties attorney Kates has observed, when laws are difficult to enforce, "enforcement becomes progressively more haphazard until at last the laws are used only against those who are unpopular with the police." Of course minorities, especially minorities who don't "know their place," aren't likely to be popular with the police, and these very minorities, in the face of police indifference or perhaps even antagonism, may be the most inclined to look to guns for protection—guns that they can't acquire legally and that place them in jeopardy if possessed illegally. While the intent of such laws may not be racist, their effect most certainly is.

Today's gun-control battle, like those of days gone by, largely breaks down along class lines. Though there are exceptions to the rule, the most dedicated and vociferous proponents of strict gun controls are urban, upper-middle-class or aspiring upper-middle-class, pro-big-government liberals, many of whom are part of the New Class (establishment intellectuals and the media), and most of whom know little or nothing about guns and the wide range of legitimate uses to which they are regularly put. Many of these elitists make no secret of their disdain for gun-owners. For instance, Gov. Mario Cuomo of New York recently dismissed those who are opposed to the Empire State's mandatory seat-belt law as "NRA hunters who drink beer, don't vote, and lie to their wives about where they were all weekend."

22   On the other hand, the most dedicated opponents of gun control are often rural- or small-town-oriented, working- or middle-class men and women, few of whom possess the means to publicize their views, but many of whom know a great deal about the safe and lawful uses of guns. To these Americans, guns mean freedom, security, and wholesome recreation. The battle over gun controls, therefore, has come about as affluent America has attempted to impose its anti-gun prejudices on a working-class America that is comfortable with guns (including handguns), seldom misuses them (most gun crime is urban), and sees them as protection against criminal threats and government oppression.

How right you are, General Lancy. "All guns laws have been enacted to control certain classes of people. . . . "   ❖

Questions for Meaning

1   Why does Tonso object to New York state's Sullivan Law?
2. What led England to adopt gun control in the 1920s?
3. According to this essay, what are the political motives that lead to gun control?
4. What does Tonso mean by "transference" in paragraph 19?
5. What is wrong with a law that is selectively enforced?
6. Vocabulary: impeccable (5), emancipated (5), agrarian (5), impotently (8), authoritative (10), collectivist (15), vociferous (21).

Questions about Strategy

1. Why do you think Tonso chose to begin this essay with a reference to General Laney when he realized that his audience was probably unfamiliar with this man?
2. Consider Tonso's use of sources in this essay. How well are they incorporated into Tonso's own argument? Which source is the most effective in your opinion?
3. Why does Tonso discuss both English and Japanese history?
4. How does Tonso characterize his opponents? Does he treat them fairly? What is the quotation from Mario Cuomo meant to illustrate?

ONE STUDENT'S ASSIGNMENT

Summarize William Tonso's "White Man's Law" in 500 words or less. Be sure to include the most important points made in Tonso's article and to accurately convey its thesis. Be careful not to let your own opinions interfere with your summary of Tonso's views.

A Summary of William Tonso's "White Man's Law"
Sara Jenkins

History shows that governments have repeatedly sought to restrict gun ownership to social elites. In 1541, the English government restricted handgun ownership to people who earned more than one hundred pounds a year (which was a great deal of money at the time). European aristocrats were concerned about guns because these weapons threatened the established social order. The rulers might have horses and fancy armor, but bullets could pierce right through armor.

2   A similar pattern can be found in American history. Gun control was initially favored by those in power. Cheap guns could be purchased by poor people, and the ruling class was afraid of what could happen if too many poor people had guns.

The first gun control laws were passed in the south soon after the Civil War. Tennessee, Arkansas, South Carolina, Alabama, and Texas all sought to restrict gun ownership by allowing only for the legal purchase of expensive guns or by putting heavy taxes on the sale of handguns. As a result, poor whites and blacks could not afford to own handguns legally. Some southern states even banned black people from owning any kind of gun.

4   In the north, gun control was inspired by similar thinking. In 1911, New York passed the Sullivan Law, which required would-be gun owners to get a police permit. Although this law may not have been designed specifically to keep African Americans from owning guns, it did have the effect of granting the police the power of giving permits only when they wanted. Minorities—especially immigrants from countries that were not popular at the time—were discriminated against. Today, most permits in New York go to the rich and influential.

More recent gun control laws have also been inspired by fear of minorities. The Gun Control Act of 1968 was passed only one year after riots broke out in big cities because of conditions in the ghettos. And since then much attention has been given to the "Saturday Night Special"—the sort of cheap gun that poor people are most likely able to afford. "Saturday Night Specials" are blamed for crime, but research shows that they are not used in crimes any more often than expensive guns are used. So once again, government seems to want to keep poor people unarmed—even if they need guns to defend themselves.

6   Liberals who are in favor of gun control probably don't understand the history of gun control. They may also be blaming guns because they are unwilling to blame the criminals who misuse guns. Unfortunately, the debate over gun control continues to show divisions along class lines. Many advocates of gun control have security and power. Many opponents do not.

SUGGESTIONS FOR WRITING

1. In the first two essays in this section, Elizabeth J. Swasey and Ruth Rosen claim that the criminal use of guns has particular significance for women, but they reach different conclusions about how women should respond to gun-related violence. Write an argument that establishes a compromise between these two positions.
2. If you have ever used a gun, or lived in a house where a gun was present, write an argument on gun control that begins with an account of your own experience.
3. Regardless of your own opinion of gun control, which essay in this section is the most persuasive? Write an analysis of this argument, evaluating the techniques the writer used.
4. Write an essay explaining why advocates of gun control are especially concerned about handguns.
5. Write an argument for or against taxing bullets.
6. Write an argument on behalf of the right to own a rifle or shotgun.
7. Drawing on the arguments by Roger Koopman and Daniel Polsby, write a paper defining the extent to which the Second Amendment guarantees a right to bear arms.
8. William Tonso takes the position that gun control is racist. Write a paper arguing that it is racist *not* to control guns.
9. Synthesize the arguments for and against gun control.

COLLABORATIVE PROJECT

How are guns used in your community? Form a writing team from your class and investigate violence in your city or county. Sources to consider include gun clubs, gun dealers, the police department, the sheriff's office, the district attorney's office, the coroner's office, the health department, and indexes to local newspapers. Divide research and writing responsibilities among teammates but use the entire team to compose the paper in which you report your findings.

SECTION 2

IMMIGRATION: WHO GETS TO BECOME AN AMERICAN?

EMMA LAZARUS

THE NEW COLOSSUS

Emma Lazarus (1849–1887) was a Russian-born poet who settled in New York. Her works include *Admetus and Other Poems* (1871), *Alide* (1874), *Songs of the Semite* (1882), and *By the Waters of Babylon* (1887). But of all her works, none is so famous as her sonnet to the Statue of Liberty. Now carved on the statue's pedestal, the poem was first published in 1883. As you read it, note the pattern with which lines are rhymed.

1
    Not like the brazen giant of Greek fame,
    With conquering limbs astride from land to land;
    Here at our sea-washed, sunset gates shall stand
    A mighty woman with a torch, whose flame
5
    Is the imprisoned lightning, and her name
    Mother of Exiles. From her beacon-hand
    Glows world-wide welcome; her mild eyes command
    The air-bridged harbor that twin cities frame.
    "Keep, ancient lands, your storied pomp!" cries she
10
    With silent lips. "Give me your tired, your poor,
    Your huddled masses yearning to breathe free,
    The wretched refuse of your teeming shore.
    Send these, the homeless, tempest-tost to me,
    I lift my lamp beside the golden door!"

Questions for Meaning

1. Lazarus calls her poem "The New Colossus" and begins by contrasting the Statue of Liberty with "the brazen giant of Greek fame." To what is she alluding?
2. Although the Statue of Liberty is on the American east coast, Lazarus associates it with "sunset gates." From what point of view would New York be associated with the setting sun rather than the rising sun?

3. In the final line, Lazarus makes "golden door" a metaphor for New York harbor. In what sense then can arrival in America be seen as reaching a "golden door"?

4. Vocabulary: astride (line 2), beacon (line 6), pomp (line 9), teeming (line 12).

Questions about Strategy

1. Lazarus composed her poem as a sonnet: a fourteen-line poem expressing a complete thought written with a fixed number of stressed and unstressed syllables in each line and divided into an octave (eight lines) and a sextet (six lines). In this form, the end of the first line rhymes with the end of the fourth, fifth and eighth lines; the second line rhymes with the third, sixth, and seventh; and, in the sextet, two new sounds are introduced, with every other line rhyming. Does her use of this poetic form contribute to the argument made by the poem?

2. In line 6, Lazarus renames the Statue of Liberty. The statue's actual name is "Liberty Enlightening the World." Lazarus calls it "Mother of Exiles." How do these names differ, and how does the change reveal the poet's purpose in this poem?

MICHAEL KINSLEY

GATECRASHERS

Responding to growing concerns about immigration, Michael Kinsley published the following editorial on December 28, 1992. A Harvard-educated attorney who was cohost of CNN's *Crossfire,* Kinsley is senior editor of *The New Republic,* a magazine that usually reflects liberal political opinions.

A new Census Bureau report predicts that there will be 383 million Americans in the year 2050. That's 128 million more than there are now, and 83 million more than the bureau was predicting just four years ago, when it appeared that the U.S. population would peak and stabilize at around 300 million.

2   Part of the startling upward revision reflects an unexpected increase in the birthrate. But most of it is due to an increase in immigration. The Census Bureau expects an average of 880,000 new arrivals a year, legal and illegal. By 2050 a fifth of the American population will be folks who arrived here after 1991 and their children. Almost half the population (47 percent) will be "minority"—black, Asian, Hispanic, Native American—compared with just a quarter today.

Immigration has not been much of a political issue lately. In fact a 1990 law increasing the annual legal quota by 40 percent passed almost unnoticed. And there's been little fuss over the total failure of the hotly contested 1986 immigration reform—which for the first time made it a crime to employ illegal aliens—to achieve its purpose of reducing illegal immigration.

4   But the politics of immigration may be heating up. And the political coloration of anti-immigrant sentiment may be changing too. Despite the traditional association of the Democratic Party with immigrant groups, what little opposition there has been to immigration in recent years has come vaguely from the left. Some environmentalists believe that immigrants contribute to overpopulation and strain the nation's natural resources. And some blacks (and white sympathizers) worry that immigrants are stealing opportunities from America's oldest and still most down-trodden minority.

What's new, though, is the re-emergence of anti-immigrant sentiment on the right. Here it takes the traditional form of concern about the nation's ethnic character. This fits in with other social concerns about matters like multiculturalism and even gay rights: a sense that some classic and comfortable image of America is being changed before our eyes.

6   Presidential candidate Pat Buchanan sometimes included immigration in his riffs on this general theme. And the *National Review* (edited by an immigrant—although only from Britain) ran a long cover story (by another immigrant from Britain) condemning immigration as a liberal elitist plot and predicting an America of "ethnic strife . . . dual loyalties . . . collapsing like the Tower of Babel" if the foreign hordes aren't kept out. ("Tired? Poor? Huddled? Tempest-Tossed?" asked the witty cover. "Try Australia.") Free market capitalism itself, the author suggests at one point, may depend on the continued predominance of Anglo-Saxon stock.*

There have been Americans who feared that our country is "running out of room" since the frontier closed off more than a century ago. Although 128 million extra people in the next six decades sounds like an awful lot, that is no greater than the population increase over the past six decades. (And it's a much smaller proportional increase.) Only environmentalist zealots could believe that America would be better off if our population were still only 125 million—even accepting the complacent assumption that everyone reading this column would be one of the lucky 125 million.

8   There is no answer to the argument that "at some point" the country becomes too crowded, but there's no particular reason to believe we're at that point yet. Germany, with less than a third of America's population in a far smaller area, is currently accepting new arrivals in almost the same volume.

Germany may not seem the happiest example for my side of the immigration argument. There, immigration is straining the social fabric and producing riots and violence by neo-Nazi punks. Not to defend such

---

* An excerpt from this article (by Peter Brimelow) appears on pages 219–223.

xenophobic outrages, but Germany is different from the United States. Like most countries in the world (Israel, to pick a sensitive example), its sense of nationhood has a large ethnic component. This is neither good nor evil; it's just a fact. Although any civilized nation should be prepared to take in refugees from oppression, the "otherness" of foreigners will always be more vivid elsewhere than in America. In other countries, concern about diluting the nation's ethnic stock even has a certain validity.

10   Such concerns have no validity in America. In fact, they are un-American. If applied in earlier times, when they were raised with equal passion, they would have excluded the ancestors of many who make the ethnic/cultural preservation argument today. The anti-immigration literature seems to regard this point as some kind of cheap shot. But I cannot see why.

On the economic effects of immigration, there are studies to suit every taste. Immigrants take jobs from poor Americans; or they go on welfare and bloat the tax bill; or both; or neither. Basic economic logic suggests that even when a new arrival "takes" a job, the money he earns and spends will in turn create a job or so. The more the merrier is a tenet of capitalism dating back to Adam Smith, and nothing I've seen disproves it.

12   The propaganda from FAIR (Federation for American Immigration Reform, the liberal anti-immigration lobby) on these issues is unpersuasive because it tends to "prove too much," as the lawyers say. With a straight face, FAIR compares immigration to slavery and child labor, as if the trouble with these practices were the burden they placed on rival sources of labor. In one recent broadside FAIR's executive director, Dan Stein, suggests that America should have curtailed immigration after the Civil War in order to increase economic opportunities for ex-slaves. Whether this would actually have benefited blacks or not, it might have spared us Dan Stein.

The emerging case for curtailing immigration has many byways. There's the argument that we need "time to digest" the immigrant wave of the past couple of decades, just as previous waves were followed by periods of low immigration. There's the argument that today's ethnic assertiveness and social welfare apparatus mean that the machinery of assimilation no longer works to turn immigrants into middle-class Americans. There's the undeniable fact that instant communication and cheap transportation have eroded the natural restraints of distance and ignorance on the demand for places in America.

14   There are counterarguments to all these points, and others. And counter-counterarguments. No one can know the effect of future large-scale immigration on our country. It has always been beneficial in the past, but that's no guarantee it will be so in the future. The previous tenant of this column, the late Richard Strout believed passionately that America's achievement of a liberal welfare state depended on levels of both affluence and social cohesion that were threatened by large-scale immigration.

Immigration is a subject, I suspect, of which very few opinions are changed because of arguments or statistics. It's almost a matter of faith.

Your views of immigration depend on your sense of what makes America America. For some it's endless open spaces. For some it's a demographic image frozen in time. For some that stuff on the Statue of Liberty still plucks a chord. All these visions of America have a large component of fantasy. But I know which fantasy I prefer. ❖

Questions for Meaning

1. How is the American population likely to change in the next half-century?
2. Kinsley claims that concern about "the nation's ethnic stock" is less pressing in the United States than in other countries. Why does he believe this?
3. According to Kinsley, how is the debate over immigration changing?
4. In paragraph 12, Kinsley introduces the idea that an argument can be unpersuasive if it proves too much. How could this be?
5. Vocabulary: riffs (6), elitist (6), complacent (7), xenophobic (9), curtailed (12), assimilation (13).

Questions about Strategy

1. Kinsley opens his argument by emphasizing that the U.S. population is increasing and that recent Census Bureau reports were apparently inaccurate. How does this opening contribute to the argument that follows?
2. In paragraph 5, Kinsley associates immigration with such controversial issues as multiculturalism and gay rights. Is the association appropriate?
3. At the beginning of paragraph 9, Kinsley concedes, "Germany may not seem the happiest example for my side of the immigration argument." If Germany is *not* a good example, should he have used it?
4. Consider the use of "fantasy" in paragraph 15, especially in the last sentence. Does it leave Kinsley open to counterargument?

GARY S. BECKER

ILLEGAL IMMIGRATION: HOW TO TURN THE TIDE

The winner of the 1992 Nobel Prize in economics, Gary S. Becker teaches at the University of Chicago. He is also a Fellow of the Hoover Institution at Stanford University. Drawing on his knowledge of economics, Becker has written on the costs of current immigration policies. He first published this article in *BusinessWeek* in 1993.

The uproar over White House nominees for Attorney General who had employed illegal aliens has focused attention once again on unlawful entry of workers from poor countries. This is a perplexing issue not only for the U.S. but also for France, Germany, Italy, Japan, and other prosperous, democratic countries. I believe such immigration can be effectively discouraged by sizably increasing the number of legal immigrants and at the same time punishing more severely the illegal entrants or those who hire them.

2   Given the yawning gap between the incomes of rich and poor countries, the issue will not simply go away—as long as it remains so easy to enter prosperous countries illegally or on tourist visas. Workers are attracted to rich countries because the jobs available there are much better-paying than anything they can find in their homelands. And that's true even though they are usually employed as low-paid, unskilled labor in restaurants, households, agriculture, or, in a few cases, manufacturing industry.

Since illegal aliens mainly take jobs shunned by native workers, some economists oppose punishing them. Instead, they advocate what amounts to "benign neglect"—especially if the immigrants are not eligible for tax-supported benefits. But democracies find it politically impossible to deny them health care, education for their children, and other benefits paid for by the taxpayer. And when the number of illegals in a country gets large, political pressure often mounts to grant them amnesty, as happened in the 1980s in the U.S. I am troubled, too, by the morality of a policy that encourages violations of the law by employers and illegal immigrants, while entry is denied to millions who stoically wait their turn for the right to enter legally.

Seldom Penalized

4 This is why democratic countries must take stronger steps than simply shipping illegal entrants who get caught back to where they came from. Entry cannot be reduced without effective punishment of either illegal aliens or their companies. Employers will not stop hiring illegal aliens on their own, because they do not believe they are doing anything wrong. The 1986 U.S. Immigration Control and Reform Act includes penalties for companies that

hire illegal aliens, but households and very small businesses have seldom
been penalized. Even though domestic help is believed to account for a considerable fraction of all off-the-books workers, Zoë Baird's household appears to be the first one fined.

The reasons I have given for greater restrictions on illegal entrants
should be distinguished from erroneous claims that they take jobs from native workers or that they are often exploited. Research has found that the
employment prospects of native workers are only slightly reduced when immigrants enter a local labor market. And although some illegal workers are
afraid to complain about bad treatment—because they may be deported—
there isn't room for extensive exploitation in the highly competitive labor
markets where most illegals find jobs. For example, those households and
small companies that do not pay Social Security and unemployment compensation taxes for illegal employees are forced by the competition for labor
to pay higher wages than if these taxes were paid. In a study of apprehended
illegal workers, economist Barry R. Chiswick of the University of Illinois at
Chicago found that their average pay was in fact well above the minimum
wage.

Same Asylum

6   I am not advocating the erection of a wall against immigration. Instead a
more generous immigration policy should go hand in hand with greater
punishment of illegal entrants, including fines and possibly jail terms.
Greater legal immigration is not only desirable in its own right but would
also reduce the number who seek to enter illegally. Not surprisingly, illegal
entry generally expands when a country contracts the number of immigrants accepted.

France, Germany, and other countries are mistaken if they believe
that they can reduce their immigration problem by cutting back on the
right to political asylum or other legal means of entry. When legal immigration is curtailed, the number who sneak in or seek work after entering
on a tourist visa will expand—unless a country is willing to punish effectively either the illegal entrants or the households and small companies
that hire them.

8   I suggested in an earlier column that the most rational approach would
be to sell the right to immigrate, but a less radical method of improving
present policy and combating illegal immigration would be to allow a larger
number of skilled and young people to enter legally. To prevent immigrants
from taking advantage of government handouts, however, they should not
be eligible for welfare, food stamps, government-financed health care, or
certain other benefits until they become naturalized citizens. Politicians on
both sides of the debate might well support this requirement, because it
would not permanently exclude legal immigrants from taxpayer-financed
benefits. Meanwhile, it would give them an incentive to become citizens as
soon as they could. ❖

Questions for Meaning

1. What is Becker's thesis and where does he state it?
2. On what grounds is U.S. immigration policy morally questionable? Is it questionable on any other grounds?
3. According to Becker, what happens when legal immigration is restricted?
4. Does Becker make any distinction between the rights of immigrants and the rights of citizens?
5. Vocabulary: shunned (3), benign (3), stoically (3), erroneous (5), compensation (5).

Questions about Strategy

1. Becker opens his argument by referring to a controversy in the news. (President Clinton had nominated Zoë Baird for U.S. Attorney General. During her confirmation hearing, Baird admitted hiring illegal aliens for whom she did not pay Social Security taxes.) How would this opening have benefited Becker in 1993? Is this strategy still effective?
2. Does Becker make any concessions that are likely to appeal to readers who are opposed to immigration?
3. In his concluding paragraph, Becker refers to an earlier article in which he advocated a different approach to immigration. What does he achieve by making this reference? Is there any risk to this strategy?

PETER BRIMELOW

A NATION OF IMMIGRANTS

Born and educated in Great Britain, Peter Brimelow now lives and works in the United States. His books include *The Patriot Game: Canada and the Canadian Question Revisited* (1986) and *The Wall Street Game* (1988). "A Nation of Immigrants" is an editor's title for the following short excerpt from a long, controversial article on immigration that Brimelow published in *National Review* in 1992. Founded by William F. Buckley Jr., *National Review* is a monthly magazine that reflects politically conservative opinions.

Everyone has seen a speeded-up film of the cloudscape. What appears to the naked eye to be a panorama of almost immobile grandeur writhes into wild life. Vast patterns of soaring, swooping movement are suddenly discernible. Great towering cumulo-nimbus formations boil up out of nowhere, dominating the sky in a way that would be terrifying if it were not, in real life, so gradual that we are barely aware that anything is going on.

2   This is a perfect metaphor for the development of the American nation. America, of course, is exceptional. What is exceptional about it, however, is not the way in which it was created, but the speed.

"*We are a nation of immigrants.*" No discussion of U.S. immigration
policy gets far without someone making this helpful remark. As an immigrant myself, I always pause respectfully. You never know. Maybe this is
what they're taught to chant in schools nowadays, a sort of multicultural
Pledge of Allegiance.

4   But it secretly amuses me. Do they really think other nations sprouted
up out of the ground? ("Autochthonous" is the classical Greek word.) The
truth is that *all* nations are nations of immigrants. But the process is usually
so slow and historic that people overlook it. They mistake for mountains
what are merely clouds.

This is obvious in the case of the British Isles, from which the largest
single proportion of Americans are still derived. You can see it in the place-
names. Within a few miles of my parents' home in the north of England, the
names are Roman (Chester, derived from the Latin for camp), Saxon (anything ending in *-ton*, town, like Oxton), Viking (*-by*, farm, like Irby), and
Norman French (Delamere). At times, these successive waves of peoples
were clearly living cheek by jowl. Thus among these place-names is Walle-
sey, Anglo-Saxon for "Island of the Welsh"—Welsh being derived from the
word used by low-German speakers for foreigners wherever they met them,
from Wallonia to Wallachia. This corner of the English coast continued as
home to some of the pre-Roman Celtic stock, not all of whom were driven
west into Wales proper as was once supposed.

6   The English language that America speaks today (or at least spoke
until the post-1965 fashion for bilingual education) reflects the fact that the
peoples of Britain merged, eventually; their separate contributions can still
be traced in it. Every nation in Europe went through the same process. Even
the famously homogeneous Japanese show the signs of ethnically distinct
waves of prehistoric immigration.

But merging takes time. After the Norman Conquest in 1066, it was
nearly three hundred years before the invaders were assimilated to the point
where court proceedings in London were again heard in English. And it was
nearly nine centuries before there was any further large-scale immigration
into the British Isles—the Caribbean and Asian influx after World War II.

8   Except in America. Here the process of merging has been uniquely
rapid. Thus about 7 million Germans have immigrated to the U.S. since the
beginning of the nineteenth century. Their influence has been profound—
to my British eye it accounts for the odd American habit of getting up in the
morning and starting work. About 50 million Americans told the 1980 Census that they were wholly or partly of German descent. But only 1.6 million
spoke German in their homes.

So all nations are made up of immigrants. But what is a nation—the end-
product of all this merging? This brings us into a territory where words are

weapons, exactly as George Orwell pointed out years ago. "Nation"—as suggested by its Latin root *nascere,* to be born—intrinsically implies a link by blood. A nation is an extended family. The merging process through which all nations pass is not merely cultural, but to a considerable extent biological, through intermarriage.

10   Liberal commentators, for various reasons, find this deeply distressing. They regularly denounce appeals to common ethnicity as "nativism" or "tribalism." Ironically, when I studied African history in college, my politically correct tutor deprecated any reference to "tribes." These small, primitive, and incoherent groupings should, he said, be dignified as "nations." Which suggests a useful definition: tribalism/nativism is nationalism of which liberals disapprove.

American political debate on this point is hampered by a peculiar difficulty. American editors are convinced that the term "state" will confuse readers unless reserved exclusively for the component parts of the United States—New York, California, etc. So when talking about sovereign political structures, where the British would use "state," the Germans "*Staat,*" and the French "*l'état,*" journalists here are compelled to use the word "nation." Thus in the late 1980s it was common to see references to "the nation of Yugoslavia," when Yugoslavia's problem was precisely that it was not a nation at all, but a state that contained several different small but fierce nations— Croats, Serbs, etc. (In my constructive way, I've been trying to introduce, as an alternative to "state," the word "polity"—defined by Webster as "a politically organized unit." But it's quite hopeless. Editors always confuse it with "policy.")

12   This definitional difficulty explains one of the regular entertainments of U.S. politics: uproar because someone has unguardedly described America as a "Christian nation." Of course, in the sense that the vast majority of Americans are Christians, this is nothing less than the plain truth. It is not in the least incompatible with a secular *state* (polity).

But the difficulty over the N-word has a more serious consequence: it means that American commentators are losing sight of the concept of the "nation-state"—a sovereign structure that is the political expression of a specific ethno-cultural group. Yet the nation-state was one of the crucial inventions of the modern age. Mass literacy, education, and mobility put a premium on the unifying effect of cultural and ethnic homogeneity. None of the great pre-modern multinational empires have survived. (The Brussels bureaucracy may be trying to create another, but it has a long way to go.)*

14   This is why Ben Wattenberg is able to get away with talking about a "Universal Nation." On its face, this is a contradiction in terms. It's possible, as Wattenberg variously implies, that he means the diverse immigrant groups will eventually intermarry, producing what he calls, quoting the English poet John Masefield a "wondrous race." Or that they will at least be

* Brussels is the administrative site of the European Community, which governs the Common Market, among other responsibilities.

assimilated by American culture, which, while globally dominant, is hardly "universal." But meanwhile there are hard questions. What language is this "universal nation" going to speak? How is it going to avoid ethnic strife? dual loyalties? collapsing like the Tower of Babel? Wattenberg is not asked to reconcile these questions, although he is not unaware of them, because in American political discourse the ideal of an American nation-state is in eclipse.

Ironically, the same weaknesses were apparent in the rather similar concept of "cultural pluralism" invented by Horace M. Kallen at the height of the last great immigration debate, before the Quota Acts of the 1920s. Kallen, like many of today's pro-immigration enthusiasts, reacted unconditionally against the cause for "Americanization" that the 1880-to-1920 immigrant wave provoked. He argued that any unitary American nationality had already been dissipated by immigration (sound familiar?). Instead, he said the U.S. had become merely a political state (polity) containing a number of different nationalities.

16   Kallen left the practical implications of this vision "woefully undeveloped" (in the words of the *Harvard Encyclopedia of American Ethnic Groups*). It eventually evolved into a vague approval of tolerance, which was basically how Americans had always treated immigrant groups anyway—an extension, not coincidentally, of how the English built the British nation.

But in one respect, Kallenism is very much alive: he argued that authentic Americanism was what he called "the American Idea." This amounted to an almost religious idealization of "democracy," which again was left undeveloped but which appeared to have as much to do with non-discrimination and equal protection under the law as with elections. Today, a messianic concern for global "democracy" is being suggested to conservatives as an appropriate objective for U.S. foreign policy.

18   And Kallenism underlies the second helpful remark that someone always makes in any discussion of U.S. immigration policy: "*America isn't a nation like the other nations—it's an idea.*"

Once more, this American exceptionalism is really more a matter of degree than of kind. Many other nations have some sort of ideational reinforcement. Quite often it is religious, such as Poland's Roman Catholicism; sometimes cultural, such as France's ineffable Frenchness. And occasionally it is political. Thus—again not coincidentally—the English used to talk about what might be described as the "English Idea": English liberties, their rights as Englishmen, and so on. Americans used to know immediately what this meant. As Jesse Chickering wrote in 1848 of his diverse fellow-Americans: "English laws and institutions, adapted to the circumstances of the country, have been adopted here. . . . The tendency of things is to mold the whole into one people, whose leading characteristics are English, formed on American soil."

20   What is unusual in the present debate, however, is that Americans are now being urged to abandon the bonds of a common ethnicity and instead

to trust entirely to ideology to hold together their state (polity). This is an extraordinary experiment, like suddenly replacing all the blood in a patient's body. History suggests little reason to suppose it will succeed. Christendom and Islam have long ago been sundered by national quarrels. More recently, the much-touted "Soviet Man," the creation of much tougher ideologists using much rougher methods than anything yet seen in the U.S., has turned out to be a Russian, Ukrainian, or Kazakh after all.

Which is why Shakespeare has King Henry V say, before the battle of Agincourt, not "we defenders of international law and the dynastic principle as it applies to my right to inherit the throne of France," but

We few, we happy few, we band of brothers.

However, although intellectuals may have decided that America is not a nation but an idea, the news has not reached the American people—especially that significant minority who sternly tell the Census Bureau their ethnicity is "American." (They seem mostly to be of British origin, many generations back.) And it would have been considered absurd throughout most of American history.

22   John Jay in *The Federalist Papers* wrote that Americans were "one united people, a people descended from the same ancestors, speaking the same language, professing the same religion, attached to the same principles of government, very similar in their manners and customs." Some hundred years later, Theodore Roosevelt in his *Winning of the West* traced the "perfectly continuous history" of the Anglo-Saxons from King Alfred to George Washington. He presented the settling of the lands beyond the Alleghenies as "the crowning and greatest achievement" of "the spread of the English-speaking peoples," which—though personally a liberal on racial matters—he saw in explicit terms: "it is of incalculable importance that America, Australia, and Siberia should pass out of the hands of their red, black, and yellow aboriginal owners, and become the heritage of the dominant world races."

Roosevelt himself was an example of ethnicities merging to produce this new nation. He thanked God—he teased his friend Rudyard Kipling—that there was "not a drop of British blood" in him. But that did not stop him from identifying with Anglo-Saxons or from becoming a passionate advocate of an assimilationist Americanism, which crossed ethnic lines and was ultimately to cross racial lines.

24   And it is important to note that, at the height of the last great immigration wave, Kallen and his allies totally failed to persuade Americans that they were no longer a nation. Quite the contrary: once convinced that their nationhood was threatened by continued massive immigration, Americans changed the public policies that made it possible. While the national-origins quotas were being legislated, President Calvin Coolidge put it unflinchingly: "America must be kept American."

Everyone knew what he meant. ❖

Questions for Meaning

1. Why does Brimelow question the value of asserting that the United States is a nation of immigrants?
2. How does Brimelow distinguish between "nation" and "state"? Why does he believe that the distinction is important?
3. According to Brimelow, how has the debate over immigration changed? Why is he concerned about this change?
4. In paragraph 21, Brimelow alludes to the battle of Agincourt. When was this battle fought? Who won? And why was this outcome significant?
5. Vocabulary: writhes (1), discernible (1), homogeneous (6), deprecated (10), sundered (20), incalculable (22).

Questions for Strategy

1. How effective is the comparison Brimelow makes between a speeded-up film of clouds and the development of American history?
2. How would you describe the tone of this article? Can you point to specific lines that support your view?
3. Consider paragraphs 22 and 23. Has Brimelow strengthened his case by appealing to American figures of historical importance? Has he left himself open to counterargument?
4. Brimelow concludes by stating that "everyone" knew what it meant to be American back in the 1920s. What is Brimelow implying here? How does this implication affect you?

Denise Topolnicki

MAKING IT BIG IN AMERICA

This argument first appeared in a 1995 issue of *Money*, a magazine that frequently publishes success stories and other articles focused on how to generate and preserve personal wealth. As you read, note how staff writer Denise Topolnicki draws attention to numerous individuals who seem to represent the American dream that financial success comes to those who are unafraid of opportunity and prepared to work hard.

A lot of the angry Californians who helped pass Proposition 187—to deny costly welfare, health care and public education to undocumented aliens—probably had someone like Hilda Pacheco in mind when they pulled the lever in November. Pacheco, 32, entered the state illegally from Mexico in 1978, never finished high school and is the single mother of two children. People like her, the argument goes, are draining $2.3 billion a year from

California's strained health care, prison and education systems while also filling some of the relatively few jobs available in the state's recessionary economy. What's more, they lack the skills ever to contribute as much as they will take. *People like her should go home.*

2   Such anti-immigrant sentiments echo well beyond California's borders today. Arizona, California, Florida, New Jersey and Texas are suing the federal government for a collective $14 billion—the states' estimate of their outlay to support, educate, hospitalize and imprison illegal aliens. In Washington, the Commission on Immigration Reform, headed by former Democratic Rep. Barbara Jordan, urged Congress to create a national registry of legal workers, effectively barring jobs from the estimated 200,000 to 300,000 undocumented immigrants each year. And the new Republican majority in Congress has gone further, threatening to cut off welfare benefits even for legal immigrants, except for refugees and those over age 75.

Before you reach your own conclusion about these initiatives, you may want to learn more about people like Hilda Pacheco. What you discover may not conform to the talk radio image of immigrants as leeches. Rather than being a drag on the economy, Pacheco—like most immigrants—is making it in America. She has never been on welfare, has attained legal status and has elevated herself from a subminimum-wage job at a hamburger stand 16 years ago to her current $50,000-a-year managerial position at a worker-training firm. "I'm sure that illegals pay more taxes than they get credit for," Pacheco says.

4   With immigrants entering the U.S. at a rate of 1 million a year, foreign-born residents—legal and illegal—now represent 8.5% of the U.S. population, nearly twice the percentage (4.7%) in 1970. And in California, where fully 40% of recent immigrants settle, 22% of the population was born outside the U.S. Still, foreign-born residents today make up a much smaller portion of the U.S. population than they did following the great wave of immigration at the start of the century, when foreign-born residents peaked at 15%.

People who criticize today's immigrants, however, contend that as a whole, the current newcomers are fundamentally different from the 13 million Eastern and Southern Europeans who immigrated to the U.S. in the first half of this century. They surely are different in at least one sense: Just 38% of today's arrivals are white, compared with 88% of those who came before 1960. Critics also argue that our high-tech economy now demands brains, not brawn, which means poorly educated and unsophisticated immigrants have little hope of following their predecessors into the middle class.

6   If you look at the research on immigrants, however, you'll find that much of the pessimism is unwarranted. Contrary to what many Americans believe:

   • The vast majority of today's immigrants—legal and illegal—are doing well, or at least striving to pave the way for their children to live better lives. Figures from the Census Bureau reveal that immigrants who arrived in the

U.S. before 1980 actually boast higher average household incomes ($40,900) than all native-born Americans ($37,300).

• Few immigrants come here to get on welfare. In reality, working-age, nonrefugee immigrants are less likely than their native-born counterparts to be on the dole.

• Immigrant children aren't gobbling up precious educational dollars, either. In fact, only 4% of the $227 billion we spend to educate our children is spent educating legal immigrant children and just 2% is spent on the estimated 648,000 kids who are here illegally.

• Immigrants are not long-term drains on our economy. Yes, the estimated 3.8 million illegal immigrants cost us about $2 billion a year, chiefly because many work in low-wage jobs and often don't pay income taxes. But over time, immigrants become productive. As a group, the foreign-born pay $25 billion to $30 billion a year *more* in taxes than they consume in government services, says the Urban Institute.

Like yesterday's immigrants, the newcomers choose America because it offers a chance to prosper. Jeffrey S. Passel, the Urban Institute's director of immigration research and policy, is optimistic about their prospects. "The very act of pulling up stakes and moving to a foreign country indicates that you have initiative and want to better yourself," he says.

8   The successes of today's immigrants hold lessons for us all, whether our ancestors came here on the Mayflower, in slave ships, on a turn-of-the-century steamer or on a jetliner.

Jobs, Not Welfare

Immigration's foes are fond of pointing out that 9% of immigrant households collect cash welfare benefits, compared with only 7% of households headed by native-born Americans. But that single statistic paints a misleading picture. Welfare use is high almost exclusively among legal refugees from war-torn or Communist countries, including Cambodia (50% of all households), Laos (46%), Vietnam (26%), the former Soviet Union (17%) and Cuba (16%). Unlike other immigrants, these favored refugees are immediately entitled to public assistance. As a result, 16% of the refugees, in contrast to only 3% of other immigrants, who came here during the 1980s, get public aid.

10   The notion that illegal immigrants come to the U.S. to obtain welfare benefits is a myth. Illegals already are barred from all public assistance except for emergency medical care under Medicaid and the women, infants and children (WIC) nutrition program. Further, even a legal immigrant who goes on the dole during his five years in the U.S. risks deportation. Though few actually get the boot, the law still acts as a deterrent because an immigrant on welfare would have difficulty getting the approvals necessary to sponsor relatives for residency in the U.S., which is a prime goal for many immigrants.

Thirty-two-year-old Iraji Khiar reflects the prevalent immigrant attitude toward welfare. He fled war-torn Ethiopia in 1977 and spent the next
10 years with family friends in the Sudan before being sponsored for U.S.
entry by a cousin who had come a few years earlier. But when Khiar arrived
in San Diego in 1987, he couldn't locate his relative, and in order to survive,
he accepted the Catholic Church's help in signing him up for welfare—for
all of four weeks. At that point, Khiar refused further aid, insisting that he
wanted to earn his keep "with my own sweat." He began working as a high
school janitor at $7.75 an hour and attending classes toward an associate's
degree in business administration from San Diego City College. He later
went into the food business with another cousin and her brother. Today the
trio typically work 141 hours a week at the Maryam Sambussa Factory,
which bakes savory East African pastries, and the Sphinx International
Restaurant, which serves up a multiethnic stew of East African and African
American foods. The Sphinx features African and American music—when
it's not karaoke night.

The Dream Is Alive

12   Academics have found that the longer immigrants are here, the more likely
they are to have obtained two staples of the American dream: a home and
their own business. For example, among immigrants who have lived here
five to nine years, 44% own their own homes. That figure rises to 55% after
at least 10 years.

Some scholars believe that immigrants eventually pull ahead of natives
in the income race because their work habits aren't constricted by our notions
of the typical eight-hour workday. Further, a willingness to strike out on their
own has allowed many immigrants to earn more money sooner than they
would have in the corporate world, given their often limited command of
English. Overall, the same portion (7%) of immigrants as native-born Americans are self-employed, and both groups of entrepreneurs earn, on average,
about $30,000 a year. Yet for some ethnic groups, self-employment rates are
significantly higher, particularly for Koreans (18%) and Iranians (12%). Immigrants also are well represented in highly skilled professional and technical
jobs. Two of every 10 U.S. physicians are foreign-born, for example, as is one
in eight engineers.

14   Nevertheless, some immigration experts argue that immigrants who
arrived here *after* 1980 will never do as well as natives because they're
more likely than their predecessors to have come from Third World nations. Only time will tell whether recent immigrants' median household
income of $31,100 will rise. Still, a closer look at the facts reveals that these
newcomers aren't as disadvantaged as they first appear. Explains University of Texas sociologist Frank D. Bean: "To say that today's immigrants are
of lower quality than their predecessors puts an unfair onus on them.
They actually have more education than immigrants who came here 20

years ago." Indeed, between 1970 and 1990, the percentage of immigrants with college degrees climbed from 19% to 27%. Meanwhile, the portion of immigrants who dropped out of high school fell to 37% from 48%. (By comparison, 15% of native-born Americans are high school dropouts and 27% are college graduates.) Nearly half (47%) of African immigrants hold college degrees.

Even if you assume that most immigrants who lack college degrees will never earn much in today's demanding job market, it's wrong to presume that they won't become taxpayers or that their children will get stuck in low-wage jobs. As Michigan State sociologist Ruben C. Rumbaut, an expert on recent immigrants, reminds us: "At the turn of the century, many people argued that the U.S. was attracting immigrants who had little education and few job skills. But the fact that you came here as a peasant didn't mean that your children would forever be part of the unwashed underclass."

Immigrant Kids: Moving to the Head of the Class

16   The widely held belief that most immigrant kids demand to be taught in their native languages indefinitely is also dead wrong, as is the notion that we are spending a ton of money on bilingual education. Federal spending on bilingual education, adjusted for inflation, actually *fell* 48% during the 1980s, despite a 50% increase in the number of public school children with limited proficiency in English. In addition, studies show that English is the language of choice for the children of immigrants, no matter what their nationality. The experience of the Rev. Nancy C. Moore, senior pastor of Faith United Presbyterian Church in Los Angeles' predominantly Hispanic Highland Park neighborhood, is instructive. Since most of the 72 children who signed up for Sunday School two years ago were Hispanic, Mrs. Moore decided to assign two teachers to each classroom, one who spoke English, another who spoke Spanish. She dropped the plan, however, when she discovered that 69 of the kids already knew English and that the three who didn't wanted to be taught in their adopted language, not their parents' tongue.

There's also plenty of evidence that immigrants' children are performing well academically, despite poverty, poorly educated parents and discrimination—problems often associated with underachievement in native-born Americans. Even children who missed years of school while detained in refugee camps abroad do amazingly well. In one study, for example, University of Michigan researchers tracked 536 Vietnamese, Laotian and Chinese-Vietnamese children who attended public schools in low-income sections of Boston, Chicago, Houston, Orange County, Calif., and Seattle during the early 1980s. Most were B students, more than a quarter regularly got A's, and only 4% had grade point averages at or below C. They also did better than average on a standardized achievement test: in math, an impressive 27% ranked in the top 10% nationwide.

18   Why do these kids remind us of Horatio Alger rather than Bart Simpson? Because their parents preached a mantra that has served immigrants

for generations: Control your destiny through education. The kids, in turn, relish the chance to learn; in their homelands, education is generally reserved for the wealthy. As a result, families gather around their kitchen tables on weeknights, with older children expected to assist younger siblings. The University of Michigan researchers found that, on average, immigrant grade school students studied two hours and five minutes a night, while high school kids hit the books three hours and 10 minutes. The typical American junior or senior high school student studies only an hour and a half per day. Unfortunately, other researchers have found that when immigrant kids' grades falter, it is often because of overassimilation into American culture. In other words, the longer they live here, the more television they watch and the less homework they do—results that reflect more poorly on us than them.

Another myth: Success is limited to Asian kids. A study of Salvadoran, Guatemalan and Nicaraguan illegals who attended overcrowded, violence-plagued schools in the San Francisco area found that they were the academic stars of otherwise dismal institutions. Although two-thirds of the 50 Central American students surveyed worked 15 to 30 hours a week to supplement their families' income, half made the honor roll.

20   The most astonishing achievements, however, belong to the Hmong, people who were subsistence farmers and CIA operatives in the mountains of northern Laos during the Vietnam War. Many adult Hmong are not literate even in their native language, and a disturbing three-quarters of their households are on welfare. Yet studies of Hmong schoolkids in San Diego and St. Paul conducted during the past four years reveal that they earn better grades than native-born white children. Ruben Rumbaut is still haunted by one San Diego teenager he interviewed a few years ago. The girl's mother had died giving birth to her eighth child; her father remarried and had six more children. In the U.S., the family of 16, joined by the girl's maternal grandparents, squeezed into two apartments. The girl was responsible for keeping house, so she usually couldn't start studying until midnight. Yet she scored 1216 on the SAT (the national average is 902). Muses Rumbaut: "Whenever I think of that girl, I know it's unwise to make pronouncements about the future success of immigrants' children simply by looking at aggregate census data on recent immigrants' education and income."

Yet despite immigrant accomplishments, some Americans seem determined to keep whispering: *No matter what, they'll never be real Americans.* They'll keep their strange customs, congregate in ethnic enclaves, and as their numbers and economic well-being increase, they will demand political power.

22   And if they do, well, they won't be very much unlike the largely unschooled, ragtag ethnic tribes that landed on our shores three or four generations ago and still insist on clinging to such rituals as polka dancing, playing boccie and marching in the St. Patrick's Day parade. Aren't we better off for having let them in?   ❖

Questions for Meaning

1. What do the statistics in paragraph 4 reveal about U.S. history in the twentieth century?
2. According to this argument, how are today's immigrants affecting the U.S. economy?
3. What factors can explain the financial success of many of today's immigrants?
4. What would be the purpose of establishing a national registry of legal workers?
5. Vocabulary: unwarranted (6), dole (10), median (14), onus (14), mantra (18), falter (18), aggregate (20).

Questions about Strategy

1. What does Topolnicki achieve by opening with the example of Hilda Pacheco?
2. Where does Topolnicki recognize the views of people who question the value of today's immigrants? How effectively does she respond to these concerns?
3. How credible are the sources cited in this argument?
4. This essay concludes with a rhetorical question. How does the author expect readers to answer this question? Is this a reasonable expectation?

George J. Borjas

THE NEW ECONOMICS OF IMMIGRATION

A professor of Economics at the University of California at San Diego, George J. Borjas has emerged as a prominent voice in public debate over American immigration policy. His books include *Hispanics in the U.S. Economy* (1985), *Friends or Strangers: The Impact of Immigrants on the U.S. Economy* (1990), and *Immigration and the Work Force* (1992). In the following argument, first published by the *Atlantic Monthly* in 1996, Borjas discusses the effects of recent immigration on the economy as a whole and argues that immigration is making some Americans richer and others poorer.

The United States is on the verge of another great debate over immigration. Thus far the focus of this still-inchoate debate has been on illegal immigration or welfare benefits to legal immigrants, not on the larger issue of the character and consequences of the current high levels of legal immigration. Economic factors by themselves should not and will not decide the outcome of this debate. But they will play an important role. Economics helps us to frame answerable questions about immigration: Who gains by it? Who loses? And in light of the answers to these questions, what should U.S. immigration policy be?

2   There have been two major shifts in immigration policy in this century. In the twenties the United States began to limit the number of immigrants admitted and established the national-origins quota system, an allocation scheme that awarded entry visas mainly on the basis of national origin and that favored Germany and the United Kingdom. This system was repealed in 1965, and family reunification became the central goal of immigration policy, with entry visas being awarded mainly to applicants who had relatives already residing in the United States.

The social, demographic, and economic changes initiated by the 1965 legislation have been truly historic. The number of immigrants began to rise rapidly. As recently as the 1950s only about 250,000 immigrants entered the country annually; by the 1990s the United States was admitting more than 800,000 legal immigrants a year, and some 300,000 aliens entered and stayed in the country illegally. The 1965 legislation also led to a momentous shift in the ethnic composition of the population. Although people of European origin dominated the immigrant flow from the country's founding until the 1950s, only about 10 percent of those admitted in the 1980s were of European origin. It is now estimated that non-Hispanic whites may form a minority of the population soon after 2050. More troubling is that immigration has been linked to the increase in income inequality observed since the 1980s, and to an increase in the costs of maintaining the programs that make up the welfare state.

4   These economic and demographic changes have fueled the incipient debate over immigration policy. For the most part, the weapons of choice in this debate are statistics produced by economic research, with all sides marshaling facts and evidence that support particular policy goals. In this essay I ask a simple question: What does economic research imply about the kind of immigration policy that the United States should pursue?

A Formula for Admission

Every immigration policy must resolve two distinct issues: how many immigrants the country should admit and what kinds of people they should be.

6   It is useful to view immigration policy as a formula that gives points to visa applicants on the basis of various characteristics and then sets a passing grade. The variables in the formula determine what kinds of people will be let into the country, and the passing grade determines how many will be let into the country. Current policy uses a formula that has one overriding variable: whether the visa applicant has a family member already residing in the United States. An applicant who has a relative in the country gets 100 points, passes the test, and is admitted. An applicant who does not gets 0 points, fails the test, and cannot immigrate legally.

Of course, this is a simplistic summary of current policy. There are a lot of bells and whistles in the immigration statutes (which are said to be only slightly less complex than the tax code). In fact the number of points a person gets may depend on whether the sponsor is a U.S. citizen or a permanent resident, and whether the family connection is a close one (such as a parent, a spouse, or a child) or a more distant one (a sibling). Such nuances help to determine the speed with which the visa is granted. A limited number of visas are given to refugees. Some are also distributed on the basis of skill characteristics, but these go to only seven percent of immigrants.

8   Although the United States does not officially admit to using a point system in awarding entry visas, other countries proudly display their formulas on the Internet. A comparison of these point systems reveals that the United States is exceptional in using essentially one variable. Canada, Australia, and New Zealand have more-complex formulas that include an applicant's educational background, occupation, English-language proficiency, and age along with family connections.

Sometimes a host country awards points to people who are willing to pay the visa's stated price. Canada, for example, has granted entry to virtually anyone who would invest at least $250,000 in a Canadian business. Although this "visas-for-sale" policy is a favorite proposal of economists (if we have a market for butter, why not also a market for visas?), it is not taken very seriously in the political debate, perhaps because policymakers feel a repugnance against what may be perceived as a market for human beings. I will therefore discuss the implications of economic research only for policies in which points are awarded on the basis of socioeconomic characteristics, not exchanged for dollars.

What Have We Learned?

10   The academic literature investigating the economic impact of immigration on the United States has grown rapidly in the past decade. The assumptions that long dominated discussion of the costs and benefits of immigration were replaced during the 1980s by a number of new questions, issues, and perceptions.

Consider the received wisdom of the early 1980s. The studies available suggested that even though immigrants arrived at an economic disadvantage, their opportunities improved rapidly over time. Within a decade or two of immigrants' arrival their earnings would overtake the earnings of natives of comparable socioeconomic background. The evidence also suggested that immigrants did no harm to native employment opportunities, and were less likely to receive welfare assistance than natives. Finally, the children of immigrants were even more successful than their parents. The empirical evidence, therefore, painted a very optimistic picture of the contribution that immigrants made to the American economy.

12   In the past ten years this picture has altered radically. New research has established a number of points.

- The relative skills of successive immigrant waves have declined over much of the postwar period. In 1970, for example, the latest immigrant arrivals on average had 0.4 fewer years of schooling and earned 17 percent less than natives. By 1990 the most recently arrived immigrants had 1.3 fewer years of schooling and earned 32 percent less than natives.
- Because the newest immigrant waves start out at such an economic disadvantage, and because the rate of economic assimilation is not very rapid, the earnings of the newest arrivals may never reach parity with the earnings of natives. Recent arrivals will probably earn 20 percent less than natives throughout much of their working lives.
- The large-scale migration of less-skilled workers has done harm to the economic opportunities of less-skilled natives. Immigration may account for perhaps a third of the recent decline in the relative wages of less-educated native workers.
- The new immigrants are more likely to receive welfare assistance than earlier immigrants, and also more likely to do so than natives: 21 percent of immigrant households participate in some means-tested social-assistance program (such as cash benefits, Medicaid, or food stamps), as compared with 14 percent of native households.
- The increasing welfare dependency in the immigrant population suggests that immigration may create a substantial fiscal burden on the most-affected localities and states.
- There are economic benefits to be gained from immigration. These arise because certain skills that immigrants bring into the country complement those of the native population. However, these economic benefits are small—perhaps on the order of $7 billion annually.
- There exists a strong correlation between the skills of immigrants and the skills of their American-born children, so that the huge skill differentials observed among today's foreign-born groups will almost certainly become tomorrow's differences among American-born ethnic groups. In effect, immigration has set the stage for sizable ethnic differences in skills and socioeconomic outcomes, which are sure to be the focus of intense attention in the next century.

The United States is only beginning to observe the economic consequences of the historic changes in the numbers, national origins, and skills of immigrants admitted over the past three decades. Regardless of how immigration policy changes in the near future, we have already set in motion circumstances that will surely alter the economic prospects of native workers and the costs of social-insurance programs not only in our generation but for our children and grandchildren as well.

Whose Interests Will We Serve?

14   If economic research is to play a productive role in the immigration debate, research findings should help us to devise the formula that determines admission into the United States. We need to decide what variables are to be

used to award points to applicants, and what is to be the passing grade. Before we can resolve these issues, however, we have to address a difficult philosophical question: What should the United States try to accomplish with its immigration policy?

The answer to this question is far from obvious, even when the question is posed in purely economic terms. We can think of the world as composed of three distinct groups: people born in the United States (natives), immigrants, and people who remain in other countries. Whose economic welfare should the United States try to improve when setting policy—that of natives, of immigrants, of the rest of the world, or of some combination of the three? The formula implied by economic research depends on whose interests the United States cares most about.

16   Different political, economic, and moral arguments can be made in favor of each of the three groups. I think that most participants in the U.S. policy debate attach the greatest (and perhaps the only) weight to the well-being of natives. This is not surprising. Natives dominate the market for political ideas in the United States, and most proposals for immigration reform will unavoidably reflect the self-interest and concerns of native voters.

Immigration almost always improves the well-being of the immigrants. If they don't find themselves better off after they enter the United States, they are free to go back or to try their luck elsewhere—and, indeed, some do. A few observers attach great weight to the fact that many of the "huddled masses" now live in relative comfort.

18   As for the vast populations that remain in the source countries, they are affected by U.S. immigration policy in a number of ways. Most directly, the policy choices made by the United States may drain particular skills and abilities from the labor markets of source countries. A brain drain slows economic growth in the source countries, as the entrepreneurs and skilled workers who are most likely to spur growth move to greener pastures. Similarly, the principles of free trade suggest that world output would be largest if there were no national borders to interfere with the free movement of people. A policy that restricts workers from moving across borders unavoidably leads to a smaller world economy, to the detriment of many source countries.

The three groups may therefore have conflicting interests, and economics cannot tell us whose interests matter most. The weight that we attach to each of the three groups depends on our values and ideology. For the sake of argument I will assume a political consensus that the objective of immigration policy is to improve the economic well-being of the native population.

20   Beyond that, we have to specify which dimension of native economic well-being we care most about: per capita income or distribution of income. As we shall see, immigration raises per capita income in the native population, but this does not mean that all natives gain equally. In fact some natives are likely to see their incomes greatly reduced. We must therefore be able to judge an immigration policy in terms of its impact on two different economic dimensions: the size of the economic pie (which economists call

"efficiency") and how the pie is sliced ("distribution"). The relative weights that we attach to efficiency and distribution again depend on our values and ideology, and economics provides no guidance on how to rank the two.

For the most part, economists take a very narrow approach: policies that increase the size of the pie are typically considered to be better policies, regardless of their impact on the distribution of wealth in society. We shall begin our construction of an immigration policy by taking this narrow approach. In other words, let's assume that immigration policy has a single and well-defined purpose: to maximize the size of the economic pie available to the native population of the United States. We shall return to the distributional issues raised by immigration policy later on.

The Economic Case for Immigration

22 To see how natives gain from immigration, let's first think about how the United States gains from foreign trade. When we import toys made by cheap Chinese labor, workers in the American toy industry undoubtedly suffer wage cuts and perhaps even lose their jobs. These losses, however, are more than offset by the benefits accruing to consumers, who enjoy the lower prices induced by additional competition. An important lesson from this exercise, worth remembering when we look at the gains from immigration, is that for there to be gains from foreign trade for the economy as a whole, some sectors of the economy must lose.

Consider the analogous argument for immigration. Immigrants increase the number of workers in the economy. Because they create additional competition in the labor market, the wages of native workers fall. At the same time, however, native-owned firms gain, because they can hire workers at lower wages; and many native consumers gain because lower labor costs lead to cheaper goods and services. The gains accruing to those who consume immigrants' services exceed the losses suffered by native workers, and hence society as a whole is better off.

24 Immigration therefore has two distinct consequences. The size of the economic pie increases. And a redistribution of income is induced, from native workers who compete with immigrant labor to those who use immigrants' services.

The standard economic model of the labor market suggests that the net gain from immigration is small. The United States now has more than 20 million foreign-born residents, making up slightly less than 10 percent of the population. I have estimated that native workers lose about $133 billion a year as a result of this immigration (or 1.9 percent of the gross domestic product in a $7 trillion economy), mainly because immigrants drive down wages. However, employers—from the owners of large agricultural enterprises to people who hire household help—gain on the order of $140 billion (or 2.0 percent of GDP*). The net gain, which I call the immigration

---

* GDP is an abbreviation used by economists for gross domestic product.

surplus, is only about $7 billion. Thus the increase in the per capita income of natives is small—less than $30 a year. But the small size of this increase masks a substantial redistribution of wealth.

26   My calculation used the textbook model of a competitive labor market: wages and employment are determined in a free market that balances the desires of people looking for work with the needs of firms looking for workers. In this framework an increase in the number of workers reduces wages in the economy—immigrants join natives in the competition for jobs and bid down wages in the process. There is a lot of disagreement over how much native wages fall when immigrants enter the labor market. Nevertheless, a great deal of empirical research in economics, often unrelated to the question of immigration, concludes that a 10 percent increase in the number of workers lowers wages by about three percent.

If we accept this finding, we can argue as follows: We know that about 70 percent of GDP accrues to workers (with the rest going to the owners of companies), and that natives make up slightly more than 90 percent of the population. Therefore, native workers take home about 63 percent of GDP in the form of wages and salaries. If the 10 percent increase in the number of workers due to immigration has lowered wages by three percent, the share of GDP accruing to native workers has fallen by 1.9 percentage points (or 0.63×0.03). Thus my conclusion that in a $7 trillion economy native earnings drop by $133 billion.

28   Those lost earnings do not vanish into thin air. They represent an income transfer from workers to users of immigrants' services—the employers of immigrants and the consumers who buy the goods and services produced by immigrants. These winners get to pocket the $133 billion—and then some, because the goods produced by immigrant workers generate additional profits for employers. Under the assumption that a 10 percent increase in the number of workers reduces wages by three percent, it turns out that the winners get a windfall totaling $140 billion. Hence the $7 billion immigration surplus.

We can quibble about assumptions, but the rigor of economic theory suggests that this nitpicking may not alter our conclusions much. For example, one could argue—and many do—that immigrants do not reduce the earnings of native workers. If we wished to believe this, however, we would also be forced to conclude that natives do not benefit from immigration at all. If wages do not fall, there are no savings in employers' payrolls and no cost savings to be passed on to native consumers. Remember the lesson from the foreign-trade example: no pain, no gain.

30   One could also argue that immigration has reduced the earnings of natives very substantially—by, say, 10 percent. The immigration surplus would then be about $25 billion annually. The net gain from immigration, therefore, remains small even with an unrealistically high estimate of the impact of immigration on native earnings. Imagine what U.S. policy would look like today if our earnings had fallen by 10 percent as a result of past immigration.

The immigration surplus has to be balanced against the cost of providing services to the immigrant population. Immigrants have high rates of welfare recipiency. Estimates of the fiscal impact of immigration (that is, of the difference between the taxes paid by immigrants and the cost of services provided to them) vary widely. Some studies claim that immigrants pay $25–30 billion more in taxes than they take out of the system, while other studies blame them for a fiscal burden of more than $40 billion on natives.

32   It is doubtful that either of these statistics accurately reflects the gap between taxes paid and the cost of services provided. Studies that claim a beneficial fiscal impact tend to assume that immigrants do not increase the cost of most government programs other than education and welfare. Even though we do not know by how much immigrants increase the cost of police protection, maintaining roads and national parks, and so forth, we do know that it costs more to provide these services to an ever larger population. However, studies that claim a large fiscal burden often overstate the costs of immigration and understate the taxes paid. As a result, estimates of the fiscal impact of immigration should be viewed with suspicion. Nevertheless, because the immigration surplus is around $7 billion, the net benefit from immigration after accounting for the fiscal impact is very small, and could conceivably be a net loss.

How Many and Whom Should We Admit?

In principle, we should admit immigrants whenever their economic contribution (to native well-being) will exceed the costs of providing social services to them. We are not, though, in a position to make this calculation with any reasonable degree of confidence. In fact, no mainstream study has ever attempted to suggest, purely on the basis of the empirical evidence, how many immigrants should be admitted.

34   This unfortunate lack of guidance from economic research has, I believe, led to sudden and remarkable swings in policy proposals. As recently as 1990 Congress legislated an increase in the number of legal immigrants of about 175,000 people annually. Last year the Commission on Immigration Reform, headed by Barbara Jordan, recommended that legal immigration be cut by about 240,000 people a year—a proposal that was immediately supported by President Clinton. (The Clinton Administration, however, successfully resisted congressional efforts to follow up on the commission's recommendations.)

    Although we do not know how many immigrants to admit, simple economics and common sense suggest that the magic number should not be an immutable constant regardless of economic conditions in the United States. A good case can be made for linking immigration to the business cycle: admit more immigrants when the economy is strong and the unemployment rate is low, and cut back on immigration when the economy is weak and the unemployment rate is high.

36   Economic research also suggests that the United States may be better off if its policy of awarding entry visas favors skilled workers. Skilled immigrants earn more than less-skilled immigrants, and hence pay more in taxes, and they are less likely to use welfare and other social services.

Depending on how the skills of immigrants compare with the skills of natives, immigrants also affect the productivity of the native work force and of native-owned companies. Skilled native workers, for example, have much to gain when less-skilled workers enter the United States: they can devote all their efforts to jobs that use their skills effectively while immigrants provide cheap labor for service jobs. These gains, however, come at a cost. The jobs of less-skilled natives are now at risk, and these natives will suffer a reduction in their earnings. Nonetheless, it does not seem far-fetched to assume that the American work force, particularly in comparison with the work forces of many source countries, is composed primarily of skilled workers. Thus the typical American worker would seem to gain from unskilled immigration.

38   How does immigration affect companies' profits? Companies that use less-skilled workers on the production line gain from the immigration of the less-skilled, who reduce the earnings of less-skilled workers in favor of increasing profits. However, other companies—perhaps even most—might be better off with skilled immigrants. Many studies in economics suggest that skilled labor is better suited to the machines that are now used widely in the production process. Most companies would therefore gain more if the immigrant flow were composed of skilled workers.

Most workers prefer unskilled immigrants, whereas most companies prefer skilled immigrants. This conflict can be resolved only by measuring how much native workers gain from unskilled immigration and how much companies gain from skilled immigration, and comparing the two. Although there is a lot of uncertainty in the academic literature, we do know that the productivity of capital is very responsive to an influx of skilled workers. The large increase in the profits of the typical company, and the corresponding reduction in the cost of goods produced by skilled workers, suggest that the United States might be better off with a policy favoring skilled immigrants.

40   The gains from skilled immigration will be even larger if immigrants have "external effects" on the productivity of natives. One could argue, for example, that immigrants may bring knowledge, skills, and abilities that natives lack, and that natives might somehow pick up this know-how by interacting with immigrants. It seems reasonable to suspect that the value of these external effects would be greater if natives interact with highly skilled immigrants. This increase in the human capital of natives might offset—and perhaps even reverse—the harm that immigration does to the wages of competing workers.

Although such effects now play a popular role in economic theory, there is little empirical evidence supporting their existence, let alone measuring their magnitude. I find it difficult to imagine that interaction with immigrants entering an economy as large as that of the United States could have a measurable effect. Nevertheless, if external effects exist, they reinforce the argument that the United States would gain most from skilled immigrants.

Efficiency versus Distribution

42 Participants in the immigration debate routinely use the results of economic research to frame the discussion and to suggest policy solutions. Perhaps the most important contributions of this research are the insights that immigration entails both gains and losses for the native population, that the winners and the losers are typically different groups, and that policy parameters can be set in ways that attempt to maximize gains and minimize losses. If the objective of immigration policy is to increase the per capita income of the native population, the evidence suggests that immigration policy should encourage the entry of skilled workers. It is important to remember, however, that even though the immigration of skilled workers would be beneficial for the United States as a whole, the gains and losses would be concentrated in particular subgroups of the population.

As we have seen, the net gains from current immigration are small, so it is unlikely that these gains can play a crucial role in the policy debate. Economic research teaches a very valuable lesson: the economic impact of immigration is essentially distributional. Current immigration redistributes wealth from unskilled workers, whose wages are lowered by immigrants, to skilled workers and owners of companies that buy immigrants' services, and from taxpayers who bear the burden of paying for the social services used by immigrants to consumers who use the goods and services produced by immigrants.

44 Distributional issues drive the political debate over many social policies, and immigration policy is no exception. The debate over immigration policy is not a debate over whether the entire country is made better off by immigration—the gains from immigration seem much too small, and could even be outweighed by the costs of providing increased social services. Immigration changes how the economic pie is sliced up—and this fact goes a long way toward explaining why the debate over how many and what kinds of immigrants to admit is best viewed as a tug-of-war between those who gain from immigration and those who lose from it.

History has taught us that immigration policy changes rarely, but when it does, it changes drastically. Can economic research play a role in finding a better policy? I believe it can, but there are dangers ahead. Although the pendulum seems to be swinging to the restrictionist side (with ever louder calls for a complete closing of our borders), a greater danger to the national interest may be the few economic groups that gain much from immigration. They seem indifferent to the costs that immigration imposes on other segments of society, and they have considerable financial incentives to keep the current policy in place. The harmful effects of immigration will not go away simply because some people do not wish to see them. In the short run these groups may simply delay the day of reckoning. Their potential long-run impact, however, is much more perilous: the longer the delay, the greater the chances that when immigration policy finally changes, it will undergo a seismic shift—one that, as in the twenties, may come close to shutting down the border and preventing Americans from enjoying the benefits that a well-designed immigration policy can bestow on the United States. ❖

Questions for Meaning

1. What two major shifts in twentieth-century immigration policy are identified by Borjas?
2. What basic issues must be considered when determining immigration policy?
3. According to Borjas, who is most likely to gain from the immigration of low-skilled workers and who is most likely to suffer?
4. Why is Borjas concerned with both the size of the "economic pie" and the way it is sliced? What would be the effect of an immigration policy that focused on only one of these concerns?
5. What kind of immigration does Borjas favor? Does he make any specific recommendations?
6. Vocabulary: inchoate (1), demographic (3), incipient (4), repugnance (9), empirical (11), assimilation (12), parity (12), correlation (12), detriment (18), accrues (27), immutable (35), entails (42), parameters (42), seismic (45).

Questions about Strategy

1. Consider the summary of immigration policy in paragraph 6, a summary that Borjas calls "simplistic" in paragraph 7. To what extent does paragraph 7 improve the summary? What is the advantage of beginning with a simplification and then admitting complications? What are the risks of this strategy?
2. How reliable is the evidence Borjas provides to support his case? Does he provide sufficient evidence to be convincing?
3. In paragraph 9, Borjas makes an assumption that is important for the rest of his argument. Is this assumption reasonable? Is anyone likely to disagree?
4. How effective is the analogy, in paragraphs 22–23, between immigration and foreign trade?
5. Does Borjas ever respond to arguments that could be made against his own?
6. What assumptions has Borjas made about his audience? Does he explain economic concepts so that they can be understood by readers who lack his expertise, or does he envision an audience of his peers?

Weston Kosova

THE INS MESS

Weston Kosova is an associate editor at Washington's City Paper. *He was formerly a reporter and researcher for* The New Republic, *which published "The INS Mess" in 1992. You will find references to the Bush Administration, which was still in power when Kosova wrote. But do not assume this material is dated. The Immigration and Naturalization Service (INS) continues to be a large government bureaucracy that has difficulty meeting the many demands made of it. As you read, imagine that you are seeking to immigrate legally to the United States.*

"No, no, I do not know what is the number of the form. It is the one for a person who has a family to bring to the country. Do you have that one? The one for relatives? . . . No. I tell you. I do not know the number of the form."

2   It was early afternoon on a Wednesday in December, and the line at the United States Immigration and Naturalization Service's regional office in Northern Virginia was backed up to the door. A fortyish man at the head of the line, a Pakistani, had been pleading his case for nearly five minutes to an agitated clerk, who shifted on her stool behind the high counter.

"Sir, like I told you, you've got to give me more to go on than that," the clerk said. "You see how many forms I've got sitting back here? I need the *number*." She called the next person in line.

4   Despite her insistence, the clerk did know which form the man wanted: after the line dissipated, I walked up to the same window and, in flawless Midwestern, asked for "the form you need to bring a family member here from another country to live." Without so much as a question she reached back to the stack of papers behind her and handed over INS I-130, Petition for Alien Relative—the most commonly requested of INS forms.

Incidents like this are familiar to anyone who has encountered the Immigration and Naturalization Service. Mention the INS to a recent immigrant or someone trying to get a green card or work permit and you will see eyes roll. Xenophobic paper pushers are just a small part of the problem. Every immigrant has his own tales of lost forms, ill-trained inspectors, usurious fees, arbitrarily enforced rules, and notoriously sluggish bureaucracy.

6   In November 1990 the General Accounting Office issued a scathing, 177-page report on the INS that laid bare the Justice Department agency's negligence. "Over the past decade weak management systems and inconsistent leadership have allowed serious problems to go unresolved," the GAO charged. The report revealed how INS employees rigged their work schedules, allowing them to take home as much as $20,000 a year in overtime pay. It described an INS office in Los Angeles that deposited the thousands of dollars in fees it took in each day by mailing the cash to the bank.

The GAO scolding was issued a year after Raymond Momboisse, a senior INS attorney, quit after penning a twenty-two-page internal memo in which he described the agency as "totally disorganized." Among other things, Momboisse revealed that the INS regularly shifted funds from office to office to cover nearly $40 million in overspending, and that it deliberately overhired border patrol guards as a way to pressure Congress for more money.

8   Momboisse's memo came on the heels of yet another investigation of the INS that had been ordered by then Attorney General Richard Thornburgh. This inspection foreshadowed many of the abuses that the GAO would detail in its report a year later. Thornburgh discovered that the INS had lost 23,059 certificates of citizenship with "an estimated street value ranging from $11 million to $115 million." The Justice Department also charged that INS "data reported for applications received, applicants interviewed, and fees collected were inaccurate and unreliable at all organizational levels."

Shortly after the Justice Department audit, INS director Alan C. Nelson was forced to resign. In his place, President Bush appointed Gene McNary, a St. Louis County executive (and county chairman of Bush's 1988 presidential campaign). At a press conference the day after his confirmation, McNary pledged to clean up the agency and overhaul its management. "I intend to see that it is brought under control and that it is centralized," he said. In the months that followed, McNary pored over the Justice Department report and the Momboisse memo. He ordered the INS's four regional managers to review the offices under their jurisdictions. He acquainted himself with the workings of the vast, 16,000-employee, $1 billion agency.

10   Yet now, more than two years later, McNary and his crew haven't even begun to reform the INS. McNary came up with a few nutty, ill-fated proposals—requiring all Americans and residents over age 16 to carry national worker-identification cards, offering Nicaraguan refugees cash "loans" to leave the country—but nothing resembling the plan he promised would bring the agency "under control."

Even if McNary were to set about gauging the immigration service's various management sores, however, the frustrations immigrants face wouldn't ease. Immigrants are treated shabbily by the INS not only because the agency is careless and inept, but because, despite its name, "immigration" and "naturalization" are not really its first concerns; the INS is far more interested in tracking down and expelling illegal aliens.

12   "The internal mentality of the INS continues to be one of [law] enforcement, while at the same time the INS tries to maintain a p.r. [public relations] image of providing public services and immigration benefits," says Ignatius Bau of the San Francisco-based Coalition for Immigration Reform. Among immigration lawyers like Bau, this is commonly referred to as the "cop mentality," an attitude that is borne out in McNary's own assessment of his agency's purpose. In a *Washington Post* profile, McNary said that his top five priorities are: to "gain control of the southern border;

increase efforts to deport criminal aliens; put into effect new regulations on granting asylum; enforce sanctions against employers who hire illegal aliens; and update the data processing system." In other words, he considers the INS to be at least four-fifths a police agency.

As a result, the agency's enforcement details are watched closely by top management. The INS maintains twenty-four-hour armed patrols along every open yard of the U.S. border. Under the 1986 Federal Immigration Reform and Control Act, businesses that hire illegal aliens now risk draconian fines. Swift deportation awaits those nabbed without proper papers. Last year the INS rounded up and expelled nearly 1 million illegals.

14 In contrast to its concerted enforcement effort, the INS only grudgingly administers the other, more mundane half of its responsibility. Since navigating incoming legal immigrants through the labyrinth of immigration laws is of comparatively little concern to agency brass, they don't bother to keep a close watch on how immigration benefits are handled. Instead, INS regional offices around the country are granted virtually a free hand in deciding for themselves how and to whom they should give out green cards, visas, and work permits. Predictably, the result is chaos. In his parting memo, Momboisse compared the INS to "a feudal state with each region, district, and sector acting independently to give its own interpretation to the law."

For example, the city of Chevy Chase sits on the border between Washington, D.C., and Maryland, and is divided by Western Avenue. One side of Western Avenue is considered Chevy Chase, D.C., and falls under the control of the INS regional office in Arlington, Virginia. The other side is considered Chevy Chase, Maryland, and falls under the jurisdiction of the INS office in Baltimore.

16 Suppose, for instance, that you are a non-American who married a U.S. citizen, which makes you automatically eligible for permanent residence status. If your spouse lives in Chevy Chase, Maryland, you must travel to Baltimore, file the proper documents, and wait nine to twelve months (or longer, depending on the time of year) for an interview from an INS inspector before you will be granted permanent residence papers. During that time, you cannot leave the country for any reason or else you lose your eligibility to return. If, however, your spouse lives across Western Avenue in Chevy Chase, D.C., you will be interviewed by an INS inspector in Arlington the same day that you file your papers. In Baltimore you cannot submit papers without attaching a copy of a birth certificate. In Arlington they don't even ask to see a birth certificate.

Each regional office also decides how many applications it will process a day. The Arlington office typically hands out numbers to the first 125 people in line when it opens in the morning, and turns everyone else away. Lines usually start forming for the next day soon after the office closes in the evening. Other offices compound the problem by accepting applications only two or three days a week. Still others are open during business hours every day and take all comers.

18   And the rules vary not only from office to office, but often from inspector to inspector within the same office. One recent immigrant from the
Philippines told me that after waiting in line from two in the morning until
noon to file naturalization papers, he was finally seen by an inspector. "The
lady told me that my application was no good," he said. "She told me that I
needed to show her my birth certificate, but I didn't have it." The inspector
informed him that he would have to come back with his birth certificate before he could file his papers. So the following week he once again waited in
line for nearly ten hours. This time he brought his birth certificate and presented it to the inspector—a different one from the week before. "She said I
don't need it," he says. "She didn't look at it, even."

Some immigrants especially those whose English is poor, have taken to hiring lawyers to accompany them to their meetings with INS inspectors, precisely to avoid this sort of frustration. But many immigrants can't afford the
immigration service's prohibitive filing fees, let alone attorney's fees. Every
INS form has a fee, and every fee must be paid up front. Except under very
limited circumstances, there are no waivers of fees for people who cannot
afford to pay. And fees are not refunded, even if the application is rejected.

20   Coming to America isn't cheap. Filing an application with the INS for
naturalization costs $90. Becoming a permanent resident runs $120. Requesting permission to bring a foreign relative runs $75. For a work permit,
add $50 more. Add to that fees for fingerprinting and photographs that are
required for many applications, and in some cases the total for the application alone can top $500 to $600, says Bau, and sometimes reaches into the
thousands.

Last year the INS attempted to charge Salvadoran refugees fees total-
ing $380 when they applied for temporary resident status under a special
amnesty program. A family of five or more was subject to $1,435 in fees.
But under pressure from immigration groups and Joe Moakley, a Democratic representative from Massachusetts, the INS scaled back the fees to $75
per person, $225 for a family of three or more. In order to remain in the
country, however, Salvadorans must renew their status every six months, at
a cost of $60 per person. And, true to form, the INS refused to pay refunds
to those refugees who paid the original $380.

22   For those who can afford the filing fees, there is still the matter of figuring
out which combination of forms is required. There are dozens of combinations governing every possible circumstance under which a person could
immigrate.

"How do you immigrate to the United States? A very good question,"
says INS spokesman Duke Austin. "Very difficult to answer. . . . I mean,
we're talking hundreds of pages of legislation." Indeed, immigration laws
are needlessly, often mindlessly, complex. Every few years, in a fit of immigration "reform," Congress trowels a new layer of benefits and restrictions
on top of existing legislation, making it more difficult both for immigrants

trying to figure out if they qualify to enter the country and for the INS. "I've been working at it for fifteen years," admits Austin, "and there are things that even I don't understand about the law."

24   For example, under the law there are three broad categories of people who are allowed to immigrate: (1) family members of U.S. citizens or legal permanent residents; (2) people found eligible to work in the United States; and (3) political refugees. A would-be immigrant who doesn't fall into one of these three categories can't immigrate. But even immigrants who do appear to meet the requirements still may not be allowed to enter.

Take the first category. The INS claims that keeping families together is a primary concern, so immediate family members of American citizens or permanent legal residents are eligible for visas without waiting. However, what you consider to be your immediate family and what the immigration laws consider it to be are probably very different. The INS, for instance, does not count brothers or sisters as immediate family. It does not recognize a child either, if he or she is married or over 21. Neither does it consider a husband or wife immediate family if, as INS documents put it, "you were not both physically present at the marriage ceremony, and the marriage was not consummated." The INS considers these family members "restricted."

26   The distinction is important. While an unlimited number of "immediate" family members are allowed to immigrate each year, "restricted" family are subject to quotas and long waits. Under new immigration laws that went into effect last October, a total of approximately 25,000 restricted family members from each country will be allowed to immigrate this year (up from 20,000 previously). When their eight-digit visa number comes up, they can enter the country. But from many countries thousands more than the limit apply each year, resulting in huge backlogs. For most countries, the wait for restricted relatives now stands at about three years. From Mexico, the wait is nine years. The Philippines tops the list with 12.5 years.

Equally quirky rules apply to immigrants who come to the United States to work. Not everyone is eligible. Immigrant workers must fall under one of the agency's three work "preference" classes. "First Preference" workers, according to the INS, are "aliens with extraordinary ability in the arts, sciences, education, business, or athletics which has been demonstrated by sustained national or international acclaim, or outstanding professors or researchers or certain multinational executives and managers." "Second Preference" workers are essentially the same as First Preference workers but not as famous. "Third Preference" workers are skilled and unskilled laborers, such as fruit pickers, who perform usually low-paying, menial jobs that employers can't find enough Americans to do.

28   But an immigrant who meets the INS's requirements might still be prevented from immigrating. Suppose that a catering company in New York has its eye on a famed Turkish ice sculptor and wants to hire her full time. She would be eligible to enter the United States under the "extraordinary ability" category, right? Probably not. Because as defined by the immigration laws, extraordinary skills aren't skills that are extraordinary in

themselves, but those that no other person in the United States possesses. This means that before a company may bring a foreign citizen here to work, it must prove that it has searched for an American to do the job and failed, usually by posting notices and advertising in newspapers. And the United States already has its share of ice sculptors, many of whom doubtless are unemployed. Even if the ice sculptor is found eligible to immigrate, that still isn't a guarantee she'll get in, since the INS puts a yearly cap of 40,000 on immigrant workers (with the exception of Third Preference workers, who are admitted only when shortages of laborers arise).

Similarly, immigrants applying for green cards as political refugees may be rejected even if technically they are eligible under the law. According to INS Form I-589, Request for Asylum in the United States, "The burden of proof is upon you to establish that you have a well-founded fear of persecution on account of your race, religion, nationality, membership in a particular social group, or political opinion." The INS defines persecution as "to pursue; to harass in a manner designed to injure, grieve, or afflict; to oppress; specifically, to cause or put to death because of belief."

30   Sounds fair enough, but that isn't the definition that the government actually applies in deciding who is granted political refugee status. If it were, President Bush wouldn't be summarily turning away the latest wave of Haitian boat refugees, many of whom would qualify. Rather, political refugee status is largely granted not on the basis of persecution itself, but on the basis of which country is doing the persecuting. A 1987 GAO study revealed that the government was far more likely to grant political asylum to refugees from countries hostile to the United States than those from friendly countries. Thus, the administration granted asylum to scores of refugees from Afghanistan during the 1980s and to refugees who escaped from Cuba in a helicopter last year, but refused thousands from El Salvador and Guatemala.

There are still further immigration restrictions. Under the law, not even an extraordinarily skilled, politically persecuted husband of an American citizen can immigrate to the United States if he is or was at any time in the previous ten years a member of the Communist Party. Under federal law, this prohibition is supposed to be illegal. In 1987 Congress passed legislation reforming the 1952 McCarren–Walter Act, which barred Communists from entering the United States. The new law prohibits the government from shunning people who hold political beliefs that, for an American citizen, would be legal. But that hasn't stopped the INS from requiring immigration applicants to "list your present and past membership in or affiliation with every organization, association, fund, foundation, party, club, society, or similar group in the United States or any other place," including "location, dates of membership, and the nature of the organization." Write down "Communist Party" and you won't get in. The INS also maintains a "lookout list" of people from various countries who, because of their political beliefs, would be rejected out of hand if they attempted to immigrate. The list, which dates back to 1904, contains more than 350,000 names; 250,000 of them were added after 1980.

32   Otherwise qualified applicants are also prohibited from immigrating if they are infected with what the government terms a "highly communicable disease" and thereby pose a health risk to Americans. The administration's definition of this term, however, is strangely selective. As Donald Goldman, a member of the National Commission on AIDS, points out, "Tuberculosis isn't included on the government's list of infectious diseases. Neither is bubonic plague." In practice, the term "highly communicable disease" has become a euphemism for AIDS. The administration claims that HIV and AIDS carriers are barred because the government cannot afford health care for infected indigent immigrants. This is a specious argument. After all, the government doesn't stop terminal cancer patients at the border.

There is one way under the new immigration laws that a lucky few can circumvent all these nitpicky regulations and enter the country whether they're eligible to or not. For the first time, the INS is holding a lottery this year that will grant green cards to a total of 40,000 people. For four days last October, applicants were allowed to mail in as many entry forms as they wanted. There were only three restrictions. Applicants couldn't be Communists. They couldn't be "highly communicable." And they couldn't be from Mexico. Or the Philippines. Or China. Or from any country other than thirty-three mostly white, mostly European nations chosen to participate. It is probably no coincidence that many of the excluded countries are the same non-white nations on which the United States had severe immigration restrictions before country-by-country quotas were abolished in 1965. And it is certainly not a coincidence that fully 40 percent of the 40,000 lottery winners have to be from Ireland. Edward Kennedy, who sits on the Senate's Immigration and Refugee Affairs Subcommittee, wrote the requirement into the bill.

34   Immigration law is excessively complex because Congress has no incentive to make it more simple. From the standpoint of Capitol Hill, there's no percentage in immigration. The people affected by the immigration laws aren't citizens, and noncitizens don't vote. Yet it wouldn't require a midnight session of Congress to reform the laws enough so that immigrating to America would become a less harrowing experience:

Split the agency in two. Even in the face of the INS's elaborate defense machinery, the number of people attempting to sneak into the United States these days isn't dwindling. While the estimated number of illegal immigrants declined between 1986 and 1988, a December INS newsletter reports that in the past two years, the numbers have once again hit pre-1986 levels. The number of illegal aliens in this country is now about 4.5 million.

36   Granted, controlling the borders is an impossible task. But in its zeal to catch every illegal, the INS regards everyone on the other side with suspicion. To the service, a legal immigrant is merely an illegal alien with papers.

The logical way to ease the agency's internal conflict is to form two agencies: a true Immigration and Naturalization Service, concerned with assisting eligible applicants, and an Identification and Expulsion Service to police the borders and remove illegals.

Get rid of the forms. The INS could easily get by with one or two well-designed application forms. Current forms are endlessly redundant, requiring the same information line after line. The only purpose multiple forms serve is to justify the agency's fees—which wouldn't be needed if there weren't so many forms.

38   *Gut the immigration laws.* Start by tossing out the lookout list, ending restrictions on AIDS carriers, and getting rid of all others you can't explain in one breath.

Reforming the INS not only would benefit legal immigrants, it would also bring closer to truth a chapter in American mythology. The agency that ushered millions of eager immigrants through the gates of Ellis Island and into the promised land has been transformed into an impenetrable army of cops and bureaucrats. The INS should at least try to live up to the "give us your poor" refrain.

40   Meanwhile, America's huddled masses can find the agency's new face reflected on TV. Recently, ABC bumped its long-running sitcom "Perfect Strangers," about a wide-eyed island immigrant who comes to America to live with his cousin. Taking over the same time slot is "Billy," a sitcom about a Scottish college professor whose visa runs out. In "Perfect Strangers," the foreign cousin finds family, adventure, and a beautiful American bride. In "Billy," the professor marries a student to avoid being deported by the INS. ❖

Questions for Meaning

1. According to Kosova, what is the primary concern of the United States Immigration and Naturalization Service?
2. How expensive is it to be a legal immigrant to this country? Can you imagine other expenses besides those stated in this article?
3. What categories of people are allowed to immigrate legally?
4. How does immigration law define "immediate family"?
5. Does INS policy and procedure reveal any evidence of racism?
6. Vocabulary: dissipated (4), usurious (5), scathing (6), draconian (13), mundane (14), labyrinth (14), euphemism (32), specious (32).

Questions about Strategy

1. Consider the story with which this article begins. What does it illustrate? Why does Kosova point out that INS I-130 is "the most commonly requested of INS forms"?

2. In paragraph 16, Kosova asks readers to imagine that they are applying for permanent resident status. Why does he use the second person in this paragraph?
3. In paragraph 31, Kosova points out that 250,000 out of 350,000 names on a list dating back to 1904 were added after 1980. What is he implying here?
4. The article concludes with three specific recommendations for reform. Has Kosova prepared the way for them? Now that you have read the argument that precedes them, do these proposals seem reasonable to you?
5. What is Kosova suggesting when he uses his conclusion to briefly contrast two television shows?

ONE STUDENT'S ASSIGNMENT

Drawing on recent data, revise the student essay on immigration that appears in the current edition of *The Informed Argument*.* Discuss your plans with the author of that essay, and share drafts with him as you revise. The final essay should be a collaborative effort that satisfies both of you.

Another Look at the Economics of Immigration
Janelle Anderson and Christopher J. Lovrien

America has long been called a nation of immigrants. It has been said so many times that it has become a cliché. Yet the fact remains, the United States' 200-year rise from newborn to superpower was made possible largely because of the skills and ambitions of immigrants. Chinese immigrants helped build the railroads that were essential to our country's economic growth. Italian stone masons helped create many of our most important public buildings. Andrew Carnegie, one of the greatest philanthropists in our history, was born in Scotland, and, more recently, Irish-Americans like the Kennedys have provided vital national leadership. It is not surprising then that our current Secretary of State, Madeleine Albright, was born in Czechoslovakia. Immigrants have long brought vitality to this nation and that is why we should continue to encourage legal immigration.

---

* Christopher J. Lovrien wrote the essay published in the Fourth Edition when he was my student in 1994. I wanted to keep Chris's argument in the Fifth Edition but saw that it needed updating. Janelle Anderson took the same course with me in 1996, when this Fifth Edition was being prepared. Knowing that Janelle and Chris were in frequent communication, I offered them this assignment as a collaborative project.—Robert K. Miller

2   However, many Americans seem to want immigration to be restricted. Barbara Jordan, the head of the Commission on Immigration Reform, recommended that immigration "be curbed by 240,000 people a year" (Borjas 237). As the economy took a downturn in the early 1990s and unemployment rose, some cried out that immigrants were taking jobs from low-skilled Americans. While this may be true in the short term, immigrants positively affect the economy in the long run. More immigrants means not only more workers but also more consumers. In economic terms, this means an increase in demand and the creation of more jobs. Economists will tell you that the number of jobs in an economy is not finite. Although research shows that less-skilled native workers' employment opportunities may be slightly reduced when immigrants enter a local labor market (Borjas 238), immigrants are still consumers. Additionally, immigrants can bring special skills that complement natives' skills.

        Another concern about the influx of immigrants is the extra burden they are said to place on the welfare system. This concern is understandable in light of the deficit and the ongoing debate on cutting social programs. It is argued that the government spends federal funds not only on those who come in legally, but also on those who enter illegally. This is not the case, however; illegal immigrants are already banned from assistance except in the case of emergency medical assistance (Topolnicki 226). Welfare benefits that immigrants do receive are awarded almost exclusively to political refugees. The truth is that immigrants pay $25–30 billion more in taxes than they use in government services (Topolnicki 226). Quite simply, most immigrants are not leeching off the system. Even though an immigrant, particularly a political refugee, may need and receive welfare when she enters America, this does not necessarily mean a continued dependence on welfare. While some immigrants do receive welfare benefits, most contribute more money to social programs through taxes than they withdraw through government assistance.

4   So what should the U.S. policy on immigration be? We should be conscious that immigration is a tremendous tool for improving our country. Americans should also keep in mind that, with the exception of Native Americans, everyone in this country has descended from immigrants. If earlier family members had not been allowed to immigrate to the United States, our citizens would not be able to call America "home" today. If we allow, or even seek out immigrants, especially skilled immigrants, the government can direct immigration to help strengthen the United States.

        The first step is to ensure that the government knows who is entering the country. This means illegal immigration must be curbed. The best way to do this is to increase legal immigration. Currently, the government allows between 800,000 and one million immigrants to legally enter the country each year. It is estimated that another 300,000 enter illegally. Statistics show that when legal immigration is cut, illegal immigration generally increases. Increasing the quota of legal immigrants could decrease the number entering illegally (Becker 218). The same number of people would be entering the country, but the government would have more control over who they are. A higher quota of legal immigrants would mean we could allow more people with special skills and education to enter the country.

6   Immigrants who are educated and have special skills are an asset to the United States. All immigrants are an asset to the country because they are consumers, but those with education and special skills are particularly beneficial to America. Economic research shows that our country will be better off favoring entry of skilled workers. These skilled immigrants generally are able to get higher-paying jobs, and therefore pay more in taxes. Also, these immigrants do not need to use welfare or any other social services (Borjas 238). The immigrants who have come to the United States since 1980 actually have more education than the immigrants who came here before 1980. Today, 27 percent of the immigrants have college degrees when they arrive. Two out of every ten U.S. physicians are foreign-born, as is one out of every eight engineers (Topolnicki 227). There is no doubt in our minds that these people constitute an asset for the United States. They are the people who are living out the American Dream. After they have lived here for ten years, 55 percent of the immigrants own their own homes (Topolnicki 227). This is the ultimate example of what the American Dream is about: bettering oneself and the country.

Looking at the history of opposition to immigration, we see some interesting trends. There seems to always have been those who felt that certain immigrants were going to ruin the country. When the Germans began immigration to America, some "ethnic" Americans said they would cause the breakdown of America. In fact, the country became stronger. When the potato famine drove a wave of Irish immigrants to America, some Americans (including some of the new German-Americans) said they would ruin the country. They were wrong. The country became stronger and the Irish-Americans eventually flourished despite initial prejudice toward them. With history as a precedent, why is there any reason to believe that this new wave of immigrants will be anything but good for America? People argue that these new immigrants are "different" from the 13 million Eastern and Southern Europeans who immigrated to the United States in the first half of the twentieth century. This is true in one sense only: Of today's immigrants, only 38 percent are white; 88 percent of those who came before 1960 were white (Topolnicki 225). We certainly hope the value of new immigrants is not being judged on the basis of skin-color prejudices. When people like Peter Brimelow say that large-scale immigration will cause America to lose its culture, they fail to realize that American culture has not only been immensely enriched by other ethnic cultures, but these "other cultures" are the basis for what Americans call our culture.

8   Why are immigrants to America often able to do so well in their new country and add so much to it? In no small part, it's because of their character. Immigrants must be ambitious enough to leave their native country. As Jeffrey S. Passel, director of the Urban Institute's immigration research and policy, says, "The very act of pulling up stakes and moving to a foreign country indicates that you have initiative and want to better yourself" (qtd. in Topolnicki 226). By increasing legal immigration and selecting skilled people, we can make sure that we do get well-educated and highly ambitious people who are the most likely to prosper in society and to benefit it.

This proposal is in no way saying that we must restrict immigration only to those who are already affluent or skilled. The current immigration policy recognizes the importance of reunifying families, and this should continue. The United States also accepts those who have been politically oppressed. We must continue to do this for obvious humane reasons. But even in the case of political refugees, the government must realize and be selective about who is coming into the country. In the case of political refugees, the government will be able to help them initially so they can begin to realize the American Dream for themselves.

10   America has had a long history of welcoming talented immigrants. Legal immigrants are taxpayers and consumers. Therefore, immigrants help our country not only by expanding its culture but also by contributing new skills that help America's economy. The next great physicist might very well be arriving in New York or San Francisco right now, and whether she is European, Asian, or African, we hope the border guards will not send her away. ❖

Suggestions for Writing

1. Is the United States "a nation of immigrants"? Does our country have a special responsibility to accept "huddled masses yearning to breathe free"? Write an essay focused on how traditional American values—as you define them—should determine our immigration policy.
2. Kinsley (paragraph 9) draws attention to neo-Nazi violence directed against immigrants to Germany. Look for articles published within the last few years on this topic and report your findings.

3. Locate the earlier column to which Becker refers at the end of his article. Compare his recommendation in that column with the position he takes in "Illegal Immigration: How to Turn the Tide." Then argue on behalf of the position you prefer.
4. Becker, Topolnicki, and Borjas all focus on the economic consequences of immigration. Drawing on these sources, write an argument for or against the belief that immigration causes harm to the American economy.
5. Write an essay comparing U.S. and Canadian immigration laws.
6. Write an argument for or against increasing the number of legal immigrants from Mexico.
7. How should the American government respond when illegal immigrants arrive safely in America after a dangerous voyage? Should these aliens be returned to the country from which they fled? Or should they be allowed to remain within the United States?
8. Drawing on the article by Kosova, write an argument recommending a specific change in procedures followed by the U.S. Immigration and Naturalization Service.
9. Is U.S. immigration policy racist? Write an essay attempting to answer this question. Draw on information provided by Brimelow and Kosova, and do additional research if necessary.
10. Write an essay defining the meaning of *asylum* and the extent to which the United States should accept foreigners seeking political asylum. Draw on at least three sources that you have discovered on your own.

COLLABORATIVE PROJECT

Interview immigrants living in your own community as well as any local officials who have responsibility for immigrants. Evaluate whether new arrivals are being treated fairly in your area. Then write a report that identifies anything you discover that is positive. Suggest any changes that you believe are necessary.

SECTION 3

SAME-GENDER MARRIAGE: WHAT IS A FAMILY?

LISA BENNETT

WHY CAN'T WE GET MARRIED?

Although the issue of same-gender marriage has far-reaching implications for the sort of country the United States will be in the twenty-first century, the people most immediately affected by this debate are those couples who are seeking the right to marry. The following argument, which was first published by *Mademoiselle* in 1996, draws heavily on personal experience. As you read, think about how you would respond to Bennett if she shared her story with you as a friend.

I am in love, and I want to get married. She is the daughter of an Ivy League philosophy professor; I am the daughter of a banker. She is a native of Manhattan's Upper West Side; I am from Long Island. She is Jewish. I am Irish Catholic. She is beautiful: a showstopper with long, curly black hair and the facial structure of an ancient Egyptian. I am not so bad.

2   We have known each other for five years and came together as a couple a little more than two years ago—on the night of February 14, 1994, to be exact. We never expected it to happen. She had been married before. I had spent 15 years dating men. But it happened.

It happened as naturally as love ever happens. Conversations became more intimate. Trust grew. Spending time together became more and more important—the most important thing in life.

4   It took her six months to reconcile herself to this so-called "alternative lifestyle." She had recently left her marriage—a brief, mistaken one undertaken chiefly because it had seemed time. I had recently been in my first same-sex relationship and already passed through the initial stages of: Is this the end of my life? Will family and friends and society shun me?

It pained me to see her go through all that, but she did it. She talked to her family, talked to herself and rose to the fact that her truth—that she loved me and wanted to be with me—was more important than society's judgments about love like ours.

6 We moved in together, and about three months later, a funny thing happened. One night, I kissed her and felt something rise in me that I never could have predicted: It was a feeling, a conviction, an irrepressible desire to say, *I want to marry you.*

Love had taken me to this place. Clearly, not society. I didn't even know then about the debate over the right of same-sex couples to marry. I just loved her—so much, and so definitively, that the words came out, as if by some biological impulse.

8 *I want to marry you.*

Tears came to her eyes. *But we are not allowed,* she said.

10 She was right, of course. So we decided to exchange rings. We saved ourselves from a rebuff at Tiffany's, headed downtown and ordered two gold and platinum bands with a small diamond in the middle. The night we picked them up, we drove out to Jones Beach, both in dresses, with a bottle of red wine, some cheese and crackers. We spread a blanket by the surf, watched the sun go down, and committed our life's love to each other.

The Parks man who just then drove by in a Jeep, telling us it was time to go, came as a bit of ironic comic relief. We finished our wine and went home.

12 It's been a year now since that date: a year in which my heart has been tumbling between my throat and my stomach with each day's news about the controversy over same-sex marriage. First, I heard that the state supreme court of Hawaii is expected to rule that same-sex couples have the constitutional right to marry, and I walked around town positively blissful. I imagined us getting on a plane to Honolulu the day the decision is announced (legal experts say, in about two years). I told friends how hard it is to wait.

Then I heard that the U.S. Congress was expected to pass a so-called Defense of Marriage Act, which would undercut Hawaii's ruling by allowing states to ignore same-sex marriages performed in that or any other state, and I alternately screamed and sobbed.

14 As I write this, 15 states (Tennessee, North Carolina and Delaware, most recently) have already acted to ban gay marriage. Three more states (California, Pennsylvania and New Jersey) have anti-gay legislation pending. And now President Clinton, who came into office a supporter of gay rights, has vowed to sign the Defense of Marriage bill—I can only imagine, to appease the religious right.

What the people who have the power to rule on same-sex marriage know of a relationship like mine, I cannot say. I know they claim that our marriage would make a mockery of theirs; they warn that our families would cause the decline of the American family; and they label our love immoral, disgusting, even dangerous.

16 The shocking thing is that before I knew what it meant to fall in love with a person of the same sex, I might have agreed with them. But now,

having been on both sides of the fence, I know that to understand a life that is different from the life lived by most people takes time—and an open mind.

Like everybody else I know, I want to get married because I was raised to believe that marriage is how we best honor a lifelong relationship. I want to feel the support from family and society that marriage brings. And I want the Parks man to know he cannot interfere: Love is love. In whatever shape it comes, it deserves respect. ❖

Questions for Meaning

1. In her opening paragraph, Bennett contrasts herself with her partner. How different are they from one another? To what extent are they similar?
2. Why does Bennett want to get married?
3. What does Bennett mean when she describes the end of her commitment ceremony as "a bit of ironic comic relief"? What does this reveal about her state of mind?
4. According to Bennett, what do people need in order to understand lives different from their own? Do you agree?

Questions about Strategy

1. Bennett begins her essay by announcing that she is in love and then goes on to report additional information about her relationship. Is her use of personal experience persuasive? Or is this essay too personal to be persuasive?
2. To what extent is gender an issue in this argument? Would you respond differently to it if it were written by a man about the man he loves?
3. Paragraph 8 consists of a single sentence, which first appeared in paragraph 6. Why does Bennett repeat this line? What does she achieve by setting it apart in a separate paragraph?
4. According to Bennett, "Love is love. In whatever shape it comes, it deserves respect." What kind of people are likely to agree with this view? Is anyone likely to disagree?

Lisa Schiffren

GAY MARRIAGE, AN OXYMORON

An oxymoron is a two-word paradox, or two words that apparently make no sense when used together. By using that word in her title, Lisa Schiffren signals that she is opposed to same-gender couples coming together in marriage. Schiffren was a speechwriter for Vice President Dan Quayle, a conservative Republican. As you read the following argument, which was first published by the *New York Times* in 1996, note how Schiffren is not concerned with the happiness of specific individuals so much as she is concerned with the social benefits of marriage for our country as a whole.

As study after study and victim after victim testify to the social devastation of the sexual revolution, easy divorce and out-of-wedlock motherhood, marriage is fashionable again. And parenthood has transformed many baby boomers into advocates of bourgeois norms.

2   Indeed, we have come so far that the surprise issue of the political season is whether homosexual "marriage" should be legalized. The Hawaii courts will likely rule that gay marriage is legal, and other states will be required to accept those marriages as valid.

Considering what a momentous change this would be—a radical redefinition of society's most fundamental institution—there has been almost no real debate. This is because the premise is unimaginable to many, and the forces of political correctness have descended on the discussion, raising the cost of opposition. But one may feel the same affection for one's homosexual friends and relatives as for any other, and be genuinely pleased for the happiness they derive from relationships, while opposing gay marriage for principled reasons.

4   "Same-sex marriage" is inherently incompatible with our culture's understanding of the institution. Marriage is essentially a lifelong compact between a man and woman committed to sexual exclusivity and the creation and nurture of offspring. For most Americans, the marital union—as distinguished from other sexual relationships and legal and economic partnerships—is imbued with an aspect of holiness. Though many of us are uncomfortable using religious language to discuss social and political issues, Judeo-Christian morality informs our view of family life.

Though it is not polite to mention it, what the Judeo-Christian tradition has to say about homosexual unions could not be clearer. In a diverse, open society such as ours, tolerance of homosexuality is a necessity. But for many, its practice depends on a trick of cognitive dissonance that allows people to believe in the Judeo-Christian moral order while accepting, often with genuine regard, the different lives of homosexual acquaintances. That is why, though homosexuals may believe that they are merely seeking a small expansion of the definition of marriage, the majority of Americans perceive this change as a radical deconstruction of the institution.

6   Some make the conservative argument that making marriage a civil right will bring stability, an end to promiscuity and a sense of fairness to gay men and women. But they miss the point. Society cares about stability in heterosexual unions because it is critical for raising healthy children and transmitting the values that are the basis of our culture.

    Whether homosexual relationships endure is of little concern to society. That is also true of most childless marriages, harsh as it is to say. Society has wisely chosen not to differentiate between marriages, because it would require meddling into the motives and desires of everyone who applies for a license.

8   In traditional marriage, the tie that really binds for life is shared responsibility for the children. (A small fraction of gay couples may choose to raise children together, but such children are offspring of one partner and an outside contributor.) What will keep gay marriages together when individuals tire of each other?

    Similarly, the argument that legal marriage will check promiscuity by gay males raises the question of how a "piece of paper" will do what the threat of AIDS has not. Lesbians seem to have little problem with monogamy, or the rest of what constitutes "domestication," despite the absence of official status.

10   Finally, there is the so-called fairness argument. The Government gives tax benefits, inheritance rights and employee benefits only to the married. Again, these financial benefits exist to help couples raise children. Tax reform is an effective way to remove distinctions among earners.

    If the American people are interested in a radical experiment with same-sex marriages, then subjecting it to the political process is the right route. For a court in Hawaii to assume that it has the power to radically redefine marriage is a stunning abuse of power. To present homosexual marriage as a fait accompli, without national debate, is a serious political error. A society struggling to recover from 30 years of weakened norms and broken families is not likely to respond gently to having an institution central to most people's lives altered. ❖

Questions for Meaning

1. How does Schiffren define marriage?
2. According to Schiffren, what is the most important reason for marriage?
3. An oxymoron is a two-word figure of speech in which words apparently contradict each other. Why does Schiffren believe "gay marriage" is an oxymoron?
4. What does Schiffren mean, in paragraph 5, by "cognitive dissonance"?

Questions about Strategy

1. Schiffren writes that the question of gay marriage is "the surprise issue of the political season." Would all readers be equally surprised by this issue? What kind of reader is most likely to be surprised?
2. In support of her case, Schiffren cites "Judeo-Christian morality," and implies that such morality clearly opposes homosexual unions. Do you agree with this claim? Is there any risk in using it as grounds for opposing civil marriage?
3. Where does Schiffren respond to views other than her own? How effectively does she do so?
4. What kind of assumptions has Schiffren made about gay men?

ANDREW SULLIVAN

SIMPLE EQUALITY

A graduate of Oxford and Harvard universities, Andrew Sullivan has been a leading advocate of same-gender marriage. From 1991 to 1996, he was editor of *The New Republic,* a widely respected magazine with a liberal editorial policy. In 1995, he published *Virtually Normal: An Argument about Homosexuality,* a book described by the *New York Times* as a "model of civil discourse." The following argument was first published that same year. As you read, note how Sullivan treats marriage as a civil rights issue.

"A state cannot deem a class of persons a stranger to its laws," declared the Supreme Court recently.

2   It was a monumental statement. Gay men and lesbians, the conservative court said, are no longer strangers in America.

They are citizens, entitled, like everyone else, to equal protection—no special rights, but simple equality.

4   For the first time in Supreme Court history, gay men and women were seen not as some powerful lobby trying to subvert America, but as the people we truly are—the sons and daughters of countless mothers and fathers, with all the weaknesses and strengths and hopes of everybody else.

And what we seek is not some special place in America but merely to be a full and equal part of America, to give back to our society without being forced to lie or hide or live as second-class citizens.

6   That is why marriage is so central to our hopes. People ask us why we want the right to marry, but the answer is obvious. It's the same reason anyone wants the right to marry.

At some point in our lives, some of us are lucky enough to meet the person we truly love. And we want to commit to that person in front of our family and country for the rest of our lives.

8   It's the most simple, the most natural, the most human instinct in the world. How could anyone seek to oppose that?

Yes, at first blush, it seems like a radical proposal, but, when you think about it some more, it's actually the opposite. Throughout American history, to be sure, marriage has been between a man and a woman, and in many ways our society is built upon that institution.

10   But none of that need change in the slightest. After all, no one is seeking to take away anybody's right to marry, and no one is seeking to force any church to change any doctrine in any way. Particular religious arguments against same-sex marriage are rightly debated within the churches and faiths themselves.

That is not the issue here: There is a separation between church and state in this country. We are asking only that when the government gives out civil marriage licenses, those of us who are gay should be treated like anybody else.

12   Of course, some argue that marriage is by definition between a man and a woman. But for centuries, marriage was by definition a contract in which the wife was her husband's legal property. And we changed that. For centuries, marriage was by definition between two people of the same race.

And we changed that. We changed these things because we recognized that human dignity is the same whether you are a man or a woman, black or white. And no one has any more of a choice to be gay than to be black or white or male or female.

14   Some say that marriage is only about raising children, but we let childless heterosexual couples be married (Bob and Elizabeth Dole, Pat and Shelley Buchanan, for instance). Why should gay couples be treated differently?

Others fear that there is no logical difference between allowing same-sex marriage and sanctioning polygamy and other horrors. But the issue of whether to sanction multiple spouses (gay or straight) is completely separate from whether, in the existing institution between two unrelated adults, the government should discriminate between its citizens.

16   This is, in fact, if only Bill Bennett* could see it, a deeply conservative cause. It seeks to change no one else's rights or marriages in any way. It seeks merely to promote monogamy, fidelity and the disciplines of family life among people who have long been cast to the margins of society.

And what could be a more conservative project than that? Why indeed would any conservative seek to oppose those very family values for gay people that he or she supports for everybody else? Except, of course, to make gay men and lesbians strangers in their own country, to forbid them ever to come home.   ❖

---

* A counter argument by Bill Bennett begins on p. 261.

Questions for Meaning

1. According to Sullivan, why do gay men and lesbians want to be able to legally marry their partners?
2. What does Sullivan mean when he writes, in paragraph 11, "There is a separation between church and state in this country"? Where does this "separation" come from?
3. Why does Sullivan believe that his support for same-gender marriage is "deeply conservative"?
4. In his conclusion, Sullivan appeals to "family values." How would you define such values?

Questions about Strategy

1. To begin an essay with a quotation is a common writing strategy. What does Sullivan achieve by opening with the specific quotation he chose?
2. Consider how Sullivan defines homosexuals, in paragraph 4, as "the sons and daughters of countless mothers and fathers, with all the weaknesses and strengths and hopes of everybody else." To what kind of values is this definition designed to appeal?
3. How does Sullivan respond to opponents of same-gender marriage?
4. How does the last sentence of this argument help to unify it?

WILLIAM J. BENNETT

AN HONORABLE ESTATE

A former Secretary of Education, William Bennett has also served as Chairman of the National Endowment for the Humanities and as Director of the Office of National Drug Control Policy. He has a PhD from the University of Texas as well as a law degree from Harvard, and he speaks frequently on behalf of conservative causes. "An Honorable Estate" is an editor's title for the following argument, which was first published in 1996 as part of a debate with Andrew Sullivan (pages 259–260), which was distributed by the New York Times to newspapers around the country. As you read, note how Bennett appeals to traditional values.

There are at least two key issues that divide proponents and opponents of same-sex marriage.

2 The first is whether legally recognizing same-sex unions would strengthen or weaken the institution.

The second has to do with the basic understanding of marriage itself.

4   The advocates of same-sex marriage say that they seek to strengthen and celebrate marriage. That may be what some intend.

But I am certain that it will not be the reality.

6   Consider: The legal union of same-sex couples would shatter the conventional definition of marriage, change the rules which govern behavior, endorse practices which are completely antithetical to the tenets of all of the world's major religions, send conflicting signals about marriage and sexuality, particularly to the young, and obscure marriage's enormously consequential function—procreation and child-rearing.

Broadening the definition of marriage to include same-sex unions would stretch it almost beyond recognition—and new attempts to expand the definition still further would surely follow.

8   On what principled ground can Andrew Sullivan exclude others who most desperately want what he wants: legal recognition and social acceptance?

Why on earth would Sullivan exclude from marriage a bisexual who wants to marry two other people? After all, exclusion would be a denial of that person's sexuality. The same holds true of a father and daughter who want to marry. Or two sisters.

10   Or men who want (consensual) polygamous arrangements. Sullivan may think some of these arrangements are unwise. But having employed sexual relativism in his own defense, he has effectively lost the capacity to draw any lines and make moral distinctions.

Forsaking all others is an essential component of marriage. Obviously it is not always honored in practice. But it is the ideal to which we rightly aspire, and in most marriages the ideal is in fact the norm.

12   Many advocates of same-sex marriage simply do not share this ideal; promiscuity among homosexual males is well known.

Sullivan himself has written that gay male relationships are served by the "openness of the contract" and that homosexuals should resist allowing their "varied and complicated lives" to be flattened into a "single, moralistic model."

14   But that "single, moralistic model" has served society exceedingly well. The burden of proof ought to be on those who propose untested arrangements for our most important institution.

A second key difference I have with Sullivan goes to the very heart of marriage itself. I believe that marriage is not an arbitrary construct which can be redefined simply by those who lay claim to it.

16   It is an honorable estate, instituted of God and built on moral, religious, sexual and human realities. Marriage is based on a natural teleology, on the different, complementary nature of men and women—and how they refine, support, encourage and complete one another.

It is the institution through which we propagate, nurture, educate and sustain our species.

18   That we have to engage in this debate at all is an indication of how steep our moral slide has been.

Worse, those who defend the traditional understanding of marriage are routinely referred to (though not to my knowledge by Sullivan) as "homophobes," "gay-bashers," "intolerant" and "bigoted." Can one defend an honorable, 4,000-year-old tradition and not be called these names?

20   This is a large, tolerant, diverse country. In America people are free to do as they wish, within broad parameters. It is also a country in sore need of shoring up some of its most crucial institutions: marriage and the family, schools, neighborhoods, communities.

But marriage and family are the greatest of these. That is why they are elevated and revered. We should keep them so.   ❖

Questions for Meaning

1. According to Bennett, what are the main issues in the debate over same-gender marriage?
2. On what grounds does Bennett object to same-gender marriage?
3. What does Bennett mean, in paragraph 10, by "sexual relativism"?
4. How does Bennett define marriage?

Questions about Strategy

1. What does Bennett achieve in paragraph 6 by appealing to "the tenets of all of the world's major religions"? Is there any risk to this strategy?
2. How does Bennett characterize gay men, and how does this characterization serve his purpose?
3. In paragraph 18, Bennett claims, "That we have to engage in this debate at all is an indication of how steep our moral slide has been." Does this claim help his argument?
4. Objecting to words like "homophobes" and "intolerant," Bennett asks, "Can one defend an honorable, 4,000-year-old tradition and not be called these names?" How does he expect readers to answer this question? Judging from his essay, would it be unfair to apply such language to Bennett?

FENTON JOHNSON

WEDDED TO AN ILLUSION

This argument was the cover story of *Harper's* magazine in November 1996—the national election year during which Congress passed the Defense of Marriage Act, a bill that defined marriage as the union of a man and a woman. Johnson draws attention to this legislation but then focuses on the meaning of marriage, the persons it benefits, and how it might work better in the future. As you read, note how Johnson combines scholarship and personal experience when arguing for a new understanding of marriage. If you are interested in learning more about his experience, read his memoir *Geography of the Heart* (1996).

Last summer, when American politicians underwent yet another of their periodic convulsions over the status of gays and lesbians, I found myself pondering the evolving history of marriage. In response to the possible recognition of same-gender marriages by the state of Hawaii, Congress overwhelmingly passed the Defense of Marriage Act, which reserves federal benefits and rights for male-female couples and permits states not to recognize same-gender marriages performed in other states. Sponsored in the House of Representatives by Bob Barr (three marriages) and endorsed by then Senator Bob Dole (two marriages), the bill was called "gay baiting" by the White House and "unnecessary" by President Clinton (he of the colorful personal life), who signed it nonetheless in late September. The law might appear to be only so much election-year positioning and counter-positioning, but long after this year's political season is forgotten, we will be agonizing over the questions implicit in the legislation. As a married, straight friend cracked to me, "If marriage needs Congress to defend it, then we know we're in trouble."

2   *Marriage.* What does it mean these days? Peau de soie, illusion veil, old, new, borrowed, blue? Can it mean the same thing to a heterosexual couple, raised to consider it the pinnacle of emotional fulfillment, as to a same-gender couple, the most conventional of whom must find the label "married" awkward? Can it mean the same thing to a young lesbian—out since her teens, occasionally bisexual, wanting a child, planning a career—as to me, a forty-plus shell-shocked AIDS widower? And in an era of no-fault divorce, can it mean to any of us what it meant to our parents?

The unacceptability of gay marriages may have bloomed with sudden propitiousness on the agendas of Clinton and Dole, but the issue has been steadily moving into the legal conversation across the last twenty-five years. In 1991 three Hawaiian couples—two lesbian, one gay-male—sued the state over the denial of their applications for marriage licenses; on principle, a heterosexual ACLU attorney took the case. Two years later, to everyone's amazement, the Hawaii Supreme Court ruled, in *Baehr* v. *Lewin,* that the state's denial of licenses violated the Hawaii constitution's equal-rights protections. The court took care to note that the sexual orientation of the plaintiffs was irrelevant. At issue instead was discrimination based on gender: the state discriminates by offering benefits (including income tax, worker's compensation, retirement, welfare, and spousal support) to married men and women that it denies to exclusively male or female couples.

4   This is no minor point. What the court ruled on in Hawaii was not *gay* marriage but simply *marriage:* whether the union of two people of the same gender qualifies for the benefits the state offers to mixed-gender couples, no matter if the spouses marry for love or children or Social Security benefits, no matter if they are gay or straight or celibate—in other words, all those reasons, good and bad, for which men and women now marry.

The Hawaii justices remanded the case to a lower court, challenging the attorney general to justify gender discrimination in marriage benefits. The plaintiffs' attorneys currently expect the State Supreme Court to allow the issuance of marriage licenses to same-gender couples by late 1997, though more litigation seems as likely, given the determination and financing of the opposition. If the state court acts as the plaintiffs anticipate, the matter will surely reach the federal level. Contrary to widespread reporting and rhetoric, Article IV of the U.S. Constitution does not necessarily require states to recognize marriages performed in other states; interstate recognition of marriage remains largely unexplored legal terrain.[1] If a couple marries in Hawaii, then moves to New York or Georgia, can those states refuse to recognize the marriage? Under the Defense of Marriage Act, the answer is yes, though some legal experts argue that states already have this right, while other experts contend that the act is unconstitutional. Either way the issue invokes a resonant precedent: as recently as 1967, sixteen states refused to recognize mixed-race marriages legally performed elsewhere. Those antimiscegenation laws were struck down that same year by the U.S. Supreme Court in *Loving* v. *Virginia,* a landmark case that the Hawaii court cited at length in *Baehr* v. *Lewin.*

6   At stake first and foremost are the rights of gays and lesbians to assume the state-conferred benefits of marriage. The assumption of these rights is controversial enough, but *Baehr* has still larger implications for an institution that has historically served as the foundation of a male-dominated society. It's instructive to recall that in the late 1970s Phyllis Schlafly and her anti-Equal Rights Amendment (ERA) allies predicted that the codification of the equality of women and men, as embodied in a federal ERA, would lead to gay marriage, presumably because they felt that to codify the equality of

---

[1] States have always established their own standards for the recognition of marriage; no consistent, nationwide definition of marriage has ever existed. Currently, a few states (e.g., Pennsylvania) still recognize common-law marriages, though for such marriages to be recognized in a non-common-law state, participants must usually submit to some official procedure. Some states allow first cousins to marry, some do not, and the minimum age for legal marriage varies from state to state, as does the recognition of such contracts across state lines.

women and men would undermine the values upon which traditional marriage rests. The federal amendment failed, but Hawaii (along with several other states) adopted its own ERA; and here we are, just as Schlafly predicted—right in the place, I argue, where we ought to be. For this is the profound and scary and exhilarating fact: to assume the equality of women and men is to demand rethinking the institution that more than any other defines how men and women relate.

Marriage has always been an evolving institution, bent and shaped by the historical moment and the needs and demands of its participants. The Romans recognized the phenomenon we call "falling in love," but they considered it a hindrance to the establishment of stable households. Marriages certified by the state had their foundations not in religion or romance but in pragmatics—e.g., the joining of socially prominent households. Divorce was acceptable, and women were generally powerless to influence its outcome; the early Catholic Church restricted divorce partly as a means of protecting women and children from easy abandonment.

8   At the beginning of the thirteenth century, facing schisms and heresies, and seeking to consolidate its power, the Catholic Church institutionalized marriage, confirming it as a sacrament and requiring that a priest officiate—a crucial step in the intrusion of organized religion into what had previously been a private transaction. Several centuries later, the conception of "family" began to be transformed from an extended feudal unit that often included cousins, servants, and even neighbors to a tightly knit nuclear unit composed of parents and children and headed by a man. With marriage as its cornerstone, this idealized unit forms the foundation for virtually all American legislation concerning the family.

Throughout these developments, one aspect of marriage remained consistent: even as women were idealized, they were widely regarded as chattel—part of the husband's personal property; marriage was state certification of that ownership. With the women's suffrage movement came a growing acceptance of the equality of women and men, along with the principle that the individual's happiness is of equal or greater importance than the honoring of social norms, including the marriage contract. Divorce became both common and accepted, to the point that even the woman who marries into wealth gains little economic security (absent a good lawyer or a prenuptial agreement).

10   Women have arguably gotten the worst of both worlds: Men may more easily leave their wives, but women are nowhere near achieving earning parity, so that now they must cope with economic insecurity as well as the fear of being dumped. For every woman who revels in freedom and the income from a fulfilling career, many more face supporting themselves and often their children on welfare or at a low salary with few benefits and no job security, dependent on child support or alimony often in arrears. No wonder that almost a third of babies are now born out of wedlock, a figure that has risen consistently since the 1950s. Some of these mothers (more than a few

of them lesbians) are building matriarchal families, but many are giving birth to unplanned and probably unwanted children. Whether by design or by happenstance, these unmarried women are the primary force in changing the profile of the family; any discussion about contemporary marriage that excludes them is pointless.

Both our culture and its couples are searching for some new thinking, informed by the understanding that what is at stake is our perception of the marriage contract and women's role in defining it. Understandably, advocates of same-gender marriage have shied away from territory so daunting, focusing on the narrower civil-rights issues—the need to extend, as required by our American commitment to equal treatment before the law, the invitation to another class of people to participate in the same troubled ritual, with one tangible result being a bonanza for attorneys specializing in gay divorce.

12   That fight is important, but in the long run the exclusive focus on civil rights minimizes the positive implications of the social transformation lesbians and gays are helping to bring about. For centuries gay and lesbian couples, along with significant numbers of unmarried heterosexuals, have formed and maintained relationships outside legislative and social approval that have endured persecution and duress for this simple reason: love. This is not to downplay the importance of the marriage license, which comes with rights and responsibilities without which gays and lesbians will never be considered full signatories to the social contract; nor is it to imply that these relationships are perfect. It is rather to point out the nature of gay couples' particular gift, the reward of those lucky enough to be given the wits and courage to survive in the face of adversity. Many of us know as much or more about partnering than those who have fallen into it as a given, who may live unaware of the degree to which their partnerships depend on the support of conventions—including the woman's acceptance of the man's primacy.

Baehr v. Lewin represents the logical culmination of generations of challenge, by feminists joined later by gay and lesbian activists, to an institution once almost exclusively shaped by gender roles and organized religion. As such, it presents an historic opportunity to reexamine the performance and practice of the institution on which so many of our hopes, rituals, and assumptions are based; to reconsider what we are institutionalizing and why.

14 Seeking to provide a legally defensible justification for limiting benefits to mixed-gender marriages, the Hawaii attorney general, after years of research, has thus far only confirmed this insurmountable reality: if one subscribes to the principles that government should not serve specific religious agendas and that it should not discriminate on the basis of gender, there is no logical reason to limit marriage benefits to mixed-gender couples. Opponents of same-gender marriage argue that it contradicts the essential purpose of the institution, which is procreation; but the state does not ask

prospective mixed-gender spouses if they intend to have children, and the law grants a childless married couple the same rights and benefits as their most prolific married neighbors. Invoking the nation's Judeo-Christian heritage is no help; even if one believes that Christians and Jews should dictate government policy, a few of the more liberal denominations have already endorsed same-gender marriage, and the issue is under serious debate in mainstream churches.[2] How may the state take sides in a theological debate, especially when the parties to the debate are so internally divided? In 1978, the Supreme Court established in *Zablocki* v. *Redhail* that a citizen's right to marry is so fundamental that it cannot be denied even to individuals who have demonstrated that they are inadequate to the task. Given that the law guarantees the right of deadbeat dads and most prison inmates to marry, what could be the logic for denying that right to two men or two women who are maintaining a stable, responsible household?

The strongest argument against same-gender marriage is not logical but arbitrary: society must have unambiguous definitions to which it turns when faced with conflicts between the desires of its citizens and the interests of its larger community. Marriage is a union between a man and a woman because that is how most people define the word, however unjust this may be for same-gender couples who wish to avail themselves of its rights.

16   Advocates of same-gender marriage respond that "the interests of the larger community" is an evolving concept. That an institution embodies social norms does not render it immune to change—slavery was once socially accepted, just as mixed-race marriages were widely forbidden and divorce an irreparable stigma. The rebuttal is accurate, but it evades the question of where the state draws the line in balancing individual needs and desires against the maintenance of community norms. Why should the state endorse same-gender couples but not (as opponents of same-gender marriage argue will result) polygamists or child spouses? The question is now more pressing because of the prevailing sense of accelerated cultural breakdown, wherein nothing seems secure, not even the definition of . . . well, marriage.

Surely the triumph of Reaganomics and corporate bottom-line thinking is more responsible for this breakdown of the social contract than the efforts of an ostracized minority to stabilize its communities. In any case marriage and the family began their transformation long before the gay civil-rights movement. By 1975, only six years after the Stonewall rebellion that marked the first widespread public emergence of lesbians and gays, half of all marriages ended in divorce. But in uncertain times people search for scapegoats, and unless gays and lesbians can make a convincing case for

---

[2] Many gay Protestant congregations, Reform Jews, Unitarians, and a number of Quaker congregations have endorsed and/or performed same-gender marriage. Presbyterians recently passed a resolution urging the national office to explore the feasibility of filing friend-of-the-court briefs "in favor of giving civil rights to same-sex partners," and the Episcopal Church is studying the blessing of same-sex unions. In addition, Hawaii's Buddhist bishops have announced their support of same-gender marriage.

the positive impact of our relationships, we are not likely to persuade any but the already converted.

18 Tellingly enough, male writers have been more passionate than women in their attachment to traditional marriage forms. Among gay male writers, Andrew Sullivan *(Virtually Normal)* and William Eskridge Jr. *(The Case for Same-Sex Marriage)* have written excellent supporting arguments.[3] Both consider legalization of same-gender marriage a means toward encouraging same-gender couples to model themselves on heterosexual marriage.

Sullivan makes an eloquent case for gay marriage but gives only a nod to the high failure rate of heterosexual marriages. Eskridge is sensitive to the women's issues inherent in marriage, but like Sullivan he endorses the institution as it exists, albeit alongside other options for partnering. Along the way he endorses the myth that marriage conveys the means to control extra-marital sexual behavior to men (or women) otherwise unlikely to achieve such control, as well as the myth that gay men are more promiscuous than their straight counterparts.[4] More discouraging is Eskridge's acceptance of the assumption that sexual desire is the beast lurking in our social jungle, whose containment is a prerequisite for a moral civilization (he subtitles his book *From Sexual Liberty to Civilized Commitment,* epitomizing in a phrase the puritanical impulse to make bachelorhood equivalent to moral lassitude, where all sexual expression outside wedlock is morally tainted).

20 That sexuality and morality are intimately linked I take as a given; one loses sight of this connection at the risk of one's self-respect and, by extension, one's ability to love others. We are surrounded by evidence of that loss of respect, particularly in television and advertising, whose relentless promotion of amoral heterosexual sex is surely the greatest factor in breaking down public and private morality. But to presume that morality follows on marriage is to ignore centuries of evidence that each is very much possible without the other.

Among heterosexual male writers, even the most intelligent dwell in fantasy logic; when they arrive at a difficult point they invoke God (an unanswering authority), or homophobic bombast, or both. James Q. Wilson, management and public policy professor at UCLA, is among the more reasonable, but even he attacks (with no apparent irony) the "overeducated," whom he accuses of "mounting a utilitarian assault on the family." As the ninth of nine children of a rural, blue-collar family whose parents (married forty-seven years) sacrificed a great deal to educate their children, I note that the only "overeducated" people I have met are those who take as

---

[3] By contrast, *Virtual Equality,* lesbian activist Urvashi Vaid's 440-page treatment of gay and lesbian civil rights, mentions same-gender marriage only glancingly, by way of offering a generalized endorsement.

[4] Since great numbers of gay men remain partly or wholly in the closet, there's no accurate way to measure or compare gay male and straight male experiences. But generalizations about gay male life based on behavior in bars and sex clubs are surely no more accurate than generalizations about heterosexual male behavior drawn from visiting America's red-light districts.

gospel the rules they have been taught rather than open their eyes to the reality in which they live, who witness love and yet deny its full expression.

22 Not all men and women fall into marriage unconscious of role models, of course. But it's hard work to avoid a form shouted at all of us daily in a million ways, whereas for same-gender partnerships to fall into that form requires deliberate denial. For same-gender relationships to endure, the partners have to figure out that we are required to make them up as we go along. This does not mean that we are always adequate to the task, which is why my friend Frederick Hertz, an Oakland attorney specializing in same-gender partnerships, originally opposed same-gender marriage. "Marriage as it exists imposes a legal partnership on people that is seldom in sync with how they think about their relationship," he tells me. "Marriage is designed to take care of dependent spouses, people who stay home to take care of the children, as well as to compensate for economic inequalities between genders. The idea of supporting a spouse for the rest of his or her life is totally contrary to the way most people nowadays think." Hertz (a partner in a fourteen-year relationship) resists the "couple-ism" that he perceives arising among gays and lesbians because he believes it imitates a heterosexual world in which women whose partners die or abandon them are left with almost no social support. "I talk to straight divorced women in their forties and fifties," he says. "They have a lack of self-worth that's devastating. My single gay friends have a hard enough time—imagine what things would be like for them if marriage were the norm."

Then the realities of working with gay and lesbian couples struggling without social approval brought Hertz to an uneasy support of the battle for same-gender marriage rights. Unlike most advocates, however, he qualifies his endorsement by adding that "while we're working for gay-marriage rights we should also be talking about issues of economic and emotional dependency among couples. . . . A partner can contribute emotional support to a relationship that is as valuable to its sustenance as an economic contribution. We need to find legal ways to protect those dependent spouses." To that end Hertz argues for a variety of state-endorsed domestic-partnership arrangements in addition to marriage, noting that although such categories may create a kind of second-class relationship, they're a step toward the state offering options that reflect contemporary life. "I want to go to the marriage bureau and have options among ways of getting married," he says. "I want the social acceptance of marriage but with options that are more appropriate for the range of couples' experiences—including same-gender childless couples."

24 In other words, rather than attempt to conform same-gender couplings to an institution so deeply rooted in sexism, why not consider ways of incorporating stability and egalitarianism into new models of marriage? Rather than consider the control of sexual behavior as a primary goal of marriage, why not leave issues of monogamy to the individuals and focus

instead on marriage as the primary (though not the only) means whereby two people help each other and their dependents through life?

Invoking the feminist writer Martha Fineman, American University law professor Nancy Polikoff argues that organizing society around sexually connected people is wrong; the more central units are dependents and their caretakers. Extrapolating from this thinking, one can imagine the state requiring that couples, regardless of gender, take steps toward attaining the benefits currently attached to marriage. Under this model the state might restrict the most significant of marriage's current benefits to those couples who demonstrate stability. The government might then get out of the marriage-certification business altogether; Hawaii governor Ben Cayetano, among others, has suggested as much. Government-conferred benefits currently reserved for married couples would instead be allocated as rewards for behavior that contributes to social stability. Tax breaks would be awarded, regardless of marital status, to stable lower- and middle-income households financially responsible for children, the elderly, or the handicapped. Other state- or federally conferred privileges—such as residency for foreign spouses, veteran's benefits, tax-free transfer of property, and the right to joint adoption—would be reserved for couples who had demonstrated the ability to sustain a household over two to five years. The decision to assume the label "marriage" would be left to the individuals involved, who might or might not seek ratification of their decision by a priest or minister or rabbi. The motivation behind such changes would be not to eliminate marriage but to encourage and sustain stable households, while leaving the definition and sustenance of marriage to the partners involved, along with their community of relatives, friends, and—if they so choose—churches.

26 In the most profound relationship I have known, my partner and I followed a pattern typical of an enduring gay male relationship. We wrangled over monogamy, ultimately deciding to permit safe sex outside the relationship. In fact, he never acted on that permission; I acted on it exactly once, in an incident we discussed the next day. We were bound not by sexual exclusivity but by trust, mutual support, and fidelity—in a word, love, only one manifestation of which is monogamy.

Polikoff tells of another model, unconventional by the standards of the larger culture but common among gay and lesbian communities: A friend died of breast cancer; her blood family arrived for the funeral. "They were astounded to discover that their daughter had a group of people who were a family—somebody had organized a schedule, somebody brought food every night," she says. "In some ways it was the absence of marriage as a dominant institution that created space for the development of a family defined in much broader ways." I find it difficult to imagine either of these relationships—mine or that described by Polikoff—developing in the presence of marriage as practiced by most of our forebears; easier to imagine

our experiences influencing the evolution of marriage to a more encompassing, compassionate place.

28   Earlier I called myself an "AIDS widower," but I was playing fast and
loose with words; I can't be a widower, since my partner and I were never
married. He was the only child of Holocaust survivors, and he taught me, an
HIV-negative man preoccupied with the future, the lessons his parents had
taught him: the value of living fully in the present and the power of love.

        He fell ill while we were traveling in France, during what we knew
would be our last vacation. After checking him into a Paris hospital, I had
to sneak past the staff to be at his side; each time they ordered me out,
until finally they told me they would call the police. Faced with the threat
of violence, I left the room. He died alone as I paced the hall outside his
door, frantic to be at his side but with no recourse—I was, after all, only his
friend.

30   At a dinner party not long ago I asked a mix of gay and heterosexual guests
to name ways society might better support the survival of gay and lesbian
relationships. A beat of silence followed, then someone piped up: "You
mean, the survival of *any* relationships." Everyone agreed that all relationships are under stress, that their dissolution had become an accepted, possibly assumed part of the status quo.

        The question is not, as opponents would have us believe, will marriage
survive the legalization of same-gender partnerships? Instead, the questions
are how do society and the state support stable households in a world where
the composition of families is changing, and how might same-gender relationships contribute to that end?

32   Denied access to marriage, lesbians and gays inevitably idealize it, but
given the abuse the dominant culture has heaped on the institution, maybe
it could use a little glamour. In my more hopeful moments, I think gays and
lesbians might help revitalize and reconceptualize marriage by popularizing
the concept of rich, whole, productive couplings based less on the regulation of sexual behavior and the maintenance of gender roles than on the
formation of mutually respectful partnerships. *Baehr* v. *Lewin* presents us
with a chance to conceive of a different way of coupling, but only if we recognize and act on its implications. Otherwise the extension (if achieved) to
same-gender couples of the marital status quo will represent a landmark
civil-rights victory but a subcultural defeat in its failure to incorporate into
the culture at large lessons learned by generations of women and men—lesbian or gay or straight—who built and sustained and fought for partnerships outside the bounds of conventional gender roles.

In *Word Is Out*, a 1977 documentary portraying lesbian and gay lives, come-
dienne Pat Bond described butch and femme role-playing among lesbians
in the 1950s, roles as unvarying as those of Ozzie and Harriet. "Relationships that lasted twenty or thirty years were role-playing," she says. "At least
in that role-playing you knew the rules, you at least knew your mother and

father and you knew what they did and you tried to do the same thing. . . . Now you say, 'Okay, I'm not butch or femme, I'm just me.' Well, who the hell is me? What do I do? How am I to behave?"

34   To heterosexuals who feel as if the marriage debate is pulling the rug of certainty from beneath them, I say, Welcome to the club. Gays' and lesbians' construction of community—which is to say, identity—is the logical culmination of the American democratic experiment, which provides its citizens with an open playing field on which each of us has a responsibility to define and then respect his or her boundaries and rules. Human nature being what it is, the American scene abounds with stories of people unable, unwilling, or uninterested in meeting that challenge—people who fare better within a package of predetermined rules and boundaries. For those people (so long as they are straight), traditional marriage and roles remain. But for the questioning mind and heart, the debate surrounding marriage is only the latest intrusion of ambiguity into the artificially ordered world of Western thinking.

And Western culture has never tolerated ambiguity. The Romans placed their faith in the state; the Christians, in God; the rationalists, in reason and science. But in marked contrast to Eastern religions and philosophy, all have in common their search for a constant governing structure, a kind of unified field theory for the workings of the heart. The emergence of gays and lesbians from the closet (a movement born of Western religious and rationalist thinking) is only one among many developments that reveal the futility of that search—how it inevitably arrives at the enigma that lies at the heart of being.

36   But the rules are so comforting and comfortable! And it is easier to oppress some so that others might live in certainty, ignoring the reality that the mystery of love and life and death is really grander and more glorious than human beings can grasp, much less legislate. ❖

Questions for Meaning

1. Why is it significant that the Hawaii Supreme Court focused its decision on gender rather than sexual orientation?
2. According to Johnson, why has marriage benefited men more than women? Why does he believe same-gender marriage will foster more equality between men and women?
3. What's wrong, in Johnson's view, with considering same-gender marriage solely as a civil rights issue? What other issues does he want people to consider?
4. Why might some gay and lesbian couples hesitate to marry even if they are deeply committed to each other?
5. The federal government currently extends tax benefits to married couples simply because they are married. Who should be entitled to such benefits, according to Johnson?

6. Vocabulary: propitiousness (3), remanded (5), pragmatics (7), schisms (8), chattel (9), denominations (14), epitomizing (19), lassitude (19), extrapolating (25), enigma (35).

Questions about Strategy

1. Why does Johnson cite the number of times the House sponsor and the Senate endorser of the Defense of Marriage Act have been married? Is he making an ad hominem argument or pointing to a real inconsistency?
2. Does Johnson ever recognize arguments that can be made against same-gender marriage? How fairly does he treat people with whom he disagrees?
3. Johnson draws on personal experience at several points in this essay. How successfully has he incorporated his own experience into his argument?
4. In paragraph 31, Johnson seeks to redefine the debate over same-gender marriage. What happens if you agree with the way he has redefined the question?
5. The last four paragraphs of this essay contrast ambiguity with certainty. Why does Johnson try to persuade readers to accept living with ambiguity? How effective is this conclusion?

JEAN BETHKE ELSHTAIN

ACCEPTING LIMITS

Centennial Professor of Political Science at Vanderbilt University, Jean Bethke Elshtain has written extensively on American culture for many years. Her books on the family include *The Family in Political Thought* (1982) and *Rebuilding the Nest: A New Commitment to the American Family* (1990). Her most recent works include *Democracy on Trial* (1995) and *Augustine and the Limits of Politics* (1995). This argument (and the one by Brent Hartinger, which follows) was first published in 1991 as part of a discussion in *Commonweal*. As you read, note how Elshtain defines the purpose of marriage and the state's responsibility to protect it.

Every society embraces an image of a body politic. This complex symbolism incorporates visions and reflections on who is inside and who is outside; on what counts as order and disorder; on what is cherished and what is despised. This imagery is fluid but not, I will argue, entirely up for grabs. For without some continuity in our imagery and concern, we confront a deepening nihilism. In a world of ever-more transgressive enthusiasms, the individual—the self—is more, not less, in thrall to whatever may be the reigning ethos. Ours is a culture whose reigning ethic is surely individual-ism and freedom. Great and good things have come from this stress on freedom and from the insistence that there are things that cannot and must not be done for me and to me in the name of some overarching collective. It is, therefore, unsurprising that anything that comes before us in the name of "rights" and "freedom" enjoys a *prima facie** power, something akin to political grace.

2   But perhaps we have reached the breaking point. When Madonna pro-claims, in all sincerity, that mock masturbation before tens of thousands is "freedom of expression" on a par, presumably, with the right to petition, as-semble, and protest, something seems a bit out of whack—distorted, quirky, not-quite-right. I thought about this sort of thing a lot when I listened to the stories of the "Mothers of the Disappeared" in Argentina and to their in-vocation of the language of "human rights" as a fundamental immunity— the right not to be tortured and "disappeared." I don't believe there is a slippery slope from queasiness at, if not repudiation of, public sexual acts for profit, orchestrated masturbation, say, and putting free speech as a fun-damental right of free citizens in peril. I don't think the body politic has to be nude and sexually voracious—getting, consuming, demanding pleasure. That is a symbolism that courts nihilism and privatism (however publicly it may be trumpeted) because it repudiates intergenerational, familial, and communal contexts and believes history and tradition are useful only to be trashed. Our culture panders to what social critic John O'Neill calls the "li-bidinal body," the body that titillates and ravishes and is best embodied as young, thin, antimaternal, calculating, and disconnected. Make no mistake about it: much of the move to imagery of the entitled self and the aspira-tions to which it gives rise are specifically, deeply, and troublingly anti-natal—hostile to the regenerative female body and to the symbolism of social regeneration to which this body is necessarily linked and has, histori-cally, given rise.

Don't get me wrong: not every female body must be a regenerative body. At stake here is not mandating and coercing the lives of individuals but pondering the fate of a society that, more and more, repudiates gener-ativity as an animating image in favor of aspiration without limit of the contractual and "wanting" self. One symbol and reality of the latter is the search for intrusive intervention in human reproducing coming from those able to command the resources of genetic engineers and medical re-production experts, also, therefore, those who have more clout over what gets lifted up as our culture's dominant sense of itself. One finds more and more the demand that babies can and must be made whenever the want is there. This demandingness, this transformation of human procrea-tion into a technical operation, promotes a project Oliver O'Donovan calls

* Latin for "at first appearance."

"scientific self-transcendence." The technologizing of birth is antiregenera-
tive, linked as it is to a refusal to accept any natural limits. What technology
"can do," and the law permits, we seem ready to embrace. Our ethics rushes
to catch up with the rampant rush of our forged and incited desires.

4   These brief reflections are needed to frame my equally brief comments
on the legality, or not, of homosexual marriage. I have long favored domestic partnership possibilities—ways to regularize and stabilize commitments
and relationships. But marriage is not, and never has been, primarily about
two people—it is and always has been about the possibility of generativity.
Although in any given instance, a marriage might not have led to the raising
of a family, whether through choice or often unhappy recognition of, and
final reconciliation to, the infertility of one or another spouse, the symbolism of marriage-family as social regenesis is fused in our centuries-old experience with marriage ritual, regulation, and persistence.

The point of criticism and contention runs: in defending the family
as framed within a horizon of intergenerationality, one privileges a restrictive ideal of sexual and intimate relations. There are within our society, as I already noted, those who believe this society can and should stay
equally open to all alternative arrangements, treating "life-styles" as so
many identical peas in a pod. To be sure, families in modernity coexist
with those who live another way, whether heterosexual and homosexual
unions that are by choice or by definition childless; communalists who
diminish individual parental authority in favor of the preeminence of the
group; and so on.

6   But the recognition and acceptance of plural possibilities does not mean
each alternative is equal to every other with reference to specific social
goods. No social order has ever existed that did not endorse certain activities and practices as preferable to others. Ethically responsible challenges to
our terms of exclusion and inclusion push toward a loosening but not a
wholesale negation in our normative endorsement of intergenerational
family life. Those excluded by, or who exclude themselves from, the familial intergenerational ideal, should not be denied social space for their own
practices. And it is possible that if what were at stake were, say, seeking out
and identifying those creations of self that enhance an aesthetic construction of life and sensibility, the romantic bohemian or rebel would get
higher marks than the Smith family of Remont, Nebraska. Nevertheless, we
should be cautious about going too far in the direction of a wholly untrammeled pluralism lest we become so vapid that we are no longer capable
of distinguishing between the moral weightiness of, say, polishing one's
Porsche and sitting up all night with an ill child. The intergenerational
family, as symbolism of social regenesis, as tough and compelling reality, as
defining moral norm, remains central and critical in nurturing recogni-
tions of human frailty, mortality, and finitude and in inculcating moral
limits and constraints. To resolve the untidiness of our public and private

relations by either reaffirming unambiguously a set of unitary, authoritative norms or eliminating all such norms as arbitrary is to jeopardize the
social goods that democratic and familial authority, paradoxical in relation
to one another, promise—to men and women as parents and citizens and
to their children. ❖

Questions for Meaning

1. According to Elshtain, what values now seem most important in the
   United States?
2. Why is Elshtain willing for gay and lesbian couples to be recognized
   as "domestic partners" but not as married couples?
3. What is the meaning of the "libidinal body," and why does Elshtain
   believe this concept is relevant to the issue of gay marriage?
4. Why does Elshtain believe that a distinction can be made between
   recognizing different alternatives and giving equal consideration to
   each?
5. Vocabulary: nihilism (1), transgressive (1), thrall (1), voracious (2),
   antinatal (2), generativity (4), pluralism (6), vapid (6), inculcating
   (6).

Questions about Strategy

1. What is Elshtain's purpose in contrasting a Madonna concert with
   Argentine mothers who waged a public protest against a military dictatorship?
2. Why does Elshtain discuss the ethics of human reproduction before
   addressing the question of gay marriage?
3. Does Elshtain make any concessions to readers who have values different from her own?
4. In paragraph 6, consider how Elshtain contrasts the life of a "romantic bohemian" with "the Smith family of Remont, Nebraska" and "the
   moral weightiness of, say, polishing one's Porsche and sitting up all
   night with an ill child." Do these contrasts help her argument?

BRENT HARTINGER

A CASE FOR GAY MARRIAGE

When it was assumed that same-gender marriage was not politically feasible, gay rights activists campaigned successfully for legal recognition of "domestic partnership"—a term applied to couples who are living together without being married, share expenses, and wish to make a public commitment. Such couples can be either heterosexual or homosexual. But, as Brent Hartinger demonstrates in this argument, marriage confers benefits that domestic partnership does not. Hartinger was a freelance writer in Seattle when he published "A Case for Gay Marriage" in 1991 in *Commonweal,* as part of the discussion in which the preceding argument by Jean Bethke Elshtain also first appeared.

In San Francisco this year, homosexuals won't just be registering for the draft and to vote. In November 1990, voters approved legislation which allows unmarried live-in partners—heterosexual or homosexual—to register themselves as "domestic partners," publicly agreeing to be jointly responsible for basic living expenses. Like a few other cities, including New York and Seattle, San Francisco had already allowed bereavement leave to the domestic partners of municipal employees. But San Francisco lesbians and gays had been trying for eight years to have some form of partnership registration—for symbolic reasons at least—ever since 1982 when then-mayor Diane Feinstein vetoed a similar ordinance. A smattering of other cities provide health benefits to the domestic partners of city employees. In 1989, a New York court ruled that a gay couple is a "family" in that state, at least in regard to their rent-controlled housing (the decision was reaffirmed late last year). And in October of 1989, Denmark became the first industrialized country to permit same-sex unions (since then, one-fifth of all marriages performed there have been homosexual ones).

2   However sporadic, these represent major victories for gay men and lesbians for whom legal marriage is not an option. Other challenges are coming fast and furious. Two women, Sandra Rovira and Majorie Forlini, lived together in a marriage-like relationship for twelve years—and now after her partner's death, Rovira is suing AT&T, Forlini's employer, for refusing to pay the death benefits the company usually provides surviving spouses. Craig Dean and Patrick Gill, a Washington, D.C., couple, have filed a $1 million discrimination suit against that city for denying them a marriage license and allegedly violating its human rights acts which outlaw discrimination on the basis of sexual orientation; the city's marriage laws explicitly prohibit polygamous and incestuous marriages, but not same-sex ones.

Legally and financially, much is at stake. Most employee benefit plans—which include health insurance, parental leave, and bereavement leave—extend only to legal spouses. Marriage also allows partners to file joint income taxes, usually saving them money. Social Security can give extra payment to qualified spouses. And assets left from one legal spouse to the other after death are not subject to estate taxes. If a couple splits up, there is the issue of visitation rights for adopted children or offspring conceived by artificial insemination. And then there are issues of jurisprudence (a legal spouse cannot be compelled to testify against his or her partner) and inheritance, tenancy, and conservatorship: pressing concerns for many gays as a result of AIDS.

4   In terms of numbers alone, a need exists. An estimated 10 percent of the population—about 25 million Americans—is exclusively or predominantly homosexual in sexual orientation, and upwards of 50 percent of the men and about 70 percent of the women are in long-term, committed relationships. A 1990 survey of 1,266 lesbian and gay couples found that 82 percent of the male couples and 75 percent of the female ones share all or part of their incomes.

As a result, many lesbians and gays have fought for "domestic partnership" legislation to extend some marital and family benefits to unmarried couples—cohabiting partners either unwilling or, in the case of homosexuals, unable to marry. In New York City, for example, unmarried municipal workers who have lived with their partners at least a year may register their relationships with the personnel department, attesting to a "close and committed" relationship "involving shared responsibilities," and are then entitled to bereavement leave.

6   But such a prescription is inadequate: the protections and benefits are only a fraction of those resulting from marriage—and are available to only a small percentage of gays in a handful of cities (in the above-mentioned survey, considerably less than 10 percent of lesbian and gay couples were eligible for any form of shared job benefits). Even the concept of "domestic partnership" is seriously flawed. What constitutes a "domestic partner"? Could roommates qualify? A woman and her live-in maid? It could take an array of judicial decision making to find out.

Further, because the benefits of "domestic partnership" are allotted to couples without much legal responsibility—and because the advantages of domestic partnership are necessarily allowed for unmarried heterosexual partners as well as homosexual ones—domestic partnership has the unwanted consequence of weakening traditional marriage. Society has a vested interest in stable, committed relationships—especially, as in the case of most heterosexual couples, when children are concerned. But by eliminating the financial and legal advantages to marriage, domestic partnership dilutes that institution.

8   Society already has a measure of relational union—it's called marriage, and it's not at all difficult to ascertain: you're either married or you're not.

Yet for unmarried heterosexual couples, marriage is at least an option. Gay couples have no such choice—and society also has an interest in committed, long-lasting relationships even between homosexuals. An estimated 3 to 5 million homosexuals have parented children within heterosexual relationships, and at least 1,000 children were born to lesbian or gay couples in the San Francisco area alone in just the last five years. None of the recent thirty-five studies on homosexual parents has shown that parental sexual orientation has any adverse effect on children (and the children of gays are no more likely to be gay themselves). Surely increased stability in the relationships of lesbians and gay men could only help the gays themselves and their many millions of children.

10   Some suggest that legal mechanisms already exist by which lesbian and gay couples could create some of the desired protections for their relationships: power-of-attorney agreements, proxies, wills, insurance policies, and joint tenancy arrangements. But even these can provide only a fraction of the benefits of marriage. And such an unwieldy checklist guarantees that many lesbian and gay couples will not employ even those available.

There is a simpler solution. Allow gay civil marriage. And throw the weight of our religious institutions behind such unions.

12   In 1959, Mildred Jeter and Richard Loving, a mixed-race Virginia couple married in Washington, D.C., pleaded guilty to violating Virginia's ban on interracial marriages. Jeter and Loving were given a suspended jail sentence on the condition that they leave the state. In passing the sentence, the judge said, "Almighty God created the races white, black, yellow, Malay, and red, and he placed them on separate continents. And but for the interference with his arrangements, there would be no cause for such marriages. The fact that he separated the races shows that he did not intend for the races to mix." A motion to overturn the decision was denied by two higher Virginia courts until the state's ban on interracial marriage was declared unconstitutional by the United States Supreme Court in 1967. At the time, fifteen other states also had such marital prohibitions.

Clearly, one's sexual orientation is different from one's race. While psychological consensus (and compelling identical and fraternal twin studies) force us to concede that the homosexual *orientation* is not a choice (nor is it subject to change), homosexual behavior definitely is a choice, very unlike race. Critics maintain that gays can marry—just not to members of their same sex.

14   But with regard to marriage, whether homosexual behavior is a choice or not is irrelevant, since one's marriage partner is *necessarily* a choice. In 1959, Richard Loving, a white man, could have chosen a different partner to marry other than Mildred Jeter, a black woman; the point is that he did not. The question is whether, in the absence of a compelling state interest, the state should be allowed to supersede the individual's choice.

Some maintain that there are compelling state interests to prohibiting same-sex marriages: that tolerance for gay marriages would open the door for any number of unconventional marital arrangements—group marriage, for example. In fact, most lesbian and gay relationships are probably far more conventional than most people think. In the vast majority of respects, gay relationships closely resemble heterosexual ones—or even actually improve upon them (gay relationships tend to be more egalitarian than heterosexual ones). And in a society where most cities have at least one openly gay bar and sizable gay communities—where lesbians and gays appear regularly on television and in the movies—a committed relationship between two people of the same sex is not nearly the break from convention that a polygamous one is. More important, easing the ban on same-sex marriage would make lesbians and gays, the vast majority of whom have not chosen celibacy, even more likely to live within long-term, committed partnerships. The result would be more people living more conventional lifestyles, not more people living less conventional ones. It's actually a conservative move, not a liberal one.

16   Similarly, there is little danger that giving legitimacy to gay marriages would undermine the legitimacy of heterosexual ones—cause "the breakdown of the family." Since heterosexuality appears to be at least as immutable as homosexuality (and since there's no evidence that the prevalence of homosexuality increases following the decriminalization of it), there's no chance heterosexuals would opt for the "homosexual alternative." Heterosexual marriage would still be the ultimate social union for heterosexuals. Gay marriage would simply recognize a consistent crosscultural, transhistorical minority and allow that significant minority to also participate in an important social institution. And since marriage licenses are not rationed out, homosexual partnerships wouldn't deny anyone else the privilege.

Indeed, the compelling state interest lies in *permitting* gay unions. In the wake of AIDS, encouraging gay monogamy is simply rational public health policy. Just as important, gay marriage would reduce the number of closeted gays who marry heterosexual partners, as an estimated 20 percent of all gays do, in an effort to conform to social pressure—but at enormous cost to themselves, their children, and their opposite-sex spouses. It would reduce the atmosphere of ridicule and abuse in which the children of homosexual parents grow up. And it would reduce the number of shameful parents who disown their children or banish their gay teen-agers to lives of crime, prostitution, and drug abuse, or to suicide (psychologists estimate that gay youth comprise up to 30 percent of all teen suicides, and one Seattle study found that a whopping 40 percent of that city's street kids may be lesbian or gay, most having run away or been expelled from intolerant homes). Gay marriage wouldn't weaken the family; it would *strengthen* it.

18   The unprecedented social legitimacy given gay partnerships—and homosexuality in general—would have other societal benefits as well: it would dramatically reduce the widespread housing and job discrimination, and verbal and physical violence experienced by most lesbians and gays, clear moral and social evils.

Of course, legal and religious gay marriage wouldn't, as some writers claim, "celebrate" or be "an endorsement" of homosexual sexual behavior—any more than heterosexual marriage celebrates heterosexual sex or endorses it; gay marriage would celebrate the loving, committed relationship between two individuals, a relationship in which sexual behavior is one small part. Still, the legalization of gay marriage, while not making homosexual sexual behavior any more prevalent, would remove much of the stigma concerning such behavior, at least that which takes place within the confines of "marriage." And if the church sanctions such unions, a further, moral legitimacy will be granted. In short, regardless of the potential societal gains, should society and the church reserve a centuries-old moral stand that condemns homosexual sexual behavior?

20   We have no choice; the premises upon which the moral stand are based have changed. Science now acknowledges the existence of a homosexual sexual *orientation,* like heterosexuality, a fundamental affectional predisposition. Unlike specific behaviors of, say, rape or incest, a homosexual's sexual behavior is the logical expression of his or her most basic, unchangeable sexual make-up. And unlike rape and incest, necessarily manifestations of destruction and abuse, sexual behavior resulting from one's sexual orientation can be an expression of love and unity (it is the complete denial of this love—indeed, an unsettling preoccupation with genital activity—that make the inflammatory comparisons of homosexual sex to rape, incest, and alcoholism so frustrating for lesbians and gays).

      Moral condemnation of homosexual sexual behavior is often founded on the belief that sex and marriage are—and should be—inexorably linked with child-rearing; because lesbians and gay men are physiologically incapable of creating children alone, all such sexual behavior is deemed immoral—and gays are considered unsuitable to the institution of marriage. But since moral sanction is not withheld from infertile couples or those who intend to remain childless, this standard is clearly being inconsistently—and unfairly—applied.

22 Some cite the promiscuity of some male gays as if this is an indication that all homosexuals are incapable or undeserving of marriage. But this standard is also inconsistently applied; it has never been seriously suggested that the existence of promiscuous heterosexuals invalidate all heterosexuals from the privilege of marriage. And if homosexuals are more likely than heterosexuals to be promiscuous—and if continual, harsh condemnation hasn't altered that fact—the sensible solution would seem to be to try to lure gays back to the monogamous fold by providing efforts in that direction with some measure of respect and social support: something gay marriage would definitely provide.

      Human beings are sexual creatures. It is simply not logical to say, as the church does, that while one's basic sexual outlook is neither chosen nor sinful, any activity taken as a result of that orientation is. One must then ask exactly where does the sin of "activity" begin anyway? Hugging a person of the same sex? Kissing? Same-sex sexual fantasy? Even apart from the practical impossibilities, what about the ramifications of such an attempt? How does the homosexual adolescent formulate self-esteem while being told that *any* expression of his or her sexuality *ever* is unacceptable—or downright evil? The priest chooses celibacy (asexuality isn't required), but this *is* a choice—one made well after adolescence.

24   Cultural condemnations and biblical prohibitions of (usually male) homosexual behavior were founded upon an incomplete understanding of human sexuality. To grant the existence of a homosexual orientation requires that there be some acceptable expression of it. Of course, there's no reason why lesbians and gays should be granted moral leniency over heterosexuals—which is why perhaps the most acceptable expression of same-sex sexuality should be within the context of a government sanctioned, religiously blessed marriage. But before we can talk about the proper way to get two brides or two grooms down a single church aisle, we have to first show there's an aisle wide enough to accommodate them.   ❖

Questions for Meaning

1. What kind of benefits would gay and lesbian couples enjoy if allowed to marry? Which of these benefits is most important in Hartinger's view?
2. Why does Hartinger find "domestic partnership" status an unacceptable alternative to marriage?
3. Could the legalization of gay marriage provide any benefits for society as a whole?
4. According to Hartinger, how should marriage be viewed? When seen in these terms, how important is the nature or frequency of sexual activity within a marriage?
5. Vocabulary: polygamous (2), attesting (5), supersede (14), immutable (16), transhistorical (16), stigma (19), ramifications (23)

Questions about Strategy

1. Consider the statistics provided in paragraphs 4, 9, and 17. What is Hartinger trying to establish through these statistics? In your opinion, which are the most important?
2. In paragraph 15, why is it useful for Hartinger to present gay marriage as "a conservative move, not a liberal one"?
3. What does the case of Mildred Jeter and Richard Loving illustrate? To what extent is their situation analogous to the situation of men and women who are currently unable to marry someone of their own gender?
4. According to Hartinger, in paragraph 24, "To grant the existence of a homosexual orientation requires that there be some acceptable expression of it." Do you agree with his reasoning?
5. Hartinger concludes his argument by suggesting that two brides or two grooms might walk down a church aisle together. In what sense would the "aisle" need to be "wide enough to accomodate them"?

One Student's Assignment

Recognizing that there are sharply divided opinions on the subject of same-gender marriage, write a Rogerian argument that will help conflicting parties find common ground. Your essay should demonstrate that you have paid close attention to views different from your own and have considered why they deserve to be taken seriously. Introduce your own views only after you have given fair consideration to the ideas of people you hope to persuade. Draw on the sources gathered in *The Informed Argument*—and your own experience, if you wish. Use MLA-style documentation.

Speak Now or Forever Hold the Past
Dana Simonson

My parents eloped 25 years ago last June. To them, it was their best and only option; they were in love. My parents are *still* in love and married, even though my mother's parents objected to the marriage. After coming to understand their deep commitment, my grandparents became supportive of my parents' marriage. Like most Americans, they realize that faithfulness in relationships promotes healthy living and that marriage is the clearest way for couples to confirm their commitment to each other alone. However, not all Americans enjoy the same opportunities to marry. In the past, my grandparents—and others of their generation—may not have considered men marrying men and women marrying women, but the time has come to discuss this possibility.

2   Opponents of same-gender marriage often cite personal religious beliefs, arguing that marriage is primarily a religious institution. "It is an honorable estate, instituted of God and built on moral, religious, sexual and human realities" from which homosexuals should be excluded because "the legal union of same-sex couples . . . endorse[s] practices which are completely antithetical to the tenets of all of the world's major religions" (W. Bennett 262). They assert that gays and lesbians can, indeed, be married, only not to a person of the same gender. I also perceive that they have a concern that homosexuals are trying to achieve special rights and privileges and that allowing them to marry would cause "a radical deconstruction of the institution [of marriage]" (Schiffren 258). Moreover, many people are concerned about the place of children in same-gender marriages, believing that heterosexuality "is critical for raising healthy children and transmitting the values that are the basis of our culture" (Schiffren 258).

I commend these citizens for upholding their religious ideals, since individuals tend to lose hope if they do not believe in values which endure. Opponents of same-gender marriage also reveal a concern for fairness insomuch as a certain group of people may be aspiring for special privileges from which others might be excluded. I also share the concern for the future of children involved in same-gender marriages. Above all, I agree with the concern that the government has a responsibility to provide a healthy society.

4   Nevertheless, I propose that the marriage decision belongs to individual citizens. Couples who are publicly ready to commit themselves to fidelity should have the authority to make their own decisions. My main interest is that insofar as Americans do not equally share the *option* of marriage, we are creating a divided society. This separation is worsening because "in uncertain times people search for scapegoats" (Johnson 268).

   The convictions held by those opposed to same-gender marriage, understandable though they are, restrict the rights of others. Although these citizens have a right to their religious beliefs, they do not have the right to impose these beliefs on others. Heterosexual couples can be legally married even if they are not religious. Why should not homosexual couples—many of whom are religious—enjoy the same opportunity? Today we are discussing the civil, not religious, right of same-gender couples to marry the individuals they love.

6   Same-gender couples are recommending equality rather than special privileges. "[W]hat we seek is not some special place in America but merely to be a full and equal part of America, to give back to our society without being forced to lie or hide or live as second-class citizens" (Sullivan 259). Married, same-gender couples would indeed receive benefits equal to, but no greater than, those of heterosexual couples. We would all be subject to the same marriage laws, such as a consenting adult age limit, prohibition of polygamy, and required child support.

   Without the option of marriage, same-gender couples might encounter financial stress because of unshared health, insurance, retirement and inheritance benefits and the inability to file joint income taxes. Why should any couple, with or without children, suffer financially after they are not allowed the right to marriage? Financial stress might also hurt the children of same-gender couples, possibly depriving them of college-education savings.

8   Many would agree that raising children within a marriage is not only a great struggle, but also an immense privilege. To take part in this experience, some couples choose to adopt children. As marriage is fulfilling in itself, other married, heterosexual couples choose not to have children. Like heterosexual couples, each homosexual couple will have to make their own decision. In fact, many same-gender couples have already made the decision to raise children, but these families do not enjoy the full protection and rights they deserve; marriage often leads to higher social

acceptance of a couple's children. The possible stigma children face because their parents cannot be married is damaging.

In order to have a healthy society, same-gender couples need to have the option of marriage. Couples themselves would benefit through control of their lives. Also, the children of couples would gain security as part of a socially recognized, stable family unit because their parents are married. Moreover, we would all partake in the benefits because "Society has a vested interest in stable, committed relationships" (Hartinger 279). Most important is the knowledge that marriage should be based on love; since all humans are capable of love, we are all eligible for marriage. Rather than realizing and accepting change, "it is easier to oppress some so that others might live in certainty, ignoring the reality that the mystery of love and life and death is really grander and more glorious than human beings can grasp, much less legislate" (Johnson 273). Not all couples in love will choose to be married, but we should all have the option.

10   If we put forth the imaginary effort to understand a same-gender couple who wishes to be married, would we not be supportive of their commitment? One writer in a same-gender relationship inspires us to put forth the effort, "I know that to understand a life that is different from the life lived by most people takes time—and an open mind" (L. Bennett 256). It took my grandparents two years to accept my parents' marriage. Although my grandfather has since passed away, my grandmother helped organize my parents' 25th anniversary party last summer. Today, my grandmother also understands and is supportive of her grandson's same-gender relationship. In defense of their love and their struggle for the equal right for same-gender couples to be married, my grandmother spoke out, "They're no different than you or me . . . they have a kitchen and cook together." Times have changed and my grandmother exclaimed, "They even have a cappuccino maker!"

Suggestions for Writing

1. "Love is love," writes Lisa Bennett. "In whatever shape it comes, it deserves respect." But should anyone in love be able to get married? Write an argument on behalf of what you believe a successful marriage requires.
2. How important is the sexual orientation of parents? Write an essay defining what you think parents should offer their children.
3. Andrew Sullivan argues that conservatives should support same-gender marriage; William Bennett argues that they should not. Write an essay defining what it means to be a conservative.

4. Imagine that you have been asked to moderate the debate between Andrew Sullivan and William Bennett, whose arguments have been included in this section. Write an essay designed to help them heal their differences.
5. Write an argument for or against the legalization of same-gender marriage in your state.
6. Drawing on the essay by Fenton Johnson, and other sources if you wish, write a paper about how marriage between men and women has changed during the twentieth century.
7. Should couples live together before they get married, or do such arrangements weaken the institution of marriage? Write an argument for or against cohabitation.
8. Write an essay defining "domestic partnership."
9. Should American corporations extend benefits to domestic partners as well as to spouses? Write an essay about how you think businesses should respond to employees who are partnered to someone of their own gender.
10. Imagine that a close friend has just come out to you, revealing that she is in love with another woman. You were shocked when she told you, and you didn't know what to say. Now, feeling that you let your friend down, you decide to write her a letter explaining your response. Write a letter that will both convey your beliefs and preserve your friendship.

COLLABORATIVE PROJECT

Interview a diverse group of people to learn what they think of marriage. Try to include married couples, couples who are living together without being married, couples who are dating but not living together, and both single men and single women. Be sure to include people of different ages and different cultural backgrounds—as well as people who are heterosexual, homosexual, or bisexual—so that you can gather a range of views. If possible, interview people, such as clergy and social workers, who are experienced in counseling couples. Then write a report that provides an analysis of the data you have gathered.

SECTION 4

SEXUAL HARASSMENT: DEFINING THE BOUNDARIES

ANNE B. FISHER

SEXUAL HARASSMENT: WHAT TO DO?

How should businesses respond to the problem of sexual harassment in the workplace? And what does "sexual harassment" mean? Anne B. Fisher explores these and other questions in the following 1993 article from *Fortune* magazine, a well-respected business monthly. As you read, note what Fisher reports about the law and how it is changing.

Tailhook. New rules on college campuses against romances between professors and students. A controversial book that purports to tell the real story of Anita Hill and Clarence Thomas. And of course that staple of late-night-TV jokes, Senator Bob Packwood.* In the shift and glimmer of the media kaleidoscope, sexual harassment is a constant glinting shard.

2   Yet no headline-making subject in recent memory has stirred so much confusion. No doubt you've read your company's policy statement and, from just under its surface, you feel the legal eagles' gimlet stare. But what does sexual harassment really mean? Managers of both sexes are sifting through the past and fretting about next week. Was it all right to say I liked her dress? Is it okay to ask him out to lunch to talk about that project? Should I just stop touching anybody, even if it's only a congratulatory pat on the back? For that big client meeting in Houston, wouldn't it be less risky to fly out with Frank than with Francine? Or, for female managers, vice versa?

If you think you've got reason to worry, you probably don't; the ones who do are usually unaware they have a problem. But right in your own organization, maybe even in your own department, your hallway, your pod, somebody may be so befuddled and self-destructive as to miss the point entirely. Sexual harassment is not really about sex. It's about power—more to the point, the abuse of power.

---

* Senator Bob Packwood of Oregon was accused of sexually harassing many of the women who worked in his office. He was widely criticized and eventually resigned from office after the Senate Ethics Committee voted to expel him.

4   Imagine it this way. Suppose one of your most senior and valued people has a little problem. Great producer, terrific salesperson, meets every goal, exceeds every guideline, but, well, there's this one glitch: He steals things. Every time he leaves an office he takes something with him—a pen, a coffee mug, a book, some change that was lying around. He's been at it a long time, can't seem to help it and, anyway, he's a good guy, a *great* guy. You're his boss. What are you going to do when he walks off with somebody's $3,000 notebook computer? That's grand larceny, and the victim is hopping mad.

        For more and more managers these days, the analogy fits. Let's suppose the fellow isn't stealing material things but rather chipping away at the human dignity and professional self-respect of other people. Can't seem to resist patting fannies and whispering innuendoes. Told a subordinate he'd like to negotiate her raise at the local No-Tell Motel. Cornered a female colleague and loudly compared her physical attributes with those of the current Playmate of the Month. All the time he's producing great stuff. But the whispering behind his back is getting louder; the troops are murmuring about calling the lawyers and human resources people. What do you do with this guy? (Alas, despite a much publicized $1 million jury award in May to a male plaintiff harassed by his female boss in Los Angeles, harassers are, in nine cases out of ten, guys.)

6   Talk to him, of course. If that doesn't work, and odds are it won't, turn him in to the human resources person in charge of these matters. And do it pronto. Otherwise you could be liable along with your employer. Unsolicited, unwelcome, and downright extortionate sexual demands are as illegal as stealing computers. So are purposeful and repeated efforts to intimidate colleagues by transforming the office into a remake of *Animal House*—what the law calls "hostile environment" harassment. He who steals my briefcase, to paraphrase Shakespeare, steals trash. But the loss of someone's dignity, productivity, and eagerness to come to work in the morning is a theft not only from the person robbed of it, but from the company too.

        Sexual harassment is not a compliment on anyone's wardrobe or a friendly pat on the shoulder. It is not the occasional tasteless remark or careless quip. It is not even asking someone for a date the second time, when she's already said no once. To stand up in court, a harassment charge must rest on either a persistent and calculated pattern of antisocial behavior or a single *quid pro quo*—"You'll never get anywhere in this company unless you sleep with me"—that is so egregious as to leave no room for misinterpretation.

8   The courts have recognized sexual harassment as an offense under Title VII since 1977. But the number of complaints filed with the Equal Employment Opportunity Commission has nearly doubled in the past five years, to 10,532 in 1992. It's debatable whether that rise occurred because instances of harassment increased or whether events like the Hill–Thomas hearings* encouraged people who had long remained silent to speak up. The EEOC doesn't keep a record of how many cases end up in litigation;

---

* For Anita Hill's analysis of these hearings, see pp. 301–316.

many are settled on the courthouse steps. One thing is certain. The consequences for corporations are costly.

Research by Freada Klein Associates, a workplace-diversity consulting firm in Cambridge, Massachusetts, shows that 90 percent of Fortune 500 companies have dealt with sexual harassment complaints. More than a third have been sued at least once, and about a quarter have been sued over and over again. Klein estimates that the problem costs the average large corporation $6.7 million a year.

10   Bettina Plevan, an attorney at Proskauer Rose Goetz & Mendelsohn in New York City, specializes in defending companies against sexual harassment lawsuits. She says employers spend an average of $200,000 on each complaint that is investigated in-house and found to be valid, whether or not it ever gets to court. Richard Hafets, a labor lawyer at Piper & Marbury in Baltimore, believes sexual harassment could be tomorrow's asbestos, costing American business $1 billion in fees and damages in the next five years.

         But the costs of sexual harassment go well beyond anything that can be measured on a profit-and-loss statement. Women, often still treated like interlopers in the office, say they feel vulnerable to the myriad subtle—and not so subtle—sexual power trips some men use to keep them in their place. At an Aetna Life & Casualty golfing party last September, four executives vented their resentment of female managers' presence at what had traditionally been an all-male event. Their mildest offense—and the only one we're halfway willing to describe in a magazine your kids might see—was calling women executives "sluts." In response Aetna demoted two of the men and asked the two others to resign.

12   Jeannine Sandstrom, a senior vice president of the executive recruiting firm Lee Hecht Harrison in Dallas, knows of instances where harassers were caught because they sent X-rated messages to their victims via voice mail or E-mail. Marvels Sandstrom: "How self-destructive do you have to be to do something like this, knowing how easy it is to trace?"

         In most cases harassment is more subtle—and far more difficult to prove. As agonizing as it may be, women have an obligation to speak up and tell someone who is hounding them to stop it. Although federal law defines sexual harassment as "unwelcome" behavior, the courts say it doesn't count as such unless the offender knows it's unwelcome. Yet a 1991 study by two professors at the University of St. Thomas in St. Paul, Minnesota, revealed that, among women in a nationwide survey who said they had been victims of sexual harassment, only 34 percent told the harasser to knock it off; just 2 percent filed a formal complaint.

14   With the economy in its current shaky state, many women may be too fearful of losing their jobs to speak up. Or they may be reluctant to be seen as whiners, either by their peers or by the people above them. But if a woman wants to file a grievance, it's important to be able to prove that she told the perpetrator to back off. Some experts suggest tape-recording the

conversation or sending a registered letter (return receipt requested) detailing the offending behavior and declaring it not OK. This helps in any follow-up by human resources or legal staff, even in cases where witnesses or other direct proof of the harassment are available.

As for men, the majority of whom wouldn't dream of harassing anybody, they are terrified of being falsely accused—with some reason. "What I'm seeing lately is that companies are overreacting, and accusers are believed on the basis of very little evidence or none at all," says Ellen Wagner, an attorney and author who specializes in labor law. "And the ultimate punishment, termination, is a first resort rather than a last one."

16   Consider the case of Louis Kestenbaum. From 1977 to 1984, Kestenbaum was vice president in charge of guest operations at a secluded ranch and spa that Pennzoil operated in northern New Mexico. In January 1984, someone wrote an anonymous letter to Pennzoil's top management accusing Kestenbaum of sexual harassment and other misdeeds. Kestenbaum denied the allegations but was fired anyway. He sued Pennzoil and won $500,000 in damages for wrongful discharge. The reason? Pennzoil's in-house investigator admitted in court that she had relied on rumor and innuendo in compiling the sexual-harassment report that got Kestenbaum the ax. "No attempt was made to evaluate the credibility of the persons interviewed," wrote the judge.

Both sexes sometimes feel they're stumbling around in a minefield, lost in enemy territory without a helicopter. What makes the terrain so treacherous is that people have an inconvenient way of seeing the same behavior quite differently. Margaret Regan is a Towers Perrin partner who has conducted a senior-management training program called Respect at Work for dozens of corporations. She points out that some of what might look like sexual harassment is in reality an innocent error arising from past experience. "My favorite example is when we ask a group of men and women, "How many times is it all right to ask someone out after they've said no once?" says Regan. "In one class I led, one of the men said, 'Ten.' The women were appalled. They said, '*Ten times?* No way! Twice is enough!' "

18   It turned out, when he got a chance to explain his answer, that the offending fellow had to ask 10 or 12 times before the girl of his dreams agreed to go to the senior prom with him in 1959. It worked out fine: They've been married for 32 years. "Naturally ten times seemed reasonable to him," says Regan. "So much of what people think about these things comes from stuff they grew up with—and just never had any reason to question."

Consultants who design sexual harassment workshops, and managers who have attended them, agree on one thing: The best training gives participants a chance to talk to each other, instead of just listening to a lecture or watching a film. In classes where men and women are asked to compare their impressions of the same hypothetical situation, real revelations can occur.

20   Perhaps not surprisingly, Aetna has stepped up its training program since the infamous golfing incident last fall. Anthony Guerriero, 34, a pension

consultant at the company, took the course in January. He says, "The guys in the class were absolutely not resistant to it, not at all. In fact, it's a relief to have someone spell out exactly what sexual harassment is. The men in my session were all saying, 'It's about time.' "

Male managers aren't the only ones who benefit from the classes. Women are sometimes startled to find how widely their perceptions differ from those of other women. Janet Kalas, 45, director of Medicare administration at Aetna, has 300 people reporting to her. "What startled me about the training was how tolerant I am," she says. In one group-discussion exercise, the instructor described an imaginary scenario in which a male and a female colleague, both married to others, are out of town on business. Late in the evening, they're still working on a client presentation for the next morning, and they decide to finish it in the female manager's hotel room. Recalls Kalas, "My reaction was, Well, that's practical. What's the big deal? But other people, men and women both, were saying, 'My gosh, don't do that, it's like an *invitation* to this guy.' I was surprised."

22   Towers Perrin recently queried executives at 600 major U.S. companies and found that about half planned to increase the amount of sexual harassment training they give managers and employees. A dozen or so big corporations have already built shining reputations among consultants and researchers for the quality, creativity, and overall earnestness of their training programs. Among them: Du Pont, Federal Express, General Mills, Levi-Strauss, Merck, and Syntex. But will they talk about what they're doing? Not a chance. "Nobody likes to acknowledge that this problem even exists," says Robert Steed, who runs a consulting firm in Westchester County, New York, that specializes in sexual-harassment training. "It makes people queasy. So their view is, the less said the better." Adds a public relations manager at a Fortune 500 company: "The general feeling is, what if we get written up somewhere as having this terrific training program—and then we get sued a week later? In other words, no comment."

For a company's policy to do any good, much less be taken seriously in a courtroom, employees have to understand it. Barbara Spyridon Pope, the Navy assistant secretary who almost single-handedly exposed the Tailhook scandal, recently established a consulting firm in Washington, D.C., to advise corporate clients on how to communicate their sexual-harassment guidelines to the troops. Her surveys show that 60 percent to 90 percent of U.S. workers know there is a policy but haven't the foggiest what it says. "Having a policy is fine, but by itself it isn't enough," says Pope. "The Navy had a policy too."

24   Sitting people down to discuss their differences on this issue is more than a therapeutic parlor game. Case law over the past decade has established that a company with a well-defined anti-sexual-harassment stance can escape liability for hostile-environment harassment. No wonder, then, that you keep getting all those policy memos and invitations to sign up for workshops. But

to prevail in court, companies must also have clear procedures for handling complaints when they arise. Typically, employers choose an impartial ombudsperson, usually in the human resources department, to hear and investigate charges before the lawyers get into the act. If the complaint seems legitimate, the company must then take what the judge in a pivotal 1986 case, *Hunter* v. *Allis-Chalmers,* called "immediate and appropriate action." Depending on the circumstances, this might range from transferring the harassed or the harasser to a different department, to docking the harasser a couple of weeks' pay, to firing the guilty party outright.

This fall the Supreme Court will hear *Harris* v. *Forklift Systems,* its first sexual harassment case since 1986. The suit was filed by Teresa Harris, who left her job at a Nashville truck-leasing company after months of crude remarks and propositions from the firm's president. The matter was dismissed by a federal judge in Tennessee and ended up in federal appeals court in Cincinnati, where the dismissal was upheld. Reason: Ms. Harris had not proven that she was psychologically damaged by her boss's behavior.

26   If psychological damage becomes the new standard in harassment cases, which is what the high court has agreed to decide, plaintiffs will have a far harder time winning. Says Anne Clark, an attorney for the National Organization for Women: "You shouldn't have to suffer a nervous breakdown before you can make a claim." Lawyers who represent companies reply that a decision in favor of the psychological-damage standard would cut down on frivolous suits. To which working women are apt to say: "Frivolous? Nobody in her right mind would have her name dragged through the dirt over a frivolous charge!"

No matter how the court rules, managers and employees would do well to keep their own responsibilities in mind. For actual or potential harassers that means: Watch it, buster. For women, it means: Speak up. For their bosses, the best advice is: Get help. Says Susan Crawford, a partner at Holtzmann Wise & Shepard in Palo Alto, California: "I've found that managers too often are reluctant to refer a complaint to human resources. Instead they try to handle it themselves. But bosses need to see that this is a complicated issue with a lot of pitfalls, and it is not a sign of failure on their part to say, 'Hey, I need help with this. I'm not the expert here.' " The people in your company who really know where all the pitfalls are—and who will try to be fair to everybody—are not in your department. They are probably upstairs somewhere. Call them.

28   For all the seriousness of the issue, it would be a great pity if men and women got to the point of giving up on workplace friendships altogether— a point some men say privately they've already reached. Remember Rob, Buddy, and Sally on the old *Dick Van Dyke Show*? Okay, it was way back in the supposedly benighted early Sixties, but those three were a great professional team, and they were pals. For men and women in corporate America, there could be far worse role models. It will be a sad day, if it ever comes, when people are too nervous to ask a pal out for a drink. ❖

Questions for Meaning

1. According to Fisher, what is sexual harassment ultimately about?
2. What quotation from Shakespeare is paraphrased in paragraph 6?
3. If a woman is being harassed by a man, why is it important that she make it clear to him that she finds his behavior objectionable?
4. What kind of training is most likely to help men and women avoid harassment in the workplace?
5. Why is it advantageous for companies to have clearly defined harassment policies?
6. Vocabulary: gimlet (2), innuendoes (5), extortionate (6), quip (7), egregious (7), interlopers (11), myriad (11), infamous (20), ombudsperson (24), pivotal (24), benighted (28).

Questions about Strategy

1. Consider the analogy in paragraph 4. Fisher states that it works for many managers. Does it work for you?
2. What is the implication of the statistics quoted in paragraph 13?
3. How reputable are the sources cited in this article?
4. How appropriate is the allusion in paragraph 28? Who is most likely to understand it? What does this allusion reveal about Fisher's sense of audience?

Ellen Frankel Paul

BARED BUTTOCKS AND FEDERAL CASES

What kinds of legal protection can people expect from behavior they find offensive? According to Ellen Frankel Paul, "A distinction must be restored between morally offensive behavior and behavior that causes serious harm." As you read her article, note the distinction that she makes. Paul teaches political science at Bowling Green State University. Her books include *Property Rights and Eminent Domain* (1987) and *Equality and Gender: The Comparable Worth Debate* (1988). The following article was first published in *Society* in 1991.

Women in American society are victims of sexual harassment in alarming proportions. Sexual harassment is an inevitable corollary to class exploitation; as capitalists exploit workers, so do males in positions of authority exploit their female subordinates. Male professors, supervisors, and apartment managers in ever increasing numbers take advantage of the financial dependence and vulnerability of women to extract sexual concessions.

2   These are the assertions that commonly begin discussions of sexual harassment. For reasons that will be adumbrated below, dissent from the prevailing view is long overdue. Three recent episodes will serve to frame this disagreement.

Valerie Craig, an employee of Y & Y Snacks, Inc., joined several co-workers and her supervisor for drinks after work one day in July of 1978. Her supervisor drove her home and proposed that they become more intimately acquainted. She refused his invitation for sexual relations, whereupon he said that he would "get even" with her. Ten days after the incident she was fired from her job. She soon filed a complaint of sexual harassment with the Equal Employment Opportunity Commission (EEOC), and the case wound its way through the courts. Craig prevailed, the company was held liable for damages, and she received back pay, reinstatement, and an order prohibiting Y & Y from taking reprisals against her in the future.

4   Carol Zabowicz, one of only two female forklift operators in a West Bend Co. warehouse, charged that her co-workers over a four-year period from 1978–1982 sexually harassed her by such acts as: asking her whether she was wearing a bra; two of the men exposing their buttocks between ten and twenty times; a male co-worker grabbing his crotch and making obscene suggestions or growling; subjecting her to offensive and abusive language; and exhibiting obscene drawings with her initials on them. Zabowicz began to show symptoms of physical and psychological stress, necessitating several medical leaves, and she filed a sexual harassment complaint with the EEOC. The district court judge remarked that "the sustained, malicious, and brutal harassment meted out . . . was more than merely unreasonable; it was malevolent and outrageous." The company knew of the harassment and took corrective action only after the employee filed a complaint with the EEOC. The company, was, therefore, held liable, and Zabowicz was awarded back pay for the period of her medical absence, and a judgment that her rights were violated under the Civil Rights Act of 1964.

On September 17, 1990, Lisa Olson, a sports reporter for *The Boston Herald,* charged five football players of the just-defeated New England Patriots with sexual harassment with making sexually suggestive and offensive remarks to her when she entered their locker room to conduct a post-game interview. The incident amounted to nothing short of "mind rape," according to Olson. After vociferous lamentations in the media, the National Football League fined the team and its players $25,000 each. The National Organization for Women called for a boycott of Remington electric shavers because the owner of the company, Victor Kiam, also owns the Patriots and allegedly displayed insufficient sensitivity at the time when the episode occurred.

6   All these incidents are indisputably disturbing. In an ideal world—one needless to say far different from the one that we inhabit or are ever likely to inhabit—women would not be subjected to such treatment in the course of their work. Women, and men as well, would be accorded respect by co-workers and supervisors, their feelings would be taken into account, and

their dignity would be left intact. For women to expect reverential treatment in the workplace is utopian, yet they should not have to tolerate outrageous, offensive sexual overtures and threats as they go about earning a living.

One question that needs to be pondered is: What kinds of undesired sexual behavior women should be protected against by law? That is, what kind of actions are deemed so outrageous and violate a woman's rights to such extent that the law should intervene, and what actions should be considered inconveniences of life, to be morally condemned but not adjudicated? A subsidiary question concerns the type of legal remedy appropriate for the wrongs that do require redress. Before directly addressing these questions, it might be useful to diffuse some of the hyperbole adhering to the sexual harassment issue.

8   Surveys are one source of this hyperbole. If their results are accepted at face value, they lead to the conclusion that women are disproportionately victims of legions of sexual harassers. A poll by the Albuquerque *Tribune* found that nearly 80 percent of the respondents reported that they or someone they knew had been victims of sexual harassment. The Merit Systems Protection Board determined that 42 percent of the women (and 14 percent of men) working for the federal government had experienced some form of unwanted sexual attention between 1985 and 1987, with unwanted "sexual teasing" identified as the most prevalent form. A Defense Department survey found that 64 percent of women in the military (and 17 percent of the men) suffered "uninvited and unwanted sexual attention" within the previous year. The United Methodist Church established that 77 percent of its clergywomen experienced incidents of sexual harassment, with 41 percent of these naming a pastor or colleague as the perpetrator, and 31 percent mentioning church social functions as the setting.

A few caveats concerning polls in general, and these sorts of polls in particular, are worth considering. Pollsters looking for a particular social ill tend to find it, usually in gargantuan proportions. (What fate would lie in store for a pollster who concluded that child abuse, or wife beating, or mistreatment of the elderly had dwindled to the point of negligibility!) Sexual harassment is a notoriously ill-defined and almost infinitely expandable concept, including everything from rape to unwelcome neck massaging, discomfiture upon witnessing sexual overtures directed at others, yelling at and blowing smoke in the ears of female subordinates, and displays of pornographic pictures in the workplace. Defining sexual harassment, as the United Methodists did, as "any sexually related behavior that is unwelcome, offensive or which fails to respect the rights of others," the concept is broad enough to include everything from "unsolicited suggestive looks or leers [or] pressures for dates" to "actual sexual assaults or rapes." Categorizing everything from rape to "looks" as sexual harassment makes us all victims, a state of affairs satisfying to radical feminists, but not very useful for distinguishing serious injuries from the merely trivial.

10   Yet, even if the surveys exaggerate the extent of sexual harassment, however defined, what they do reflect is a great deal of tension between the sexes. As women in ever increasing numbers entered the workplace in the last two decades, as the women's movement challenged alleged male hegemony and exploitation with ever greater intemperance, and as women entered previously all-male preserves from the board rooms to the coal pits, it is lamentable, but should not be surprising, that this tension sometimes takes sexual form. Not that sexual harassment on the job, in the university, and in other settings is a trivial or insignificant matter, but a sense of proportion needs to be restored and, even more importantly, distinctions need to be made. In other words, sexual harassment must be de-ideologized. Statements that paint nearly all women as victims and all men and their patriarchal, capitalist system as perpetrators, are ideological fantasy. Ideology blurs the distinction between being injured—being a genuine victim—and merely being offended. An example is this statement by Catharine A. MacKinnon, a law professor and feminist activist:

> Sexual harassment perpetuates the interlocked structure by which women have been kept sexually in thrall to men and at the bottom of the labor market. Two forces of American society converge: men's control over women's sexuality and capital's control over employees' work lives. Women historically have been required to exchange sexual services for material survival, in one form or another. Prostitution and marriage as well as sexual harassment in different ways institutionalize this arrangement.

Such hyperbole needs to be diffused and distinctions need to be drawn. Rape, a nonconsensual invasion of a person's body, is a crime clear and simple. It is a violation of the right to the physical integrity of the body (the right to life, as John Locke or Thomas Jefferson would have put it). Criminal law should and does prohibit rape. Whether it is useful to call rape "sexual harassment" is doubtful, for it makes the latter concept overly broad while trivializing the former.

12   Intimidation in the workplace of the kind that befell Valerie Craig—that is, extortion of sexual favors by a supervisor from a subordinate by threatening to penalize, fire, or fail to reward—is what the courts term *quid pro quo** sexual harassment. Since the mid-1970s, the federal courts have treated this type of sexual harassment as a form of sex discrimination in employment proscribed under Title VII of the Civil Rights Act of 1964. A plaintiff who prevails against an employer may receive such equitable remedies as reinstatement and back pay, and the court can order the company to prepare and disseminate a policy against sexual harassment. Current law places principal liability on the company, not the harassing supervisor, even when higher management is unaware of the harassment and, thus, cannot take any steps to prevent it.

* Latin for "one thing in return for another."

Quid pro quo sexual harassment is morally objectionable and analogous to extortion: The harasser extorts property (i.e., use of the woman's body) through the leverage of fear for her job. The victim of such behavior should have legal recourse, but serious reservations can be held about rectifying these injustices through the blunt instrument of Title VII: In egregious cases the victim is left less than whole (for back pay will not compensate her for ancillary losses), and no prospects for punitive damages are offered to deter would-be harassers. Even more distressing about Title VII is the fact that the primary target of litigation is not the actual harasser, but rather the employer. This places a double burden on a company. The employer is swindled by the supervisor because he spent his time pursuing sexual gratification and thereby impairing the efficiency of the workplace by mismanaging his subordinates, and the employer must endure lengthy and expensive litigation, pay damages, and suffer loss to its reputation. It would be fairer to both the company and the victim to treat sexual harassment as a tort—that is, as a private wrong or injury for which the court can assess damages. Employers should be held vicariously liable only when they know of an employee's behavior and do not try to redress it.

14   As for the workplace harassment endured by Carol Zabowicz—the bared buttocks, obscene portraits, etc.—that too should be legally redressable. Presently, such incidents also fall under the umbrella of Title VII, and are termed hostile environment sexual harassment, a category accepted later than *quid pro quo* and with some judicial reluctance. The main problem with this category is that it has proven too elastic: cases have reached the courts based on everything from off-color jokes to unwanted, persistent sexual advances by co-workers. A new tort of sexual harassment would handle these cases better. Only instances above a certain threshold of egregiousness or outrageousness would be actionable. In other words, the behavior that the plaintiff found offensive would also have to be offensive to the proverbial "reasonable man" of the tort law. That is, the behavior would have to be objectively injurious rather than merely subjectively offensive. The defendant would be the actual harasser not the company, unless it knew about the problem and failed to act. Victims of scatological jokes, leers, unwanted offers of dates, and other sexual annoyances would no longer have their day in court.

A distinction must be restored between morally offensive behavior and behavior that causes serious harm. Only the latter should fall under the jurisdiction of criminal or tort law. Do we really want legislators and judges delving into our most intimate private lives, deciding when a look is a leer, and when a leer is a Civil Rights Act offense? Do we really want courts deciding, as one recently did, whether a school principal's disparaging remarks about a female school district administrator was sexual harassment and, hence, a breach of Title VII, or merely the act of a spurned and vengeful lover? Do we want judges settling disputes such as the one that arose at a car dealership after a female employee turned down a male co-worker's offer of a date and his colleagues retaliated by calling her offensive names and embarrassing her in front of customers? Or another case in which a female shipyard worker complained of an "offensive working environment" because of the prevalence of pornographic material on the docks? Do we want the state to prevent or compensate us for any behavior that someone might find offensive? Should people have a legally enforceable right not to be offended by others? At some point, the price for such protection is the loss of both liberty and privacy rights.

16   Workplaces are breeding grounds of envy, personal grudges, infatuation, and jilted loves, and beneath a fairly high threshold of outrageousness, these travails should be either suffered in silence, complained of to higher management, or left behind as one seeks other employment. No one, female or male, can expect to enjoy a working environment that is perfectly stress-free, or to be treated always and by everyone with kindness and respect. To the extent that sympathetic judges have encouraged women to seek monetary compensation for slights and annoyances, they have not done them a great service. Women need to develop a thick skin in order to survive and prosper in the workforce. It is patronizing to think that they need to be recompensed by male judges for seeing a few pornographic pictures on a wall. By their efforts to extend sexual harassment charges to even the most trivial behavior, the radical feminists send a message that women are not resilient enough to ignore the run-of-the-mill, churlish provocation from male co-workers. It is difficult to imagine a suit by a longshoreman complaining of mental stress due to the display of nude male centerfolds by female co-workers. Women cannot expect to have it both ways: equality where convenient, but special dispensations when the going gets rough. Equality has its price and that price may include unwelcome sexual advances, irritating and even intimidating sexual jests, and lewd and obnoxious colleagues.

        Egregious acts—sexual harassment per se—must be legally redressable. Lesser but not trivial offenses, whether at the workplace or in other more social settings, should be considered moral lapses for which the offending party receives opprobrium, disciplinary warnings, or penalties, depending on the setting and the severity. Trivial offenses, dirty jokes, sexual overtures, and sexual innuendoes do make many women feel intensely discomfited, but, unless they become outrageous through persistence or content, these too should be taken as part of life's annoyances. The perpetrators should be either endured, ignored, rebuked, or avoided, as circumstances and personal inclination dictate. Whether Lisa Olson's experience in the locker room of the Boston Patriots falls into the second or third category is debatable. The media circus triggered by the incident was certainly out of proportion to the event.

18   As the presence of women on road gangs, construction crews, and oil rigs becomes a fact of life, the animosities and tensions of this transition period are likely to abate gradually. Meanwhile, women should "lighten up," and even dispense a few risqué barbs of their own, a sure way of taking the fun out of it for offensive male bores. ❖

Questions for Meaning

1. Explain the analogy in paragraph 1. What parallel can be drawn between sexual harassment and "class exploitation"?
2. Which of the cases discussed in paragraphs 3 through 5 are clearly illegal in Paul's view?
3. Why is Paul skeptical of statistics gathered by pollsters?
4. According to Paul, why has sexual harassment in the workplace become evident?
5. Why does Paul question prosecuting sexual harassment cases under Title VII of the Civil Rights Act of 1964?
6. On what grounds does Paul argue that women should be prepared to accept a degree of inappropriate behavior in the workplace?
7. Vocabulary: corollary (1), adumbrated (2), malevolent (4), vociferous (5), hyperbole (8), hegemony (10), patriarchal (10), proscribed (12), extortion (13), egregious (13), scatological (14), churlish (16), opprobrium (17).

Questions about Strategy

1. Paul opens her argument with the views she challenges. What is the advantage of this strategy?
2. Does Paul treat sexual harassment lightly, or does she recognize that women have cause for concern?
3. Consider paragraphs 8 and 9. How effectively does Paul challenge statistics showing a high rate of sexual harassment?
4. In paragraph 15, Paul asks, "Do we want the state to prevent or compensate us for any behavior that someone might find offensive?" What answer does she expect to this question? Has she brought you to the point where you are prepared to give it?

ANITA FAYE HILL

MARRIAGE AND PATRONAGE IN THE EMPOWERMENT AND DISEMPOWERMENT OF AFRICAN AMERICAN WOMEN

A lawyer and professor of law, Anita Hill achieved national prominence in 1991 when she gave public testimony against the nomination of Clarence Thomas to the Supreme Court, alleging that Thomas had sexually harassed her when she worked for him at the Office of Civil Rights in the Department of Education. The televised Senate Judiciary Committee hearings drew an enormous audience and prompted a national debate about the credibility not only of Thomas and Hill, but also of the senators conducting the hearings. The youngest of thirteen children, Hill is a graduate of Yale Law School. Honored as "Woman of the Year" by the American Bar Association's Commission on Women in 1992, Hill taught law at the University of Oklahoma until 1996. In this article, first published in *Race, Gender, and Power in America* (1995), Hill argues that racism and sexism were only two of the factors that kept her testimony from being taken seriously by the U.S. Senate. Clarence Thomas's nomination was upheld; he is now a Supreme Court Justice.

Reallocation of power is what confronting racism is about. Throughout the history of this country, African Americans have sought to obtain those things which lead to economic, political, and social power. African American women share with Black men the goal of attaining power, but often we seek it in ways culturally dictated by our gender. Black women also differ from Black men in that the power we seek is denied us because of both our race and our gender. We have sought education, employment, marriage, family, and other group associations, including religious affiliations, in efforts to centralize ourselves in a society that often views us as marginal[1] and our experiences as unessential to the definitions of race and gender.[2]

2   In ways that cannot be measured ... my dual status as Black and as female impaired my ability to present my story to the Senate Judiciary Committee and later to the public. Because of my gender and because of my race, I was then and continue to be on the fringe of what defines the African American community and the community of women.

On October 6, 1991, the press carried reports about the conduct to which I had been subjected by President George Bush's nominee to the Supreme Court, Judge Clarence Thomas. On October 11, 1991, I testified in further detail about this conduct, which I considered relevant to Thomas's competence to hold the position of associate justice of the Supreme Court. The exact sequence of events that led to the publication of my story and to my testimony at a public hearing remains a mystery to me.[3] Yet this much I do know. After inquiries from Senate staffers, I made a statement to the Judiciary Committee. I was assured that my statement would be confidential, used only for purposes of the investigation of Judge Thomas and for the committee's consideration. I never anticipated that once I issued the statement to the committee, I would have no power to control this information about my own experience, its use or its handling. Without my knowledge the statement was apparently leaked to members of the press, who then contacted me for comment and verification. After the press coverage I was contacted by and ultimately subpoenaed to appear before the Judiciary Committee for a public hearing.

4   The decision to hold a hearing about the charges, and in particular a public hearing, was made by the Senate. I had no control over the forum, its focus, its procedures, or its quality, even though it purported to be a hearing about my experience with sexual harassment. The entire structure was set by the Senate committee, the definitive insiders, and I, clearly an outsider, was forced to explain myself. Against this backdrop, it should come as no surprise that the investigation into my statement and the "fact-finding" hearing quickly turned into a "fake trial," in the words of Dennis Curtis.[4] Because of the clearly political focus of the individual senators and the absence of any established rules of procedure, the burden of proof shifted to me. I had to prove myself worthy to speak before the committee; to prove, beyond any doubt, that my testimony was true; and to prove that my experience should matter to the Senate in its capacity to advise and consent on Supreme Court nominations.

In short, I was required to validate myself and my experience within the experiential realm of the members of the Judiciary Committee. The fact that the senators were all men, all White, all powerfully connected, all insiders, and that I, with no political connections, was a dual outsider by virtue of race and gender, made the likelihood of my success remote—and all the more so as I had only two and a half days to prepare for the hearing.

6   In going before the committee, I came face to face with the history of exclusion from power. Notwithstanding many advances over the past three decades, it is hard to deny that as a group African Americans, and in particular African American women, at best can only associate with or approach power. Power and prestige are only given to African American women by license, not ownership, and that license is easily revoked. I cite my treatment by the Judiciary Committee as an example of the limits of power achieved through education or employment. At the beginning of the hearing, as for the previous ten years, I was viewed as a person holding a position of relative social respectability, a law professor at a state university. The rhetoric used to discuss my claim of harassment made my credentials irrelevant. Through their "cross-examination," the senators attempted to show their power in relationship to my powerlessness. In the end I was characterized as a contemptible threat, a vindictive pawn of radical feminists, a victim of erotomania, someone to be viewed at best with pity, at worst with disdain.[5]

The ease with which I was transformed from respected academician to malicious psychotic in the eyes of the public illustrates the tenuousness of my association with power. In sum, my license to speak before the committee as a credible witness was revoked by the tribunal and the process. I was cast as just another African American woman who was not to be trusted to describe her own experiences truthfully and who had no place in the decidedly political arena of the moment. To paraphrase Adele Logan Alexander's discussion, I was no law professor; I was a "niggress."[6]

8   My reality was so different from that of the members of the Senate Judiciary Committee that they found it incomprehensible.[7] They failed or refused to relate to almost every dimension of my race and gender, in combination with my education, my career choice, and my demeanor. Senators Simpson and Specter epitomized this incomprehension. They could not understand why I was not attached to certain institutions, notably marriage, which has traditionally defined the relationship between men and women, and the patronage system, which has often defined the relationship between African Americans and Whites. Because they misunderstood the nature of sexual harassment, the senators raised questions about my sexuality.[8] Because they were unaccustomed to issues presented without official endorsement, they searched for the senator who might have been the sponsor of the claim.

In examining the Judiciary Committee's response to my testimony, it is useful to borrow the terminology of some legal philosophers and literary critics. Through questioning on the first day of the hearing, the senators attempted to "deconstruct" my "narrative," and in the days that followed, to "construct" their own "narratives" to explain what had occurred. Richard Delgado has argued that "narratives are powerful means for destroying mindset—the bundle of presuppositions, received wisdom, and shared understandings against a background of which legal and political discourse take place"; but narratives can also be used, perhaps even more effectively, to maintain prevailing mindsets, as Charles R. Lawrence points out in his discussion of the "Master Narrative," and that is how they functioned during the hearing.[9] Indeed, many senators were simply maintaining a point of view they held even before they heard my testimony, as Charles J. Ogletree notes.[10] Because my narrative did not comport with their mindset, their assumptions about what was true and real, it had to be reconstructed—a task they undertook with assistance from the press, Thomas supporters, and Thomas witnesses. The senators claimed they had no experience with the kind of behavior I described. Thus, rather than entertain the idea that I was telling the truth, they concluded that I must be lying, and concocted an explanation based on their understanding of race and gender relationships.

10   According to the reality of the committee, "women are married, or have been, or plan to be, or suffer from not being."[11] In the senators' narrative, therefore, I was single because I was unmarriageable or opposed to marriage, the fantasizing spinster or the man-hater.

According to the reality of the committee, every opposition is politically motivated. In the senators' narrative, therefore, I was part of a left-wing conspiracy to "Bork" the Thomas nomination.*

12   According to the reality of the committee, every Washington outsider worthy of interest has a patron to confer legitimacy at official proceedings like the hearings and to navigate the corridors of power. Clarence Thomas had such a patron in Senator Danforth. The fact that I had none, and chose to speak for myself, aroused suspicion. In the senators' narrative, therefore, I was acting at the urging of Democrats who opposed Thomas or as an agent for radical feminists.

According to the reality of the committee, sexual harassment is a rare phenomenon, and in the few instances where it does occur outside the imaginations of delusional or vindictive women, it is committed only by depraved, easily identified males. In the senators' narrative, therefore—because Thomas was not identifiably depraved, and despite the scientific data about the prevalence of sexual harassment in the workplace and the rarity of false claims—I was the spiteful, spurned woman who was suffering romantic disappointment or the pathetic erotomaniac who was so deluded as to actually believe what she said.

14   According to the reality of the committee, my career success as an African American and as a woman had nothing to do with my qualifications and everything to do with the myth of the double advantage enjoyed by women of color.[12] In the senators' narrative, therefore, I was aloof and ambitious, an incompetent product of affirmative action and an ingrate who betrayed the man who had done me a favor by hiring me.

According to the reality of the committee, and of much of society, women, particularly African American women, cannot be trusted to tell the truth in matters concerning sexual misconduct. In the senators' narrative, therefore (within the framework first introduced by Freud to explain female patients' stories of incest), my story became a fantasy fueled by desire for the object of the story, "stuff . . . from the moon" and at the same time "stuff" from *The Exorcist*.[13]

16   It was this reconstruction of me—a portrait of a dangerous, unbelievable, ambitious, disappointed woman—that the senators used to justify the warning to "watch out for Anita Hill." The portrait was further reinforced by the retelling of the stories of Janet Cooke and Tawana Brawley by some commentators and editorial writers.[14] Various senators and their collaborators struggled to place me as far outside the norms of proper behavior as they could, painting me as simultaneously prudish yet lewd, easily duped yet shrewd and ambitious, fantasizing yet calculating, pathetic yet evil.[15]

The irrelevance of the narrative the senators constructed would have been apparent had they taken an honest look at the workplace and power relationships and explored the assumptions their insider status made invisible

---

* The 1987 nomination to the Supreme Court of Robert H. Bork was defeated by critics who found his views too conservative.

to them. Other contributors to this collection have written about some of these assumptions and their impact on African Americans and women. On the issue of sexual harassment, for instance, Susan Deller Ross has discussed its pervasiveness and the difficulty of bringing forth and pursuing charges; Adele Logan Alexander has delineated the multilayered reality of Black women's lives and the stereotypes against which they must struggle.[16] Had the senators availed themselves of the information on the nature of sexual harassment prepared for them by experts in the social sciences like Dr. Louise Fitzgerald, instead of excluding it from the record, they might have recognized the seriousness of sexual harassment as a social problem. Had they or their staffers even a rudimentary familiarity with the case law on sexual harassment, they would have understood that the language and behavior I described are common in many modern work settings and that the standards and procedures adopted by the committee were neither legally acceptable nor helpful in getting to the truth. Had the senators paid more than perfunctory attention to gender issues, as Judith Resnik explains, they might have understood the relevance of Thomas's behavior and views on gender subordination to his fitness to serve on the Supreme Court.[17] Had they been aware of the complex resonance of a claim of sexual misconduct raised by a Black woman, they might have stopped trying to invent a stereotypical and untrue portrait of me against which I was forced to defend myself.

18   The hearings indeed brought to the surface many negative preconceptions about African Americans in general and African American women in particular (though the senators' concerns about stereotyping were confined to negative stereotypical assumptions about Black males[18]). In the limited space of this paper I want to focus on two strategies that Black Americans, especially Black women as outsiders, have adopted to attain insider status in the face of these preconceptions: patronage and marriage. I want to address the cultural and social price one may pay for rejecting those institutions as the basis of one's identity. Specifically, I argue that my unwillingness to establish an association with power through marriage and patronage reduced my credibility in the eyes of the Senate Judiciary Committee and the public. Finally, I assert that Black women must claim our experiences and develop a sense of power based on the value of those experiences.

Patronage

One of the ways African Americans associate with power is by acquiring a patron, or in some cases having a patron imposed on them. Patronage, seemingly a universal concept, has had some peculiar manifestations in African American history. It has been argued that patronage in the slave South was part of the slaveholder's paternalistic vision of himself as an "authoritarian father," and that Blacks shared or endorsed this vision—ideas perhaps impossible to verify in the context of slavery.[19] Whether the active or the passive interpretation more accurately describes the interaction between African

Americans and Whites, patronage is part of the history of race relations in this country.

20   During slavery African Americans relied on the patronage of slave-holders for their very survival, both physical and economic. The slave codes stipulated that slaves could not leave a plantation without permission, and that if they did, any White person finding them could turn them over to public officials. When insurrections were rumored, vigilante committees randomly murdered and lynched African Americans, both slave and free, both male and female.[20] In some states the codes were more elaborate and severe than in others. In Georgia, for example, "slaves could not travel out-side Savannah or their own plantation without a ticket or letter from their master. Nor could they travel in groups of more than seven slaves without a 'white person.' They could not carry firearms during the week without . . . the supervision of a white person."[21] Thus, the patronage system was in-jected into the culture by statute.

    Since the only penalties against killing a slave were tied to interference with the slaveowner's property rights, it was incumbent on slaves outside the plantation to establish their owners' patronage. Those who could not were presumed to be runaways, and since there were no penalties for killing runaways, proof of patronage became crucial. Physical survival compelled slaves to seek the protection of their owners. And for both the enslaved and the free African American, economic survival often depended on patronage as well. Slaves had no right to interest in property, whether real, personal, or intellectual. Slaves could not own the expression of their ideas. "Slaves could not 'buy, sell, or exchange any goods, wares, provisions, grains, victuals, or commodities' of any sort without a special license." Slave inventors were ini-tially prohibited from applying for patents in their own names or even in the name of their owner, but in 1861 the Confederate Congress passed a provision allowing a patent to be issued to the owner if he "took an oath that his slave had actually invented a device."[22] Even early slave narratives had to be sanctioned by or "told to" a White patron; without a patron the text was assumed to have no validity.[23]

22   Vestiges of the patronage relationship between African Americans and Whites can be seen in recent stories of African Americans who have been stopped by law enforcement officials, questioned, and even arrested because they were alone in White neighborhoods and could not explain why they were there. Derrick Bell, in *And We Are Not Saved*, describes the sense of powerlessness experienced by a young African American military officer who wandered into an unfamiliar area. Ultimately his military uniform per-suaded a state trooper that he was not the suspect wanted by local law offi-cials. Later in life, a respected attorney and law professor, the man relives this experience when he has to invoke the name of a law school dean and a university president before a police officer will let him counsel a woman stopped for speeding. His patronage is established by professional associa-tions and by dress, but he bitterly resents that it remains a necessity of his existence.[24]

For many individuals the struggle to attain power begins with seeking education and powerful associations, but for African American women, because of our unique history, established institutions and networks take on greater significance as we attempt to overcome society's negative presumptions about us. Despite apparent gains and the myth of the double advantage, Black women are overrepresented in service occupations: private household worker, cook, housekeeper, welfare aide, and other jobs that offer little autonomy and are subject to high levels of personal control by individual employers.[25] Not only is it harder for Black women to attain certain educational, workplace, social, and cultural positions of status, but when we do, we are not rewarded commensurately. According to the 1989 census figures, Black women earned 60.9 cents for every dollar earned by a White male, compared to 68.5 cents earned by White females. Moreover, the difference in earnings cannot be explained by education alone. In 1985 the Census Bureau reported that differences in education, labor force experience, and commitment accounted for only 14.6 percent of the wage gap between women and men.[26]

24 In modern educational training and professional life, the role of the patron cannot be underestimated. No matter how impressive their credentials, individuals of all races, female and male, need sponsors in business and mentors in academia. Inside the beltway, patronage is part of the political culture and is critical to political survival. The political patrons of Washington, D.C., sponsor bills, programs, and individuals. It is understood that as the patron goes, so goes the beneficiary.[27] At least one commentator has attributed some of the problems in Lani Guinier's failed nomination as assistant attorney general for civil rights to her lack of a patron. "On Capitol Hill," Mark Shields remarked, "it's better to have one tiger than a hundred pussycats—in other words, one legislator who feels that his or her fate, fortune, or future is tied to her cause. Lani Guinier lacked that."[28]

Patronage in education, politics, and the professional sphere helps to establish an individual's relationship to the powerful, though it may not confer insider status. For African American women, the ultimate outsiders, participation in patronage relationships is crucial. However, the patronage system can be a double-edged sword. For a Black woman who attempts to make it on her own, whatever her class or position, refusing a patron can be as harmful as having one can be beneficial. And aligning herself with the wrong patron, one who harbors negative presumptions about race or gender can be even more devastating.

26 The story of Sofia in Alice Walker's *The Color Purple* vividly illustrates the problem of refusing patronage. In a key scene, two White characters, the Mayor and his wife, Millie, encounter Sofia, her friend the prizefighter, and Sofia's children on the street. "All these children. . . . Cute as little buttons though . . . and such strong teeth," says Millie. She looks at Sofia and the prizefighter, at his car and Sofia's wristwatch, remarks that Sofia's children are "so clean," and asks if Sofia would like to be her maid. Sofia emphatically rejects the offer: "Hell no." In response, the Mayor strikes Sofia, and then

she knocks him down. In the ensuing fight Sofia is brutally beaten by six policemen. She is later imprisoned.[29]

In prior passages Walker has made it clear that Sofia is no stereotypical "lazy Black." Sofia enjoys work. She is seen working in the fields, cleaning and cutting shingles to repair the roof. What Sofia rejects is not the work of being the maid for the Mayor and Millie but their patronage and the patronizing behavior toward her and her children.

28   Sofia's refusal is viewed as a threat to her would-be patrons; to contain that threat she has to be beaten and imprisoned both physically and psychologically. It seems she also poses a threat to other Blacks who feel a stake in the patronage system. When Sofia's father-in-law, a man who "know he colored," is sent as an envoy to plead with the sheriff to allow Sofia visitors, he agrees with the sheriff's description of Sofia as crazy, tries to excuse her on the grounds that she comes from a crazy family, and adds that the sheriff "know how women is."[30] In sum, when Sofia challenges the patronage system, White society punishes her, and in response her family must disavow her behavior to assure those in power that Sofia is wrong (crazy) and that the system is correct.

Most evident from the televised Judiciary Committee hearings was the fact that I sat in that hearing room without a patron on the panel. That image still resonates. My sin was not simply that I did not have a patron. Nor was it simply that I rejected patronage offered to me, since none was offered. My initial sin in the eyes of the senators was that I dared to come to the body on my own, that I did not actively pursue patronage at the outset. No senator, either Democrat or Republican, acted on behalf of my right to speak before the committee. None was sought. As Judith Resnik notes, I was allowed to speak only after public pressure made it nearly impossible for the Senate to ignore my statement.[31] I and then the public challenged the senators' system.

30   As the process continued and I prepared for the "fact-finding" hearing, my counsel and I did not focus on getting a key senator to act as my advocate; instead we relied on the weight of my testimony and the fairness of the process as we thought it should be. Again I unwittingly denied the patronage system, which is an entrenched part of Washington's political culture. In refusing to rely on this system, I implicitly questioned it and posed a challenge to those invested in it. The response was to strike back at me, the challenger. Even neutral commentators have criticized my counsel for not having organized in more political terms.[32] I thus wandered into Washington, D.C., without a patron or even a proper letter of introduction, and with no apparent explanation of how I came to be there; like the slave who wandered off the plantation, I was without my papers, so to speak. Though I was able to gain a forum without the patronage of a committee member, it quickly became clear that I would be punished for my temerity as Senator Simpson threatened me with "plain old Washington variety harassment" for raising the issue of sexual harassment,[33] and as the senators struggled to regain the control and power they perceived they had lost during the events that led to the second round of hearings.

Marriage

Marriage, as described by Simone de Beauvoir, is a form of patronage, but a distinct form. In *The Second Sex* de Beauvoir says that "for girls marriage is the only means of integration in the community" and that it is a joint enterprise with man as "the economic head through which woman gets some share in the world as her own." Of marriage in America, de Beauvoir writes, "A single woman in America . . . is a socially incomplete being even if she makes her own living; if she is to attain the whole dignity of a person and gain her full rights, she must wear a wedding ring."[34] In other words, marriage provides a way for a woman to establish her social, economic, and cultural insider status.

32   More recently Susan Faludi has debunked some of the many myths about modern marriage and shown the power of marital status as a social weapon used against single working women. Faludi traces the characterization of the single woman as "social misfit" from the Victorian press into the 1980s. She cites *Newsweek*'s unbalanced coverage of two conflicting stories about the demographics of marriage in the United States. An unpublished study that foretold "The Spinster Boom" was given greater play than a contradictory Census Bureau study because the former confirmed "impressions [the editorial staff] already had" that single women, among other things, "are more likely to be killed by a terrorist" than to marry. *Newsweek* went on to give further space to the lamentable plight of the single woman.[35]

As insightful as de Beauvoir's and Faludi's observations are, they are based on the White American model of marriage and its role in American culture.* That model is helpful in that it is the model many slaves and freedmen and their descendants were urged to follow, but marriage in this country has also been a "peculiar institution" for African Americans.[36] Though marriage between slaves was prohibited in some states and not legally recognized in others, historians believe that "the slave family was a viable institution."[37] Despite formal and informal opposition, African Americans embraced marriage as an institution during slavery. After the Civil War, former slaves sought to legalize unions made during slavery and to establish new marriages. Nevertheless, the model of a marriage with the husband working outside the home and the wife working only in the home was irrelevant to the slave experience, and has been largely irrelevant to the situation of many African Americans ever since. For them, the economic struggle was and is a shared experience.[38]

34   Work patterns among African American couples were not the only point of deviation from the White American model of marriage. In some instances African American attitudes about female subordination in marriage differed from the model as well. Though some freedmen urged their brethren "to get the woman in the proper place" for the good of the race, others advocated the full partnership of women in the struggle for equality.[39] Some African American women preferred the traditional concept of

* For an alternative discussion of this model, see pp. 264–273.

marriage because it exempted them from the double duty of working out-side and within the home, while others, unaccustomed to domination by a male partner during slavery, were not disposed to "subordination to mascu-line authority" in the post-slavery period.[40] At times the insistence on male dominance within the African American marriage took on a physical ex-pression in the form of wife beating.[41]

Derrick Bell captures the ambivalence about marriage in today's African American community in a chapter of *And We Are Not Saved* entitled "The Race-Charged Relationship between Black Men and Black Women: Chronicle of the Twenty-Seven-Year Syndrome." The female protagonist of Bell's book, Geneva Crenshaw, rejects the ideals of patriarchy as an answer to problems in Black female–male relationships, though the author seems to embrace them. He describes a disease contracted only by Black women who have achieved above-average educational or professional status. Those af-flicted by this disease, the Twenty-Seven-Year Syndrome, fall into a sleep and awaken after four to six weeks to find that they have lost their professional skills and have to be retrained for the workplace. No cure is found, but the disease can be prevented if a woman in the susceptible category marries a Black male before reaching the age of twenty-seven. "Women who were or had been married to, or who had received a serious offer of marriage from, a black man, seemed immune to the strange malady."[42] Though Geneva Cren-shaw makes compelling arguments against the author's choice of solutions to the problem of the Twenty-Seven-Year Syndrome, in the end Bell argues that maintaining "traditional" male–female relationships is crucial for African Americans and ultimately necessary to achieve racial justice.[43]

36   Along with its obvious benefits, the difficulties of modern marriage have been widely publicized. Despite these difficulties, those who reject tradi-tional marriage as an institution based on female-to-male subordination have been criticized from within and outside the African American community, and some analysts and public officials have suggested that many social and economic problems would be solved if women married before having chil-dren. They have even placed the responsibility for urban violence and unrest, delinquency, crime, and drug use on single mothers, who bear two out of three African American children, according to recent census statistics. Or-lando Patterson, for one, argues that the problems of young Black males are largely attributable to their mothers.[44] For all the debates, marriage continues to reflect a measure of social and economic success within the Black commu-nity. Though only one in four Black females below the age of forty is married, marriage is still equated with sexual desirability and sexual preference.[45]

During the Judiciary Committee hearings, as the legal burden of proof was either ignored, misunderstood, or deliberately misstated, it was left to me to prove myself politically and socially acceptable. Much was made in the press of the fact that I was single, though the relevance of my marital status to the question of sexual harassment was never articulated. Some of this attention was provoked by the insinuations of Clarence Thomas, Sena-tor Simpson, and journalist William Safire. Simpson tried to discredit my claim by referring to my sexual "proclivities," and Safire later elaborated upon the phrase.[46]

38 In raising questions about my marital status, the senators were apparently attempting to establish a relationship between marriage, values, and credibility. The scrutiny of my marital status caused people to wonder in an uninformed way why I, a thirty-five-year-old Black woman, had chosen to pursue a career and to remain single—an irrelevant shift of focus that contributed to the conclusion that I was not to be believed. This conclusion about credibility not only required a leap of logic but an ignorance of the facts of my existence. Though neither logic nor facts should have been forgone by the committee, both were. As the youngest of thirteen children, I have long embraced family values. The extended family is part of our tradition, as it is for many African Americans. Though we respect marriage, being single does not exile me from my family and its values, or from African American culture. Nor does being single in today's America equate with the rejection of values, traditional or otherwise. Linking credibility in questions of sexual harassment to marriage presumes that single women are not sexually harassed or that they should carry an extra burden of proving that they are. Marital status should never be a factor in assessing anyone's veracity, but the hearing turned into an exercise in measuring veracity by social and political clout. And as both de Beauvoir and Faludi point out, marriage is a symbol of power for many.

If my lack of a husband preoccupied certain members of the committee and the press, there was another dynamic at work in the African American community. To some Blacks, neither the truth of my claim nor the illegality of harassment mattered; the central issue was that I had violated a spoken or unspoken norm of the African American community—what Emma Jordan calls "gag order" placed on African American women who suffer abuse at the hands of African American men.[47] In the eyes of some, a declaration of such abuse diminishes the Black community in relation to the White community. This violation damned me in the eyes of many Blacks whose profound experiences of racism have led them to ignore within our own community what we find intolerable when committed by others against us. Because I seemed to break the racial solidarity rule, some in the African American community attempted to reconstruct me as a pawn of radical feminists, even though I had no contact at all with "the feminists" before the hearings. Though mostly concerned with what they viewed as the political problems I created by coming forward, partisan detractors eventually exploited my breach of the norm of the African American community in their efforts to discredit me. I had disrupted the regrettably politicized process *and* created community disharmony by giving harmful testimony against the president's nominee, a Black judge.

40 A passage from Zora Neale Hurston's *Their Eyes Were Watching God* perhaps best illustrates my feelings when I came before the Judiciary Committee, having challenged the norms of that body, of society, and of the Black community. Hurston's protagonist, Janie, has also committed a list of

sins according to the standards of her community. Ultimately her transgressions involve the legal system as well, when she is tried for the murder of her
third husband, Tea Cake, an act committed in self-defense. Hurston describes Janie's trial as follows:

> The court set and Janie saw the judge who had put on a great robe to listen
> about her and Tea Cake. And twelve more white men had stopped whatever
> they were doing to listen and pass on what happened. That was funny too.
> Twelve strange men who didn't know a thing about people like Tea Cake and
> her were going to sit on the thing. . . .
>   Then she saw all of the colored people standing up in the back of the
> courtroom. . . . They were all against her, she could see. So many were there
> against her that a light slap from each one of them would have beat her to
> death.[48]

Janie recognizes her dual role. First she has to prove that she has operated within the constraints of a legal system that was not established with
her and her experiences in mind, and then she has to prove herself and her
acts socially acceptable to a community concerned with its own established
norms of behavior. Likewise, before a Senate committee that understood
neither the experience nor the law of sexual harassment, I was forced to
make my case. And before a community that cared less about gender subordination and harassment than about a definition of racial survival driven by
racism, I had to atone for my sin of "bringing down a brother."

42   Though Janie strikes the reader of *Their Eyes Were Watching God* as an
individual who wrestles for control of her life and destiny, in the end she is
judged under circumstances beyond her control. For deviating from certain
societal expectations, Janie is first tried by a court made up of those who
cannot relate to her experience and then ostracized by her peers who will
not. Though Janie is ultimately forgiven and brought back into the fold, the
pain of the initial rejection and distrust of her story remains with her and
with her community.

Through Whose Eyes, in Whose Voice: The Telling of African American Women's Stories

As the hearings came to a close, many commentators expressed concern that
women would be less likely to file harassment claims because of the committee's harsh treatment of me and the dismissal of my complaint. The
commentators were wrong; ironically, the hearings had the opposite effect
as record numbers of women came forward with sexual harassment complaints in their aftermath.

44   Ultimately the committee's characterization of me as just another
woman who was to be viewed with immediate skepticism allowed other
women to relate to me and my experience. Though the senators claimed to
be shocked by the possibility of the behavior I described, many working
women of color and White working women knew the scenario well. Many

had had similar experiences, some much more egregious; most had never complained, as the senators were sure they would have if the harassment had really occurred, and even fewer had documented it, except in memory. The senators' incredulous reaction painfully reminded women of that incongruous, though typical, gender-biased response to any woman who reports a sexual assault: "It couldn't have happened. What did you do to provoke it?" And while the racial implications of the senators' incredulity were not fully explored by the press, they did not escape many Black women.

Just as the members of the Senate Judiciary Committee told their narratives about the experience of harassment, so did those of us who were outsiders to the political maneuvering that marked the hearing. Our narratives were often in conflict with the senators' and were often unspoken in all but the most private of conversations. Since the hearings, we have begun to tell the stories of those "whose voice and perspective—whose consciousness (and experiences)—have been suppressed, devalued and abnormalized."[49] And finally we have begun to go public with those stories. Adele Logan Alexander has shown how pervasively and effectively African American women have been silenced.[50] Now it is our responsibility to share our own narratives lest the world conclude that our unique experiences do not count in defining what it means to be a woman or what it means to be African American. In seeking to understand gender, our history, our received wisdom, and our shared perceptions must not be omitted or lost in the outpouring of other voices. In describing the impact of race and racism on the African American community, our peculiar pain must be acknowledged if the story is to be complete. We must claim the right to speak of both race and gender. We must not contribute to our own trivialization by remaining silent about our existence. Any achievement of real power for all African Americans and for all women requires no less.

46   The imagery presented by the hearings has given us new impetus and opportunity to refute the stereotypes that are part of our culture and that were reinforced by the scene in the Judiciary Committee hearing room. We can now stop deluding ourselves about how far we have come on race and gender issues and take a good long look at where African American women are and how we got here. We can make the examination without the filter of old sexually charged stereotypes and modern myths about the political and cultural benefits of our dual status. We can replace the stock images with new ones that do not depend on association with power in some of its traditional forms.[51] We can tell our stories.

One of the most poignant expressions of the beginnings of our willingness to share our narratives was an advertisement taken out by African American women from all over the country in various publications, including the *New York Times*.[52] The women's statement called attention to the painful part of our history that perpetuates the abuse and demeaning of African American women in general, and in particular when they raise claims of sexual misconduct. The women vowed that they would not "tolerate this type of dismissal of any one Black woman's experience or this attack upon our collective character without protest, outrage, and resistance." Their piercing observations are a clarion call for African American women to introduce our narratives into the discourse that ultimately defines the normative universe in which we reside.[53] A group of African American men also issued a statement warning against the misuse of the history of Black people for political gain, and asserting that the committee's failure to "thoroughly investigate Professor Hill's claim" would be a fundamental insult to all Black women.[54] I would add that it was an insult to the African American community and the community of all women.

48   Ironically, we must share our history, through narrative, with the often resistant African American community as well as the larger American society. Yet I believe that our credibility as a community turns on our willingness to address wrongs within as well as outside it. Equality begins at home.[55] Racial equality cannot be gained at the expense of gender equality. Reallocation of power is what including African American women in the confrontation with racism is about. ❖

Notes

1. Kimberlé Crenshaw, "Demarginalizing the Intersection of Race and Gender in Antidiscrimination Law, Feminist Theory, and Antiracist Politics," 1989 *Chicago Legal Forum* 139.
2. Angela Harris, "Race and Essentialism in Feminist Legal Theory," 42 *Stanford L. Rev.* 581 (1990).
3. See the accounts in Timothy Phelps and Helen Winternitz, *Capitol Games,* 229–33 (1992); and Jane Mayer and Jill Abramson, *Strange Justice: The Selling of Clarence Thomas* (1994), chap. 12, "The Leak."
4. Dennis E. Curtis, "The Fake Trial," 65 *So. Calif. L. Rev.* 1523 (1992).
5. Senator Simpson claimed to have devastating information about me yet later refused to make the information public or be more specific about it. See "The Thomas Nomination; Senator Simpson Refuses to Make Public Letters He Says Criticize Hill," *N.Y. Times,* October 14, 1991.
6. Adele Logan Alexander, " 'She's No Lady, She's a Nigger,' " in *Race, Gender, and Power in America,* ed. Anita Faye Hill and Emma Coleman Jordan, 18 (1995).
7. This parallels the experience of many women of color who are met with confusion and disbelief in the professional world. See Constance Baker Motley's essay in Goldman and Gallen, *Thurgood Marhsall: Justice for All,* 162 (1992).
8. See note 46, *infra.*
9. Richard Delgado, "Storytelling for Oppositionists and Others: A Plea for Narrative," 87 *Michigan L. Rev.* at 2413 (1989); Charles R. Lawrence, "The Message of the Verdict," in *Race, Gender, and Power in America,* 107–11 (1995).
10. Charles J. Ogletree, "The People vs. Anita Hill," in *Race, Gender, and Power in America,* 143–44 (1995). (Citing statements by Senators Hatch and Simpson on October 8 indicating that they did not believe me.)
11. Simone de Beauvoir, *The Second Sex,* 474 (1953).
12. See Pamela Smith, "We Are Not Sisters: African American Women and the Freedom to Associate and Disassociate," 66 *Tulane L. Rev.* 1467 (1992).
13. Recall from the hearings that Senator Hatch accused me of inventing my story based on a passage from *The Exorcist.* Senator Simpson described my testimony in the following manner: "And the stuff we listened to, I mean, you know, come on—from the moon." *Nomination of Judge Clarence Thomas to Be Associate Justice of the Supreme*

Court, Hearings before the Committee on the Judiciary, 102d Cong., 1st Sess. (Committee Print Draft), October 11–13, 1991, at 191–92, 235.

14. See Dickerson, "Why Is Anita Hill Out to Get Judge Thomas?" *Atlanta Constitution,* October 11, 1991, at A12. Janet Cooke is a journalist who invented characters in a prize-winning story that was published as nonfiction. Tawana Brawley accused law enforcement officers of a grotesque and racially motivated sexual assault and abduction. Investigators later concluded that the accusation was false. Cooke and Brawley are both African American women.
15. See Patricia J. Williams, "The Bread and Circus Literary Test," *Ms.,* January–February 1992.
16. Susan Deller Ross. "Sexual Harassment Law in the Aftermath of the Hill-Thomas Hearings," in *Race, Gender, and Power in America,* 228–41 (1995); Alexander, " 'She's No Lady, She's a Nigger,' " in *Race, Gender, and Power in America,* 3–25 (1995).
17. Judith Resnik, "From the Senate Judiciary Committee to the Country Courthouse," in *Race, Gender, and Power in America,* 177–227 (1995).
18. See the statements of Senators Hatch and Simpson, *Hearings, supra* note 13, at 187–89, 235.
19. See Herbert G. Gutman, *The Black Family in Slavery and Freedom, 1750–1925* (1976).
20. See Franklin and Moss, *From Slavery to Freedom,* 6th ed., 122–25 (describing the slave codes throughout the South) (1988).
21. A. Leon Higginbotham, Jr., *In the Matter of Color: Race and the American Legal Process—The Colonial Period,* 258 (1978).
22. *Id.*
23. See, e.g., Harriet Jacobs, *Incidents in the Life of a Slave Girl* (1861), which was sponsored by white abolitionist Lydia Maria Child.
24. Derrick Bell, *And We Are Not Saved: The Elusive Quest for Racial Justice,* 181–84 (1987).
25. See National Committee on Pay Equity, "The Wage Gap: Myths and Facts," reprinted in Rothenberg, *Race, Class, and Gender in the United States,* 129–36 (1992).
26. *Id.* See also Staff Report, United States Commission on Civil Rights, *The Economic Status of Black Women: An Exploratory Investigation* (1990).
27. See Phelps and Winternitz, *supra* note 3, for a discussion of John Danforth's role as Clarence Thomas's patron.
28. Mark Shields, *MacNeil/Lehrer News Hour,* PBS, June 4, 1993.
29. Alice Walker, *The Color Purple,* 75–76 (1982).
30. *Id.* at 77–79.
31. Resnik, "From the Senate Judiciary Committee to the Country Courthouse," in *Race, Gender, and Power in America,* 178 (1995).
32. See Phelps and Winternitz, *supra* note 3, at 306: "What Hill really needed was a political advance team, but there had been neither the time nor the inclination to assemble one."
33. *Cong. Rec.,* Senate 14545–46, October 8, 1991.
34. De Beauvoir, *supra* note 11, at 477–80.
35. Susan Faludi, *Backlash: The Undeclared War against American Women,* 95–101 (1991).
36. See generally Gutman, *supra* note 19, who dismisses the impact of African history and tradition on slave culture and on the slave marriage and family.
37. See Franklin and Moss, *supra* note 20, at 127 (citing John Blassingame and Herbert Gutman).
38. Franklin and Moss suggest that the stability of the slave marriage "depended on the extent to which the couple had an opportunity to work together and live together so that through common experiences they could be drawn closer together." *Id.* Ironically, Aburdene and Naisbitt report that the collaborative couple that works as a team on an economic enterprise is "making creative partnerships a new paradigm for the 21st century." *Megatrends for Women,* 165 (1992).

39. Paula Giddings, *When and Where I Enter: The Impact of Black Women on Race and Sex in America,* 58 (1984).

40. *Id.*

41. *Id.* at 64.

42. Bell, *supra* note 24, at 199.

43. Other scholars disagree. See Angela Davis, *Women, Culture, and Politics,* 75 (1989): ". . . to focus myopically on family problems as the basis for the oppression of the Afro-American community—as if setting the family in order will automatically eradicate poverty—is to espouse the fallacious 'blame the victim' argument."

44. Orlando Patterson, "The Crisis of Gender Relations among African Americans," in *Race, Gender, and Power in America,* 56–104 (1995).

45. See Davis, *supra* note 43, 75–76.

46. William Safire, "The Plot to Savage Thomas," *N.Y. Times,* October 14, 1991; and "About Men: Cordialities and Crushes," *N.Y. Times Magazine,* November 3, 1991, 18. In both pieces Safire mentions Senator Simpson's references to information about my "proclivities" received in "letters and faxes." Safire goes further than Simpson to explain that the term "was used sneakily—to hint at homosexuality," and goes on to admonish Simpson that "if he has evidence that the accuser's sexual preference is related to her reluctance to bring a charge of sexual harassment, let him make the case or shut up." Safire's remarks were read as veiled approval couched in the form of a reprimand of Simpson. Interestingly, Safire not only assumed that Simpson had information but also presumed the validity of the unsworn "letters and faxes" and of Simpson's conclusion about my sexual preference. At the same time, Safire expressed complete disbelief in my sworn testimony and statements.

47. Emma Coleman Jordan, "The Power of False Racial Memory," in *Race, Gender, and Power in America,* 37–55 (1995).

48. Zora Neale Hurston, *Their Eyes Were Watching God,* at 89 (1937; reprint, 1978).

49. Delgado, *supra* note 9, at n. 29.

50. Alexander, " 'She's No Lady, She's a Nigger,' " in *Race, Gender, and Power in America,* 3–25 (1995).

51. Many who believed me were persuaded by my association with traditional values, education, middle-class economic status, and religion. The significance of these factors for them has not gone unnoticed by me. Their significance for me is that they illustrate that like most people, I am not a monolithic stereotype. The stereotype of the superwoman is just as unyielding and unrealistic as that of the welfare queen. The image of the African American woman I hope for will reflect the multiple dimensions of our lives.

52. Reprinted in Chrisman and Allen, eds., *Court of Appeal: The Black Community Speaks Out on the Racial and Sexual Politics of Thomas vs. Hill,* 292 (1992).

53. See generally Cover, "The Supreme Court Forward: Nomos and Narrative," 97 *Harvard L. Rev.* 40.

54. Statement of Concern of African American Men, October 13, 1991 (on file with the author).

55. In the summer of 1995 a group of African American women protested the endorsement of violence against Black women symbolized by the tickertape homecoming parade planned for convicted rapist Mike Tyson. Though many in the community decried the women's protest as "Black male bashing," eventually they were heard. The parade was cancelled.

Questions for Meaning

1. Why does the status of black women in the United States differ from that of black men? What does Hill mean by "the myth of the double advantage"?

2. Under what circumstances did Hill initially agree to offer testimony about Clarence Thomas? Did she have any say in the decision to televise her testimony?
3. What did the members of the Senate Judiciary Committee have in common? According to Hill, what were their limitations?
4. What does Hill mean by "narrative"?
5. Does the legitimacy of a sexual harassment complaint depend in any way on the marital status of the people involved? Would Hill have been treated differently if she had been married at the time of her testimony?
6. How did other African Americans respond to Hill's testimony against Clarence Thomas?
7. Did Hill's experience with the Senate Judiciary Committee have any effect on the willingness of other women to speak openly about sexual harassment?
8. Vocabulary: reallocation (1), experiential (5), erotomania (6), presuppositions (9), comport (9), prudish (16), paternalistic (19), vestiges (22), invoke (22), commensurately (23), resonates (29), temerity (30), debunked (32), ostracized (42), egregious (44), clarion (47).

Questions about Strategy

1. Hill writes about her own personal experience, knowing that many Americans disbelieved her testimony before the Senate Judiciary Committee. What strategies does she use in this essay to establish her credibility?
2. Hill devotes six paragraphs (10–15) to describing what she calls "the reality of the committee," and each of these paragraphs begins with the same phrase. How does this strategy affect you? What would be the effect of combining these paragraphs into a single paragraph?
3. Why does Hill discuss slavery? Is this discussion relevant to the issue of sexual harassment in the workplace?
4. Hill draws on two novels by African American women, Alice Walker's *The Color Purple*, and Zora Neale Hurston's *Their Eyes Were Watching God*. How useful is fiction as evidence for her case?
5. Consider the use of "we" and "our" in paragraphs 45 and 46. What conclusions can you make about Hill's sense of audience?

HARSH LUTHAR AND ANTHONY TOWNSEND

MAN HANDLING

"Man Handling" was first published in *The National Review,* a monthly magazine known for advocating politically conservative positions. When it appeared there in 1995, Harsh Luthar was an assistant professor of management at Bryant College and Anthony Townsend was an assistant professor of management at the University of Nevada, Las Vegas. As you read, consider how helpful their ideas would be for people preparing to supervise other people in the workplace.

Although a popular success, *Disclosure* was derided by feminists who considered its premise—sexual harassment of a man by a woman—silly at best, dangerous at worst. After all, everyone knows sexual harassment is something a man does to a woman. That assumption is reflected in the Equal Employment Opportunity Commission's guidelines on sexual harassment, where the harasser is always a "he" and the victim a "she." You have to refer to a footnote to verify that the law, in theory, protects men as well as women.

2   Most of the published research on sexual harassment agrees: women are victims; men are harassers. In surveys, some 40 per cent of women report being harassed at work, compared to a negligible proportion of men. When men do report harassment, their harassers are often other men.

But these indicators may not give us an accurate picture of what is going on. To begin with, the leading sexual-harassment researchers are feminist ideologues who are mainly concerned with finding evidence of patriarchal oppression. They design their studies accordingly: most of the research does not even include male subjects.

4   More to the point, most men would not recognize sexual harassment if it hit them in the face. Ask a number of men if they have been harassed, and nine out of ten, will say, "No, but I'd like to be." Men generally do not consider teasing, sexual jokes, and lewd innuendoes from female co-workers harassment; they are not upset by the kinds of comments and incidents that have brought female plaintiffs millions of dollars in awards for "hostile environment" claims. In a recent lawsuit against the Jenny Craig diet organization by several male employees, one of the plaintiffs said he initially liked it when the women he worked with told him he had a nice body. He and the others did not file suit until they were denied promotions, were assigned to poor sales territories, or were terminated from the organization. After examining their complaint, the Massachusetts Commission Against Discrimination found probable cause of gender bias in the organization's actions against the men.

Since men are not sensitive to harassing behavior that women (or at least feminists) construe as harassment, it's not surprising that they are not filing many harassment complaints. Consider a scenario. A young man gets a job as an assistant manager in a bank. His boss, a member of the National Association of Bank Women, often talks about the importance of mentoring young women and complains that men have created a glass ceiling that oppresses female managers. Her coffee mug is emblazoned with an anti-male statement. To top it off, she and the other women who work in the branch often tell dirty jokes in which men are portrayed derogatorily. There's little question that this man is the victim of a "hostile environment," one that may well interfere with his ability to perform his duties. But if you ask him whether he has been sexually harassed, he will probably say no.

6   To get beyond this barrier, male subjects in harassment surveys should be asked not whether they have been sexually harassed but whether certain kinds of behavior have occurred. When we ask male undergraduates if they have ever been sexually harassed by a female instructor, almost all of them say no. But when we ask if they have experienced specific types of treatment in a female instructor's classroom, such as derogatory or off-color comments about men, some 60 per cent of them report such incidents.

As for "sleep with me or else" harassment—the kind dramatized in *Disclosure*—we are starting to see court cases indicating that some men (and women) have been pressured into sex by a predatory female boss. There is every reason to believe that more such cases will appear as more women assume positions of power.

8   Yet most people still snicker about female harassment of males. Several men who claimed to have been sexually harassed appeared recently on *Donahue*. Between the host's eye rolling and the audience's derision, you would have though these men were reporting encounters with UFOs. Sometimes even juries do not take the subject seriously. In a 1991 case in Michigan, the jury agreed that a man had endured repeated fondling by his female co-workers but awarded him only $100 in damages. Compare that to the hundreds of thousands of dollars regularly awarded to female plaintiffs.

Men are doubly penalized by the current alarm about sexual harassment. On the one hand, they are weakened in any office encounter with a woman because she always holds the harassment trump card. On the other hand, the current interpretation of harassment law gives women license to say and do things in the workplace to which men cannot respond in kind. There is an open hostility toward men in many workplaces, and no one is rushing to document or change it.

10   Business, which should have an interest in finding out the truth, has instead swallowed whole the received wisdom on sexual harassment and acted on it swiftly and thoroughly. Companies spend millions of dollars on "harassment training," hoping that putting employees through these programs will stave off potential problems or at least inoculate them against major liability. Although some of the harassment training is of passable quality (given the flawed evidence on which it is based), too much of the training results in resentment by male employees and "over-empowerment" of female employees. In a recent case, a group of male air-traffic controllers filed charges against the Federal Aviation Administration, claiming they

were forced to observe photos of male sex organs and let female participants fondle them during harassment training.

Sexually harassed men face skepticism from both sides of the political spectrum. On the Left, no one is seriously challenging the anti-male feminist paradigm. On the Right, commentators have cautioned that men should not succumb to the harassment hysteria. Yet conservatives in particular should take a more active interest in setting the record straight, given the costs and public-policy ramifications of current erroneous theories.

Workplace Tensions

12   The current approach to sexual harassment has clearly hurt working relationships between men and women. Men are retreating to the safety of their offices, avoiding private contact with female co-workers, and carefully censoring their speech. Although the evidence has not yet been collected, it seems likely that male harassment victims, like their female counterparts, are more likely to be absent from work, to be less productive, and to leave the organization. In addition, men confronted by a sexually hostile environment may lash out against female co-workers, thereby prompting sexual-harassment complaints.

Trying to document a large, invisible mass of harassed men in the work force, however, does not mean advocating a new set of entitlements. On the contrary, recognizing that women are also harassers will help control the hysteria. Public policy, judicial interpretation, and popular sentiment have been swayed by statistics fraught with paradigmatic prejudice and methodological error. It is time for responsible researchers to begin an objective reexamination of the way that men and women treat each other at work. If the research shows that both men and women are experiencing harassment, then judicial remedy and public policy can be adjusted, and the idea of a harassing class and a victim class can be discarded.

14   It may also be time to reconsider the extent to which government can or should try to assure a comfortable working environment. People often receive treatment at work they do not like. The problem may lie in how the individual interprets the treatment.

Differing male and female interpretations of harassing behavior led the federal courts to establish the "reasonable woman" standard in 1991. This codified what we have known all along: men and women see things differently. According to the ruling, behavior that a man considers acceptable can constitute harassment if it is offensive to a "reasonable woman." In other words, decades of evolving feminist theory have led us back to a Victorian vision of woman; she cannot endure what a man can and must be protected.

16   Most of the outcry over sexual harassment is not about bosses demanding sex but about men doing and saying things that some women find offensive. Perhaps women are behaving just as offensively, but men have learned to live with it. The real answer to the "hostile environment" problem may be that women should learn to live with it too.   ❖

Questions for Meaning

1. According to this article, how do men and women differ in their response to sexual harassment?
2. Why do the authors believe that men are "doubly penalized" by current attitudes toward sexual harassment?
3. How does sexual harassment affect performance in the workplace?
4. On what grounds do Luthar and Townsend object to businesses training employees to avoid sexual harassment?
5. Vocabulary: derided (1), innuendoes (4), construe (5), paradigm (11), ramifications (11).

Questions about Strategy

1. How useful is the opening allusion to *Disclosure,* a film that appeared shortly before this article was first published? Do the authors provide sufficient information so that you can understand what this film was about if you were not already familiar with it?
2. The authors claim that "leading sexual-harassment researchers are feminist ideologues." What evidence do they provide to support this claim?
3. Consider the scenario described in paragraph 5. Is it believable?
4. How would you describe the tone of this argument?

STEPHANIE RIGER

GENDER DILEMMAS IN SEXUAL HARASSMENT POLICIES AND PROCEDURES

Discussion of sexual harassment often reveals that men and women have a different understanding of what kind of behavior constitutes harassment. Recognizing these differences may be essential in designing policies and programs to prevent the problem from occurring. The nature of these differences is the focus of this article by Stephanie Riger, Professor of Psychology and Women's Studies at the University of Illinois, Chicago. With Margaret T. Gordon, she coauthored *The Female Fear* (1988). "Gender Dilemmas in Sexual Harassment Policies and Procedures" was first published by *American Psychologist* in 1991. You will find that Riger draws on an extensive body of scholarship and uses APA-style documentation to identify her sources.

———————————— Abstract ————————————

Many organizations have established policies and procedures to deal with sexual harassment, yet few complaints are reported. Some have suggested that the lack of complaints is due to the absence of a problem, or the timidity or fearfulness of victims. This article proposes that the reasons for the lack of use of sexual harassment grievance procedures lie not in the victims, but rather in the procedures themselves. Women perceive sexual harassment differently than men do, and their orientation to dispute-resolution processes is likely to differ as well. The way that policies define harassment and the nature of dispute resolution procedures may better fit male than female perspectives. This gender bias is likely to discourage women from reporting complaints.

Sexual harassment—unwanted sexually oriented behavior in a work context—is the most recent form of victimization of women to be redefined as a social rather than a personal problem, following rape and wife abuse. A sizeable proportion of women surveyed in a wide variety of work settings reported being subject to unwanted sexual attention, sexual comments or jokes, offensive touching, or attempts to coerce compliance with or punish rejection of sexual advances. In 1980 the U.S. Merit Systems Protection Board (1981) conducted the first comprehensive national survey of sexual harassment among federal employees: About 4 out of 10 of the 10,648 women surveyed reported having been the target of sexual harassment during the previous 24 months. A recent update of this survey found that the frequency of harassment in 1988 was identical to that reported earlier: 42% of all women surveyed in 1988 reported that they had experienced some form of unwanted and uninvited sexual attention compared to exactly the same percentage of women in 1980 (U.S. Merit Systems Protection Board, 1988).

2   Women ranging from blue-collar workers (LaFontaine & Tredeau, 1986; Maypole & Skaine, 1982) to lawyers (Burleigh & Goldberg, 1989) to airline personnel (Littler-Bishop, Seidler-Feller, & Opaluch, 1982) have reported considerable amounts of sexual harassment in surveys. Among a random sample of private sector workers in the Los Angeles area, more than one half of the women surveyed by telephone reported experiencing at least one incident that they considered sexual harassment during their working lives (Gutek, 1985). Some estimate that up to about one third of women in educational institutions have experienced some form of harassment (Kenig & Ryan, 1986). Indeed, Garvey (1986) stated that "Unwanted sexual attention may be the single most widespread occupational hazard in the workplace today" (p. 75).

It is a hazard faced much more frequently by women than men. About 40% of the women in the original U.S. Merit Systems Protection Board survey reported having experienced sexual harassment, compared with only 15% of the men (U.S. Merit Systems Protection Board, 1981). Among working people surveyed in Los Angeles, women were nine times more likely than men to report having quit a job because of sexual harassment, five times more likely to have transferred, and three times more likely to have lost a job (Konrad & Gutek, 1986). Women with low power and status, whether due to lower age, being single or divorced, or being in a marginal position in the organization, are more likely to be harassed (Fain & Anderton, 1987; LaFontaine & Tredeau, 1986; Robinson & Reid, 1985).

4   Sex differences in the frequency of harassment also prevail in educational environments (Fitzgerald et al., 1988). A mailed survey of more than 900 women and men at the University of Rhode Island asked about a wide range of behavior, including the frequency of respondents' experience of sexual insult, defined as an "uninvited sexually suggestive, obscene or offensive remark, stare, or gesture" (Lott, Reilly, & Howard, 1982, p. 309). Of the female respondents, 40% reported being sexually insulted occasionally or often while on campus, compared with 17% of the men. Both men and women reported that women are rarely the source of such insults. Similar differences were found in a survey of social workers, with 2½ times as many women as men reporting harassment (Maypole, 1986).

Despite the high rates found in surveys of sexual harassment of women, few complaints are pursued through official grievance procedures. Dzeich and Weiner (1984) concluded, after reviewing survey findings, that 20% to 30% of female college students experience sexual harassment. Yet academic institutions averaged only 4.3 complaints each during the 1982–1983 academic year (Robertson, Dyer, & Campbell, 1988), a period roughly consecutive with the surveys cited by Dzeich and Weiner. In another study conducted at a university in 1984, of 38 women who reported harassment, only 1 reported the behavior to the offender's supervisor and 2 reported the behavior to an adviser, another professor, or employer (Reilly, Lott, & Gallogly, 1986). Similar findings have been reported on other college campuses (Adams, Kottke, & Padgitt, 1983; Benson & Thompson, 1982; Brandenburg, 1982; Cammaert, 1985; Meek & Lynch, 1983; Schneider, 1987).

6   Low numbers of complaints appear in other work settings as well. In a survey of federal workers, only about 11% of victims reported the harassment to a higher authority; and only 2.5% used formal complaint channels (Livingston, 1982). Similarly, female social workers reacted to harassment by avoiding or delaying the conflict or attempting to defuse the situation rather than by adopting any form of recourse such as filing a grievance (Maypole, 1986). The number of complaints alleging sexual harassment filed with the Equal Employment Opportunity Commission in Washington, DC, has declined since 1984, despite an increase in the number of women in the workforce during that time (Morgenson, 1989), and surveys that suggest that the rate of sexual harassment has remained relatively stable (U.S. Merit Systems Protection Board, 1981, 1988).

It is the contention of this article that the low rate of utilization of grievance procedures is due to gender bias in sexual harassment policies that discourages their use by women. Policies are written in gender-neutral language and are intended to apply equally to men and women. However, these policies are experienced differently by women than men because of gender differences in perceptions of harassment and orientation toward conflict. Although victims of all forms of discrimination are reluctant to pursue grievances (Bumiller, 1987), women, who are most likely to be the victims of sexual harassment, are especially disinclined to pursue sexual harassment grievances for at least two reasons. First, the interpretation in policies of what constitutes harassment may not reflect women's viewpoints, and their complaints may not be seen as valid. Second, the procedures in some policies that are designed to resolve disputes may be inimical to women because they are not compatible with the way that many women view conflict resolution. Gender bias in policies, rather than an absence of harassment or lack of assertiveness on the part of victims, produces low numbers of complaints.

Gender Bias in the Definition of Sexual Harassment

8   The first way that gender bias affects sexual harassment policies stems from differences between men and women in the interpretation of the definition of harassment. Those writing sexual harassment policies for organizations typically look to the courts for the distinction between illegal sexual harassment and permissible (although perhaps unwanted) social interaction (see Cohen, 1987, for a discussion of this distinction in legal cases). The definition of harassment in policies typically is that provided by the U.S. Equal Employment Opportunity Commission (1980) guidelines:

> Unwelcome sexual advances, requests for sexual favors, and other verbal or physical conduct of a sexual nature constitute sexual harassment when (1) submission to such conduct is made either explicitly or implicitly a term or condition of an individual's employment, (2) submission to or rejection of such conduct by an individual is used as the basis for employment decisions affecting such individual, or (3) such conduct has the purpose or effect of unreasonably interfering with an individual's work performance or creating an intimidating, hostile, or offensive working environment. (p. 74677)

The first two parts of the definition refer to a *quid pro quo* relationship involving people in positions of unequal status, as superior status is usually necessary to have control over another's employment. In such cases bribes, threats, or punishments are used. Incidents of this type need happen only once to fall under the definition of sexual harassment. However, courts have required that incidents falling into the third category, "an intimidating, hostile, or offensive working environment," must be repeated in order to establish that such an environment exists (Terpstra & Baker, 1988); these incidents must be both pervasive and so severe that they affect the victim's psychological well-being (Trager, 1988). Harassment of this type can come from peers or even subordinates as well as superiors.

In all three of these categories, harassment is judged on the basis of conduct and its effects on the recipient, not the intentions of the harasser. Thus, two typical defenses given by accused harassers—"I was just being friendly," or "I touch everyone, I'm that kind of person"—do not hold up in court. Yet behavior may have an intimidating or offensive effect on some people but be inoffensive or even welcome to others. In deciding whose standards should be used, the courts employ what is called the *reasonable person rule,* asking whether a reasonable person would be offended by the conduct in question. The dilemma in applying this to sexual harassment is that a reasonable woman and a reasonable man are likely to differ in the judgements of what is offensive.

10   Definitions of sexual harassment are socially constructed, varying not only with characteristics of the perceiver but also those of the situational context and actors involved. Behavior is more likely to be labelled harassment when it is done by someone with greater power than the victim (Gutek, Morasch, & Cohen, 1983; Kenig & Ryan, 1986; Lester et al., 1986; Popovich, Licata, Nokovich, Martelli, & Zoloty, 1987); when it involves physical advances accompanied by threats of punishment for noncompliance (Rossi & Weber-Burdin, 1983); when the response to it is negative (T. S. Jones, Remland, & Brunner, 1987); when the behavior reflects persistent negative intentions toward a woman (Pryor & Day, 1988); the more inappropriate it is for the actor's social role (Pryor, 1985); and the more flagrant and frequent the harasser's actions (Thomann & Wiener, 1987). Among women, professionals are more likely than those in secretarial–clerical positions to report the more subtle behaviors as harassment (McIntyre & Renick, 1982).

The variable that most consistently predicts variation in people's definition of sexual harassment is the sex of the rater. Men label fewer behaviors at work as sexual harassment (Kenig & Ryan, 1986; Konrad & Gutek, 1986; Lester et al., 1986; Powell, 1986; Rossi & Weber-Burdin, 1983). Men tend to find sexual overtures from women at work to be flattering, whereas women find similar approaches from men to be insulting (Gutek, 1985). Both men and women agree that certain blatant behaviors, such as sexual assault or sexual bribery, constitute harassment, but women are more likely to see as harassment more subtle behavior such as sexual teasing or looks or gestures (Adams et al., 1983; Collins & Blodgett, 1981; Kenig & Ryan, 1986; U.S. Merit Systems Protection Board, 1981). Even when they do identify behavior as harassment, men are more likely to think that women will be flattered by it (Kirk, 1988). Men are also more likely than women to blame women for being sexually harassed (Jensen & Gutek, 1982; Kenig & Ryan, 1986).

12   These gender differences make it difficult to apply the reasonable person rule. Linenberger (1983) proposed 10 factors that permit an "objective" assessment of whether behavior constitutes sexual harassment, regardless of the perception of the victim and the intent of the perpetrator. These factors range from the severity of the conduct to the number and frequency of encounters, and the relationship of the parties involved. For example, behavior is less likely to be categorized as harassment if it is seen as a response to provocation from the victim. But is an objective rating of provocation possible? When gender differences are as clear-cut and persistent as they are in

the perception of what behavior constitutes sexual harassment, the question is not one of objectivity, but rather of which sex's definition of the situation will prevail. Becker (1967) asserted that there is a "hierarchy of credibility" in organizations, and that credibility and the right to be heard are differently distributed: "In any system of ranked groups, participants take it as given that members of the highest group have the right to define the way things really are" (p. 241). Because men typically have more power in organizations (Kanter, 1977), Becker's analysis suggests that in most situations the male definition of harassment is likely to predominate. As MacKinnon (1987) put it, "objectivity—the nonsituated, universal standpoint, whether claimed or aspired to—is a denial of the existence or potency of sex inequality that tacitly participates in constructing reality from the dominant point of view," (p. 136). "The law sees and treats women the way men see and treat women" (p. 140). This means that men's judgments about what behavior constitutes harassment, and who is to blame, are likely to prevail. Linenberger's 10 factors thus may not be an objective measure, but rather a codification of the male perspective on harassment. This is likely to discourage women who want to bring complaints about more subtle forms of harassment.

Sex Differences in the Attribution of Harassment

Attribution theory provides an explanation for the wider range of behaviors that women define as harassment and for men's tendency to find women at fault (Kenig & Ryan, 1986; Pryor, 1985; Pryor & Day, 1988). Attribution theory suggests that people tend to see their own behaviors as situationally determined, whereas they attribute the behaviors of others to personality characteristics or other internal causes (E. E. Jones & Nisbett, 1971). Those who see sexual harassment through the eyes of the actor are likely to be male. As actors are wont to do, they will attribute their behaviors to situational causes, including the "provocations" of the women involved. They will then not perceive their own behaviors as harassment. In fact, those who take the perspective of the victim do see specific behaviors as more harassing than those who take the perspective of the actor (Pryor & Day, 1988). Women are more likely to view harassment through the eyes of the victim; therefore they will label more behaviors as harassment because they attribute them to men's disposition or personality traits. Another possibility is that men, as potential harassers, want to avoid blame in the future, and so shift the blame to women (Jensen & Gutek, 1982) and restrict the range of behaviors that they define as harassment (Kenig & Ryan, 1986). Whatever the cause, a reasonable man and a reasonable woman are likely to differ in their judgments of whether a particular behavior constitutes sexual harassment.

14   Men tend to misinterpret women's friendliness as an indication of sexual interest (Abbey, 1982; Abbey & Melby, 1986; Saal, Johnson, & Weber, 1989; Shotland & Craig, 1988). Acting on this misperception may result in

behavior that is harassing to women. Tangri, Burt, and Johnson (1982) stated that "Some sexual harassment may indeed be clumsy or insensitive expressions of attraction, while some is the classic abuse of organizational power" (p. 52). Gender differences in attributional processes help explain the first type of harassment, partially accounting for the overwhelming preponderance of sexual harassment incidents that involve a male offender and a female victim.

Gender Bias in Grievance Procedures

Typically, procedures for resolving disputes about sexual harassment are written in gender-neutral terms so that they may apply to both women and men. However, men and women may react quite differently to the same procedures.

16   Analyzing this problem requires looking at specific policies and procedures. Educational institutions will serve as the context for this discussion for three reasons. First, they are the most frequent site of surveys about the problem, and the pervasive nature of harassment on campuses has been well documented (Dzeich & Weiner, 1984). Second, although sexual harassment is harmful to women in all occupations, it can be particularly devastating to those in educational institutions, in which the goal of the organization is to nurture and promote development. The violation of relationships based on trust, such as those between faculty and students, can leave long-lasting and deep wounds, yet many surveys find that those in positions of authority in educational settings are often the source of the problem (Benson & Thomson, 1982; Fitzgerald et al., 1988; Glaser & Thorpe, 1986; Kenig & Ryan, 1986; Maihoff & Forrest, 1983; Metha & Nigg, 1983; Robinson & Reid, 1985; K. R. Wilson & Kraus, 1983). Third, educational institutions have been leaders in the development of sexual harassment policies, in part because of concern about litigation. In *Alexander v. Yale University* (1977) the court decided that sexual harassment constitutes a form of sex discrimination that denies equal access to educational opportunities, and falls under Title IX of the Educational Amendments of 1972. The Office of Civil Rights in the U.S. Department of Education now requires institutions that receive Title IX funds to maintain grievance procedures to resolve complaints involving sexual discrimination or harassment (M. Wilson, 1988). Consequently, academic institutions may have had more experience than other work settings in developing procedures to combat this problem. A survey of U.S. institutions of higher learning conducted in 1984 (Robertson et al., 1988) found that 66% of all responding institutions had sexual harassment policies, and 46% had grievance procedures specifically designed to deal with sexual harassment complaints, with large public schools more likely to have them than small private ones. These percentages have unquestionably increased in recent years, given the government funding regulations. Although the discussion here is focused on educational contexts, the problems identified in sexual harassment policies exist in other work settings as well.

Many educational institutions, following guidelines put forward by the American Council on Education (1986) and the American Association of University Professors (1983), have established policies that prohibit sexual harassment and create grievance procedures. Some use a formal board or hearing, and others use informal mechanisms that protect confidentiality and seek to resolve the complaint rather than punish the offender (see, e.g., Brandenburg, 1982; Meek & Lynch, 1983). Still others use both types of procedures. The type of procedure specified by the policy may have a great impact on victims' willingness to report complaints.

Comparison of Informal and Formal Grievance Procedures

18 Informal attempts to resolve disputes differ from formal procedures in important ways (see Table 1; for a general discussion of dispute resolution systems, see Brett, Goldberg, & Ury, 1990). First, their goal is to solve a problem, rather than to judge the harasser's guilt or innocence. The assumptions underlying these processes are that both parties in a dispute perceive a problem (although they may define that problem differently); that both share a common interest in solving that problem; and that together they can negotiate an agreement that will be satisfactory to everyone involved. Typically, the goal of informal processes is to end the harassment of the complainant rather than judge (and punish, if appropriate) the offender. The focus is on what will happen in the future between the disputing parties, rather than on what has happened in the past. Often policies do not specify the format of informal problem solving, but accept a wide variety of strategies of reconciliation. For example, a complainant might write a letter to the offender (Rowe, 1981), or someone might talk to the offender on the complainant's behalf. The offender and victim might participate in mediation, in which a third party helps them negotiate an agreement. Many policies accept a wide array of strategies as good-faith attempts to solve the problem informally.

In contrast, formal procedures generally require a written complaint and have a specified procedure for handling cases, usually by bringing the

TABLE 1
A Comparison of Formal and Informal Grievance Procedures

	Procedures	
Elements	*Informal*	*Formal*
Purpose	Problem solving or reconciliation	Judge guilt or innocence
Time Focus	What will happen in the future	What happened in the past
Format	Usually unspecified	Usually specified
Completion	When complainant is satisfied	When hearing board decides
Control	Complainant	Hearing board
Compliance	Voluntary	Punishment is binding

complaint to a group officially designated to hear the case, such as a hearing board. The informal process typically ends when the complainant is satisfied (or decides to drop the complaint); the formal procedure ends when the hearing board decides on the guilt or innocence of the alleged harasser. Thus, control over the outcome usually rests with the complainant in the case of informal mechanisms, and with the official governance body in the case of a hearing. Compliance with a decision is usually voluntary in informal procedures, whereas the decision in a formal procedure is binding unless appealed to a higher authority. Formal procedures are adversarial in nature, with the complainant and defendant competing to see whose position will prevail.

20   A typical case might proceed as follows: A student with a complaint writes a letter to the harasser (an informal procedure). If not satisfied with the response, she submits a written complaint to the sexual harassment hearing board, which then hears both sides of the case, reviews available evidence, and decides on the guilt or innocence of the accused (a formal procedure). If the accused is found guilty, the appropriate officer of the institution decides on punishment.

Gender Differences in Orientation to Conflict

Women and men may differ in their reactions to dispute resolution procedures for at least two reasons. First, women typically have less power than men in organizations (Kanter, 1977). Using a grievance procedure, such as appearing before a hearing board, may be inimical because of the possibility of retaliation for a complaint. Miller (1976) suggested that differences in status and power affect the way that people handle conflict:

> As soon as a group attains dominance it tends inevitably to produce a situation of conflict and . . . it also, simultaneously, seeks to suppress conflict. Moreover, subordinates who accept the dominant's conception of them as passive and malleable do not openly engage in conflict. Conflict . . . is forced underground. (p. 127)

22   This may explain why some women do not report complaints at all. When they do complain, however, their relative lack of power or their values may predispose women to prefer informal rather than formal procedures. Beliefs about the appropriate way to handle disputes vary among social groups (Merry & Silbey, 1984). Gilligan's (1982) distinction between an orientation toward rights and justice compared with an emphasis on responsibilities to others and caring is likely to be reflected in people's preferences for ways of handling disputes (Kolb & Coolidge, 1988). Neither of these orientations is exclusive to one sex, but according to Gilligan, women are more likely to emphasize caring. Women's orientation to caring may be due to their subordinate status (Miller, 1976). Empirical support for Gilligan's theories is inconclusive (see, e.g., Mednick, 1989, for a summary of criticisms). Yet the fact that most victims of sexual harassment state that they simply

want an end to the offending behavior rather than punishment of the offender (Robertson et al., 1988) suggests a "caring" rather than "justice" perspective (or possibly, a fear of reprisals).

In the context of dispute resolution, an emphasis on responsibilities
and caring is compatible with the goals of informal procedures to restore
harmony or at least peaceful coexistence among the parties involved,
whereas that of justice is compatible with formal procedures that attempt to
judge guilt or innocence of the offender. Thus women may prefer to use informal procedures to resolve conflicts, and indeed most cases in educational
institutions are handled through informal mechanisms (Robertson et al.,
1988). Policies that do not include an informal dispute resolution option are
likely to discourage many women from bringing complaints.

Problems with Informal Dispute-Resolution Procedures

24   Although women may prefer informal mechanisms, they are problematic
for several reasons (Rifkin, 1984). Because they do not result in punishment, offenders suffer few negative consequences of their actions and may
not be deterred from harassing again. In institutions of higher learning, the
most common form of punishment reported is a verbal warning by a supervisor, which is given only "sometimes" (Robertson et al., 1988). Dismissal
and litigation are almost never used. It seems likely, then, that sexual harassment may be viewed by potential harassers as low-risk behavior, and that
victims see few incentives for bringing official complaints.

The confidentiality usually required by informal procedures prevents
other victims from knowing that a complaint has been lodged against a
multiple offender. If a woman knows that another woman is bringing a
complaint against a particular man who has harassed both of them, then she
might be more willing to complain also. The secrecy surrounding informal
complaint processes precludes this information from becoming public and
makes it more difficult to identify repeat offenders. Also, complaints settled
informally may not be included in reports of the frequency of sexual harassment claims, making these statistics underestimate the scope of the problem. Yet confidentiality is needed to protect the rights of the accused and
may be preferred by those bringing complaints.

26   These problems in informal procedures could discourage male as well
as female victims from bringing complaints. Most problematic for women,
however, is the assumption in informal procedures that the complainant
and accused have equal power in the process of resolving the dispute. This
assumption is likely to put women at a disadvantage. Parties involved in sexual harassment disputes may not be equal either in the sense of formal position within the organization (e.g., student versus faculty) or status (e.g.,
female versus male students), and position and status characteristics that
reflect levels of power do not disappear simply because they are irrelevant to
the informal process. External status characteristics that indicate macrolevel
social stratification (e.g., sex and age) help explain the patterns of distribution of sexual harassment in the workplace (Fain & Anderton, 1987). It

seems likely that these external statuses will influence the interpersonal dynamics within a dispute-resolution procedure as well. Because women are typically lower than men in both formal and informal status and power in organizations, they will have less power in the dispute resolution process.

When the accused has more power than the complainant (e.g., a male faculty member accused by a female student), the complainant is more vulnerable to retaliation. Complainants may be reluctant to use grievance procedures because they fear retaliation should the charge be made public. For example, students may fear that a faculty member will punish them for bringing a complaint by lowering their grades or withholding recommendations. The person appointed to act as a guide to the informal resolution process is usually expected to act as a neutral third party rather than advocate for the complainant, and may hold little formal power over faculty: "Relatively few institutions have persons empowered to be (nonlegal) advocates for the complainants; a student bringing a complaint has little assurance of stopping the harassment and avoiding retaliation" (Robertson et al., 1988, p. 801). The victim then is left without an advocate to face an opponent whose formal position, age, and experience with verbal argument is often considerably beyond her own. The more vulnerable a woman's position is in her organization, the more likely it is that she will be harassed (Robinson & Reid, 1985); therefore sexual harassment, like rape, involves dynamics of power and domination as well as sexuality. The lack of an advocate for the complainant who might equalize power between the disputing parties is particularly troubling. However, if an advocate is provided for the complainant in an informal process, fairness and due process require that the defendant have an advocate as well. The dilemma is that this seems likely to transform an informal, problem-solving process into a formal, adversarial one.

Other Obstacles to Reporting Complaints

Belief That Sexual Harassment of Women Is Normative

28   Because of differences in perception of behavior, men and women involved in a sexual harassment case are likely to have sharply divergent interpretations of that case, particularly when a hostile environment claim is involved. To women, the behavior in question is offensive, and they are likely to see themselves as victims of male actions. The requirement that an attempt be made to mediate the dispute or solve it through informal processes may violate their perception of the situation and of themselves as victims of a crime. By comparison, a victim of a mugging is not required to solve the problem with the mugger through mediation (B. Sandler, personal communication, 1988). To many men, the behavior is not offensive, but normative. In their eyes, no crime has been committed, and there is no problem to be solved.

Some women may also consider sexual harassment to be normative. Women may believe that these sorts of behaviors are simply routine, a commonplace part of everyday life, and thus not something that can be challenged. Younger women—who are more likely to be victims (Fain & Anderton, 1987; LaFontaine & Tredeau, 1986; McIntyre & Renick, 1982)— are more tolerant of harassment than are older women (Lott et al., 1982; Reilly et al., 1986). Indeed, Lott et al. concluded that "younger women in particular have accepted the idea that prowling men are a 'fact of life' " (p. 318). This attitude might prevent women from labeling a negative experience as harassment. Surveys that ask women about sexual harassment and about the frequency of experiencing specific sexually harassing behaviors find discrepancies in responses to these questions (Fitzgerald et al., 1988). Women report higher rates when asked if they have been the target of specific harassing behaviors than when asked a general question about whether they have been harassed. Women are also more willing to report negative reactions to offensive behaviors than they are to label those behaviors as sexual harassment (Brewer, 1982).

30   Normative beliefs may deter some male victims of harassment from reporting complaints also, because men are expected to welcome sexual advances if those advances are from women.

Negative Outcomes for Victims Who Bring Complaints

The outcome of grievance procedures does not appear to provide much satisfaction to victims who bring complaints. In academic settings, despite considerable publicity given to a few isolated cases in which tenured faculty have been fired, punishments are rarely inflicted on harassers, and the punishments that are given are mild, such as verbal warnings (Robertson et al., 1988). Among federal workers, 33% of those who used formal grievance procedures to protest sexual harassment found that it "made things worse" (Livingston, 1982). More than 65% of the cases of formal charges of sexual harassment filed with the Illinois Department of Human Rights involved job discharge of the complainant (Terpstra & Cook, 1985). Less than one third of those cases resulted in a favorable settlement for the complainant, and those who received financial compensation got an average settlement of $3,234 (Terpstra & Baker, 1988). Similar findings in California were reported by Coles (1986), with the average cash settlement there of $973, representing approximately one month's pay. Although a few legal cases have resulted in large settlements (Garvey, 1986), these studies suggest that typical settlements are low. Formal actions may take years to complete, and in legal suits the victim usually must hire legal counsel at considerable expense (Livingston, 1982). These small settlements seem unlikely to compensate victims for the emotional stress, notoriety, and financial costs involved in filing a public complaint. Given the consistency with which victimization falls more often to women than men, it is ironic that one of the largest settlements awarded to an individual in a sexual harassment case ($196,500 in damages) was made to a man who brought suit against his female supervisor (Brewer & Berk, 1982), perhaps because sexual aggression by a woman is seen as especially egregious.

Emotional Consequences of Harassment

32 In academic settings, harassment can adversely affect students' learning, and therefore their academic standing. It can deprive them of educational and career opportunities because they wish to avoid threatening situations. Students who have been harassed report that they consequently avoid taking a class from or working with a particular faculty member, change their major, or leave a threatening situation (Adams et al., 1983; Lott et al., 1982). Lowered self-esteem follows the conclusion that rewards, such as a high grade, may have been based on sexual attraction rather than one's abilities (McCormack, 1985). Decreased feelings of competence and confidence and increased feelings of anger, frustration, depression, and anxiety all can result from harassment (Cammaert, 1985; Crull, 1982; Hamilton, Alagna, King, & Lloyd, 1987; Livingston, 1982; Schneider, 1987). The psychological stress produced by harassment is compounded when women are fired or quit their jobs in fear or frustration (Coles, 1986).

Meek and Lynch (1983) proposed that victims of harassment typically go through several stages of reaction, at first questioning the offender's true intentions and then blaming themselves for the offender's behavior. Women with traditional sex-role beliefs are more likely to blame themselves for being harassed (Jensen & Gutek, 1982). Victims then worry about being believed by others and about possible retaliation if they take formal steps to protest the behavior. A victim may be too frightened or confused to assert herself or punish the offender. Psychologists who work with victims of harassment would do well to recognize that not only victims' emotional reactions but also the nature of the grievance process as discussed in this article may discourage women from bringing formal complaints.

Prevention of Sexual Harassment

34 Some writers have argued that sexual harassment does not occur with great frequency, or if it once was a problem, it has been eliminated in recent years. Indeed, Morgenson (1989), writing in the business publication *Forbes,* suggested that the whole issue had been drummed up by professional sexual harassment counselors in order to sell their services. Yet the studies cited in this article have documented that sexual harassment is a widespread problem with serious consequences.

Feminists and union activists have succeeded in gaining recognition of sexual harassment as a form of sex discrimination (MacKinnon, 1979). The law now views sexual harassment not as the idiosyncratic actions of a few inconsiderate males but as part of a pattern of behaviors that reflect the imbalance of power between women and men in society. Women in various occupations and educational settings have sought legal redress for actions of supervisors or coworkers, and sexual harassment has become the focus of numerous organizational policies and grievance procedures (Brewer & Berk, 1982).

36   Well-publicized policies that use an inclusive definition of sexual harassment, include an informal dispute resolution option, provide an advocate for the victim (if desired), and permit multiple offenders to be identified seem likely to be the most effective way of addressing claims of sexual harassment. However, even these modifications will not eliminate all of the problems in policies. The severity of the consequences of harassment for the victim, coupled with the problematic nature of grievance procedures and the mildness of punishments for offenders, makes retribution less effective than prevention of sexual harassment. Organizational leaders should not assume that their job is completed when they have established a sexual harassment policy. Extensive efforts at prevention need to be mounted at the individual, situational, and organizational level.

In prevention efforts aimed at the individual, education about harassment should be provided (e.g., Beauvais, 1986). In particular, policymakers and others need to learn to "think like a woman" to define which behaviors constitute harassment and recognize that these behaviors are unacceptable. Understanding that many women find offensive more subtle forms of behavior such as sexual jokes or comments may help reduce the kinds of interactions that create a hostile environment. Educating personnel about the punishments involved for offensive behavior also may have a deterring effect.

38   However, education alone is not sufficient. Sexual harassment is the product not only of individual attitudes and beliefs, but also of organizational practices. Dziech and Weiner (1984, pp. 39–58) described aspects of educational institutions that facilitate sexual harassment, including the autonomy afforded the faculty, the diffusion of authority that permits lack of accountability, and the shortage of women in positions of authority. Researchers are beginning to identify the practices in other work settings that facilitate or support sexual harassment, and suggest that sexual harassment may be part of a pattern of unprofessional and disrespectful attitudes and behaviors that characterizes some workplaces (Gutek, 1985).

Perhaps the most important factor in reducing sexual harassment is an organizational culture that promotes equal opportunities for women. There is a strong negative relationship between the level of perceived equal employment opportunity for women in a company and the level of harassment reported (LaFontaine & Tredeau, 1986): Workplaces low in perceived equality are the site of more frequent incidents of harassment. This finding suggests that sexual harassment both reflects and reinforces the underlying sexual inequality that produces a sex-segregated and sex-stratified occupational structure (Hoffman, 1986). The implementation of sexual harassment policies demonstrates the seriousness of those in authority; the language of the policies provides some measure of clarity about the types of behavior that are not acceptable; and grievance procedures may provide relief and legitimacy to those with complaints (Schneider, 1987). But neither policies nor procedures do much to weaken the structural roots of gender inequalities in organizations.

40   Reforms intended to ameliorate women's position sometimes have unintended negative consequences (see Kirp, Yudof, & Franks, 1986). The
presence of sexual harassment policies and the absence of formal complaints might promote the illusion that this problem has been solved. Assessment of whether organizational policies and practices promote or
hinder equality for women is required to insure that this belief does not prevail. A long-range strategy for organizational reform in academia would
thus attack the chilly climate for women in classrooms and laboratories
(Project on the Status and Education of Women, 1982), the inferior quality
of athletic programs for women, differential treatment of women applicants, the acceptance of the masculine as normative, and a knowledge base
uninfluenced by women's values or experience (Fuehrer & Schilling, 1985).
In other work settings, such a long-range approach would attack both sex-
segregation of occupations and sex-stratification within authority hierar-
chies. Sexual harassment grievance procedures alone are not sufficient to
insure that sexual harassment will be eliminated. An end to this problem
requires gender equity within organizations. ❖

References

Abbey, A. (1982). Sex differences in attributions for friendly behavior: Do males misper-
ceive females' friendliness? *Journal of Personality and Social Psychology, 42,* 830–838.

Abbey, A., & Melby, C. (1986). The effects of nonverbal cues on gender differences in perceptions of sexual intent. *Sex Roles, 15,* 283–298.

Adams, J. W., Kottke, J. L., & Padgitt, J. S. (1983). Sexual harassment of university students. *Journal of College Student Personnel, 23,* 484–490.

Alexander et al. v. Yale University, 459 F. Supp. 1 (D. Conn. 1977), affirmed 631 F.2d 178
(2nd Cir. 1980).

American Association of University Professors (1983), Sexual harassment: Suggested
policy and procedures for handling complaints. *Academe, 69,* 15a–16a.

American Council on Education. (1986). *Sexual harassment on campus: Suggestions for reviewing campus policy and educational programs.* Washington, DC: Author.

Beauvais, K. (1986). Workshops to combat sexual harassment: A case study of changing
attitudes. *Signs: Journal of Women in Culture and Society, 12,* 130–145.

Becker, H. S. (1967). Whose side are we on? *Social Problems, 14,* 239–247.

Benson, D. J., & Thomson, G. (1982). Sexual harassment on a university campus: The
confluence of authority relations, sexual interest and gender stratification. *Social
Problems, 29,* 236–251.

Brandenburg, J. B. (1982). Sexual harassment in the university: Guidelines for establishing
a grievance procedure. *Signs: Journal of Women in Culture and Society, 8,* 320–336.

Brett, J. M., Goldberg, S. B., & Ury, W. L. (1990). Designing systems for resolving disputes
in organizations. *American Psychologist, 45,* 162–170.

Brewer, M. (1982). Further beyond nine to five: An integration and future directions.
Journal of Social Issues, 38, 149–157.

Brewer, M. B., & Berk, R. A. (1982). Beyond nine to five: Introduction. *Journal of Social Issues, 38,* 1–4.

Bumiller, K. (1987). Victims in the shadow of the law: A critique of the model of legal
protection. *Signs: Journal of Women in Culture and Society, 12,* 421–439.

Burleigh, N., & Goldberg, S. (1989). Breaking the silence: Sexual harassment in law firms. *ABA Journal, 75,* 46–52.

Cammaert, L. P. (1985). How widespread is sexual harassment on campus? *International Journal of Women's Studies, 8,* 388–397.

Cohen, C. F. (1987, November). Legal dilemmas in sexual harassment cases. *Labor Law Journal,* 681–689.

Coles, F. S. (1986). Forced to quit: Sexual harassment complaints and agency response. *Sex Roles, 14,* 81–95.

Collins, E. G. C., & Blodgett, T. B. (1981). Some see it . . . some won't. *Harvard Business Review, 59,* 76–95.

Crull, P. (1982). The stress effects of sexual harassment on the job. *American Journal of Orthopsychiatry, 52,* 539–543.

Dziech, B., & Weiner, L. (1984). *The lecherous professor.* Boston: Beacon Press.

Fain, T. C., & Anderton, D. L. (1987). Sexual harassment: Organizational context and diffuse status. *Sex Roles, 5/6,* 291–311.

Fitzgerald, L. R., Schullman, S. L., Bailey, N., Richards, M., Swecker, J., Gold, Y., Ormerod, M., & Weitzman, L. (1988). The incidence and dimensions of sexual harassment in academia and the workplace. *Journal of Vocational Behavior, 32,* 152–175.

Fuehrer, A., & Schilling, K. M. (1985). The values of academe: Sexism as a natural consequence. *Journal of Social Issues, 41,* 29–42.

Garvey, M. S. (1986). The high cost of sexual harassment suits. *Labor Relations, 65,* 75–79.

Gilligan, C. (1982). *In a different voice: Psychological theory and women's development.* Cambridge, MA: Harvard University Press.

Glaser, R. D., & Thorpe, J. S. (1986). Unethical intimacy: A survey of sexual contact and advances between psychology educators and female graduate students. *American Psychologist, 41,* 43–51.

Gutek, B. A. (1985). *Sex and the workplace.* San Francisco: Jossey-Bass.

Gutek, B. A., Morasch, B., & Cohen, A. G. (1983). Interpreting social-sexual behavior in a work setting. *Journal of Vocational Behavior, 22,* 30–48.

Hamilton, J. A., Alagna, S. W., King, L. S., & Lloyd, C. (1987). The emotional consequences of gender-based abuse in the workplace: New counseling programs for sex discrimination. *Women and Therapy, 6,* 155–182.

Hoffman, F. L. (1986). Sexual harassment in academia: Feminist theory and institutional practice. *Harvard Educational Review, 56*(2), 107–121.

Jensen, I. W., & Gutek, B. A. (1982). Attributions and assignment of responsibility in sexual harassment. *Journal of Social Issues, 38,* 121–136.

Jones, E. E., & Nisbett, R. E. (1971). *The actor and the observer: Divergent perceptions of the causes of behavior.* Morristown, NJ: General Learning Press.

Jones, T. S., Remland, M. S., & Brunner, C. C. (1987). Effects of employment relationship, response of recipient and sex of rater on perceptions of sexual harassment. *Perceptual and Motor Skills, 65,* 55–63.

Kanter, R. M. (1977). *Men and women of the corporation.* New York: Basic Books.

Kenig, S., & Ryan, J. (1986). Sex differences in levels of tolerance and attribution of blame for sexual harassment on a university campus. *Sex Roles, 15,* 535–549.

Kirk, D. (1988, August). *Gender differences in the perception of sexual harassment.* Paper presented at the Academy of Management National Meeting, Anaheim, CA.

Kirp, D. L., Yudof, M. G., & Franks, M. S. (1986). *Gender justice.* Chicago: University of Chicago Press.

Kolb, D. M., & Coolidge, G. G. (1988). *Her place at the table: A consideration of gender issues in negotiation* (Working paper series 88-5). Harvard Law School, Program on Negotiation.

Konrad, A. M., & Gutek, B. A. (1986). Impact of work experiences on attitudes toward sexual harassment. *Administrative Science Quarterly, 31,* 422–438.

LaFontaine, E., & Tredeau, L. (1986). The frequency, sources, and correlates of sexual harassment among women in traditional male occupations. *Sex Roles, 15,* 433–442.

Lester, D., Banta, B., Barton, J., Elian, N., Mackiewicz, L., & Winkelried, J. (1986). Judgments about sexual harassment: Effects of the power of the harasser. *Perceptual and Motor Skills, 63,* 990.

Linenberger, P. (1983, April). What behavior constitutes sexual harassment? *Labor Law Journal,* 238–247.

Littler-Bishop, S., Seidler-Feller, D., & Opaluch, R. E. (1982). Sexual harassment in the workplace as a function of initiator's status: The case of airline personnel. *Journal of Social Issues, 38,* 137–148.

Livingston, J. A. (1982). Responses to sexual harassment on the job: Legal, organizational, and individual actions. *Journal of Social Issues, 38*(4), 5–22.

Lott, B., Reilly, M. E., & Howard, D. R. (1982). Sexual assault and harassment: A campus community case study. *Signs: Journal of Women in Culture and Society, 8,* 296–319.

MacKinnon, C. A. (1979). *Sexual harassment of working women: A case of sex discrimination.* New Haven, CT: Yale University Press.

MacKinnon, C. A. (1987). Feminism, Marxism, method and the state: Toward feminist jurisprudence. In S. Harding (Ed.), *Feminism and methodology: Social science issues.* Bloomington: Indiana University Press.

Maihoff, N., & Forrest, L. (1983). Sexual harassment in higher education: As assessment study. *Journal of the National Association for Women Deans, Administrators, & Counselors, 46,* 3–8.

Maypole, D. E. (1986). Sexual harassment of social workers at work: Injustice within? *Social Work, 31,* 29–34.

Maypole, D. E., & Skaine, R. (1982). Sexual harassment of blue-collar workers. *Journal of Sociology and Social Welfare, 9,* 682–695.

McCormack, A. (1985). The sexual harassment of students by teachers: The case of students in science. *Sex Roles, 13,* 21–32.

McIntyre, D. I., & Renick, J. C. (1982). Protecting public employees and employers from sexual harassment. *Public Personnel Management Journal, 11,* 282–292.

Mednick, M. T. (1989). On the politics of psychological constructs: Stop the bandwagon, I want to get off. *American Psychologist, 44,* 1118–1123.

Meek, P. M., & Lynch, A. Q. (1983). Establishing an informal grievance procedure for cases of sexual harassment of students. *Journal of the National Association for Women Deans, Administrators, & Counselors, 46,* 30–33.

Merry, S. E., & Silbey, S. S. (1984). What do plaintiffs want? Reexamining the concept of dispute. *Justice System Journal, 9,* 151–178.

Metha, J., & Nigg, A. (1983). Sexual harassment on campus: An institutional response. *Journal of the National Association for Women Deans, Administrators, & Counselors, 46,* 9–15.

Miller, J. B. (1976). *Toward a new psychology of women.* Boston: Beacon Press.

Morgenson, G. (1989, May). Watch that leer, stifle that joke. *Forbes,* 69–72.

Popovich, P. M., Licata, B. J., Nokovich, D., Martelli, T., & Zoloty, S. (1987). Assessing the incidence and perceptions of sexual harassment behaviors among American undergraduates. *Journal of Psychology, 120,* 387–396.

Powell, G. N. (1986). Effects of sex role identity and sex on definitions of sexual harassment. *Sex Roles, 14,* 9–19.

Project on the Status and Education of Women. (1982). The campus climate: A chilly one for women? Washington, DC: Association of American Colleges.

Pryor, J. B. (1985). The lay person's understanding of sexual harassment. *Sex Roles, 13,* 273–286.

Pryor, J. B., & Day, J. D. (1988). Interpretations of sexual harassment: An attributional analysis. *Sex Roles, 18,* 405–417.

Reilly, M. E., Lott, B., & Gallogly, S. (1986). Sexual harassment of university students. *Sex Roles, 15,* 333–358.

Rifkin, J. (1984). Mediation from a feminist perspective: Promise and problems. *Mediation, 2,* 21–31.

Robertson, C., Dyer, C. E., & Campbell, D. (1988). Campus harassment: Sexual harassment policies and procedures at institutions of higher learning. *Signs: Journal of Women in Culture and Society, 13,* 792–812.

Robinson, W. L., & Reid, P. T. (1985). Sexual intimacy in psychology revisited. *Professional Psychology: Research and Practice, 16,* 512–520.

Rossi, P. H., & Weber-Burdin, E. (1983). Sexual harassment on the campus. *Social Science Research, 12,* 131–158.

Rowe, M. P. (1981, May–June). Dealing with sexual harassment. *Harvard Business Review,* 42–46.

Saal, F. E., Johnson, C. B., & Weber, N. (1989). Friendly or sexy? It may depend on whom you ask. *Psychology of Women Quarterly, 13,* 263–276.

Schneider, B. E. (1987). Graduate women, sexual harassment, and university policy. *Journal of Higher Education, 58,* 46–65.

Shotland, R. L., & Craig, J. M. (1988). Can men and women differentiate between friendly and sexually interested behavior? *Social Psychology Quarterly, 51,* 66–73.

Tangri, S. S., Burt, M. R., & Johnson, L. B. (1982). Sexual harassment at work: Three explanatory models. *Journal of Social Issues, 38,* 33–54.

Terpstra, D. E., & Baker, D. D. (1988). Outcomes of sexual harassment charges. *Academy of Management Journal, 31,* 185–194.

Terpstra, D. E., & Cook, S. E. (1985). Complainant characteristics and reported behaviors and consequences associated with formal sexual harassment charges. *Personnel Psychology, 38,* 559–574.

Thomann, D. A., & Wiener, R. L. (1987). Physical and psychological causality as determinants of culpability in sexual harassment cases. *Sex Roles, 17,* 573–591.

Trager, T. B. (1988). Legal considerations in drafting sexual harassment policies. In J. Van Tol (Ed.), *Sexual harassment on campus: A legal compendium* (pp. 181–190). Washington, DC: National Association of College and University Attorneys.

U.S. Equal Employment Opportunity Commission. (1980, November 10). Final amendment to guidelines on discrimination because of sex under Title VII of the Civil Rights Act of 1964, as amended. 29 CFR Part 1604. *Federal Register, 45,* 74675–74677.

U.S. Merit Systems Protection Board. (1981). *Sexual harassment in the federal workplace: Is it a problem?* Washington, DC: U.S. Government Printing Office.

U.S. Merit Systems Protection Board. (1988). *Sexual harassment in the federal government: An update.* Washington, DC: U.S. Government Printing Office.

Wilson, K. R., & Kraus, L. A. (1983). Sexual harassment in the university. *Journal of College Student Personnel, 24,* 219–224.

Wilson, M. (1988). Sexual harassment and the law. *The community psychologist, 21,* 16–17.

Questions for Meaning

1. How does Riger define "sexual harassment"?
2. Why are women more likely than men to be victims of sexual harassment?
3. Why are women reluctant to report incidents of sexual harassment?
4. What is meant by "the reasonable person rule"? Why does Riger find this rule problematic?
5. How do formal and informal grievance procedures differ? What are the disadvantages of an informal procedure?
6. According to Riger, what may be the best way of preventing sexual harassment?
7. Vocabulary: prevail (4), respondents (4), pervasive (8), noncompliance (10), nonsituated (12), wont (13), inimical (21), stratification (26), normative (28), idiosyncratic (35), ameliorate (40).

Questions about Strategy

1. As called for by the *Publication Manual of the American Psychological Association,* Riger prefaces her article with an abstract. What is the advantage in doing so? Is there any risk?
2. How would you describe the tone of this article? Is it appropriate for the topic and audience?
3. How does Riger justify her decision to focus on educational institutions?
4. Riger first states her thesis at the beginning of paragraph 7. What does she achieve by reserving her thesis until this point? How would the article change if Riger decided to include her thesis in the opening paragraph?
5. Riger draws on a large number of sources. How effectively has she drawn on them? When you encounter a reference list such as Riger's, how do you respond as a reader?

Kingsley R. Browne

TITLE VII AS CENSORSHIP: HOSTILE-ENVIRONMENT HARASSMENT AND THE FIRST AMENDMENT

Arguments of considerable length and complexity appear regularly in
law journals, as legal scholars argue on behalf of new interpretations of
the law, clarify prevailing interpretations, or demonstrate the need for
new rulings. Kingsley R. Browne teaches law at Wayne State University,
and "Title VII as Censorship" is part of a much longer argument he
published in the *Ohio State Law Journal* in 1991. In order to make this
work more accessible for college students, the seventy-four footnotes in
the following version have been edited down, with Browne's permission,
from 408 in the original version. Even so, you may find Browne's work
challenging because of the extensive research upon which it draws. As
you prepare to read, note how the argument is divided into separate
sections and plan to read one section at a time.

I. Introduction

"Women do not belong in the medical profession; they should stay home and
make babies!" Is such a statement occurring in the workplace a constitutionally protected expression of a currently unfashionable social view, or is it sexual harassment in violation of Title VII of the Civil Rights Act of 1964? If it
violates Title VII, is Title VII to that extent inconsistent with the first amendment? Many courts and commentators have addressed the first question—that
is, the contours of "hostile environment" harassment—but few have acknowledged the possibility of constitutional protection for such statements. The
purpose of this Article is to examine the extent to which the broad definition
of "hostile work environment" adopted by the courts in harassment cases establishes a content-based—even viewpoint-based—restriction of expression
that is inconsistent with contemporary first amendment jurisprudence. To the
extent that it does establish such a restriction Title VII must be given a narrowing construction in order to avoid a finding of invalidity.

2   Recent attention to the first amendment implications of racist and
sexist speech has focused largely on attempts by colleges and universities to
regulate such speech and the application of general tort doctrine to such
speech. It is not surprising that scholars have been particularly interested in
regulation of speech in their own bailiwick. Yet the amount of attention
paid university policies prohibiting racist and sexist speech seems out of
proportion to their global importance since these policies seem to be the
product of a temporary aberration that would burn itself out probably
sooner than later even without any kind of legal intervention. Like the

Indianapolis anti-pornography ordinance, regulation of offensive speech on campus probably generates far more expression than it regulates. Moreover, when legal intervention did occur, in the form of *Doe v. University of Michigan*[1] and *American Booksellers Ass'n v. Hudnut*,[2] the courts' responses were sure and decisive: the first amendment prohibits regulation of racist and sexist speech on the basis of the viewpoint expressed.

In contrast with the immediate rejection of regulation of campus speech and pornography that was deemed to convey a "wrongheaded" view about women, regulation of offensive speech in the workplace has been proceeding apace virtually without comment for well over a decade. Although it has resulted in suppression of a vast amount of expression, objections from the traditional defenders of free speech have not been forthcoming. An optimist might suggest that the concern over free speech in the academy is simply the opening skirmish in a broader battle to challenge regulation of offensive speech everywhere; the champions of the first amendment are simply attempting to get their own house in order before taking on the rest of the world. The indications are otherwise, however. Even the *Doe* court suggested that "speech which creates a hostile or abusive working environment on the basis of race or sex" is unprotected by the first amendment.[3] It is difficult to avoid the conclusion that some who would protect the speech of students and faculty but not the speech of workers possess an elitist perspective that simply values the former group of speakers more than the latter. The lack of value of the speech of workers seems to be based upon one or more of the following opinions: (1) when workers speak they do not convey ideas; (2) ideas are not important to workers; (3) the ideas of workers are not important to us. These judgments can form no part of a first amendment jurisprudence.

4   Regulation of speech in the workplace that is deemed "harassing" is pervasive. The Guidelines of the Equal Employment Opportunity Commission provide the most commonly accepted definition of "sexual harassment," a definition that courts have adapted to fit cases of racial harassment as well: "verbal or physical conduct of a sexual nature [that] has the purpose or effect of unreasonably interfering with an individual's work performance or creating an intimidating, hostile, or offensive work environment,"[4] Although the Guidelines purport to regulate only "verbal or physical *conduct*," the concept of "verbal conduct" has no obvious meaning, and courts have consistently interpreted it to mean "verbal expression." Relying on the EEOC's definition of hostile-environment harassment, courts, both state and federal, have found employers liable for "conduct" ranging from clearly unprotected forcible sexual assault and other unwanted sexual touching to "obscene propositions," sexual vulgarity (including "off color" jokes) and "sexist" remarks, some of which are almost certainly protected by the first amendment. Similarly, racial jokes, slurs, and other statements deemed derogatory to minorities have served as the basis for claims of racial harassment.

The restrictions on expression created by harassment regulation are not merely incidental; indeed, courts have recognized that the very purpose of the law is to "prevent . . . bigots from expressing their opinions in a way that abuses or offends their co-workers."[5] Moreover, protected expression[6] is often a substantial, if not the primary, basis for imposing liability. That is, the trier of fact is offended by the implicit or explicit message of the expression—for example, that women should be sexual playthings for men, that women (or blacks) do not belong in the workplace, or that they should hold an inferior position in our society. Yet, the right to express one's social views is generally considered to be at or near the core of the first amendment's protection of free expression.

6   A broad definition of sexual and racial harassment necessarily delegates broad powers to courts to determine matters of taste and humor, and the vagueness of the definition of "harassment" leaves those subject to regulation without clear notice of what is permitted and what is forbidden. The inescapable result is a substantial chilling effect on expression. Holding employers liable for the offensive speech of their employees exacerbates that chilling effect, because fear of litigation and liability creates a powerful incentive for employers—which in the private sector are not subject to the constraints of the first amendment—to censor the speech of their employees. Employers have responded to these incentives by substantially overregulating the speech of their employees.

Although with only one apparent exception[7] no reported harassment decision has imposed liability solely on the basis of arguably protected expression, it does not follow that hostile-environment claims therefore pose little threat to first amendment rights. First, when protected expression is excluded from the liability calculus, the remaining unprotected expression or conduct, though of a harassing nature, may not be sufficiently severe or pervasive on its own to support a judgment. Second, even if sufficient unprotected conduct or expression is present so that a trier of fact *could* find against the defendant, a risk that liability may be imposed based in part on protected speech is intolerable under the first amendment. Third, under the doctrine of overbreadth, a legal scheme that reaches a substantial amount of protected speech cannot be applied to reach even unprotected expression.[8] Therefore, evidence of protected speech should not be admitted at trial to support a claim of hostile environment.

8   The first amendment does not insulate all speech from legal regulation, but in order for speech to be regulated on the basis of content, it must fall within some recognized exception to the first amendment—such as defamation, obscenity, or "fighting words"—or a new exception must be recognized. Although some "harassing speech"[9] falls neatly within existing exceptions, much does not, and the Title VII standard is sufficiently broad that it covers both protected and unprotected speech. . . .

II. The Theory of Harassment Under Title VII

Title VII expressly prohibits neither sexual nor racial harassment. Instead, it generally provides that it is an unlawful employment practice for an employer "to discriminate against any individual with respect to his compensation, terms, conditions, or privileges of employment because of such individual's race, color, religion, sex, or national origin."[10] Nonetheless, courts have identified two forms of sexual harassment that violate Title VII—"*quid pro quo*" and "hostile work environment" harassment. "*Quid pro quo*" harassment typically involves a claim that an employee, usually female, was required to submit to sexual advances as a condition of receiving job benefits or that her failure to submit to such advances resulted in a tangible job detriment, such as discharge or failure to receive a promotion. "Hostile work environment" harassment involves the claim that the workplace is so "polluted" with sexual hostility toward women—or racial hostility to other races—that it discriminatorily alters the "terms and conditions of employment" within the meaning of the statute.[11] The hostility may be expressed either through conduct or through speech. The focus of this Article is limited to hostile-environment harassment and then only to the extent that the hostile environment is created in whole or in part by expression.[12]

10   The first case to recognize a hostile-environment theory under Title VII was a race case. In *Rogers v. EEOC,* Judge Goldberg stated:

> [E]mployees' psychological as well as economic fringes are statutorily entitled to protection from employer abuse, and . . . the phrase "terms, conditions, or privileges of employment" in Section 703 is an expansive concept which sweeps within its protective ambit the practice of creating a working environment heavily charged with ethnic or racial discrimination.[13]

Numerous cases since *Rogers* have relied upon this broad conception of the phrase "terms, conditions, or privileges of employment" to hold that a racially or sexually hostile atmosphere violates Title VII even absent any discrimination in wages, job assignments, or other tangible benefits, and *Rogers* was a major impulse behind the EEOC's promulgation of its Guidelines. In *Meritor Savings Bank, FSB v. Vinson,* the Supreme Court, in recognizing a cause of action for sexual harassment leading to non-economic injury, quoted the EEOC Guidelines approvingly, stating that in adopting those Guidelines, "the EEOC drew upon a substantial body of judicial decisions and EEOC precedent holding that Title VII affords employees the right to work in an environment free from discriminatory intimidation, ridicule, and insult."[14] The Court announced that "a requirement that a man or woman run a gauntlet of sexual abuse in return for the privilege of being allowed to work and make a living can be as demeaning and disconcerting as the harshest of racial epithets."[15] The Court emphasized, however, that "not all workplace conduct that may be described as 'harassment' affects a 'term, condition, or privilege' of employment within the meaning of Title VII."[16] Rather, for harassment to be actionable under Title VII, "it must be sufficiently severe or pervasive 'to alter the conditions of [the victim's] employment and create an abusive working environment.' "[17] The Court in

Vinson had no trouble finding sufficient allegations of hostile environment, because the plaintiff alleged that she had been forcibly raped.

The reported cases reveal that the definitions of sexual and racial harassment under Title VII are at the same time broader and narrower than the conventional definition of "harassment," which generally connotes a pattern of conduct aimed at a particular person and intended to annoy. The statutory definition is broader in that expression can constitute "harassment" even when it is not directed toward the plaintiff and not intended to annoy, and narrower in that it includes only harassment based upon protected status and, even then, only harassment that is sufficiently severe or pervasive as to alter the terms and conditions of employment.

12   Although some courts have stated that a plaintiff must show a "pattern of harassment," rather than "a few isolated incidents," others have expressly rejected that distinction and suggested that the plaintiff "need not prove that the instances of alleged harassment were related in either time or type,"[18] and others have suggested that it is error for a court to conclude that harassment did not exist simply because very few incidents were alleged.[19] Conduct need not be overtly sexual or racial to be actionable; other hostile conduct directed against the victim because of the victim's race or sex is also prohibited.

Ironically, though couched in terms of discriminatory treatment, the real claim in many harassment cases is that the work atmosphere did *not* change in response to the addition of women (or minorities) to the environment. The rationale is that conduct that appears harmless to men may be offensive to women, although such reasoning seems inconsistent, at least superficially, with the view that Title VII "rejects the notion of 'romantic paternalism' towards women."[20] For example, the court in *Andrews v. City of Philadelphia*[21] rejected the argument that the environment was not a hostile one because "a police station need not be run like a day care center," stating that neither should it have "the ambience of a nineteenth-century military barracks," although an all-male police station having such an ambience would certainly not violate Title VII. The court also noted that although men might find the obscenity and pornography that pervaded the workplace "harmless and innocent," women might well "feel otherwise," and such expression may be "highly offensive to a woman who seeks to deal with her fellow employees and clients with professional dignity and without the barrier of sexual differentiation and abuse." As a consequence, a locker room atmosphere that was perfectly legal before the entry of women into the job becomes illegal thereafter.

14   The extent to which courts will be willing to pursue the above logic remains to be seen. Suppose, for example, an employer had a policy of imposing discipline against any employee who used profanity in front of a woman. The assumption that women as a group may be more offended by profanity than men as a group seems like just the sort of stereotype that Title VII was intended to erase. Just as it may be empirically true that women as a group are more offended by profanity than men, it also may be

empirically true that women as a group are more nurturant than men, but courts have interpreted Title VII to prohibit reliance on the latter generalization, and it is unclear why the two generalizations should enjoy a different status.

Because harassment claims rest upon a discrimination theory, a number of courts have suggested that where sexual conduct is equally offensive to males and females there is no actionable harassment. Similarly, where supervisors are abusive to all employees, many courts have rejected racial and sexual harassment claims. Other courts have allowed such claims, however, where the harassment of the plaintiff took a sexual or racial form. The latter cases seem inconsistent with the underlying theory of Title VII harassment, which is that the employee suffers an adverse working environment because of race or sex. A supervisor who refers to subordinates by terms such as "dumb bastard," "dumb bitch," "fat bastard," "red-headed bastard," and "black bastard" cannot fairly be said to have discriminated against the woman and the black in favor of the fat, dumb, and red-headed employees. All were subjected to an abusive environment, and unless the black and the woman would have been spared the abuse but for their race and sex, they are not victims of discrimination. By similar reasoning, when harassment is directed against an individual because of a personal grudge, it should not be actionable even if it takes a racial or sexual form, though the cases come out the other way. Conversely, of course, where the harassment does not take a sexual or racial form but is aimed at the victim because of the victim's race or sex, harassment on the prohibited basis exists.

16   The Supreme Court has not yet wholly defined the extent of an employer's liability for harassment by its employees. In *quid pro quo* cases, which by definition involve supervisory employees, courts generally apply automatic vicarious liability on the theory that such behavior is like any other form of prohibited discrimination, where the employer is liable irrespective of whether it knew of the particular discriminatory conduct by one of its agents or had a policy against it.[22] The scope of employer liability for hostile-environment harassment is not as well settled and may depend upon whether the harasser is a supervisor or a co-worker. Although the EEOC Guidelines provide that an employer is automatically liable in all cases of sexual harassment,[23] the Supreme Court in *Vinson* rejected that standard.[24] The Court declined, however, to articulate any standard in its place, although it did suggest that courts should look to general agency principles and consider the following factors: (1) whether the employer has a policy prohibiting sexual harassment; (2) whether the policy was communicated to employees; (3) whether the employer had notice of the harassment; and (4) whether the employer's response upon learning of the harassment was adequate.[25] However, the Court noted that "absence of notice to an employer does not necessarily insulate that employer from liability."[26] Courts since *Vinson* are split on whether notice is required in supervisor cases, but in cases involving co-workers most courts have required that the plaintiff show that the employer knew or should have known of the

harassment and failed to take adequate remedial steps.[27] There is no need, however, for the employee to show that the failure of the employer to remedy the situation was discriminatory. An employer that routinely tells employees to work out their problems with their co-workers is liable for harassment if it applies the same rule to complaints of harassment.

Reported decisions under Title VII have found a wide variety of speech to constitute or contribute to a sexually or racially hostile working environment. In many of the cases discussed below, additional facts contributed to the decision. The point of the illustrations is not that only protected expression was involved or that the ultimate conclusions by the courts were necessarily wrong. Rather, the examples show that pure expression plays a large role in many of the decisions, a conclusion having substantial first amendment implications.

III. Title VII as a Viewpoint-Based Restriction on Expression

18 Expression contributing to harassment claims comes in a variety of forms. While much of it is exceedingly crude and probably outside the protection of the first amendment, some is merely uncivil, some at most insensitive, and some perhaps wholly harmless. As the description of the cases below reveals, speech that is only arguably sexist, sexual, or racist may form the basis for a claim of harassment. Central to a finding of unlawful harassment is often a conclusion by the court that the message is "offensive," "inappropriate," or even "morally wrong." Even if the employer ultimately prevails in such cases, it must incur a high cost in litigation fees for declining to regulate the speech of employees. Because the underlying objection to sexist or sexual speech and to racist speech* is sometimes different, the two forms of harassment will be considered separately. . . .

There are two primary messages conveyed by the expression that leads to sexual harassment complaints. The first is a message of unwelcomeness or hostility; expressions that women do not belong in the workplace or scornful or derisive statements about women would fall in this class. The second is a message that the harasser views the plaintiff in particular or women in general in a sexual light. For sake of discussion, the former will be called the "hostility message," while the latter will be called the "sexuality message."

20 Many sexual harassment cases have involved the use of "bad words" of a sexual nature. Crude or otherwise inappropriate language referring to or addressing women is commonly present in hostile-environment cases, though it is not generally by itself enough to establish a claim of harassment. The terms complained of are primarily of two kinds, and they convey both of the above-described messages: (1) the "hostility message" is conveyed by terms of derision, such as "broad," "bitch," and "cunt;"[28] and (2) the "sexuality message" is conveyed by terms of "endearment," such as "honey,"[29] "sweetie," and "tiger."

---

* This abridged version of Browne's argument does not include his discussion of racist speech.

The complained-of terms may refer to women in general, particular women other than the plaintiff, or they may refer to the plaintiff herself and be addressed either to her or to others while referring to her.

At least with respect to the most vulgar expressions, arguably it is just the use of "indecent" words—words that are "beyond the pale" of what can be spoken in polite society—that is being regulated. That, of course, would justify viewing the most vulgar terms as contributing to a hostile environment, but it would not justify reliance on milder terms, such as "broad." But Title VII is not a "clean language act,"[30] and bad language conveying no idea is not the target of the harassment cases. Thus, the court in *State v. Human Rights Commission*,[31] distinguished between "gender-specific" terms, such as "cunt," "bitch," "twat," and "raggin' it"—which constitute "conduct of a sexual nature"—and "general sexual" terms, such as "fuck" and "motherfucker" used as expletives, which do not. The court held that a supervisor's reference to women's physical appearance and his reference to women by "gender-specific" derogatory terms constituted sexual harassment because it was an "expression of animosity" toward women.[32] The finding of harassment was not based primarily on one-to-one expressions of hostility by the supervisor toward the employee, but instead on the general disrespect he showed women in his conversations with others.

22 More explicit expressions of "Neanderthal" attitudes toward women have also been held to support a claim of hostile environment. Thus, in *Lipsett v. University of Puerto Rico*,[33] a female medical resident claimed that one of her fellow residents told her that women should not become surgeons "because they need too much time to bathe, to go to the bathroom, to apply makeup, and to get dressed," and she frequently heard other comments to the effect that women did not belong in surgery.[34] Although these statements were "not explicitly *sexual*," the court concluded that they were "charged with anti-female animus" because they "challenged their capacity as women to be surgeons" and "questioned the legitimacy of their being in the Program at all."[35] As a result, they could contribute to the hostile environment. Rejecting the defendant's argument that many of the comments were jokes, the court observed that "[b]elittling comments about a person's ability to perform, on the basis of that person's sex, are not funny."[36]

Plaintiffs in sexual harassment cases also frequently challenge the exhibition of written or pictorial material that they believe is demeaning or mocking toward women. Pin-ups or "girlie magazines" in the workplace have been the subject of innumerable sexual harassment claims.[37] The conflicting approaches to the problem of sexually oriented displays are revealed by the majority and dissenting opinions in *Rabidue v. Osceola Refining Co.*[38] The majority rejected a claim that was based upon anti-female language and pin-ups, stating:

> The sexually oriented poster displays had a *de minimis* effect on the plaintiff's work environment when considered in the context of a society that condones and publicly features and commercially exploits open displays of

written and pictorial erotica at the newsstands, on prime-time television, at the cinema, and in other public places.[39]

24   On the other hand, Judge Keith's frequently cited dissent would have found that the alleged harasser's "misogynous language" combined with the pin-ups constituted a Title VII violation because they "evoke and confirm the debilitating norms by which women are primarily and contemptuously valued as objects of male sexual fantasy."[40] In the dissent's view, the "precise purpose" of Title VII was to prevent sexual jokes, conversations, and literature from "poisoning the work environment."[41] Two of the displays that Judge Keith seemed to find particularly reprehensible were a poster showing a woman in a supine position with a golf ball on her breasts and a man standing over her, golf club in hand, yelling "Fore" and a supervisor's desk plaque declaring "Even male chauvinist pigs need love."[42]

The message restricted by exclusion of pin-ups is the "sexuality message." Kathryn Abrams describes that message as follows:

> Pornography on an employer's wall or desk communicates a message about the way he views women, a view strikingly at odds with the way women wish to be viewed in the workplace. Depending on the material in question, it may communicate that women should be objects of sexual aggression, that they are submissive slaves to male desires, or that their most salient and desirable attributes are sexual. Any of these images may communicate to male coworkers that it is acceptable to view women in a predominantly sexual way.[43]

26   The very recent case of *Robinson v. Jacksonville Shipyards, Inc.*,[44] which adopted the view of both the *Rabidue* dissent and the Abrams article, was apparently the first reported decision to impose liability for sexual harassment based entirely on the pervasive presence of sexually oriented magazines, pin-up pictures—such as *Playboy* foldouts and tool-company calendars—and "sexually demeaning remarks and jokes" by male coworkers; the plaintiff complained of neither physical assaults nor sexual propositions.[45] Some of the pictures were posted on walls in public view, but included within the category of sexually harassing behavior were incidents where male employees were simply reading the offending magazines in the workplace[46] or carrying them in their back pockets.[47] The court rejected the suggestion of *Rabidue* that sexually oriented pictures and comments standing alone cannot form the basis for Title VII liability, stating that "[e]xcluding some forms of offensive conduct as a matter of law is not consistent with the factually oriented approach" required by Title VII.[48]

A desire not to be viewed as a "sex object" also underlies the objection to sexual propositions in the workplace. Sexual harassment cases have often involved sexual propositions of varying degrees of vulgarity. For example, in *Continental Can Co. v. State*,[49] an employee's coworkers told her how they could "make her feel sexually" and that they could make her want to leave her husband.[50] In another case, male workers told dirty jokes, suggested that plaintiff participate in a sexually explicit home video, and one worker suggested that she "sit on [his] face."[51] In yet another, the plaintiff alleged that the message, "How about a little head?" appeared on the screen of her computer terminal.[52] Although sometimes the advances are crude and explicit, that is not always the case. For example, in *Zowayyed v. Lowen Co.*, the plaintiff alleged that the company president wrote a note to her reading, "You have very playful eyes. Do you play?" and the next day said to her, "If you don't bait the hook, you can't catch the fish."[53] Sometimes the assertion goes beyond what the alleged harasser has said to what the harasser is thinking. Thus, plaintiffs in sexual harassment cases have relied on both the tone of voice[54] and the look on a face.

28   A recent Ninth Circuit case held that the plaintiff had established a prima facie case of sexual harassment based on what can only be described as a pathetic romantic overture by a coworker.[55] The accused harasser, a revenue agent of the Internal Revenue Service named Gray, had asked the plaintiff, a fellow agent, out for a drink after work. The plaintiff declined but suggested that they have lunch the following week. The next week, Gray asked the plaintiff out for lunch, but she declined. The following week, Gray handed the plaintiff a note stating:

> I cried over you last night and I'm totally drained today. I have never been in such constant term oil [sic]. Thank you for talking with me. I could not stand to feel your hatred for another day.[56]

Plaintiff left the room and asked a male coworker to tell Gray that she was not interested in him and to leave her alone. The next week, Gray sent plaintiff a three-page letter stating in part:

> I know that you are worth knowing with or without sex. . . . Leaving aside the hassles and disasters of recent weeks. I have enjoyed you so much over these past few months. Watching you. Experiencing you from O so far away. Admiring your style and elan. . . . Don't you think it odd that two people who have never even talked together, alone, are striking off such intense sparks . . . I will [write] another letter in the near future.[57]

The letter also said, "I am obligated to you so much that if you want me to leave you alone I will. . . . If you want me to forget you entirely, I can not do that."[58] The Ninth Circuit reversed the district court's grant of summary judgment, rejecting the lower court's conclusion that the incident was "isolated and genuinely trivial"[59] and holding that "Gray's conduct was sufficiently severe and pervasive to alter the conditions of [plaintiff's] employment and create an abusive working environment."[60]

     Not all cases involve statements of views about women in general; sometimes the displays are more focused. For example, a female firefighter established a claim of sexual harassment based in large part upon the appearance of "blatant sexual mockery" in the form of graffiti and cartoons on the communal bulletin boards and living space of the firehouse.[61] A display that the court seemed to find among the more offensive was a cartoon posted in the firehouse depicting a woman firefighter at a men's urinal,[62] though the message seems quite "political" in the context of a fire department under orders to set positions aside for women.[63] The term "political" is used here and throughout the Article in its broad sense—that is, pertaining to matters of social policy. Speech expressing views about matters of social policy—such as the proper role of the races and sexes—should be considered political in the same sense that speech advocating nondiscriminatory treatment should be. The most obvious interpretation of the *Berkman* cartoon is that it is a negative comment on the notion of sexual integration of the fire department.

30   The importance of an anti-female message in harassment cases is starkly revealed by *Goluszek v. Smith*,[64] in which a male plaintiff claimed that male coworkers had harassed him. The plaintiff was an unsophisticated man who apparently was quite sensitive to comments about sex. His coworkers showed him pictures of nude women, told him they would get him "fucked," and poked him in the buttocks with a stick,[65] all conduct that most courts would find constituted sexual harassment if directed toward women. Although the court acknowledged that Goluszek was harassed because he was a male,[66] it held that the harassment was not actionable under Title VII. Unlike this case, said the court, in a valid Title VII harassment case, "the offender is saying by words or actions that the victim is inferior because of the victim's sex."[67] Because Goluszek was a male in a male-dominated environment, the court reasoned that the harassment could not have embodied the message that he was inferior because of his sex. . . .

VIII. Conclusion

The impulse to censor is a powerful one, and it has been given free rein under Title VII. Not only has "targeted vilification" been regulated, but much less harmful and less invidiously motivated expression has been restricted as well. That so much speech has been stifled without substantial outcry is in large measure a reflection of the powerful current consensus against racism and sexism. But it is precisely when a powerful consensus exists that the censorial impulse is most dangerous and, ironically, least necessary. The primary risk of censorship in our society today is not from a government fearful of challenge, but from majorities seeking to establish an orthodoxy for all society. When the orthodoxy is one of "equality," that risk is at its highest.

32   The definition of "harassment" contained in the EEOC Guidelines and applied by the courts, combined with vicarious employer liability, creates a substantial chilling effect on discussion in the workplace of matters even tangentially dealing with sex and race. Acting pursuant to those Guidelines, courts have displayed remarkably little discernment among

examples of expression. Once they have been labelled as racist or sexist, all such expression has been deemed regulable. Although much of the speech that has been described in this Article arguably may be regulated through appropriately narrow and specific legislation that is viewpoint neutral, the Guidelines are not the appropriate vehicle, and, in fact, are so vague and so overbroad that they may not be applied even to unprotected speech consistent with the Constitution.

The current approach to regulation of offensive speech is directly contrary to the traditional notion that noxious ideas should be countered through juxta-position with good ideas in the hope that the bad ideas will lose out in the marketplace of ideas. To a degree perhaps unprecedented, the current attempt to stifle offensive speech can be viewed as an attempt to achieve not only an egalitarian orthodoxy of speech and action but an orthodoxy of thought itself. Consider, for example, prohibitions against employees' having sexually explicit pictures on the inside of their lockers or their reading *Playboy* (or worse) in the workplace. The justification for such regulation is not that women of delicate sensibilities might see the material and be shocked by it. Rather, the basis for the prohibition is that some people, mostly women, are offended by what the employee is thinking while he is looking at the pictures; they are offended by the way he "views"—that is, "thinks about"—women.

34   An apparently growing number of academics and judges explicitly defend limitations of expression on the ground that restricting expression will modify beliefs. Thus, Delgado states, "a tort for racist speech will discourage such speech, establish a new public conscience, and ultimately change attitudes.[68] It should not be concluded that the censorship advocated is solely for protection of the target; Delgado seeks also to protect the speaker. In a passage reminiscent of the Soviet attempt to label political dissidents mentally ill, he argues: "Bigotry harms the individuals who harbor it by reinforcing rigid thinking, thereby dulling their moral and social senses and possibly leading to a 'mildly . . . paranoid' mentality."[69]

The "thought-control" rationale for restricting expression is not confined to academic commentary. A similar justification for limitation of speech was provided by the Sixth Circuit in *Davis v. Monsanto Chemical Co.*:[70] "By informing people that the expression of racist or sexist attitudes in public is unacceptable, people may eventually learn that such views are undesirable in private, as well. Thus, Title VII may advance the goal of eliminating prejudices and biases in our society." Thus is the "freedom to think as you will and to speak as you think," so celebrated by Justice Brandeis,[71] converted to a duty to think as you are told and to speak as you are told to think.

36   It is but a small step from requiring a person to refrain from expressing beliefs in the hope that he will cease to hold them to requiring a person to express beliefs in the hope that he will begin to hold them. If the state may justify a prohibition on a person's saying "blacks are inferior" by pointing to the effect of the prohibition on a person's beliefs, the state should have

equivalent power to require that a person affirm a belief in racial equality on the ground that repeated affirmation will cause the person to come to believe it, and, once having come to believe it, to conform his actions to his newly acquired beliefs. Thus, the state could require as a condition of holding public employment—or attending public school—that an applicant sign an "equality oath," affirming a belief in the equality of the races and sexes.

In addition to its Orwellian overtones, the assumption that beliefs can be altered by forbidding expression is probably wrong. As Paul Chevigny has suggested in the context of the debate over pornography regulation, propaganda—whether in the form of "anti-female" pornography or racist expression—appeals only to those whose systems of belief make them receptive to the representations.[72] Suppressing pornography (or racist speech) is "beside the point in a cognitive world where we can interpret new experience only through existing patterns."[73] The only effective method of altering a world view that is deemed pernicious is to provide a persuasive response—that is, "more speech." "Shut up!" is not a persuasive response.

38   Although the contrary is sometimes asserted, challenging censorship is not to cast one's lot with those censored or to minimize the substance of the opinions of those urging censorship. Instead it is to accept the fundamental *constitutional* truth that the government may not establish a fundamental *moral* truth through suppression of expression. Probably everyone reading this Article would agree that the world would be a better place without much of the expression that is described in the harassment cases. It does not follow, however, that the world would be a better place if elimination of such expression is compelled by the threat of governmental sanctions. Persuasion that the offensive views are wrong or that they not be expressed where they are unwelcome is a far better solution than "silence coerced by law—the argument of force in its worst form."[74] ❖

Notes

1. 721 F. Supp. 852 (E.D. Mich. 1989) (striking down the University of Michigan offensive-speech policy).
2. 771 F.2d 323, 331 (7th Cir. 1985). aff'd, 475 U.S. 1001 (1986) (striking down the Indianapolis anti-pornography ordinance).
3. Doe v. University of Michigan, 721 F. Supp. 852, 863 (E.D. Mich. 1989).
4. 29 C.F.R. § 1604.11(a)(3). Because the EEOC lacks the authority to promulgate substantive regulations, the Guidelines lack the force of law. However, federal courts, including the Supreme Court, have uniformly relied upon them, *see, e.g.,* Meritor Sav. Bank, F.S.B. v. Vinson, 477 U.S. 57, 65 (1986), and many state statutes and regulations have adopted the EEOC language, *see, e.g.,* ILL. REV. STAT. ch. 68, § 2–101(E); MICH. COMP. LAWS § 37.2103(h).
5. Davis v. Monsanto Chemical Co., 858 F.2d 345, 350 (6th Cir. 1988), *cert. denied,* 109 S. Ct. 3166 (1989). Andrews v. City of Philadelphia, 895 F.2d 1469, 1486 (3d Cir. 1990) (quoting *Davis,* 858 F.2d 345).
6. The terms "protected expression" and "protected speech" are used in this Article because they are commonly used in the literature. There is, of course, no expression that is protected or unprotected under all circumstances. A political speech

may be prohibited by regulations prohibiting noise in an intensive-care unit, and obscenity may not be prohibited by a law that distinguishes among obscene expressions based upon their political content. Thus, it may actually be more meaningful to speak in terms of "prohibited regulation" than in terms of "protected speech."

7. Robinson v. Jacksonville Shipyards, Inc., 1991 U.S. Dist. LEXIS 794 (M.D. Fla. 1991).

8. Broadrick v. Oklahoma, 413 U.S. 601, 615 (1973).

9. The term "harassing speech" is used to describe speech that courts have held to contribute to a finding of harassment under Title VII, without regard to whether the speech by itself would be actionable or whether the speaker intended to annoy the listener.

10. 42 U.S.C. § 2000c.

11. The distinction between the two kinds of harassment is not always clear, and some courts have criticized attempts to draw such distinctions. For example, in Mitchell v. OsAir, Inc., 629 F. Supp. 636, 643 (N.D. Ohio 1986), the court, referring to a hostile environment, stated that "[t]he threat of loss of work explicit in the quid pro quo may only be implicit without being any less coercive."

12. A somewhat different form of hostile-environment claim is that consensual sexual relationships of other persons create an offensive sexually charged environment. In Broderick v. Ruder, 685 F. Supp. 1269, 1280 (D.D.C. 1988), the court held that the plaintiff proved a sexually hostile work environment by demonstrating the existence of pervasive consensual sexual conduct in the office. See also Drinkwater v. Union Carbide Corp., 904 F.2d 853, 862 (3d Cir. 1990) (acknowledging the theory, but rejecting the argument because there was no evidence that romantic relationships were "flaunted" or prevalent).

13. 454 F.2d 234, 238 (5th Cir. 1971), cert. denied, 406 U.S. 957 (1972).

14. 477 U.S. 57, 65 (1986). See also Scott v. Sears, Roebuck & Co., 798 F.2d 210, 213 (7th Cir. 1986) ("After Meritor there is no mistaking the acceptability of the EEOC definition (and verbiage) found at § 1604.11(a)").

15. 477 U.S. at 67 (quoting Henson v. City of Dundee, 682 F.2d 897, 902 (11th Cir. 1982)).

16. 477 U.S. at 67 (citing Rogers v. EEOC, 454 F.2d 234, 238 (5th Cir. 1971) ("mere utterance of an ethnic or racial epithet which engenders offensive feelings in an employee" would not affect the conditions of employment to sufficiently significant degree to violate Title VII)), cert. denied, 406 U.S. 957 (1972); Henson v. City of Dundee, 682 F.2d at 904 (quoting Rogers, 454 F.2d 234).

17. 477 U.S. at 67 (quoting Henson v. City of Dundee, 682 F.2d at 904). See also Anderson v. Chicago Housing Authority, 1988 U.S. Dist. LEXIS 14454, *20 (N.D. Ill. 1988) (rejecting claim based on "a few isolated incidents of sexual harassment" on ground that it was not enough to characterize workplace as "abusive working environment").

18. Davis v. Monsanto Chem. Co., 858 F.2d 345, 349 (6th Cir. 1988), cert. denied, 109 S. Ct. 3166 (1989). See also Waltman v. Int'l. Paper Co., 875 F.2d 468, 475 (5th Cir. 1989) ("focus is whether [plaintiff] was subjected to recurring acts of discrimination, not whether a given individual harassed [plaintiff] recurrently.").

19. King v. Board of Regents, 898 F.2d 533, 537 (7th Cir. 1990) ("although a single act can be enough, . . . generally repeated incidents create a stronger claim of hostile environment, with the strength of the claim depending on the number of incidents and the intensity of each incident"); Vance v. Southern Bell Tel. & Tel. Co., 863 F.2d 1503, 1510 (11th Cir. 1989) ("the determination of whether the defendant's conduct is sufficiently 'severe or pervasive' to constitute racial harassment does not turn solely on the number of incidents alleged by plaintiff.").

20. United States v. City of Buffalo, 457 F. Supp. 612, 629 (W.D.N.Y. 1978) (quoting Rosen v. Public Serv. Elec. & Gas Co., 328 F. Supp. 454, 464 (D.C. N.J. (1990)). See also Note, Sexual Harassment and Title VII: A Better Solution, 30 B.C. L. REV. 1071 (1989) (arguing that sexual harassment is not really discrimination and urging enactment of separate sexual harassment legislation).

21. 895 F.2d 1469, 1486 (3d Cir. 1990).
22. Lipsett v. University of Puerto Rico, 864 F.2d 881, 901 (1st Cir. 1988); Sparks v. Pilot Freight Carriers, Inc., 830 F.2d 1554, 1564 n.22 (11th Cir. 1987); Horn v. Duke Homes, Div. of Windsor Mobile Homes, Inc., 755 F.2d 599, 605 (7th Cir. 1985); Katz v. Dole, 709 F.2d 251, 256 n.6 (4th Cir. 1983); McCalla v. Ellis, 180 Mich. App. 372, 379–80, 446 N.W.2d 904, 909 (1989).
23. 29 C.F.R. § 1604.11(c).
24. 477 U.S. 59, 72 (1986).
25. *Id.* at 71–72.
26. *Id.* at 72.
27. *Lipsett* at 902 (1st Cir. 1988); Davis v. Monsanto Chem. Co., 858 F.2d 345, 349 (6th Cir. 1988).
28. Some words, primarily those relating to female sexual anatomy, may actually convey a dual message by showing contempt for women by equating them with their sex organs.
29. Robinson v. Jacksonville Shipyards, Inc., 1991 U.S. Dist. LEXIS 794, at *27 (M.D. Fla. 1991).
30. Katz v. Dole, 709 F.2d 251, 256 (4th Cir. 1983).
31. 178 Ill. App. 3d 1033, 1046, 534 N.E.2d 161, 170 (1989).
32. *Id.* at 1049, 534 N.E.2d at 171. Comments similar to those in this case were not considered enough to create a hostile environment by the court in Rabidue v. Osceola Ref. Co., 805 F.2d 611 (6th Cir. 1986), *cert. denied,* 481 U.S. 1041 (1987).
33. 864 F.2d 881 (1st Cir. 1988).
34. *Id.* at 887. Another supervisory resident justified his assigning plaintiff menial tasks by asserting that women should not be surgeons because they could not be relied upon while they were menstruating or, as he put it, "in heat." *Id. See also* Arnold v. City of Seminole, 614 F. Supp. 853, 862–63 (N.D. Okla. 1985) (comments that women are not fit to become police officers; picture of a nude woman posted on a locker door with words "Do women make good cops—No - No - No.").
35. 864 F.2d at 905 (emphasis in original).
36. *Id.* at 906.
37. Andrews v. City of Philadelphia, 895 F.2d 1469, 1472 (3d Cir. 1990) ("pornographic" pictures of women were displayed in the locker room on the inside of a locker that was generally kept open); Waltman v. International Paper Co., 875 F.2d 468, 471 (5th Cir. 1989) (sexually oriented calendars on walls and in lockers); Bennett v. Corroon & Black Corp., 845 F.2d 104, 105 (5th Cir. 1988) (presence of "obscene cartoons" bearing plaintiff's name), *cert. denied,* 489 U.S. 1020 (1989); Lipsett v. University of Puerto Rico, 864 F.2d 881 (1st Cir. 1988) (*Playboy* centerfolds displayed by male residents in rest facility); Rabidue v. Osceola Ref. Co., 805 F.2d 611 (6th Cir. 1986), *cert. denied,* 481 U.S. 1041 (1987); Sanchez v. City of Miami Beach, 720 F. Supp. 974, 977 n.9 (S.D. Fla. 1989) ("various pictures from *Playboy, Penthouse,* and other publications were posted in the station."); Robinson v. Jacksonville Shipyards, Inc., 1991 U.S. Dist. LEXIS 794 (M.D. Fla. 1991) ("allegation that the pervasive presence of pornography in the workplace is offensive to female employees generally and plaintiff in particular."); Barbetta v. Chemlawn Servs. Corp., 669 F. Supp. 569 (W.D.N.Y. 1987) (presence of "pornographic" magazines and sexually oriented pictures and calendars); Brown v. City of Guthrie, 1980 WL 380, *3 (W.D. Okla. 1980) (presence of magazines containing photographs of nude women in police dispatcher's desk for policemen to look at during their spare time).
38. 805 F.2d 611 (6th Cir. 1986), *cert. denied,* 481 U.S. 1041 (1987).
39. *Id.* at 622.
40. *Id.* at 627 (Keith, J., dissenting). Barbetta v. Chemlawn Servs. Corp., 669 F. Supp. 569, 573 (W.D.N.Y. 1987) (explicitly rejecting *Rabidue* majority opinion and adopting position of *Rabidue* dissent that "sexual posters and anti-female language can seriously affect the psychological well-being of the reasonable woman and interfere with her

ability to perform her job," *id.* at 573 n.2 (quoting *Rabidue,* 805 F.2d at 627 (Keith, J., dissenting)), and may "create an atmosphere in which women are viewed as men's sexual playthings," *Barbetta,* 669 F. Supp. at 573); Robinson v. Jacksonville Shipyards, Inc., 1991 U.S. Dist. LEXIS 794 (M.D. Fla. 1988) ("To the extent that *Rabidue* holds that some forms of abusive, anti-female behavior must be tolerated in the work environment because the behavior is prominent in society at large, the case conflicts with the established law in this Circuit") (citation omitted).

41. 805 F.2d at 626.

42. Rabidue v. Osceola Ref. Co., 805 F.2d at 624 (Keith, J., dissenting). (M.D. Fla. 1991) (Title VII prohibits speech that is "disproportionately more offensive or demeaning to one sex . . . because it conveys the message that they do not belong, that they are welcome in the workplace only if they will subvert their identities to the sexual stereotypes prevalent in that environment").

43. Abrams, *Gender Discrimination and the Transformation of Workplace Norms,* 42 VAND. L. REV. 1183, 1212 n.118 (1989). Abrams' categorical assertion that the message of pornography is "strikingly at odds with the way women wish to be viewed in the workplace" seems overbroad and based not on an empirical judgment that all women object to being viewed in a sexual manner in the workplace, but rather on the normative judgment that women *should* object. Moreover, not all women object to pornographic materials, even in the workplace, and many who do object do so on grounds having nothing to do with views of "sexual subordination."

44. 1991 U.S. Dist. LEXIS 794 (M.D. Fla. 1991).

45. *Id.* at 90.

46. *Id.* at 18, 25.

47. *Id.* at 37.

48. *Id.* at 120–23. The court also examined, albeit superficially, the argument that the first amendment imposes limits on the kind of activity that can be the subject of sexual harassment claims. *Id.* at 154–62.

49. 297 N.W.2d 241, 245 (Minn. 1980).

50. *Id.* at 245. One coworker told her that "he wished slavery days would return so that he could sexually train her and she would be his bitch." *Id.* at 246. Coworkers also told her that women who worked at factories were "tramps." *Id.*

51. Egger v. Local 76, Plumbers & Pipefitters Union, 644 F. Supp. 795, 797 n.3, 799 (D. Mass. 1986).

52. Monge v. Superior Court, 176 Cal. App. 3d 503, 507, 222 Cal. Rptr. 64, 65 (1986).

53. 735 F. Supp. 1497, 1499 (D. Kan. 1990). *See also* Scott v. Sears, Roebuck & Co., 798 F.2d 210, 211 (7th Cir. 1986) (plaintiff alleged that she had been "propositioned," which turned out on deposition to mean that the alleged harasser had asked to take her to a restaurant for drinks after work; not sufficient to create actionable hostile environment).

54. Andrews v. City of Philadelphia, 895 F.2d 1469, 1474 (3d Cir. 1990) (plaintiff asserted that alleged harasser spoke to her in "seductive tones").

55. Ellison v. Brady, 924 F.2d 872 (9th Cir. 1991).

56. *Id.* at 874.

57. *Id.* at 874 n.1.

58. *Id.* Shortly thereafter, Gray transferred to a different office, but almost immediately filed a union grievance requesting a return to his original office. The IRS and the union settled the grievance by allowing Gray to retransfer, provided he spend four more months in the new office and promise not to bother the plaintiff. When plaintiff learned that Gray was returning, she filed a charge of sexual harassment.

59. *Id.* at 876.

60. *Id.* at 878.

61. Berkman v. New York, 580 F. Supp. 226, 231 (E.D.N.Y. 1983), *aff'd,* 755 F.2d 913 (2d Cir. 1985).

62. *Berkman,* 580 F. Supp. at 232 n.7.

63. *Id.* at 228.

64. 697 F. Supp. 1452 (N.D. Ill. 1988).

65. *Id.* at 1454.

66. *Id.* at 1456. The court also noted that if Goluszek were a woman, defendant would have taken action to stop the harassment. *Id.*

67. *Id.*

68. *Professor Delgado Replies,* at 595. R. George Wright suggests a similar justification: "Assuming that legal restraints on legal speech deter racist speech, genuine social gains may result. Enforced behavioral change, in the form of avoiding racist speech, may tend to produce genuine attitudinal change, as persons bring their attitudes into line with their non-racist speech."

Wright, at 23–24. Mari Matsuda also would justify regulation on the basis of its impact on beliefs: "Racism as an acquired set of behaviors can be dis-acquired, and law is the means by which the state typically provides incentives for changes in behavior." Matsuda, at 2361.

69. Delgado, at 140. Delgado also argues: "[b]igotry, and thus the attendant expression of racism, stifles, rather than furthers, the moral and social growth of the individual who harbors it." *Id.* at 176.

Of course, if all it took to justify regulation of speech was a determination that it "stifles . . . the moral and social growth of the individual," we could limit expression of any ideas that we did not value. Some might argue that Marxism stifles the moral and social growth of the individual, while others might argue that laissez-faire capitalism does the same. Educators across the country believe that Bart Simpson stifles the moral and social growth of the individual, although the Neilsen ratings suggest that a substantial segment of the population either does not agree or does not care. *See A Giant Case of Simpsonitis,* Chicago *Tribune,* Style Section, at 12 (June 13, 1990).

70. 858 F.2d 345, 350 (6th Cir. 1988).

71. Whitney v. California, 274 U.S. 357, 375 (1927) (Brandeis, J., concurring).

72. Chevigny, *Pornography and Cognition: A Reply to Cass Sunstein,* 1989 DUKE L.J. 420, 432.

73. *Id.*

74. Whitney v. California, 274 U.S. 357, 375–76 (1927) (Brandeis, J., concurring).

Questions for Meaning

1. Why is the first amendment relevant to the discussion of sexual harassment in the workplace?

2. In paragraph 13, what does the term "romantic paternalism" mean?

3. According to Browne, what are the two main messages conveyed by sexual harassment complaints?

4. Consider the cartoon described in paragraph 29. Why could a cartoon like this be considered "political"? If defined as political speech, would the cartoon be allowed to remain or would it have to be removed?

5. Given the risk of litigation, how are employers most likely to frame regulations governing speech at work?

6. How much free speech should men and women enjoy in the workplace? Does Browne support any restrictions on speech at work?

7. Vocabulary: aberration (2), exacerbates (6), ambience (13), empirically (14), vicarious (16), animus (22), reprehensible (24), plaintiff (26), actionable (30), discernment (32).

Questions about Strategy

1. How do you respond to the questions Browne poses at the beginning of his opening paragraph? Does this response suit Browne's purpose in raising these questions?
2. Browne opens his argument by contrasting attempts to regulate speech on college campuses with attempts to do so in the workplace. What does this contrast establish, and why is it useful for Browne's purpose?
3. Compare the examples in paragraphs 27 and 28. Do they seem equally serious? What does Browne achieve by using these examples?
4. How sympathetic is Browne to the kind of speech he wants to protect? Does he ever concede that unregulated speech can be harmful?
5. In his conclusion (paragraph 36), Browne claims, "It is but a small step from requiring a person to refrain from expressing beliefs in the hope that he will cease to hold them to requiring a person to express beliefs in the hope that he will begin to hold them." Do you agree?

ONE STUDENT'S ASSIGNMENT

Write a synthesis of the material on sexual harassment included in *The Informed Argument*. When writing, imagine an audience that consists either of managers who need to be briefed on the principal issues in the debate over harassment in the workplace, or of employees who need to decide what kind of behavior is appropriate at work. Use APA-style documentation.

> What Managers Need to Know: A Synthesis of Arguments
> Concerning Sexual Harassment in the Workplace
> Jessica Cozzens

Sexual harassment is one of the most controversial topics currently facing the American workforce. In fact, a study performed in 1986 suggests: "Unwanted sexual attention may be the single most widespread occupational hazard in the workplace today" (Riger, 1991, p. 322). An additional study performed in 1988 indicates that 42% of all the women surveyed "reported that they had experienced some form of unwanted and uninvited sexual attention . . ." (Riger, 1991, p. 322). In 1992 the Equal Opportunity Employment Commission reported that the number of complaints filed within a five-year period had doubled (Fisher, 1993, p. 289). Unfortunately, these statistics only serve to fuel the growing controversy regarding sexual harassment in the workforce.

2   On one hand we have individuals such as Fisher (1993), Hill (1995), and Riger (1991), who define sexual harassment in traditional terms where women, in nine cases out of ten (Fisher, 1993, p. 289), are the victims, often afraid to stand up for their rights and then abused when they do come forward. Studies

conducted in 1982 and 1992 show that only 2–3% of harassment victims actually file complaints through formal channels (Fisher, 1993; Riger, 1991). Furthermore, Fisher (1993) reported that only 34% of the victims surveyed felt confident enough to confront the offender and request that the offensive action be terminated (p. 290). A study conducted in 1988 among Federal workers found that 33% of those who filed formal complaints claimed that it "made things worse" (Riger, 1991, p. 332). When these victims finally do confront their harassers, they are often met with further abuse and ridicule. The Hill–Thomas hearings of 1991 can be offered as an example. During the course of the hearings Anita Hill was portrayed as "prudish yet lewd, easily duped yet shrewd and ambitious, fantasizing yet calculating, pathetic yet evil" (Hill, 1995, p. 304), a view quite different from how Anita Hill sees herself. Fisher (1993) points out that these conflicts are often fueled by the simple fact that individuals often see certain types of behavior quite differently. Riger (1991) takes this issue a step further in claiming that these conflicting viewpoints are primarily gender-based; men and women tend to have very different ways of looking at the world.

On the other side of the spectrum are individuals such as Browne (1991), Paul (1991), and Luthar and Townsend (1995), who believe that the sexual harassment controversy has been blown out of proportion. They believe that in order to make it into the court system the "behavior would have to be objectively injurious rather than merely subjectively offensive" (Paul, 1991, p. 298). These advocates are calling for a distinction "between morally offensive behavior and behavior that causes serious harm" (Paul, 1991, p. 298). Browne (1991) emphasizes that the constitutional right to free speech should not be jeopardized by sexual harassment litigation. Luthar and Townsend (1995) agree, pointing out that women often find men's behavior offensive and claim that "the real answer to the 'hostile environment' problem [a basis for harassment suits] may be that women should learn to live with it too" (p. 320). Paul (1991) adds only that women should "lighten up, and even dispense a few risqué barbs of their own" (p. 299).

4   Title VII of the Civil Rights Act as well as the guidelines from the Equal Employment Opportunity Commission provide the foundation for sexual harassment cases today. They provide for two types of sexual harassment: *Quid pro quo,* which is equivalent to "Sleep with me, or else," and conduct that "has the purpose or effect of unreasonably interfering with an individual's work performance or creating an intimidating, hostile, or offensive working environment" (Riger, 1991, p. 324). While there is universal consensus regarding quid pro quo harassment, other types of abuse are more difficult to address. In order to interpret the standards defining a hostile working environment, courts have devised the "reasonable person rule," which

basically asks whether a reasonable person would be offended by the behavior in question (Browne, 1991; Luthar & Townsend, 1995; Riger, 1991). The question then becomes: What is a reasonable person, and how is this different for men and women? Riger believes that "Men tend to find sexual overtures from women at work to be flattering, whereas women find similar approaches from men to be insulting" (p. 325). She believes that these problems stem from imbalances in the workforce and wants to promote "gender equity within organizations" (Riger, 1991, p. 335), eliminating the need for employers to distinguish between a "reasonable man" and a "reasonable woman." Luthar and Townsend (1995) dislike the reasonable woman theory, feeling that it has "led us back to a Victorian vision of woman; she cannot endure what a man can and must be protected" (p. 320). Browne (1991) and Paul (1991) both question the practicality of Title VII itself, and argue that *quid pro quo* places an unfair burden on the employer to prevent the offensive action. Paul also argues against Title VII maintaining that monetary compensation does not compensate the victim for his or her mental distress.

Employer responsibility is one of the central themes within the sexual harassment debate. Title VII currently provides that the burden of protection actually falls on the employer (Browne, 1991; Fisher, 1993; Paul, 1991; Riger, 1991). Both Fisher (1993) and Riger (1991) stress that, for their own protection, employers are expected to not only develop and aggressively enforce an aggressive sexual harassment policy, but also promote an extensive education program clearly defining the policy. Luthar and Townsend (1995), however, question the value of such education programs. Furthermore, Browne (1991) believes that employers are virtually coerced into overregulating free speech in an attempt to protect themselves from liability. This overregulation often leads directly to violations of the First Amendment's guarantee of freedom of expression. Rather than the current system of penalizing the employer, or Riger's proposal of increased education and clearly defined policies, Browne (1991) maintains that the world is not made a better place through elimination of free expression with employer threats or government sanctions. Instead, Browne proposes that the only solution is to persuade the offender that his or her views are wrong, thereby preserving the constitutional rights of the general public. Paul (1991) takes quite a different approach and proposes that sexual harassment should be treated by the courts as a tort, or a personal injury. If sexual harassment is treated as a tort, employers would no longer be held liable for an employee's actions unless they were aware of the harassment and failed to act on their knowledge. Furthermore, harassers would be held personally responsible for damages assessed by the courts, perhaps thereby deterring potential harassers (Paul, 1991).

6   It is clear that there will be no easy solution to end this debate. Whether the courts continue to uphold the *quid pro quo* and hostile

work environment premises, or one day declare sexual harassment to be a tort, it is unlikely that an absolute consensus will ever be reached. One thing both sides can agree on, however, is that this debate has led to increased pressure and tension in offices around the country. Men and women everywhere admit to withdrawing from the social work environment for fear of committing an unforgivable and potentially prosecutable social blunder, a trend which, if continued, can only result in a further lowering of the work morale across America.

SUGGESTIONS FOR WRITING

1. Draw on your knowledge of your own gender and write an essay explaining what you think "the other gender" most needs to understand about sexual harassment.
2. Does your school or workplace have a policy against sexual harassment? If so, obtain a copy and write an evaluation of it.
3. Drawing on the articles by Anne B. Fisher and Ellen Frankel Paul, write a grievance procedure for sexual harassment in the workplace.
4. Write an argument defining how much freedom of speech people should enjoy in the workplace.
5. Write a summary of the article by Stephanie Riger.
6. Do research on the confirmation hearings of Clarence Thomas in 1991, and then write an essay focused on whether the evidence you have discovered indicates that Anita Hill was sexually harassed by Thomas.
7. Drawing on the argument by Anita Hill, write an essay focused on how race can be a factor in sexual harassment.
8. Reread the argument by Harsh Luthar and Anthony Townsend and write a response to it.
9. Obtain the full version of Kingsley R. Browne's "Title VII as Censorship: Hostile-Environment Harassment and the First Amendment." Write a summary of those parts (iv–vii) omitted from the abridged version published in this book.
10. Research recent cases involving sexual harassment in the military, and make a written recommendation for how this problem should be treated.

COLLABORATIVE PROJECT

Write a code of conduct that defines acceptable behavior when persons are trying to initiate a personal relationship with someone they have met at work or in class. Indicate also the behavior that is unacceptable. Be sure to consider the views of people of different gender and different sexual orientation, as well as other cultural differences such as age, race, and social class. Include specific recommendations for how someone can clearly indicate that personal overtures are unwelcome.

SECTION 5

SURFING THE WEB:
WHO CONTROLS INFORMATION?

JON KATZ

THE RIGHTS OF KIDS IN
THE DIGITAL AGE

What happens when a world of information, much of it potentially disturbing to children, becomes accessible from the home computer tucked in the corner of a child's bedroom? Should children be denied access to pornography and adult discussion groups? Or should they be free to learn how to make their own decisions regarding the responsible use of technology. In the following argument, first published in a 1996 issue of *Wired* magazine, Jon Katz argues that children have a moral right to information. Drawing on the work of John Locke, a seventeenth-century philosopher whose ideas influenced the founders of our country, Katz structures his argument like the U.S. Constitution by dividing it into a series of "articles." Katz is a contributing editor of *Wired* and the author of *Virtuous Reality* (1997). Address: jdkatz@aol.com

Article I
Children Lead the Revolution

Children are at the epicenter of the information revolution, ground zero of the digital world. They helped build it, and they understand it as well or better than anyone. Not only is the digital world making the younger more sophisticated, altering their ideas of what culture and literacy are, it is connecting them to one another, providing them with a new sense of political self. Children in the digital age are neither unseen nor unheard; in fact, they are seen and heard more than ever. They occupy a new kind of cultural space. They're citizens of a new order, founders of the Digital Nation.

2   After centuries of sometimes benign, sometimes brutal, oppression and regulation, kids are moving out from under our pious control, finding one another via the great hive that is the Net. As digital communications flash through the most heavily fortified borders and ricochet around the world independent of governments and censors, so can children for the first time reach past the suffocating boundaries of social convention, past their elders'

rigid notions of what is good for them. Children will never be the same; nor will the rest of us.

The young are the last significant social entity in America perceived to be under the total control of others. Although in recent years society has finally moved to protect kids against exploitation and physical abuse, they make up the only group in our so-called democracy with no inherent political rights, no voice in the political process. Teenagers in particular, so close to adulthood, are subjected to sometimes intolerable controls over almost every aspect of their lives.

4   In part, that's because fears for children are manifold, ranging from real danger (assault, molestation, kidnapping) to such perceived—but often unprovable—perils as the alleged damage caused by violent or pornographic imagery, the addictive nature of some new technology, the supposed loss of civilization and culture.

In some parts of America, particularly amid the urban underclass where violence and economic hardship are epidemic, those fears for children seem not only valid, but understated. But for middle-class families that consume much of this controversial popular culture, such fears seem misplaced, exaggerated, invoked mostly to regain control of a society changing faster than our ability to comprehend it.

6   The idea that children are moving beyond our absolute control may be the bitterest pill for many to swallow in the digital era. The need to protect children is reflexive, visceral, instinctive. All the harder, then, to change.

Article II
A New Social Contract

Three centuries ago, a stunning new idea was introduced to the world: No one has the right of absolute control over others. People have the inherent right to some measure of freedom. Rules should be agreed upon, not imposed. Although this notion has become our most cherished political value, in the 17th century it existed in practice nowhere on the planet. When it did spread, slowly, it was first applied to men, usually white men. Bit by bloody bit, the idea has encompassed other groups, but it has yet to be applied at all to children.

8   John Locke, the 17th-century English philosopher and essayist, is most remembered for that influential political argument: People have some say in the way they are governed. Locke preached that people naturally possess certain rights—life, liberty, and property. Rulers, he wrote, derive their power only from the consent of the people they rule. Government, then, is essentially a Social Contract: subjects give up certain freedoms and submit to the authority of government in return for just rule, the safeguarding of what is rightfully theirs. The ruler holds power only so long as he uses it justly. If that sounds familiar, it's because Locke's intellectual fingerprints are all over the Declaration of Independence and the Constitution.

Locke's contract requires mutual responsibility. If the government violates the trust placed in it by the people, if rulers "endeavor to take away and destroy the power of the people or to reduce them to slavery," then government forfeits the power the people have placed in it. An arbitrary or destructive ruler who does not respect his subjects' rights is "justly to be esteemed the common enemy and pest of mankind and is to be treated accordingly."

10   The idea of a Social Contract emphasizing mutual responsibility rather than arbitrary power seems especially relevant to the rights of children and the extent of parental authority, particularly in the midst of our raging civil war over culture and media.

Children are being subjected to an intense wave of censorship and control—V-Chips, blocking software, ratings systems on everything from movies and music to computer games. Cultural conservatives like Bob Dole and William Bennett* are forging a national political movement out of their desire to put cultural blinders on the young. President Clinton has enthusiastically embraced the idea that parents should have the right to block kids' TV programs. In this struggle, the young are largely alone; few political, educational, or social entities have lent support or defense.

12   Locke challenged the belief, widespread then and now, that the power of parents over children is "absolute." In his *Two Treatises on Government* and the essay "Some Thoughts Concerning Education," Locke argued for the moral education of children rather than the arbitrary imposition of rules. Children, like adults, were entitled to some measure of freedom because that was appropriate to their status as rational human beings. Parents' authority should not be severe or arbitrary, he wrote, but used only for the help, instruction, and preservation of their offspring. It is eventually to be relinquished.

The adult world seized on Locke's basic concepts of individual liberty and over time established political and legal rights. The French and American Revolutions transformed the politics of the world in ways that are still being played out today. But children have lived almost completely outside these notions—and for understandable reasons. Children's rights are, in fact, vastly more complicated.

14   Any sort of legislated political emancipation for the young is almost out of the question. Children are unlikely to win the sweeping legal protections granted other minorities. But some of the most powerful movements in our political history—civil rights, feminism, gay emancipation—were moral as well as legal struggles. With children, the idea of expanded freedom also begins as a moral issue.

The lives of children are far too complex to generalize about. Degrees of maturity, emotional stability, rates of development and learning, and the level of parents' patience, thoughtfulness, and resources vary too widely

---

* For an argument by William Bennett, see pp. 261–263.

to set forth strict rules. Five-year-olds aren't like 15-year-olds. And when it comes to culture, at least, boys are often not like girls.

16   But that's why the notion that all children possess some basic rights in the digital age is critical. Their choices ought not to be left completely to the often arbitrary and sometimes ignorant whims and fancies of individual educators, religious leaders, or parents, any more than people ought to be subject to the total control of kings. Parents who thoughtlessly ban access to online culture or lyrics they don't like or understand, or parents who exaggerate and distort the dangers from violent and pornographic imagery are acting out of their own anxiety and arrogance, imposing brute authority. Rather than preparing kids for the world they'll have to live in, these parents insist on preparing them for a world that no longer exists.

The young have a moral right of access to the machinery and content of media and culture. It's their universal language. It's their means of attaining modern literacy, which in the next millennium will surely be defined as the ability to access information, rather than to regurgitate the names of the presidents. It may mean the difference between economic well-being and economic hardship.

18   Blocking, censoring, and banning should be the last resort in dealing with children, not the first. Particularly if children have been given the chance to develop a moral and responsible ethic and are willing—as in Locke's notion of the Social Contract—to meet their responsibilities.

Article III
The Responsible Child

The cultural disputes between children and their families cannot be solved by extending the legal system into the home. No legislator can define every circumstance in which a child is entitled to assume more responsibility for his or her decisions. And wildly varying family values make it difficult to spell out universal rights.

20   But we as adults and parents can start to understand what a new Social Contract with children looks like—beginning with the notion of the Responsible Child. He or she is a teenager, or almost one, who meets certain criteria:

• She works to the best of her ability in school. She's reasonably responsible about her education and functions successfully in a classroom.

• She's socially responsible. She avoids drug and alcohol abuse and understands the health dangers of smoking.

• She does not harass, steal from, or otherwise harm people, including siblings, friends, fellow students.

• She carries her weight at home. She does the tasks and chores she has agreed on or has been assigned to do.

The Responsible Child is not the embodiment of some utopian vision; she can at times be difficult, rebellious, obnoxious, moody. But she makes a good-faith effort to resolve differences rationally and verbally. Saintliness is not required.

Article IV
The Moral Foundation

22 The Responsible Child does not appear miraculously but emerges as a result of years of preparation and education. Her conscience and sense of responsibility don't spontaneously form at the legal age of adulthood. They are built into her life early through thoughtful parenting and a complex series of relationships.

The vast literature on children and child psychology contains arguments about every conceivable child-rearing issue. But respected experts conclude nearly unanimously that dominant character traits don't just appear during the teen years. They get formed much earlier, from the interactions and environment provided since infancy.

24 If parents spend time with their children, form strong attachments with them, teach them morals, live moral lives, discourage and punish immoral behavior, and treat their children in a moral way, then the moral issues their children face later are much more likely to be resolved.

As parents define permissible behavior and limits, as they explain them again and again, the child gradually incorporates these rules into her own reflexive behavior. This becomes the formation of conscience and individual value systems.

26 The idea that a TV show or a lyric can transform a healthy, connected, grounded child into a dangerous monster is absurd, an irrational affront not only to science but to common sense and to what we know about children in our own lives. It is primarily the invention of politicians (who use it to frighten or rally supporters), of powerful religious groups (that can't teach dogma to the young without control), and of journalism (which sees new media and new culture as menaces to its own once-powerful and highly profitable position in American society).

As powerful as they are, media and culture—or the sometimes offensive imagery transmitted by them—can't form our children's value systems or provide the building blocks of conscience. Only we can do that.

Article V
The Rights of Children

28 The Responsible Child has certain inalienable rights, not conferred at the caprice of arbitrary authority, but recognized by a just society as inherently belonging to every person. As we enter the digital age, this recognition is inevitable, a powerful idea that will bring children into the vast community of people who have, or are battling for, some control over their lives.

• Children have the right to be respected, to be accorded the same sensitivity that other disenfranchised minorities have grudgingly been granted by the rest of society. They should not be viewed as property or as helpless to participate in the decisions affecting their lives.

• Children should not be branded ignorant or inadequate because their educational, cultural, or social agenda is different from that of previous generations. They have the right to help redefine what education, literacy, and civic-mindedness are.

• Children have a right to two-way communications with the politicians, clergy, and educational leaders who claim to know what is best for them. Children have a right to help shape discussions about their moral lives.

• Children of various socioeconomic levels ought to have equal exposure to the new technologies—multimedia, cable channels, the Net—that deliver information, education, and culture. They have a right to have new media and technology included in their school curricula.

• Children who meet their personal and educational responsibilities ought to have nearly unrestricted access to their culture—particularly if they demonstrate an ability to maintain balance in their lives.

• Children have the right to assemble online, to form groups, and to communicate with like-minded communities through Web sites and home-pages, online services, email, and the range of possibilities created by the Net.

• Children have a right to challenge the use of blocking software and other technologies, like the V-Chip, that arbitrarily deny them choice, exposure to ideas, and freedom of speech.

Children's rights are not synonymous with permissiveness. Scholars of childhood agree that children need clear boundaries and occasional discipline. But if children have the opportunity from an early age to make informed decisions about themselves—what to eat, when to sleep, what to wear—they will be able to take a measure of control of their cultural lives by their teens.

30   These rights are not a gift conferred out of the goodness of our hearts, but the fulfillment of the most basic responsibility of parents: to prepare children for the world they will live in.

Article VI
Negotiating the Social Contract

How would a Social Contract about media and culture—a truce between adults and children—work?

32   The model envisioned by Locke applies eerily well to kids. By definition, a contract is agreed upon, not imposed. Its power comes not from arbitrary authority but from a moral base, a desire to do the right thing for everyone, to respect and understand the rights and needs of all parties. Parents and children would both have to want an agreement that ratifies the children's rights and makes responsible parents yield some of their power while feeling safe about it.

The rational adult has to begin by accepting that censorship and arbitrary controls don't work, that he or she has to thrash out a shared value system with his or her children. Attempting to censor children can undermine authority and values rather than affirming them. Since most older children and their friends can circumvent almost all censorious technology, and since much of the digital world is beyond the comprehension of most parents anyway, mere authority becomes limited, sometimes meaningless. Children will learn not how to form value systems, but how their moral guardians can't make their dictums stick.

34   So, family members need to think through their own notions about children and culture. How much power and control are the elders willing to cede? A parent would spell out how much TV or online time he finds appropriate and define what else is expected from the child: domestic chores, school performance, religious obligations.

The child would spell out what access to culture she wants: which TV shows, which CDs, how much time online. And she has to specify what she's willing to do in exchange. She must agree to follow rules of safety: not giving out telephone numbers or home addresses to strangers online, and telling parents about "pornographic" contacts, such as files with sexual content. Media access is granted as a right, but it's subject to some conditions.

36   There would probably be as many different kinds of contracts as there are families. But if children meet their end of the Social Contract, then parents would concede that their children have a moral right to access the TV programs they want, the CDs they want to hear, the online services they choose and can afford. Families could begin to rely on trust, negotiation, and communication rather than phobias, conflict, and suspicion.

It has to be a good-faith contract. Parents who ask too much will lose their moral authority to make an arrangement like this. Kids willing to do too little will jeopardize it as well. Some parties will probably have to set aside their broken contracts and keep on fighting.

38   Naturally, if either side violates its agreement—if kids fail in school, harm other people, start drinking heavily—then the contract is null and void. Children who can't or won't behave rationally forfeit the right to rational understandings and will return themselves to a state of diminished freedom.

But millions of American kids who can handle a racy chat room or an episode of *NYPD Blue* won't be denied cultural freedom because of their parents' fears about the kids who can't.

Article VII
Test Case

40 As it happens, for years my own household has operated under a form of Social Contract—not that we called it that or thought much about John Locke. I have seen that it can work. My wife and I have a 14-year-old daughter, who is comfortable with my writing about her cultural rights, though not about other details of her personal life.

Believing that culture is the language and currency of her generation, we've always encouraged her to understand it. She played Nintendo, watched cable, loved the *Teenage Mutant Ninja Turtles.* Now, she watches *ER, Homicide: Life on the Street,* and *The X-Files,* plus old musicals on cable and the occasional dumb sitcom after a tough week.

42   She can see virtually any movie she wants, although sometimes there is some discussion about it. If she is shocked, upset, or otherwise uncomfortable, she feels free to leave. The Motion Picture Association of America's parental rating system is an absurd guide to what children can or cannot handle and has never been the criterion in our family. When my daughter was younger, if there were serious questions about the violence, sexual content, or emotional intensity of a movie, my wife and I would sometimes see it first, then take our daughter. The ability to tell an 8-year-old when to close her eyes is a helpful thing. Now, of course, we don't have to.

She has been online since she was 10. We have never thought of acquiring blocking software, which would be offensive and demeaning to her, but she's been taught not to pass around her name, address, or phone number—and to pass problems or unsettling experiences on to us.

44   She hasn't had many. She has encountered occasional creeps and a few disturbed people online—boys who want to talk dirty, men who want to send her explicitly sexual files—and she's learned important phrases like No and Get lost. Despite the enormous publicity those kinds of contacts generate, they have been relatively rare. She does have online friendships, few of which I know anything about.

We trust her implicitly, until she provides a reason to be regarded differently. So far, so good: she does well in school, has healthy friendships, sings in a demanding chorale, has shown little interest in violence, drugs, or alcohol. She's developed a high level of common sense and analytic thoughtfulness about the culture she uses. But new media haven't supplanted old—she reads a lot, and writes, and talks. In fact, it was she, I hereby acknowledge, who first pointed out to me that my thoughts about children's rights related directly to this John Locke guy she'd learned about in her history class.

46   I have no illusions that she is a "typical" child, if there is such a thing. As an only child, she's easier to monitor. As a middle-class family, we can provide a computer, books, and an allowance high enough to cover movie tickets.

Still, she—and we—live very much according to Locke's idea of a Social Contract. It is understood and articulated that as long as she does as well as she's doing, she has the right to her culture and to her own rational judgments about it without interference, ridicule, or censorship.

48   We all understand that she needs to be different from us. Her culture is perhaps the most important way she has of separating, of differentiating herself from us.

So far, the contract holds.

Article VIII
The Political Power of Children

50 Cultural conservatives, politicians, parents, teachers, adults in general—and especially journalists—have greatly underestimated just how political an issue this assault on kids' culture has become.

In topics online, on Web sites, in countless live chats, the young vent their anger at the pious efforts of the adult world to "safeguard" them, at congressional efforts to legislate "decency" on the Internet, and to curb free speech in this freest of environments. They're generating email, firing up online discussions, bordering Web pages in black.

52 This is as intensely aroused and political as kids have been since the '70s. Plus this digital generation has an organizational weapon no previous generation had: the ability to find and talk to distant allies just a modem away. Easily able to measure their own lives against others, to compare their own experience with rhetoric, these kids know their culture isn't dangerous. Their tactics, occurring almost completely out of sight of parents and beyond the consciousness of journalists and politicians, could transform the politics of the young.

Journalists have underreported the extent to which culture is politics to young people, and how they resent suggestions that culture is rendering them stupid, indifferent, and violence-prone. Since children are almost voiceless in media and in the political debates on issues affecting them, it's not surprising that their outrage goes largely unnoticed.

54 But the traditional, hidebound press is learning the high cost of relentlessly patronizing and offending kids—it has alarmingly few young consumers. Politicians may soon be learning the same lesson. The battles over new media are likely to spark youthful politicization reminiscent of the movements launched by racial minorities, women, and gays.

Under the noses of their guardians, the young are now linked to one another all over the world. They already share their culture online, trading information about new movies, TV shows, and CDs, warning one another about viruses, sharing software and tech tips. At times, they band together to chastise or drive out aggressive, obnoxious, or irresponsible digital peers. They steer one another to interesting Web sites.

56 But children, perhaps more than any other oppressed minority, have a long way to go to become politically organized. And they can't engage in political struggle by themselves.

By now, they should have had some help. Some online benefactor should fund something like a Children's Digital Freedom Center, similar to the Electronic Frontier Foundation. It could provide children with truthful information about violence, pornography, and online safety with which they could educate their classmates and confront ignorance and misinformation about their youth culture. It could also provide legal support to young people penalized for free expression online, or those unfairly denied their right of access to culture.

58   Instead, what children have received from the digital community is a deafening yawn.

Article IX
The Hypocrisy of the Digital World

Above almost all things, the digital culture prides itself on the notion that information should be free, that this new culture should remain unfettered and unobstructed. Efforts at corporate and governmental control and the promotion of so-called "decency" standards are the subject of ferocious debate online and political lobbying offline.

60   But the culture is either silent or supportive of the attempts to block children's access. The EFF wholeheartedly supports limiting children's access to the Net and even has links from its Web site to publishers of blocking software. Even on libertarian-minded conferencing systems like The Well, it's mostly taken for granted that children can be denied the freedom of speech for which everyone else is so willing to fight.

Citizens of the Digital Nation, so quick to hit the barricades when Congress attempts to cut back on their freedom of speech, seem happy to embrace the new raft of blocking software. They seem quite willing to trade children's rights for their own freedom of expression. Don't take us, take our kids.

62   No one in the highly sensitive and politicized adult digital world blinks when the media cheerfully talk about blocking software as the clear alternative to censoring the Internet. No one minds when reviews recommend programs such as Cybersitter, SurfWatch, Net Nanny, and Cyber Patrol. The very names of the programs are patronizing and demeaning.

This approach is the antithesis of trust and rational discourse between adults and children and more evidence of the growing need to protect children not from smut, but from adult abuses of power. Blocking software is noxious and potentially unlimited. Some of these programs have thousands of potentially forbidden categories, going far beyond sex and violence. Once applied, censoring and restrictions inevitably will spread into other areas that adults want to place off-limits: political topics that differ from their own values, music and movie forums that don't conform to their adult tastes, online friends that don't meet their approval, Darwinian theory.

64   Although it's being introduced in America as a means of protecting children, as this technology evolves it could easily become the tyrant's best techno-pal, offering ever more ingenious ways to control speech and thought. Some children reared on this stuff will inevitably grow up thinking that the way to deal with topics we don't like is to block them—remove them from our vision and consciousness. In any other context, defenders of free speech would be bounding off the walls.

Like the movie industry's silly ratings code, blocking software gives the illusion of control. It doesn't ensure safety since sophisticated evildoers will circumvent it even more quickly than kids. And it doesn't teach citizenship in the digital world.

66   As parents withdraw, secure in the belief that the Net Nanny will do the work they should be doing, count on this: children, many of whom helped build the digital culture, will swiftly transcend this software. They would be much better off if parents accompanied them when they first set out online, showing them what is inappropriate or dangerous.

Blocking deprives children of the opportunity to confront the realities of new culture: some of it is pornographic, violent, occasionally even dangerous. They need to master those situations in a rational, supervised way to learn how to truly protect themselves.

68   The urge to block presumes that exposure to certain topics is intrinsically dangerous. But only an infinitesimally small number of kids have been lured into potentially dangerous situations as a result of online encounters—fewer than 25, according to the National Center for Missing and Exploited Children. That's a tiny figure given the billions of online encounters.

The digital world owes it to children to defend their rights as zealously as it defends its own. So far, it has failed, betraying its own heritage and, worse, its future.

Article X
What Children Need in the 21st Century

70 Children need to get their hands on the new machines. They need equal access to the technology of culture, research, and education. Poor and working-class families have few computers compared with the affluent middle class. And we are learning that some minority children are resisting computers as the toys of the white nerd.

But if new technology can create a gap between haves and have-nots, it can also narrow it. Cheap, portable PCTVs—televisions with computers and cable modems—would help equalize the digital revolution in a hurry. Hastening the arrival of such equal access should be the first and most pressing moral issue of the digital generation.

72   Children also need to learn to use the machinery of culture safely and responsibly. That means grasping the new rules of community in the online world, transcending the often abrasive, pointlessly combative tone that permeates many online discussions. They need to learn how to research ideas and history as well as to chat, mouth off, and download games.

Children need help in becoming civic-minded citizens of the digital age, in figuring out how to use the machinery in the service of some broader social purpose than simple entertainment. They need guidance in managing their new ability to connect instantly with other cultures. They need reminders about how to avoid the dangers of elitism and arrogance.

74   But more than anything else, it's time to extend to children the promise of the fundamental idea that Locke, Thomas Paine, Thomas Jefferson, and others introduced to the world three centuries ago: That everyone has rights. That everyone should be given as great a measure of freedom as possible. That all should get the opportunity to rise to the outer limits of their potential.

We need to teach ourselves how to trust children to make rational judgments about their own safety. We see their world as a dark and dangerous place, even as they see it as challenging, entertaining, and exciting. We patronize them in the belief that they don't have the character, common sense, or conscience to withstand the dangers of their vastly expanding cultural universe. And now we try to block them from that world.

76 We haven't got a chance. Like Locke's ideas of emancipation, children's lives are taking on a momentum of their own, moving rapidly past our anxious and fearful grasp. Their emancipation is as inevitable as our own.

Since Locke's time, democracy has inexorably advanced as monarchies and authoritarian regimes have increasingly failed. They have been undermined by new ideas riding on the back of new technologies that now extend to every corner of the world. Oppressive authority and censorship seem increasingly anachronistic amidst the porous borders of the emerging digital era.

78 The approaching millennium is more than a historical landmark. It's the right time to liberate our children from the heavy hands of history. Most of us recognize that our children are moving into a miraculous new era. They will, like everyone else, take risks and face dangers. They will also reap great rewards.

Children have the chance to reinvent communications, culture, and community. To address the problems of the new world in new ways. To do better than we did. Instead of holding them back, we should be pushing them forward. Instead of shielding them, we should take them by the hands, guide them to the gates, and cheer them on. ❖

Questions for Meaning

1. How are children changing, according to Katz, and how do these changes affect their relationships with adults?
2. What is the meaning of Locke's "Social Contract"? How can it be applied to children?
3. Why does Katz believe that children need to be able to access information electronically?
4. How do children learn to make responsible choices?
5. How should adults respond to children who make irresponsible choices?
6. Vocabulary: epicenter (1), benign (2), visceral (6), caprice (28), dictums (33), patronizing (62), inexorably (77), anachronistic (77).

Questions about Strategy

1. Katz has organized his argument into a series of "articles" imitating the plan used by the framers of the U.S. Constitution. Does this plan work?
2. This argument is based on the idea that children have a "moral right" to access information. How does Katz go about establishing

3. In Article VII, Katz writes about his daughter. To what extent is this example persuasive? Under what conditions can this "test case" be considered representative of other children?

4. Katz argues, in paragraph 63, that censorship inevitably leads to additional censorship. Is this reasoning persuasive?

Paul F. Burton

FREE OR FETTERED?

One of the great advantages of doing research through the Internet is that computer technology provides access to material from around the world—as suggested by the phrase *World Wide Web*. But when material is being produced in one country and being read in dozens of others, what are the implications for governments that want to control information access? How can the censorship laws of one country be applied to what is being written in another? And how can any government restrict information access within its boundaries when personal computers are owned by many of its citizens? These are among the questions addressed here by Paul Burton. His argument was first presented as a paper at an international conference in London in 1996. Burton is a professor of Information Science at the University of Strathclyde in Scotland. Address: paul@dis.strath.ac.uk

──────────── Abstract ────────────

This paper examines the nature of the problem caused by potentially offensive material on the Internet and summarizes current efforts to regulate content, along with reactions to those efforts. (Figures quoted without attribution are from the author's own research data.)

1. Introduction: What Is the Problem?

Earlier last year, you could have been forgiven for believing that the world had just discovered the Internet, and that it had, in the process, concluded that the Internet was awash with pornographic images, drugs information and general threats to the safety and good order of society. What was worse, it seemed, was that nobody appeared to be in charge of this new phenomenon; indeed, it was proudly proclaimed that "No one owns the Internet," except perhaps the millions of people throughout the world who contribute to it in various ways. This is seen in many quarters as its major benefit—freely available information ("Information wants to be free" is another common cry) from numerous sources—but it has also come rapidly to be regarded in some quarters as its most worrying feature. Everyone with access to the required technology is free to make material available via the Internet, and there appears to be no control over that material—and so the "cyberporn debate," amongst others, began on the WWW, in the media, and in legislatures (especially in the USA).

2   As a result, suggestions have appeared which link the use of the Internet with the Oklahoma bombing, extremist political groups, the manufacture of ecstasy and other drugs, and with the ready availability of pornographic images—and these are all problems which public libraries and schools are concerned about as they move towards Internet provision. There were also fears that it was too easy to find this material *inadvertently* (as distinct from consciously searching it out); again it was felt that there was a threat to the innocent and the unwary, although an investigation, reported in the *Guardian* newspaper, estimated (Holderness, 1995) that "[t]he odds against finding a random pornographic image thus seem to be worse than 70,000:1."

     Given that a well-known British broadsheet newspaper recently listed the URL* of a World Wide Web (WWW) site which included links to eight so-called "top-shelf" magazines,* inadvertent discovery can be regarded as a problem, although some commentators have denied this, saying that it requires effort to find these sites and to download images and so on. Inadvertent retrieval of offensive material is also less likely, due to the increasing use of warnings placed at the start of WWW pages. My recent research suggests that the number of these warning signs appears to have grown considerably—of 81 sites investigated, 45% now have a warning notice which, amongst other things, requires users to be over the age of either 18 or 21. In some cases, users are required first to register by quoting a credit card number (this is not used to charge for access, but simply to verify age), and a few sites have now begun to quote the *Communications Decency Act* (see below) as a reason for requiring proof of age. Few if any of the other sites actively prevent under-age users from accessing the pages, but at least there is no excuse for not knowing what the site contains. Of course, many would argue that such warnings will only serve to encourage access, especially by children and young people.

4   It is not particularly difficult to find this material if one is *consciously* looking. The "adult" bulletin board systems (BBS) advertise freely in many magazines, including some of the now well-established journals for the Internet, while telephone numbers of BBS and network addresses circulate freely in the newsgroups. On the WWW, the various search engines will retrieve Web pages with little difficulty, using keywords in sophisticated search strategies. Professor Harold Thimbleby (1995) suggested at last year's

---

*URL is an acronym for Uniform Resource Locator, the full set of characters for reaching an electronic address: the protocol being used (such as http://), the Internet address and domain name, and the path to the file.

*Normally kept out of the reach of children, "top-shelf magazine" is a British euphemism for pornography.

British Association meeting in Newcastle that "47% of the 11,000 most often repeated searches were pornographic," though it is very important to note that this does not indicate what proportion of the total number of searches this represents. Unfortunately, Lycos will not release this information, so it is impossible to judge the relative extent of such searches (Whitney, 1996).

Thus, enter the word "sex" on the Lycos search engine (which indexes over 130 million unique URLs) and you will be told that there are 30,976 documents containing that term (at the time of writing). However, of the first 50 URLs listed, 27 (54%) appeared *not* to contain pornographic images, but were instead either serious discussions of sexual matters, duplicate entries, lists of newsgroups, etc. (Three were, in fact, "spoofs," pages that used the word "sex" to encourage users to link to them. One of these gave every appearance of being a research programme.)

6   Similarly, a search on "drugs" found 92% of the first 50 sites (17,504 were found) could not be considered as actively encouraging drug use, and of the first 50 documents listed under "explosives," 60% stemmed from organizations with a legitimate interest in explosives (professional institutions, etc.), although a number of the remaining sites were parts of *The Terrorist's Handbook*, which does give recipes for bomb making.

The problem of accurately calculating the relative volume of potentially offensive material has bedevilled the Internet since its growth first became noticeable. It is too easy to generate figures and then to extrapolate from them to the whole of the Internet to create completely the wrong impression, but it is often this false perception which generates so much concern in parents and legislators. This was a major criticism of the study by Marty Rimm last year, which was featured so prominently in TIME Magazine and was also used by US Senators pushing through the Communications Decency Bill. Rimm's 1995 study was interpreted by US Senators as proving that 83.5% of the Internet consisted of pornographic images, when in fact he only analyzed the adult BBS and then extended his conclusion to the entire Internet. Examining only adult BBS, it was hardly surprising that he could claim to have found a large percentage of such images, though even these data have been widely criticized. In fact, a more accurate figure has been calculated by Hoffman and Novak (1995), who point out that "less than one-half of 1% (3% of 11%) of the messages on the Internet are associated with newsgroups that contain pornographic imagery." The point appears to be that, while this material is available over the Internet, it is not there in the quantities which some people fear, though it is very difficult to change entrenched attitudes. A good friend, who is a school librarian, told me recently that she is being given every encouragement to provide Internet access, "But how do I stop the pupils finding all the pornography?".

8   Once one page with the sought-after material has been found, it is usually possible to link from that page to others on the same theme, just as one can follow citations in a journal article. Some WWW pages are simply that: links to other related pages, like bibliographies of their subject.

The conclusion is that material which could give offense and which legislators in the UK, USA, Australia, Canada, Germany and New Zealand (to name but some of the countries actively investigating Internet content) are concerned about is there, but not in the quantities which some branches of the popular media (and some politicians) would have us think. Having said that, it does appear that a lot of use is made of these sites, especially those providing the alleged pornographic images, though last year the *Guardian* also found that the pornographic newsgroups generated much less traffic than, say, a group listing job opportunities (Holderness, 1995). In a recent analysis, I found a high of 58,198 accesses per day and a low of 198 for 12 randomly chosen sites: the average daily figure for these sites was 14,578 accesses. Again, this figure must be treated cautiously, as it may not, in every case, represent the number of *individuals* accessing the site, but rather the number of times text or an image was downloaded. (Some accesses may result in multiple downloads.) Some sites claim accesses far in excess of this: one million-plus in a few months has been seen.

10   This high level of demand is also a contributory factor in the rapid turnover of sites, which close down or are closed down regularly. The most frequent reason for closure is sheer overload on the server involved, which causes problems for other users: 41% of sites closed down in the course of one investigation and the single most frequently cited reason (58% of cases) was system overload. Concern over legal action or breaches of acceptable use policy tend to be less frequently cited as reasons for closure. The *JANET Acceptable Use Policy* in the UK already prohibits the use of JANET for a range of materials, including the obscene, libel and copyright infringement (UKERNA, 1995). We might also note that such sites have a relatively short life span: 87% had been closed down within 6 months of start-up, and 43% lasted only 2 months or less.

So far, we have considered Internet access to the material that has caused most reported concern to various groups, but if we are considering the question of free or fettered access to networked resources, we might also look at a wide range of material that could be subject to criticism on completely different grounds, if only because of the rapidly increasing demands being placed on the Internet bandwidth. Given that the *original* purpose of the Internet was academic research, why should such recreational material as home pages for football clubs, popular music groups, television, or a student's interest and hobbies be allowed space on servers? Somewhere on the Internet, I'm told, is a list of one young man's CD collection. Is this a sensible use of the resource? In the United States at least, the continuation of such sites (as well those containing the potentially more offensive material) is justified under the First Amendment, and they are symptomatic of the change in the nature of the Internet from academic research tool to multimedia information resource.

12   I want simply to raise the question here because it is part of the wider question of Internet regulation—some universities do not permit students to maintain their own home pages because it is an "inappropriate use of

university resources." A further step in this direction has been taken by one British university, which logs the thirty most popular URLs each week. The resulting list is examined, and access to any sites that contravene user regulations may be blocked. This includes those sites which it is felt constitute a waste of university computing resources, and "deliberate or reckless overloading of access links or of switching equipment" is prohibited under the *UKERNA JANET Acceptable Use Policy.*

I suspect, however, that the availability of recreational sites will become less of a relevant question as the Internet becomes progressively commercialised and as more and more people use Internet service providers from systems in their homes. Service providers will, in general terms, be happy to accept anything for which they receive income (though they will still have to pay attention to the law of the land).

14   So, to summarize this first part, we can say that there is material available over the Internet which causes concern in some quarters, either because of its content or because it is seen as a less-than-appropriate use of computing resources. We can also note that some degree of regulation is already in effect, especially in the university sector, though, increasingly, service providers are taking note of the problem. While this paper was in preparation, CompuServe announced that it was blocking access to some 200 newsgroups, following complaints from the German Government about obscene materials that were being accessed from Germany. CompuServe says that there is no way in which they can selectively prevent access by users in one country, so the action applies to all CompuServe users. In addition, the German Land of Baden-Wÿrttemburg is investigating Duetsche Telekom to see if it can be considered as assisting in the dissemination of the views of a US-based neo-Nazi (Schofield, 1996).

In the USA, legislation was passed at the beginning of February 1996 which makes it illegal to distribute certain types of material over computer networks, and the UK, Canada, Australia and New Zealand are all actively examining the problem with a view to defining its size and the nature of their response. In the UK, for example, the CCTA's Ethics Open Collaborative Group (1995) is looking at ethical issues in the use of the information superhighway, and its 1995 report contains statements on censorship. It is also looking at technical options, such as limiting access to approved sites, or prohibiting access to banned addresses. Following a meeting between the UK Home Office and Internet service providers, the UK government is looking towards a code of conduct from providers. In Australia, a Computer Bulletin Board Task Force is examining the regulatory options for BBSs, in the light of community concern over offensive materials online (Federal Department of Communications and the Arts, 1995), and the Canadian Government has already issued a background paper on the topic of illegal and offensive content on the information highway (Sansom, 1995). The final report of the Canadian Information Highway Advisory Council (1995) makes a number of recommendations, though none goes so far as to advocate new Canadian legislation.

2. Is the Internet So Different?

16 If offensive material is there on the Internet, are we in fact facing a radically new situation, or is it simply a case of old wine in new bottles? Does the fact that a new medium is involved warrant new legislation of the type currently before the US Senate, or can existing laws deal with this material? What, in a word, is different about the Internet? For many observers, the answer is "nothing." They would claim that current laws are perfectly adequate to control material judged to be offensive by national legislation, whether this relates to possession or distribution or both, not least because it would appear that much of the offensive material is in fact digitized from original print versions. (This, I suspect, is not a situation which will always pertain, however; new material which has never existed (and may never exist) in print form is appearing regularly on the Internet and the WWW.) The argument is that the Internet is just another medium, and that we must not allow ourselves to be dazzled by the technology into creating a whole new set of laws, most of which, as we shall see, might not be enforceable. At most, all that is required is an amendment to existing legislation which will cover digital media and computer networks.

Other commentators, however, claim that there are differences in the way in which this material is distributed which are inherent in the Internet and that it does therefore create new problems. Firstly, there is that fact that access to this material is easier. There is no longer a need to have contacts or to go looking for this material; the search engines will find it for you (as we saw earlier). Thus, individuals who might otherwise have been protected from offensive material by simply not knowing how to find it can now actively seek it out from a desktop terminal (admittedly, one does require access to the technology, but that is becoming less and less of a problem).

18 Secondly, since this is access from a desktop terminal, access is less public. There is no need to risk the embarrassment of buying a top-shelf magazine in the local newsagent, or of trying to find *The Terrorist's Handbook* in a bookshop, or of being seen with known members of neo-Nazi groups—all of this can be downloaded in the (relative) privacy of one's room.

However, the biggest difference which the nature of the Internet makes is in its international nature, and the potential this creates for breaches of national legislation. We have already mentioned the demands of the German Government to CompuServe and the problems these have created, and this is only the latest instance of the problem to surface. It is now well-known that material prohibited in one country can be stored on a server in another and then accessed from the first and that, at present, there is little that governments can do about this. It cannot be stopped at the frontier, as print can. This may not always be an overt attempt to evade one country's laws, but there are instances where information is located on a server in one country specifically to avoid legislation in another. It is, however, accessible to all who seek it out, even if it is forbidden to some. Can country A put pressure on country B in some way, and how would country B react? How, for example, would the Netherlands, with its more relaxed attitude to soft drugs, feel if the UK asked it to close down WWW sites containing information on marijuana, because British residents were accessing the information? If it is not illegal in the Netherlands, would the Dutch Government have any right to accede to such a request? The Chinese government is very concerned about this aspect of Internet provision, and is attempting to centralize control of Internet usage by requiring all users to register with the police. Its concern is over both pornographic material and information which threatens the security of the Chinese government. Singapore has recently announced that it too will seek to control access to politically sensitive and sexually oriented material (*The Guardian*, 1996).

20   The answer, it may appear obvious, is to create new international legislation, but as we shall see, this too is fraught with problems. In many cases, it appears that all that can be done is to request cooperation between states to establish which nationals have accessed the prohibited material and then to take action internally, but that too may involve breaches of constitutional rights of privacy and/or freedom of speech.

3. What Should We Control?

Can we then look at the problem of what should be controlled on an international basis, so that some level of multilateral agreement is hammered out? What Internet content could the international community agree to prohibit universally, so that there is no uncertainty?

22   I asked this question of almost 100 students during a seminar just over a year ago. Many suggestions were forthcoming from individuals, but we could not agree on one single topic which should be universally prohibited. In many cases, the attitude was, "I don't want to look at this material, but I appreciate that others will." Others pointed out that no one was forced to look at this material; as with television, one could always use the equivalent of the "Off" switch. Now, while a straw poll like this cannot be said to be representative, it does indicate the problem, perhaps best summarized as "One man's terrorist is another's freedom fighter"—what offends me may not offend you, so have I the right to say you should not view it or read it? Attitudes toward material that could be deemed offensive are often part of a nation's culture, and so will differ widely. Consider the example of the Netherlands, given earlier, or the difference between Scandinavian and Middle Eastern attitudes toward nudity. Jack Schofield (1996) has recently raised similar questions: Could fundamentalists ban discussion on theories of evolution, or could the Vatican seek to ban sites on birth control? Can we hope to find common ground on which all could agree, and if we did, would the result be so bland and anodyne that it would, in effect, regulate nothing?

Somewhere in the vast amount of information currently circulating on the Internet—I have seen it suggested that daily traffic is around 30 terabytes or 30 million million bytes of information (Merel, 1995)—there will be something to offend someone or some group. How can we hope to stop it all, any more than we have been able to stop all of the same material circulating in print form? Let us not forget that, thanks to its Cold War origins, the Internet is designed to overcome "blockages." It interprets them as damage and finds another way round (the newsgroups are a difficult case, and can be stopped if necessary). So would international legislation be effective, even if there was agreement? Indeed, should we try to regulate all of it, or should our main concern be the freedom of information and of "speech," even in an electronic environment? Societies do not generally try to control everything that is published just because it offends one group or another. We are free to argue the case for and against abortion, the legalization of soft drugs, and so on, and the Internet provides us with another medium in which to carry on our discussions.

24   Many commentators fear that legislation of any sort against offensive material like pornography or drugs information will simply be the thin end of the wedge: it is, they feel, only a short step from there to controlling or censoring other types of material that upset national governments (witness the efforts of China and Singapore) or big business and commercial interests—a fear that will, I believe, only grow with the progressive privatization of the network. Once commercial interests operate the Internet, will they use their power to prohibit access to, for example, environmental groups critical of their operations?

There is a further danger that, in seeking to control the Internet, any national or international legislation would be so blunt that it would prohibit access to genuine, serious material (on admittedly controversial topics) along with the offensive. Let me give a personal example. I maintain a set of WWW pages on Internet regulation, and, since pornography is the main topic of concern at present, the word "pornography" occurs frequently in the annotations, etc. As a result, if you search for "pornography" you will find my pages, whether you are looking for serious discussions or pin-up pictures. The corollary of this is, of course, that if you seek to ban sites containing the word pornography, my site would disappear as well! This is one of the problems encountered by the various software programs (discussed below) that are intended to control access to the Internet.

26   Of course, any such legislation would be doomed to failure from the start, because all that would be needed is to remove the offending words, and legislators would be back to trying somehow to examine content, an equally impossible task given the huge volume of material flowing daily over the network.

The Internet is clearly in a state of flux at present, and we will have to wait and see what develops, but for many Internet users that too is fraught with danger. They argue that we must take action now to prevent governments' legislating on Internet content, otherwise it will be too late.

4. How Can We Control the Internet?

28   With that in mind, let us turn to ways in which some form of control can be exercised over the material that is currently found on the Internet.

4.1 Self-Regulation

The most time-honored method is that of *self-regulation:* individuals or (more usually) systems managers and administrators control what is made available from the systems under their control. It is they who have been responsible for most of the closures of sites that I mentioned earlier, primarily because of the load such sites place on the server, or because the material does not accord with an acceptable use policy. Many systems administrators admit, however, that it is technically very difficult to control which sites their users *access* (as distinct from the material users place online), though acceptable use policies are similarly relevant and there is some evidence of various monitoring procedures (which are made known to users) to ensure that use policies are adhered to. It would appear from a 1992 study, however, that obscene or harassing material is not the primary concern of systems administrators. The most frequently occurring incidents are virus infection and the printing of nonacademic materials on university-owned printers (Stager, 1992). Complaints that, for example, the contents of BBS were obscene were mentioned by less than one-third of the computer center directors in this survey. There is also, as Stager has pointed out, a potential source of confusion in the minds of computer center directors. More than two-thirds of those asked agreed that university-operated bulletin boards are subject to restrictions if their content is clearly libellous or obscene, but less than half agreed that they had a "general understanding of what my campus community considers obscene." Again, we have the problem of defining our terms.

30   I have already mentioned the growing use of warning signs as an example of self-regulation. They do not prohibit access, but no one can be under any illusion about the content of such sites. Acceptable use policies on the part of organisations (such as universities and private sector companies) and of service providers must also count as self-regulation, and there are instances where these have been used to prohibit access to, and provision of, material judged to be offensive and/or illegal. The UKERNA guidelines are an example, since, as a result of these, many UK universities block access to the more controversial newsgroups, but many such institutions and providers have developed similar policies, and many of these are available on the WWW. The British Computer Society's Schools Committee (1995) has produced guidelines to prevent computer misuse which recognize the existence of potentially offensive material and give advice on the development of a suitable policy.

For many Internet and WWW users, self-regulation is the only way to control content, anything else being seen as an infringement of freedom of speech or civil liberty (especially in the United States). In the United

Kingdom, this seems, for the moment, to be the route which will be taken by Government, which feels that *a code of conduct* is the best route forward, and presumably the Internet industry will now sit down to establish that code, preventing the storage and distribution of offensive material.

4.2 Parental/Teacher Control

32   As Internet access becomes a growing feature of schools and homes (as distinct from universities and other institutions), parents worry about what their children are seeing and reading in class or in the privacy of their rooms, and teachers are concerned about the implications if, during one of their classes, a pupil stumbles across (or goes looking for) a pornographic image, a discussion on abortion rights, or where to buy marijuana.

Many have argued that, rather than introduce sweeping legislation which will, it is claimed, be the end of the Internet, parents (and to a lesser extent, teachers) should take responsibility for their children's actions. The analogy is often drawn with teaching our children to cross the road safely and to deal with traffic: we don't let them wander off on their own, but we show them the dangers and how to avoid them. Gradually, as they learn and mature, they are allowed to do things on their own. Similarly, it is argued, parents should accompany their children on their first Internet surfings, pointing out the dangers in the process.

34   To help parents and teachers in this, a number of software packages have been developed to shut out access to the more offensive material. Programs like *NetNanny, CyberSitter, SurfWatch* and *Internet Filter* block access to sites containing certain listed words. This stop list comes "built-in" to the software, but it can be added to by parents to suit specific requirements. In some cases, attempts to access prohibited sites are logged and can be inspected by a parent or teacher, who could then help to stop such attempts. There is even a version for business use; presumably, it could also be used to prevent staff from wasting time surfing the Net!

4.3 Government Legislation

Anyone who has kept an eye on the scene over the past twelve months will be aware that the big (and now rather complicated) story in controlling the Internet is the passage of the Communications Decency Act (CDA) through the US Senate, initially accompanied by two other broadly similar bills, plus a fourth which is believed to take a slightly different line and could be more acceptable to the majority of Internet users. The amended CDA was passed by a single vote in a House/Senate conference committee and became effectively an amalgam of two bills passed by the House and the Senate respectively. The three most restrictive bills, which have come in for the most criticism, all seek to make it illegal to transmit *indecent* material and would make both online service providers and content providers liable. The fourth bill was thought to avoid such action and to empower parents and teachers to control Internet access.

36   The CDA was passed at the beginning of February 1996, and signed into law on 8 February. It was immediately the subject of a lawsuit to the US

Attorney General by the American Civil Liberties Union and 19 other complainants, who have succeeded in having some parts of the Act declared unconstitutional; as a result, it is in abeyance at the time of writing. A similar
suit has been filed by a coalition of industry and online organizations, including the American Library Association.

The chief criticism directed at the Act relates to its attempts to make
service providers liable and to the fact that, at the last minute, the word "indecent" was substituted for the word "obscene." The argument against this
development is that the concept of "indecent material" is vague but more
wide-ranging than "obscene," and that it would include not only sexually
explicit material but texts that are now regarded as classics of literature. The
oft-quoted example is that this bill would prohibit the distribution of such
classic works of fiction as *Catcher in the Rye* or *Lady Chatterley's Lover,*
when most thought that this was a battle already won. The bill would also
give the US Federal Communications Commission some authority to regulate online speech.

38   It should be noted that opposition to the CDA is not limited to the online community and such organisations as Computer Professionals for Social Responsibility, the American Civil Liberties Union, or the Center for
Democracy and Technology. Newt Gingrich has already suggested that such
efforts are unconstitutional and the US Justice Department has said that the
legislation is unnecessary (it believes it has all the legislation needed to
prosecute where necessary). Other opponents have said that such legislation
will only result in the creation of an underground Internet, where the material objected to will still circulate freely and could still be accessed by those
in the know.

Not only would this legislation prohibit literary works, but also the serious discussions of many topics and problems to do with sexual matters.
There would be a threat to AIDS information, mutually supportive discussions of abuse and many other online forums which, enthusiasts claim, can
be very important to those affected. Its effects on discussions of abortion
rights have already been challenged as a breach of the US Constitution.

40   This is currently the only impending legislation that seeks to control
content on the Internet. Many other countries are investigating the question, and the UK government, for example, would prefer to establish a code
of conduct, as I indicated earlier. However, I think we can be sure that, if the
USA passes this or similar legislation, many other countries will face considerable pressure to do likewise. The pressure is already there in the French
efforts to introduce European legislation.

5. Conclusion

The question of a free or fettered Internet is not an easy one: so many variables come into play, and in many instances we can have only a personal
reaction to the problem of offensive material on computer networks. The
overwhelming majority of Internet users agree on the need to protect
our young people from this material, but the way to do so, they argue, is to

involve parents and teachers and to educate our children, just as we educate them about the dangers of road traffic. The problem, it is argued, is not as serious as some would have us think, and legislation is too big a hammer for this particular nut: it would destroy more than it would protect. The next few months are going to be both interesting and crucial to the future shape of the Internet. ❖

References

(More links to relevant material are available from *Censorship and the Internet.*)

British Computer Society Schools Committee (1995). *Preventing the misuse of computers in schools.* Swindon: British Computer Society.

CCTA Ethics Collaborative Open Group (1995). *Superhighways Ethics Project: Report.*

Federal Department of Communications and the Arts, Australia (1995). *Consultation paper on the regulation of on-line information services, 7 July 1995.*

The Guardian (1996). Singapore to censor Internet. 6 March, 12.

Hoffman, D., and Novak, T. (1995). *A detailed analysis of the conceptual, logical, and methodological flaws in the article: Marketing pornography on the information super-highway.*

Holderness, M. (1995). In search of a sea of sex. *The Guardian,* 2 August, 19. (Also available through the *Guardian Online Archives search facility.*)

Information Highway Advisory Council (1995). *Connection, community, content: The challenge of the information highway.* Final report of the Information Highway Advisory Council, Ottawa, Industry Canada.

Merel, P. (1995). *Response to consultation paper on the regulation of on-line information services,* Electronic Frontiers, Australia.

Rimm, M. (1995). *Marketing pornography on the information superhighway: A survey of 917,410 images, descriptions, short stories and animations downloaded 8.5 million times by consumers in over 2000 cities in forty countries, provinces and territories.*

Sansom, G. (1995). *Illegal and offensive content on the information highway: A background paper.* Ottawa, Industry Canada; Spectrum, Information Technologies and Telecommunications Sector.

Schofield, J. (1996). *This comment is free for now, The Guardian Online,* 26 January.

Stager, S.F. (1992). *Computer ethics violations: More questions than answers. EDUCOM Review, 27*(4), 1992.

Thimbleby, H. (1995). *Problems in the global village.*

UKERNA (1995). *JANET acceptable use policy,* London, UKERNA.

Whitney, T. (1996). Personal communication, 18 January.

Questions for Meaning

1. Why is it unlikely that anyone will download pornography accidentally?
2. On what grounds does Burton question the research that influenced U.S. senators when designing the Communications Decency Act?
3. Why would it be a mistake to assume that the number of times a site is accessed is the same as the number of individuals using that site?

4. Why is it difficult for any one government to control the availability of material on the Internet?
5. According to Burton, what are the three ways through which we can attempt to regulate the Internet? Which of these does he favor?
6. Vocabulary: bedevilled (7), extrapolate (7), entrenched (7), contravene (12), dissemination (14), fraught (20), corollary (25), amalgam (35), abeyance (36).

Questions about Strategy

1. Where does Burton recognize views that are different from his own?
2. How useful is the straw poll discussed in paragraph 22? Would you be able to use similar data in an argument of your own?
3. What strategies does Burton use to help readers keep track of the different points he makes in this argument?
4. This argument is a revision of a paper presented in London. What aspects of it would appeal to a British audience? How do these aspects affect your own response? Does Burton make any attempt to address the concerns of people in other countries?

MAY KADI

WELCOME TO CYBERBIA

Is access to a world of information really as empowering as computer enthusiasts seem inclined to believe? And is the Internet making people more connected to others or more isolated? These are among the questions addressed by May Kadi in this argument published in 1995 by zine h2so4. As you read, consider how Kadi would respond to the way you yourself use the computer—if you are using one at all.

> Computer networking offers the soundest basis for world peace that has yet been presented. Peace must be created on the bulwark of understanding. International computer networks will knit together the peoples of the world in bonds of mutual respect; its possibilities are vast, indeed.
> —*Scientific American*, June 1994

Computer bulletin board services offer up the glories of e-mail, the thought provocation of Newsgroups, the sharing of ideas implicit in public posting, and the interaction of real-time chats. The fabulous, wonderful, limitless world of Communication is just waiting for you to log on. Sure. Yeah. Right.

2   I confess, I am a dedicated cyber-junkie. It's fun. It's interesting. It takes me places where I've never been before. I sign on once a day, twice a

day, three times a day, more and more; I read, I post, I live. Writing an article on the ever-expanding, ever-entertaining, ever-present world of online
existence would have been easy for me. But it would have been familiar,
perhaps dull; and it might have been a lie. The world does not need another
article on the miracle of online reality; what we need, what I need, what this
whole delirious, inter-connected, global-community of a world needs, is a
little reality check.

To some extent the following scenario will be misleading. There *are*
flat rate online services (Netcom for one) which offer significant connectivity for a measly 17 dollars a month. But I'm interested in the activities and
behavior of the private service users who will soon comprise a vast majority
of online citizens. Furthermore, let's face facts, the U.S. government by and
large foots the bill for the Internet, through maintaining the structural
(hardware) backbone, including, among other things, funding to major
universities. As surely as the Department of Defense started this whole
thing, AT&T or Ted Turner is going to end up running it so I don't think it's
too unrealistic to take a look at the Net as it exists in its commercial form[1] in
order to expose some of the realities lurking behind the regurgitated media
rhetoric and the religious fanaticism of net junkies.

Time and Money

4   The average person, the normal human, J. Individual, has an income. Big
or small, how much of J. Individual's income is going to be spent on Computer Connectivity? Does 120 dollars a month sound reasonable? Well,
you may find that number a bit too steep for your pocket book, but the
brutal fact is that 120 dollars is a "reasonable" amount to spend on
monthly connectivity. The major online services have a monthly service
charge of approximately $15. 15 dollars to join the global community,
communicate with a diverse group of people and access the world's largest
repository of knowledge since the Alexandrian Library* does not seem unreasonable, does it? But don't overlook the average per-hour connectivity
rate of an additional $3 (which can skyrocket upwards of $10, depending
on your modem speed and service). You might think that you are a crack
whiz with your communications software—that you are rigorous and
stringent and never, ever respond to e-mail or a forum while online, that
you always use your capture functions and create macros, but let me tell
you that no one, and I repeat, no one, is capable of logging on this efficiently every time. 30 hours per month is a realistic estimate for online
time spent by a single user engaging in activities beyond primitive e-mail.

---

[1] techno concession: I know that the big three commercial services are not considered part of the
Internet property, but they (Prodigy, CompuServe and AOL) are rapidly adding real Net access and
considering AOL just bought out Netcom—well just read the article.

*The library in Alexandria, Egypt, housed one of the most important collections of manuscripts in
the ancient world. After flourishing for almost six hundred years, it was destroyed in the third century AD.

Now consider that the average, one-step-above-complete neophyte user has at least two distinct BBS accounts, and do the math: Total Monthly Cost: $120. Most likely, that's already more than the combined cost of your utility bills. How many people are prepared to double their monthly bills for the sole purpose of connectivity?

In case you think 30 hours a month is an outrageous estimate, think of it in terms of television. (OK, so you don't own a television, well, goody-for-you—imagine that you do!) 30 hours, is, quite obviously, one hour a day. That's not so much. 30 hours a month in front of a television is simply the evening news plus a weekly Seinfeld/Frasier hour. 30 hours a month is less time than the average car-phone owner spends on the phone while commuting. Even a conscientious geek, logging on for e-mail and the up-to-the-minute news that only the net services can provide is probably going to spend 30 hours a month online. And, let's be truthful here, 30 hours a month ignores shareware downloads, computer illiteracy, real-time chatting, interactive game playing and any serious forum following, which by nature entail a significant amount of scrolling and/or download-ing time.

6 If you are really and truly going to use the net services to connect with the global community, the hourly charges are going to add up pretty quickly. Take out a piece of paper, pretend you're writing a check, and print out "One hundred and twenty dollars—" and tell me again, how diverse is the online community?

That scenario aside, let's pretend that you're single, that you don't have children, that you rarely leave the house, that you don't have a TV and that money is not an issue. Meaning, pretend for a moment that you have as much time and as much money to spend online as you damn-well want. What do you actually do online?

8 Well, you download some cool shareware, you post technical questions in the computer user group forums, you check your stocks, you read the news and maybe some reviews—Hey, you've already passed that 30-hour limit! But, of course, since "computer networks make it easy to reach out and touch strangers who share a particular obsession or concern," you are participating in the online forums, discussion groups, and conferences.

Let's review the structure of forums. For the purpose of this essay, we will examine the smallest of the major user-friendly commercial services— America OnLine (AOL). There is no precise statistic available (at least none that the company will reveal—you have to do the research by HAND!!!) on exactly how many subject-specific discussion areas (folders) exist on AOL. Any online service is going to have zillions of posts pertaining to computer usage (e.g., the computer games area of AOL breaks into five hundred sepa-rate topics with over 100,000 individual posts), so let's look at a less popular area: the "Lifestyles and Interests" department.

10 For starters, there are 57 initial categories within the Lifestyles and In-terests area. One of these categories is Ham Radio. Ham Radio? How can

there possibly be 5,909[2] separate, individual posts about Ham Radio? 5,865 postings in the Biking (and that's just bicycles, not motorcycles) category. Genealogy—22,525 posts. The Gay and Lesbian category is slightly more substantial—36,333 posts. There are five separate categories for political and issue discussion. The big catch-all topic area, The Exchange, has over 100,000 posts. Basically, service wide (on the smallest service, remember) there are over a million posts.

So, you want to communicate with other people, join the online revolution, but obviously you can't wade through everything that's being discussed—you need to decide which topics interest you, which folders to browse. Within The Exchange alone (one of 57 subdivisions within one of another 50 higher divisions) there are 1,492 separate topic-specific folders—each containing a rough average of 50 posts, but with many containing close to 400. (Note: AOL automatically empties folders when their post totals reach 400, so total post numbers do not reflect the overall historical totals for a given topic. Sometimes the posting is so frequent that the "shelf life" of a given post is no more than four weeks.)

12   So, there you are, J. Individual, ready to start interacting with folks, sharing stories and communicating. You have narrowed yourself into a single folder, three tiers down in the AOL hierarchy, and now you must choose between nearly fifteen hundred folders. Of course, once you choose a few of these folders, you will then have to read all the posts in order to catch up, be current, and not merely repeat a previous post.

A polite post is no more than two paragraphs long (a screenful of text, which obviously has a number of intellectually negative implications). Let's say you choose ten folders (out of 1,500). Each folder contains an average of 50 posts. Five hundred posts, at, say, one paragraph each, and you're now looking at the equivalent of a two-hundred-page book.

14   Enough with the stats. Let me back up a minute and present you with some very disturbing, but rational, assumptions. J. Individual wants to join the online revolution, to connect and communicate. But, J. Individual is not going to read all one million posts on AOL. (After all, J. Individual has a second online service.) Exercising choice is J. Individual's god-given right as an American, and, by gosh, J. Individual is going to make some decisions. So, J. Individual is going to ignore all the support groups—after all, J. is a normal, well-adjusted person, and all of J.'s friends are normal, well, adjusted individuals, what does J. need to know about alcoholism or incest victims? J. Individual is white. So, J. Individual is going to ignore all the multi-cultural folders. J. couldn't give a hoot about gender issues; does not want to discuss religion or philosophy. Ultimately, J. Individual does not

---

[2] Statistics obtained in June 1994. Most of these numbers have increased by at least 20% since that time, owing to all the Internet hoopla in the media, the consumer desire to be "wired" as painlessly as possible, and AOL's guerrilla marketing tactics.

engage in topics which do not interest J. Individual. So, who is J. meeting? Why, people who are *just like* J.

J. Individual has now joined the electronic community. Surfed the Net. Found some friends. *Tuned in, turned on, and geeked out.* Travelled the Information Highway and, just off to the left of that great Infobahn, J. Individual has settled into an electronic suburb.

16   Are any of us so very different from J. Individual? It's my time and my money and I am not going to waste any of it reading posts by disgruntled Robert-Bly drum-beating Men's-Movement boys who think that they should have some say over whether or not I choose to carry a child to term simply because a condom broke. I know where I stand. I'm an adult. I know what's up and I am not going to waste my money arguing with a bunch of neanderthals.

Oh yeah; I am so connected, so enlightened, so open to the opposing viewpoint. I'm out there, meeting all kinds of people from different economic backgrounds (who have $120 a month to burn), from all religions (yeah, right, like anyone actually discusses religion anymore from a user-standpoint), from all kinds of different ethnic backgrounds and with all kinds of sexual orientations (as if any of this ever comes up outside of the appropriate topic folder).

18   People are drawn to topics and folders that interest them and therefore people will only meet people who are likewise interested in the same topics in the same folders. Rarely does anyone venture into a random folder just to see what others (The Others?) are talking about. This magazine being what it is, I can assume that the average reader will most likely not be as narrow-minded as the average white collar worker out in the burbs—but still, I think you and I are participating in the wide, wide world of online existence only insofar as our already existing interests and prejudices dictate.

Basically, between the monetary constraints and the sheer number of topics and individual posts, the great Information Highway is not a place where you will enter an "amazing web of new people, places, and ideas." One does not encounter people from "all walks of life" because there are too many people and too many folders. Diversity might be out there (and personally I don't think it is), but the simple fact is that the average person will not encounter it because with one brain, one job, one partner, one family, and one life, no one has the time!

20   Just in case these arguments based on time and money aren't completely convincing, let me bring up a historical reference. Please take another look at the opening quote of this essay from *Scientific American*. Featured in their "50 Years Ago Today" column, where you read "computer networks," the original quote contained the word "television." Amusing, isn't it?

Moving beyond the practical obstacles mentioned above, let's assume that the Internet is the functional, incredible information tool that everyone says it is. Are we really prepared to use it?

Who, What, Where, When and Why?

22 School trained us to produce answers. It didn't matter if your answer was right or wrong, the fact is that you did the answering while the teacher was the one asking the questions, writing down the equations, handing out the topics. You probably think that you came up with your own questions in college. But did you? Every class has its theme, its reading list, its issues; you chose topics for papers and projects keeping within the context set by your professors and the academic environment. Again, you were given questions, perhaps more thinly disguised than the questions posed to you in fourth grade, but questions nevertheless. And you answered them. Even people focusing on independent studies and those pursuing higher degrees, still do very little asking, simply because the more you study, the more questions there seem to be, patiently waiting for you to discover and answer them.

These questions exist because any contextual reality poses questions. The context in which you exist defines the question, as much as it defines the answer. School is a limited context. Even life is a limited context. Well, life was a limited context until this Information Highway thing happened to us. Maybe you think that this Infobahn is fabulous; fabulous because all that information is out there waiting to be restructured by you into those answers. School will be easier. Life will be easier. A simple tap-tap-tap on the ol' keyboard brings those answers out of the woodwork and off the Net into the privacy of your own home.

24 But this Information Highway is a two-way street and as it brings the world into your home it brings you out into the world. In a world filled with a billion answers just waiting to be questioned, expect that you are rapidly losing a grip on your familiar context. This loss of context makes the task of formulating a coherent question next to impossible.

The questions aren't out there and they never will be. You must make them.

26 Pure information has no meaning. I would venture to assert that a pure fact has no meaning; no meaning, that is, without the context which every question implies. In less than fifteen minutes I could find out how much rain fell last year in Uzbekistan, but that fact, that answer, has no meaning for me because I don't have or imagine or know the context in which the question is meaningful.

No one ever taught me how to ask a question. I answered other people's questions, received a diploma, and now I have an education. I can tell you what I learned, and what I know. I can quantify and qualify the trivia which comprises my knowledge. But I can't do that with my ignorance. Ignorance, being traditionally "bad," is just lumped together and I have little or no skills for sorting through the vast territory of what I don't know. I have an awareness of it—but only in the sense that I am aware of what I don't know about the topics which I already know something about in the first place.

28   What I mean to say is, I don't know what I don't know about, say, miners in China because I don't know anything about China, or what kinds of minerals they have, or where the minerals are, or the nature of mining as a whole. Worse yet, I don't have a very clear sense of whether or not these would be beneficial, useful, enlightening things for me to know. I have little sense of what questions are important enough for me to ask, so I don't know what answers, what information to seek out on the Internet.

      In this light, it would seem that a massive amount of self-awareness is a prerequisite for using the Internet as an information source—and very few people are remotely prepared for this task. I believe that most people would simply panic in the face of their own ignorance and entrench themselves even more firmly into the black holes of their existing beliefs and prejudices. The information is certainly out there, but whether or not any of us can actually learn anything from it remains to be seen.

Fly, Words, and Be Free

30 The issues pertaining to time, money and the fundamental usefulness of pure information are fairly straightforward when contrasted with the issues raised by e-mail. E-mail is the first hook and the last defense for the Internet and computer-mediated communication. I would like to reiterate that I am by no means a Luddite when it comes to computer technology; in fact, because of this I may be unqualified to discuss, or even grasp, the dark side of electronic communication in the form of e-mail.

      The general quality of e-mail sent by one's three-dimensional[3] friends and family is short, usually funny, and almost completely devoid of thoughtful communication. I do not know if this is a result of the fact that your 3-d friends already "know" you, and therefore brief quips are somehow more revealing (as they reflect an immediate mental/emotional state) than long, factual exposés, or if this brevity is a result of the medium itself. I do not know if I, personally, will ever be able to sort this out, owing to the nature of my friends, the majority of whom are, when all is said and done (unlike myself, I might add), Writers.

32   Writers have a reverence for pen and paper which does not carry over well into ASCII.* There is no glorified history for ASCII exchange and perhaps because of this fact my friends do not treat the medium as they would a hand-written letter. Ultimately, there is very little to romanticize about e-mail. There is decidedly a lack of sensuality, and perhaps some

---

[3] So sue me for being a nerd. Personally, I find referring to friends one has made outside of the cyber world as one's "real" friends, or one's "objective" friends, to be insulting and inaccurate. Certainly one's cyber friends are three-dimensional in a final sense, but the "3-d" adjective is about the only term I have come up with which doesn't carry the negative judgmental weight of other terms so over-used in European philosophy. Feel free to write me if you've got a better suggestion. Better yet, write me in the appropriate context: flox@netcom.com.

* ASCII is an abbreviation used by computer specialists for American Standard Code for Information Interchange.

lack of realism. There is an undeniable connection between writers and their written (literally) words. This connection is transferred via a paper letter in a way that can never be transferable electronically. A hand-written letter is physically touched by both the sender and the receiver. When I receive an electronic missive, I receive only an impression of the mind, but when I receive a hand-written letter, I receive a piece, a moment, of another's physical (real?) existence; I possess, I own, that letter, those words, that moment.

Certainly there is a near-mystical utopianism to the lack of ownership of electronic words. There is probably even an evolution of untold consequences. Personally, I do not think, as so many do, that a great democracy of thought is upon us—but there is a change, as ownership slips away. While this is somewhat exciting, or at least intriguing, insofar as public communication goes, it is sad for private correspondence. To abuse a well-known philosopher, there is a leveling taking place: The Internet and the computer medium render a public posting on the nature of footwear and a private letter on the nature of one's life in the same format, and to some extent this places both on the same level. I cannot help but think that there is something negative in this.

34   Accessibility is another major issue in the e-mail/handwritten letter debate. Text sent via the Net is instantly accessible, but it is accessible only in a temporal sense. E-text is inaccessible in its lack of presence, in its lack of objective physicality. Even beyond this, the speed and omnipresence of the connection can blind one to the fact that the author/writer/friend is not physically accessible. We might think we are all connected, like an AT&T commercial, but on what level are we connecting? A hand-written letter reminds you of the writers' physical existence, and therefore reminds you of their physical absence; it reminds you that there is a critical, crucial component of their very nature which is not accessible to you; e-mail makes us forget the importance of physicality and plays into our modern belief in the importance of time.

Finally, for me, there is a subtle and terrible irony lurking within the Net: the Net, despite its speed, its exchange, ultimately reeks of stasis. In negating physical distance, the immediacy of electronic transfers devalues movement and the journey. In one minute a thought is in my head, and the next minute it is typed out, sent, read, and in your head. The exchange may be present, but the journey is imperceptible. The Infobahn hype would have us believe that this phenomenon is a fast-paced dynamic exchange, but the feeling, when you've been at it long enough, is that this exchange of ideas lacks movement. Lacking movement and the journey, to me it loses all value.

36   Maybe this is prejudice. Words are not wine, they do not necessarily require age to improve them. Furthermore, I have always hated the concept that Art comes only out of struggle and suffering. So, to say that e-mail words are weaker somehow because of the nature, or lack, of their journey, is to romanticize the struggle. I suppose I am anthropomorphising text too much—but I somehow sense that one works harder to endow one's handwritten words with a certain strength, a certain soul, simply because those

things are necessary in order to survive a journey. The ease of the e-mail journey means that your words don't need to be as well-prepared, or as well-equipped.

Electronic missives lack time, space, embodiment and history (in the sense of a collection of experiences). Lacking all these things, an electronic missive is almost in complete opposition to my existence and I can't help but wonder what, if anything, I am communicating. ❖

Questions for Meaning

1. What limits restrict the extent to which the average person can access information through the Internet?
2. What is the difference between a folder and a post?
3. Why would it be "polite" to limit a post to two paragraphs, or a screenful of text? What would be the "intellectually negative implications" of this convention?
4. According to Kadi, why is the information superhighway more likely to take us to "an electronic suburb" than to a truly diverse community?
5. Why does Kadi believe that the effective use of the Internet for research requires "a massive amount of self-awareness"?
6. How is reading an electronic message different from reading a handwritten letter? Which does Kadi seem to prefer? Which do you prefer to receive?

Questions about Strategy

1. Consider the quotation from *Scientific American*, which Kadi cites at the beginning of her article and then discusses in paragraph 20. How useful is it, given the purpose of this argument?
2. When calculating the monthly cost of computer networking, Kadi imagines someone using the Internet for thirty hours a month. Does this estimate seem reasonable? How important is this estimate to her case as a whole?
3. Paragraphs 8–13 are devoted to describing how information is organized on an online service and how someone would proceed when searching through this information. What is the purpose of this description?
4. Kadi urges readers to "face facts." To what extent has she provided facts that are useful to face? Does she rely on opinion as well as fact?
5. How does Kadi present herself as an individual? What kind of limitations does she acknowledge? What role does her self-presentation play in her argument?

ERIK NESS

BIGBROTHER@CYBERSPACE

As the world becomes increasingly wired and more transactions take place through computer networks, will much of our private lives become known to people we've never met or even thought about? And how will these strangers use the information about us that is now at their disposal? Invoking the idea of Big Brother, the totalitarian ruler in George Orwell's *1984,* Erik Ness argues that the Internet poses a potential danger to civil liberty. His argument first appeared in a 1994 issue of *The Progressive,* a monthly periodical known for advocating liberal political opinions. Ness is editor of The Progressive Media Project.

In its popular series of futuristic commercials, AT&T paints a liberating picture of your not-too-distant life, when the information superhighway will be an instrument of personal freedom and a servant to your worldly needs and desires. But is the future of cyberspace really so elegant, so convenient? Or does it represent a serious threat to your privacy and your freedom?

2   The information superhighway is at least a decade away for most of us, but whether you know it or not, you already exist in cyberspace—through credit and other electronic records, your phone line, and your cable television. Constitutional scholar Laurence Tribe has argued that "without further thought and awareness . . . the danger is clear and present" that the Constitution's core values will be compromised "in the dim reaches of cyberspace."

When you visit your doctor, it is increasingly likely that your medical records are kept on a computer. Many of the health-care bills introduced in Congress this year called for a national medical database to link these records. Unfortunately, law-enforcement officers could gain access to those files without even obtaining a warrant. President Nixon's henchmen had to break into Daniel Ellsberg's psychiatrist's office to pull his files. Using a national medical database, they would need only to press a button.

4   Of course, the Government already has large stores of sensitive personal information at its disposal. In July of this year, Senator John Glenn, Ohio Democrat, released Internal Revenue Service papers showing that its employees were using IRS computers to prowl through the tax files of family, friends, neighbors, and celebrities. Since 1989, the IRS says, the agency has investigated more than 1,300 of its employees for unauthorized browsing; more than 400 employees have been disciplined.

But even seemingly benign information—your address in a government computer, for example—can betray you. Chris Criner volunteers as an escort for an abortion clinic in Tustin, California. After a Saturday morning of escort work in November 1992, Criner returned home to find a note on his door reading, "Hi. We came by for coffee. We'll be back." One week later,

Operation Rescue picketed his apartment. Criner was mystified; after clinic work he always went shopping or took a different route home to shake any over-zealous pursuers.

6   Criner had noticed a new protester lately—a man scribbling notes on a clipboard. Then one protester asked about Criner's wife, a clinic worker, using her given name—not the one she was known by. On a hunch, Criner and others at the clinic filed a complaint with the California Department of Motor Vehicles and found that four of their license plates had been illegally traced within an hour of each other at the Anaheim Police Department.

A former police employee eventually confessed to intruding into the restricted files. But Criner is still chilled by the incident—particularly after the shooting deaths of two abortion providers and a clinic escort in Pensacola, Florida. "Who knows where this information went besides this one little picket group?" he wonders. "Maybe it's on a computer bulletin board somewhere, or in some militant pro-life newsletter. Should I worry about my wife getting shot in the back of the head as she walks up to our front door because they know where we live?"

8   Businesses, government officials, activists, engineers, and intellectuals are busily defining cyberspace, and with various goals. Their divergent interests meet on the National Information Infrastructure, the so-called information superhighway. This cable—capable of delivering voice, data, and video images at high speed—is eventually supposed to connect every home and business in the United States and the world to an ever-growing web of electronic services ranging from stock quotations to movies on demand. The buzzword for this change is "convergence"—the melding of telephone, computer, and television technologies into the foundation of an information economy.

The Clinton Administration, particularly Vice President Al Gore, is a self-proclaimed champion of this information age. The business world is salivating over potential profits in the information economy. Meanwhile, consumer advocates and privacy experts warn that, without proper safeguards, this potential global village could become George Orwell's *1984*.

10   The National Information Infrastructure is projected to cost between $400 billion and $700 billion. During the 1992 Presidential campaign, Gore called for a major Government role in its development, but high Federal debt has led the Administration to favor private-sector design and operation instead. This shift has placed an even bigger burden on Congressional efforts this year to restructure the nation's $170 billion telecommunications industry, consisting of local telephone companies (worth $90 billion), long-distance carriers ($60 billion), and cable television industry (worth $20 billion).

The basic goal was to allow phone and cable operators to compete with each other locally, while preventing a total monopoly of both by any one company in one area and developing a new definition of universal service. Regulators and activists alike have long been leery of allowing a monopoly of the wires going into the American home, and their apprehensions have been heightened as electronic communication and commerce increasingly become central parts of our lives.

12   But even as telephone companies and cable television were eager to compete with each other for emerging markets, their rivalry got the better of them, killing telecommunications restructuring in the Senate. "Much of this battle is over who will control the television of the future," explains Jeff Chester of the Washington-based Center for Media Education. One example, he says, was NBC's effort to create a competitor for Ted Turner's twenty-four-hour Cable News Network. John Malone, president of TCI—who has a financial stake in CNN—controlled enough of the cable market that he was able to force NBC to turn a hard-news service into a softer, infotainment-oriented channel. "Their principal focus is profit, not the currency of democracy, not the diversity of ideas," warns Chester.

"We're in real danger of having a handful of giant, global communications corporations controlling the public mind," says Chester, whose organization filed a thirty-eight-page brief with the FCC opposing last year's mega-deal between Bell Atlantic and cable giant Telecommunications, Inc. The deal broke down, but that has not slowed the pace of consolidation: In the last year, AirTouch Communication acquired U.S. West (a deal worth $13.5 billion), AT&T Corporation merged with McCaw Cellular Communications, Inc. (a $12.6 billion value), and Viacom bought Blockbuster Entertainment ($7.97 billion).

14   "There is a direct relationship between the health of our democracy and the diversity of our communications system," says Chester. "I think one reason why the body politic is so ill can be traced back to problems with the media system and the institutions which are part of it."

If we're not careful, he says, today's captive consumer of telephone and cable television will become tomorrow's totally exposed consumer. "We're turning over the info superhighway to Madison Avenue, so they can better, more effectively serve the needs of advertisers to target individuals in discrete demographic groups."

16   As if to emphasize this, no sooner had the telecommunications restructuring bill died for the year than the computer service American Online ignited a fresh battle in cyberspace when it advertised its "upscale" subscriber list in a direct-mail trade publication. "America Online members are computer and modem owners who pay up to $200 a month to enjoy hundreds of entertaining and informative services," the ad promised. "Credit-worthy—over 85 per cent pay by credit card. . . . Mail Order Buyers!"

The popular online service drew fire from Massachusetts Representative Edward Markey, chairman of the House Subcommittee on Telecommunications and Finance, who fired off a letter to America Online president Steve Case, arguing that "comprehensive privacy protections must become part of the electronic ethics of companies doing business on the information superhighway and a fundamental right of all its travelers."

18   According to David Banisar, staff attorney for the Electronic Privacy Information Center, the America Online controversy is important because commerce on the Internet is in danger of becoming more like a shopping mall than a public street. "In shopping malls, the owners can pretty much do what they want," he warns, "and those same shopping malls are going to be collecting reams, if I can use an old-fashioned term, of personal data." With more transactions taking place over the net, more personal information about you enters cyberspace. "Even if you go into a store," says Banisar, "the odds are it's going to transfer transaction information via the same superhighway to its suppliers, to its deliverers, and to its main offices."

        America Online was not unique. As Case pointed out, CompuServe, another online service, had been renting its list for years. In fact, the mailing-list business is a refined industry; lists can include explicit and implicit demographic information ranging from income to political preference to your favorite television shows. But these are relatively primitive compared to what advancing computer technology could produce: complete profiles of consumers, including brand-name inclinations, credit histories, and shopping habits. Many supermarkets already use check-cashing cards that, in conjunction with computerized scanners, keep detailed records of consumer spending habits. Will your insurance company someday be able to learn whether or not you buy beer and cigarettes?

20 First Amendment rights are already at issue in cyberspace. One major concern is whether commercial online companies deserve the broad protection of telephone companies, which have no responsibility for the content of conversations on their wires, and bookstores, which are also broadly protected, or are like publishers and broadcasters, who are held accountable for libel and other transgressions.

        CompuServe, the oldest and largest online service, appears to want it both ways. In 1990, an online journal called Rumorville, produced under contract for CompuServe, published allegedly defamatory remarks about a competitor, Skuttlebut. When Skuttlebut sued for libel in a New York district court, CompuServe argued that it was more like a bookstore than a publisher, and therefore subject to a different standard of libel. The court agreed, saying a "computerized database is the functional equivalent of a more traditional news vendor." Because it did not exercise control over editorial content, it was not held liable for defamation.

22   But last year, CompuServe took a different approach toward Richard Patterson, a computer programmer and CompuServe member who believes—and claimed online—that the company had infringed on his trademark. CompuServe asked a Federal court to resolve the trademark dispute, but warned Patterson that if he discussed the suit online it would sever his CompuServe access.

        This contradictory strategy indicates the general confusion over what rights and privileges are accorded in the commercial online environment. Because the services are private, they are not automatically obligated to respect constitutional rights of privacy and freedom of expression. Several years ago, Prodigy, another service, booted subscribers who tried to fight a rate hike, and censored anti-Semitic comments in online forums. Just this year, America Online closed several feminist discussion forums for fear that young girls might stumble upon adult discussions.

24   Censorship can take insidious forms online. Users do not always understand the different regions of cyberspace, which is divided into loosely overlapping sectors ranging from the commercial services to the Internet to underground bulletin boards trafficking in stolen credit card numbers. Usenet, for example, is a sprawling electronic forum with more than 8,000 discussion groups ranging from alt.fan.NoamChomsky to alt.tv-dinosaurs .barney.die.die.die.

      CompuServe and America Online both offer access to Usenet, but restrict areas—largely those dealing with sexuality—that they deem objectionable. On CompuServe, you can't subscribe to a newsgroup deemed objectionable by the company unless you know the exact title. Since many people choose their newsgroups by scanning for key words, the company automatically reserves full access for the initiated. America Online does not provide access at all to what it decides are objectionable groups. Both companies promised to provide me with the list of excluded discussion groups, but did not.

26   Less-restricted portions of the net are also censored, though generally with a lighter touch. Working within established and respected community guidelines, some Usenet groups are moderated to keep discussions focused. It's easy to appreciate the utility of the policy—communication on the net is often hailed for its casual intelligence and its potential to build community. But if every keystroke of every person who had ever surfed the net were saved in perpetuity, it would quickly drown in its own chatter.

      Of more immediate concern these days is the increasingly unruly environment as new members unfamiliar with traditions flood the net. The Internet actually began as a military research project, but when scientists discovered its usefulness for exchanging data and computer power, the National Science Foundation took over administration. It grew largely unregulated into what has been called the largest functioning anarchy, with users establishing protocols and "netiquette."

28   Within this intellectual framework of self-governance, the move toward commercialism has met vociferous resistance. Last April, the Phoenix immigration law firm of Canter & Segal advertised its services on Usenet by placing messages in thousands of forums, the vast majority of which had no relationship to immigration. While informational postings in related areas have been tolerated on Usenet, the indiscriminate Canter & Segal posting drew a furious response. Outraged "netizens" deluged the company with angry e-mail messages called "flames." Undeterred by the communal outrage, Canter & Segal ventured onto the net again in June, drawing the ire of a Norwegian programmer who devised a search-and-destroy program, or

"cancelbot" to wipe out the firm's transmissions. As the net becomes more crowded and contentious, the specter of vigilante censors seems quite real.

Despite the phenomenal growth of computer networks, relatively few people are actually online. Some five million subscribe to commercial services, while as many as twenty million gain access to the Internet through universities or work. Online computing has sparked such interest because it is the most likely model for the emerging information economy. In the future, your telephone, computer, and television will all be linked, and you'll gain access to everything from the latest rap video to maps of Virginia in the 1600s stored in the Library of Congress, using the kinds of graphical interfaces being pioneered by America Online and CompuServe. But while the media hype a Golden Age of democracy spurred by the free flow of information, commercial online services resemble nothing so much as the current offerings of television and newsstands: *Time, The Atlantic,* ABC, DC Comics, the *Chicago Tribune,* Associated Press, and Reuters.

30   What would it take for a publication like *The Progressive* to get online? Brian Jaffe, director of online publications for CompuServe, the country's largest commercial online service, is firm about its priorities. "We're in business to make money," he explains. "The overall tone is going to be: You have to sell me on you."

First, *The Progressive* would have to show CompuServe that it would "add value to the service" by providing the demographic makeup of the people it was planning to reach online. Second, Jaffe looks at brand-name awareness. "When you pop up in our WHAT'S NEW—our intrusive marketing area—and I see *The Progressive* is online, come visit our area, I don't know what type of emotion that's going to stir in our two-and-a-quarter million users." Finally, Jaffe looks at "comarketing opportunities"—basically, what kind of new members *The Progressive* would offer to CompuServe—an evaluation driven by circulation and demographics. "We are an extremely powerful marketing entity," says Jaffe, citing CompuServe's phenomenal growth rate of 85,000 new members a month. Next to this, *The Progressive's* 32,000 circulation is relatively small, a factor that he says doesn't work in its favor.

32   Still, you may yet find publications like *The Progressive* available from commercial online services. "I'm never going to turn a deaf ear, because I never know when the next winner is going to come around," says Jaffe. But, he cautions, "You're right, we don't have a lot of political-type publications online. To be quite honest with you—maybe you can convince me otherwise—but it doesn't quite fit in with the publishing formula that I'm looking for in a successful online product."

The clout of these commercial services already intimidates small publications. As a staff member from one alternative periodical said after discussing its efforts to get online. "Don't say anything about us being critical of them that could hurt their willingness to sign us on in the future."

34   This clout will only increase as the Internet moves from the public to the private sector. More than half of it is now commercial in origin, and the National Science Foundation is passing management of the remainder into private hands. The Internet has thrived in part because its flat-rate pricing has made it possible for individuals and nonprofits to take full advantage of electronic communications. Eventually, the net will abandon flat-rate pricing, which could curtail open participation as costs rise. The booming media interest in the Internet may also be more cloud than silver lining: "It's clear to me the media industries want to use the Internet as another programming channel that they control," says Chester.

While the Clinton Administration has won praise for its information-age advocacy, it has taken a beating on privacy. "The Clinton Administration has paid some lip service to privacy issues, but it's really done almost nothing," explains Dave Banisar of the Electronic Privacy Information Center.

36   Bill Clinton's first mistake was the hugely unpopular Clipper chip proposal. Clipper is a computer chip that scrambles a message using a classified mathematical function.

Users would have numerical keys to encode and decode messages, but two agencies—the Treasury Department and the National Institute of Standards and Technology—would hold copies of the keys in escrow, providing Government access as needed. Clipper was the response of law-enforcement and national-security officials who see cheap and powerful computers making it easier for criminals and spies to break the law.

38   Many cryptographers worried that Clipper, classified and developed in secret by the National Security Agency, might not be secure, and would not sufficiently protect privacy. To get your key, law officers would not have to present a warrant—they would only have to fax a request claiming they had a warrant. Safeguards against dissemination of the key and guaranteeing destruction once the order had expired were also deemed insufficient.

The keys for every Clipper chip would be available to only a handful of people, but if these individuals were corrupted, the whole system would be compromised. NSA involvement also worried some people: Had the agency built a trapdoor into the system that would allow it special access?

40   Even the Office of Technology Assessment criticized the agency's involvement in Clipper, concluding it was "part of a long-term control strategy intended to retard the general availability of 'unbreakable' or 'hard-to-break' cryptography within the United States."

Clipper has been essentially abandoned for data encryption, but is still on the table as a standard for voice encryption. Gore is currently working to develop a compromise, but has said that the White House will not yield on the proposed key escrow, though the Government would not have to be the escrow agent.

42   Clipper is only one part of vigorous efforts by the authorities to protect their eavesdropping rights. "If you think crime is bad now, just wait and

see what happens if the FBI one day is no longer able to conduct court-approved electronic surveillance," FBI director Louis Freeh told an audience last May soon after the reintroduction of his agency's Digital Telephony in Congress.

First proposed by the Bush Administration and one of the few bills successfully pushed through the last Congress by Clinton, digital telephony requires common carriers—telephone companies—to help law-enforcement officers with appropriate court orders to listen to your conversations. It would also make transactional data—who's calling whom—easily available to law-enforcement officers. To do this, the phone companies need special equipment to ensure access to their new digital switches—equipment the legislation would buy for $500 million.

44   But is this cost-effective law enforcement? Freeh testified before the Senate in March that not a single wiretap order has been hindered by advancing technology. Since the 1968 passage of wiretap legislation, there have been about 900 Federal and state wiretaps per year, costing an average of $46,492 per tap in 1992.

Why should law-abiding citizens be concerned with wiretaps, codes, and scrambled conversations? The British royal family is certainly the most public example of the hazards of unsecured communications, but Philip Zimmermann, a cryptographic-software designer, told Congress last year that technological advances made possible massive Government intrusions on privacy. "Today," Zimmermann warned, "electronic mail is gradually replacing conventional paper mail, and is soon to be the norm for everyone, not the novelty it is today.

46   "Unlike paper mail," he added, "e-mail messages are just too easy to intercept and scan for interesting key words. This can be done easily, routinely, automatically, and undetectably on a grand scale. This is analogous to drift net fishing—making a quantitative and qualitative Orwellian difference to the health of democracy."

Among the rationales for increased electronic-monitoring powers is the need to fight computer crime. Law-enforcement officials cite a burgeoning traffic in pornography, illegally copied software, and stolen credit information, but often they have been too trigger-happy in policing a world they don't fully understand. Specific targets have been computer bulletin boards, which people dial into to obtain information or to talk.

48   Police in Munroe Falls, Ohio, confiscated the $3,000 computer of Mark Lehrer, charging that kids had seen pornography on his bulletin board, Akron Anomaly. Lehrer did have some X-rated files, but access was restricted—users had to send a copy of their driver's license to get in. A few explicit photos were in common space—Lehrer claims a filing error—so local police recruited a fifteen-year-old to gain access to the files, then busted Lehrer. But with no complaints from local parents, the charge didn't stick. Police filed new charges alleging that other photos—not even available on the bulletin board, but seized with the computer—could have depicted minors.

Lacking the money for expert testimony, Lehrer entered a guilty plea to a misdemeanor charge of possessing a criminal tool—his computer. But confiscating the computer for a misfiled picture is akin to seizing a convenience store for a misfiled copy of *Penthouse*. An *Akron Beacon* editorial asked "whether the police were protecting against a child pornographer or using the intimidating power of the police and judicial system to help themselves to a nice hunk of expensive machinery."

50   Michael Elansky ran the Ware House bulletin board in West Hartford, Connecticut. Elansky was arrested in August 1993, when police found files on his bulletin board explaining in detail the construction of various explosive devices. The files had been written four years earlier by a fifteen-year-old, and contained constitutionally protected information widely available in sources ranging from chemistry textbooks to *The Anarchist Cookbook*.

Elansky's case was compounded by his previous scrapes with the law—he eventually entered guilty pleas to parole violations—but the charges relating to the bulletin board files were never dropped. Activists maintain that his arrest and detention (Elansky could not post the $500,000 bond) were a violation of First Amendment rights and do not bode well for free speech in cyberspace.

52   "I don't think it's a police conspiracy to chill the whole net," says Banisar of such crackdowns, "but it certainly has that result." Banisar says the most closely watched legal contest in cyberspace is that of Robert Alan Thomas and his wife, Carleen, who live in Milpitas, California, where they ran the Amateur Action Bulletin Board Service. Subscribers—3,600 in the United States and Europe—paid $99 a year, using their computers to call the Amateur Action computer and download pornographic photographs, chat with other members, and order explicit videotapes.

Then a Tennessee hacker broke into the system. Disturbed by the hardcore content, the intruder alerted the Memphis authorities, who began a sting operation. The Thomases were busted and saddled with eleven Federal obscenity charges—not in California but in Tennessee, the heart of the Bible belt. For the first time a bulletin-board operator was prosecuted where the obscene material was received instead of at its point of origin. The Thomases were convicted; the case is on appeal and could end up in the Supreme Court.

54   At issue is the Supreme Court's 1973 ruling that obscenity be judged by local community standards. This time, the Court would have to answer a new question: Where are you when you're in cyberspace? "Whatever your view of looking at nudie pictures, this is pretty chilling for everybody in the rest of the country that doesn't want to be subject to Tennessee morals," says David Banisar of the Electronic Privacy Information Center. "If I wanted to be subject to Tennessee morals, I'd move to Tennessee."

Just as Al Gore is playing an important role in the National Information Infrastructure, his father helped create the interstate highway system in the 1950s. The interstate, while it ushered in an era of great prosperity, has also been blamed for the decline of the cities and the loss of services to poor and minority communities. Many advocates fear that a poorly designed information superhighway could lead to further marginalization of the underprivileged in society.

56   The big telecommunications players are at pains to promise this won't happen, and both Pacific Telesis and AT&T-McCaw have signed commitments with community groups in California to ensure that the state's minority, low-income, inner-city and disabled populations are wired into the electronic future. But a recent study of early plans for advanced communications networks by a coalition of groups (including the National Association for the Advancement of Colored People, the Consumer Federation of America, and the Center for Media Education) suggests that poor and minority neighborhoods are already becoming victims of "electronic redlining."

"Everyone is going to need affordable access to interactive communications services to ensure that the public has access to a basic range of information," explains Jeffrey Chester. He says it's conceivable that the media could evolve so that C-SPAN is the only source of information for what's going on in Congress, making a lower-cost tier of information services vital for democracy.

58   "We don't know what a Twenty-first Century version of public television will look like, but we can start thinking about it when we look at the Internet and freenet and community radio stations," he suggests. Freenets, for example, provide access to e-mail, computer databases, and the Internet in such cities as Buffalo, Cleveland, and Seattle, through libraries and other outreach programs. "Those services are not going to become a part of the information superhighway without a real public policy to ensure that they are a viable—not marginal—part of the media system," warns Chester.

Another access question raised by the information economy is that when information is bought and sold in units, you can only know as much as you can afford. The commercial databases used by large corporations, law firms, and news services are expensive. In legal cases, in particular, this puts the well-heeled at a distinct advantage. Most of the material in legal databases consists of case law and judicial decisions in the public domain, but such companies as West Publishing maintain that they own the copyright for the page numbers of the decisions, giving them an effective monopoly in the legal database market for many states and Federal courts. Furthermore, local, state, and federal Governments maintain many valuable databases which are not currently accessible to their putative owners—the general public.

60 While this is a dark rendering of tomorrow, the future of cyberspace could be a lot more promising. Activists worldwide are already using advanced computer networks to share information and coordinate strategies. And citizens across the country could instantaneously gather information from a variety of sources uncensored by the corporate media.

But the perils of the Information Age are broad. In his book, *The Cult of Information,* Theodore Roszak reminds us that information cannot replace—

and may even obscure—knowledge, insight, and wisdom. "Every mature technology brings an immediate gain followed by enormous long-term liabilities," he writes. "How things will balance out is a matter of vigilance, moral courage, and the distribution of power."

62   Consider the story of Philip Zimmermann, a software engineer who believes in "freeware"—software given away to help people better use their computers. In 1991, Zimmermann released an encryption program called Pretty Good Privacy (PGP) to help protect electronic mail; since then it has spread all over the world. On the day that Boris Yeltsin went to war against his own parliament, Zimmermann received an e-mail message from Latvia: "Phil I wish you to know: Let it never be, but if dictatorship takes over Russia your PGP is widespread from Baltic to Far East now and will help democratic people if necessary. Thanks." But despite the worldwide availability of PGP and other encryption tools, this technology is still controlled by national-security interests. The U.S. Customs Service is currently investigating how PGP was exported.

Testifying last year before the House Subcommittee for Economic Policy, Trade, and the Environment, Zimmermann worried that "some elements of the Government" were intent on denying citizens their privacy. "This is unsettling because in a democracy, it is possible for bad people to occasionally get elected—sometimes very bad people," said Zimmermann. "Normally, a well-functioning democracy has ways to remove these people from power. But the wrong technology infrastructure could allow such a future government to watch every move anyone makes to oppose it. It could very well be the last government we ever elect." ❖

Questions for Meaning

1. What is the relationship between privacy and democracy? How has the information superhighway made privacy more difficult to preserve?
2. Who has a stake in defining cyberspace? How might their goals differ?
3. Why have so many people been able to gain relatively easy access to the Internet?
4. Who is at risk in the electronic future? Who might be denied access to advanced communications networks?
5. Will all information become available electronically, or is some information unlikely to go online?
6. Vocabulary: convergence (8), demographic (15), defamation (21), insidious (24), vociferous (28), cryptographers (38), encryption (41), rendering (60).

Questions about Strategy

1. Consider the picture of the information superhighway with which Ness opens his essay—a picture that he then challenges. Does it fairly state a commonly held view?

2. What kind of political values does Ness invoke in this argument? What do these values reveal about the audience for whom he originally wrote?
3. How does Ness expect readers to respond to the question at the end of paragraph 19? What are the implications of this answer?
4. Ness ends his argument by suggesting that American democracy is at risk. Within the context of this essay, does this claim seem plausible?

NANCY WILLARD

PORNOGRAPHY ON THE INTERNET

Can the problem of pornography on the Internet be resolved through technology, or is it part of a larger social problem that must be addressed in our own homes and communities? Nancy Willard, author of *The Cyberethics Reader* (1996), published the following editorial on an Internet home page in 1995, attaching the following note: "I just completed this article and submitted it to our local newspaper as a guest editorial—don't know whether they will run it. As will be evident, it is addressed to those who might not have an in-depth understanding of Internet technology and the issues around pornography. I hope that it provides some helpful ideas for your thinking and discussions with people in your community." Address: nwillard@ordata.com

The issue of pornography on the Internet has received much attention lately. Unfortunately, some of the media coverage has been misleading, the technical issues are confusing, accurate information is sparse, and the issue is being sensationalized by some politicians.

2   On one hand, the extent of the problem has been greatly overexaggerated. Within the scope of all of the incredible resources that are available through the Internet, pornography is a tiny portion and quite easy to avoid. The Internet provides access to a vast amount of information and communication that is highly beneficial to our society. The Internet is not a place to be feared or avoided.

On the other hand, pornography on the Internet is clearly a problem that we must find a way to resolve. A disturbingly high amount of this pornography is not erotica, but sexual violence—images and text that glorify the sadistic sexual torture of women and the exploitation of children. It is depraved, warped, vile. While there are legitimate concerns about the extent to which government ought to dictate what people can read and see, there are limits to acceptability and much of this stuff crosses the limits. Just because some depraved individuals have the ability through new technologies to more freely share their depravity, does not mean that we, in the name of free speech, have the obligation to provide them with a conduit to our homes and communities.

4   Imposing government control through new laws will be extremely difficult. Internet technology is called open systems technology and it is just that, open and virtually impossible to control. A popular saying on the Internet is "the Internet interprets censorship as damage and routes around it." The Internet is also global, so whatever laws that might be passed in the U.S. will not have any effect beyond our borders.

       Some technical background may be helpful to your understanding. There are two basic ways that you can access pornography on the Internet. Some pornography is stored on remote computers that are located somewhere on the Internet, anywhere in the world. To get to this material you either use telnet, which allows you to login to the remote computer or you use FTP or World Wide Web to send commands to the remote computer telling it to send selected material to you.

6   The other way that pornography is transmitted is through USENET newsgroups. Newsgroups are global discussion groups that cover a wide range of topics. The newsgroup data is transmitted throughout the world. The data is downloaded by your Internet provider and is stored on their computer in a revolving manner—new data comes in, the old data moves off. The pornography is found in a hierarchy of newsgroups called "alt.sex"— alt.sex.bestiality, alt.sex.pedophilia, etc. The pornography is in the form of both text and images.

       While the number of alt.sex newsgroups is small, the amount of computer data traffic they account for is high. It is estimated that 20–22% of the USENET newsgroup data feed—the data being downloaded into the local computer—is pornography. A significant portion of the alt.sex images are "teasers" that are posted as advertisements for commercial BBSs that sell pornography images. Studies on the use of the Internet have consistently shown that several of the alt.sex newsgroups are among the most popular newsgroups.

8   An Internet provider has the ability to select which newsgroups they will download. My local Internet provider does not download the alt.sex newsgroups because of the drain it would place on his resources and because his clientele are businesspeople. Schools that provide Internet access also do not download the pornographic newsgroups. Schools also block access to any known remote pornography sites and monitor students when they are accessing the Internet.

       Congressional action is pending that addresses this issue. The Senate is acting in a reactionary fashion and has proposed legislation that is considered by many people to be unconstitutional and unworkable in the Internet environment—but it makes for good public posturing. The House appears to be backing legislation that instructs the Department of Justice to do more research and propose some legal and enforceable solutions. Hopefully, the House legislation will prevail. What is not needed at this time is legislation that is ill-considered and quite likely to be rejected by the courts. The issues are complex and we need to take some time to fully understand them.

10   New software is coming on the market that can assist in blocking access. The software prevents access to the alt.sex newsgroups and to any of the known remote sites that host pornography. Obviously, since new sites are always being found or being established, the list of blocked sites must be kept updated.

But there are many unanswered questions. A partial list includes: Who is going to be responsible for making decisions about what is or is not pornography? How do we decide what should be allowed but only for adult access (erotica) and what is totally beyond the bounds of acceptability (sexual violence)? Should discussion groups related to gay and lesbian issues or safe sex be inaccessible to minors? Should all of these decisions be made in the home with no role for government or does government have some responsibility with respect the regulation of materials that are truly unacceptable or the safety of minors? Should you impose liability on a system administrator who may not have actual knowledge that pornography has been placed on their system? The current legal test for pornography includes reference to "community standards." Whose community—where the material is located or where the recipient lives? Should our universities—tax-supported institutions—be downloading pornography on systems that are established to support education and research objectives? How do we limit the transmission of truly objectionable material, while preserving open expression?

12   Most of the recent attention has been focused on the issue of preventing access by minors. But clearly the problem is much more than this. Sexual violence is the fastest growing violent crime in the U.S. Family violence and child abuse are destroying the lives of many innocent people. Being able to restrict your 14-year-old daughter's access to pornography will not address the kinds of attitudes or physical abuse she may be exposed to in the "real world."

As a society we must recognize and address the fact that there are a significant number of people, primarily men, who believe that the sexual abuse and exploitation of women and children is acceptable behavior.

14   What is becoming ever more clear throughout this debate is that laws and technical fixes will only provide partial answers. What is lacking is the most significant potential restraint, namely moral and ethical values enforced by individual and organizational conscience and social rebuke. What is required is that we, as a society, and as individuals in society, internalize a set of values that embody a higher level of respect for others. This issue will not be resolved without each of us taking responsibility for our actions and calling upon other individuals and organizations within our realm of influence to also demonstrate responsible behavior.

So where can you start?

16   With yourself. Look closely inside, what are your values? Do you treat other people with respect? Do you stand up for what you know is right and

challenge what you know is wrong? Do you rely on what other people think or tell you to think or do you have an internal value system that guides your actions? Are your actions consistent with your words?

If you are a man, what is your opinion of women? Do you treat the women, your wife, your partner, your co-workers, with respect? Do you engage in sex primarily for mutual enjoyment or primarily for your own physical satisfaction? Have you ever forced or pressured a woman to engage in sex when she was not interested? What are your thoughts about young women?

18 If you are a woman, do you respect yourself enough to be assertive about your rights and needs? Or do you give in to keep the peace?

With your family. Do you talk about values with your children and are your actions in accordance with your words? Do you demonstrate to them on a daily basis your respect for others, your respect for them, and your respect for yourself? Do you expect them to obey you because you are the "boss" (external control) or do you assist them in learning how to make appropriate decisions for themselves (internal control)? Do you avoid so-called entertainment that is violent or prurient in nature and do you discuss with your children why such material is not acceptable? Do you allow your children to demonstrate lack of respect or violence towards others?

20 In your community. Are you respectful of all people regardless of their gender, color, race, religion, physical status, or sexual preference? Do you speak up when you are concerned about the actions of individuals or organizations in your community? Do you contribute time and money to those organizations that are seeking to make your community a better place for all to live in? Do you work to ensure that the children in your community have the opportunity to grow up in a happy and healthy environment? Do you support your schools and ensure that they have sufficient resources to accomplish their very vital tasks?

In cyberspace. Have you selected an Internet or online services provider that is acting responsibly and is exerting reasonable editorial control? Has the provider provided you with information and services to assist you in protecting your children from danger or from access to inappropriate material? Does the provider respond promptly to any concerns you may have? Does the provider use its resources to provide access to material that is unacceptable (i.e., is your money going to support access to the alt.sex newsgroups)? Have you taken the time to discuss with your children the dangers they may face in cyberspace and how to protect themselves and how you expect they will conduct themselves online? Have you taken the time to have your children show you the sites on the Internet that excite them and introduce you to their online friends? Do you, yourself, avoid materials that promote sexual or other forms of violence? Do you behave responsibly, respectfully, and demonstrate good netiquette, while you are online? ❖

Questions for Meaning

1. Why does Willard believe that fears about the availability of pornography on the Internet are exaggerated?
2. How does Willard distinguish between "pornography" and "erotica"? Why might it be useful to make this distinction?
3. Why is government censorship unlikely to eliminate pornography from the Internet?
4. How does Willard want readers to respond to the availability of pornography on the Internet? What does she recommend we do?
5. Vocabulary: conduit (3), pedophilia (6), reactionary (9), downloading (11), prurient (19).

Questions about Strategy

1. How does Willard establish her reason for writing? Why is it useful for her to make this reason clear?
2. In paragraph 11, Willard raises a series of questions that she does not answer. What does she achieve by raising these questions?
3. According to Willard (in paragraph 13), "we must recognize and address the fact that there are a significant number of people, primarily men, who believe that the sexual abuse and exploitation of women and children is acceptable behavior." What does Willard gain by calling attention to gender? Would her statement be more persuasive, or less, if she eliminated the reference to men?
4. How useful is the advice with which Willard concludes her argument? Does her essay persuade you to follow this advice?

Robert F. Goldman

THE EFFECT OF APPLYING CURRENT ANTI-OBSCENITY LAWS TO ONLINE COMMUNICATIONS

As more and more information emanates from personal computer screens to other terminals worldwide, attorneys are confronted with the legal implications of information transfer. One of the issues that needs to be resolved is the extent to which current obscenity laws—which were framed to apply to print and film distribution—are applicable to cases in which individuals download pornography within the privacy of their own homes. To the ongoing discussion among attorneys, Robert F. Goldman contributed the following argument, which was first published in a 1995 issue of the *Georgia Law Review*. As a courtesy to readers, Goldman divided his argument into several separate sections. Given the length of this material, try reading one section at a time—but be alert to how each section is related to the others.

> [A]lthough . . . media have acquired the functions of the press, they have not yet obtained the rights of the press. The rate of technological change has outstripped the ability of the law, lurching from one precedent to another, to address new realities. Novel communications are pressed into service while still in their infancy, and the legal system's initial encounters with these newborns have a lasting influence. As one astute observer has explained, "[t]echnical laymen, such as judges, perceive the new technology in that early, clumsy form, which then becomes their image of its nature, possibilities, and use. This perception is an incubus on later understanding."[1]

Just how relevant is modern law to electronic networks? The Internet is perhaps the best known electronic network. It is the "granddaddy" of computer networks; it is the "network of networks."[2] What are judges and legislators hearing about the Internet in the Press? Smut, anarchy, stalking, pirating, terrorist groups, defamation, cybersex . . . . One is led to think the Internet is laying the foundation for the Apocalypse.

2   What is any right-minded jurist to think other than the worst? A not-so-insignificant portion of the Internet's users say their electronic

---

[1] Laurence Tribe, American Constitutional Law § 12-25, at 1007 (2d ed. 1988) (citation omitted).
[2] *See infra* notes 11–51 and accompanying text (explaining technical aspects of Internet).

community is the last frontier; anarchy does and should continue to reign supreme.[3] It may be hard to believe, but the frontier-types and anarchists may have a point; from a legal perspective, believing that the same rights that apply to other forms of communication should apply to online communication misses the mark. Not only are all other forms of media not treated equally, but different aspects of the Internet mimic different media. For example, should electronic words speeding across "cyberspace" into "mailboxes" be treated as mail or as phone calls? Should bulletin boards where users leave messages for the general public be treated the same as electronic mail? Are the differences between the aspects of the Internet significant enough to demand individualized treatment, or should they all be treated consistently?

I. A Plausible Scenario

Imagine a scenario in which a young woman named Diane is a nude performance artist in New York City. She packs audiences in a squalid Times Square lounge where she performs under the stage name of "Lotus Flower" and is practically famous for her on-stage contortions. Because her show caters to those who are familiar with what Americans may refer to as "Far Eastern culture," the audience typically consists of South Asian émigrés and businessmen; they are the ones who appreciate the art in her performance. In fact, before going on stage, Diane will practice yoga to limber herself and to clear her head of emotional trauma that living in New York causes.

4   Diane's husband, Jack, is a professor of South Asian studies at Pacific Northwest College in Seattle, Washington. They met backstage after one of her performances and found they had much in common. His doctorate thesis was on the impact of the Kama Sutra on Indian culture, and Diane had performed nearly all of the positions described in the writings. They soon married. However, because there are very few South Asian studies programs in the country and even fewer openings, Jack took the first position he could find, which was in Seattle. He had to leave suddenly, and he temporarily left his new bride behind while he saved enough money to support them. Additionally, there is no real market for Diane's work in Seattle, and she is reluctant to leave her work behind.

---

[3] *See, e.g.,* John Markoff, *The Rise and Swift Fall of Cyber Literacy,* N. Y. TIMES, Mar. 13, 1994, at A4 (noting Berkeley history professor's statement that Internet is similar to anarchy of French Revolution); James Srodes, *Business Class in Cyberspace?,* FIN. WORLD, Oct. 25, 1994, at 16 (noting that Internet is like anarchy in "Mad Max" movie, "not some happy town square"); Susan Watts, *Internet vs. the Invaders; Users Fight On-Line Publicists,* THE INDEPENDENT, Oct. 23, 1994, at 4 (depicting users as thinking "of the Net as an anarchic web of computer networks linked haphazardly, with nobody in control, no fixed rules, and nobody making money from it").

In order to save money, Diane and Jack correspond by e-mail,[4] using the Internet[5] as their medium. After discovering that he could send photographs over the Internet, Jack scanned a copy of his smiling face onto his computer, addressing it to Diane's e-mail box. Diane decided to "one-up" him: She scanned a photograph of herself while in one of her famed positions and sent it to Jack's e-mail box. In some, if not most, circles, such a photograph would be considered obscene. However, Jack is a professional and sees beauty in Diane's pose.

6   Jack realized that many of his colleagues around the country would appreciate his wife's artistry. After gaining her permission to do so, he posted the image at the electronic bulletin board for those interested in South Asian issues, which is called "SEASIA-L."[6] His posting began with the following message: "The following image is not for the 'faint of heart.' If you do not appreciate the artistic beauty of the naked human body, DO NOT DOWNLOAD THIS IMAGE }:(."[7] Any interested user of the bulletin board could download the image to the user's own computer by copying the binary picture contained in the file.

Jack saw nothing wrong with his actions and took steps to protect those who might be offended. The image is representative of a millennium of Indo-Asian culture; it is not strictly erotic to him or to the readers of his bulletin board. Although Jack could not be sure who would use the bulletin board, he knew children never use SEASIA-L because it is, after all, for South Asian studies professorial communications. The chances a child would accidentally stumble across his wife's picture are practically nil. In any event, someone looking for sexy photos would invariably search in the "alt.binary.pictures.erotica" area of the Internet[8] and not SEASIA-L. Additionally, because he followed Internet protocol by giving potential viewers ample warning of the nature of the image, Jack felt totally innocent.

8   Likewise, the operator of the bulletin board where Jack posted the image probably felt innocent of any wrongdoing. First of all, the operator

---

[4] E-mail is shorthand for "electronic mail" and is described as being like regular mail, only faster. It is also like a phone call, only without the "telephone tag" or the expense. ADAM GAFFIN, EFF's Guide to the Internet (formerly the Big Dummy's Guide to the Internet) 22 (1994), *AVAILABLE IN* FTP.EFF.ORG (Electronic Frontier Foundation's FTP site on Internet) [hereinafter BIG DUMMY'S GUIDE]; *see infra* notes 54–58 (analyzing legal implications of e-mail).

[5] "Internet" is a term that will be used loosely throughout the remainder of this Note. While in the context of this document the term refers to almost all communications that are transmitted using an electronic network, a more accurate description would be that the "Internet" is only one of many networks. However, it is the largest, is government-funded, and is the most widely used. By analogy, reference to the Internet in the Note is akin to calling the winners of the Superbowl "World Champions" when in fact there are many football leagues around the world that do not compete with the National Football League.

[6] *See infra* notes 63–67 and accompanying text (discussing electronic bulletin boards in greater detail, including description of "SEASIA-L").

[7] Internet users are fond of using syntax marks, such as the semicolon and parens, to create facial expressions. Turning the page clockwise 90°, the reader can see the stern face Jack created at the end of his warning. Another example is a smiley face: ":)".

[8] HARLEY HAHN & RICK STOUT, INTERNET YELLOW PAGES 282 (1994) [hereinafter INTERNET YELLOW PAGES].

does not check other people's postings because he does not want to act as a censor. He also thinks the rightful purpose of the Internet is the free exchange of ideas. Moreover, not only is he unwilling to take on the role of censor, but he lacks the manpower to do so. Screening every posting on his bulletin board would take a large amount of time, and running the bulletin board is just a hobby for him.

Despite feelings of innocence—or pride in having contributed to a civic forum—Jack and the bulletin board operator should begin looking for ways to mitigate their criminal sentences. Jack could go to jail for his acts and could bring the administrator of the bulletin board down with him. In the modern world of Internet anarchy, such fears of liability by bulletin board operators have led to various forms of censorship, raising serious constitutional questions about when such censorship goes too far.

10   This Note focuses on the problems depicted in this scenario. These problems center primarily on the application of current obscenity law to communications on the Internet and other electronic networks. Part II of this Note presents a detailed description of the history of the Internet and explains how one puts a photograph into cyberspace and where an image is located when it is on the Internet. This explanation is necessary to understand the circumstances surrounding online pornography and indecency.[9]

The remainder of this Note involves the application of obscenity law to online communications. Part III covers the history of obscenity law and its treatment of a variety of media. Part IV analyzes the potential application of obscenity laws to the Internet and discusses likely outcomes of the continuation of current policies. This Note then recommends possible solutions to the enigma presented in applying obscenity laws to the Internet and finds that enlightened legislation is needed that will treat the Internet as what it is: A new and unique communications medium that does not fit within the current statutory framework proscribing the distribution of obscene material.

II. "The Granddaddy of Computer Networks"[10]

A. Internet's Exponential Growth: Building a Mountain Out of a Molehill

12   1. Internet's Historical Background. It may come as no surprise that the Internet's start-up, which took place during the 1960s—a period in which technological innovation was a national security imperative[11]—was sponsored by the United States military.[12] Commentators suggest that the ability

---

[9] Since regulation of child pornography stems from different public policy considerations and is governed by a different statutory framework, it is beyond the scope of this Note.

[10] DANIEL C. LYNCH & MARSHALL T. ROSE, INTERNET SYSTEM HANDBOOK 4 (1993) [hereinafter INTERNET HANDBOOK].

[11] See ROBERT A. DIVINE, THE SPUTNIK CHALLENGE (1993) (tracing political history of United States during post-Sputnik era).

[12] BIG DUMMY'S GUIDE, supra note 4, at 17.

to survive an atomic war was a critical criterion of the Internet.[13] With military sponsorship, the network became a functional source for the transmission of data by 1968.[14] The Internet's etymology traces its roots to the very idea of a "network" of computers.[15]

Computing power did not come cheaply in the 1960s. Therefore, linking together a variety of computers from around the country, each with its own specialty,[16] would be an efficient use of time and resources.[17]

14   The Advanced Research Projects Agency (ARPA), an agency of the Department of Defense, through the work of elite scientists from the RAND Corporation, MIT, and other scientific laboratories, developed a system called "ARPAnet."[18] The major problem with computer design in the 1960s was that engineers produced computers without considering the possibility that they might someday be networked; therefore, transferring programs from one mainframe to another required extensive program modifications.[19] ARPAnet employed new technology[20] to allow its users on one networked computer to utilize a program on any other networked computer without first jumping through hoops to make the programs compatible.[21] In 1968, the scientists participating in ARPAnet linked geographically dispersed, dissimilar computers using telephone lines.[22] By October 1971, experimenters were logging onto each others' sites, a feat worthy of "a place in the interoperability history books."[23]

Within a decade after these first experiments, networks around the world were communicating with one another using the same rules, or protocols, developed in 1968.[24] However, it was not until the mid 1980s—when the National Science Foundation (NSF) took control of ARPAnet—that use of the network expanded beyond the laboratories of the government agencies and a few elite universities.[25] NSF envisioned a network of "backbone" supercomputer centers that would interconnect with autonomous networks serving different communities of researchers, government agencies, and

---

[13] INTERNET HANDBOOK, *supra* note 10, at 9; BIG DUMMY'S GUIDE, *supra* note 4, at 18.

[14] INTERNET HANDBOOK, *supra* note 10, at 9.

[15] *See infra* note 21 and accompanying text (discussing etymological roots of "network").

[16] An example would be linking one computer that could retrieve data to another that was proficient at sorting data.

[17] INTERNET HANDBOOK, *supra* note 10, at 6.

[18] *Id.* at 5; BIG DUMMY'S GUIDE, *supra* note 4, at 18.

[19] INTERNET HANDBOOK, *supra* note 10, at 4.

[20] BIG DUMMY'S GUIDE, *supra* note 4, at 18.

[21] The first study of the possibility of "networking" resulted in a report released in 1965, entitled *A Cooperative Network of Time-Sharing Computers, reprinted in* INTERNET HANDBOOK, *supra* note 10, at 5. Interestingly, under the word "network," the Oxford English Dictionary cites the first known use of "network" in computer terminology as occurring in 1972. The ARPA report predates the Oxford English Dictionary by seven years. 10 OXFORD ENGLISH DICTIONARY 346 (2d ed. 1989).

[22] INTERNET HANDBOOK, *supra* note 10, at 6.

[23] *Id.* at 10.

[24] *Id.;* BIG DUMMY'S GUIDE, *supra* note 4, at 18.

[25] INTERNET HANDBOOK, *supra* note 10, at 12.

university campus networks.[26] By the 1980s, some systems on the NSFnet, the "network of networks,"[27] had gone public, and anyone with a computer and a modem could communicate world-wide, just as researchers had done for nearly two decades.[28]

16   The NSFnet, now called Internet, has enjoyed an exponential growth rate.[29] The Internet's *monthly* growth rate of new "host" computers—those that operate as storage sites for traffic on the Internet—is estimated at ten to fifteen percent while the traffic rate of growth on the major routes of the Internet exceeds twenty-five percent each month.[30] It is possible to project the staggering future growth potential of the Internet by considering the following numbers: With somewhere between 5 and 10 million users in 1992, "the number of computers connected to the Internet has been doubling every 8 to 15 months."[31] The exponential growth of the Internet may make quantification of users impossible: "[T]he Internet . . . is growing so rapidly that estimates of 'the size of the Internet' are obsolete long before they can be published."[32] Projections for early next century reasonably predict one billion online computers.[33]

      2. Where You Go When You're in Cyberspace. Throughout the Internet's exponential growth, its protocols[34] have remained constant.[35] The three most commonly used Internet protocols are (1) telnet, the remote login to another, or dispersed, computer;[36] (2) file transfer protocol, or FTP, the transfer of actual computer files among networked computers;[37] and (3) electronic mail, or e-mail.[38] This discussion concentrates on the latter two aspects of the Internet foundation, as they are the ones most likely to be central to legal issues involving obscenity.

---

[26] *Id.*

[27] BIG DUMMY'S GUIDE, *supra* note 1077, at 18.

[28] *Id.*

[29] *Id.*

[30] INTERNET HANDBOOK, *supra* note 10, at 13.

[31] Herb Brody, *Of Bytes and Rights; Freedom of Expression and Electronic Communications,* 95 TECH. REV. 22, 27 (1992).

[32] INTERNET HANDBOOK, *supra* note 10, at 708.

[33] *Id.*

[34] "Protocol" is defined as "[t]he rules and technical standards to be observed to perform a transaction between two computers." DON MACLEOD, THE INTERNET GUIDE FOR THE LEGAL RESEARCHER 294 (1995).

[35] *See supra* notes 11–33 and accompanying text (discussing origins of Internet).

[36] *See* MARK VELJKOV & GEORGE HARTNELL, POCKET GUIDES TO THE INTERNET, VOL. 1: TELNETTING (1994). Telnet is a program available for many Internet users. It connects them to databases, library catalogs, and other sources of information around the globe, from up-to-the-minute information on the Shuttle astronauts to ski conditions. BIG DUMMY'S GUIDE, *supra* note 4, at 78.

[37] *See generally,* MARK VEJKOV & GEORGE HARTNELL, POCKET GUIDES TO THE INTERNET, VOL. 2: TRANSFERRING FILES WITH FILE TRANSFER PROTOCOL (FTP) 20 (1994) (explaining FTP) [hereinafter POCKET FTP].

[38] "[E-mail] wasn't even in the original plan—it was an afterthought! Around 1971, two programmers . . . decided to send each other messages, not just data. Before that, the true purpose of the network was strictly resource sharing—passing data files back and forth . . . ." INTERNET HANDBOOK, *supra* note 10, at 9.

18   *a. File Transfer Protocol.* An FTP user is basically a visitor in some- one else's hard drive.[39] The owner of the FTP site has stored files on his or her computer's hard drive. By connecting the computer to the Internet by modem, the owner of the site has opened up the hard drive to users of the Internet.[40]

     Operators of FTP sites give each file a name that identifies for users the type of information contained within each file.[41] Certain signals indi- cate whether the file is a graphic, text, or a user's guide to that FTP. Graph- ics, while increasingly popular, take up much more space on a hard drive and require special software, so they are limited to FTP sites with above av- erage memory capacity.[42]

20   For example, a user familiar with the "protocol" of cyberspeak may, while browsing through one of one of NASA's numerous FTP sites, en- counter the file named *ftp.nau.edu.shuttlelaunch.gif.*[43] That user could im- mediately discern that the file contained a graphic image of a shuttle launch and that the image was in the "GIF" style of graphics format. By simply typ- ing "GET" and the filename, the user could download the image.[44]

     The greatest problem with FTP is the difficulty users have locating the files that they want.[45] Previously, Internet users had to learn the cumbersome DOS-oriented language of a database system called "Archie."[46] However, for

---

[39] *See* Big Dummy's Guide, *supra* note 4, at 85. There are rules of etiquette for visiting another's hard drive. For example, it is bad form to connect to most FTP sites during business hours because transferring files takes up a great deal of computing power, detracting from that computer's main function. *Id.*

[40] *Id.* at 85–92.

[41] *Id.*

[42] The cost of software for operating an FTP site runs from fifty dollars into the thousands, but set- ting up an FTP site is hardware-intensive. Erik Delfino, *The Basics on Setting up an Electronic Bul- letin Board System,* Online, Mar. 1993, at 90. In addition, IRCs (Internet relay chats) create "chat rooms," where people can type something on their computer and have it instantly sent around the globe to whoever happens to be in that chat room at the moment. Big Dummy's Guide, *supra* note 4, at 123–26. Commercial ventures, such as America Online, Compuserv, and Prodigy, market these chat rooms as allowing users to visit simulated bars, join political debates, or even enjoy "cybersex" with other users, while onlookers watch. Matthew Childs, *Lust Online; Computer User Groups for Sex,* Playboy, Apr. 1994, at 94. In chat rooms, about half of the users claim to be female, but they generally are almost entirely an all-male audience. *Id.* Gender verification can occur through off- line phone calls in which a disinterested third party will call the alleged impostor to determine his or her gender. *Id.*

     The Internet can also be used for more noble purposes. For example, when Russian lawmakers barricaded themselves inside the Russian Parliament building in 1993, Russians and Americans set up an IRC that gave news accounts of what was happening. Big Dummy's Guide, *supra* note 4, at 129. Such capabilities may make the Internet a valuable source to those who live under a regime that suppresses other avenues of information.

[43] Internet Yellow Pages, *supra* note 8, at 312.

[44] Pocket FTP, *supra* note 37, at 35.

[45] Finding the bulletin board you are looking for can be difficult if you do not already have an ad- dress. Indexing the sites on the Internet has become a priority. Ed Krol, author of The Hitchhiker's Guide to the Internet, discussed the Internet's beginnings: "What we had was a library where all the books were dumped in the floor and there was no card catalog." Joshua Quittner, *Getting up to Speed on the Computer Highway: Overcoming Real Problems in a Virtual World,* Newsday, Nov. 3, 1992, at 51.

[46] Big Dummy's Guide, *supra* note 4, at 85–87.

those who either are not interested or are not capable of learning the intricacies of DOS-style commands, new software, known as the World Wide Web, has integrated use of the mouse in a "point-and-click" windows environment with search services that previously would have required greater computer knowledge.[47] This easier access to searching techniques for the mass of computer novices may expand the Internet's prominence in the coming decades.[48]

22   *b. Electronic Mail.*[49] The primary difference between e-mail and FTP is that an e-mail message, while being more interactive, is less intrusive upon someone else's hard drive. E-mail is *sent;* in FTP, the user *goes and gets.*

An important part of e-mail is the form of the message. Commentators have suggested that e-mail is changing the way we communicate with one another. The lack of things like voice inflection in cyberspace makes humor or sarcasm difficult to convey. The standard format for an e-mail message includes a "FROM" line, a "TO" line, and a message field for the user to fill in.[50] The rest of the message is controlled by the communications software. Therefore, stylistic machinations are practically non-existent. Moreover, the quickness with which the message can be sent gives it an oral quality.[51] While the "ephemeral" quality of e-mail messages may seem tangential to the legal implications of online obscenity, it is important to recognize that e-mail is similar to many common forms of communication—phone calls, letters, and face-to-face conversations—but it is also very distinct. An e-mail message does not fit accurately into any existing category of communication.

---

[47] *Id.* at 108–112.

[48] PLAYBOY magazine appears to have recognized the future of communications, as it has a site accessible through the World Wide Web that displays both clothed and nude images of each month's centerfold. These images are available to anyone with access to the World Wide Web, regardless of the user's age.

[49] "E-mail is like a phone call, only written. It's like a paperless letter, but faster. It's like a casual conversation, or a postcard, or a scribbled note to a classmate in the middle of class. It's all of the above, and . . . none of them." Jacques Leslie, *Mail Bonding: E-mail Is Creating a New Oral Culture,* WIRED, Mar. 1994, at 42.

[50] The user can overcome the generic format through the use of tabs, quotes, and other individualizing techniques within the message field.

[51] An interesting legal question that this Note does not address is whether a defamatory e-mail communication is slander (oral) or libel (written). *See* W. PAGE KEETON ET AL., PROSSER AND KEETON ON THE LAW OF TORTS § 112, at 786 (5th ed. 1984) (noting difference between libel and slander is uncertain).

The oral quality of an e-mail message is summed up best in the following passage:

> E-mail is written, yet its language typically embodies a shift toward oral speech patterns. It is the most ephemeral of written mediums, lacking the material form of books and letters and capable of being erased in a keystroke, yet it can be archived and retrieved with unprecedented ease.

Leslie, *supra* note 49.

B. Erotica at Your Finger-Tips

24   The modern computer owner with a modem (or access to a university computer network), some patience, and an active libido can easily access erotic language and images on the Internet[52] using e-mail, FTP, or Usenet.[53] Commercial enterprises and even non-commercial, amateur bulletin boards may contain differing levels of "smut opportunity" for an Internet "surfer's" erotic stimulation. This subsection reviews the methods of interaction between the Internet user and the data stored on networks. Where and how a user garners that data can have a great impact on the legal consequences to the user and to the operator of the system providing the user with access.

    1. E-mail. Jack and Diane, the protagonists of this Note, communicated with one another using e-mail. Because e-mail entries often sound like they belong in a diary[54] (generally because of the quickness with which they are entered), these private [55] messages are likely to be more interesting

---

[52] The process by which users will have Internet access is becoming increasingly simple. More companies are offering access, and as they do, users need to know less about technical commands because they can access the Internet through their computer's windows application. Laurie Flynn, *Browsers Make Navigating the World Wide Web a Snap,* N.Y. TIMES, Jan. 29, 1995, § 3, at 8 (reporting on Microsoft's entry into Internet access market). The number of users on the Internet is also sure to continue growing due to new technology providing World Wide Web access. *Id.; see infra* note 68 and accompanying text (discussing World Wide Web).

[53] Usenet is the Internet equivalent of a global bulletin board. While often confused with the Internet, the Usenet is really a separate system. BIG DUMMY'S GUIDE, *supra* note 4, at 37. The Usenet's popularity stems from the ease in which its index allows users to find discussion groups fitting their interests. The top ten discussion groups for April, 1994 were:

	newsgroup	estimated number of readers
1.	news.announce.newusers	800,000
2.	alt.sex.stories*	500,000
3.	alt.binaries.pictures.erotica*	450,000
4.	alt.sex*	440,000
5.	news.answers	420,000
6.	rec.humor.funny	380,000
7.	rec.arts.erotica*	370,000
8.	misc.jobs.offered	370,000
9.	clari.news.briefs	360,000
10.	misc.forsale	360,000

Wired Top 10, WIRED, Aug. 1994, at 36 (citing as source post on news.list newsgroup by Brian Reid, Digital Equipment Corp.).

*Note that greater than one-half of the total volume of Usenet's top ten groups are erotica-based.

[54] Leslie, *supra* note 49.

[55] Messages are not as private as one might hope. *See* Jaleen Nelson, Comment, *Sledge Hammers and Scalpels: The FBI Digital Wiretap Bill and Its Effect on Free Flow of Information and Privacy,* 41 UCLA L. REV. 1139 (1994). Nelson's Comment discusses a bill that would allow the FBI to require manufacturers of digital communication equipment to install what is referred to as a "Trap Door," a means for the FBI to eavesdrop on encrypted communications, some of which use an encryption code so sophisticated (called a "Clipper Chip") that the communication is indecipherable to all but those who have the keys. *Id.; see also* Digital Telephone Bill: Hearings on H.R. 4922, S. 2375 Before Joint Session of Subcomm. on Civil and Const. Rights of the House Comm. on the Judiciary, and the Subcomm. on Law and Tech. of the Senate Comm. of the Judiciary, 101st Cong., 2d Sess. (1994) (testimony of Jerry Berman, Policy Director, Electronic Frontier Foundation) (commending

to sociologists and psychologists than to lawyers and lawmakers, at least in the context of obscenity/pornography. This occurs because messages contained within e-mail generally are not meant for "distribution," as the term is identified for prosecution purposes.[56] Instead, the very intimacy of the messages is often the issue. Some of the most recent cases involving the expressions made in the course of an e-mail message involve stalking[57] and assault[58] crimes.

26   *2. Usenet/Bulletin Board Systems.* There are close to 5,000 newsgroups on the Usenet, each offering an area of special interest where like-minded users can read and respond to messages ranging from highly technical computer-related topics to art and sex.[59] Some Usenets are devoted exclusively to erotica;[60] some are devoted to the discussion of sex in a therapeutic sense;[61] and some may not be devoted to sex at all but still can contain large amounts of pornography.[62]

One would think that the 5,000 Usenet newsgroups would satisfy the demand of hobbyists and researchers looking for individuals with similar interests. However, there are also a large number of what are called "Bulletin Board Systems," or BBSs, that are accessible through telnet.[63] These systems frequently are not available through the Internet.[64]

28   For example, the hypothetical situation described at the beginning of this Note portrayed a posting of a potentially pornographic image onto a bulletin board using telnet. When Jack posted the picture of his wife in the South Asia bulletin board, he actually was creating a file that contained an arguably obscene image on someone's hard drive without the consent or knowledge of the system operator.[65]

Congress for reworking and narrowing scope of bill, thereby affording greater protection to electronic communications users' right to privacy).

[56] *See infra* note 185 and accompanying text (noting that distribution requirement of many federal anti-pornography statutes may require more formal means of carriage than e-mail messages provide).

[57] Marianne Lavelle, *U.S. Sees Computer Crime as Threat*, NAT'L L.J., July 25, 1994, at A21 (describing Massachusetts man who first met children he allegedly raped by exchanging computer messages with them).

[58] Megan Garvey, *Crossing the Line on the Info Highway; Jake Baker Fantasized on the Internet. Then He Ran Smack Into Reality*, WASH. POST, Mar. 11, 1995, at H1 (concerning college student charged with violation of federal statutes proscribing transmission of threatening letters across state lines).

[59] *See supra* notes 45–48 and accompanying text (discussing methods of finding sites on Internet); *see also* TONY ABBOTT, ED., INTERNET WORLD'S ON INTERNET 94 (1994); ERIC BRAUN, THE INTERNET DIRECTORY (1994) (compiling Internet bulletin boards and user groups).

[60] For example, "alt.sex.bestiality" is a user group devoted to discussing sex involving animals. INTERNET YELLOW PAGES, *supra* note 8, at 282.

[61] For example, "SSSSTALK" is a discussion group centered on the field of sexuality. Access is limited to clinicians, researchers, educators, and students in that field. ABBOTT, *supra* note 59.

[62] *See* Adam S. Bauman, *Computer at Nuclear Lab Used for Access to Porn*, L.A. TIMES, July 12, 1994, at A1 (reporting on discovery of hard-core pornography at Lawrence Livermore National Laboratory).

[63] BIG DUMMY'S GUIDE, *supra* note 4, at 79–81; *see also supra* note 36 (explaining telnet).

[64] BIG DUMMY'S GUIDE, *supra* note 4, at 79–81.

[65] While the introductory situation was purely hypothetical, the SEASIA-L bulletin board Jack used is real. It is physically located in an office in the journalism department of Michigan State University in Lansing, Michigan. It is sponsored by the Center for Asian Studies of Michigan State and is

Some commercial networks take the bulletin board to the next level. Users gain access by using their modem, dialing the host computer directly, and paying a fee by typing their credit card number. Then, they can retrieve and download even more erotic images and text than can be found on the Internet. The commercial operators in these situations scan images and input text onto the host computer, storing the images and text for users. However, the operators of these boards do not have complete control over what users can access. Some users will not only read what is on these commercial BBSs and copy files from it, but they also will leave files containing text, images, or programs[66] that they think would interest other users. The files placed on the bulletin board could come from Internet users in any one of the 107 or so countries with Internet access.[67] After all, the idea of the Internet generally—and a BBS specifically—is the free and open exchange of data and ideas between interested users.

30   *3. FTP and World Wide Web.* FTP sites offer a similar opportunity for gathering smut from online but have a different twist. In the FTP and World Wide Web setting, the user is visiting the hard drive in such a way that posting a message like Jack did in the opening scenario would not be possible.[68] Those users with slightly advanced software on their own computers can easily view text and images simultaneously; they can listen to music and can even view video images. As a result, an FTP site may represent the purest form of distribution of arguably obscene images because the pictures, text, video, and sound conveniently convey a message that impacts the user on all sensory levels.[69]

III. Brief History of Obscenity

The Internet has changed the way people communicate ideas. From the technology that has developed over the past few decades has emerged not only a new medium for expression but also a new way of expressing oneself. By combining pictures and stream-of-consciousness text, users of the Internet have a tool to better express visceral reactions. Obscenity is a visceral communication that greatly benefits from this new medium.

32   Starting with the historical treatment of obscene materials, this section seeks to examine ways in which the law has typically treated obscenity. Landmark judicial decisions regarding obscenity shed light on how the

open to all interested parties. It is not, however, to be confused with the South Asian women's net, which is available only to women and only by request. Abbott, *supra* note 59.
[66] *See* Pamela Samuelson & Robert Glushko. *Intellectual Property Rights for Digital Library and Hypertext Publishing Systems,* 6 Harv. J. Law and Tech. 237 (1993) (discussing copyright issues that have arisen on electronic information systems).
[67] *See supra* notes 29–33 and accompanying text (discussing raw numbers of Internet users).
[68] *See supra* notes 39–48 and accompanying text (discussing technology of FTP and World Wide Web).
[69] *See infra* notes 175–192 and accompanying text (detailing framework of federal statutes regulating obscenity).

Internet may be treated in the future, particularly in regard to for-profit distribution of pornographic materials.

A. Historical Definition of Obscenity

There is a tradition-rich history of court's treatment of obscenity.[70] The guiding principle when applying obscenity laws to online communications is that the First Amendment guarantee of free speech does not extend to obscene material. While the constitution dictates that "Congress shall make no law . . . abridging the freedom of speech . . .",[71] Congress does make laws and regulations, in some instances, that limit the rights of speakers.[72] To discover what is obscene, one must address the Supreme Court's interpretation of the boundaries of protected speech under the First Amendment, including what factual settings may lead to a finding that certain speech is unprotected.

B. The Miller Test

34   In the landmark case for modern obscenity laws, *Miller v. California*,[73] the defendant was convicted under California law for mailing unsolicited brochures that advertised various publications the defendant offered for sale. The brochures contained photographic depictions of young men and women engaging in sex acts. The images included prominent displays of genitalia.[74]

---

[70] More detailed analyses of obscenity law's history are widely available. *See* LAURENCE H. TRIBE, AMERICAN CONSTITUTIONAL LAW § 12-16 (2d ed. 1988) (offering one of best histories of obscenity). The Supreme Court delineated a less than comprehensive history of American obscenity law in Miller v. California, 413 U.S. 15 (1973) and Erznoznik v. City of Jacksonville, 422 U.S. 205 (1975). Law review articles that detail the history of certain areas of obscenity law abound. *See, e.g.,* Diane L. Hofbauer, *"Cableporn" and the First Amendment: Perspectives on Content Regulation of Cable Television,* 35 FED. COMM. L.J. 139 (1983) (addressing early cable-access pornography); Linda N. Woito & Patrick McNulty, *The Privacy Disclosure Tort and the First Amendment: Should the Community Decide Newsworthiness?,* 64 IOWA L. REV. 185, 221–31 (1979) (comparing obscenity with newsworthiness to establish that privacy should depend on community mores); P. Heath Brockwell, Comment, *Grappling with* Miller v. California: *The Search for an Alternative Approach to Regulating Obscenity,* 24 CUMB. L. REV. 131 (1994) (urging conduct-based approach); John V. Edwards, Note, *Obscenity in the Age of Direct Broadcast Satellite: A Final Burial for* Stanley v. Georgia, *a National Obscenity Standard, and Other Miscellany,* 33 WM. & MARY L. REV. 949 (1992) (noting new technology of direct satellite broadcasts requires a fresh look at obscenity regulation); Philip H. Miller, Note, *New Technology, Old Problem: Determining the First Amendment Status of Electronic Information Services,* 61 FORDHAM L. REV. 1147 (1993) (surveying general First Amendment considerations for electronic information superhighway); Elise M. Whitaker, Note, *Pornography Liability for Physical Harms Caused by Obscenity and Child Pornography: A Tort Analysis,* 27 GA. L. REV. 849, 858–59 (1993) (stating that "pornography liability will encourage media distributors to take adequate precaution to prevent the dissemination of obscenity and child pornography").

[71] U.S. CONST. amend. I, § 1.

[72] *See infra* notes 174–193 and accompanying text (discussing federal law that prohibits obscene phone calls, interstate mail, and ostensibly, electronic transmission); *see also* Roth v. United States, 354 U.S. 476, 487 (1957) (holding obscene material is that "which deals with sex in a manner appealing to prurient interest").

[73] 413 U.S. 15 (1973).

[74] *Id.* at 18.

The jury in *Miller* convicted the defendant of the misdemeanor crime of knowingly distributing obscene material. The California statute he violated essentially codified a test developed by the Supreme Court[75] in *Roth v. United States,* which asked "whether to the average person, applying contemporary community standards, the dominant theme of the material taken as a whole appeals to prurient interest."[76]

36   Therefore, in *Miller,* the Court really was reviewing the definition of obscenity it had established in *Roth.* This definition had caused so many dissenting opinions that there was no true consensus about what constituted obscenity.[77] While the *Roth* decision focused on finding some prurient appeal,[78] the *Miller* Court further reduced the breadth of First Amendment protection.

In short, the Court announced that the method for determining whether material is obscene was to be a modified three-step process, based primarily on the *Roth* test. First, the fact-finder should determine "whether 'the average person, applying contemporary community standards' would find the work, taken as a whole, appeals to the prurient interest."[79] Second, the fact-finder must establish "whether the work depicts or describes, in a patently offensive way, sexual conduct specifically defined by the applicable state law."[80] Third, the fact-finder must find "whether the work, taken as a whole, lacks serious literary, artistic, political, or scientific value."[81] The Court, therefore, narrowed the scope of First Amendment protection by allowing the prohibition of works that contained some value; so long as the work, "taken as a whole," lacked serious value, it would be unprotected.[82]

---

[75] *See* A Book Named "John Cleland's Memoirs of a Woman of Pleasure" v. Attorney General of Massachusetts, 383 U.S. 413 (1966) (applying test of *Roth* as delineated/described/applied? in subsequent cases) [hereinafter *Memoirs v. Massachusetts*].

[76] *Roth,* 354 U.S. at 489.

[77] *See* Stone et al., Constitutional Law 1209 (2d ed. 1991) (noting breakdown of consensus among Supreme Court Justices between 1957 and 1973); *see also Miller,* 413 U.S. at 41. In his dissent in *Miller,* Justice Douglas quoted from Justice Harlan's concurrence in Interstate Circuit, Inc. v. Dallas, 390 U.S. 676, 707 (1967), in which Harlan stated that "[t]he upshot of all this divergence in viewpoint is that anyone who undertakes to examine the Court's decisions since *Roth* which have held particular material obscene or not obscene would find himself in utter bewilderment." *Id.*

[78] *Roth,* 354 U.S. at 484–85; *see also* Tribe, *supra* note 70, § 12-16, at 908 (analyzing *Miller* test).

[79] *Miller,* 413 U.S. at 24 (quoting Kois v. Wisconsin, 408 U.S. 229, 230 (1972); *Roth,* 354 U.S. at 489). The first step in the *Miller* analysis basically adopts the *Roth* test.

[80] *Id.*

[81] *Id.* This final step appears to be an attempt at consensus building, as Chief Justice Burger admitted that the Court's previous attempt at developing a "social value" aspect of obscenity in *Memoirs v. Massachusetts* proved unworkable. *Id.* at 24–25. In *Memoirs,* only three Justices approved the use of "utterly without redeeming social value" as the third prong of the test. A Book Named "John Cleland's Memoirs of a Woman of Pleasure" v. Attorney General of Massachusetts, 383 U.S. 413 (1966). A variety of concurrences and dissents added to the confusion that the Court ultimately alleviated with the *Miller* test. *See supra* note 77 and accompanying text (quoting Justice Harlan on Court's lack of consensus on obscenity).

[82] Tribe, *supra* note 70, § 12-16, at 909.

38   The crux of the *Miller* test as it may be applied to the Internet is the "contemporary community standards" portion of the test.[83] In *Miller,* the Court established the meaning of this element by explaining what it does *not* mean: "[C]ontemporary community standards" are "not 'national standards.'"[84] The Court was unwavering in its depiction of national standards as contrary to its intent in *Miller:* "It is neither realistic nor constitutionally sound to read the First Amendment as requiring that the people of Maine or Mississippi accept public depiction of conduct found tolerable in Las Vegas, or New York City."[85] With that pronouncement, the Court firmly established the mechanism by which courts evaluate obscenity and, by extension, obscenity on the Internet.[86]

C. Miller and Regulatory Schemes

While rejecting the notion that it was proposing a regulatory scheme for the states,[87] the Supreme Court was explicit in describing what state statutes prohibiting obscene material can proscribe: "Patently offensive representations or descriptions of ultimate sexual acts, . . . masturbation, excretory functions, and lewd exhibition of the genitals."[88] Essentially, the Court carved out "hard-core" pornography from the body of protected First Amendment speech.[89] Since *Miller,* the Court has struck down state statutes that are "overly broad" despite their narrow judicial construction[90] as well as statutes that are "content based."[91]

40   The Supreme Court also has demonstrated a willingness to examine for-profit distribution of pornography with heightened scrutiny. This treatment effectively singles out the "prurient interest" portion of the *Miller* test as an element deserving careful attention.

---

[83] *See, e g,* Judge Joseph T. Clark, *The "Community Standard" in the Trial of Obscenity Cases—A Mandate for Empirical Evidence in Search of the Truth,* 20 OHIO N.U.L. REV. 13 (1993) (concluding that litigants in obscenity trial should produce expert testimony to determine appropriate contemporary community standards); Edwards, *supra* note 70 (recommending that Supreme Court adopt alternative to current community standards rule to deal with new communications technology).

[84] *Miller,* 413 U.S. at 37.

[85] *Id.* at 32. One attorney-activist, in reaction to the Federal District Court for the Western District of Tennessee's imposition of the contemporary community standards test to material found on the Internet, stated: "This . . . case has one community attempting to dictate standards for the whole country." *Computer Operators Convicted on Federal Obscenity Charges,* THE LEGAL INTELLIGENCER, at 8 (1994).

[86] *See infra* notes 161–173 and accompanying text (discussing recent obscenity trial employing community standards test in context of Internet).

[87] *Miller,* 413 U.S. at 25.

[88] *Id.*

[89] *Id.* at 26.

[90] New York v. Ferber, 458 U.S. 747, 768 (1982) (noting overbreadth doctrine is predicated on sensitive nature of protected speech; fear of prosecution may lead to refraining from expression of protected speech); *see also,* Broadrick v. Oklahoma, 413 U.S. 601 (1973) (landmark case on overbreadth doctrine).

[91] *See, e.g.,* Erznoznik v. City of Jacksonville, 422 U.S. 205 (1975) (holding that regulating movies displaying nudity at drive-in theater for safety considerations and not other movies which could cause same risk to passing traffic is impermissible content-based regulation).

In *Ginzburg v. United States*,[92] the Court held that lower courts should consider commercial exploitation when deciding whether material is obscene. In *Ginzburg*, the defendant mass-mailed three types of publications that contained sexually explicit material. The Court found "abundant evidence" proving that the publications were part of a "pandering" trade;[93] as stated in Justice Warren's concurrence in *Roth*, they were part of a "business of purveying textual or graphic matter openly advertised to appeal to the erotic interest of their customers."[94] Thus, obscenity laws may be tougher on those who are panderers even though in other contexts the material they distribute would not be obscene.[95]

D. Applying Obscenity Definition

42 The *Miller* obscenity test is not readily applicable to criminal obscenity charges resulting from distribution of pornography on the Internet. Defendants seemingly will have to guess how the court they face will apply the *Miller* obscenity definition to electronic networks. Because rules are often made by analogy, the court may determine which media best corresponds to the Internet and follow previous decisions in that area.

In applying obscenity laws to various media, courts have shown a tendency to treat each one uniquely, depending, in no small part, on the medium's potential for intrusiveness. Media to which courts apply obscenity laws include television,[96] radio,[97] cable television,[98] telephones,[99] books,[100]

---

[92] 383 U.S. 463 (1966).

[93] *Id.* at 467.

[94] *Id.* (citing Roth v. United States, 354 U.S. 476, 495–96 (1957)).

[95] *Id.* at 476.

[96] *E.g.,* Monroe Communications Corp. v. FCC, 900 F.2d 351 (D.C. Cir. 1990) (holding that FCC should consider station's broadcasting of obscene material as evidence when deciding whether to grant renewal license or should give better explanation of why FCC did not consider obscenity broadcasts in that determination proceeding). The FCC is empowered by statute to revoke a television station's license for a violation of federal obscenity laws. 47 U.S.C. § 312(a)(6) (1988); *see also* 18 U.S.C. § 1464 (1988) (criminalizing obscene radio broadcasts); *infra* notes 175–192 and accompanying text (discussing federal obscenity statutes).

[97] *E.g.,* FCC v. Pacifica Found., 438 U.S. 726 (1978); *see infra* notes 111–114 and accompanying text (discussing indecency standard and Supreme Court's struggle to find workable standards in radio context).

[98] *See, e.g.,* Cruz v. Ferre, 755 F.2d 1415 (11th Cir. 1985) (holding that Miami ordinance regulating distribution of indecent material through cable television was unconstitutionally overbroad and violated due process requirements); Community Television of Utah, Inc. v. Wilkinson, 611 F. Supp. 1099 (D. Utah 1985) (holding Utah state law giving state authorities power to bring nuisance actions against breaches of indecency statute unconstitutionally overbroad and preempted by Cable Communications Policy Act of 1984), *aff'd sub nom.* Wilkinson v. Jones, 480 U.S. 926 (1987); Home Box Office, Inc. v. Wilkinson, 531 F. Supp. 987 (D. Utah 1983) (finding application of *Pacifica* decision to cable television inappropriate, as cable television does not compare to radio's pervasiveness).

[99] *E.g.,* Carlin Communications, Inc. v. Mountain States Tel. & Tel. Co., 827 F.2d 1291, 1297 (9th Cir. 1987) (holding that regional telephone company, despite status as public utility, may refuse to carry salacious matter on dial-a-message network because censorship exercised could not be categorized as "power traditionally exclusively reserved" to government), *cert. denied,* 485 U.S. 1029 (1988).

[100] *E.g.,* Memoirs v. Massachusetts, 383 U.S. 413 (1966) (holding that court must consider entirety of book to establish whether it meets obscenity test threshold).

newspapers,[101] magazines,[102] movies,[103] bookstores,[104] sound recordings,[105] amplified speech,[106] and even wearing a jacket in a courthouse.[107]

44   When these media present obscene material according to the *Miller* test, the First Amendment does not protect the speech; therefore, they are subject to regulation by state or federal laws.[108] The courts, however, do not apply obscenity laws to each medium equally. Courts have allowed the government to regulate the broadcast media much more heavily then the print media, possibly because of the print media's historical significance.[109] Courts also have generally advocated that the willingness and age of the audience is more relevant to determining the constitutionality of obscenity

---

[101] *E.g.*, Papish v. Board of Curators of the Univ. of Mo., 410 U.S. 667 (1973) (per curiam) (holding that expulsion of student for distributing on-campus newspaper containing indecent speech was violation of First Amendment since "conventions of decency" test used by University in expulsion proceeding was "no justification for denial of constitutional rights"); Kois v. Wisconsin, 408 U.S. 229 (1972) (per curiam) (holding that newspaper photograph of nude male and female embracing, accompanying text entitled "Sex Poem," was not obscene); United States v. Head, 317 F. Supp. 1138 (E.D. La. 1970) (ruling that all of newspaper's contents must be considered to determine whether newspaper is obscene).

[102] *E.g.*, Penthouse Int'l., Ltd. v. McAuliffe, 610 F.2d 1353 (5th Cir.) (granting relief to publishers of magazines whose distributors in Fulton County, Georgia were being arrested for violating Georgia anti-pornography laws, on grounds that police were making warrantless arrests and did not have authority to determine whether magazines were obscene and holding that entire magazine must be considered when determining whether magazine possesses serious value), *cert. dismissed*, 447 U.S. 931 (1980).

[103] *E.g.*, Young v. American Mini Theaters, Inc., 427 U.S. 50 (1976) (holding that city may create restrictive zoning ordinances limiting number of adult theaters in certain neighborhoods); Erznoznik v. City of Jacksonville, 422 U.S. 205 (1975) (finding Jacksonville, Florida ordinance, making it public nuisance for drive-in theaters to exhibit films containing nudity, unconstitutional because it discriminated among movies solely on basis of content that would otherwise be protected speech); Paris Adult Theater I v. Slaton, 413 U.S. 49 (1973) (ruling that films exhibiting "hard-core" pornography are not entitled to First Amendment protection and are subject to state limitations).

[104] *E.g.*, American Booksellers v. Webb, 919 F.2d 1493 (11th Cir. 1990) (holding Georgia statute, banning distribution or display of sexually explicit materials "harmful to minors," constitutional when narrowly construed and that exemption granted to libraries was not in violation of Equal Protection Clause), *cert. denied*, 500 U.S. 942 (1991).

[105] *E.g.*, Soundgarden v. Eikenberry, 871 P.2d 1050 (Wash.) (holding state statute that required labeling of all erotic sound recordings was unenforceable because it placed prior restraint on adults' protected speech and was overbroad), *cert. denied sub nom.* Soundgarden v. Gregoire, 115 S. Ct. 663 (1994).

[106] *E.g.*, Reeves v. McConn, 631 F.2d 377, 387 (5th Cir. 1980) (holding Houston, Texas ordinance prohibiting amplification of "obscene slanderous" words was not constitutionally vague or overbroad based on its failure to limit excluded speech to erotic or hard-core sounds).

[107] *E.g.*, Cohen v. California, 403 U.S. 15, 26 (1971) (holding that slogan "Fuck the Draft," worn on back of jacket, was protected speech because it was attempt at communicating through "emotive function" of speech).

[108] TRIBE, *supra* note 70, § 12-25, at 1002–1010.

[109] *Id.; see infra* notes 132–135 and accompanying text (addressing traditional importance of print journalism in comparison to computer communications). Comparing the result in FCC v. Pacifica Found., 438 U.S. 726 (1978), with that in Smith v. California, 361 U.S. 147 (1959), demonstrates the disparate treatment afforded the two sectors: While the FCC has broad discretionary power to regulate indecency in radio broadcasts, booksellers are not even required to check the content of the books they offer to the public to determine whether they are obscene.

laws than other characteristics.[110] Because different media approach and reach different audiences, determining the constitutionality of applying obscenity laws to the various media has not been uniform.

The Supreme Court's decision in *FCC v. Pacifica Foundation*[111] provides a good example of the line-drawing courts must perform in distinguishing among the intrusiveness of different media. In this decision, the Court distinguished between "indecent" material and "obscene" material.[112] A sharply divided Court held that a radio station that played George Carlin's "Filthy Words" comedic monologue at two o'clock in the afternoon had violated a federal law prohibiting the broadcast of indecent language. The Court considered the "pervasiveness" of the radio medium and the time of day during which the station aired the Carlin monologue to be key aspects of the determination that the speech in question was indecent.[113]

46   Had this monologue been aired under different circumstances—for example, on pay-per-view television or on the radio at a later hour—the Court may have reached a very different conclusion. The decision was not based on the perception that Carlin's "bathroom humor" should be censored but on the belief that his material was inappropriate for *that* medium at *that* particular time.[114]

Another Supreme Court decision established a limit on the government's power to proscribe admittedly obscene material. In *Stanley v. Georgia*,[115] police officers entered Stanley's house with a search warrant based on his alleged book-making activities. While in his bedroom, they discovered movies that a jury subsequently found to be obscene. The Court held that the private possession of these obscene materials was not a punishable offense. More specifically,

---

[110] In the Supreme Court's decision in *Miller,* for example, an important aspect of the State's interest was the "prohibiti[on of] dissemination or exhibition of obscene material when the mode of dissemination carries with it a significant danger of offending the sensibilities of unwilling recipients or of exposure to juveniles." Miller v. California, 413 U.S. 15,.18–19 (1973) (citations omitted).

[111] 438 U.S. 726 (1978).

[112] *Id.* at 748–50. The Court ultimately concluded that the material was indecent but, nonetheless, fell under the regulatory authority of the Federal Communications Commission. *Id.*

[113] *Id.*

[114] Professor Tribe, in commenting on communication that obscenity laws can regulate, notes:

> There is little likelihood that this area [obscenity laws in general] has reached a state of rest—or that it will ever do so until the Court recognizes that obscene speech *is* speech nonetheless, although it is subject—as is all speech—to regulation in the interests of unwilling viewers, captive audiences, young children, and beleaguered neighborhoods—but *not* in the interest of a uniform vision of how human sexuality should be regarded and portrayed.

TRIBE, *supra* note 70, § 12-16, at 909–10 (emphasis in original). Thus, of the potential rationales for obscenity laws that Tribe identifies, he considers only the first to have merit; to regulate based on excluding unsolicited obscenity from the eyes and ears of an unwilling public is rational. However, laws that paternalistically treat otherwise consenting adults the same way as they treat children often lead to conflicting judicial opinions and laws that do not provide flexibility for the varying media.

[115] 394 U.S. 557 (1969).

[w]hatever may be the justifications for other statutes regulating obscenity, we do not think they reach into the privacy of one's own home. If the First Amendment means anything, it means that a State has no business telling a man, sitting alone in his own house, what books he may read or what films he may watch.[116]

Mere possession of obscene material is, therefore, outside the reach of anti-obscenity laws; such laws can regulate only the distribution of obscene material.

48   In sum, obscenity laws are not some unwavering maxim; *Pacifica* demonstrates that what is obscene on the radio is not necessarily obscene on dial-a-porn telephone calls. Courts and legislatures consider the pervasiveness of the medium, its accessibility to minors, whether the material is actually being distributed, and whether its distribution is for profit. These nuances must be retained when applying obscenity laws to the Internet.

E. Censorship's Legal Background

The final question in the Supreme Court's rulings regarding obscenity is *who* decides whether material is obscene. The Supreme Court is definitive on this issue. In *Freeman v. Maryland*,[117] the Court held that the proper forum for the determination of obscenity is a courtroom. More specifically, the Supreme Court held that certain procedural safeguards were needed to ensure that censorship boards acted expeditiously and under the close scrutiny of the judiciary.[118] In *Freedman*, the State convicted a theater operator for exhibiting a motion picture without submitting it to the state board of censors for prior approval.

50   The Court's (and commentators') concerns over censorship stem from a fear that an administrative censor will be less sensitive to the constitutional values of freedom of expression than the judiciary.[119] The problem with administrative censorship is not that it gives authority to an administrator to make decisions regarding whether the speech at issue deserves First Amendment protection. Instead, the Court is concerned that such authority, either when accompanied by the power to make a final determination without an opportunity for a timely judicial appeal[120] or when leaving "unbridled discretion in the hands of a government official or agency,"[121] makes the enjoyment of the freedom of expression guaranteed by the First Amendment dependent on the "uncontrolled will of a [public] official."[122] The Supreme Court, therefore, has remained firm in requiring procedural

---

[116] *Id.* at 565.

[117] 380 U.S. 51 (1965).

[118] *Id.* at 58–60.

[119] TRIBE, *supra* note 70, § 12-38, at 1055–57.

[120] *Id.; see also* Vance v. Universal Amusement Co., 445 U.S. 308 (1980) (holding statute that restrained speech for indefinite duration unconstitutional).

[121] Lakewood v. Plain Dealer Publishing Co., 486 U.S. 750, 757 (1988).

[122] Paris Adult Bookstore II v. City of Dallas, 493 U.S. 215, 226 (1990) (citations omitted).

safeguards when a state administrative official has censorship authority. The settled rule in this area is that "[w]hile prior restraints are not unconstitutional per se . . . any system of prior restraint . . . comes to this Court bearing a heavy presumption against its constitutional validity."[123]

The tension between obscenity and censorship comes into sharp focus on the Internet. The Internet, as a communications medium, provides an as yet unrivalled forum for distributing obscene material. The question then turns to how to stop the flow of this material. Past Supreme Court decisions demonstrate an intolerance for government censorship, and stopping online obscenity with prior restraint of its distribution may conflict with clear Supreme Court precedent.

IV. Online Obscenity Liability Issues

52   As the hypothetical involving Jack and Diane demonstrated, those who post obscenity are not the only individuals facing liability for the posting of the images. The operators of bulletin boards where images such as the ones Jack put in his favorite user group appear also to be liable under the obscenity framework established by Supreme Court cases such as *Miller*. Faced with potential liability for such postings, operators, in order to avoid liability, are edging closer to the legal realm of censorship.[124]

First, this Section deals with the liability of electronic bulletin board operators. It addresses both who can be liable for the posting of hard-core images on a bulletin board and what will actually trigger that liability. This Section then discusses the very real problem of online censorship and offers some suggestions for preventing censorship from becoming a structural part of the Internet.

A. Who can be Liable?

54   *1. Reason for Liability Concerns.* Liability for obscenity is a reasonable fear of system operators, or sysops.[125] One issue that causes concern for sysops is their degree of liability for the obscene material someone else puts on the sysops' bulletin boards. Physically, the obscene material is in a file on a hard drive in a sysop's possession, but the sysop may not know the material is there.[126] While the sysop could not be prosecuted on the basis of possession alone,[127] he might be subject to prosecution for its distribution.

---

[123] Southeastern Promotions, Ltd. v. Conrad, 420 U.S. 546, 558 (1975) (citations omitted).

[124] *See supra* notes 117–123 and accompanying text (discussing legal background of censorship).

[125] In Fort Wayne Books, Inc. v. Indians, 489 U.S. 46 (1989), the Supreme Court held that operators of adult book stores could be prosecuted under a state RICO statute for substantive obscenity violations. This decision certainly would apply to system operators if convicted of similar obscenity crimes.

[126] Encryption codes are available that would make reading the file almost completely impossible without a decoding key. James Fallows, *Open Secrets; Clipper Chip and Electronic Security*, The Atlantic, June 1994, at 46 (reporting on encryption codes).

[127] The system operator who possesses, but does not distribute, obscene materials cannot be prosecuted. Stanley v. Georgia, 394 U.S. 557 (1969); *see supra* notes 115–116 and accompanying text

Under the Supreme Court's decision in *Smith v. California*,[128] however, the sysop may be protected from liability for being an unknowing conduit for distribution of obscenity. In *Smith,* the Court struck down a Los Angeles ordinance making it unlawful for a bookseller to possess obscene or indecent writing, regardless of the seller's knowledge of the obscene nature of the work.[129] The Court reasoned that by eliminating the scienter requirement, the ordinance severely limited the public's access to constitutionally protected material.[130] The Court stated that because of the ordinance, a bookseller might "tend to restrict the books he sells to those he has inspected . . . . The bookseller's self-censorship, compelled by the State, would be a censorship affecting the whole public, hardly less virulent for being privately administered."[131] Therefore, *Smith* stands for the proposition that distributors of large amounts of written material should not be held liable for random amounts of obscenity contained therein. In the Supreme Court's view, demanding that merchants, such as booksellers, conduct such an obscenity search would cause overbroad censorship.

56   Courts may not be willing to draw the analogy between booksellers and operators of electronic bulletin boards for several reasons. First, technology that would allow sysops to screen out obscene transmissions to their bulletin board is available and is currently being applied to some types of electronic networks.[132] Second, electronic data does not have the storied tradition that books have: Books have been burned and banned throughout history in attempts to thwart dissemination of ideas counter to those in power[133] and also have been central to the American system of democracy.[134] Streams of computer data simply do not have the same history of being subjected to suppression, and therefore, sysops may not be afforded the protection that booksellers receive.[135]

(discussing *Stanley*). In *Stanley*, the Supreme Court held the right to possess obscene material in one's own home is constitutionally protected. *Id.* Thus, a sysop with obscene materials on the system he maintained seemingly would be on safe ground as long as the materials were not accessible by outsiders who logged onto the system.

[128] 361 U.S. 147 (1959).

[129] *Id.* at 154–55.

[130] *Id.* at 150–54.

[131] *Id.* at 153–54.

[132] *See infra* note 194 and accompanying text (discussing screening role of commercial Internet access-providers).

[133] *See* MARK DROGAN, BIBLIOCLASM 81–103 (1989) (tracing history of book burnings).

[134] *E.g.,* THE FEDERALIST PAPERS (Clinton Rossiter ed., 1961).

[135] Professor Tribe notes that the Supreme Court has been willing to make a similar distinction between the printed press and the broadcast media:

> [B]roadcast regulation has proceeded on the premise that, since government must somehow carve up the electromagnetic spectrum so as to prevent interference among broadcast frequencies, those who are permitted to use the public airwaves may be selected on criteria, and subject to controls, that would be unacceptable in the case of the print media.

TRIBE, *supra* note 70, § 12-25, at 1004. *See also supra* note 42 (referring to use of Internet in Russian Parliament barricade and other quasi-revolutions).

In addition to the protection that *Smith* may provide them, sysops have good reason *not* to know[136] what is in the files on their bulletin boards: The Electronic Communications Privacy Act of 1986 (ECPA)[137] provides that a system operator[138] is not entitled to divulge data contained in an "electronic communication service"[139] to any outside source. Bulletin board operators could argue that the Act reflects the federal government's policy of not inquiring into what has been posted on their bulletin boards. Because the sysop has a legal obligation not to *divulge* what is on his or her bulletin board, it would be logical to assume that the best way to fulfill that obligation is not to inquire into what users have been posting. Obviously, such a "don't ask, don't tell" policy by sysops may not be the best approach because it indicates that the sysop has taken an apathetic approach to possibly obscene postings—an approach courts seem to disfavor.[140]

58   *2. Application of Current Liability Schemes to Access-Providers.* Many sysops will want to take an active approach to resolving the liability issue instead of hoping that, by ignoring it, the problem will disappear. Cases concerning operators of information-carrying "utilities" may foretell how courts will treat sysops who actively try to screen out obscene material but are unsuccessful.[141] In a related area, a recent New York state court decision[142] found that Prodigy could be sued for libel as if it were a newspaper or broadcaster because it exercised editorial control over one of its electronic bulletin boards.[143] Prodigy's "hands-on" approach to regulating the

---

[136] Federal laws proscribing the distribution of obscene materials contain a "knowing" requirement. *See infra* notes 175–192 and accompanying text (detailing federal anti-pornography laws).

[137] 18 U.S.C. §§ 2701–2711 (1988).

[138] An operator of an electronic bulletin board is within the statutory definition of "remote computing service." 18 U.S.C. § 2702(a)(2) (1988); *see* Steve Jackson Games, Inc. v. United States Secret Serv., 816 F. Supp. 432 (W.D. Tex. 1993) (finding Secret Service's seizure of computer bulletin board contained within seized computer's hard drive, despite its having obtained search warrant, was violation of Act).

[139] 18 U.S.C. § 2701(a)(1) (1988).

[140] *See, e.g.,* Playboy v. Frena, 839 F. Supp. 1552 (M.D. Fla. 1993) (holding a context of trademark infringement that sysop was partially liable even though he did not know trademark-bearing material had been posted by user).

[141] Sysops can try to avoid liability for exposing minors to indecent material by following the guidelines promulgated by the FCC in regards to dial-a-porn operators. 47 C.F.R. § 64.201 (1994). These rules require that dial-a-porn operators: (1) notify the phone company of the kind of service they are providing; (2) require payment by credit card; (3) give users an access code they must repeat before the transmission of an indecent message after the operator has "reasonably" verified through a written application that the user is not a minor; and (4) have a procedure to quickly cancel access numbers when they have been used by minors or otherwise tainted (or scramble the message). *Id.*

Encoding the message may be the most reliable technique for an operator of an "indecent" BBS. Keys to decoding the files could be distributed only to users who have properly established their age. However, dial-a-porn regulations lose their effectiveness when images are distributed in an encoded format because it would be impossible for a sysop to look at images to decide whether they are pornographic. *See supra* note 55 (discussing FBI wiretap bill).

[142] Stratton Oakmont, Inc., v. Prodigy Servs. Co., No. 31063/94, 1995 N.Y. Misc. LEXIS 229 (N.Y. Sup. Ct. May 26, 1995).

[143] *Id.* at *3.

content of its users' communications opened the company up to liability even though it did not have knowledge of the communication at issue.[144]

This is a question courts will continue to have to address to determine under what standard network operators will be treated.[145] The nature of this issue changes somewhat when the access-provider is a public institution.[146] Furthermore, while actual pandering may be missing for both types of access-providers, their for-profit motives may distinctly handicap private providers.[147]

60   One plausible judicial response is to treat access-providers as analogous to common carriers:[148] "[T]he definitions of the term 'common carrier' are legion, and invariably include the concept of one holding himself out to the public as engaged in the business of carrying persons or things for hire."[149] Thus, universities and other non-profit access-providers do not succinctly fall within the definition of "common carrier" because they are not "for hire."[150] However, commercial enterprises that offer their services for money, such as Compuserv and Prodigy, may fall under the broad definition courts and legislatures have given common carriers.[151]

An element of determining whether a field of communication is a common carrier is the presence of free competition.[152] With the current limited access to the Internet, a court might determine that these services—and any other access-provider who is for hire—are common carriers. Therefore, Internet access-providers might be held to higher standards of conduct, possibly including routine screening of all files transmitted through their systems.

[144] Matthew Goldstein, *On-Line Service Held in Libel Suit; Editorial Control Cited in State Ruling*, N.Y. L. J., May 26, 1995, at 1.

[145] Randolph S. Sergent, Note, *Sex, Candor, and Computers: Obscenity and Indecency on the Electronic Frontier*, 10 J.L. & POL. 703 (1994) (recommending that information services not be held responsible for all material posted on their service).

[146] *See infra* notes 199–211 and accompanying text (describing one University's reaction to threat of liability for providing minors access to Internet discussion groups possibly containing obscenity).

[147] *See supra* notes 92–95 and accompanying text (discussing landmark pandering case of *Ginzburg*).

[148] Telephone companies are treated as common carriers at the federal level, while television broadcasters are not. FCC v. Sanders Bros. Radio Station, 309 U.S. 470, 474 (1940). A Georgia court, however, has held that telephone companies are not to be treated as common carriers. Southern Bell Tel. & Tel. Co. v. Sharara, 307 S.E.2d 129 (Ga. Ct. App. 1983). The court held that without statutory authority, telephone companies are not required to exercise the extraordinary diligence required of common carriers, just ordinary care in the context of selection and retention of employees.

[149] 15A C.J.S. *Common* 18 (1967).

[150] 86 C.J.S. *Telegraphs, Telephones, Radio and Television* § 7 (1954) states that telephone companies "are not, strictly speaking, common carriers." Because they are often treated as one by statute, it can be assumed that more often than not they should be treated with the same kind of liability expectations as common carriers.

[151] *E.g.*, CAL. CIV. CODE § 2168 (West 1995) ("Everyone who offers to the public to carry persons, property, or messages, excepting only telegraphic messages, is a common carrier of whatever he thus offers to carry."); O.C.G.A. § 46-1-1(1) (Supp. 1992) ("'Carrier' means a person who undertakes the transporting of goods or passengers for compensation."). The fact that Internet access-providers are providing communications access and not goods or passengers may not remove them from the realm of common carriers.

[152] *See* United States v. RCA, 358 U.S. 334 (1959) (ruling free competition and lack of regulatory scheme make courts' intervention in broadcasting industry less destructive).

62   *3. Concluding Notes on "Who Is Liable."* At the present time, deciding who will be liable under current schemes of liability takes guesswork about which schemes courts will use and where access-providers will fall within those schemes. However, in a nutshell, it appears that sysops can avoid liability in the following ways:

    • If a sysop knows about the images stored on his or her system, then that sysop will likely avoid liability if he has taken proper precautions to limit the access of files that contain indecent or pornographic materials to adults through the use of access codes, encryption devices, and/or credit card payments;[153]

    • If images stored on the system are files placed there without the administrator's knowledge (*e.g.,* files were uploaded by a user while browsing—or "surfing"—through the bulletin board), then, after *Smith v. California,* the administrator arguably should not be liable;[154]

    • If the file that contains the obscenity is electronic mail addressed to a particular person, the administrator should not have reason to know (in fact, may have reason *not* to know) the content. Again, he should be protected from criminal liability;[155] and

    • Even if the bulletin board is the "nastiest place on Earth"[156] and is a commercial bulletin board providing users with thousands of files of "hard-core" pornography, the operators may not be liable for criminal prosecution if they can prove that they did not "distribute" pornography but merely had it on hand for users to take for their own use.[157]

B. What Triggers Liability?

Having established that the potential for liability in obscenity cases extends beyond the person who posts the transmission, the next issue is what constitutes an obscene posting in the first place. In this context, the *Miller* test, especially its "community standards" prong, will play an important role. Due to the international reach of the Internet, sysops may find that they are held liable under community standards very different from their own.

64   *1. Role of Community Standards in Triggering Liability.* Community standards take on a new importance in online obscenity cases.[158] For example, in the scenario involving Jack and Diane, the relevant community could be any one of several locations: Times Square, New York, where the photo

---

[153] *See supra* note 141 and accompanying text (discussing FCC regulations regarding dial-a-porn telephone communications).

[154] *See supra* notes 128–131 accompanying text (discussing liability of bookstore owners).

[155] *See supra* notes 137–139 and accompanying text (discussing Electronic Communications Privacy Act of 1986).

[156] *See infra* notes 161–173 and accompanying text (providing example of bulletin board claiming to be "nastiest place on Earth").

[157] *See infra* notes 175–193 and accompanying text (discussing federal anti-pornography laws).

[158] *See supra* notes 83–86 and accompanying text (discussing what Supreme Court intended by including "community standards" in *Miller* obscenity test).

was taken and the original audience resided; Seattle, Washington, the community from which Jack sent the image; Lansing, Michigan, the location of the SEASIA-L bulletin board; or any jurisdiction in which someone could download the image onto a computer.[159]

Dropping the "community standards" prong of the *Miller* test seems the obvious solution for a medium such as the Internet, which knows no geographical or jurisdictional boundaries. In fact, a number of commentators recently have argued forcefully for applying alternate standards in obscenity cases involved advanced technology media, including the Internet.[160] Presently, however, courts and legislatures have not experimented with alternative standards for advanced communications. Therefore, defendants must attempt to avoid courtrooms in which a jury's community standards do not equate with their own.

66 *2. Example of Application of Community Standards.* The obscenity case of Robert and Carleen Thomas provides an example of what can happen when federal prosecutors employ the "any jurisdiction" option mentioned above.[161] The Thomases were enterprisers selling access to a bulletin board—called "Amateur Action BBS"—to adults[162] for the purpose of providing the users with pornographic images.[163] They lived in Milpitas, California, and the hard drive containing pornographic images was in their home.[164] There was no question about the nature of the images; when users signed on to the Thomases' BBS, they were greeted with a shocking welcome: "The Nastiest Place on Earth."[165]

A Memphis, Tennessee Postal Inspector who was working undercover logged onto the Thomases' BBS[166] from his computer terminal and downloaded images of obscenity from their hard drive.[167] Later, the Postal Inspector's Office mailed child pornography to the Thomases' house in

---

[159] *See supra* Section I (presenting hypothetical situation in which two characters send arguably pornographic material via Internet).

[160] TRIBE, *supra* note 70, § 12-25, at 1007; *see also* Edwards, *supra* note 70 (urging national standard or some alternative); Sergent, *supra* note 145 (recommending national standards for Internet services).

[161] *See* David Plotnikoff, *Putting Couple on Trial Constitutes Real Obscenity*, PHOENIX GAZETTE, August 29, 1994, at C6 (reporting discussion groups' rage about chilling effect *Thomas* decision may have on Internet traffic).

[162] Those familiar with the case indicate that the Thomases adhered to FCC Rules regarding dial-a-porn by requiring all users to pay for use of their bulletin board with credit cards. Telephone Interview with Keith Henson, computer hacker; member of *Electronic Frontier Foundation* (Oct. 8, 1994).

[163] Elizabeth Weise, *Ruling Sends a Chill Through the Infobahn*, THE SAN FRANCISCO EXAMINER, Aug. 8, 1994, at D1. The author notes, "The fear is that almost every computer network, conferencing system, bulletin board and mailing list in the United States would be vulnerable to such a suit because they might carry material that someone, somewhere, might find offensive." *Id.*

[164] Joshua Quittner, *Computers in the 90's; Life in Cyberspace, the Issue of Porn on Computers*, NEWSDAY, Aug. 16, 1994, at B28.

[165] Telephone Interview with Keith Henson, computer hacker; Member of *Electronic Frontier Foundation* (Oct. 8, 1994).

[166] The Thomases' BBS was not on the Internet. Like many others, it was a BBS operated by self-proclaimed amateur operators to make some money and to play with the electronic gadgets required to run such a BBS.

[167] Quittner, *supra* note 164, at B27.

Milpitas. Minutes after the child pornography was delivered,[168] federal agents entered the Thomases' house and charged them with violating federal anti-obscenity laws. Because images of child pornography were in their possession at the time, the agents also charged the couple with violating federal anti-child pornography laws.[169]

68   Since the postal inspector was sitting in Memphis when he browsed the Thomases' BBS, the trial was held in Memphis. A jury returned a guilty verdict in July 1994 against Robert Thomas for interstate distribution of obscenity.[170] The jury relied on the community standards of Memphis[171] in determining that the computer images in question were pornographic.[172] However, the jury found Thomas innocent of the child pornography charge.[173]

3. How Federal Laws Would Create Liability. Community standards are not the end of the discussion regarding what triggers liability. They are merely one of the judicial elements required to find a violation of a legislatively-created anti-obscenity law. This sub-section delves into the legislative element of a finding of obscenity: the policy behind federal laws regarding obscenity[174] and the specific language of the federal laws. It then addresses how online activities can be conduct proscribed by federal law.

---

[168] Chris Conley, *Pornography Co-Defendant Says Clients Were a Club,* Com. Appeal (Memphis), July 26, 1994, at 1B.

[169] *Id.*

[170] *Id.*

[171] One journalist has noted the degree to which the Memphis court's liberal use of community standards negatively affected the Thomases' defense since, unlike Tennessee, "California law and courts generally have allowed such fare [graphic sexual pictures] in bookstores, adult theaters, and among consenting adults." James Crawley, *Memphis Porn Decisions is Far-Reaching: Ruling Raises Concerns About Rights of Online Computer Users,* San Diego Union-Trib., Aug. 16, 1994, at 9.

[172] United States v. Thomas, No. 94-20019 (W.D. Tenn. July 1994).

[173] While, for the most part, child pornography is beyond the scope of this note, 18 U.S.C.A. § 2252(a) states:

> Any person who . . . (2) knowingly receives, or distributes, any visual depiction that has been mailed, or has been shipped or transported in interstate or foreign commerce, or which contains materials which have been mailed or so shipped or transported, *by any means including by computer,* or knowingly reproduces any visual depiction for distribution in interstate or foreign commerce *by any means including by computer* or through the mails, if—
> (A) the producing of such visual depiction involves the use of a minor engaging in sexually explicit conduct; and
> (B) such visual depiction is of such conduct;
> . . . shall be punished as provided in subsection (b) of this section.

18 U.S.C.A. § 2252(a) (West 1994) (emphasis added). This statute has been updated to include the prohibition of distribution of child pornography by computer, and consequently, it may support the argument that because other statutes have not been similarly adjusted, those statutes do not intend to encompass interstate distribution of hard-core pornography by computer. *See infra* notes 175–193 and accompanying text (referring to question of reach of current federal statutes concerning pornography).

[174] Although state laws also will apply in such a situation, those laws generally mimic the federal laws and would otherwise require extensive and, to a large extent, redundant analysis of the issues at hand. *See, e.g.,* O.C.G.A. § 16-12-80 (1992) (representing state statute that follows pattern of federal laws, including heavy reliance on the *Miller* test).

70   The current federal anti-pornography statute applicable to Internet users and system operators is based on a turn of the century statute which itemized all material considered obscene. Obscene materials consisted of any "filthy book, pamphlet, picture, paper, letter, writing, print, or other publication matter of indecent character."[175] In 1950, the Supreme Court determined that phonographic recordings fell within the scope of the anti-pornography statute.[176] At the urging of the Postmaster General, Congress in 1955 changed the wording of the anti-pornography laws to make them independent of specific media.[177] The Senate Judiciary Committee included the following in its statement on the purpose of the legislation:

> The subcommittee of this Committee on the Judiciary investigating juvenile delinquency in the United States reports that the nationwide traffic in obscene matter is increasing year by year and that a large part of that traffic is being channeled into the hands of children. That subcommittee recommended implementation of the present statute so as to prevent the using of the mails in the trafficking of all obscene matter.[178]

Thus, the language of Section 1461 was changed to its current state: "Every obscene, lewd, lascivious, indecent, filthy or vile article, matter, thing, device, or substance . . . [i]s declared to be nonmailable matter and shall not be conveyed in the mails or delivered from any post office or by any letter carrier."[179] The purpose of this change was, ostensibly, for the protection of our nation's young people—the same public policy driving other federal anti-obscenity (or, more precisely, anti-distribution-of-obscenity) laws.

       As they now stand, federal laws concerning obscenity contain a built-in flaw regarding distribution of obscene images online. That is, while the sections of the code dealing with obscenity were purposefully altered in 1950 to reflect a broad prohibition, they are still very much medium-related. Thus, the prohibition does not clearly apply to a new and different medium such as the Internet. Federal statutes, which are generally medium-based, simply do not, without prosecutorial creativity and a "sideways look" on the part of judges and juries, apply to the Internet.

72   With a little coaxing, Internet postings could fall within a number of federal anti-pornography statutes. For example, Section 1460 prohibits the possession of obscene material with the intent to distribute,[180] and Section 1462 prohibits the distribution or reception of obscene materials in interstate

---

[175] Act of Mar. 4, 1909, ch. 321, § 211, 35 Stat. 1429 (current version at 18 U.S.C. § 1461 (1988)).

[176] United States v. Alpers, 338 U.S. 680 (1950).

[177] S. Rep. No. 113, 84th Cong., 1st Sess. (1955), reprinted in 1955 U.S.C.C.A.N. 2210, 2211. The Congress added the Postmaster General's letter to the legislative history of the bill. The letter stated, in part, "It is obscene matter which the Congress seeks to prohibit whether it be photographs or phonograph records or some other article or thing not yet described." Id.

[178] Id.

[179] 18 U.S.C. § 1461.

[180] 18 U.S.C. § 1460 (1988).

or foreign commerce through a common carrier.[181] Section 1463 recognizes as criminal any obscene material on the wrappers of "otherwise mailable" goods,[182] while Section 1464 makes it a crime to broadcast "obscene, indecent, or profane" language.[183] Sections 1465 and 1466 make it a crime to knowingly transport[184] or otherwise be "engaged in the business of selling or transferring obscene matter,"[185] or "knowingly receive[] or possess[] with intent to distribute any obscene book, magazine, picture, paper, film, videotape, or phonograph or other audio recording, which has been shipped or transported in interstate or foreign commerce."[186] To be "engaged in the business of selling" is to have the objective of earning a profit.[187]

So far it appears that the statutory framework encompasses sysops, but the "knowing" requirement could provide an escape clause for many network operators, because strict reading of that element would not appear to require any active screening for hard-core pornography. Also, the distribution element is an obvious area of ambiguity when the system operator merely provides a medium through which obscene material travels. It is questionable that anything is being "distributed," in the strict sense of the word.

74   These present laws are, quite simply, comprehensive anti-distribution-of-obscenity statutes. One might argue that they are inclusive and that Congress intended to leave out what is not in them.[188] Because the electronic distribution of obscenity is not on the list of prohibited items, it is not prohibited.

Until Congress addresses the issue, Section 1462 may prove the most useful anti-obscenity law for purposes of regulating online obscenity. It provides the broadest framework for prosecuting the distribution of obscenity through electronic means. Section 1462 prohibits distribution of obscene material through the use of a "common carrier."[189] As discussed above, a technical reading of "common carrier" would exclude the phone companies through which online distribution of obscenity occurs, but

---

[181] 18 U.S.C. § 1462 (1988).

[182] 18 U.S.C. § 1463 (1988).

[183] 18 U.S.C. § 1464 (1988).

[184] 18 U.S.C. § 1465 (1988). These sections of federal anti-pornography laws employ an apparently inclusive list of items that are non-transportable. *See infra* note 186 (discussing Congress's return to use of such inclusive lists).

[185] 18 U.S.C. § 1466(a) (1988).

[186] *Id.* This relatively new piece of legislation has returned to the inclusive list of what is obscene matter and away from the less limiting definition of obscenity Congress passed with its 1955 amendment. Congress seems to be experiencing an institutional forgetfulness. Consequently, the specter of *Alpers* may haunt the modern day Congress if, for example, a court finds, in a plain language reading of the statute, that the inclusive list of § 1466 excludes computer files.

[187] 18 U.S.C. § 1466(b).

[188] For example, child pornography statutes have been updated to include electronic distribution of child pornography. That may provide more support for the assertion that if Congress wanted anti-pornography statutes to encompass electronic distributions, it would have done so. *See supra* note 173 and accompanying text (describing child pornography statute).

[189] 18 U.S.C. § 1462.

courts regularly place telephone companies within that category.[190] Similarly, courts could find that Internet access-providers are analogous to common carriers, even if they do not meet the technical definition of common carriers. Thus, they could fall within the provisions of Section 1462.

76   Another statute under which federal agencies could regulate obscenity on the Internet is 47 U.S.C. § 223 that states, in part:

> Whoever—(1) in the District of Columbia or in interstate or foreign communication by means of telephone—(A) makes any comment, request, suggestion or proposal which is obscene, lewd, lascivious, filthy, or indecent; . . . [or] (2) knowingly permits any telephone facility under his control to be used for any purpose prohibited by this section, shall be fined . . . or imprisoned . . . ."[191]

Since electronic communications invariably use phones, via modem, to transmit and receive messages, the statute appears applicable to bulletin board operators.

      The question however, is how strictly a court will read the statute: Bulletin board operators do not "make" obscene phone calls. First, they are not actually placing a call; someone is calling them and "browsing" through their hard drive. Second, the legislative intent of Section 223 certainly did not encompass the use of telephones to transmit images.[192] "Obscene phone calls" equate with juveniles and jilted boyfriends.[193] Bulletin board operators and users simply do not fall within the intent of Section 223.

78   Ultimately, the determination that sysops are "distributors" of hardcore pornography is hampered by the technology of the Internet: *Users* place the phone calls; *uses* decide which files they want; and *users* take the files. In many respects, online obscenity defies the definition of what is obscene material under federal law.

C. Censorship

Because they are afraid of liability if others post files containing obscene images on their systems, sysops screen—or chill—items posted on their bulletin boards. For example, two major commercial online enterprises, Prodigy and Compuserv, scan every message their customers post.[194] Their

---

[190] *See supra* notes 148–152 and accompanying text (discussing whether Internet access-providers will fall under common carrier definition).

[191] 47 U.S.C. § 223 (1988); *see* Carlin Communs. v. FCC, 749 F.2d 113 (2d Cir. 1984) (holding that FCC regulations developed in response to statute placing certain requirements on dial-a-porn services would be reviewed under "compelling government interest" standard and not reasonableness standard); *see also supra* note 141 (discussing details of FCC regulations regarding dial-a-porn).

[192] The legislative intent of section 223 indicates that its purpose was to guard against "placing" of threatening telephone calls "(most of which are anonymous)" to unsuspecting victims. The Legislators believed that people could use the telephone as a "weapon" to harass others. H.R. REP. No. 1109, 90th Cong., 2d Sess. 2 (1968), *reprinted in* 1968 U.S.C.C.A.N. 1915.

[193] Stalking cases involving the Internet may be good cases for applying 47 U.S.C. § 223 to online communications. *See supra* note 57 and accompanying text (discussing Internet stalking case).

[194] *New Technology, New Controversies*, THE PLAIN DEALER, July 15, 1993, at 2F.

systems are designed to screen out profanities and "red flag" any questionable entries.[195] They employ a full-time staff devoted to looking at the red
flags to determine whether the messages should be posted.[196] While the
Supreme Court has not addressed the range of editorial control of a licensed
member of the broadcast media,[197] private enterprises, such as Compuserv
and Prodigy, are probably within their rights in censoring their customers'
messages.[198]

80   Bulletin Board operators' role as censors forces them into a position
for which they are ill-equipped: deciding whether material posted meets the
three prong *Miller* test.[199] Naturally, the administrator will err on the side of
caution, thus deleting more than is actually obscene. This form of censorship was the very kind the Supreme Court sought to prevent in the area of
bookselling in *Smith v. California*.[200] This Section looks at a variety of ways
access-providers find themselves censoring the material to which their users
have access, with special attention directed toward recent decisions by universities to limit student-users' access to certain online bulletin boards.

The University of Georgia provides a prime example of the type of
censorship occurring at universities across the nation. The school provides
its students with access to the Internet, including e-mail accounts and FTP,
and access to the Usenet. The University has established an advisory board
for the computing operations, called the "Computer Information and Technology Forum" (the "Forum"). In 1993, the Forum met to discuss what level
of access they should allow users of the Usenet newsgroups.[201] The board,
considering a new Georgia anti-obscenity law,[202] wrangled over whether the
University would violate the law by providing Usenet newsgroups such as
"alt.sex" or "alt.binaries.erotica."[203] Ultimately, the Forum decided to limit

---

[195] *Id.*

[196] How the red flag "checkers" become experts at determining whether a certain message does or
does not pass the "community standards" test and which community they use is unclear. Most likely,
however, the checkers are trained to err on the side of excluding the image. *See infra* notes 199–211
and accompanying text (surveying conservative stance taken by University of Georgia officials in
determining what Internet discussion groups University students could access).

[197] Schneider v. Indian River Community College Found., 875 F.2d 1537 (11th Cir. 1989).

[198] The Supreme Court's recent labor law decision in Lechmere, Inc. v. NLRB, 502 U.S. 527 (1992),
may indicate the direction the Court is heading in the area of private enterprisers' property rights.
In the case, the Court held that the owner of a supermarket and adjoining stores could demand
that union organizers not leave leaflets on cars parked in the parking lot adjacent to the stores. Because that case involved a labor union and its statutory interest in being able to distribute information, it appears that a customer of an Internet access-provider lacks sufficient interest to
overcome the access-provider's property interest. However, if the First Amendment right the access-provider is impinging on is sufficiently substantial, a court could find for the customer.

[199] *See supra* notes 73–86 and accompanying text (discussing *Miller* test); *see also supra* note 194
and accompanying text (concerning private access-provider's use of red-flagging).

[200] 361 U.S. 147 (1959); *see supra* notes 128–131 and accompanying text (discussing *Smith* decision).

[201] *See supra* note 53 and accompanying text (describing Usenet).

[202] O.C.G.A. § 16-12-100.1 (Supp. 1994); *see infra* note 220 and accompanying text (regarding
1993 revision of Georgia Code making it a misdemeanor to knowingly furnish obscene material to
minors electronically).

[203] The minutes of the pertinent Forum discussion are as follows:

> In order to increase the number of Internet information resources available to the
> campus, the UCNS [University Computing and Network Service] has implemented

the use of these discussion groups to users who signed waivers saying they were not minors and were aware of the Georgia obscenity statute.[204]

82   Two months after the decision, however, the procedure allowing those who had signed waivers to use the discussion groups was abandoned. Minutes from the October 2, 1993 meeting of the Forum indicate that the University's Office of Legal Affairs had overruled the previous decision.[205] The new rules dictated that "access to those specific discussion groups in question must be unconditionally restricted."[206] Thus, University of Georgia students may no longer access these discussion groups, even through a waiver procedure.

         While it is difficult to argue that University students have the right to review online smut, it does appear that the University of Georgia's self-censorship creates a legal liability for the school—exactly what it was trying to avoid through censoring in the first place. The problem is that if courts treat the discussion groups in question as they would licensing arrangements and treat the Forum as acting in its capacity as a public official, the University's policy appears to be overbroad censorship. The policy not only prohibits the dissemination of obscene material, but also whatever protected material is contained within the newsgroups.[207] The discussion groups banned by the University's actions include those dedicated to issues of psychological sexual hang-ups and sex techniques, both of which are arguably protected speech.[208] In its eagerness to maximize its liability protection, the University created a potentially unconstitutional pre-screening.[209] While it is true, as one of the members of the Forum pointed out, that

a public news server to carry USENET discussion groups. Proposed procedures to control access to certain discussion groups which are generally recognized to contain obscene materials were presented. *The requirement to control access to these discussion groups is deemed necessary because of existing Georgia law which makes it a misdemeanor to electronically furnish obscene materials to minors . . .*

     In general, the procedures would make the full USENET feed available to individuals, if the individual signs a form stating that they are not a minor and that they have read and understand the pertinent Georgia law . . . .

     A lengthy discussion of the issues ensued, including claims that the existing Georgia laws would not endure the test of court scrutiny; that censorship under certain circumstances is permitted; that eliminating institutional liability was the essential consideration; and that the Forum and Policy Board were not the appropriate bodies to decide on such matters.

     Ultimately, a vote was taken . . . [t]wenty one members voted to endorse the proposed procedures, one objected, and four abstained.

Memorandum obtained from Dennis Griffeth, University of Georgia Law School Director of Computer Services (Sept. 29, 1993) (emphasis added).

[204] *Id.*

[205] Memorandum obtained from Dennis Griffeth, University of Georgia Law School Director of Computer Services (Oct. 27, 1993).

[206] *Id.*

[207] *See supra* notes 128–131 (listing cases where Supreme Court has found that censorship of published material should only be allowed when, in aggregate, publication lacks serious value).

[208] *See* INTERNET YELLOW PAGES 282–290, 375 (listing all "alt.sex" groups on Internet and their content).

[209] *See supra* notes 117–123 and accompanying text (discussing legal issues involving censorship). The members of the Forum appear to have been acting in their capacity as state officials.

"censorship under certain circumstances is permitted,"[210] those "certain circumstances" are sharply limited by Supreme Court decisions. The University policy appears to be a classic example of unconstitutional censorship because it places unbridled discretion to decide what is obscene in the hands of a public official.[211]

84   Debate stemming from another university's decision to limit access to Usenet accounts crystallizes the issues involved in the University of Georgia's self-censorship. Carnegie Mellon University announced in late October 1994 that it would eliminate access to the Internet discussion groups dedicated to sexuality from its network.[212] Pennsylvania laws proscribe distribution of obscenity to minors in much the same manner as Georgia's.[213] Public reaction to the decision has been resoundingly negative,[214] indicating that had the University of Georgia made its decision public, the same concern over loss of free speech through censorship would have been expressed. Carnegie Mellon, unlike some other universities, has stood by its decision to eliminate access to some discussion groups.[215]

The type of overreaction demonstrated by the University of Georgia is occurring all over the country and will continue to occur until legislatures consider the effects of current anti-obscenity laws on the Internet. Legislatures who truly respect the importance of a free and open exchange of ideas will recognize the implications of forcing universities to eliminate certain discussion groups altogether. Universities, in particular, should regard shutting off access to bulletin boards as an evil on par with the distribution of pornography.

D. Recommendations

86   There are strong reasons supporting Congress's update of the obscenity laws. First, Internet hackers boast of the lawlessness of their network.[216] Federal laws making it clear that obscenity laws apply to distributors of obscenity over networks like the Internet would serve to remind Internet users

---

[210] Memorandum obtained from Dennis Griffeth, University of Georgia Law School Director of Computer Services (Sept. 29, 1993).

[211] See Freedman v. Maryland, 380 U.S. 51 (1965) (holding that discretionary authority granted to public official is unconstitutional when official acts with unbridled discretion and without timely review by judiciary); see also supra notes 117–123 (discussing cases involving censorship).

[212] John Schwartz, School Gives Computer Sex the Boot; Carnegie Mellon University Taking Discussion Groups Off Its Network, Wash. Post, Nov. 6, 1994, at A26 (taking note that Carnegie Mellon's action "casts a long shadow" as leader in computer technology).

[213] 18 Pa. Cons. Stat. Ann. § 5903 (1990).

[214] See Editorial, Why It Matters, Pittsburgh Post-Gazette, Nov. 27, 1994, at F3 (arguing that private university's removal of all forums that exist for pictures which might be considered erotica is hypocritical when university claims to respect free expression); Reid Kanaley, Some Say Computer Porn Is Putting Free Speech on the Line, Philadelphia Inquirer, Dec. 13, 1994, at B1 (reporting Carnegie Mellon's decision has sent shock waves through academia).

[215] Schwartz, supra note 212, at A26 (reporting that Stanford University removed access to sex newsgroups and bulletin boards for jokes in 1989, but later reopened them and established campus committee to deal with problem.)

[216] See supra note 3 and accompanying text (noting declaration of Internet users that anarchy reigns online).

that their rights are no greater or less online than they are elsewhere.[217] Second, the federal government should be aware of the government funding being used by the National Science Foundation to maintain the Internet backbone.[218] Carefully crafted obscenity laws might, therefore, prevent public outrage[219] over the government subsidizing a medium for obscenity distributors.

Just as importantly, legislatures, including Congress, should address online obscenity in a way that will eliminate the confusion that is creating the current environment of unconstitutional censorship. The state legislatures that have attempted to address obscene online communications have not yet succeeded in alleviating the confusion.[220] The current failure to address this issue successfully will lead to continued overreaction by bulletin board operators who fear criminal prosecution for "distributing" obscene matter posted on their bulletin boards, despite the fact that they have reasons not to inquire into what is being posted.[221]

88   Over the last few months, Congress has revisited the anti-obscenity laws in an effort to make them encompass electronic communications. The two types of bills that have come out of Congress's deliberations evince the problems that arise when the government tries to regulate the transmission of obscene materials.

On the one hand, the Senate passed a bill introduced by Senator Exon referred to as the "Communications Decency Act," which established fines and criminal penalties for individuals and companies who transmit obscene materials.[222] Alternatively, Representatives Cox and Wyden offered the "Internet Freedom and Family Empowerment Act" which would exempt network operators from coverage under the laws.[223] Congress has taken no final action on the bills.

---

[217] See All Things Considered: Interview (NPR radio broadcast Oct. 15, 1994) (referring to American University professor's urging for "Bill of Rights" for electronic networking community).

[218] See supra notes 11–33 and accompanying text (presenting technical background of Internet). In testimony before the House Science and Technology Committee, the acting assistant director of NSF asked for $329 million to fund its high performance computer and communications program, a sizable amount of which is earmarked for maintaining the Internet. Testimony of Dr. Melvyn Ciment, FEDERAL DOCUMENT CLEARING HOUSE CONGRESSIONAL TESTIMONY, May 10, 1994, available in LEXIS, News Library, Curnws File.

[219] See, e.g, Mike McManus, Controversy Continues over NEA Grant to Artist, DURHAM MORNING HERALD, Apr. 1, 1990, at C9 (reporting on criticism of NEA for funding controversial projects like Mapplethorpe homoerotic exhibit).

[220] See, e.g., O.C.G.A. § 16-12-80 (1992) (prohibiting electronic furnishing of indecent materials to minors); see supra notes 199 211 and accompanying text (portraying reaction to enactment of law by University of Georgia officials).

[221] See supra notes 137–139 and accompanying text (discussing factors that would keep bulletin board operators from knowing what is in files on bulletin boards).

[222] Elizabeth Corcoran, Legislation to Curb Smut On-Line Is Introduced, WASH. POST, July 1, 1995, at F2. One newspaper article was critical of the piece of legislation because the word "transmit" means a great deal more to access-providers for Internet e-mail accounts than it does to others in the communications field, and could force access-providers to monitor every transmission. Hobbling the Internet, WASH. POST, Feb. 26, 1995, at C6. Thus, his proposal has lead to even greater confusion about the current state of federal laws.

[223] Corcoran, supra note 222.

90   These two legislative proposals illustrate the dilemma the government faces in trying to stop the flow of obscenity. Making network operators liable puts an incentive on the companies with the technological know-how to stop the distribution. However, as this Note has demonstrated, the current framework of laws prohibiting distribution of obscenity does not lend itself to Internet communications, especially if transmissions made on the networks are encoded.

Furthermore, *any* regulation of the Internet will be subject to judicial review under the prior restraint doctrine. Since either government or Internet-industry censorship of obscene material will inevitably proscribe some transmissions that are not obscene, any law passed by Congress likely will have to withstand a prior restraint challenge in court. As with many controversial issues, the electronic transmission of obscenity may ultimately be decided by the United States Supreme Court. Network operators will respond to ambiguous legislation in two different ways: (1) by shutting down their bulletin board altogether (or severely limiting its access to known users, *i.e.,* establishing a password or encryption code) or (2) searching every file and deleting those that the administrator believes contain obscene material. Either of these actions will have the effect of eviscerating the very intent of the bulletin boards: free and open exchange of ideas. This race to overzealous censorship, even by leading universities in the computer field, is compounded by statutes that are unclear in their reach and purpose.

92   Unconstitutional censorship is sure to flourish in the current environment of unclear statutes and seemingly unfair enforcement of obscenity. It appears from the minutes of the University of Georgia's Forum that they did not want to eliminate access to all files related to sexual material but that they felt they had no other choice in light of the uncertain legal climate. Until lawmakers settle this area of the law, access-providers will continue to limit user's access to certain bulletin boards, even though they may contain constitutionally-protected material.

Not all attempts at clearing up this area of the law will be successful. Inevitably, early legislation will lead to even greater confusion. However, as Justice Ginsburg suggested in her dissenting opinion in *Arizona v. Evans,*[224] when "frontier legal problems are presented," it is best to allow "percolation" at the state level.[225]

94   Two non-legislative solutions are also available to control the flow of obscenity. To address the concern that the most damaging thing about pornography is its effect on children, some computer software firms are offering relatively inexpensive programs that will provide parents and schools control over what files children can access.[226] This solution is preferable to a legislative one because it keeps the government out of having to censor online

---

[224] 115 S. Ct. 1185 (1995).

[225] *Id.* at 1198 n.1.

[226] *See generally New Software Will Help Block Computer Pornography* (NPR radio broadcast, July 10, 1995), *available in* LEXIS, NEWS Library, NPR File (reporting on software developed by California firm to help parents control what young people can get online).

transmissions. It also allows more flexibility over control at the most local level, thus effectuating more fully the community standard prong of the *Miller* test. Each home could fine-tune the restrictions to its own standard.[227]

Another solution is allowing self-regulation. One such proposal is currently being worked on by an Internet industry group. Ideas that group is considering include parental control software like that discussed above, a rating system, an education campaign, and industry-wide standards and a code indicating which networks meet those standards.[228] Another possible answer would be to create a code of conduct, not unlike that which controls the legal profession, with a sanctioning body to enforce the self-regulation.

96   Both of these suggestions illustrate an important point: The Internet is in its infancy. Trying to fashion solutions to the various problems that will arrive on the Internet, including obscenity, will take time. There will be successes and failures, and all of the good ideas will not emanate from Congress. However, the sooner legislatures start trying to resolve these problems, the sooner a solution will be discovered.

Part of the Internet's problem is that different states have different community standards for what is obscene, and a user's posting on any Internet newsgroup or bulletin board could be read in any jurisdiction in the United States. Allowing experimentation at the state level may exacerbate the already-confusing state of liability laws regarding use of the Internet. It may be more appropriate to encourage experimentation at the regulatory as well as self-regulatory level.

Conclusion

98   As the Internet emerges as a dominant communication medium, lawmakers must scramble to update obscenity laws dating from the Nineteenth Century. It is unfortunate that the laws have fallen behind the learning curve on the Internet because users will be the ones who will bear the burden of mistakes through excessive contravention of their free speech rights. The experimentation stage that Internet obscenity regulations is now entering will assuredly continue to be both controversial and explosive. However, it is better for Internet users that the debate surrounding online obscenity be rancorous because subtle, yet overzealous, self-censorship would certainly be more injurious to users' rights.

The Internet is still in a clumsy form, technologically speaking, and it would be futile to attempt to foretell what it will look like in the coming decades. While waiting for its final form, legislatures should enact legislation that provide the greatest personal freedom for adults while limiting children's access. Legislators must keep in clear focus the two policies driving the need to curb online obscenity—protecting minors and/or paternalistically

---

[227] *Id.*
[228] *See generally Industry Task Force to Study Ways to Control Obscenity on Computer Systems,* (NPR radio Broadcast, June 29, 1995), *available in* LEXIS, NEWS Library, NPR File (reporting on task force looking at options for self-regulation).

protecting society as a whole—and remember that while the former policy can be effectuated in a variety of ways, the latter policy may prove more difficult to enforce without broad censorship of inoffensive material.

100   Also, if the problem is that these images are hard-core pornography, then legislatures and courts should *let the communities where the individual who is distributing the obscene material resides* make the decision. This approach will be effective because (1) fairness dictates that just as New York should not set the community standards for Memphis, neither should Memphis set the community standards for the rest of the country; and (2) allowing prosecutors to forum shop hurts the credibility of otherwise worthwhile laws. The country should not have its social mores dictated by its one or two most conservative jurisdictions.

The media response to the *Thomas* case was indicative of the deteriorating respect for federal anti-obscenity laws: Articles ignored the fact that this defendant was distributing some very objectionable material, even by California standards. Allowing prosecutors to forum shop in online cases fosters antagonism which, in the end, works against enforcement of the laws the prosecutors are trying to uphold.

102   The Internet currently is a fairly closed community, one which will require cooperation from its users for meaningful enforcement of obscenity laws. If the intent of the *Thomas* prosecution was to inspire fear in the users of a largely unregulated medium, the United States Attorney's Office may have won a short-lived victory. However, if the intent was to direct attention to abuses being carried out on the Internet and gain public support to combat those abuses then it was no victory at all.   ❖

Questions for Meaning

1. What is a "protocol"? What protocols are most commonly used on the Internet?
2. How does the nature of communication by e-mail differ from other types of communication?
3. Why are courts concerned with the kind of media through which "obscene material" is distributed? To what extent is current law useful for determining the legality of transmitting or receiving "obscene material" through the Internet?
4. What process should be used to determine whether material is obscene?
5. According to Goldman, who should decide whether material is obscene? Why would it be problematic to give this authority to others?
6. What is the significance of "community standards"? In a case involving the Internet, what community should be at issue: the community from which material is distributed or the community in which it is received?
7. Why does Congress have legitimate reason for regulating the Internet? Can Congress do so on its own?

Questions about Strategy

1. Consider the scenario presented in paragraphs 3–9. Is it plausible? How effectively does it illustrate the issues Goldman subsequently discusses?
2. Although Goldman calls this article a "Note," many readers are likely to find it long and complex. What strategies does Goldman use to help readers follow his argument?
3. On what principles has Goldman built his case? What kind of audience is likely to share these principles?
4. Which of Goldman's examples were most useful for you?
5. What is the effect of reading an argument with so many citations? What conclusions can you draw from recognizing this effect?

ONE STUDENT'S ASSIGNMENT

Write an argument focused on whether access to the Internet should be restricted, either by the government or by service providers, in order to protect users from pornography and other disturbing material. Follow the plan for classical arrangement: begin by catching the attention of your audience, then provide background information on your subject, indicate your position, provide proof for your position, respond to views different from your own, and conclude by summarizing your main points. Use MLA-style documentation.

Regulation of the Internet
B. J. Nodzon

It's one o'clock in the morning, and you have a sociology paper discussing sexually transmitted diseases due at 8:00 A.M. Other assignments consumed your time; consequently, you failed to conduct any research beyond what was available in your textbook. You still need more current, in-depth information, but the library is closed at this late hour. As you panic over this dilemma, it hits you: the Internet. You quickly start your computer and log onto the University's system only to find that your search cannot be conducted because you used the word *sexually.* Frantically, you call a friend who lives off-campus and ask him to conduct a search on his computer, which uses a different service provider. Your friend exhausts every possible search engine for information on STDs; however, the material is restricted.

2   This scenario could easily occur since many universities block a number of entries into the Internet (Goldman 440). Many high schools also limit access to reduce the possibility of students' encountering offensive material. Access to Internet information

outside of universities and schools has been threatened since the U.S. Senate narrowly passed the Communications Decency Act. The Act has been called unconstitutional because its vague language apparently bans classic pieces of literature and prohibits certain topics for discussion groups. Other attempts to regulate the Internet have been made by service providers. For example, CompuServ blocked access to 200 newsgroups because of complaints from the German government about obscene content (Burton 377). Similarly, fearful that young girls might accidentally discover sexually explicit discussions, America Online dropped a number of feminist discussion forums (Ness 398). These acts have caused great debate about who should regulate the Internet—if it should be regulated at all.

Certainly, some material on the Internet is not suitable for children to view; however, this does not mean the material should be banned. I believe free speech and freedom of information should be embraced on the Internet; neither the government nor the global service providers should regulate or censor the content of the Internet. The only acceptable type of regulation is local self-regulation conducted by parents who want to monitor their children's access and by universities and schools that do not want students to use school computers for accessing nonacademic material. To help minimize illegal activity on the Internet, current obscenity and liability laws need only an amendment that will cover digital and computer networks (Burton 378).

4 The hypothetical scenario described earlier demonstrates the need for access to updated information during all hours of the day. With updated information, students and researchers can learn more about their topics and can provide their readers with current information. Even a good library cannot provide as much current material as the Internet can. Through accessible information on the Internet, students and researchers who are pressed for time will no longer be constricted by the hours of the library or the limits of its collection. The Internet also assists people in the American workforce. For instance, doctors can obtain updated medical information and view reports from other physicians around the country, and businesspeople can search for financial and stock information. All of these people utilize the Internet's advancements in the accessing and distribution of information—and no one can accurately predict what information will need to be consulted in the future.

The new technology of the Internet also helps Americans practice our historically important right to free speech. People now have a new medium to view a wide range of opinions and ideas, which helps them discover, learn, and formulate their own opinions on important issues. Even people with established ideas need to examine opposing viewpoints in order to evolve or embrace new ideas. Through the global reaches of the Internet, people have an opportunity to research controversial issues and become more informed, active participants in national and international society.

6   Some people argue that the federal government should apply legislation prohibiting offensive material on the Internet. However, the global reaches of the Internet make any form of government legislation difficult to enforce. "(M)aterial prohibited in one country can be stored on a server in another and then accessed from the first and . . ., at present, there is little that governments can do about this" (Burton 378). International legislation is also unworkable because each country holds different standards when considering offensive material.

Since international legislation is impossible, many people suggest that global service providers should regulate the Internet. However, this causes many of the same concerns expressed with government legislation because service providers cannot prohibit access to material deemed offensive in a specific country. Once again, this causes problems because different standards prevail in different countries. Furthermore, with the power to regulate the Internet, service providers have the opportunity to block material for self-serving purposes. Hypothetically, America Online could block a discussion group that criticizes the increased prices of the service. This type of control violates free speech and places too much responsibility on the server.

8   Service providers have a legitimate concern that they might be found guilty of distributing offensive material over the Internet. Unfortunately, many service providers overcompensate by blocking material and discussion groups that are perfectly legal. However, the Supreme Court's decision in *Smith v. California* illustrates the Court's belief that distributors of large amounts of information should not be held liable for any random amounts of offensive material contained therein (Goldman 429). Furthermore, the Electronic Communications Privacy Act of 1986 gives systems operators a legal reason not to know the content of the files on their bulletin boards. The Act states that a system operator is not entitled to divulge data contained in an electronic communication service to any outside source (Goldman 430). Service providers are also not guilty of distribution because the people who access the offensive material are actively seeking it. Systems operators merely make the material available for users to take (Goldman 432). Therefore, service providers cannot be held liable and should not make themselves responsible for the content of the Internet.

I agree that service providers should not ignore users' complaints about offensive material. If someone notifies the service provider about offensive or illegal material on the Internet, then the service provider is obligated to notify the FCC. I also concede that there are legitimate reasons why service providers can prohibit material from the Internet. For instance, many operators are forced to shut down web pages and discussion groups because of viruses or systems overload. These are acceptable reasons to block access to material on the Internet. However, the content of a web page or discussion group should never be the reason for a service provider to block access.

10   I am sympathetic to many people's concerns about the welfare of children and what they might encounter on the Internet. Children should not be exposed to or accidentally stumble upon material unsuitable for their age. Therefore, special programs, such as NetNanny, CyberSitter, and SurfWatch, can be utilized by parents to prohibit content that may be unsuitable for their children (Burton 382). This type of regulation begins with the user and does not require regulation from the government or service providers. This local regulation by individuals will not interfere with the millions of other Internet users and will help protect children.

I also understand the schools' and universities' wish to limit access to nonacademic material on the Internet. Some aspects of the Internet are unsuitable in an academic environment and may cause extra strain on the local system. Therefore, future software will almost certainly be designed for universities to restrict access from school facilities. The standards and type of regulation will be decided by each university and will not interfere with the millions of other Internet users.

12   The wish to regulate the Internet is valid. However, how we regulate the Internet could change our ideas of free speech and freedom of information. Regulation by a single government or by a single global service provider is impossible due to the global reaches of the Internet. Strict regulation of the Internet is also potentially unconstitutional in America because it could violate our constitutional guarantee of free speech. Current obscenity laws will sufficiently govern the Internet; however, some offensive, yet legal, material will still circulate on it. Therefore, current software and soon-to-be-developed programs can be utilized by parents and universities to block unsuitable material. Regulation standards must be set locally, or our freedom of speech and information will be compromised.

Suggestions for Writing

1. In response to the argument by Jon Katz, write a Bill of Rights for parents.
2. Drawing on Burton, Willard, and Goldman, write an argument focused on eliminating pornography from the Internet.

3. Write an essay defining "obscenity."
4. Drawing on Kadi and Ness, write an essay describing problems on the information superhighway.
5. Kadi describes herself as a "cyber-junkie." Write an essay defining what this term means to you.
6. Interview the systems operator at your school or workplace and then report what you learn about the nature of the computer system you access when at school or at work.
7. Using three different search engines, do research on regulating the Internet and then write an essay comparing your results.
8. Visit a high school in your area and interview students and teachers about the quality of the school's computer resources. What kind of computer instruction is available there? Write an evaluation of how well students at the school are being prepared to access information electronically.
9. Summarize the argument by Robert F. Goldman.
10. Write an essay in which you teach how to find information on the Internet. Assume that your audience can get access to a network but has never previously used a computer for anything besides word processing. Technology makes this audience nervous, so try to be re-assuring.

COLLABORATIVE PROJECT

Investigate how much information about the members of your writing team is available to anyone with access to a computer and your Social Security numbers, phone numbers, driver's license numbers, medical record numbers, or electronic addresses. Check such sources as the records office at your school, the personnel department of your employer, the Department of Motor Vehicles, your banks, and a credit bureau. If you receive unsolicited catalogs in the mail, find out how these companies got your mailing address. Report your findings in an essay focused on the nature of privacy in an electronic age.

SECTION 6

CULTURE AND CURRICULUM: WHAT SHOULD STUDENTS BE TAUGHT?

Hugh B. Price

MULTICULTURALISM: MYTHS AND REALITIES

Hugh B. Price is vice president of the Rockefeller Foundation, one of the country's most prestigious sources of funding for research. Trying to clarify the debate over multiculturalism and reduce misunderstanding of its purpose, Price published this article in a 1992 issue of *Phi Delta Kappan*. As you read it, note how Price draws on his own experience as an African American who attended segregated schools.

Academe is in high dudgeon these days over multiculturalism—what it means and what are its appropriate curricular manifestations. It's a fascinating debate and in many respects an exasperating one, especially with regard to K–12 education. It is being carried out on the ideological extremes, but the issues are seldom discussed from the perspective of students and teachers inside the classroom. Usually the argument centers on whether Western culture and history should dominate instruction. Are school curricula sufficiently sensitive to multicultural perspectives? Are Afrocentrism and other "centrisms" appropriate responses to perceived insensitivity on the part of curriculum designers?

2   These questions, which are the ones we hear most often, raise an intriguing set of subsidiary issues that are seldom discussed in depth but that may actually lie at the core of the debate. Is there even such a thing as objective history? Should schools attempt to instill self-esteem? And what metaphor most appropriately characterizes what America actually is and what it ought to be—a melting pot or a mosaic?

But first, a warning. I am neither a scholar nor an educator, neither a participant in the debate over multiculturalism nor an ideologue. I am only a captivated and sometimes puzzled observer of the furor, who happens also to be a colored/black/Negro/Afro/African-American. I have borne each of these labels during my nearly five decades on this earth. I wonder what new label awaits me this decade.

4   Now, the issue of history. Many scholars and educators are up in arms over demands that school curricula be revised and over the denunciation of Western civilization courses as instruments of cultural imperialism. And, for that matter, many are upset over the rejection of the so-called canon (or list of essential books) as an instrumentality of the entrenched power structure. Advocates of the ascendancy of Western values argue that there is a disinterested Western cultural tradition that is rooted in a commitment to rational inquiry, that is governed by rigorous standards of evidence, and that has, over the centuries, converged on the truth. Yet minorities and women argue that history texts have not gone nearly far enough in portraying their cultures and contributions. They say the texts are rife with glaring omissions, cultural stereotypes, and misrepresentations of their histories.

These accusations ring true. I, for one, was an adult before I learned that Pushkin, the celebrated Russian poet, and Alexandre Dumas, the noted French author, were black. No one in secondary school or college taught me those salient facts. Why was there no mention in the standard literary anthologies?

6   This pattern of denial helps explain the deep-rooted suspicions among minorities and women about the accuracy of history as taught in the schools. And these suspicions have been both the driving force behind the Afrocentrist movement, which has spawned a new body of scholarship by black authors on the African-American cultural heritage, and the impetus for much of the other pressure for multicultural education in this country. There is emerging research that suggests that ancient Egypt was to a large extent a black African society. According to Asa Hilliard of Georgia State University, school curricula should teach that Africa is the birthplace of mankind and thus of the arts, the sciences, mathematics, and the great philosophies.

Some scholars take issue with that assertion, of course. They contend that many of the purported contributions of the Egyptians are inflated and that some claims are downright false. And they contend that Hilliard's view of history has not been confirmed by recognized scholars from major universities.

8   Rather than foam at the mouth, as the protagonists on both sides of the issue are prone to do, why not find out whether these exciting and provocative assertions are well-founded? Defenders of traditional Western content argue that history must meet the highest standards of accuracy and integrity as an intellectual discipline based on commonly accepted standards of evidence. They contend that revision of history occurs not as a result of political imposition, but because better history corrects and improves on previous research and teachings. Is this really so?

I grew up in Washington, D.C., and am old enough to have attended segregated schools and to have witnessed the onset of integration. In the early Fifties we learned one version of the Civil War—the Southern version. Yet there was another, Northern version of the war that we weren't taught.

Those contrasting versions of the Civil War were clearly products of conscious decisions by historians to codify, of textbook publishers to disseminate, and of schoolteachers to teach one as opposed to the other.

10   Are historians entirely objective when they write about the past? An
article in the *Chronicle of Higher Education* suggests that history isn't the ex-
acting, disinterested discipline that it is reputed to be.[1] Ever since the 19th
century, mainstream historians have argued that historical interpretation is
an objective, unbiased, and accurate reflection of the past. But that belief is
now being shattered by the fragmentation of historical research and by
emerging theories that knowledge is indeed subjective. According to Peter
Novick, author of *That Noble Dream: The Objectivity Question and the
American Historical Profession*, "What has come under attack among historians is not the commitment to amassing evidence, but the notion that there
is one right version of history, a single truth about the past." Novick continues, "There is a distinction between upholding singular factualities, like saying I am wearing a red tie, and larger questions of synthesis."[2]

J. H. Hexter, professor emeritus of history at Washington University,
distinguishes between writing history with a capital *H* and writing history
with a small *h*. The former deals with what Hexter characterizes as major
trends, large movements, deep-running tides, and portentous rumbles. It's
impossible, he says, to write capital *H* history objectively. However, according to Hexter, many historians believe they can answer the small *h* questions
objectively, using accepted standards of evidentiary accuracy.[3]

12   But even small *h* history can befuddle historians on occasion. An interesting article appeared in the *New York Times* not long ago that illumi-
nated the perils faced by historians. The article was headlined "Vienna
Takes Aim at Myths About Mozart." Supposedly Mozart died of poisoning
while working on a requiem mass that was commissioned by a "gray-
cloaked stranger." The article went on: "Too poor to buy even a proper
coffin, his wife supposedly buried the composer in an unmarked pauper's
grave with four other bodies." Viennese historians now have second
thoughts. Contemporary researchers have concluded, according to the article, that Mozart probably died of the effects of a bloodletting administered
to counter acute rheumatic fever. And he almost certainly knew that the
requiem that he was working on the night of his death had been commissioned not by a stranger, but by a count.[4]

What's the moral of that revelation? Perhaps historians who attack
Afrocentrists should be humbler in their accusations. At the same time,
Afrocentrists might be more cautious in their claims. And everyone should
be more temperate in their tones.

14   The formulation of history is an evolutionary process of discovery,
argumentation, interpretation, and codification. The cycle repeats itself
over the years as investigators dig ever deeper for evidence and synthesis.
Why is it even necessary to present all history as settled truth? When there
is sharp disagreement, why not couch the issue as an unsettled question in
the quest for truth? Why not pose the contrasting positions to students as

propositions to be studied—in effect, as an exercise in inquiry-based learning? Instead of asking students to absorb history, challenge them to "do" history. Teach them how to ferret out primary sources, weigh evidence, critique arguments, and formulate their own views. This learning process would be a prelude to the kinds of judgments they will be called on to make as adults.

Next, the nettlesome issue of self-esteem. Advocates of multicultural and "centrist" curricula argue that, if students do not feel good about themselves, they will not fare well in school. They say that students do better academically when they see people like themselves represented in the curriculum. In some communities, parent groups have even gone so far as to sue on behalf of multicultural education. The parents claim that, as the result of glaring omissions in the curriculum, their children's sense of self-worth has suffered. The lack of multicultural curricula, they contend, has contributed to such problems as student disengagement and high dropout rates.

16   Proponents of this view have come under withering criticism. Their opponents say that the role of those who formulate curricula is critical analysis, accuracy, and objectivity—not making students feel better about themselves. Teaching self-esteem is not the province of schools. Russell Baker, the *New York Times* columnist, questions the notion that education has a duty to affect people's feelings in a positive way. What's depressing about the arguments over "centrism," in his view, is the indifference to the idea that education entails training people to think clearly.[5]

Is it really the case that instilling self-esteem has no place in school and is of dubious educational value? I take issue with that assertion, based on personal experience if not personal research. When I was growing up in segregated Washington, I attended B. K. Bruce Elementary School. Although most of our curriculum was standard mainstream stuff, elements of an Afrocentric curriculum were included. We were taught that Benjamin Banneker had laid out the street system in Washington, D.C.; that Ralph Bunche helped bring peace to the Middle East in the late Forties; that Charles Drew discovered blood plasma and saved the lives of many American soldiers in World War II; and, yes, that Jackie Robinson had integrated major league baseball.

18   In other words, we learned that blacks had made seminal contributions to mainstream society. We learned that we belonged intellectually as well as constitutionally and that we were of value to mainstream society, whether others thought so or not. Moreover, our families maintained close ties with Howard University, which was considered a citadel of learning with a distinguished faculty and student body.

Thus, even though we were reared in a segregated society, we were brimful of pride in our people and in our contributions to all mankind. There was never any doubt in my young mind about my self-worth or my capacity to succeed in school and beyond. Nor were there any doubts in the minds of my parents and other relatives. It's impossible to overstate the impact of this mindset on our confidence, our capacity, and our determination to succeed in school.

20   In my commonsense view, there is an unequivocal connection between self-esteem and success in life. Just imagine the handicaps that burden a child from a chronically poor family that is shut off from the mainstream—a family in which the parents harbor little hope for themselves, much less for their children. Imagine the odds against the child who lacks self-esteem and receives scant support from home.

We may argue that instilling self-esteem is no business of the schools, but we are deluding ourselves if we think there isn't a link between self-esteem and achievement—or that the close nexus between mainstream schools and well-functioning, intact families hasn't promoted the self-esteem of mainstream children all along. If schools are to succeed for millions of at-risk children who lack adequate support at home and in the community, then educators simply must fill this void in the children's lives.

22   As James Comer of Yale argues, schools must learn to respond flexibly and creatively to students' needs. When he was a youngster, three of Comer's neighborhood friends fell by the wayside. Comer succeeded largely because his parents, unlike those of his buddies, imparted the social skills and the self-confidence that enabled him to take advantage of educational opportunities.[6] These days there is a vast gulf between home and school. The lack of support for children makes such a difference that educators have to try to bridge that gulf.

What's more, Jeffrey Howard, a social psychologist who heads the Efficacy Institute in Boston, uses "attribution theory" to explain the inner governing mechanisms and external signals that influence whether or not students believe they can achieve. If students have confidence in their ability, then success or failure in school and in life is largely a function of effort. Whether children achieve is contingent on whether they possess self-esteem and confidence in their ability—and on whether their teachers share that confidence in them.[7]

24   I don't mean to suggest by citing Comer and Howard that they necessarily subscribe to Afrocentrism—or other "centrisms"—as appropriate curricular strategies. Or even that they believe Afrocentrism will instill self-esteem in minority students. I don't know how they feel about these propositions. But I do mean to suggest that their views lend credence to the argument that self-esteem and academic achievement go hand in hand. Thus, if we care about the academic development of children and if we acknowledge the reality that many at-risk children come from families and communities that don't instill the forms of self-esteem that foster school performance, then educators who teach such children must tackle self-esteem too.

The issue for me is not whether to boost students' self-esteem, but how and toward what end. It does students no favor to build self-esteem on a specious historical foundation or to use history to insulate or alienate them from others. Rather, the fundamental purpose should be to ensure that young people achieve the necessary intellectual and social development to function confidently and effectively as adults in a highly competitive world.

26   Finally, I come to the issue of "melting pot" versus "mosaic." Which is the myth and which is the reality? America has been called a great melting pot for races and ethnic groups that are constantly dissolving and re-forming. It is said that most people who have emigrated to the U.S. over the years have arrived expecting to become Americans. Their goals were deliverance from a harsh past and assimilation into a hopeful future.

The trouble is that the melting pot works only at the margins and only in some aspects of life. It seldom works socially and has succeeded in education and the labor market only under duress. It took decades of political, judicial, and legislative pressure to include some, and only some, minorities and women in the melting pot.

28   In my view, mounting economic hardship may well lie at the heart of the rising ethnic tensions that have increasingly called the melting pot metaphor into question. Note the coincidence between the erosion of earnings among working-class people—white, black, and Latino—and the rise in strident multiculturalism. The social compact in America between our society and its working people—white and minority alike—is gradually dissolving. Once upon a time, whether or not you were a capable student, if you played by the rules, worked hard, and were willing to sweat, America would reward you with a readily available, reasonably well-paying job that enabled you to be the head of your household, to support your family, to buy a car and a home, to educate your children, and to take an occasional vacation.

This simply is no longer so. Those manufacturing jobs that once provided dignity and decent wages for high school graduates and dropouts alike are vanishing. All are victims of a new world industrial order that is redistributing manufacturing jobs and redefining the economic role of our communities. It is true that the service industries have sopped up some of these workers, but in such jobs they earn much less than the factory workers of old. Families whose primary breadwinners lack high school degrees earned 30 percent less in 1987 (adjusted for inflation) than they did in 1973.[8]

30   Essentially, the income of "haves" has risen steadily while that of "have-nots" has declined alarmingly. According to Richard Freeman, a labor economist at Harvard University, "Young working people, particularly men, particularly non-college-graduate men, have taken a terrible beating in the job market over the last twenty years." Adds Arnold Packer, executive director of the Labor Department's Commission on Wages and Education, "A kid used to be able to drop out of school and get a job with his old man at General Motors. Now the old man is lucky if he can keep his job and his kid has to start somewhere else at the minimum wage."[9] To compound the problem, the Army doesn't even want dropouts anymore. Young people must pass the General Education Development exam or possess a high school diploma to get into the Army.

Millions of Americans, a disproportionate number of them minorities, are going backward, losing hope, finding it increasingly difficult to share in the American dream. How can we expect them to accept, much less treasure, Western history and values if they're incessantly under economic siege? Why, under the circumstances, are we surprised that people seek solace and security among their own and adopt an increasingly insular view of the world? Try looking at the world through their prism and wonder how long it would take before paranoia, defeatism, or even defiance would set in.

32   What then is the role of the schools in this emerging world? Irreversible demographic trends will force public institutions to respond in new ways. Schools have traditionally served to mainstream students, divesting them of the language and culture of their countries of origin. But the reality also is that schools, with their testing systems, have long performed a sorting rather than a developmental function—which is to say, they have selected out some students for advanced opportunities and shunted most others aside to the armed forces, the factories, or the farm. This sorting function has affected young people, I hasten to add, of all races.

To compete successfully in the world economy, America must revamp the way it develops *all* of its human talent. The economy needs the productivity of highly skilled workers, regardless of complexion or cultural background. Schools have to equip young people to function successfully and harmoniously in a truly new world.

34   And what is that new world? Let me cite an anecdote shared by Beverly White, superintendent of schools in rural, predominantly black Lee County, Arkansas. She told me that Sanyo, the Japanese appliance manufacturer, has opened a plant in Lee County. The local schools have no choice but to embrace multiculturalism and global education because Lee County's children will soon enter the world of work—many of them at Sanyo's plant. What's more, the adults of Lee County and the Japanese managers who reside there must learn to live with "others"—namely, each other. Ideology aside, multiculturalism is a matter of good citizenship and of survival for Lee County.

Charles Krauthammer, writing in the *Washington Post,* has expressed concern that we are witnessing the rise of tribalism, of Balkanization, and of multiculturalism. He lumped all these forces together. We see, he lamented, tribes surfacing within nations within empires. In his view, this worrisome trend should be a warning to America, which alone among multiethnic countries in the world has managed to assimilate its citizenry into a common nationality. According to Krauthammer, we risk squandering this great achievement.[10]

36   Interestingly enough, several pioneering scholars in the field of multiculturalism are also worried about the soaring decibel level of the debate. According to Henry Louis Gates, "routinized righteous indignation is being substituted for rigorous criticism." He says society simply won't survive without the values of tolerance. Perhaps, Gates suggests, we should think of American culture as a conversation among different voices, even if it is a conversation that some were able to join only recently.[11]

In 1991, Nicholas Lemann, author of *The Promised Land,* wrote in the *New York Times Magazine* of the families stranded for generations in Robert Taylor Homes, a massive public housing project in Chicago. Where there once were poor people and others in the neighborhood, there are now only poor people.[12] A week after Lemann's article appeared, Harvard University political economist Robert Reich, also writing in the *New York Times Magazine,* bemoaned the growing isolation of America's elite, who are curled up in their comfortable economic enclaves, unwilling to support those in need outside. This secession of the fortunate fifth has been encouraged by the "newest federalism," which is shifting increased responsibility to state and local governments. In Reich's view, the political challenge ahead is to reaffirm that America remains a society whose citizens have a binding obligation to one another, who honor the mutual obligations of the social compact.[13]

38   I wonder, frankly, how we can in clear conscience bewail the phenomena of tribalization and multiculturalism when we do so little to eliminate the economic and educational disparities that fuel them. The appropriate antidote for cultural insularity is a culture of inclusiveness that infuses every facet of our society. The blame for balkanization rests more with those who have the power to include but won't than with those outside who are barred entry.

In fact, economic inclusion may well be the more original, enduring, and compelling characteristic of this country. I'm no historian, but I submit it is the opportunity to breathe politically and advance economically—not a desire to assimilate—that has lured millions of immigrants to our shores for centuries and that continues to draw them to this day.

40   That is the transcendent American attribute that defines our society, that bonds us together, and that sets our nation noticeably apart from others. Were those who ardently preach American values truly to practice them, then perhaps our collective anxiety about the growing intolerance and insularity in America would, shall we say, melt away.   ❖

Notes

1. Karen J. Winkler, "Challenging Traditional Views, Some Historians Say Their Scholarship May Not Be Truly Objective," *Chronicle of Higher Education,* 16 January 1991, p. A-4.
2. Ibid.
3. Ibid.
4. "Vienna Takes Aim at Myths About Mozart," *New York Times,* 16 January 1991, p. A-5.
5. Russell Baker, "School as Spin Control," *New York Times,* 30 October 1990, p. A-25.
6. James P. Comer, *Maggie's American Dream: The Life and Times of a Black Family* (New York: NAL-Dutton, 1988).
7. Jeffrey Howard and Ray Hammond, "Rumors of Inferiority: The Hidden Obstacles to Black Success," *New Republic,* 9 September 1985, p. 17.
8. Lawrence Mishel and David M. Frankel, *The State of Working America: 1990–91 Edition* (Armonk, N.Y.: M. E. Sharpe, 1991), p. 199.

9. Peter T. Kilborn, "Youths Lacking Special Skills Find Jobs Leading Nowhere," *New York Times*, 27 November 1990, p. A-1.
10. Charles Krauthammer, "The Tribalization of America," *Washington Post*, 6 August 1990, p. A-11.
11. Karen J. Winkler, "Proponents of 'Multicultural' Humanities Research Call for a Critical Look at Its Achievements," *Chronicle of Higher Education*, 28 November 1990, p. A-5.
12. Nicholas Lemann, "Four Generations in the Projects," *New York Times Magazine*, 13 January 1991, p. 17.
13. Robert B. Reich, "Secession of the Successful," *New York Times Magazine*, 20 January 1991, p. 16.

Questions for Meaning

1. According to Price, why are minorities and women suspicious about history as it is traditionally taught?
2. How are historians reconsidering the nature of their discipline?
3. What is the difference between *History* and *history*?
4. Why does Price believe that fostering self-esteem is a legitimate mission for schools?
5. What is the difference between a "mosaic" and a "melting pot" view of America?
6. Vocabulary: dudgeon (1), subsidiary (2), imperialism (4), ascendancy (4), salient (5), impetus (6), imposition (8), codification (14), nettlesome (15), seminal (18), contingent (23), credence (24), duress (27), demographic (32), transcendent (40).

Questions about Strategy

1. In paragraph 3, Price advises readers that he is "neither a scholar nor an educator, neither a participant in the debate over multiculturalism nor an ideologue." What is the purpose of this disclaimer? How did it affect you?
2. Where does Price summarize conflicting views about the curriculum? What does he achieve by doing so?
3. How effectively does Price incorporate personal experience into his argument?
4. What is Price illustrating by his discussion of Mozart's death in paragraph 12?
5. On what basic values has Price built his argument? Are these values likely to appeal to a diverse audience?

RONALD TAKAKI

AN EDUCATED AND CULTURALLY LITERATE PERSON MUST STUDY AMERICA'S MULTICULTURAL REALITY

Professor of Ethnic Studies at the University of California at Berkeley, Ronald Takaki is the author of *Strangers from a Different Shore: A History of Asian Americans* (1989), *Iron Cages: Race and Culture in Nineteenth-Century America* (1990), *A Different Mirror: A History of Multicultural America* (1993), *From Different Shores: Perspectives on Race and Ethnicity in America* (1994), and *Hiroshima: Why America Dropped the Atomic Bomb* (1995). He first published the following article in the *Chronicle of Higher Education* in 1989.

In Palolo Valley, Hawaii, where I lived as a child, my neighbors were Japanese, Chinese, Portuguese, Filipino, and Hawaiian. I heard voices with different accents and I heard different languages. I played with children of different colors. Why, I wondered, were families representing such an array of nationalities living together in one little valley? My teachers and textbooks did not explain our diversity.

2   After graduation from high school, I attended a college on the mainland where students and even professors would ask me how long I had been in America and where I had learned to speak English. "In this country," I would reply. "I was born in America, and my family has been here for three generations."

Today, some twenty years later, Asian and also Afro-Americans, Chicano/Latino, and Native-American students continue to find themselves perceived as strangers on college campuses. Moreover, they are encountering a new campus racism. The targets of ugly racial slurs and violence, they have begun to ask critical questions about why knowledge of their histories and communities is excluded from the curriculum. White students are also realizing the need to understand the cultural diversity of American society.

4   In response, colleges and universities across the country, from Brown to Berkeley, are currently considering requiring students to take courses designed to help them understand diverse cultures.

The debate is taking place within a general context framed by academic pundits like Allan Bloom and E. D. Hirsch.* Both of them are asking: What is an educated, a culturally literate person?

---

* Educators Allan Bloom and E. D. Hirsch achieved national prominence during the 1980s by arguing that American colleges were failing to produce culturally literate citizens. Bloom is best known for *The Closing of the American Mind* (1987); Hirsch for *The Philosophy of Composition* (1981) and *Cultural Literacy: What Every American Needs to Know* (1987).

6   I think Bloom is right when he says: "There are some things one must know about if one is to be educated. . . . The university should try to have a vision of what an educated person is." I also agree with Hirsch when he insists that there is a body of cultural information that "every American needs to know."

But the question is: What should be the content of education and what does cultural literacy mean? The traditional curriculum reflects what Howard Swearer, former president of Brown University, has described as a "certain provincialism," an overly Eurocentric perspective. Concerned about this problem, a Brown University visiting committee recommended that the faculty consider requiring students to take an ethnic-studies course before they graduate. "The contemporary definition of an educated person," the committee said, "must include at least minimal awareness of multicultural reality."

8   This view now is widely shared. Says Donna Shalala, chancellor of the University of Wisconsin at Madison: "Every student needs to know much more about the origins and history of the particular cultures which, as Americans, we will encounter during our lives."

This need is especially felt in California, where racial minorities will constitute a majority of the population by 2000, and where a faculty committee at the University of California at Berkeley has proposed an "American-cultures requirement" to give students a deeper understanding of our nation's racial and cultural diversity. Faculty opposition is based mainly on a disdain for all requirements on principle, an unwillingness to add another requirement, an insistence on the centrality of Western civilization, and a fear that the history of European immigrant groups would be left out of the proposed course.

10   In fact, however, there are requirements everywhere in the curriculum (for reading and composition, the major, a foreign language, breadth of knowledge, etc.). The American-cultures requirement would not be an additional course, for students would be permitted to use the course to satisfy one of their social-sciences or humanities requirements. Western civilization will continue to dominate the curriculum, and the proposed requirement would place the experiences of racial minorities within the broad context of American society. Faculty support for some kind of mandatory course is considerable, and a vote on the issue is scheduled this spring.

But the question often asked is: What would be the focus and content of such multicultural courses? Actually there is a wide range of possibilities. For many years I have been teaching a course on "Racial Inequality in America: A Comparative Historical Perspective." Who we are in this society and how we are perceived and treated have been conditioned by America's racial and ethnic diversity. My approach is captured in the phrase "from different shores." By "shores," I intend a double meaning. One is the shores that immigrants left to go to America—those in Europe, Africa, Latin America, and Asia. The second is the different and often conflicting shores or perspectives from which scholars have viewed the experiences of racial and ethnic groups.

12   In my course, students read Thomas Sowell's *Ethnic America: A History* along with my *Iron Cages: Race and Culture in 19th-Century America*. Readings also include Winthrop Jordan on the colonial origins of racism, John Higham on nativism, Mario Barrera on Chicanos, and William J. Wilson on the black underclass. By critically examining the different "shores," students are able to address complex comparative questions: How have the experiences of racial minorities such as blacks and Asians been similar to, and different from, one another? Is "race" the same as "ethnicity?" How have race relations been shaped by economic developments, as well as by culture? What impact have these forces had on moral values about how people should think and behave, beliefs about human nature and society, and images of the past as well as the future?

        Other courses could examine racial diversity in relation to gender, immigration, urbanization, technology, or the labor market. Courses could also study specific topics such as Hollywood's racial images, ethnic music and art, novels by writers of color, the civil rights movement, or the Pacific Rim. Regardless of theme or topic, all of the courses should address the major theoretical issues concerning race and should focus on Afro-Americans, Asians, Chicanos/Latinos, and Native Americans.

14   Who would teach these courses? Responsibility could be located solely in ethnic-studies programs. But this would reduce them to service-course programs and also render even more remote the possibility of diversifying the traditional curriculum. The sheer logistics of meeting the demand generated by an institutionwide requirement would be overwhelming for any single department.

        Clearly, faculty members in the social sciences and humanities will have to be involved. There also are dangers in this approach, however. The diffusion of ethnic studies throughout the traditional disciplines could undermine the coherence and identity of ethnic studies as a field of teaching and scholarship. It could also lead to area-studies courses on Africa or Asia disguised as ethnic studies, to revised but essentially intact Western-civilization courses with a few "non-Western" readings tacked on, or to amorphous and bland "American studies" courses taught by instructors with little or no training in multicultural studies. Such courses, though well-intentioned, could result in the unwitting perpetuation of certain racial stereotypes and even to the transformation of texts by writers and scholars of color into "mistexts." This would only reproduce multicultural illiteracy.

16   But broad faculty participation in such a requirement can work if there is a sharply written statement of purpose, as well as clear criteria for courses on the racial and cultural diversity of American society. We also need interdisciplinary institutes to offer intellectual settings where faculty members from different fields can collaborate on new courses and where ethnic-studies scholars can share their expertise. More importantly, we need to develop and strengthen ethnic-studies programs and departments as academic foundations for this new multicultural curriculum. Such bases should bring together a critical mass of faculty members committed to, and

trained in ethnic studies, and should help to preserve the alternative perspectives provided by this scholarly field.

In addition, research must generate knowledge for the new courses, and new faculty members must be trained for ethnic-studies teaching and scholarship. Berkeley already has a doctoral program in ethnic studies, but other graduate schools must also help prepare the next generation of faculty members. Universities will experience a tremendous turnover in teachers due to retirements, and this is a particularly urgent time to educate future scholars, especially from minority groups, for a multicultural curriculum.

18   The need to open the American mind to greater cultural diversity will not go away. We can resist it by ignoring the changing ethnic composition of our student bodies and the larger society, or we can realize how it offers colleges and universities a timely and exciting opportunity to revitalize the social sciences and humanities, giving both a new sense of purpose and a more inclusive definition of knowledge.

If concerted efforts are made, someday students of different racial backgrounds will be able to learn about one another in an informed and systematic way and will not graduate from our institutions of higher learning ignorant about how places like Palolo Valley fit into American society.   ❖

Questions for Meaning

1. Consider the questions, in paragraph 2, that Takaki was often asked when he was a college student. What do they reveal?
2. According to Takaki, why did faculty at his school oppose a required course in American cultures?
3. In paragraph 12, Takaki asks, "Is 'race' the same as 'ethnicity'?" How would you answer this question?
4. Who should teach multicultural courses? What risks does Takaki see in giving responsibility for such courses to a single department? Why is he concerned about locating such courses within traditional academic disciplines?
5. Vocabulary: pundits (5), provincialism (7), logistics (14), amorphous (15), criteria (16).

Questions about Strategy

1. Takaki opens his essay by drawing on personal experience from twenty years ago. Is it relevant to the question at hand?
2. Why does Takaki choose Brown and Berkeley as examples of "colleges and universities across the country"?
3. Why does Takaki draw particular attention to educational needs in California?
4. What is the function of paragraph 6?
5. Consider paragraphs 12 and 13. Why does Takaki offer both a description of his own course and a list of other possibilities?

CHRISTINE E. SLEETER

WHAT IS MULTICULTURAL EDUCATION?

Professor of Teacher Education at the University of Wisconsin at Parkside, Christine E. Sleeter is the coauthor of *Making Choices for Multicultural Education* (1988), editor of *Empowerment Through Multicultural Education* (1990), and coeditor of *Multicultural Education, Critical Pedagogy, and the Politics of Difference* (1995). Her most recent book is *Multicultural Education as Social Activism* (1996). This 1992 article was published by Sleeter in *Kappa Delta Pi Record*. As its title suggests, the article attempts to define a concept that means different things to different people. As you read, note how Sleeter describes several different approaches to multicultural education.

Three teachers are sitting in a graduate course discussing their teaching. All three say they are actively involved in multicultural education, but as their discussion evolves, all three describe it differently. The first teacher says she has taught in an inner-city school for years and has learned to adapt her teaching successfully to the students; most of the students in her class score above the national average on standardized tests. The second teacher, rather surprised at that conception of multicultural education, says she has developed a series of intense units about the history of four different oppressed groups in the United States and has organized much of her instruction around these units.

2   The third teacher argues that the other teachers do not understand multicultural education. He has reconstructed his teaching in such a way that students analyze various social justice issues across different subject areas through the perspectives of diverse American sociocultural groups. He has also challenged tracking and ability grouping in his school.

Which of these conceptions of multicultural education is "correct"? All of them are, and they illustrate a few of the many conceptions of multicultural education teachers ascribe to in today's classrooms. In this article I will briefly outline five different "correct" approaches to multicultural education that many teachers use and educational theorists discuss.

4   To respond to American diversity more effectively, all five approaches involve a substantial reworking of the existing education program. However, each approach defines "effective education" differently and makes different assumptions about how it is achieved. These approaches to multicultural education have been developed in much more detail by me and Carl Grant elsewhere (Sleeter and Grant 1989; 1988).

First, let me briefly point out what these approaches have in common that makes them "multicultural education." First, each attempts to improve how schools address diversity in the United States, acknowledging that racism, sexism, and other forms of discrimination still exist and are perpetuated through "business as usual." Simply teaching a diverse class of students does not, in and of itself, constitute multicultural education. Teaching a White supremacist curriculum and maintaining relatively low expectations for minority student learning, for example, reproduces inequalities rather than confronts them. Second, each approach addresses only diversity in the United States. Some may also include international diversity, but do not equate American diversity with immigrants or international education. Some multicultural educators focus mainly on race and ethnicity, and some focus mainly on gender. My discussion will include race, ethnicity, social class, gender, and disability.

6   The *Teaching the Exceptional and Culturally Different Approach* to multicultural education aims to help students of color, low-income students, and/or special education students to achieve, assimilate, and "make it" in society as it currently exists. This approach assumes that the United States and Western culture provide abundant opportunities to citizens and show leadership in cultural development. It recognizes that students who are not achieving and succeeding may require bridges between their backgrounds and the schools to make the curriculum more "user friendly." Teachers who actually work with this approach have very high expectations for academic achievement. They believe the traditional academic curriculum is sound for all students, but that different students require different teaching approaches to connect successfully with it. Bridges may consist of instructional strategies that build on students' learning styles, culturally relevant materials, use of students' native language to teach academic content and Standard English, or compensatory programs that try to bring students up to grade-level. This approach does not advocate changing the emphasis or content of disciplines of study, only "marketing" them more effectively to a wider diversity of students.

Much research addresses how some teaching strategies either hinder or help the achievement of students who are members of groups that historically have not achieved well in schools. For example, research in anthropology and psychology documents a relationship between culture and cognitive style, suggesting that if teachers match their teaching strategies with students' learning styles, students will learn better (Shade 1989). Much work in bilingual education follows this model, providing considerable guidance for the development of school programs that build students' first language, teach new academic content and skills through the first language, and teach English as a second language (Crawford 1989; Trueba 1989).

8   Many teachers who are new to multicultural education are attracted to this approach. They are concerned about low achievement among students and believe that if students get a "boost" from the school (many regard this boost as making up for deficiencies at home) or are actually taught aspects of Western culture their parents are unable to teach, the students—regardless of their background—will be able to go on in life and achieve what they want.

One can distinguish educators who favor this approach in two ways. First, the changes they advocate in schooling are mainly or solely for members of a particular group, such as students from the inner city, bilingual students, mainstreamed special-education students, and immigrant students. If asked about parallel changes in the education of members of dominant groups, they either view few changes as needed or are not interested in expending energy trying to change the education of dominant group members. Second, advocates generally support much of the dominant discourse about the United States—that it is a free country with limitless opportunity, that its history is one of progress, and that only a few changes are needed to extend the American Dream to everyone.

10   The *Human Relations Approach* attempts to foster positive interpersonal relationships among members of diverse groups in the classroom and to strengthen each student's self-concept. Teachers who are attracted to this approach are concerned primarily with how students feel about and treat each other. The Human Relations curriculum includes lessons about stereotyping, individual differences and similarities, and contributions to society made by groups of which students are members; lessons and special events are supplemental to the main curriculum. Cooperative learning is used for the purpose of promoting student-student relationships. Much of what many schools do in the name of multicultural education is actually in reality Human Relations, such as ethnic fairs or special celebrations to feature a particular group—*Cinco de Mayo,* Asian/Pacific American Heritage Week, Black History Month, Women's History Month, etc. Usually the main purpose of such celebrations is affective—to attempt to deconstruct stereotypes students may have of each other and to help them feel good about contributions members of such groups have made.

The Human Relations Approach seems to fit particularly well with EuroAmericans' conception of their own ethnicity. Today ethnicity for EuroAmericans is acknowledged voluntarily, is connected with family history, and is acted upon mainly in the form of festivals and food (Alba 1990).

12   Like those who favor the Teaching the Exceptional and Culturally Different Approach, teachers who are attracted to the Human Relations approach generally regard American society at large as fair and open. They view disharmony among students (such as racial name-calling or social segregation on the playground) to be a result of misunderstanding and untrue stereotypes. They believe that providing positive information about groups as well as contact experiences will eliminate sources of such disharmony.

The next three approaches to multicultural education offer much stronger critiques of American society than do the first two. Educators who are sympathetic to the next three approaches usually have experienced and/or studied inequality in the United States sufficiently to appreciate the degree to which it is embedded in social institutions and perceive a need for far-reaching changes in education.

14   "Single-Group Studies" is an umbrella term for units or courses of study that focus on particular groups, such as ethnic studies, labor studies, women's studies, or disability studies. The *Single-Group Studies Approach* seeks to raise consciousness about a group by teaching its history, culture,

and contributions, as well as how that group has worked with or been oppressed by the dominant group in society. Single-Group Studies courses were created during the 1960s and 1970s as alternatives to the main curriculum of the university or school, which is strongly based on the experience of White men.

Although textbooks today may appear to be multicultural, careful analysis finds them to be still White and male-dominant and to treat other groups in a very fragmented fashion (Sleeter and Grant 1991). For example, examine several current textbooks to see how well they help answer the following questions: What historical and contemporary factors account for the persistent poverty of Mexican Americans? Why do full-time working women still earn only about 70 percent of what men earn, even with the same level of education? To what degree is wealth concentrated in a small number of hands in the United States? What insights does traditional and contemporary Native American literature give about how life should be lived? Why do persons with disabilities tend to see themselves as an oppressed minority rather than a group with a particular medical condition?

16   Often teachers attempt well-meaning lessons and units about other groups, but without realizing it, they replicate distortions, inaccuracies, or what one writer has termed "fantasies of the master race" (Churchill 1992). This happens when we ourselves have not studied another group in much depth, nor talked much with members of that group regarding the group's history or experiences. For example, I have observed units during Women's History Month that suggest sexism has been eliminated, and young girls today can simply go forth and do whatever they wish, the only remaining barrier being their own aspirations.

Most teachers have not studied an oppressed group in enough depth to realize the degree to which disciplinary knowledge is being reconstructed in Single-Group Studies departments in higher education.

18   Since the late 1960s, scholars working in university departments of ethnic studies, women's studies, and labor studies have unearthed and synthesized an enormous amount of information about particular groups of study. In addition, scholars have begun to reconceptualize fields of study based on the experiences and perspectives of previously marginalized groups. For example, Afrocentric scholars, placing people of African rather than European descent at the center of inquiry, have reconceptualized and restructured fields such as history, communication, art, and philosophy. Latino theorists question the traditional definition of "American culture" as meaning culture created within the boundaries of the United States. According to Lauter:

> One might argue that, for example, the virtual exclusion of early Spanish and French exploration texts, or of black and Indian sermons and autobiographies from received definition of "American literature" served the important ideological role of maintaining boundaries between what was truly "American," "ours," and what was "other," marginal. (1991)

Schools controlled by African Americans and Native Americans are producing excellent K–12 materials in the Afrocentric curricula and Native American curricula. Further, university libraries are housing rapidly growing collections of fascinating, vibrant work. It may be initially daunting to come to terms with how little one may know about other groups and the degree to which other groups' perspectives challenge much of what one may take for granted about the broader American society. However, there is plenty of material available to educate one's self and a fair amount available to use to educate one's students.

20   The *Multicultural Approach* to education reconstructs the entire education process to promote equality and cultural pluralism. Content in the curriculum is reorganized around the perspectives and knowledge of diverse American racial and ethnic groups (oppressed groups as well as EuroAmericans), both sexes, disability groups, and diverse social classes. A multicultural poetry unit usually features a wider variety of language use, lived experience, and perspective than does a monocultural unit, making it rich and fostering critical thinking.

The Multicultural Approach also reconstructs other processes in education that traditionally have not promoted high achievement for all students. Under this approach, tracking and ability grouping would be greatly reduced or eliminated because they are viewed as institutionalizing differential achievement and learning opportunity, which contradicts the ideal of equality. The Multicultural Approach advocates staffing schools with a diverse teaching force and breaking up traditional role designations (such as men teaching math and technical education or women working as secretaries and foreign-language teachers). It builds on students' learning styles, adapts to their skill level, and involves students actively in thinking and analyzing life situations. It encourages native language maintenance for students whose first language is not English and multilingual acquisition for all students.

22   Often teachers who are new to multicultural education confuse the Human Relations Approach with the Multicultural Approach, since both involve integrating diverse groups into the curriculum. They are quite different, however. The Multicultural Approach transforms everything in the entire school program to reflect diversity and uphold equality. The school program becomes quite rich and dynamic although not harmonious. For example, in a multicultural classroom, students would become used to considering different perspectives as "right;" they would discuss and debate different viewpoints and consider whether diversity actually means "anything goes." This approach deliberately fosters equal academic achievement across groups; achievement does not take a back seat to interpersonal relationships. Further, in the Multicultural Approach the entire curriculum is rewritten to be multicultural, drawing on content developed through Single-Group Studies; the Human Relations Approach adds on lessons without rewriting the curriculum.

The *Education that is Multicultural and Social Reconstructionist Approach* builds on the previous approaches, especially Single-Group Studies and the Multicultural Approach, teaching students to analyze inequality and oppression in society and helping them develop skills for social action. The main *raison d'être**** for multicultural education is that, while Americans espouse ideals of democracy, justice, and equality, the social system does not work—and has never worked—that way for large segments of the population. For example, the average EuroAmerican in the 1990s has greater access to a wide range of resources, such as access to jobs, decent housing, good education, and health care, than does the average American of color. Single-Group Studies focuses on a particular group, examining why this is the case historically as well as today, and exploring the creative and intellectual work of a group despite oppression. The Multicultural Approach offers a synthesis of Single-Group Studies, but one that is not overtly political.

24   The Social Reconstructionist approach begins with contemporary social-justice issues that cut across diverse groups, using disciplinary knowledge to examine them and create ways of affecting change. For example, a theme that appears in literature, art, and other creative works of oppressed groups is criticism of oppressive social structures and cultural representations. This is not generally a theme in the creative work of dominant groups, and educators who are members of dominant groups often mute or eliminate such criticism in constructing curriculum; it would, however, be a theme salient to Education that is Multicultural and Social Reconstructionist.

For example, a history course could begin with the following problem. Americans today as well as historically have proclaimed the United States stands for equality, justice, and liberty for all. Yet, one can amass abundant data illustrating great inequalities, lack of justice, and restricted liberties in the United States.

26   Historically, how have different groups defined "equality," "justice," and "liberty," and how have the different definitions been acted out and contested? Using these questions as a basis for analysis, one could then structure a fascinating examination of United States history that would connect with questions Americans today are asking.

In the Social Reconstructionist Approach, students are encouraged to learn to take action on issues. On the basis of studying an issue such as religious freedom, for example, some members of a class may decide to organize a letter-writing campaign to congressional representatives on behalf of Native American religious freedom.

28   Ultimately, I regard this last approach as the one most in keeping with American ideals of equality and democracy. But the approach takes democracy and equality very seriously, not accepting the platitudes with which we all were raised. As such, it is challenging and uncomfortable for many people. The approach also takes a good deal of work to master, since it builds on the information base of Single-Group Studies and Teaching the Exceptional and Culturally Different. There are texts available to help teachers get

---

* Justification (from the French for "reason to be").

started (Nieto 1992; Schniedewind and Davidson 1983; Sleeter 1991; Sleeter and Grant 1989 and 1988).

In the long run, I do not believe our school system, or our social institutions more broadly, will survive without radical reconstruction. While our own diversity grows, so also does the frustration of people who experience continued blocked access to the "American Dream." Some argue that multicultural education is divisive. To me, multicultural education means listening to and taking seriously what diverse Americans are saying about themselves and the conditions of their lives, then acting on what we learn, to build a better system for us all. Failure to do so is divisive. ❖

References

Alba, Richard D. *Ethnic Identity: The Transformation of White America.* New Haven, Conn.: Yale University Press, 1990.

Churchill, Ward. *Fantasies of the Master Race: Literature, Cinema and the Colonization of American Indians.* Monroe, Me.: Common Courage Press, 1992.

Crawford, Jack. *Bilingual Education: History, Politics, Theory and Practice.* Trenton, N.J.: Crane Publishing Co., 1989.

Grant, Carl A., and Christine E. Sleeter. *Turning on Learning.* Columbus, Oh.: Merrill, 1989.

Lauter, Paul. *Canons and Contexts.* New York: Oxford University Press, 1991.

Nieto, Sonia. *Affirming Diversity.* New York: Longman, 1992.

Schniedewind, Nancy, and Ellen Davidson. *Open Minds to Equality.* Englewood Cliffs, N.J.: Prentice-Hall, 1983.

Shade, Barbara J. R. *Culture, Style, and the Educative Process.* Springfield, Il: Charles C. Thomas, 1989.

Sleeter, Christine E., ed. *Empowerment Through Multicultural Education.* Albany, N.Y.: SUNY Press, 1991.

Sleeter, Christine E., and Carl A. Grant. "An Analysis of Multicultural Education in the United States," *Harvard Educational Review,* 57 (4), 421–444.

Sleeter, Christine E., and Carl A. Grant. *Making Choices for Multicultural Education.* Columbus, Ohio: Merrill, 1988.

Sleeter, Christine E., and Carl A. Grant. "Race, Class, Gender, and Disability in Current Textbooks." *The Politics of the Textbook.* Michael W. Apple and Linda K. Christian-Smith, eds. New York: Routledge, 1991, 78–110.

Trueba, Henry T. *Raising Silent Voices: Educating the Linguistic Minorities for the 21st Century.* New York: Newbury House, 1989.

Questions for Meaning

1. What do different approaches to multicultural education have in common?
2. What does Sleeter mean by "bridges," and what is their purpose?
3. Why do some educators adopt pedagogies designed to teach "the exceptional and culturally different"? On what grounds is this approach questionable?
4. What is necessary to succeed in teaching "single-group studies"?

5. How does the "human relations" approach differ from the "multicultural" approach?
6. Vocabulary: perpetuated (5), stereotyping (10), embedded (13), marginalized (18), daunting (19), pluralism (20), salient (24), platitudes (28).

Questions about Strategy

1. Sleeter opens her article with an emphasis on description. Does she confine herself to describing approaches to multicultural education or does she advocate one or more of these approaches?
2. On what basic principle does Sleeter justify the need for multicultural education?
3. Where does Sleeter advise readers of potential problems in multicultural classrooms? Why does she do this?
4. How does Sleeter respond to the argument that multicultural education is divisive?

DINESH D'SOUZA

THE VISIGOTHS IN TWEED

Born in India, Dinesh D'Souza was educated at Dartmouth, Yale, and Princeton. A critic of what he perceives as the left wing in American education, D'Souza is the author of *Illiberal Education: The Politics of Race and Sex on Campus* (1991), which argues that American higher education is dominated by radicals. His most recent book is *The End of Racism: Principles for a Multiracial Society* (1995). He published this 1991 article in *Forbes,* a widely read business magazine.

"I am a male wasp who attended and succeeded at Choate (preparatory) School, Yale College, Yale Law School, and Princeton Graduate School. Slowly but surely, however, my life-long habit of looking, listening, feeling, and thinking as honestly as possible has led me to see that white, male-dominated, western European culture is the most destructive phenomenon in the known history of the planet.

2   "[This Western culture] is deeply hateful of life and committed to death; therefore, it is moving rapidly toward the destruction of itself and most other life forms on earth. And truly it deserves to die. . . . We have to face our own individual and collective responsibility for what is happening—our greed, brutality, indifference, militarism, racism, sexism, blindness. . . . Meanwhile, everything we have put into motion continues to endanger us more every day."

This bizarre outpouring, so reminiscent of the "confessions" from victims of Stalin's show trials,* appeared in a letter to *Mother Jones* magazine and was written by a graduate of some of our finest schools. But the truth is that the speaker's anguish came not from any balanced assessment but as a consequence of exposure to the propaganda of the new barbarians who have captured the humanities, law, and social science departments of so many of our universities. It should come as no surprise that many sensitive young Americans reject the system that has nurtured them. At Duke University, according to the *Wall Street Journal,* professor Frank Lentricchia in his English course shows the movie *The Godfather* to teach his students that organized crime is "a metaphor for American business as usual."

4   Yes, a student can still get an excellent education—among the best in the world—in computer technology and the hard sciences at American universities. But liberal arts students, including those attending Ivy League schools, are very likely to be exposed to an attempted brainwashing that deprecates Western learning and exalts a neo-Marxist ideology promoted in the name of multiculturalism. Even students who choose hard sciences must often take required courses in the humanities, where they are almost certain to be inundated with an anti-Western, anticapitalist view of the world.

Each year American society invests $160 billion in higher education, more per student than any nation in the world except Denmark. A full 45 percent of this money comes from the federal, state, and local governments. No one can say we are starving higher education. But what are we getting for our money, at least so far as the liberal arts are concerned?

6   A fair question? It might seem so, but in university circles it is considered impolite because it presumes that higher education must be accountable to the society that supports it. Many academics think of universities as intellectual enclaves, insulated from the vulgar capitalism of the larger culture.

Yet, since the academics constantly ask for more money, it seems hardly unreasonable to ask what they are doing with it. Honest answers are rarely forthcoming. The general public sometimes gets a whiff of what is going on—as when Stanford alters its core curriculum in the classics of Western civilization—but it knows very little of the systematic and comprehensive change sweeping higher education.

8   An academic and cultural revolution has overtaken most of our 3,535 colleges and universities. It's a revolution to which most Americans have paid little attention. It is a revolution imposed upon the students by a university elite, not one voted upon or even discussed by the society at large. It amounts, according to University of Wisconsin—Madison Chancellor

---

* During the 1930s, Joseph Stalin conducted a massive purge of the Soviet elite. After being tortured, intellectuals, army officers, and government officials read prepared statements at staged trials before being put to death or imprisoned in concentration camps.

Donna Shalala, to "a basic transformation of American higher education in the name of multiculturalism and diversity."

The central thrust of this "basic transformation" involves replacing traditional core curricula—consisting of the great works of Western culture—with curricula flavored by minority, female, and Third World authors.

10   Here's a sample of the viewpoint represented by the new curriculum. Becky Thompson, a sociology and women's studies professor, in a teaching manual distributed by the American Sociological Association, writes: "I begin my course with the basic feminist principle that in a racist, classist, and sexist society we have all swallowed oppressive ways of being, whether intentionally or not. Specifically, this means that it is not open to debate whether a white student is racist or a male student is sexist. He/she simply is."

Professors at several colleges who have resisted these regnant dogmas about race and gender have found themselves the object of denunciation and even university sanctions. Donald Kagan, dean of Yale College, says: "I was a student during the days of Joseph McCarthy, and there is less freedom now than there was then."*

12   As in the McCarthy period, a particular group of activists has cowed the authorities and bent them to its will. After activists forcibly occupied his office, President Lattie Coor of the University of Vermont explained how he came to sign a sixteen-point agreement establishing, among other things, minority faculty hiring quotas. "When it became clear that the minority students with whom I had been discussing these issues wished to pursue negotiations *in the context of occupied offices . . .* I agreed to enter negotiations." As frequently happens in such cases, Coor's "negotiations" ended in a rapid capitulation by the university authorities.

At Harvard, historian Stephan Thernstrom was harangued by student activists and accused of insensitivity and bigotry. What was his crime? His course included a reading from the journals of slave owners, and his textbook gave a reasonable definition of affirmative action as "preferential treatment" for minorities. At the University of Michigan, renowned demographer Reynolds Farley was assailed in the college press for criticizing the excesses of Marcus Garvey and Malcolm X†; yet the administration did not publicly come to his defense.

14   University leaders argue that the revolution suggested by these examples is necessary because young Americans must be taught to live in and govern a multiracial and multicultural society. Immigration from Asia and Latin America, combined with relatively high minority birth rates, is changing the complexion of America. Consequently, in the words of University of Michigan President James Duderstadt, universities must "create a model of how a more diverse and pluralistic community can work for our society."

---

* Senator Joseph McCarthy (1908–1957) achieved great influence during the early 1950s by charging that important figures in government, the military, and the arts were communists.

† Marcus Garvey (1887–1940) was a prominent African-American leader who worked for world unity among blacks. Malcolm X (1925–1965) was one of the most important advocates for African-Americans during the 1960s.

No controversy, of course, about benign goals such as pluralism or diversity, but there is plenty of controversy about how these goals are being pursued. Although there is no longer a Western core curriculum at Mount Holyoke or Dartmouth, students at those schools must take a course in non-Western or Third World culture. Berkeley and the University of Wisconsin now insist that every undergraduate enroll in ethnic studies, making this virtually the only compulsory course at those schools.

16   If American students were truly exposed to the richest elements of other cultures, this could be a broadening and useful experience. A study of Chinese philosophers such as Confucius or Mencius would enrich students' understanding of how different peoples order their lives, thus giving a greater sense of purpose to their own. Most likely, a taste of Indian poetry such as Rabindranath Tagore's *Gitanjali* would increase the interest of materially minded young people in the domain of the spirit. An introduction to Middle Eastern history would prepare the leaders of tomorrow to deal with the mounting challenge of Islamic culture. It would profit students to study the rise of capitalism in the Far East.

But the claims of the academic multiculturalists are largely phony. They pay little attention to the Asian or Latin American classics. Rather, the non-Western or multicultural curriculum reflects a different agenda. At Stanford, for example, Homer, Plato, Dante, Machiavelli, and Locke are increasingly scarce. But often their replacements are not non-Western classics. Instead the students are offered exotic topics such as popular religion and healing in Peru, Rastafarian poetry, and Andean music.

18   What do students learn about the world from the books they are required to read under the new multicultural rubric? At Stanford one of the non-Western works assigned is *I, Rigoberta Menchú*, subtitled "An Indian Woman in Guatemala."

The book is hardly a non-Western classic. Published in 1983, *I, Rigoberta Menchú* is the story of a young woman who is said to be a representative voice of the indigenous peasantry. Representative of Guatemalan Indian culture? In fact, Rigoberta met the Venezuelan feminist to whom she narrates this story at a socialist conference in Paris, where, presumably, very few of the Third World's poor travel. Moreover, Rigoberta's political consciousness includes the adoption of such politically correct causes as feminism, homosexual rights, socialism, and Marxism. By the middle of the book she is discoursing on "bourgeois youths" and "Molotov cocktails," not the usual terminology of Indian peasants. One chapter is titled "Rigoberta Renounces Marriage and Motherhood," a norm that her tribe could not have adopted and survived.

20   If Rigoberta does not represent the convictions and aspirations of Guatemalan peasants, what is the source of her importance and appeal? The answer is that Rigoberta seems to provide independent Third World corroboration for Western left-wing passions and prejudices. She is a mouthpiece for a sophisticated neo-Marxist critique of Western society, all the more powerful because it seems to issue not from some embittered American

academic but from a Third World native. For professors nourished on the political activism of the late 1960s and early 1970s, texts such as *I, Rigoberta Menchú* offer a welcome opportunity to attack capitalism and Western society in general in the name of teaching students about the developing world.

We learn in the introduction of *I, Rigoberta Menchú* that Rigoberta is a quadruple victim. As a person of color, she has suffered racism. As a woman, she has endured sexism. She lives in South America, which is—of course—a victim of North American colonialism. She is also an Indian, victimized by Latino culture within Latin America.

22   One of the most widely used textbooks in so-called multicultural courses is *Multi-Cultural Literacy,* published by Graywolf Press in St. Paul, Minnesota. The book ignores the *The Tale of Genji,* the Upanishads and Vedas, the Koran and Islamic commentaries. It also ignores such brilliant contemporary authors as Jorge Luis Borges, V.S. Naipaul, Octavio Paz, Naguib Mahfonz, and Wole Soyinka. Instead it offers thirteen essays of protest, including Michele Wallace's autobiographical "Invisibility Blues" and Paula Gunn Allen's "Who Is Your Mother? The Red Roots of White Feminism."

One student I spoke with at Duke University said he would not study *Paradise Lost* because John Milton was a Eurocentric white male sexist. At the University of Michigan, a young black woman who had converted to Islam refused to believe that the prophet Muhammad owned slaves and practiced polygamy. She said she had taken courses on cultural diversity and the courses hadn't taught her that.

24   One of the highlights of this debate on the American campus was a passionate statement delivered a few years ago by Stanford undergraduate William King, president of the Black Student Union, who argued the benefits of the new multicultural curriculum before the faculty senate of the university. Under the old system, he said, "I was never taught . . . the fact that Socrates, Herodotus, Pythagoras, and Solon* studied in Egypt and acknowledged that much of their knowledge of astronomy, geometry, medicine, and building came from the African civilization in and around Egypt. [I was never taught] that the Hippocratic oath acknowledges the Greeks' 'father of medicine,' Imhotep, a black Egyptian pharaoh whom they called Aesculapius. . . . I was never informed when it was found that the 'very dark and wooly haired' Moors in Spain preserved, expanded, and reintroduced the classical knowledge that the Greeks had collected, which led to the 'renaissance.' . . . I read the Bible without knowing Saint Augustine looked black like me, that the Ten Commandments were almost direct copies from the 147 Negative Confessions of Egyptian initiates. . . . I

---

* Socrates (469–399 B.C.) was one of the most important theorists in the development of Western philosophy. Herodotus (484?–425? B.C.) was the first great historian in the West; Pythagoras (582?–507? B.C.) was an important Greek philosopher and mathematician best remembered today for the theorem that the square of the length of the hypotenuse of a right triangle equals the sum of the squares of the lengths of the other two sides; Solon (639?–559? B.C.) was an Athenian statesman and reformer who helped establish the fundamental principles of democracy.

didn't learn Toussaint L'Ouverture's defeat of Napoleon in Haiti directly influenced the French Revolution, or that the Iroquois Indians in America had a representative democracy which served as a model for the American system."

This statement drew wild applause and was widely quoted. The only trouble is that much of it is untrue. There is no evidence that Socrates, Pythagoras, Herodotus, and Solon studied in Egypt, although Herodotus may have traveled there. Saint Augustine was born in North Africa, but his skin color is unknown, and in any case he could not have been mentioned in the Bible; he was born over 350 years after Christ. Viewing King's speech at my request, Bernard Lewis, an expert on Islamic and Middle Eastern culture at Princeton, described it as "a few scraps of truth amidst a great deal of nonsense."

26   Why does multicultural education, in practice, gravitate toward such myths and half-truths? To find out why, it is necessary to explore the complex web of connections that the academic revolution generates among admissions policies, life on campus, and the curriculum.

American universities typically begin with the premise that in a democratic and increasingly diverse society the composition of their classes should reflect the ethnic distribution of the general population. Many schools officially seek "proportional representation," in which the percentage of applicants admitted from various racial groups roughly approximates the ratio of those groups in society at large.

28   Thus universities routinely admit black, Hispanic, and American Indian candidates over better-qualified white and Asian American applicants. As a result of zealously pursued affirmative action programs, many selective colleges admit minority students who find it extremely difficult to meet demanding academic standards and to compete with the rest of the class. This fact is reflected in the dropout rates of blacks and Hispanics, which are more than 50 percent higher than those of whites and Asians. At Berkeley a study of students admitted on a preferential basis between 1978 and 1982 concluded that nearly 70 percent failed to graduate within five years.

For affirmative action students who stay on campus, a common strategy of dealing with the pressures of university life is to enroll in a distinctive minority organization. Among such organizations at Cornell University are Lesbian, Gay & Bisexual Coalition; La Asociacion Latina; National Society of Black Engineers; Society of Minority Hoteliers; Black Students United; and Simba Washanga.

30   Although the university brochures at Cornell and elsewhere continue to praise integration and close interaction among students from different backgrounds, the policies practiced at these schools actually encourage segregation. Stanford, for example, has "ethnic theme houses" such as the African house called Ujaama. And President Donald Kennedy has said that one of his educational objectives is to "support and strengthen ethnic theme houses." Such houses make it easier for some minority students to feel comfortable but help to create a kind of academic apartheid.

The University of Pennsylvania has funded a black yearbook, even though only 6 percent of the student body is black and all other groups appeared in the general yearbook. Vassar, Dartmouth, and the University of Illinois have allowed separate graduation activities and ceremonies for minority students. California State University at Sacramento has just established an official "college within a college" for blacks.

32 Overt racism is relatively rare at most campuses, yet minorities are told that bigotry operates in subtle forms such as baleful looks, uncorrected stereotypes, and "institutional racism"—defined as the underrepresentation of blacks and Hispanics among university trustees, administrators, and faculty.

Other groups such as feminists and homosexuals typically get into the game, claiming their own varieties of victim status. As Harvard political scientist Harvey Mansfield bluntly puts it, "White students must admit their guilt so that minority students do not have to admit their incapacity."

34 Even though universities regularly accede to the political demands of victim groups, their appeasement gestures do not help black and Hispanic students get a genuine liberal arts education. They do the opposite, giving the apologists of the new academic orthodoxy a convenient excuse when students admitted on a preferential basis fail to meet academic standards. At this point student activists and administrators often blame the curriculum. They argue that it reflects a "white male perspective" that systematically depreciates the views and achievements of other cultures, minorities, women, and homosexuals.

With this argument, many minority students can now explain why they had such a hard time with Milton in the English department, Publius in political science, and Heisenberg in physics. Those men reflected white male aesthetics, philosophy, and science. Obviously, nonwhite students would fare much better if the university created more black or Latino or Third World courses, the argument goes. This epiphany leads to a spate of demands: Abolish the Western classics, establish new departments such as Afro-American Studies and Women's Studies, hire minority faculty to offer distinctive black and Hispanic "perspectives."

36 Multicultural or non-Western education on campus frequently glamorizes Third World cultures and omits inconvenient facts about them. In fact, several non-Western cultures are caste-based or tribal, and often disregard norms of racial equality. In many of them feminism is virtually nonexistent, as indicated by such practices as dowries, widow-burning, and genital mutilation; and homosexuality is sometimes regarded as a crime or mental disorder requiring punishment. These nasty aspects of the non-Western cultures are rarely mentioned in the new courses. Indeed, Bernard Lewis of Princeton argues that while slavery and the subjugation of women have been practiced by all known civilizations, the West at least has an active and effective movement for the abolition of such evils.

Who is behind this academic revolution, this contrived multiculturalism? The new curriculum directly serves the purposes of a newly ascendant generation of young professors, weaned in the protest culture of the late 1960s and early 1970s. In a frank comment, Jay Parini, who teaches English at Middlebury College, writes, "After the Vietnam War, a lot of us didn't just crawl back into our library cubicles. We stepped into academic positions. . . . Now we have tenure, and the work of reshaping the university has begun in earnest."

38   The goal that Parini and others like him pursue is the transformation of the college classroom from a place of learning to a laboratory of indoctrination for social change. Not long ago most colleges required that students learn the basics of the physical sciences and mathematics, the rudiments of economics and finance, and the fundamental principles of American history and government. Studies by the National Endowment for the Humanities show that this coherence has disappeared from the curriculum. As a result, most universities are now graduating students who are scientifically and culturally impoverished, if not illiterate.

At the University of Pennsylvania, Houston Baker, one of the most prominent black academics in the country, denounces reading and writing as oppressive technologies and celebrates such examples of oral culture as the rap group N.W.A. (Niggers With Attitude). One of the group's songs is about the desirability of killing policemen. Alison Jaggar, who teaches women's studies at the University of Colorado, denounces the traditional nuclear family as a "cornerstone of women's oppression" and anticipates scientific advances enabling men to carry fetuses in their bodies so that child-bearing responsibilities can be shared between the sexes. Duke professor Eve Sedgwick's scholarship is devoted to unmasking what she terms the heterosexual bias in Western culture, a project that she pursues through papers such as "Jane Austen and the Masturbating Girl" and "How To Bring Your Kids Up Gay."

40   Confronted by racial tension and Balkanization on campus, university leaders usually announce that, because of a resurgence of bigotry, "more needs to be done." They press for redoubled preferential recruitment of minority students and faculty, funding for a new Third World or Afro-American center, mandatory sensitivity education for whites, and so on. The more the university leaders give in to the demands of minority activists, the more they encourage the very racism they are supposed to be fighting. Surveys indicate that most young people today hold fairly liberal attitudes toward race, evident in their strong support for the civil rights agenda and for interracial dating. However, these liberal attitudes are sorely tried by the demands of the new orthodoxy: many undergraduates are beginning to rebel against what they perceive as a culture of preferential treatment and double standards actively fostered by university policies.

Can there be a successful rolling back of this revolution, or at least of its excesses? One piece of good news is that blatant forms of racial preference are having an increasingly tough time in the courts, and this has implications for university admissions policies. The Department of Education is more vigilant than it used to be in investigating charges of discrimination against whites and Asian Americans. With help from Washington director Morton Halperin, the American Civil Liberties Union has taken a strong stand against campus censorship. Popular magazines such as *Newsweek* and *New York* have poked fun at "politically correct" speech. At Tufts University, undergraduates embarrassed the administration into backing down on censorship by putting up taped boundaries designating areas of the university to be "free speech zones," "limited speech zones," and "Twilight Zones."

42   Even some scholars on the political left are now speaking out against such dogmatism and excess. Eugene Genovese, a Marxist historian and one of the nation's most respected scholars of slavery, argues that "too often we find that education has given way to indoctrination. Good scholars are intimidated into silence, and the only diversity that obtains is a diversity of radical positions." More and more professors from across the political spectrum are resisting the politicization and lowering of standards. At Duke, for example, sixty professors, led by political scientist James David Barber, a liberal Democrat, have repudiated the extremism of the victims' revolution. To that end they have joined the National Association of Scholars, a Princeton, New Jersey-based group devoted to fairness, excellence, and rational debate in universities.

But these scholars need help. Resistance on campus to the academic revolution is outgunned and sorely needs outside reinforcements. Parents, alumni, corporations, foundations, and state legislators are generally not aware that they can be very effective in promoting reform. The best way to encourage reform is to communicate in no uncertain terms to university leadership and, if necessary, to use financial incentives to assure your voice is heard. University leaders do their best to keep outsiders from meddling or even finding out what exactly is going on behind the tall gates, but there is little doubt that they would pay keen attention to the views of the donors on whom they depend. By threatening to suspend donations if universities continue harmful policies, friends of liberal learning can do a lot. In the case of state-funded schools, citizens and parents can pressure elected representatives to ask questions and demand more accountability from the taxpayer-supported academics.

44   The illiberal revolution can be reversed only if the people who foot the bills stop being passive observers. Don't just write a check to your alma mater; that's an abrogation of responsibility. Keep abreast of what is going on and don't be afraid to raise your voice and even to close your wallet in protest. Our Western, free-market culture need not provide the rope to hang itself. ❖

Questions for Meaning

1. Who were the Visigoths? What does D'Souza mean by "Visigoths in tweed"?

2. Why does D'Souza believe that the general public deserves a voice in determining college curriculums?
3. Why does D'Souza believe that universities are fostering a "contrived multiculturalism" rather than a curriculum that is truly multicultural?
4. What connection does D'Souza make between social activism in the 1960s and current interest in multicultural education?
5. What does D'Souza mean when he refers, in paragraph 40, to "Balkanization on campus"?
6. Vocabulary: indifference (2), enclaves (6), regnant (11), capitulation (12), harangued (13), pluralistic (14), indigenous (19), corroboration (20), polygamy (23), zealously (28), epiphany (35).

Questions about Strategy

1. D'Souza devotes the first two paragraphs of his argument to quoting someone with a view very different from his own. What does he achieve by this strategy?
2. In paragraph 11, D'Souza incorporates an allusion to Joseph McCarthy. What is his reason for doing so?
3. Where does D'Souza respond to arguments made by advocates of multiculturalism? Does he make any concessions?
4. In paragraphs 18 through 21, D'Souza discusses a book by Rigoberta Menchú. Why does he devote so much space to this example? Was it a wise decision?
5. According to D'Souza, "universities routinely admit black, Hispanic, and American Indian candidates over better-qualified white and Asian American applicants." How well does he support this claim?
6. Toward what kind of audience is this argument directed?
7. Paragraphs 19, 29, 33, and 34 include references to homosexuality. What role do they play in D'Souza's argument? How do they affect you?

MARILYN FRIEDMAN

MULTICULTURAL EDUCATION AND FEMINIST ETHICS

Believing that the standard curriculum was designed by men and focused almost exclusively on works written by men, feminist scholars have worked in recent decades to ensure that works by women are included in college courses. But are the interests and needs of women adequately met simply by reading works written by women? How should such material be taught? And to what extent is the feminist perspective of Western scholars applicable to the study of non-Western cultures? These are among the questions addressed here by philosopher Marilyn Friedman, in an argument first published in 1995. Friedman is the author of *What Are Friends For?: Feminist Perspectives on Personal Relationships and Moral Theory* (1993). As you read, note how Friedman examines the questions that interest her from more than one perspective.

——————————————— Abstract ———————————————

Feminist ethics supports the contemporary educational trend toward increased multiculturalism and a diminished emphasis on the Western canon. First, I outline a feminist ethical justification for this development. Second, I argue that Western canon studies should not be altogether abandoned in a multicultural curriculum. Third, I suggest that multicultural education should help combat oppression in addition to simply promoting awareness of diversity. Fourth, I caution against an arrogant moralism in the teaching of multiculturalism.

In 1993, the College of Arts and Sciences at my university, Washington University in St. Louis ("Wash. U."), doubled the number of multicultural courses required of undergraduates in Arts and Sciences. Students were formerly required to take at least one course from among these three areas of study: minority groups in the United States, non-European societies outside the United States, and gender studies.[1] Now students must take at least two courses from these three areas and from two different areas. At the same time, Wash. U. does not require its Arts and Sciences students to take any courses in Western civilization or Western classics. Such courses *may* be used to satisfy general requirements in the areas of literature, art, history, and values, but they are not required.

2   The move to double the multicultural studies requirement at Wash. U. was proposed and adopted with little controversy. Similar curricular changes at other universities, however, have caused divisive confrontations and have sparked popular debates so heated that they are often referred to

as "wars," as in "the culture wars." Over the past decade, books and articles have appeared which excoriate multicultural education with such hostile titles as *Illiberal Education: The Politics of Race and Sex on Campus* (D'Souza 1991), *Tenured Radicals: How Politics Has Corrupted Our Higher Education* (Kimball 1990), *Impostors in the Temple* (Anderson 1991), and "The Visigoths in Tweed" (D'Souza 1992).*

Feminist ethics, in its most interesting contemporary manifestations, endorses the trend toward multicultural education and toward a diminished emphasis on the study of the canonical literatures of the West. First (Section I), I outline the feminist ethical justification for this educational change. Then (Section II), I consider whether the multicultural program requires abandoning the study of the Western canon. Next (Section III), I compare two different approaches to multicultural education. Finally (Section IV), I look at some feminist complications within multiculturalism.

I. Feminist Ethics and Multicultural Education

4 The feminist ethics with which most of us in the United States are familiar is largely a Western product, with white, middle-class, and heterosexual strains predominating. White, Western, middle-class heterosexual feminist ethics draws its inspiration from at least two sources: first, those values that dominant cultures of the West have traditionally associated with the feminine, and, second, the political project of ending women's pervasive subordination to men and their oppression by systems of male power and authority.

These projects are not unrelated. One facet of the project of ending women's subordination is to reclaim those values traditionally associated with women and women's social roles but culturally devalued under systems of male power. To elevate cultural esteem for values traditionally associated (rightly or wrongly) with women will help somewhat to elevate cultural esteem for women. This is the project for which Carol Gilligan, Nel Noddings, and, with importance differences, Sara Ruddick became famous.[2] So influential have these thinkers been that, for awhile during the 1980s, "feminist ethics" meant just the values that they famously championed: care, nurturance, and an emphasis on close personal relationships. I will refer to these and related values as "care ethics," an approach that should be distinguished from the other project of feminist ethics which will be my main focus of concern. Care ethics is a legitimate part, though not the whole, of feminist ethics. The other project of feminist ethics is, in my view, more nearly definitive of feminist ethics as a whole.

6 The second source of feminist ethics is the project of ending women's subordination. This larger project puts the status of care ethics into question by promoting an attitude of *suspicion* toward the values traditionally associated with women. Those values, after all, arose out of and reflect

* For "The Visigoths in Tweed," see pp. 470–478.

women's traditionally subordinated status. To promote esteem for women as nurturers, for example, is to risk implicitly endorsing the stereotype that women are merely nurturers, a view that would reinforce social practices by which women are excluded from non-nurturing occupations and activities. To celebrate the work that women have always done to sustain intimate relationships is to risk forgetting how women are abused, exploited, or oppressed in many of those same relationships. The project of ending women's subordination calls for a vigilant attentiveness to the social context of power relations in which caring and close relationships are located and the reconceptualization of all values and practices in the light of this context. Nothing traditional, on this approach, can be taken simply at face value.

Although white, Western, middle-class feminist ethics grew out of an implicitly parochial focus on the subordination of only some classes and groups of women within certain Western societies, the scope of its vocabulary and its articulated aspirations have always been global. Presumptuous or unrealistic as it may have been, Western feminists have talked about global sisterhood and called for an end to the oppression and subordination of women in general in all human communities and subcommunities. This formidable goal requires collective action on a grand scale, a requirement which, in turn, generates the preeminent feminist value of community and solidarity among all women.

8   We are now very familiar with the argument that, despite the rhetoric of global sisterhood, women are not all the same and that the political and intellectual work of white, Western, middle-class heterosexual feminists often does not encompass other women. Some of the differences among women have to do with systems of oppression other than sex/gender, systems in which some women become oppressors toward other women as well as toward some men.

Genuine solidarity with women in general calls, at the very least, for white Western feminists to acknowledge and work to diminish the oppressive relations among women. It also provides its own rationale for solidarity with those men who have been victimized by oppressions such as racism, heterosexism, and colonialism. To be sure, efforts to form either of these sorts of community face formidable obstacles. Nevertheless, despite the failure to live up to its articulated ideals, Western feminism still *aims* for genuine solidarity among women worldwide, and perhaps for solidarity among all oppressed groups.

10   It is widespread among (Western) feminists to regard as devastating the criticism that a feminist text has ignored the perspectives or experiences of, say, lesbians or women of color. This critical strategy presupposes that white, Western, middle-class, heterosexual feminists should indeed take account of the perspectives of women different from themselves. Those women who criticize white Western (etc.) feminists in these terms are not thereby contesting the value of global solidarity among women. Their charge is, rather, that white Western (etc.) feminists fail to promote precisely this value, fail, that is, to engage in genuine dialogue and community-building with all women. The importance of worldwide solidarity among women, to the extent that it is genuinely realizable, is not itself in question.

The ideal of female global solidarity in turn suggests the importance of communication and dialogue between women worldwide. One pervasive feature of oppression is the silencing of viewpoint. Overcoming oppression must involve overcoming the silencing of the oppressed. Those engaged in a common opposition to oppression must certainly not engage in silencing each other. Communication among all women is therefore a primary concern so that we do not perpetuate oppression among women. In addition, our contributions to public political debate are important as a means by which we can fight the subordination of women. Communication aimed at public culture is one means of struggle against oppressive cultural practices.

12   A multicultural curriculum can help to promote these ends. First, it can facilitate encounters between white, Western, middle-class, heterosexual women and women (and oppressed men) of other global communities and of marginalized Western subcommunities. Such encounters will expand the possibilities for global solidarity among women (and among the oppressed in general). Second, a multicultural curriculum can help open up public cultural space for dialogue between Westerners and members of non-Western groups as well as between privileged Westerners and those Westerners who have been traditionally marginalized and silenced within Western culture. Western feminist ethics, therefore, easily endorses a multicultural curriculum.

None of this is new to feminists. There are, however, a number of unsettling—and unsettled—questions raised for feminists by multicultural education, especially when it is considered as a means of ending the oppression of women (and other overlapping groups). I now turn to some of those questions.

II. Multiculturalism Plus Western Studies

14   One set of questions revolves around this query: Should U.S. students be encouraged or required to abandon the study of the Western canon altogether and replace it entirely with multicultural studies? In my view, the answer is "no." My reasons for defending the study of the Western canon, however, are quite different from the arguments of those who promote the Western canon in the "culture wars."

Western canon promoters do so for several reasons. Their most common claims are that Western canonical works: (1) address universal human interests, (2) have extraordinary aesthetic merit, (3) constitute "our" cultural heritage, and (4) constitute the foundational values that undergird and unify "our" society.[3] Western canon promoters sometimes argue that our nation will be imperiled if the Western canon is not placed at the center of our academic curriculum (Kagan 1991). The implicit assumption of this view seems to be that familiarity with the political principles espoused in the canon will make us all "good citizens," compliant law-abiders who would never seriously disrupt U.S. political institutions.

16   All four of the above arguments for studying the Western canon have been challenged.[4] Many critics, for example, have noted the falsification

involved when works by a minuscule number of Europeans and EuroAmericans are counted as "the" intellectual heritage of all the people of the United States (see, e.g., Gates 1991). The claim that Western canonical works address universal human interests is also rather suspect, especially if made exclusively or predominantly by Westerners themselves. In response to that claim, I have elsewhere[5] offered this guideline: *No universalization without representation!*

Nevertheless, I believe that an introduction to the Western canon should be required reading for U.S. students *along with* requirements in both non-Western cultures and Western subcultures. *My* reasons are these. The intellectual heritage that is called "ours" in the United States consists of works that, in various ways, have established themselves as historically dominant in U.S. society, for example, by providing some of the intellectual rationales at the foundation of U.S. government. U.S. government and culture intrude inescapably into the lives of all those who live in the United States, even those who do not count those foundational ideals as their "own." U.S. education should certainly acquaint its students with the values and ideals underlying the government and culture that dominate life in this society.

18   In addition, familiarity with the Western canon is essential for Western feminist politics. A knowledgeable social criticism and an effective political activism require some familiarity with the dominant traditions and institutions to be contested. At the very least, anyone who publicly challenges conventional treatments of gender, race, and so on in U.S. society already risks being attacked and discredited intellectually. To display ignorance about traditional U.S. values and ideals is to intensify that risk. Even the most extreme anti-Western political activist can grasp how prudential it is to "know thine enemy."

Furthermore, many political battles in this country are still waged in the name of various classically Western ideals. The fact that those ideals are deployed as political rhetoric, however, does not entail that they are genuinely implemented in practice. Much of the public political rhetoric about rights, justice, liberty, and equality is mere symbol manipulation designed to win adherents to what are partisan political causes that do not in fact promote *for everyone* the values that they trumpet.

20   It is important for a Western feminist to determine whether women's subordination in Western society derives from the actual implementation of Western values that happen to be worthless, or, rather, from the *failure* to implement Western values that do happen to be worthwhile.[6] This complicated determination calls, at the very least, for the study of Western classics of social and political philosophy along with the study of works that explore actual conditions in contemporary society and culture. Thus, the best education for effective political struggle in the West combines the study of Western classics with contemporary nonclassical materials, at least some of which are empirically oriented. The point is that Western classics need not, indeed should not, be neglected as a foundation for Western political struggle.

It is also well to remember that even within the Western canon, there is diversity. Western cultural works do not unanimously endorse the modern "heteropatriarchal-capitalist state." Some canonical writings of the West themselves criticize the political ideals and values that ground U.S. society. Marx's critique of capitalism, to take the most obvious example, has canonical stature even in the estimation of many of his staunchest critics.

22   As feminists, we are familiar with the distortions involved when antifeminists generalize about *us* in ways that ignore the diversity among us. Similarly, it is a mistake to generalize about the Western canon in a way that ignores its diversity. Deliberate ignorance of the intellectual foundations of government and culture in the societies in which we each live and struggle would disserve our educational credibility as well as our political aspirations.

III. External Questions

The proponents of multicultural education, in general, have two aims: first, to promote diversity in U.S. education along with appreciation of the cultural achievements of societies other than the United States as well as non-dominant subcultures within the United States, and second, to challenge systems of subordination and oppression, both in the West and elsewhere.[7] These ends are not the same. Educating students to appreciate global cultural diversity *might* promote challenges to oppression in Western societies and elsewhere, but it does not necessarily do so.

24   Many promoters of the Western canon, for example, have responded to multiculturalists by conceding that knowledge of cultural diversity is, in itself, worthwhile. After all, it's a small world, isn't it? For some of these cultural diversificationists, to be sure, the aim is still ultimately to promote U.S. global power. After all, a knowledge of foreign societies is good for business. We might be more competitive internationally if we understand the customs and tastes of our global customers and competitors. Some diversificationist canon promoters, however, are not so chauvinistic. Although dedicated to emphasizing the Western canon in U.S. education, they rightly recognize that there is intrinsic value in studies that also expose U.S. students to the lives and perspectives of people beyond our borders.

Nevertheless, when Western canon promoters thus condone multicultural diversity, their concession is usually limited simply to the ideal of cultural diversity as such. Diversity, unfortunately, is a value that one can endorse without any interest whatsoever in combating gender or other oppression.[8] Those Western canon promoters who accede to multicultural education still typically continue to reject the multiculturalist idea that education should help challenge systems of human oppression.

26   This qualified response (of valuing diversity yet still opposing the educational politics of combating oppression) is more difficult for multiculturalists to contest than simple rejection. Against such opposition, the central controversy changes. Instead of debating whether *or not* to include multicultural works in the educational curriculum, we must debate *which* multicultural works to include. The non-Western works that Western canon promoters tolerate are often limited simply to non-Western classics: the

Koran, the *Analects* of Confucius, the Bhagavad Gita, and so on (see, e.g., D'Souza 1991, 73–75). The nonclassical multicultural works that focus on oppressive global practices remain just as controversial as ever.

Dinesh D'Souza, for example, approves of the study of non-Western classics, but ridicules the multiculturalists' use of such contemporary works as *I, Rigoberta Menchú: An Indian Woman in Guatemala* (Menchú 1983).[9] This book recounts the autobiographical oral narrative of Rigoberta Menchú, an illiterate Guatemalan of indigenous ancestry. According to D'Souza, Menchú does not genuinely represent Guatemalan culture. In his view, she has attracted multicultural attention only because she has been "pierced by the arrows" of racism, sexism, and colonialism. She is, in other words, a "consummate victim" who can serve as a "mouthpiece for a sophisticated left-wing critique of Western society (D'Souza 1991, 72)."

28   D'Souza's condescending first-name reference to Menchú ("Rigoberta") throughout his discussion does not inspire confidence in his analysis. Recent events have further confirmed its unreliability. D'Souza had presumed, in his 1991 best-seller, *Illiberal Education,* that the woman, Rigoberta Menchú, had no cultural importance and that her popularity with multiculturalists was a sure sign of the educational bankruptcy of multicultural studies. Menchú, however, has since become internationally renowned for her nonviolent social activism in support of indigenous peoples throughout the Americas. Indeed, she was awarded the Nobel Peace Prize for 1992 (McKeown 1992).

Menchú's award adds public credibility to multiculturalist proposals. Obviously, however, most works favored by multiculturalists have not received Nobel Prizes. Without such independent imprimaturs, it is more difficult to convince a skeptical public to study those non-Western and Western noncanonical works that *challenge* Western forms of oppression. Critics of multiculturalism can condemn such studies as exemplifying an ideological "culture of complaint,"[10] thereby trivializing the whole project of combating oppression.

30   This means that although multiculturalists (in my estimation) will likely succeed at fostering greater U.S. study of non-Western national cultures, we stand far less chance of convincing the public that culturally diverse education should aim at ending subordination and oppression. For this focus to be implemented in actual multicultural courses, those courses will have to be taught by faculty members who believe that this focus is appropriate.[11]

A related issue has to do with the *way* in which both Western and non-Western materials are taught. The teaching of a work can significantly shape the way in which the work is received by students. A teacher can employ a pedagogical style which emphasizes the importance of the work and its contribution to knowledge or which, by contrast, emphasizes the criticism of ideas presented in the work. And ideas can be criticized at their foundational levels or merely at the level of their superficial details.

32   Thus, for multicultural courses and, indeed, for courses in the Western classics, the precise works that are taught and the manner in which they are

taught become matters of the greatest urgency. This means that the staffing of such courses is an implicit site of multicultural struggle in U.S. education today. Multiculturalists could approach this problem by trying to prevent Western canon promoters from teaching non-Western courses, even when they have the right "scholarly" credentials, or by monitoring the course content and pedagogy of those canon promoters who teach non-Western (and even Western-oriented) courses. These strategies, however, would be bad ones. Interfering with the faculty autonomy of traditionalists would not only risk a backlash that could discredit the multicultural project; it would also undermine the same protection for multiculturalists. Better to let a variety of people teach non-Western courses, making sure to support teachers who do conceive of education as a means of challenging oppression—and then vigilantly guard the faculty autonomy of *those* teachers.

IV. Internal Questions

The feminist ethics most familiar to people in the United States is a Western phenomenon. The educational controversies that I am exploring pertain to innovations in the U.S. educational system at all levels. The students whose education is at stake are predominantly U.S. citizens. Many of those students who reach the postsecondary level enjoy at least some degree of class privilege, an advantage that will be further accentuated for those who complete their college degrees. Thus, multiculturalism in colleges and universities affects what is largely a cultural elite. The amount of their education that is at stake, however, is a relatively small portion. At Wash. U., as I noted earlier, only six out of a required 120 hours (and only for Arts and Sciences undergraduates) must come from the assortment of multicultural course offerings. With these limitations in mind, I will finish by identifying some areas of concern within the multicultural educational project itself.

34   Who is the "we" whose educational and cultural system is at the center of this controversy? Who is the "we" that aims to diversify U.S. education and diminish oppression within the U.S. and elsewhere? Many of "us" who promote these courses are white, middle-class, Western heterosexual feminists. When "we" promote multicultural education, we do not forsake the privilege of our status, but rather exercise it to fashion an academic curriculum that realizes our educational values. Only those with the power to influence U.S. education could have this impact on U.S. cultural life.

This does not mean that we should stop promoting the multicultural project. It does mean that we should be vigilant about how we promote it. If one major goal of the multicultural project is to diminish systems of gender (and other) oppression in the United States and elsewhere, then multicultural education is not simply an end in itself, but is also a means to at least one further end: global human betterment. The point of multicultural education is not simply for students to have the educational equivalent of a few fine meals at "ethnic" restaurants, returning home afterward to life as usual. One peril to avoid is a kind of shopping-mall consumerism that endorses multicultural studies merely for the edification, enrichment, and diversion of privileged U.S. students. The project of diminishing systems of subordination and oppression calls instead for serious commitment and engagement.

36   A different peril, however, looms for the committed opponent of oppression. Such commitments might lead to oppressive and arrogant forms of struggle *against* oppression. Practices of clitoridectomy and the veiling and confinement of women under Islam, for example, arouse the repugnance and anger of white Western middle-class feminists. It is tempting to work against such forms of oppression from the outside, even without consulting the women who endure them, much as the British did when they used their imperial power to criminalize the Hindu practice of suttee, or widow-burning, in India during the nineteenth century.[12]

These measures raise a philosophical quandary. One prominent aspect of oppression is the denial to oppressed people of the sort of daily independence and self-determination that non-oppressed or less-oppressed people enjoy in some measure. When we force someone to be "free," however, there is a sense in which we continue to deny her self-determination. There is a kind of *emancipationist imperialism* involved in "freeing" someone from conditions which she herself does not regard as seriously oppressive and would not, on her own, challenge.

38   This problem is not merely an international one; it arises as well within cultures and subcultures. Many U.S. feminists are puzzled by the women within our own communities who appear to tolerate or endorse the social practices that subordinate women to male power. With other women of my own subculture, however, I share a sociohistorical context and much common background understanding on the basis of which I can try to initiate dialogue in which we discuss and debate our contrary views. National boundaries with their frequent language barriers make such communication difficult if not impossible. Lacking sufficient dialogue with women of another society, white Western feminists are not likely to understand the whole complex of conditions in which another culture's pattern of gender oppression is located. Women living with a particular misogynist practice might, for example, regard it as the lesser of two evils; to eradicate the practice from outside might actually leave the women vulnerable to a greater evil which they have no other means to combat.

In addition, unless people are ready for a political reform, they may not be able to readjust their lives so as to take advantage of the change. Political reforms that do not arise out of indigenous struggle will probably be wasted efforts doing more harm than good. It is most respectful to women in cultures and subcultures other than my own to remind myself repeatedly that they know, as I seldom do, what it is like to live as women in their cultures. Unless very strong reasons suggest otherwise, I should, thus, avoid activities and teaching styles that challenge the practices of their lives unless invited or welcomed by them to do so. The point is even stronger for U.S. students whose acquaintance with other cultures is limited to six credit hours of undergraduate study.

40   On the other hand, to complicate matters further, I must also remember that self-determination, and its near relations of individuality, independence, and autonomy, are not the sorts of preeminent values for non-Western cultures that they are in Western traditions.[13] When I refrain from intervening in another culture's pattern of gender oppression on the grounds that I would violate the self-determination of the women in that culture, I am appealing to a value that might be of little or no concern to those women. In addition, when the gender oppression is very serious, a matter of life and death, for example, it is no longer obvious that the most respectful attitude is noninterventionist. Should the British, after all, have permitted suttee to continue?

This whole issue may well have to be resolved on a case by case basis. My point, in this essay, is not to present a solution (I have none) but rather to outline this complication in the multiculturalist educational goal of combating oppression on a global scale.

42   A second problem within multicultural education is that the word "multicultural," in contemporary Western usage, has come to demarcate anything that is not-Western, or not-canonically-Western, anything that is excluded from or marginal to whatever happens to be included in the Western canon. The West becomes the "self"-center of the discourse and whatever is not canonically Western is constituted as different, alien, or "other." Multicultural education might thereby reinforce preexisting U.S. tendencies toward cultural arrogance.

Many U.S. citizens, for instance, already believe that Western culture, especially that of the United States, is not merely one among a variety of global cultures, but is preeminent among them. The fact that, since World War II, the United States has dominated much of the globe, economically and militarily, has added to this presumption. It is all too easy for U.S. citizens to lapse into thinking that the comfort, power, and privilege from which the United States reaches out to study other cultures manifests cultural superiority. Multicultural education can seem to confirm that presumption by appearing to be an unselfish gesture of moral nobility by members of a dominant society toward the cultural backwaters of the global underclasses. Here is a Western presumption that multicultural pedagogy must take pains to avoid.

44   A third challenge posed by multicultural education is to rethink the intellectual foundations of human community. Can there be intellectually unified communities without domination? By "intellectual unity," I mean very broadly an agreement on basic values, ideals, or self-conceptions, whether based on reason or passion or both. Multiculturalists have criticized the very concept of the Western canon for elevating the intellectual works of an infinitesimally small and unrepresentative fraction of the Western population to the status of intellectual spokespersons for the whole, many members of which have not heard of, let alone read, the authors in question. Irving Howe,* for example, with no apparent sense of his own

---

* For Howe's defense of the Western Canon, see pp. 493–504.

irony, refers to the Western canon as the "classical heritage of mankind" (Howe 1992, 158, 160).[14] Less sweeping and less overtly male-biased is the common view that the Western canon is the intellectual heritage of all U.S. citizens.

The question for multiculturalists is whether there can be intellectually unified communities that are not thus dominated by a small, highly select number of unrepresentative voices. Do traditional communities such as nations have any intellectual unity at all? If not, then how do they cohere? Or do they?

46   There are several possibilities here. One is that large modern societies such as the United States do indeed cohere but not intellectually; their unity is constituted through nonintellectual means such as economic or administrative practices, social forms that each involve both power and domination. Or perhaps large modern societies are not unified at all. Any appearance of unity may be a mere illusion for privileged members of society whose advantages of class, race, gender, ethnicity, or heterosexuality insulate their self-segregated subcommunities from the true chaos and anarchy of life in a pluralist society.

This problem of unity is of special interest to feminists. The question is: Can there be a genuinely nonhierarchical women's community or feminist community without the intellectual dominance of some voices over others? If not, then how are we to understand the scope and authority of feminist politics? The debate over multicultural education and the Western canon offers us another context in which to rethink this thorny problem. ❖

Notes

1. At some universities, the term "women's studies" is used instead of "gender studies," to indicate the woman-centered focus of the interdisciplinary program in question. "Feminist studies" has a still more precise orientation. Throughout this paper, I use the term "multicultural education" to encompass all of these as well as the more recent lesbian and gay studies programs.
2. The key works are Gilligan (1982), Noddings (1984), and Ruddick (1989).
3. This is how John Searle (1992) summarizes the traditional arguments on behalf of the study of the Western canon. Several of the papers in Berman (1992) defend these arguments; see especially Kimball (1992) and Howe (1992).
4. See, for example, the multiculturalist essays in Berman (1992), Aufderheide (1992), and Gless and Smith (1992).
5. See my lead essay, "Codes, Canons, Correctness, and Feminism," Part II, in Friedman and Narveson (1995). Note that I do not deny that there is intellectual and aesthetic merit to the works included in the ever-shifting Western canon.
6. Perhaps the values are both worthless and not implemented. This possibility strengthens my argument, since, to determine this, it would still be necessary to understand the traditional values along with the actual conditions of contemporary life.
7. This distinction is based on a discussion by Blum (1991–1992).
8. A similar point is made by Gordon and Lubiano (1992).
9. D'Souza discusses this book in (1991, 71–73). I discuss D'Souza on Menchú in my "Codes, Canons, Correctness, and Feminism," Part II (Friedman and Narveson 1995).

10. This phrase appears on the cover of a *TIME* magazine issue, which announced that it was taking a "scorching look at political correctness" (Hughes 1992).

11. In Part IV of my essay, "Codes, Canons, Correctness, and Feminism" (Friedman and Narveson, 1995, n. 8), I point out that a good deal of uncontroversial academic research is directed toward changing social conditions. There is thus nothing inherently anti-academic in such an approach.

12. To be more exact, it was then governor-general of India, Lord William Bettinck, who passed an 1829 regulation that criminalized the practice of burning or burying alive Hindu widows. Until that time, British policy toward suttee had been only mildly negative at best, and Bettinck's action was opposed by many British officials. British imperial policy toward India had been dominated by the aim of preserving colonial power, and many Britons opposed intervening in Hindu religious rites, such as suttee, on the grounds that it would provoke Indian rebellion against British rule. Ironically, it may well have taken the temporary supremacy of British rule, achieved in 1818, to give any effectiveness to the prohibition. Interestingly, Bettinck's action was inspired by his strong commitment to utilitarianism, as bolstered by his contacts with Benthamites such as James Mill. See Datta (1988, esp. chaps. 1, 3).

13. I am grateful to Susan Pinkard for reminding me of this point at a crucial state in my writing of this essay.

14. Howe attributes the phrase "intellectual heritage of mankind" to George Lukacs.

References

Anderson, Martin. 1991. *Impostors in the temple.* New York: Simon and Schuster.

Aufderheide, Patricia. 1992. *Beyond p.c.: Toward a politics of understanding.* St. Paul, MN: Graywolf.

Berman, Paul. 1992. *Debating p.c.* New York: Dell.

Blum, Lawrence A. 1991–92. Antiracism, multiculturalism, and interracial community: Three educational values for a multicultural society. *Distinguished Lecture Series.* Boston: Office of Graduate Studies and Research, University of Massachusetts at Boston.

Datta, V. N. 1988. *Sati: A historical, social and philosophical enquiry into the Hindu rite of widow burning.* Riverdale, MD: Riverdale Co.

D'Souza, Dinesh. 1991. *Illiberal education: The politics of race and sex on campus.* New York: Random House.

————. 1992. The visigoths in tweed. In *Beyond p.c.* See Aufderheide 1992. Reprinted from *Forbes,* 1 April 1991.

Friedman, Marilyn. 1995. Codes, canons, correctness, and feminism. In *Political correctness: For and against.* See Friedman and Narveson 1995.

Friedman, Marilyn and Jan Narveson. 1995. *Political correctness: For and against.* Lanham, MD: Rowman and Littlefield.

Gates, Henry Louis, Jr. 1991. It's not just Anglo-Saxon. *New York Times,* 4 May, sec. A, p. 23.

Gilligan, Carol. 1982. *In a different voice.* Cambridge, MA: Harvard University Press.

Gless, Darryl J. and Barbara Herrnstein Smith, eds. 1992. *The politics of liberal education.* Durham, NC: Duke University Press.

Gordon, Ted and Wahneema Lubiano. 1992. The statement of the black faculty caucus. In *Debating p.c.* See Berman 1992. Reprinted from *The Daily Texan,* The University of Texas at Austin, 3 May 1990.

Howe, Irving. 1992. The value of the canon. In *Debating p.c.* See Berman 1992. Reprinted from *The New Republic,* 1991.

Hughes, Robert. 1992. The fraying of America. *Time,* 3 February, 44–49.

Kagan, Donald. 1991. Western values are central. *New York Times*, 4 May, sec. A, p. 23.

Kimball, Roger. 1992. The periphery v. the center: The MLA in Chicago. In *Debating p.c.* See Berman 1992. Reprinted from *The New Criterion*, February 1991.

————. 1991. *Tenured radicals: How politics has corrupted our higher education.* New York: HarperCollins.

McKeown, Clare. 1992. Rigoberta, nombre de la paz. *Oxfam America News*, Fall, 1, 4.

Menchú, Rigoberta. 1983. *I, Rigoberta Menchú: An Indian woman in Guatemala.* Ed. and intro. Elisabeth Burgos-Debray. Trans. Ann Wright. New York: Verso.

Noddings, Nel. 1984. *Caring.* Berkeley: University of California Press.

Ruddick, Sara. 1989. *Maternal thinking: Toward a politics of peace.* New York: Ballantine Books.

Searle, John. 1992. The storm over the university. In *Debating p.c.* See Berman 1992. Reprinted from *The New York Review of Books*, 6 December 1990.

Questions for Meaning

1. What are the goals of "feminist ethics"? To what extent are its two principal goals complementary?
2. Why does Friedman believe in the importance of communication among women?
3. Why does Friedman believe that feminists should read the Western canon? On what grounds does she question education that focuses exclusively on this canon?
4. According to Friedman, what are the goals of multicultural education? Why does she believe that learning to appreciate diversity is not in itself a sufficient goal?
5. What does Friedman mean by "emancipationist imperialism," and why is she concerned about it?
6. Vocabulary: excoriate (2), parochial (7), espoused (15), staunchest (21), indigenous (27), imprimaturs (29), clitoridectomy (36), quandary (37), misogynist (38).

Questions about Strategy

1. What does Friedman accomplish by opening her argument with information about her own university?
2. In paragraph 3, Friedman explains how her argument is organized. Where else does the assist readers to understand her case?
3. Consider Friedman's response to Dinesh D'Souza's views. (An argument by D'Souza immediately precedes Friedman's essay.) What is her response meant to illustrate? How fairly does Friedman treat D'Souza's views?
4. In paragraphs 36–40, Friedman identifies complications with which she struggles. Do these paragraphs make her argument more persuasive or less?
5. How effective is the conclusion of this argument?

IRVING HOWE

THE VALUE OF THE CANON

The author of numerous books on literature, politics, and ethnicity, Irving Howe has been a productive scholar for more than forty years. He has taught many courses in American literature and published works on Ralph Waldo Emerson, Sherwood Anderson, and William Faulkner. He is also known for *World of Our Fathers: The Journey of the East European Jews to America and the Life They Found and Made* (1989). His *Selected Writings: 1950–1990* were published in 1990. Drawing on his experience as a college professor, Howe published the following article in *The New Republic* in 1991.

Of all the disputes agitating the American campus, the one that seems to me especially significance is that over "the canon." What should be taught in the humanities and social sciences, especially in introductory courses? What is the place of the classics? How shall we respond to those professors who attack "Eurocentrism" and advocate "multiculturalism"? This is not the sort of tedious quarrel that now and then flutters through the academy; it involves matters of public urgency. I propose to see this dispute, at first, through a narrow, even sectarian lens, with the hope that you will come to accept my reasons for doing so.

2   Here, roughly, are the lines of division. On one side stand (too often, fall) the cultural "traditionalists," who may range politically across the entire spectrum. Opposing them is a heterogeneous grouping of mostly younger teachers, many of them veterans of the 1960s, which includes feminists, black activists, Marxists, deconstructionists, and various mixtures of these.

At some colleges and universities traditional survey courses of world and English literature, as also of social thought, have been scrapped or diluted. At others they are in peril. At still others they will be. What replaces them is sometimes a mere option of electives, sometimes "multicultural" courses introducing material from Third World cultures and thinning out an already thin sampling of Western writings, and sometimes courses geared especially to issues of class, race, and gender. Given the notorious lethargy of academic decision-making, there has probably been more clamor than change; but if there's enough clamor, there will be change.

4   University administrators, timorous by inclination, are seldom firm in behalf of principles regarding education. Subjected to enough pressure, many of them will buckle under. So will a good number of professors who vaguely subscribe to "the humanist tradition" but are not famously courageous in its defense. Academic liberalism has notable virtues, but combativeness is not often one of them. In the academy, whichever group goes on the offensive gains an advantage. Some of those who are now attacking

"traditionalist" humanities and social science courses do so out of sincere persuasion; some, from a political agenda (what was at first solemnly and now is half-ironically called p.c.—politically correct); and some from an all-too-human readiness to follow the academic fashion that, for the moment, is "in."

Can we find a neutral term to designate the antitraditionalists? I can't think of a satisfactory one, so I propose an unsatisfactory one: let's agree to call them the insurgents, though in fact they have won quite a few victories. In the academy these professors are often called "the left" or "the cultural left," and that is how many of them see themselves. But this is a comic misunderstanding, occasionally based on ignorance. In behalf of both their self-awareness and a decent clarity of debate, I want to show that in fact the socialist and Marxist traditions have been close to traditionalist views of culture. Not that the left hasn't had its share of ranters (I exclude Stalinists and hooligans) who, in the name of "the revolution," were intent upon jettisoning the culture of the past; but generally such types have been a mere marginal affliction treated with disdain.

6   Let me cite three major figures. Here is Georg Lukacs, the most influential Marxist critic of the twentieth century:

> Those who do not know Marxism may be surprised at the respect for *the classical heritage of mankind* which one finds in the really great representatives of that doctrine. [Emphasis added.]

Here is Leon Trotsky,* arguing in 1924 against a group of Soviet writers who felt that as the builders of "a new society" they could dismiss the "reactionary culture" of the past:

> If I say that the importance of *The Divine Comedy* lies in the fact that it gives me an understanding of the state of mind of certain classes in a certain epoch, this means that I transform it into a *mere historical document.* . . . How is it thinkable that there should be not a historical but a *directly aesthetic relationship* between us and a medieval Italian book? This is explained by the fact that in class society, in spite of its changeability, there are certain common features. Works of art developed in a medieval Italian city can affect us too. What does this require? . . . That these feelings and moods shall have received such broad, intense, powerful expression as to have raised them above the limitations of the life of those days. [Emphasis added.]

8   Trotsky's remarks could serve as a reply to those American professors of literature who insist upon the omnipresence of ideology as it seeps into and perhaps saturates literary texts, and who scoff that only "formalists" believe that novels and poems have autonomous being and value. In arguing, as he did in his book *Literature and Revolution,* that art must be judged by

---

* Leon Trotsky (1879–1940) was one of the leaders of the Bolshevik revolution in Russia. After Lenin's death, he lost influence and eventually his life in a power struggle with Stalin.

"its own laws," Trotsky seems not at all p.c. Still less so is Antonio Gramsci, the Italian Marxist, whose austere opinions about education might make even our conservatives blanch:

> Latin and Greek were learnt through their grammar, mechanically, but the accusation of formalism and aridity is very unjust. . . . In education one is dealing with children in whom one has to inculcate certain habits of diligence, precision, poise (even physical poise), ability to concentrate on specific subjects, which cannot be acquired without the mechanical repetition of disciplined and methodical acts.

These are not the isolated ruminations of a few intellectuals; Lukacs, Trotsky, and Gramsci speak with authority for a view of culture prevalent in the various branches of the Marxist (and also, by the way, the non-Marxist) left. And that view informed many movements of the left. There were the Labor night schools in England bringing to industrial workers elements of the English cultural past; there was the once-famous Rand School of New York City; there were the reading circles that Jewish workers, in both Eastern Europe and American cities, formed to acquaint themselves with Tolstoy, Heine, and Zola.* And in Ignazio Silone's novel *Bread and Wine* we have a poignant account of an underground cell in Rome during the Mussolini years that reads literary works as a way of holding itself together.

10   My interest here is not to vindicate socialism or Marxism—that is another matter. Nor is there anything sacrosanct about the opinions I have quoted or their authors. But it is surely worth establishing that the claims of many academic insurgents to be speaking from a left, let alone a Marxist, point of view are highly dubious. Very well, the more candid among them might reply, so we're not of the left, at least we're not of the "Eurocentric" left. To recognize that would at least help clear the atmosphere. More important, it might shrink the attractiveness of these people in what is perhaps the only area of American society where the label of "the left" retains some prestige.

What we are witnessing on the campus today is a strange mixture of American populist sentiment and French critical theorizing as they come together in behalf of "changing the subject." The populism provides an underlying structure of feeling, and the theorizing provides a dash of intellectual panache. The populism releases anti-elitist rhetoric, the theorizing releases highly elitist language.

12   American populism, with its deep suspicion of the making of distinctions of value, has found expression not only in native sages (Henry Ford: "History is bunk") but also in the writings of a long line of intellectuals—indeed, it's only intellectuals who can give full expression to

---

* Leo Tolstoy (1828–1910) was a Russian novelist whose works include *War and Peace* (1863–1869) and *Anna Karenina* (1875–1877); Heinrich Heine (1797–1856) is widely considered one of the great German poets; Émile Zola (1840–1902) was an important French novelist and social reformer best known today for *Nana* (1888) and *Germinal* (1885).

anti-intellectualism. Such sentiments have coursed through American literature, but only recently, since the counterculture of the 1960s, have they found a prominent place in the universities.

As for the French theorizing—metacritical, quasi-philosophical, and at times of a stupefying verbal opacity—it has provided a buttress for the academic insurgents. We are living at a time when all the once-regnant world systems that have sustained (also distorted) Western intellectual life, from theologies to ideologies, are taken to be in severe collapse. This leads to a mood of skepticism, an agnosticism of judgment, sometimes a world-weary nihilism in which even the most conventional minds begin to question both distinctions of value and the value of distinctions. If you can find projections of racial, class, and gender bias in both a Western by Louis L'Amour and a classical Greek play, and if you have decided to reject the "elitism" said to be at the core of literary distinctions, then you might as well teach the Western as the Greek play. You can make the same political points, and more easily, in "studying" the Western. And, if you happen not to be well informed about Greek culture, it certainly makes things still easier.

14 I grew up with the conviction that what Georg Lukacs calls "the classical heritage of mankind" is a precious legacy. It came out of historical circumstances often appalling, filled with injustice and outrage. It was often, in consequence, alloyed with prejudice and flawed sympathies. Still, it was a heritage that had been salvaged from the nightmares, occasionally the glories, of history, and now we would make it "ours," we who came from poor and working-class families. This "heritage of mankind" (which also includes, of course, Romantic and modernist culture) had been denied to the masses of ordinary people, trained into the stupefaction of accepting, even celebrating, their cultural deprivations. One task of political consciousness was therefore to enable the masses to share in what had been salvaged from the past—the literature, art, music, thought—and thereby to reach an active relation with these. That is why many people, not just socialists but liberals, democrats, and those without political tags, kept struggling for universal education. It was not a given; it had to be won. Often, winning proved to be very hard.

Knowledge of the past, we felt, could humanize by promoting distance from ourselves and our narrow habits, and this could promote critical thought. Even partly to grasp a significant experience or literary work of the past would require historical imagination, a sense of other times, which entailed moral imagination, a sense of other ways. It would create a kinship with those who had come before us, hoping and suffering as we have, seeking through language, sound, and color to leave behind something of enduring value.

16 By now we can recognize that there was a certain naïveté in this outlook. The assumption of progress in education turned out to be as problematic as similar assumptions elsewhere in life. There was an underestimation of

human recalcitrance and sloth. There was a failure to recognize what the twentieth century has taught us: that aesthetic sensibility by no means assures ethical value. There was little anticipation of the profitable industry of "mass culture," with its shallow kitsch and custom-made dreck. Nevertheless, insofar as we retain an attachment to the democratic idea, we must hold fast to an educational vision somewhat like the one I've sketched. Perhaps it is more an ideal to be approached than a goal to be achieved; no matter. I like the epigrammatic exaggeration, if it is an exaggeration, of John Dewey's remark that "the aim of education is to enable individuals to continue their education."*

This vision of culture and education started, I suppose, at some point in the late eighteenth century or the early nineteenth century. It was part of a great sweep of human aspiration drawing upon Western traditions from the Renaissance to the Enlightenment. It spoke in behalf of such liberal values as the autonomy of the self, tolerance for a plurality of opinions, the rights of oppressed national and racial groups, and soon, the claims of the women's movements. To be sure, these values were frequently violated—that has been true for every society in every phase of world history. But the criticism of such violations largely invoked the declared values themselves, and this remains true for all our contemporary insurgencies. Some may sneer at "Western hegemony," but knowingly or not, they do so in the vocabulary of Western values.

18   By invoking the "classical heritage of mankind" I don't propose anything fixed and unalterable. Not at all. There are, say, seven or eight writers and a similar number of social thinkers who are of such preeminence that they must be placed at the very center of this heritage; but beyond that, plenty of room remains for disagreement. All traditions change, simply through survival. Some classics die. Who now reads Ariosto?† A loss, but losses form part of tradition too. And new arrivals keep being added to the roster of classics—it is not handed down from Mt. Sinai or the University of Chicago. It is composed and fought over by cultivated men and women. In a course providing students a mere sample of literature, there should be included some black and women writers who, because of inherited bias, have been omitted in the past. Yet I think we must give a central position to what Professor John Searle in a recent *New York Review of Books* article specifies as "a certain Western intellectual tradition that goes from, say, Socrates to Wittgenstein in philosophy, and from Homer to James Joyce in literature. . . . It is essential to the liberal education of young men and women in the United States that they should receive some exposure to at least some of the great works of this intellectual tradition."

Nor is it true that most of the great works of the past are bleakly retrograde in outlook—to suppose that is a sign of cultural illiteracy. Bring together in a course on social thought selections from Plato and Aristotle,

---

* John Dewey (1859–1952) was an American philosopher and educator who defined basic assumptions about education that subsequently prevailed in our century.

† Ludovico Ariosto (1474–1533) was an important Italian poet, best known for *Orlando furisoso.*

Machiavelli and Rousseau, Hobbes and Locke, Nietzsche and Freud, Marx and Mill, Jefferson and Dewey, and you have a wide variety of opinions, often clashing with one another, sometimes elusive and surprising, always richly complex. These are some of the thinkers with whom to begin, if only later to deviate from. At least as critical in outlook are many of the great poets and novelists. Is there a more penetrating historian of selfhood than Wordsworth? A more scathing critic of society than the late Dickens? A mind more devoted to ethical seriousness than George Eliot? A sharper critic of the corrupting effects of money than Balzac or Melville?

20   These writers don't necessarily endorse our current opinions and pieties—why should they? We read them for what Robert Frost calls "counterspeech," the power and brilliance of *other minds,* and if we can go "beyond" them, it is only because they are behind us.

What is being invoked here is not a stuffy obeisance before dead texts from a dead past, but rather a critical engagement with living texts from powerful minds still very much "active" in the present. And we should want our students to read Shakespeare and Tolstoy, Jane Austen and Kafka, Emily Dickinson and Léopold Sénghor, not because they "support" one or another view of social revolution, feminism, and black self-esteem. They don't, in many instances; and we don't read them for the sake of enlisting them in a cause of our own. We should want students to read such writers so that they may learn to enjoy the activity of mind, the pleasure of forms, the beauty of language—in short, the arts in their own right.

22   By contrast, there is a recurrent clamor in the university for "relevance," a notion hard to resist (who wishes to be known as irrelevant?) but proceeding from an impoverished view of political life, and too often ephemeral in its excitements and transient in its impact. I recall seeing in the late 1960s large stacks of Eldridge Cleaver's *Soul on Ice* in the Stanford University bookstore. Hailed as supremely "relevant" and widely described as a work of genius, this book has fallen into disuse in a mere two decades. Cleaver himself drifted off into some sort of spiritualism, ceasing thereby to be "relevant." Where, then, is *Soul on Ice* today? What lasting value did it impart?

American culture is notorious for its indifference to the past. It suffers from the provincialism of the contemporary, veering wildly from fashion to fashion, each touted by the media and then quickly dismissed. But the past is the substance out of which the present has been formed, and to let it slip away from us is to acquiesce in the thinness that characterizes so much of our culture. Serious education must assume, in part, an adversarial stance toward the very society that sustains it—a democratic society makes the wager that it's worth supporting a culture of criticism. But if that criticism loses touch with the heritage of the past, it becomes weightless, a mere compendium of momentary complaints.

24   Several decades ago, when I began teaching, it could be assumed that entering freshmen had read in high school at least one play by Shakespeare and one novel by Dickens. That wasn't much, but it was something. These days, with the disintegration of the high schools, such an assumption can seldom be made. The really dedicated college teachers of literature feel that,

given the bazaar of elective courses an entering student encounters and the propaganda in behalf of "relevance," there is likely to be only one opportunity to acquaint students with a smattering—indeed, the merest fragment—of the great works from the past. Such teachers take pleasure in watching the minds and sensibilities of young people opening up to a poem by Wordsworth, a story by Chekhov, a novel by Ellison. They feel they have planted a seed of responsiveness that, with time and luck, might continue to grow. And if this is said to be a missionary attitude, why should anyone quarrel with it?

Let me now mention some of the objections one hears in academic circles to the views I have put down here, and then provide brief replies.

26   *By requiring students to read what you call "classics" in introductory courses, you impose upon them a certain worldview—and that is an elitist act.*

In some rudimentary but not very consequential sense, all education entails the "imposing" of values. There are people who say this is true even when children are taught to read and write, since it assumes that reading and writing are "good."

28   In its extreme version, this idea is not very interesting, since it is not clear how the human race could survive if there were not some "imposition" from one generation to the next. But in a more moderate version, it is an idea that touches upon genuine problems.

Much depends on the character of the individual teacher, the spirit in which he or she approaches a dialogue of Plato, an essay by Mill, a novel by D. H. Lawrence. These can be, and have been, used to pummel an ideological line into the heads of students (who often show a notable capacity for emptying them out again). Such pummeling is possible for all points of view but seems most likely in behalf of totalitarian politics and authoritarian theologies, which dispose their adherents to fanaticism. On the other hand, the texts I've mentioned, as well as many others, can be taught in a spirit of openness, so that students are trained to read carefully, think independently, and ask questions. Nor does this imply that the teacher hides his or her opinions. Being a teacher means having a certain authority, but the student should be able to confront that authority freely and critically. This is what we mean by liberal education—not that a teacher plumps for certain political programs, but that the teaching is done in a "liberal" (open, undogmatic) style.

30   I do not doubt that there are conservative and radical teachers who teach in this "liberal" spirit. When I was a student at City College in the late 1930s, I studied philosophy with a man who was either a member of the Communist Party or was "cheating it out of dues." Far from being the propagandist of the Party line, which Sidney Hook kept insisting was the necessary role of Communist teachers, this man was decent, humane, and tolerant. Freedom of thought prevailed in his classroom. He had, you might say, a "liberal" character, and perhaps his commitment to teaching as a vocation was stronger than his loyalty to the Party. Were such things not to happen now and then, universities would be intolerable.

If, then, a university proposes a few required courses so that ill-read students may at least glance at what they do not know, that isn't (necessarily) "elitist." Different teachers will approach the agreed-upon texts in different ways, and that is as it should be. If a leftist student gets "stuck" with a conservative teacher, or a conservative student with a leftist teacher, that's part of what education should be. The university is saying to its incoming students: "Here are some sources of wisdom and beauty that have survived the centuries. In time you may choose to abandon them, but first learn something about them."

32   *Your list of classics includes only dead, white males, all tied in to notions and values of Western hegemony. Doesn't this narrow excessively the horizons of education?*

All depends on how far forward you go to compose your list of classics. If you do not come closer to the present than the mid-eighteenth century, then of course there will not be many, or even any, women in your roster. If you go past the mid-eighteenth century to reach the present, it's not at all true that only "dead, white males" are to be included. For example—and this must hold for hundreds of other teachers also—I have taught and written about Jane Austen, Emily Brontë, Charlotte Brontë, Elizabeth Gaskell, George Eliot, Emily Dickinson, Edith Wharton, Katherine Anne Porter, Doris Lessing, and Flannery O'Connor. I could easily add a comparable list of black writers. Did this, in itself, make me a better teacher? I doubt it. Did it make me a better person? We still lack modes of evaluation subtle enough to say for sure.

34   The absence of women from the literature of earlier centuries is a result of historical inequities that have only partly been remedied in recent years. Virginia Woolf, in a brilliant passage in *A Room of One's Own*, approaches this problem by imagining Judith, Shakespeare's sister, perhaps equally gifted but prevented by the circumstances of her time from developing her gifts:

> Any woman born with a great gift in the sixteenth century would certainly have gone crazed, shot herself, or ended her days in some lonely cottage outside the village, half witch, half wizard, feared and mocked at. . . . A highly gifted girl who had tried to use her gift for poetry would have been so thwarted and hindered by other people, so tortured and pulled asunder by her own contrary instincts, that she must have lost her health and sanity. . . .

The history that Virginia Woolf describes cannot be revoked. If we look at the great works of literature and thought through the centuries until about the mid-eighteenth century, we have to recognize that indeed they have been overwhelmingly the achievements of men. The circumstances in which these achievements occurred may be excoriated. The achievements remain precious.

36   *To isolate a group of texts as the canon is to establish a hierarchy of bias, in behalf of which there can be no certainty of judgment.*

There is mischief or confusion in the frequent use of the term "hierar-chy" by the academic insurgents, a conflation of social and intellectual uses. A social hierarchy may entail a (mal)distribution of income and power, open to the usual criticisms; a literary "hierarchy" signifies a judg-ment, often based on historical experience, that some works are of supreme or abiding value, while others are of lesser value, and still others quite with-out value. To prefer Elizabeth Bishop to Judith Krantz is not of the same order as sanctioning the inequality of wealth in the United States. To prefer Shakespeare to Sidney Sheldon is not of the same order as approving the hierarchy of the nomenklatura* in Communist dictatorships.

38   As for the claim that there is no certainty of judgment, all tastes being historically molded or individually subjective, I simply do not believe that the people who make it live by it. This is an "egalitarianism" of valuation that people of even moderate literacy know to be false and unworkable—the making of judgments, even if provisional and historically modulated, is inescapable in the life of culture. And if we cannot make judgments or demonstrate the grounds for our preferences, then we have no business teaching literature—we might just as well be teaching advertising—and there is no reason to have departments of literature.

The claim that there can be value-free teaching is a liberal deception or self-deception; so too the claim that there can be texts untouched by social and political bias. Politics or ideology is everywhere, and it's the better part of hon-esty to admit this.

40   If you look hard (or foolishly) enough, you can find political and so-cial traces everywhere. But to see politics or ideology in all texts is to scruti-nize the riches of literature through a single lens. If you choose, you can read all or almost all literary works through the single lens of religion. But what a sad impoverishment of the imagination, and what a violation of our sense of reality, this represents. Politics may be "in" everything, but not everything is in politics. A good social critic will know which texts are invit-ing to a given approach and which it would be wise to leave to others.

To see politics everywhere is to diminish the weight of politics. A seri-ous politics recognizes the limits of its reach; it deals with public affairs while leaving alone large spheres of existence: it seeks not to "totalize" its range of interest. Some serious thinkers believe that the ultimate aim of pol-itics should be to render itself superfluous. That may seem an unrealizable goal; meanwhile, a good part of the struggle for freedom in recent decades has been to draw a line beyond which politics must not tread. The same holds, more or less, for literary study and the teaching of literature.

42   *Wittingly or not, the traditional literary and intellectual canon was based on received elitist ideologies, the values of Western imperialism, racism, sexism, etc., and the teaching of the humanities was marked by corresponding biases. It is now necessary to enlarge the canon so that voices from Africa, Asia, and*

* The ruling elite.

*Latin America can be heard. This is especially important for minority students
so that they may learn about their origins and thereby gain in self-esteem.*

It is true that over the decades some university teaching has reflected
inherited social biases—how, for better or worse, could it not? Most often
this was due to the fact that many teachers shared the common beliefs of
American society. But not all teachers! As long as those with critical views
were allowed to speak freely, the situation, if not ideal, was one that people
holding minority opinions and devoted to democratic norms had to accept.

44   Yet the picture drawn by some academic insurgents—that most teachers, until quite recently, were in the grip of the worst values of Western society—is overdrawn. I can testify that some of my school and college teachers
a few decades ago, far from upholding Western imperialism or white supremacy, were sharply critical of American society, in some instances from a
boldly reformist outlook. They taught us to care about literature both for its
own sake and because, as they felt, it often helped confirm their worldviews.
(And to love it even if it didn't confirm their worldviews.) One high school
teacher introduced me to Hardy's *Jude the Obscure* as a novel showing how
cruel society can be to rebels, and up to a point, she was right. At college, as
a fervent anti-Stalinist Marxist, I wrote a thoughtless "class analysis" of Edmund Spenser's poetry for an English class, and the kindly instructor, whose
politics were probably not very far from mine, suggested that there were
more things in the world, especially as Spenser had seen it, than I could yet
recognize. I mention these instances to suggest that there has always been a
range of opinion among teachers, and if anything, the American academy
has tilted more to the left than most other segments of our society. There
were of course right-wing professors too: I remember an economics teacher
we called "Steamboat" Fulton, the object of amiable ridicule among the students who nonetheless learned something from him.

Proposals to enlarge the curriculum to include non-Western writings—if made in good faith and not in behalf of an ideological campaign—
are in principle to be respected. A course in ancient thought might well
include a selection from Confucius; a course in the modern novel might
well include a work by Tanizaki or García Márquez.

46   There are practical difficulties. Due to the erosion of requirements in
many universities, those courses that survive are usually no more than a year
or a semester in duration, so that there is danger of a diffusion to the point
of incoherence. Such courses, if they are to have any value, must focus primarily on the intellectual and cultural traditions of Western society. That,
like it or not, is where we come from and that is where we are. All of us who
live in America are, to some extent, Western: it gets to us in our deepest and
also our most trivial habits of thought and speech, in our sense of right and
wrong, in our idealism and our cynicism.

As for the argument that minority students will gain in self-esteem
through being exposed to writings by Africans and black Americans, it is
hard to know. Might not entering minority students, some of them ill-
prepared, gain a stronger sense of self-esteem by mastering the arts of

writing and reading than by being told, as some are these days, that Plato and Aristotle plagiarized from an African source? Might not some black students feel as strong a sense of self-esteem by reading, say, Dostoyevsky and Malraux (which Ralph Ellison speaks of having done at a susceptible age) as by being confined to black writers? Is there not something grossly patronizing in the notion that while diverse literary studies are appropriate for middle-class white students, something else, racially determined, is required for the minorities? Richard Wright found sustenance in Dreiser, Ralph Ellison in Hemingway, Chinua Achebe in Eliot, Léopold Sénghor in the whole of French poetry. Are there not unknown young Wrights and Ellisons, Achebes and Senghors in our universities who might also want to find their way to an individually achieved sense of culture?

48   In any case, is the main function of the humanities directly to inculcate self-esteem? Do we really know how this can be done? And if done by bounding the curriculum according to racial criteria, may that not perpetuate the very grounds for a lack of self-esteem? I do not know the answers to these questions, but do the advocates of multiculturalism?

One serious objection to "multicultural studies" remains: that it tends to segregate students into categories fixed by birth, upbringing, and obvious environment. Had my teachers tried to lead me toward certain writers because they were Jewish, I would have balked—I wanted to find my own way to Proust, Kafka, and Pirandello, writers who didn't need any racial credentials. Perhaps things are different with students today—we ought not to be dogmatic about these matters. But are there not shared norms of pride and independence among young people, whatever their race and color?

50   The jazz musician Wynton Marsalis testifies: "Everybody has two heritages, ethnic and human. The human aspects give art its real enduring power. . . . The racial aspect, that's a crutch so you don't have to go out into the world." David Bromwich raises an allied question: Should we wish "to legitimize the belief that the mind of a student deserves to survive in exactly the degree that it corresponds with one of the classes of socially constructed group minds? If I were a student today I would find this assumption frightening. It is, in truth, more than a license for conformity. It is a four-year sentence to conformity."

What you have been saying is pretty much the same as what conservatives say. Doesn't that make you feel uncomfortable?

52   No, it doesn't. There are conservatives—and conservatives. Some, like the editor of *The New Criterion,* are frantic ideologues with their own version of p.c., the classics as safeguard for the status quo. This is no more attractive than the current campus ideologizing. But there are also conservatives who make the necessary discriminations between using culture, as many have tried to use religion, as a kind of social therapy and seeing culture as a realm with its own values and rewards.

Similar differences hold with regard to the teaching of past thinkers. In a great figure like Edmund Burke you will find not only the persuasions of conservatism but also a critical spirit that does not readily lend itself to ideological coarseness. Even those of us who disagree with him fundamentally can learn from Burke the disciplines of argument and resources of language.

54   Let us suppose that in University X undergoing a curriculum debate there is rough agreement about which books to teach between professors of the democratic left and their conservative colleagues. Why should that trouble us—or them? We agree on a given matter, perhaps for different reasons. Or there may be a more or less shared belief in the idea of a liberal education. If there is, so much the better. If the agreement is momentary, the differences will emerge soon enough. ❖

Questions for Meaning

1. In his opening paragraph, Howe expresses special concern for what is taught in introductory courses. Why would the content of such courses be considered particularly important in debates over the curriculum?
2. Why does Howe believe that university administrators and faculty cannot be depended on to defend "the value of the canon"?
3. Why does Howe prefer to speak of "insurgents" rather than "the cultural left"?
4. Why does Howe believe that the canon is a "precious legacy"?
5. What does Howe mean when he complains that American culture "suffers from the provincialism of the contemporary"?
6. What is the role of the teacher when helping students to understand canonical works?
7. Vocabulary: sectarian (1), lethargy (3), timorous (4), austere (8), vindicate (10), panache (11), nihilism (13), stupefaction (14), recalcitrance (16), kitsch (16), epigrammatic (16), hegemony (17), retrograde (19), ephemeral (22), patronizing (47).

Questions about Strategy

1. What does Howe achieve by quoting Lukacs, Trotsky, and Gramsci?
2. Consider Howe's use of *Soul on Ice* in paragraph 22. Is this book a good example to illustrate his point? Does it leave Howe open to counterargument?
3. How fairly does Howe restate the arguments of his opponents? How effective are his responses?
4. Does Howe make any concessions?
5. Howe draws on personal experience in paragraphs 30, 44, and 49. To what extent does this help his argument? Would he have been able to use experience as effectively if he came from a culturally privileged background?
6. Throughout his argument, Howe alludes to writers and philosophers without identifying them. What do these allusions reveal about his sense of audience? How do they make you feel?

ONE STUDENT'S ASSIGNMENT

Write an argument for retaining a Western emphasis in core courses or for making such courses multicultural. Because you are limited to a short essay of between three and four pages, you should focus your argument on a specific area of study such as literature, history, economics, or philosophy. Draw on material from *The Informed Argument,* but focus primarily on developing your own ideas. Use MLA-style documentation.

The Great Conversation
Alicia Fedorczak

Plato or Angelou?? Wordsworth or Morrison?? In recent years, universities and colleges have debated the material necessary for a strong core curriculum. Much of the battle centers around the selection of appropriate and necessary readings. On one side, many scholars seek to preserve a traditional Western canon, insisting that all students must know and understand the basic ideas of Western culture. Their opponents encourage a broader, multicultural curriculum that exposes students to the literature and thought of many overlooked minorities. Although both groups present some valid arguments, many scholars have forgotten the true purpose of literature and education. Effective education must prepare all students for success, not only as members of the work force, but most importantly as human beings. Universities must be committed to providing the best possible education, a difficult task that requires the voices of many cultures and backgrounds.

2   As new curriculums develop, educators must consider the changing needs of today's students. Deteriorating nuclear families and rising racial tensions force institutions to define new objectives in the classroom. Today, preparing students for success becomes a challenging and complicated duty. Effective education must provoke thinking, encourage cooperation, raise self-esteem, and promote the understanding and acceptance of all cultures and people. As universities attempt to produce successful students, they must employ every available resource.

Literature serves as an essential tool in the process of modern education. Literature itself is a reflection of the human spirit, a guide to understanding people and their societies. Like art or history, literature provides insight necessary for personal development and professional growth. Certainly, literature teaches a highly individualized lesson to each reader, as students discover and apply a book's wisdom in their own lives. Yet, even the best scholars have not discovered a magical equation for genius. If literature has no universal meaning, how can it have universal significance? There is no single definition of a classic, and no possible way for any person to read every great book; even critics disagree over the importance of many contributions. Therefore, no single person can determine a canon of indispensable reading. Rather, universities should focus on effectively using literature to ensure the best possible education.

4   A broad range of literature provides students with the potential for greater growth and learning. The importance of the Western canon remains, but must be supplemented with the voices of other cultures. Rather than limiting ideas, students should be exposed to a variety of viewpoints and then determine the valuable lessons of each. The integration of many authors provides strong role models, understanding of other cultures, and finally new perspectives.

     Promoting reform does not undermine the importance of Western ideas and thought. By encouraging the expansion of the curriculum, scholars do not intend to belittle or reduce the importance of Western literature. The works of the traditional canon have survived time, defining a significant piece of American culture. As universities face reform, they must retain the wisdom of the past, remembering that "the past is the substance out of which the present has been formed" (Howe 498). Western literature should remain an important component of education, simply not the only component. The point of reform is not to encourage separation or "Balkanization" (D'Souza 477), but to achieve understanding. By recognizing the importance and achievements of all groups, students may survive in a diverse society.

6   Universities must attempt to integrate both multicultural and Western literature within a single core curriculum. When administrators concentrate on the goals of education, a balanced curriculum becomes feasible. Rather than focusing on the exact percentage of minority authors on a syllabus, educators must determine how to adequately introduce a variety of perspectives. At present, scholars seem to be caught up in numbers and statistics, instead of honestly attempting to aid student success. Only a few of the best Western authors can be adequately covered in a short course, and two professors may even teach the same course with entirely different readings. By including multicultural voices, the Western sample becomes increasingly smaller. Yet, administrators should not worry about changing curriculums to include new voices. Education is not a question of numbers and quotas, but one of growth and development. Rather than placing blame and calling names, scholars must reform the process of education in an attempt to further student learning.

     At times, literature has been described as a great conversation, a significant exchange of ideas. Every great piece of writing provokes response. Authors are forced to respond to the assumptions, thoughts, and ideas of the works that exist before them. By examining this great conversation, students unlock the knowledge that literature has to share. Rather than limiting education, universities should encourage the introduction of new ideas and perspectives. As one educator suggests, "we should think of American culture as a conversation among different voices, even if it is a conversation that some were able to join only recently" (Price 456). When universities learn to put education first, the debates will cease and the great conversation may resume.

Suggestions for Writing

1. Drawing on Price, Sleeter, and Friedman, write an argument in defense of a multicultural curriculum.
2. Drawing on D'Souza and Howe, argue for a curriculum that emphasizes Western civilization.
3. Consider the five views of multicultural education described by Sleeter. Do you have a sixth view? Argue on behalf of a model of your own design.
4. Drawing on the argument by Marilyn Friedman, summarize the challenges faced by advocates of multicultural education.
5. In your opinion, which author in this section seems the most reasonable, and which author seems the most biased? Contrast these authors by showing how they differ in terms of how respectful they are of opposing points of view.
6. What, in your view, is the purpose of higher education? Write an argument on behalf of that purpose.
7. Write an essay explaining how you benefited (or failed to benefit) from a required course that you probably would not have taken as an elective.
8. Write an argument for or against studying a foreign language.
9. Write a defense of one course that you believe all students should take regardless of their major.
10. When planning a syllabus, how much attention should instructors give to the gender of the authors whose texts will be used? Does it matter to you whether you are reading a work by a man or by a woman? Write an argument for or against the consideration of gender as a factor in course design.

COLLABORATIVE PROJECT

Study the requirements at your school as described in your college catalog. Interview students and faculty to learn how much support these requirements have and to determine whether there is a desire for change.

SECTION 7

NATIONAL PARKS: WHAT IS THEIR FUTURE?

TERRY L. ANDERSON

IT'S TIME TO PRIVATIZE

It is becoming increasingly apparent that our national parks system is under strain. One problem is the popularity of the parks: the more people visit them, the more congested they become and the more damage can be done. Another problem is that park administrators have lacked sufficient funding to make necessary repairs and maintain adequate services. What, then, can be done to save the parks at a time when federal dollars are becoming harder to come by? As the title of the following argument suggests, Terry L. Anderson believes that entrepreneurs can make the park system more self-sufficient. Anderson is Executive Director of the Political Economy Research Center in Bozeman, Montana. He first published "It's Time to Privatize" in the May 1996 issue of *The World & I.*

Bumper-to-bumper traffic on Yellowstone's deteriorating roads. Closed gates at Yosemite. A 10-year wait to float through the Grand Canyon. Overcrowding of our national parks cannot be debated.

2   One way to deal with this problem is to increase the entry fees and reinvest them directly into improved management. As it is now, visitors to national parks pay almost nothing, and taxpayers, not users, bear the costs. Until that changes, we will have overcrowding and inadequate visitor service.

Low fees inevitably lead to overuse. A family of four in a Winnebago pays only $10 for a seven-day permit to visit Yellowstone, or 36 cents per person per day for use of a national treasure. With the price so low, people visit more often and stay longer than they would otherwise. Traffic congestion is commonplace, campgrounds fill up in early morning, and muddy trails erode from heavy use.

4   Low fees also mean woefully inadequate budgets. Yellowstone, the "crown jewel" of our park system, has 2.2 million acres and 3 million visitors. Yet its budget for operations is only $17 million, shameful for a park of its size, and its backlog of capital improvements exceeds $250 million.

Environmentalists often accuse commodity users such as logging companies and miners of "feeding at the government trough" through subsidies. But recreational subsidies are far worse. In fiscal year 1994, fees collected for all recreation on federal lands were only 10 percent of what the agencies spent on recreation.

6   Yellowstone Park took in only about $1.30 per visitor in 1993 but spent $6.00. Given the amount tourists spend on transportation, meals, and lodging, it is safe to say that a trip to a national park like Yellowstone is worth far more than $1.30 per person! Visitors are getting something for nothing—the definition of a subsidy.

It was not always this way, as the history of Yellowstone illustrates, and it does not have to be that way in the future.

8   The common folklore is that Yellowstone was the brainchild of far-sighted conservationists. According to the story, as they sat around one of the first campfires in the park, they pledged that these wonders of nature—the geysers, the hot springs, the geological formations that they had just explored—should be protected forever.

But the reality is quite different. Profits spawned the world's first national park. The owners of the Northern Pacific Railroad saw the tourism potential of Yellowstone. They financed the expeditions that collected information about the area and lobbied Congress to set aside the area as a park—and to do it fast, before homesteaders cut the timber or carved up the park into small tourist attractions.

10   As one railroad official put it, "We do not want to see the Falls of the Yellowstone driving the loom of a cotton factory, or the great geysers boiling pork for some gigantic packing-house, but in all the native majesty and grandeur." Because railroads had monopolies on transportation to the West and were able to take control of internal facilities, they were the driving force behind not only Yellowstone but also the Grand Canyon, Mount Rainier, and many of the other early parks.

Railroads initially wanted low or no entry fees, so they could charge the maximum for train tickets, stagecoach rides, and hotel facilities. But they also understood the importance of limiting congestion. For example, stagecoach departures were staggered to minimize dust.

12   The first meaningful entry fees for our national parks came when personal automobiles were allowed into the parks. Such fees undoubtedly were supported by railroads as a way of limiting competition. And indeed, with the first entry fees for Yellowstone set at $100 in today's dollar, some tourists would have thought twice about visiting the park.

Despite such high fees, enough people were still willing to pay so that national parks were self-sufficient. In 1917, the first year of the National Park Service's existence, fees collected in the major parks such as Yellowstone, Yosemite, Grand Canyon, and Mount Rainier exceeded operating costs.

14   At that time, entrance fees went to a special treasury account with no congressional oversight. The only role for Congress was to provide addi-

tional appropriations when capital improvement funds were needed. But this didn't last long. Congress wanted control of the agency, and controlling the purse strings was the best way. By 1918 legislation was passed requiring that all monies go to the general fund. Not surprisingly, revenues fell, because the National Park Service had little interest in collecting them.

Even so, there was support for the idea that the user should pay. As Secretary of Interior Harold Ickes put it in 1939, "Those who actually visit the national parks and monuments should make small contributions to their upkeep for the services those visitors receive which are not received by other citizens who do not visit the parks but who contribute to the support of these parks."

16   In recent years Congress has altered the fee structure for use of federal lands, in some cases raising fees and in others lowering them. Legislation enacted in 1959 required all federal agencies to set "a reasonable charge" for their services. But in 1978, when the Park Service faced large budget cuts and responded with proposals to increase fees, Congress passed a moratorium that froze fees.

In 1982, the federal Office of Management and Budget put pressure on the Park Service to obtain at least 25 percent of its operation and maintenance funds from fees. Unfortunately, such fee revenues were offset by reduced budget appropriations so the Park Service had little incentive to collect the fees.

18   Most recently, Congress allowed the Park Service to keep a share of fees to cover the costs of collection. As a result, collections went up, but the extra revenues only cover the costs of collection and do not provide better services for park visitors.

The bottom line from the history of fees is that the taxpayer heavily subsidizes the national parks. This "welfare" system for funding national parks guarantees overcrowding and underfunding, and it focuses entrepreneurial talents on Washington rather than on the ground.

20   Because budgets are enacted by congressional committees, Park Service officials pay more attention to politicians than to visitors. The number of visitors, not the quality of visits, becomes the *raison d'être* for the Park Service. The absurdity of this approach is illustrated by the fact that commuters using Rock Creek Parkway, a major arterial highway through Washington, D.C., used to be counted as national park visitors because the Park Service managed that land!

To make the park experience better for visitors, we need to raise fees and allow managers to use those fees for improving visitor services. Such a step could switch on entrepreneurship within the Park Service. Suddenly, the focus would be on quality, not quantity.

22   A study by Donald Leal of PERC, a think tank in Bozeman, Montana, suggests the positive results that could occur. Leal compared state and federal timber management of lands that are similar or even adjacent. He found that the state of Montana made $2 for every dollar it spent for timber management on state-owned lands, while the Forest Service lost $0.50 for

HOW THE PARKS CAN BE SAVED

 Raise fees and allow managers to use those fees for improving visitor services.

 Allow alternative sources of incomes. In Texas, park managers generate revenues from dances, weddings, bird-watching tours, and nature seminars.

 Cut dependency on Washington bureaucracy and handouts.

every dollar it spent on timber operations on national forests in Montana. Measures of environmental quality also show that state forests were better managed over the long haul. Why the difference?

Revenues from Montana's state forests help fund public schools. Hence parents, teachers, and school administrators become "majority stockholders" who care about the bottom line. In contrast, most revenues from national forests drain into the general treasury abyss in Washington. Hence, the Forest Service has little incentive to be economically responsible.

24   Some state park systems are also self-supporting. While national parks are severely subsidized, state parks in New Hampshire and Vermont earn sufficient revenues to cover expenses, and Texas state parks are moving in that direction. Because the parks are "profit centers," the managers are entrepreneurs. Their revenues depend on satisfied visitors, so they have an incentive to give the customer a quality experience.

In Texas, for example, park managers generate revenues from dances, weddings, bird-watching tours, nature seminars, and "Christmas in the parks." On just 500,000 acres, one-fourth the area of Yellowstone, Texas parks generate $25 million annually, compared with Yellowstone's $3 million. As one Texas park manager put it, "We were so limited by bureaucracy, but now, the sky is the limit."

26   There are several reasons why the time is right to move the Washington bureaucracy toward allowing greater self-sufficiency for the national parks. First, our national parks and their visitors are not getting what they deserve. Many people pass through the gates, but the quality of the experience is diminished by overcrowding.

Second, these days people are willing to pay to enjoy the outdoors. Large private landowners recognize this and are earning profits from recreation. For example, the International Paper Company leases land to 2,100 hunting clubs and rents small parcels where families can park their trailers and enjoy the outdoors. Private fund drives for the parks also indicate a willingness to pay. The Glacier National Park Association, for example, has started a "Backcountry Preservation Fund," asking for private contributions to fund projects that protect natural resources.

28   Finally, budgets are tight and likely to get tighter. In this fiscal setting, user fees become the only way to adequately fund the national parks.

From Yellowstone to the Grand Canyon, entrepreneurship was the original driving force behind the national park system. Restructuring the incentives by making users pay and linking each park's expenditures to gate receipts can rekindle that entrepreneurship for the sake of our national parks and their visitors. By resisting reform in the name of democracy and equal access, we are only delaying the day of reckoning. It's time to stop subsidizing our national parks to death.   ❖

Questions for Meaning

1. How does Anderson define "subsidy"? Why does he believe that visitors to our national parks are being subsidized?
2. Where did entrance fees for the parks go in 1917? What changed in 1918? What has been the consequence of this change?
3. Why has timber management in Montana been more profitable on state land than on national forests in that state?
4. What recommendations does Anderson make for reforming the administration of our national parks?
5. Why does Anderson believe that the time is right for a change in park management?

Questions about Strategy

1. Consider the sequence of sentences in Anderson's opening paragraph. Do the first three sentences provide sufficient evidence for the conclusion reached in the fourth?
2. In paragraphs 8–11, Anderson contrasts what he calls "folklore" and "reality." What advantage is there to devoting more space, in this case, to "reality"? Are you convinced that this version of "reality" is historically accurate?
3. Illustrating how park managers can make parks profitable, Anderson devotes paragraph 25 to describing the administration of parks in Texas. Does this example help his argument?
4. In his conclusion, Anderson contrasts "entrepreneurship" with "resisting reform in the name of democracy and equal access." How would you paraphrase this conflict? What kind of readers are likely to respond positively to a conflict defined in these terms?

MELANIE GRIFFIN

THEY'RE NOT FOR SALE

Melanie Griffin is Director of the Land Protection Program of the Sierra Club, one of the most influential environmental groups in the United States. "They're Not for Sale" appeared in the same 1996 issue of the magazine *The World & I* that carried the preceding argument by Terry L. Anderson. Taken together, these two pieces illustrate how differently people can respond to the same problem. As you read Griffin's argument, note how it includes both facts and appeals to commonly held values.

Most Americans cannot conceive of selling off our national park lands. And it's no wonder. Our national parks represent the heart of our nation's proud tradition of protecting special places for our children and grandchildren. Since the establishment of Yellowstone as the world's first national park in 1872, America's park system has come to represent the best of our natural and cultural heritage.

2   If you've ever stood in awe before the towering cliffs of Yosemite, or marveled at a sunset over the Grand Canyon, you know that our public lands—and particularly our national parks—represent the very best in American values. Our children can learn about freedom and democracy from the principles embodied in Independence Hall and the Statue of Liberty. They can learn about our nation's history from Valley Forge and Gettysburg, and about national pride from the Washington Monument and Mount Rushmore. And from the Everglades to the Redwoods, our national parks speak to us all of the majesty of nature.

But today, we find this legacy threatened by an extreme faction in Congress, determined to sell off our splendid natural heritage. Reps. Jim Hansen (R-Utah)and Joel Hefley (R-Colorado) have concocted a scheme to establish a Parks Closure Commission to recommend "a list of National Park System units where National Park Service management should be terminated."

4   No one but the politicians in Washington, D.C., could come up with the idea that our national park system is too large or too expensive. As the *Seattle Post-Intelligencer* editorialized, "The idea, it appears on the surface, is to make the park system pay for itself. That will never happen. It was never intended to happen. The United States' national parks are its crown jewels, held in trust by the government. The parks belong to each citizen."

A survey conducted last year by Colorado State University and released by the National Parks and Conservation Association showed that over 87 percent of those polled believe that the most important value of the national parks is to "provide an important experience for future generations." Those who would sell our national parks are clearly out of touch with America.

6   This misguided attempt to close national parks is not an isolated effort. The same people who argue that we should sell off our national parks are pushing a broader agenda of giving away our country's natural resources and public lands to the extractive industries that finance their election campaigns. Funded by narrow special-interest groups, these politicians seek to give large corporate interests supremacy over the public lands. Hunters, fishermen, families, scientists, and responsible small businesses would not get their fair share of our natural resources if these radical proposals were to become the law of the land.

As outdoor writer George Reiger told sportsmen in a recent issue of *Field and Stream* magazine:

> Many of you supported the Republican Revolution because you wanted to see the welfare state dismantled, the budget balanced, and our national debt paid down. But I don't believe many of you wanted this mandate extended to include the privatization of public rangelands, the exploitation of oil and minerals on every possible national wildlife refuge, and national forests clearcut at an accelerated rate.

8   Through decades of bipartisan cooperation, our nation has carefully crafted land-use policies that allow our public lands to be managed for multiple uses. Our parks, refuges, forests, and western public lands support commercial activity, recreation, scientific research, and wilderness values. And they are good for local economies. We must not let a few special interests and their allies in Congress upset this balance. Consider the following:

• Our 92-million-acre national wildlife refuge system provides exceptional opportunities for conservation education, scientific research, and wildlife-dependent recreation like hunting, fishing, and bird-watching. Over 30 million people visit the refuges each year, including 5.7 million

RETURN TO COMMON SENSE

🏠 Our rich legacy, from Yosemite to Independence Hall, is threatened by the present Congress, which wants to sell it off. Hunters, fishermen, families, scientists, and responsible small businesses would be hurt by such a radical proposal.

🏠 Big business, not the American taxpayer, should pay its fair share for America's public lands. If there are millions of dollars to give to politicians, business should contribute to help preserve natural resources.

🏠 The only way to ensure this priceless heritage is through responsible federal management.

anglers. Our refuges represent the most diverse network of protected fish and wildlife habitats in the entire world. Yet there are proposals in Congress that would hand over refuges to the states and allow oil drilling in the spectacular Arctic National Wildlife Refuge, which constitutes the only 5 percent of Alaska's north slope not already open to drilling.

• Our national forests contain 2 million acres of ponds and lakes and 200,000 miles of streams and rivers that support substantial commercial and subsistence fisheries. In 1988, fishermen harvested over 170 million pounds of anadromous fish that originated in the waters of our national forests. Those fish had a dockside value of more than $250 million. Yet in 1995, Congress passed a bill that allows extensive logging under a waiver of all our forest protection laws, including the Clean Water Act.

• The diverse habitats found on western lands managed by the Bureau of Land Management (BLM) support a wide array of fish and wildlife species. Ask any hunter, angler, or camper about the value of BLM lands. About 70 million people visit the BLM public lands each year, generating nearly $678 million. Yet a bill in Congress would give our vast western lands to the states, to do with what they will, including auctioning them off. And you know what that means: "Keep Out."

• The 368 diverse units of our national park system received 273 million visitors in 1993, generating over $10 billion in revenues to local communities and supporting over 200,000 jobs. And the federal cost for these national park units is just $1.5 billion, barely one-tenth of 1 percent of the entire U.S. budget.

The politicians who seek to get rid of our public lands often try to justify their arguments by citing the need to reduce the federal deficit. This argument makes little sense given the great economic value of these lands. But it becomes downright insulting when viewed in the larger context of public-lands subsidies.

10 While American families and sportsmen continue to pay their fair share through recreational fees that support the management of the lands we all use, big business interests and the extractive industries continue to exploit our natural resources at the taxpayers' expense.

American taxpayers spend billions of dollars every year to subsidize environmental destruction caused by multinational mining companies, agribusiness, and large corporate timber interests. If the politicians calling for the sale of our public lands are serious about fiscal responsibility, they should pull the plug on this welfare for rich corporations. Consider:

• Probably the most outrageous public-lands subsidy goes to the mining industry, which walks off with approximately $2–3 billion each year in publicly owned minerals from our public lands without paying the government a penny. To add insult to injury, mining companies can buy our public lands outright for $5 an acre or less. Nationally, 12,000 miles of rivers have been polluted by mining operations, and there are over 550,000 abandoned hard-rock mines, some of which are Superfund toxic waste sites. And the taxpayers are left with the cleanup bills.

• Over the last seven years, the U.S. Forest Service has lost $1.9 billion on its timber sales program, because the agency spends more to prepare timber sales than it takes in from the timber companies. The main expense is the construction of new logging roads. Thousands of miles of taxpayer-funded roads are being built in our national forests every year, causing extreme soil erosion, water pollution, and reduced fishing opportunities.

• Subsidized livestock grazing on public lands managed by the BLM and the Forest Service leads to overgrazing and severe habitat destruction on fragile western lands. According to the Competitive Enterprise Institute, the full cost of the BLM grazing management programs, not including Forest Service costs, is $200 million each year.

• Many big businesses that provide food, lodging, transportation, and gift shop services in the national parks are given lucrative contracts at taxpayer expense. Overall, park concessionaires grossed about $657 million in 1993, but they paid only $18 million in franchise fees to the government—an average of just 2.6 percent (compared to state park fees of over 10 percent).

12   Americans love their national parks. And they are willing to pay for them. Last year's poll by Colorado State University found that nearly four in five Americans would support an increase in park entry fees if 100 percent of the revenues were used to maintain the national park system. And the same number said they would make an additional contribution through their income taxes if they knew the money would go to the parks.

But let's start by making big business pay its fair share for America's public lands. If it's got millions to contribute to politicians, surely it can pitch in for the use of our natural resources.

14   The real bottom line is that Americans treasure their heritage of national parks, national forests, national wildlife refuges, and wilderness and western public lands. They recognize that these lands are an incalculable part of our nation's natural heritage and economic and ecological wealth.

We must protect our national parks, for our families and for our future. The only way that we can ensure that our priceless heritage of national parks and other public lands is still here for our grandchildren is through responsible federal management. We must not abandon the guiding principles of the national parks set down in 1916: Our parks must remain "dedicated to conserving unimpaired . . . natural and cultural resources and values . . . for the enjoyment, education and inspiration of this and future generations." ❖

Questions for Meaning

1. According to Griffin, who is most likely to suffer if public lands are sold to large corporations?
2. Consider the use of "refuges" in paragraph 8. How does Griffin seem to define the term? How would you define it?
3. Why does Griffin believe that the cost of the national park system is minimal when compared to its benefits?

4. How does Griffin want to reform the management of our national parks and forests?

Questions about Strategy

1. Griffin appeals frequently to the need to preserve parks for "our children and grandchildren." Is this appeal appropriate for an argument about natural resources? Does it exclude any readers?
2. What other values does Griffin appeal to in her argument?
3. Griffin cites two authorities in support of her case: a survey conducted by Colorado State University, and an article in *Field and Stream*. How credible are these sources? Did Griffin use any other sources?
4. How does Griffin characterize politicians who want to privatize public lands? What does she gain by presenting her opposition in these terms? What does she lose?

WILLIAM R. LOWRY

PROMISES, PROMISES

William R. Lowry worked for the National Park Service during the 1970s and now teaches political science at Washington University in St. Louis. He is the author of *The Capacity for Wonder: Preserving National Parks* (1994), which was published by the Brookings Institution, a prestigious research organization that often advocates liberal political positions. This argument was first published in 1994 in the Institution's journal, *The Brookings Review*. As you read, note how Lowry traces the national park problems to decisions made in Washington, DC.

As another summer fades, so does political attention to the plight of America's national parks. Last spring, as the thoughts of millions of Americans turned to the cool mountain air and fresh, clear streams of their parks, the Clinton Administration's spokesman, Interior Secretary Bruce Babbitt, promised to "lay out our vision of where we want to take the national parks in the next three years." That promise, and others like it, reflected another effort by the Administration to avoid neglect of the "vision thing" that plagued the Bush presidency. But what has been missing in American parks policy—and what has remained in short supply during the Clinton presidency—is not vision, but the political courage to see preservation become a reality.

2   The vision of parks as wilderness preserved under natural conditions has been explicit in American political thought since 1872. In legislation setting aside Yellowstone that year, Congress called for "the preservation,

from injury or spoliation, of all timber, mineral deposits, natural curiosities, or wonders . . . and their retention in their natural condition." In the years since, Americans have entrusted to the National Park Service more than 360 parks or other units, a small (less than 4 percent of the nation's total) but precious land area, to be preserved "unimpaired for the enjoyment of future generations."

But many of America's national parks—and indeed the Park Service itself—are now in trouble.

4   One obvious problem is lack of money. Throughout the 1980s and early 1990s, the Park Service's budget hovered around $1 billion a year, even though total visits to the parks increased more than 25 percent. As a result of increased use and simple aging, the parks now have a backlog of nearly $2.2 billion in infrastructure repairs. Park visitors, for example, find that more than one-third of all roads in the parks need repairs. Crime is also on the rise. More than 40,000 crimes, including 6,500 major ones, were committed in the parks last year. Because staffing has not grown commensurately, more and more Park Service employees must be detailed to crime prevention, and fewer are available for interpretive and preservation programs. External threats to the parks—air pollution, water pollution, commercial encroachment—have also increased dramatically. Visitors now find in the parks much of the congestion, smog, and urban blight they had hoped to leave behind. Air pollution from recently built power plants in Virginia, for example, has reduced annual average visibility on Shenandoah's Skyline Drive from a natural figure of 80 miles to today's 15.

With park entrance fees rising of late, one might have expected increased park use to provide a revenue windfall for the Park Service. Indeed, many visitors accept the higher entrance fees and inflated prices for concessions such as food and lodging, believing that they are contributing to Park Service revenue. But congressional authorization of higher entrance fees in 1986 diverted entrance fee revenue to the General Treasury Fund, where it can be used for everything from welfare to defense. And the average return to the federal government from concessions is only 2.5 percent.

6   The Park Service budget has also been stretched by haphazard expansion of the system. Often expansion is driven by politics. The classic example is Steamtown National Historic Site in Scranton, Pennsylvania. Steamtown came under the Park Service in 1986 when Scranton's congressman, Joe McDade, bypassed the formal procedures for park creation, using his clout as ranking minority member of the House Appropriations Committee to amend a pending omnibus bill. Over the next six years, nearly $70 million was appropriated to convert an abandoned railyard with no original equipment into what a panel of historians testified to Congress was "little more than a railroad theme park with an eclectic collection of trains." Meanwhile, plans to preserve natural conditions in other parks, such as the one formulated in 1980 to relieve automobile congestion in Yosemite Valley, remained unrealized for lack of money. Nor is Steamtown alone. In 1990, several Park Service personnel complained in a memo that the agency was

becoming a "repository for what are in essence economic development type projects." Indeed, a bitter standing joke inside the agency is that it would more appropriately be named the "National Pork Service."

Opportunistic expansion is not the only avenue for political meddling in Park Service business. Members of Congress and political appointees have become increasingly involved through oversight, constituent casework, financial control, manipulation of personnel, and policy decisions. Too often, as Yosemite superintendent Mike Finley told me, "Decisions are made for politics instead of for the resource." Two examples suffice. In 1974 park officials trying to improve bear management in Yellowstone proposed to remove one commercial settlement, Fishing Bridge, in prime grizzly bear habitat and, in exchange, to build a new one, also in prime bear habitat, at Grant Village. Today, commercial operations continue at both at the insistence of the Wyoming congressional delegation—what one superintendent called "policy consideration beyond Yellowstone." In 1979 the Park Service called for the complete phase-out of motorized craft from the Colorado River in the Grand Canyon. But the plan was scuttled by Senator Orrin Hatch (R-UT). The agency's own internal 1992 assessment terms the Park Service "overrun" by political intervention.

8   According to one Park Service field manager in 1992, "Morale is at an all-time low." A General Accounting Office study that same year found that 60 percent of National Park Service employee housing needed repairs—at an estimated cost of $500 million. Pay scales have stagnated while the cost of living has gone up, resulting in much higher than normal employee turnover. In their 1992 self-appraisal, Park Service employees concluded, "There is a wide and discouraging gap between the Service's potential and its current state, and the Service has arrived at a crossroads in its history."

Discouraged Park Service personnel—and park supporters generally—took heart from Clinton Administration promises of a renewed emphasis on preservation in park policy. Vice-President Gore, Interior Secretary Babbitt, and Assistant Secretary George Frampton, Jr., were all prominent environmental advocates. On appointing Babbitt, Clinton insisted, "The Secretary of the Interior must be tough enough to stand up to powerful interests." National Parks and Conservation Association president Paul Pritchard said of Babbitt, "We can count on him to care for and be committed to our national parks." Historian Robin Winks wrote in a *New York Times* editorial, "For the first time in 12 years the American people have a chance to reclaim their national parks." Editors of the *Economist* speculated that "the wilderness may flourish again."

10   Administration rhetoric has sustained that enthusiasm. Babbitt promised a "substantial increase" in the Park Service budget to go along with more emphasis on preservation and expansion. On a visit to Yosemite, he urged a return to the goals of the Park Service's 1980 plan for reducing traffic and emphasizing mass transit. Last May the administration unveiled National Park Week with numerous festivities promising greater attention to park problems.

But the Administration's record has fallen short. As in so many other issues facing the Clinton presidency, vision has often exceeded political courage. A willingness to compromise—an eagerness to please all sides— may be easy politically, but it does not undo the damage of the past.

12   Talk is cheap. Protecting parks is not. The promised "substantial" increase for the Park Service budget in 1993 was anything but. The $984 million operating budget in 1993 was slightly higher than that in 1992, but adjusted for inflation, it purchased fewer services. The 1994 operating budget saw a 9 percent increase, but that was offset by cuts in other areas such as acquisitions. The total budget grew only 3.9 percent. The proposed 1995 budget would increase operations (6 percent), but cut construction (26 percent) and acquisitions (22 percent). The small increases going to the parks are not nearly enough.

In decisions on individual parks, again, Administration performance has not matched expectations. Babbitt made several promising early decisions such as reversing construction of the Cape Hatteras National Seashore jetties approved by President Bush in the days before the 1992 election. In many parks, however, the biggest changes seen in 1993 were cutbacks in services through such means as trimming interpretive programs, reducing visitor center hours, and closing campgrounds. And even those cutbacks continue to be politically determined. For example, Shenandoah officials who proposed closing part of the Skyline Drive in winter months to save $200,000 were overruled by Virginia's congressional delegation, who were concerned about "severe economic consequences" for constituents in neighboring Front Royal. In a highly publicized case, in July of last year, the Administration released a new plan for the Everglades that it claimed would stop the devastating diversion of fresh water out of the park and reduce pollution washing in from nearby farms. In fact, the plan compromised on the timetable for pollution reduction and on the imposed costs to sugar growers. Even so, disputes over the compromise plan returned the case to court last April.

14   The morale of the Park Service has improved, but only slightly. Agency employees are thankful that problems affecting the parks are at least getting official attention. But they are still skeptical that political commitment will follow. During National Park Week, a Park Service employee grumbled, "Because this is parks week we have to put on a show, but there's nothing new to say."

Why is there nothing new to say? The anecdote about Shenandoah suggests one reason. Many of the changes expected from the Clinton Administration are beyond their control. Many policy decisions affecting parks are determined in Congress. And political manipulation of Park Service actions is not confined to Republicans. In addition, budget changes are historically incremental. Most of the shortages in Park Service financing, accumulated over decades, will not be easily remedied. Finally, changing some of the specific arrangements affecting the parks will take time. Concession contracts, for example, are issued for up to 30 years.

16   This is not to let the Administration off the hook. Clinton and his appointees have not fully used the tools available to them in attempting to change Park Service practice. Budget proposals have been less than bold. Political appointees in public lands policy have hardly been reform zealots. In itself, the selection of the Smithsonian's Roger Kennedy over the National Parks and Conservation Association's Paul Pritchard to head the Park Service signaled a backpedaling from the Administration's initial rhetoric. The most outspoken appointee in public lands policy, Bureau of Land Management Director Jim Baca, was forced to resign by Babbitt earlier this year after complaints from western ranching and farming interests, the same interests that made the Administration back down on land use fee reforms. Presidents can also propose structural reorganizations, but the Park Service remains part of the Interior Department despite calls by Pritchard and other park supporters to make it an independent agency. Indeed, the closest the Administration has come to proposing a reorganization of the Park Service has been to discuss "downsizing" the agency. Finally, the president enjoys access to the fabled "bully pulpit," but Clinton has remained largely silent on national parks issues.

        To live up to its promises to restore the original vision of the parks, the Administration can take several steps. The first is simply to reaffirm the original mandate for the Park Service, making preservation the dominant and explicit goal of the agency. Representative Bruce Vento's (D-MN) proposed National Parks and Landmarks Conservation Act will provide a good starting point. The proposal calls for a five-year term for the director of the Park Service, a commitment to a systematic research program, and explicit recognition that units of the Park Service "be accorded the highest degree of protection feasible."

18   Second, the Administration should provide the Park Service more resources. Admittedly that is a difficult proposition given the fiscal situation, but several possibilities exist. First, the existing system for awarding concessions contracts is an acknowledged mess. Contracts are awarded on a near-monopoly basis with long durations (15 to 30 years), low rates of return (a 1990 average of 2.5 percent on gross sales), and often preferential right of renewal. Senator Dale Bumpers (D-AR) has introduced legislation that would reform the system by emphasizing competitive bidding, shorter contracts, and higher returns to the government. Second, user fees are a good candidate for park revenues. The Interior Department has again proposed to raise entrance and user fees. The proposal warrants support as long as it is written to guarantee higher returns to the Park Service.

        Boondoggles like Steamtown can be avoided by using a systematic procedure for expanding the park system. The House Natural Resources Committee has proposed a long-range expansion plan using scientific analysis of potential new units. Congressional meddling with the Park Service's limited resources might also be reduced by closing the loophole in the 1935 Historic Sites Act that allows appropriations for projects not authorized through the normal committee channels.

20   Finally, the Administration would do well to consider reorganizing the environmental policy bureaucracy. As it stands, the Park Service is housed in a cabinet department with agencies whose missions are often contrary to preservation ideals. The Interior Department is now responsible not only for preserving parks (Park Service) and preserving endangered species (the Fish and Wildlife Service), but also for strip mining (Office of Strip Mining Reclamation and Enforcement), grazing (Bureau of Land Management), and Native American issues (Bureau of Indian Affairs). National forests, commonly located adjacent to parklands, are managed by the Forest Service in the Agriculture Department. Coordination of effective responses to various problems is now quite difficult. For example, imagine a river flowing through rangelands and forests before entering parklands. The Park Service has no control over pollution and use of the river outside park grounds. Rather than making the Park Service an independent agency, as some have proposed, the Administration could create a new Department of the Environment, modeled on the Canadian system. (Attempts to establish such a department were made in both the Nixon and Carter Administrations.) The department could bring together not only the Fish and Wildlife Service and the Park Service, but also the Forest Service. Coordinated actions by these agencies would help address difficult situations, including external threats such as encroachment and pollution.

        In essence, the Administration needs to find ways to give the Park Service the authority and discretion to do the job. The Canadians have recently done just that by decentralizing powers within the Canadian Parks Service. We could start with implementing the Park Service plans already existing in places like Yosemite, Grand Canyon, and Yellowstone.

22   As the Clinton Administration has learned so many times, change is never easy. Successful change requires vision and courage. With national parks, a vision has been built through a century of foresight and the desires of millions of park visitors who simply want a portion of this country to be kept as relatively natural wilderness. Seeing that vision become reality will take the courage to confront commercial operations with a vested interest in the status quo, the courage to counteract political authorities who have used the parks to satisfy the demands of specific constituencies, and the courage to seek additional funding for national parks in tough economic times. Promises won't do it.   ❖

Questions for Meaning

1. Why are national parks under strain? What signs of strain have begun to appear?
2. What political factors influence parks policy?
3. How has parks policy been affecting employee morale?
4. According to this argument, what steps should be taken to improve the condition of our national parks?

5. Vocabulary: commensurately (4), omnibus (6), opportunistic (7), suffice (7), jetties (13), incremental (15), zealots (16), boondoggles (19).

Questions about Strategy

1. In his opening paragraph, Lowry refers to the "vision thing," placing this phrase within quotation marks. What are the implications of this phrase?
2. When drawing attention to park problems, what kind of assumptions does Lowry make about his audience and what they expect of national parks?
3. Lowry presents Steamtown National Historic Site as a "classic example" and devotes most of paragraph 6 to it. What is this example meant to illustrate? How do you respond to it?
4. Although he worked for the National Parks Service during the 1970s, Lowry does not mention this experience. How else does he establish his authority to be writing on this topic?

KENNETH R. OLWIG

REINVENTING NATURE

An American scholar who is now a senior research fellow at Odense University in Denmark, Kenneth R. Olwig writes that he came to a new understanding of Yosemite, his favorite American national park, as the result of living abroad and observing how another culture responds to nature. He is the author of *Nature's Ideological Landscape* (1984) and published the original version of the following work in 1995. The version reprinted here is abridged from the original ("Reinventing Common Nature: Yosemite and Mount Rushmore—A Meandering Tale of a Double Nature") and omits the ninety-one footnotes with which Olwig provided documentation and additional discussion. As you read, you may be surprised to find Olwig discussing poetry and painting. He does so to show how national parks were created in response to ideas that were prevailing in Western culture in earlier times. Pay particular attention to Olwig's analysis of *The Deserted Village*, a poem by Oliver Goldsmith.

"Nature" has a double meaning and represents at one and the same time both a physical realm and the realm of cultural ideals and norms—all of which we lump together as the "natural." If we say that Americans "naturally" love their country we are implying that this truth about the nature of Americans is to be taken for granted. To be an American is to love one's country. Much as it would be "unnatural" for Americans not to love their country, it would be "unnatural" to call this "truth" into question. But why is it "natural" to love the "purple mountains' majesty," and what do mountains have to do with the "leaves of grass" on the "fruited plain"? Despite the fact, then, that *nature* is one of the most abstract and complicated concepts we have, nature nevertheless signifies all that is concrete, unmediated, and *naturally* given. It is this doubleness of meaning that makes the term "nature" so duplicitous that it should never be taken at face value. Yet we do so constantly, because not to do so is to challenge basic norms. The very idea of "reinventing" nature is no doubt offensive to many people because the natural is so bound up with their deepest, unreflected, individual, social, and national values. If, however, people are to become aware of the questionable ways that their concepts of nature can affect the way they act upon their physical environment, then they must question these values. They must realize that the "natural" values they find in their environment are given not by physical nature but by society.

2   This essay attempts to reinvent, or at least recover, an essentially premodern concept of nature in which people and their values do not appear to be excluded from nature. I wish to defend an older usage of the word in which nature is fundamentally a generative, creative principle. It is a principle furthermore akin to that of "love"—be it love toward an individual, "thy neighbor," or one's country. This usage of "nature" emphasizes sustainable reciprocity rather than domination and makes of nature not a spectacle but something to be dwelled within. I hope this will lead people to reflect upon that which they take most for granted—*nature*.

Yosemite and Mount Rushmore are ideal vehicles with which to approach the nature of American environmental values and behavior. Yosemite valley is where the national park idea was pioneered in 1864. It was the archetypal natural park and broke the ground for the establishment of a later system of national parks. Mount Rushmore makes a useful counterpoint to Yosemite because it expresses a transformation in the idea of nature and in ideas of the natural way for Americans to interact with each other and their environment. The comparison will point to the necessity of reinventing a "common nature." It was this idea of a common nature, I will argue, that gave rise to the idea of Yosemite as a natural park for the American people. If this natural ideal was the model for all of America, not just some of its parks, we might be able to rectify environmental policies that tend to create inviolable wilderness preserves in areas where people are largely excluded while overlooking the desecration of environments where we live and work.

4   Yosemite is not just a natural area; it is a natural "park." The Yosemite valley, with its meandering stream of the Merced River—the river of mercy—flowing through green meadows at the bottom of a rock-walled canyon, has always been immediately recognizable as a park to American visitors. According to Lafayette Bunnell, who was among the first whites to penetrate the valley, in 1851, it "presented the appearance of a well kept park." Bunnell was the diarist of Major James D. Savage's military expedition, whose

mission was to further mining interests by evicting the Ahwahneechee Indians from Yosemite. To Frederik Law Olmsted, who first visited the valley in 1864, Yosemite was a "wild park," and represented "the greatest glory of nature." He was the first chairman of the California Yosemite Park Commission, which managed the valley until 1906, when the federal government retook control of the park. As the landscape architect of what was to become a similarly encanyoned scene of meadows and winding streams—New York's Central Park—Olmsted knew what he meant by park "scenery." Even the great celebrant of a wild and sublime Yosemite—John Muir, the founding president of the Sierra Club (1892)—praised its valleys for being "a grand landscape garden." This is the term used for British landscape parks in the "natural" style, which had their heyday in the eighteenth century. The new "natural" parks were called landscape gardens to distinguish them from the formal gardens they replaced.

This seemingly automatic recognition of Yosemite as being naturally a park, much more than the persuasive abilities of particular individuals, arguably generated the national consensus that made Yosemite the pioneer national park. Drawings, paintings, and written descriptions somehow effectively transmitted the idea to the American public that Yosemite was not just natural but was and ought to be a park. This suggests that if we are to understand the "nature" of Yosemite, we will have to look much more closely at the idea of the park as it has become ingrained in Western civilization.

6   The etymologically primary meaning of the word "park," found in many early European languages, is an enclosed preserve for beasts of the chase. A "wilderness" was, in contrast, the place where the beasts (*deoren* in Old English) ran wild (wild-deer-ness), and was related to "bewilderment" and going astray. The term "park" was later extended to mean a "large ornamental piece of ground, usually comprising woodland and pasture, attached to or surrounding a country house or mansion, and used for recreation, and often for keeping deer, cattle, or sheep." Olmsted was clearly thinking of this sort of park when he described Yosemite in terms of "the most placid pools . . . with the most tranquil meadows, the most playful streams, and every variety of soft and peaceful pastoral beauty." The meandering stream of the Merced, he tells us, "is such a one as Shakespeare delighted in, and brings pleasing reminiscences to the traveller of the Avon or the upper Thames."

When woodlands are enclosed for wild game, or for the pasturage of domesticated animals in a pastoral economy, they take on a characteristically open, grassy, "parklike" appearance with scattered, "naturally" fully crowned, high-trunked trees. The "natural" appearance of parkland trees is due to the browsing of the animals, helped, perhaps, by the clearing activities of the gamekeepers, shepherds, or gardeners. This environment is ideally suited to sport and recreation and thus also for pleasure parks because people, even on horseback, can move freely and quickly after game or a ball. . . .

8   In his 1865 report to the California Park Commission for Yosemite, Olmsted makes repeated references to the recreational benefits for the upper classes of the British landscape parks. He notes the existence in Britain of "more than one thousand private parks and notable grounds devoted to luxury and recreation." These parks were so valuable that the cost of their annual maintenance was "greater than that of the national schools." He criticizes, however, the fact that the enjoyment of the "choicest natural scenes in the country" is the monopoly of "a very few, very rich people." After comparing the recreational value of this scenery to the collective value of the waters of a river, and after favorably comparing democratic America to Britain, he concludes, "It was in accordance with these views of the destiny of the New World and the duty of the republican government that Congress enacted that the Yosemite should be held, guarded and managed for the free use of the whole body of the people forever. . . . " Olmsted's grasp of what was to become the American national park ideal was seminal precisely because he had such a good grasp of American social and cultural ideals. It is therefore important to note the way Olmsted plays upon the continuities and discontinuities between American values and those of America's imperial mother country. The various metaphorical meanders by which Olmsted traces the Merced back to headwaters in England provide a useful means of understanding American ideas of nature. In following the current of these ideas back to their source, one soon discovers a vital cultural heritage that can help explain the genesis of American environmental values.

Yosemite and the Deserted Village

When Olmsted draws upon the symbolism of the English landscape park as land that has been privatized and so made inaccessible to the general public, he is striking a theme that was widely known to the educated nineteenth-century public. Among the most familiar sources would have been *The Deserted Village*, by Oliver Goldsmith, from 1770, one of the most popular English poems ever written. In it Goldsmith describes the contemporary origin of the British parks in the gentry's imparkment of English village lands. I will dwell upon this poem at some length because it so wonderfully embodies the "natural" community values that Americans (and Goldsmith) felt Britain had deserted and the American folk had rightfully inherited. These natural values, as the poem makes clear, were heavily bound up with both the idea of the "park" and that of "imparkment," by which an area is enclosed. The village common or green in the poem is thus essentially a native community park that is imparked by a man of wealth in order to exclude that very community. The distinction between the community's park and the private imparked park is critical, even though the naked eye may not be able to distinguish the grass on the village common from that appropriated for the manor's natural-style landscape garden.

10   Though the description of Goldsmith's village of "sweet Auburn" seems quite realistic, we can only guess at its actual identity, because it is a literary fiction. As fiction it is not about the historical details of actual

places but about the world of ideas attached to the long history of controversy surrounding the enclosure and imparkment of the land of the village
commoners. The commons were enclosed as part of ongoing social and economic processes that generated ever larger private estates. They were not
normally enclosed because of an ecological "tragedy of the commons" that
necessitated the land's transferal to private ownership as a result of environmental abuse by the commoners. This fact is made particularly poignant by
the irony of the enclosure of Auburn's working community commons in
order to make room for a park designed to look like a "natural" functioning
commons, but which, in reality, is an artificial construction for private pleasure. In treating the social issues generated by enclosure and imparkment,
this poem highlights the difference between the use of fiction to make people reflect upon their ideas of what is natural and the use of aesthetics to deceive by creating a scenic "virtual reality," which disguises an unnatural
world and makes it seem natural. This poem is especially relevant to our
theme because it is about the aesthetics of imparkment and "scenery"—a
term that itself derives from the realm of theatrical illusion. Guidebooks to
our national parks are full of references to vantage points from which one
might view natural "scenery." The origins of this word should alert us to the
fact that the nature we are led to see might be staged.

In his poem Goldsmith describes an environment that could be
Yosemite, with its stream and grassy lawns:

> How often have I loitered o'er thy green, . . .
> The sheltered cot, the cultivated farm,
> The never-failing brook, the busy mill,
> The decent church that topped the neighboring hill,
> The hawthorn bush, with seats beneath the shade,
> For talking age and whispering lovers made!
> How often have I blest the coming day,
> When toil remitting lent its turn to play,
> And all the village train, from labor free,
> Led up their sports beneath the spreading tree.

Yosemite, of course, is the sort of place the nation goes to take vacations on
the green beneath the park's spreading trees. Children romp and play in the
glades along the stream, and it is even possible to spy whispering lovers. It is
the sort of place where people who might have little in common in their
workaday lives share the green. The only thing that appears to be missing is
the village. Even though the Park Service has created an imitation Indian
village, it is no doubt hard for the average modern visitor to imagine a village like Goldsmith's Auburn in Yosemite! And yet, there actually once was a
village not unlike Auburn in Yosemite. It is difficult to find today because
between 1959 and 1963 the Park Service razed its buildings to the ground,
and the old village site is now the object of an extensive project to erase all
archaeological traces of its existence. Soon the village will have been entirely
rubbed out, with the exception of its 1879 church.

The church, from 1879, is all that survives from Yosemite village. The village was razed between 1959 and 1963. *(Photograph by Kenneth R. Olwig)*

The Gentrification and Appropriation of Common Nature

12   The village in Goldsmith's poem is "deserted" because it has been turned into a park for the gentry. This was done by a selfish individual who had the village enclosed and its population dispossessed to create a landscape park. The park would have been in the then popular "natural" pastoral style, which created the idealized appearance of a grazed commons while transforming the actual commons into a private pleasure park:

> The man of wealth and pride
> Takes up a space that many poor supplied;
> Space for his lake, his park's extended bounds, . . .
> His seat, where solitary sports are seen,
> Indignant spurns the cottage from the green.

The farmers must leave not just the land but England itself, and this is not all that leaves:

> E'en now, methinks, as pondering here I stand,
> I see the rural virtues leave the land.

The rural "virtues" of which Goldsmith speaks are quite similar to those which Americans think of in connection with Jeffersonian democracy:

> A time there was, ere England's griefs began,
> When every rood of ground maintained its man;
> . . . his best riches, ignorance of wealth.
>   But times are altered: trade's unfeeling train
> Usurp the land, and dispossess the swain;
> Along the lawn, where scattered hamlets rose,
> Unwieldy wealth and cumbrous pomp repose.

The meandering stream and its green meadows play an important role in this poem, as a nationally recognized symbol of community love and place that characterizes the "rural virtues" of England. The imparkment of this landscape was thus not only a means of creating an idyllic scene; it was also a means of appropriating an important symbol of natural community and thus "naturalizing" a process of enclosure that was anything but natural.

The Historical Symbolism of Common Nature

14 The stream and meadows are ideal symbols of the natural because they combine physical and spiritual elements of nature and the related idea of love. The stream and meadows are critical both to the fertility that sustains the village community physically through time and to the need for a community spirit that enables the population to manage its resources in an equitable and sustainable way. In this manner the meadow becomes a vital symbol of the brotherly love that sustains community identity. The power of the symbol depends to some degree on a historical geographical knowledge of the working relation between people and nature that, for many, has been lost. The physical and community dynamics that make the stream and meadows so historically compelling as a symbol are, in fact, quite fascinating. First the physical dynamics: the meandering of the stream causes the water flow to slow and nutrient-rich sediments to be deposited on the inside of the bend. As any canoeist knows, this causes the inside of the bend to become shallow and mucky, before it grades off into a mire of reeds and eventually grass. The fast-moving, turbulent water on the outside of the bend eats into the bank of the stream, creating sediment and causing the stream to meander further. During the spring the stream often runs over its banks, and the reeds and grass slow the water, causing it to deposit even more

sediment while cleaning the stream of sediments and nutrients that may have run off the grain fields. When the spring sun warms the soft muck, seeds germinate and feed on its nutrients, turning into a lush growth of reeds and grass in the summer. This grass makes the pastures for the keeper's game and/or the pastoralist's flocks. In a more developed agricultural economy, the manure from the grazing animals fertilizes the farmer's grain fields. It is for this reason that such meadows were often termed "the mother of the grain fields" and regarded as being the farmer's most valuable land. The grass by the meandering stream was therefore not just a comfortable place for lovers; it was, in a very concrete way, a source of the sustainable generative power of nature.

The village green with its meandering stream was also an ideal symbol of the sort of love that binds a community together. Both the meadowlands along the stream and the green surrounding the pond were community property prior to enclosure, and the village green is still community property throughout much of Europe. The water of the stream was also a vital common resource that had to be apportioned fairly. The grazing of the meadowlands thus required the villagers to agree on such issues as how many animals could be grazed, by whom, and when, so as to sustain their environmental viability. Issues of this sort were traditionally sorted out by the farmers in a kind of protodemocratic town meeting, or "moot," which was held on the green.

16   Though the village green was grazed, its primary purpose may well have been for sport and recreation and, of course, for community activities such as village meetings and fairs. The importance of the common use of grasslands both for grazing and for recreation is also attested to by the remnants of this landscape in the language we use today to express ideas of democracy and community. There is thus a close tie between the concept of the commons, commoners, and community. Even the word "fellowship" apparently derives ultimately from ancient Germanic terms referring to those who form (ship/shape) a body (*lag*—literally meaning "lay together") to share the grazing of animals (*fe*). American metaphors for democracy and community are, in fact, filled with references to the green environment characteristic of a commons. These metaphors range from Walt Whitman's "leaves of grass" to the expression "grassroots democracy." It is also for this reason that the lawn on the New England village commons is freighted with much of the same symbolic load for many Americans as the Old England village commons was for Goldsmith. The guidebook statement "To the entire world, a steepled church, set in its frame of white wooden houses around a manicured common, remains a scene which says 'New England'" thus leads the historical geographer Donald Meinig to comment,

drawing simply upon one's experience as an American (which is, after all, an appropriate way to judge a national symbol) it seems clear that such scenes carry connotations of continuity (of not just something important in our past, but a viable bond between past and present), of stability, quiet prosperity, cohesion and intimacy. Taken as a whole, the image of the New England village is widely assumed to symbolize for many people the best we have known of an intimate, family-centered, Godfearing, morally conscious, industrious, thrifty, democratic *community.*

The Washington Mall, which despite its name is not a shopping plaza, is in many respects such a common writ large, with the edifices and monuments of American democracy grouped around it.

In some ways the lawns of Yosemite were heirs to the symbolism of the community green that had wended its way from England to America along with the meandering stream. Olmsted thus not only stressed in his report on Yosemite that "the establishment by government of great public grounds for the free enjoyment of the people . . . is a political duty." He also felt that laws were necessary "to prevent an unjust use by individuals, of that which is not individual but public property." As Stephen T. Mather, the first director of the U.S. Park Service, wrote in a 1921 book on Yosemite, "our parks are not only show places and vacation lands but also vast schoolrooms of Americanism where people are studying, enjoying, and learning to love more deeply this land in which they live." The national parks were thus in many respects conceived of as a means of protecting what I would term "common nature" (or, perhaps better, "commons nature") by preserving it for use by the national community.

Was America Natural?

18   The unnaturalness of what was being done to the English national community was symbolized in Goldsmith's poem by the fact that the villagers were exiled from the garden into the wilderness. The wilderness of America! Wilderness was clearly a symbol of the unnatural. This is powerfully evident in Goldsmith's description of the New World to which his villagers are exiled:

> Ah, no. To distant climes, a dreary scene,
> Where half the convex world intrudes between,
> Through torrid tracts with fainting steps they go, . . .
> The various terrors of that horrid shore:
> Those blazing suns that dart a downward ray,
> And fiercely shed intolerable day,
> Those matted woods where birds forget to sing,
> But silent bats in drowsy clusters cling;
> Those pois'nous fields with rank luxuriance crowned, . . .
> While oft in whirls the mad tornado flies,
> Mingling the ravaged landscape with the skies.
> Far different these from every former scene,
> The cooling brook, the grassy-vested green,
> The breezy covert of the warbling grove,
> That only sheltered thefts of harmless love.

Goldsmith's poem helps explain, in a rather backhanded way, some of the motivation that led Americans to preserve the verdant meadows of Yosemite and Yellowstone as the first national parks. Americans were ashamed of the way Europeans like Goldsmith tended to depict the United States as having an unnaturally wild and unkempt scenery. When park scenery was discovered at Yosemite and Yellowstone that could rival the scenery of the natural landscape gardens of Britain, it seemed to prove that America was not by nature unnatural. It was only poetic justice to make these parklands into parks for the American people. This, in fact, is precisely the way Olmsted saw Yosemite. Olmsted's idea for Yosemite was as American as the landscape parks of England were British, or as the Parisian state monuments to nationhood were French. Writing at the close of the Civil War, Olmsted clearly envisioned the park as a monument reaffirming America's national identity. He thus presented Yosemite as being on a par with Thomas Crawford's Statue of Liberty,* New York's Central Park, Washington's Capitol dome and fresco *Westward the Course of Empire Takes Its Way,* by Emanuel Leutze.

Unnatural Scenery?

20 The bitter irony of the imparkment of the village green in Goldsmith's poem illustrates the way a natural physical scene can create an aesthetic appearance that "naturalizes" human conditions many would regard to be unnatural:

> Thus fares the land, by luxury betrayed;
> In nature's simplest charms at first arrayed;
> But verging to decline, its splendors rise,
> Its vistas strike, its palaces surprise;
> While, scourged by famine from the smiling land,
> The mournful peasant leads his humble band;
> And while he sinks, without one arm to save,
> The country blooms—a garden and a grave.

Similar rhetoric actually was used in the early disputes over Yosemite's imparkment. In 1868 Representative James A. Johnson of California thus opposed the appropriation of James Lamon's Yosemite farm and orchard by stating that the Constitution and laws of the United States made no provision "for the creation of fancy pleasure grounds by Congress out of citizens' farms." While Johnson's reaction may seem exaggerated, Yosemite did set a precedent, in principle, for the appropriation and destruction of farms that took place with the establishment of the Shenandoah National Park in the 1920s and 1930s. Some of these farms dated back to the eighteenth century, and their removal involved the uprooting of several thousand people. Early supporters of natural parks as wild scenery actually feared a public perception

---

* The American sculptor Thomas Crawford (1814–1857) is best known for his statue of freedom which sits on top of the U.S. Capitol Building. Also known as "Armed Freedom," it is not be confused with the large Statue of Liberty in New York harbor.

of Yosemite valley as an agricultural landscape, rather than as untouched natural scenery. In their publications they therefore sought to give the impression that the rural cultural landscape did not exist, or sought to have it removed altogether.

The tendency to define a landscape as being either natural, in which case it is ideally untrammeled virgin wilderness, or cultural is perhaps typically American. "It is no accident," as David Lowenthal puts it, "that God's own wilderness and His junkyard are in the same country." He is referring to the American tendency to dichotomize landscapes into natural and wild ones, which are strictly protected against human development, and human ones, which tend to be poorly protected and regulated. In Denmark, by contrast, the nature preservation movement has largely opposed setting aside nature in enclosed parks. Danes have essentially preferred to treat the entire nation as a park. They do this, in part, by regulating land use in areas considered by experts and community representatives to be important examples of "nature." Few such areas would meet American standards for wilderness, yet, as the example of Yosemite shows, American "natural" landscapes may not be as wild as they appear. England now has national natural parks that, unlike the aristocracy's landscape gardens, are expressly open to the entire nation. They are not, furthermore, pastoral paradises preserved from evidence of human labor, but working agrarian landscapes. Unlike their American counterparts, they tend to be conserved precisely because of their evidence of ancient habitation and stewardship, and it is widely recognized that the landscape must continue to be worked by the local community if it is to exist.

22   The vistas of the gentlemen's park in Goldsmith's poem offer striking but deceptive surprises. At the same time as the prospect pleases, the working landscape, with its green and stream, is neglected. The overgrown state of a once sustainably productive environment is used to symbolize the unnaturalness of the rulers of the English nation:

> And desolation saddens all thy green:
> One only master grasps the whole domain,
> And half a tillage stints thy smiling plain;
> No more thy grassy brook reflects the day,
> But, choked with sedges, works its weedy way.

Much of the symbolism of Goldsmith's poem can be traced back to sources in the classical literary pastoral. But we are also dealing with what might be termed a "natural" symbol, because it is born out of basic forms of human environmental activity such as hunting, pastoralism, and agriculture. The Indian woman Totuya thus immediately remarked upon the deterioration of the Yosemite valley in 1929 when she returned for the first time since she had been driven out by Savage's troops in 1851. The granddaughter of Chief Tenaya, she was now the sole survivor of the band of Ahwahneechee Indians that had dwelled in the valley. The nature purists, such as Muir and his backers in the Sierra Club, who had opposed attempts to graze and burn the area "Indian style," were at least partially responsible for its becoming overgrown with vegetation. It was conceptually impossible, of course, for the park to be both a wild scenic expression of U.S. values and an Indian cultural landscape. But the fact remained that the Yosemite that was "discovered" in 1852 "presented the appearance of a well kept park" because it was a park in the original sense of the word. The Indian gamekeepers burned it to promote, among other things, the growth of grass for game and black oaks for acorns. The open environment was also ideal for Indian field games. According to Lafayette Bunnell, in 1855 "there was no undergrowth of young trees to obstruct clear open views in any part of the valley from one side of the Merced River across to the base of the opposite wall." The extent of "clear open meadow land . . . was at least four times as large" as in 1894, when he made these comments. The result of the white man's neglect was an environment that led Totuya to shake her head and exclaim, "Too dirty; too much bushy."

Totuya's "aesthetic" judgment was based on an environmental stewardship that sought to sustain the ability of the tribe to reproduce itself. This use-oriented aesthetic is foreign to the visually oriented, scenic aesthetic of the champions of the natural park. Olmsted, for example, made a point of arguing that "savages" were little affected by "the power of scenery," and he decried the Indians' burning. The problem, unfortunately, is that when the park is not regularly burned and cleared, the accumulation of detritus and bush ultimately makes for much more violent fires, which can also destroy the ancient forest that preservationists are so anxious to save. Ironically, the lack of burning also means that the very scenic views from the valley bottom that Olmsted so prized become obliterated by vegetation. This suggests that Olmsted's British landscape garden ideal is insufficient as a model for natural parks. A better ideal might be landscapes showing forms of sustainable community stewardship. This, however, would mean accepting the natural priority of the Indian cultural landscape, not as a visual scene, but as a place of dwelling.

Raw Nature, Raw Power

24   After the designation of Yellowstone as a national park in 1872, more than twenty years went by before the next parks were named. Many of these new parks were characterized solely by wild infertile environments, with no counterbalancing green meadows, meandering streams, and pools such as are found at both Yosemite and Yellowstone. It is as if the ideal symbol of the natural has shifted focus from the valley bottom of Yosemite to the rugged walls and high mountains that surround it.

In some ways this change in focus reflects the difference in scenic values between Olmsted and Muir, a more transitional figure. Olmsted clearly saw Yosemite as a beautiful recreative park for the general population, and he emphasized the experience of the *ensemble* formed by the encompassing scenery surrounding the "native" vegetation at the valley bottom. He was not so interested in particular sights. For him it was "conceivable that any one or all of the cliffs of the Yo Semite might be changed in form and color, without lessening the enjoyment which is now obtained from the scenery." The cascades were "scarcely to be named among the elements of the scenery," and he actually preferred the park when the cascades were dry!

26   Muir, on the other hand, was emphatically a cliff and cascade man who climbed the valley's walls alone and preferred the view from the top down. The elite who followed in his singular footsteps traditionally have looked down on the hoi polloi flocked below, and the two differing points of view have made of the park contested territory. As a club member wrote in 1919, "to a Sierran bound for the high mountains the human noise and dust of Yosemite [Valley] seem desecration of primitive nature." Though he was concerned about the living nature of the valley bottom, Muir was particularly interested in reading the "glacial hieroglyphics," written in the stone of the valley walls, "whose interpretation is the reward of all who devoutly study them."

The Nature of Mount Rushmore

The change in prevailing ideas of the natural, as reflected in the difference between the original American natural parks and the newer variety, can perhaps best be symbolized by the figures on Mount Rushmore. They look out from a mountainside not unlike the walls of Yosemite, but they do not look down on an enclosed green and watered valley.

28   At Mount Rushmore we have graven, into a South Dakotan mountain, images intended to express American national values by their creator, Gutzon Borglum. According to Borglum's wife, who acted as the sculptor's spokesman, the effigies expressed a "sincere patriotic effort to preserve and perpetuate the ideals of liberty and freedom on which our government was established and to record the territorial expansion of the Republic." These values are not only jackhammered and dynamited into the commonly owned physical nature of the nation; they represent, as it were, a vision of its shared spiritual nature. This was a vision of manifest destiny believed to have come to Borglum when he first stood on the crest of the mountain and was overwhelmed by the magisterial view "out over a horizon level and beaten like the rim of a great cartwheel 2,000 feet below."

      Mount Rushmore belongs to a later era of parks and monuments when barren cliffs did not need to be contrasted with fertile meadows in order to conjure up a picture of nature. One can imagine that Teddy Roosevelt, the favorite of Borglum and a friend of Muir, is quite happy on his cliff, spying out over the wilderness. He had a hunting lodge in the Dakotas, and this was an area where he loved to test his masculinity against a rugged nature. This rough-riding warrior, outdoorsman, big-game hunter, and father of American imperial expansion, would probably look down his long stony nose at the soft nature lovers in Yosemite valley. His national values are more like those expressed by William C. Everhart, an official in the National Park Service, when he described the parks as preserving the memory of an era in American history when the "exemplary virtues of rugged individualism and free enterprise were the foremost commandments of Manifest Destiny."

30   If Teddy is happy with the magisterial view from Mount Rushmore, Jefferson and Washington are no doubt longing for the grassy lawns of Monticello or Mount Vernon (which despite their names are on hills, *not* mountains). Abraham Lincoln probably identified more with the leaves of prairie grass and the lilac-bedecked dooryards of prime midwestern farm

houses. Honest Abe, too, is no doubt wondering what he is doing carved
into a mountain, alone in a wilderness with three other men. In the period
between Jefferson and Roosevelt a sea change occurred in prevailing ideas
of nature and the natural. Though this change had been brewing since the
Renaissance, it is during the nineteenth century that we see a virtual reversal
in the symbolism of the natural. The wild, which had once been the epitome
of the unnatural, now becomes a natural ideal.

The Idolization of the Wilderness

In times past the wilderness was associated with demons—the most famous, of course, being the devil himself. It is in the wilderness that Jesus,
the prophet of love, is be*wild*ered and tempted by Satan. Wild environments are places where one "strays from the path" and becomes lost both
physically and spiritually. The meaning of the word "diabolic" (from which
the word "devil" derives) is highlighted when it is contrasted to that of
"symbolic." A symbol is something that stands for something else. The
Greek and Latin prefix "sym" means "together," suggesting that a symbol
brings meanings together. The word "diabolic," by contrast derives from
Greek and Latin words that literally mean "thrown across," which suggests
that the symbolic and the diabolic might be at cross-purposes. The diabolic
is thus typically identified with the graven image or idol, which does not
stand, symbolically, for the abstract idea of God, but which is treated as
being itself a god. The graven image or idol is diabolic because it blocks or
confuses meaning when it no longer stands for the abstract divine nature of
the Godhead, but is seen to be the Godhead itself.

32   "In the beginning was the Word," according to the word of the Scrip-
ture, "and the Word was God." The message of God was to be found not in
the pantheism and graven images of the pagans but in the intangible symbolic expression of the word with which God ordered and created nature. If
you followed that holy word, and loved thy neighbor as thyself, you would
live as in a garden paradise. And the physical "nature" of that garden would
be a physical symbolic expression of the spiritual "nature" of that love. The
reverse, however, is not true. People do not necessarily love one another because they live in a paradisiacal garden. It would be diabolic, and contrary to
the word of the Bible, to confuse the biblical ideal of a natural state of
human affairs with the physical nature that symbolizes that state. This, however, is just the sort of confusion that is generated when we treat concrete
wild nature as something that is in and of itself holy. People or businesses do
not necessarily become moral or natural because they preserve nature. Natural environments are generated and preserved because people act morally
or naturally. The central point here, however, is not moral or religious,
though it derives historically from arguments couched in moral and religious terms. It is simply that meaning is confused when physical nature is
not seen to be an expression of human values but rather is seen to embody
values in and of itself. The values that humans place in physical nature are
displaced and obscured when they are made to appear to derive from the

objective authority of that nature rather than from a subjective human source. It then becomes difficult to discern the true origin and meaning of these values, and the resulting confusion can be quite diabolical.

A painting that captures the new idolization of wilderness is Caspar David Friedrich's depiction of a lone figure staring across a sea of clouds

Caspar David Friedrich's early-nineteenth-century painting of a lone wanderer above a sea of clouds, entitled *Wanderer über dem Nebelmeer*, emphasizes the grandeur of nature and the relative insignificance of the individual. *(Courtesy Hamburger Kunsthalle, Hamburg, Germany)*

and mountaintops from around 1818 called *Wanderer über dem Nebelmeer.* In this painting nature becomes something raw and rugged that lies opposite the lone viewer, who gazes upon it across a chasm of space. For people like Friedrich the sublime wild mountain scenery was sacred. It was this sort of nature that the transcendental philosopher Ralph Waldo Emerson was looking for, bearing a German dictionary and a work by Johann Wolfgang Goethe, when he visited John Muir at Yosemite in May 1871.

34   Muir himself had originally gone to Yosemite in 1868 in search of "any place that is wild." Encountering the wild was, for him, a religious experience, and he heard a "sublime psalm" in the "pure wildness" of a cataract. At Yosemite he found a 2,500-foot-high "grand Sierra Cathedral," built by "nature," where one could worship. Yosemite, for him, was a place where "no holier temple has ever been consecrated by the heart of man." For Emerson and Muir alike the most sublime aspect of the park was the magisterial views downward from the valley walls. The religious power of Yosemite is a theme that was also picked up by the National Park Service. We find this sentiment expressed in 1926 by Stephen Mather when he wrote, "from Nature can be learned the scheme of creation and the handiwork of the Great Architect as from no other source." These sentiments persist, as one can see by the way quasi-religious statements like the above are used to adorn the interpretive sepulcher of many modern national parks.

The Demon in the Wild

However grateful we might be to Muir and others for their religious efforts to preserve the glories of Yosemite, a dark side to the venture reveals the dangers of idolizing wilderness as nature. When wildness is sanctified, it is difficult to interpret the theology expressed by the "hieroglyphics" of its landscape scenery. Muir's temple was bloodied from the start by the violent eviction of the native Indians. This tale is not made prettier by stories of false treaties of sale and suggestions of wanton murder and rape. Such stories also abound, of course, in the vicinity of Mount Rushmore, where Wounded Knee and Custer State Park are located. Questions are raised, too, by the odd alliance between wilderness preservers and industrial interests, particularly the railroads, which were not otherwise noted for their environmental concerns. We must even confront the schism, on the personal level, between Muir the wilderness purist and Muir the Yosemite sawmill operator at the base of Yosemite falls, producing lumber for tourist development. Finally, there is the troubling support by the wilderness preservationists for militarizing the park. As Muir wrote in 1895, "The effectiveness of the War Department in enforcing the laws of Congress has been illustrated in the management of Yosemite National Park." He was impressed by the army's work because "the sheep having been rigidly excluded, a luxuriant cover has sprung up on the desolate forest floor, fires have been choked before they could do any damage, and hopeful bloom and beauty have taken the place of ashes and dust." To him, "one soldier in the woods, armed with authority and a gun, would be more effective in forest preservation than millions of forbidding notices." Such words are in the worst tradition of the British park and game wardens, who were known for their use of violence. This cannot have been what the pacifist and lazy man's gardener Henry David Thoreau had in mind when he made the oft-abused statement "In Wildness is the preservation of the world!"

36   The point in noting this dark side of the wilderness preservation movement is neither to discredit important prophets of the environmental movement nor to decry the existence of the American national parks. It is rather to encourage us to rethink the nature of these parks and to find the place where our modern concept of nature may bewilder us and lead us astray. It is time, I believe, to reconsider the idolization of wilderness. It is one thing to respect and fear a wilderness conceived as something "wholly other," like the biblical Leviathan. This beast is a symbol of that wildness which is beyond the limits of human comprehension or control, which we neither can nor should attempt to fathom, tame, or worship. It can be useful to learn to respect human limitations and to fear the consequences of environmental hubris. It is quite another thing, however, to sanctify a wilderness that symbolizes not American community values but a rugged, misanthropic individualism that, in the face of historical evidence, often assumes the "tragedy of the commons" to be a foregone conclusion. In this case the wilderness is not "wholly other" but "wholly us," and to idolize such a wilderness is to idolize, unwittingly, ourselves. . . . ❖

Questions for Meaning

1. According to Olwig, how has the Western conception of nature changed since the late eighteenth century? Why does he want to defend an older conception of nature?
2. Why did the Yosemite valley appeal to influential Americans in the nineteenth century? How did their values differ from those of the native Americans who were evicted from the park that was established there?
3. Why does Olwig object to the term "scenery" when applied to nature?
4. What do the village green and the meandering system symbolize for Olwig? Why are these symbols significant for understanding the founding of Yosemite National Park?
5. What does Mount Rushmore reveal about American values?
6. What are the implications of this argument for the designation and management of national parks?
7. Vocabulary: reciprocity (2), counterpoint (3), etymologically (6), seminal (8), imparkment (9), aesthetics (10), dichotomize (21), pastoral (21), desecration (26), exemplary (29), pantheism (32), sepulcher (34), schism (35).

Questions about Strategy

1. Why does Olwig discuss an eighteenth-century poem when writing about our national parks? Are the quotations from *The Deserted Village* necessary for his purpose?
2. What does Olwig accomplish by contrasting Yosemite with Mount Rushmore?
3. Why does Olwig discuss a painting by Caspar David Friedrich? How does he tie this painting to Yosemite?
4. Consider the information included in paragraph 35. What is it meant to establish?
5. What kind of values does Olwig appeal to when arguing for a premodern concept of nature?

WILLIAM CRONON

THE TROUBLE WITH WILDERNESS

William Cronon is Frederick Jackson Turner Professor of History, Geography, and Environmental Studies at the University of Wisconsin. His works on environmental history include *Changes in the Land: Colonists, and the Ecology of New England* (1983), *Nature's Metropolis: Chicago and the Great West* (1991), and *Uncommon Ground: Toward Reinventing Nature* (1995). In the following essay, Cronon explores the meaning of "wilderness," showing how this concept has changed during the past two centuries. A careful scholar, Cronon included forty-three footnotes when he published this essay in *Uncommon Ground*—notes providing documentation and additional discussion. These notes have been omitted from the version reprinted here in order to conserve space. As you read, note how Cronon's reservations about prevailing attitudes toward "wilderness" are linked to his concern about the quality of the environment as a whole.

The time has come to rethink wilderness.

2   This will seem a heretical claim to many environmentalists, since the idea of wilderness has for decades been a fundamental tenet—indeed, a passion—of the environmental movement, especially in the United States. For many Americans wilderness stands as the last remaining place where civilization, that all too human disease, has not fully infected the earth. It is an island in the polluted sea of urban-industrial modernity, the one place we can turn for escape from our own too-muchness. Seen in this way, wilderness presents itself as the best antidote to our human selves, a refuge we must somehow recover if we hope to save the planet. As Henry David

Thoreau* once famously declared, "In Wildness is the preservation of the World."

But is it? The more one knows of its peculiar history, the more one realizes that wilderness is not quite what it seems. Far from being the one place on earth that stands apart from humanity, it is quite profoundly a human creation—indeed, the creation of very particular human cultures at very particular moments in human history. It is not a pristine sanctuary where the last remnant of an untouched, endangered, but still transcendent nature can for at least a little while longer be encountered without the contaminating taint of civilization. Instead, it is a product of that civilization, and could hardly be contaminated by the very stuff of which it is made. Wilderness hides its unnaturalness behind a mask that is all the more beguiling because it seems so natural. As we gaze into the mirror it holds up for us, we too easily imagine that what we behold is Nature when in fact we see the reflection of our own unexamined longings and desires. For this reason, we mistake ourselves when we suppose that wilderness can be the solution to our culture's problematic relationships with the nonhuman world, for wilderness is itself no small part of the problem.

4   To assert the unnaturalness of so natural a place will no doubt seem absurd or even perverse to many readers, so let me hasten to add that the nonhuman world we encounter in wilderness is far from being merely our own invention. I celebrate with others who love wilderness the beauty and power of the things it contains. Each of us who has spent time there can conjure images and sensations that seem all the more hauntingly real for having engraved themselves so indelibly on our memories. Such memories may be uniquely our own, but they are also familiar enough to be instantly recognizable to others. Remember this? The torrents of mist shoot out from the base of a great waterfall in the depths of a Sierra canyon, the tiny droplets cooling your face as you listen to the roar of the water and gaze up toward the sky through a rainbow that hovers just out of reach. Remember this too: looking out across a desert canyon in the evening air, the only sound a lone raven calling in the distance, the rock walls dropping away into a chasm so deep that its bottom all but vanishes as you squint into the amber light of the setting sun. And this: the moment beside the trail as you sit on a sandstone ledge, your boots damp with the morning dew while you take in the rich smell of the pines, and the small red fox—or maybe for you it was a raccoon or a coyote or a deer—that suddenly ambles across your path, stopping for a long moment to gaze in your direction with cautious indifference before continuing on its way. Remember the feelings of such moments, and you will know as well as I do that you were in the presence of something irreducibly nonhuman, something profoundly Other than yourself. Wilderness is made of that too.

* Henry David Thoreau (1817–1862) was an American naturalist, political activist, and writer. His account of living simply in the woods near Walden Pond has moved many generations of readers.

And yet: what brought each of us to the places where such memories became possible is entirely a cultural invention. Go back 250 years in American and European history, and you do not find nearly so many people wandering around remote corners of the planet looking for what today we would call "the wilderness experience." As late as the eighteenth century, the most common usage of the word "wilderness" in the English language referred to landscapes that generally carried adjectives far different from the ones they attract today. To be a wilderness then was to be "deserted," "savage," "desolate," "barren"—in short, a "waste," the word's nearest synonym. Its connotations were anything but positive, and the emotion one was most likely to feel in its presence was "bewilderment"—or terror.

6   Many of the word's strongest associations then were biblical, for it is used over and over again in the King James Version to refer to places on the margins of civilization where it is all too easy to lose oneself in moral confusion and despair. The wilderness was where Moses had wandered with his people for forty years, and where they had nearly abandoned their God to worship a golden idol. "For Pharaoh will say of the Children of Israel," we read in Exodus, "They are entangled in the land, the wilderness hath shut them in." The wilderness was where Christ had struggled with the devil and endured his temptations: "And immediately the Spirit driveth him into the wilderness. And he was there in the wilderness for forty days tempted of Satan; and was with the wild beasts; and the angels ministered unto him." The "delicious Paradise" of John Milton's Eden* was surrounded by "a steep wilderness, whose hairy sides / Access denied" to all who sought entry. When Adam and Eve were driven from that garden, the world they entered was a wilderness that only their labor and pain could redeem. Wilderness, in short, was a place to which one came only against one's will, and always in fear and trembling. Whatever value it might have arose solely from the possibility that it might be "reclaimed" and turned toward human ends—planted as a garden, say, or a city upon a hill. In its raw state, it had little or nothing to offer civilized men and women.

But by the end of the nineteenth century, all this had changed. The wastelands that had once seemed worthless had for some people come to seem almost beyond price. That Thoreau in 1862 could declare wildness to be the preservation of the world suggests the sea change that was going on. Wilderness had once been the antithesis of all that was orderly and good—it had been the darkness, one might say, on the far side of the garden wall—and yet now it was frequently likened to Eden itself. When John Muir arrived in the Sierra Nevada in 1869, he would declare, "No description of Heaven that I have ever heard or read of seems half so fine." He was hardly alone in expressing such emotions. One by one, various corners of the American map came to be designated as sites whose wild beauty was so spectacular that a growing number of citizens had to visit and see them for themselves. Niagara Falls was the first to undergo this transformation, but it

---

* One of the greatest of all English poets, John Milton (1608–1674) describes Eden in *Paradise Lost.*

Thomas Cole, *Expulsion from the Garden of Eden*, 1827–28. (Gift of Mrs. Maxim Karolik for the M. and M. Karolik Collection of American Paintings, 1815–1865, courtesy Museum of Fine Arts, Boston)

was soon followed by the Catskills, the Adirondacks, Yosemite, Yellowstone, and others. Yosemite was deeded by the U.S. government to the state of California in 1864 as the nation's first wildland park, and Yellowstone became the first true national park in 1872.

8   By the first decade of the twentieth century, in the single most famous episode in American conservation history, a national debate had exploded over whether the city of San Francisco should be permitted to augment its water supply by damming the Tuolumne River in Hetch Hetchy valley, well within the boundaries of Yosemite National Park. The dam was eventually built, but what today seems no less significant is that so many people fought to prevent its completion. Even as the fight was being lost, Hetch Hetchy became the battle cry of an emerging movement to preserve wilderness. Fifty years earlier, such opposition would have been unthinkable. Few would have questioned the merits of "reclaiming" a wasteland like this in order to put it to human use. Now the defenders of Hetch Hetchy attracted widespread national attention by portraying such an act not as improvement or progress but as desecration and vandalism. Lest one doubt that the old biblical metaphors had been turned completely on their heads, listen to John Muir attack the dam's defenders. "Their arguments," he wrote, "are curiously like those of the devil, devised for the destruction of the

first garden—so much of the very best Eden fruit going to waste; so much of the best Tuolumne water and Tuolumne scenery going to waste." For Muir and the growing number of Americans who shared his views, Satan's home had become God's own temple.

The sources of this rather astonishing transformation were many, but for the purposes of this essay they can be gathered under two broad headings: the sublime and the frontier. Of the two, the sublime is the older and more pervasive cultural construct, being one of the most important expressions of that broad transatlantic movement we today label as romanticism; the frontier is more peculiarly American, though it too had its European antecedents and parallels. The two converged to remake wilderness in their own image, freighting it with moral values and cultural symbols that it carries to this day. Indeed, it is not too much to say that the modern environmental movement is itself a grandchild of romanticism and post-frontier ideology, which is why it is no accident that so much environmentalist discourse takes its bearings from the wilderness these intellectual movements helped create. Although wilderness may today seem to be just one environmental concern among many, it in fact serves as the foundation for a long list of other such concerns that on their face seem quite remote from it. That is why its influence is so pervasive and, potentially, so insidious.

10   To gain such remarkable influence, the concept of wilderness had to become loaded with some of the deepest core values of the culture that created and idealized it: it had to become sacred. This possibility had been present in wilderness even in the days when it had been a place of spiritual danger and moral temptation. If Satan was there, then so was Christ, who had found angels as well as wild beasts during His sojourn in the desert. In the wilderness the boundaries between human and nonhuman, between natural and supernatural, had always seemed less certain than elsewhere. This was why the early Christian saints and mystics had often emulated Christ's desert retreat as they sought to experience for themselves the visions and spiritual testing He had endured. One might meet devils and run the risk of losing one's soul in such a place, but one might also meet God. For some that possibility was worth almost any price.

By the eighteenth century this sense of the wilderness as a landscape where the supernatural lay just beneath the surface was expressed in the doctrine of the *sublime,* a word whose modern usage has been so watered down by commercial hype and tourist advertising that it retains only a dim echo of its former power. In the theories of Edmund Burke, Immanuel Kant, William Gilpin,* and others, sublime landscapes were those rare places on earth where one had more chance than elsewhere to glimpse the face of God. Romantics had a clear notion of where one could be most sure of having this experience. Although God might, of course, choose to show Himself

---

* Edmund Burke (1729–1797), English statesman and author; Immanuel Kant (1724–1804), German philosopher; and William Gilpin (1724–1804), English travel writer and essayist, all fostered new ways of viewing the natural world.

anywhere, He would most often be found in those vast, powerful landscapes where one could not help feeling insignificant and being reminded of one's own mortality. Where were these sublime places? The eighteenth-century catalog of their locations feels very familiar, for we still see and value land-scapes as it taught us to do. God was on the mountaintop, in the chasm, in the waterfall, in the thundercloud, in the rainbow, in the sunset. One has only to think of the sites that Americans chose for their first national parks—Yellowstone, Yosemite, Grand Canyon, Rainier, Zion—to realize that virtually all of them fit one or more of these categories. Less sublime landscapes simply did not appear worthy of such protection; not until the 1940s, for instance, would the first swamp be honored in Everglades Na-tional Park, and to this day there is no national park in the grasslands.

12   Among the best proofs that one had entered a sublime landscape was the emotion it evoked. For the early romantic writers and artists who first began to celebrate it, the sublime was far from being a pleasurable experience. The classic description is that of William Wordsworth* as he recounted climbing the Alps and crossing the Simplon Pass in his autobiographical poem *The Prelude*. There, surrounded by crags and waterfalls, the poet felt himself literally to be in the presence of the divine—and experienced an emo-tion remarkably close to terror:

> The immeasurable height
> Of woods decaying, never to be decayed,
> The stationary blasts of waterfalls,
> And in the narrow rent at every turn
> Winds thwarting winds, bewildered and forlorn,
> The torrents shooting from the clear blue sky,
> The rocks that muttered close upon our ears,
> Black drizzling crags that spake by the way side
> As if a voice were in them, the sick sight
> And giddy prospect of the raving stream,
> The unfettered clouds and region of the Heavens,
> Tumult and peace, the darkness and the light—
> Were all like workings of one mind, the features
> Of the same face, blossoms upon one tree;
> Characters of the great Apocalypse,
> The types and symbols of Eternity,
> Of first, and last, and midst, and without end.

This was no casual stroll in the mountains, no simple sojourn in the gentle lap of nonhuman nature. What Wordsworth described was nothing less than a religious experience, akin to that of the Old Testament prophets as they conversed with their wrathful God. The symbols he detected in this

---

* Like other Romantic poets, William Wordsworth (1770–1850) celebrated the beauty and power of nature in his work.

wilderness landscape were more supernatural than natural, and they inspired more awe and dismay than joy or pleasure. No mere mortal was meant to linger long in such a place, so it was with considerable relief that Wordsworth and his companion made their way back down from the peaks to the sheltering valleys.

Lest you suspect that this view of the sublime was limited to timid Europeans who lacked the American know-how for feeling at home in the wilderness, remember Henry David Thoreau's 1846 climb of Mount Katahdin, in Maine. Although Thoreau is regarded by many today as one of the great American celebrators of wilderness, his emotions about Katahdin were no less ambivalent than Wordsworth's about the Alps.

> It was vast, Titanic, and such as man never inhabits. Some part of the beholder, even some vital part, seems to escape through the loose grating of his ribs as he ascends. He is more lone than you can imagine. . . . Vast, Titanic, inhuman Nature has got him at disadvantage, caught him alone, and pilfers him of some of his divine faculty. She does not smile on him as in the plains. She seems to say sternly, why came ye here before your time? This ground is not prepared for you. Is it not enough that I smile in the valleys? I have never made this soil for thy feet, this air for thy breathing, these rocks for thy neighbors. I cannot pity nor fondle thee here, but forever relentlessly drive thee hence to where I *am* kind. Why seek me where I have not called thee, and then complain because you find me but a stepmother?

This is surely not the way a modern backpacker or nature lover would describe Maine's most famous mountain, but that is because Thoreau's description owes as much to Wordsworth and other romantic contemporaries as to the rocks and clouds of Katahdin itself. His words took the physical mountain on which he stood and transmuted it into an icon of the sublime: a symbol of God's presence on earth. The power and the glory of that icon were such that only a prophet might gaze on it for long. In effect, romantics like Thoreau joined Moses and the children of Israel in Exodus when "they looked toward the wilderness, and behold, the glory of the Lord appeared in the cloud."

14   But even as it came to embody the awesome power of the sublime, wilderness was also being tamed—not just by those who were building settlements in its midst but also by those who most celebrated its inhuman beauty. By the second half of the nineteenth century, the terrible awe that Wordsworth and Thoreau regarded as the appropriately pious stance to adopt in the presence of their mountaintop God was giving way to a much more comfortable, almost sentimental demeanor. As more and more tourists sought out the wilderness as a spectacle to be looked at and enjoyed for its great beauty, the sublime in effect became domesticated. The wilderness was still sacred, but the religious sentiments it evoked were more those of a pleasant parish church than those of a grand cathedral or a harsh desert retreat. The writer who best captures this late romantic sense of a domesticated sublime is undoubtedly John Muir, whose descriptions of Yosemite

and the Sierra Nevada reflect none of the anxiety or terror one finds in earlier writers. Here he is, for instance, sketching on North Dome in Yosemite
Valley:

> No pain here, no dull empty hours, no fear of the past, no fear of the future.
> These blessed mountains are so compactly filled with God's beauty, no petty
> personal hope or experience has room to be. Drinking this champagne water
> is pure pleasure, so is breathing the living air, and every movement of limbs
> is pleasure, while the body seems to feel beauty when exposed to it as it feels
> the campfire or sunshine, entering not by the eyes alone, but equally
> through all one's flesh like radiant heat, making a passionate ecstatic plea-
> sure glow not explainable.

The emotions Muir describes in Yosemite could hardly be more different from Thoreau's on Katahdin or Wordsworth's on the Simplon Pass. Yet
all three men are participating in the same cultural tradition and contributing to the same myth: the mountain as cathedral. The three may differ in the
way they choose to express their piety—Wordsworth favoring an awe-filled
bewilderment, Thoreau a stern loneliness, Muir a welcome ecstasy—but
they agree completely about the church in which they prefer to worship.
Muir's closing words on North Dome diverge from his older contemporaries only in mood, not in their ultimate content:

> Perched like a fly on this Yosemite dome, I gaze and sketch and bask, often-
> times settling down into dumb admiration without definite hope of ever
> learning much, yet with the longing, unresting effort that lies at the door of
> hope, humbly prostrate before the vast display of God's power, and eager to
> offer self-denial and renunciation with eternal toil to learn any lesson in the
> divine manuscript.

Muir's "divine manuscript" and Wordsworth's "Characters of the great
Apocalypse" were in fact pages from the same holy book. The sublime
wilderness had ceased to be a place of satanic temptation and become instead a sacred temple, much as it continues to be for those who love it today.
16   But the romantic sublime was not the only cultural movement that
helped transform wilderness into a sacred American icon during the nineteenth century. No less important was the powerful romantic attraction of
primitivism, dating back at least to Rousseau*—the belief that the best antidote to the ills of an overly refined and civilized modern world was a return to simpler, more primitive living. In the United States, this was
embodied most strikingly in the national myth of the frontier. The historian Frederick Jackson Turner wrote in 1893 the classic academic statement
of this myth, but it had been part of American cultural traditions for well
over a century. As Turner described the process, easterners and European

---

* The French philosopher, Jean Jacques Rousseau (1712–1778), argued that human beings were essentially good in a primitive state but become corrupted by social influences.

immigrants, in moving to the wild unsettled lands of the frontier, shed the trappings of civilization, rediscovered their primitive racial energies, reinvented direct democratic institutions, and thereby reinfused themselves with a vigor, an independence, and a creativity that were the source of American democracy and national character. Seen in this way, wild country became a place not just of religious redemption but of national renewal, the quintessential location for experiencing what it meant to be an American.

One of Turner's most provocative claims was that by the 1890s the frontier was passing away. Never again would "such gifts of free land offer themselves" to the American people. "The frontier has gone," he declared, "and with its going has closed the first period of American history." Built into the frontier myth from its very beginning was the notion that this crucible of American identity was temporary and would pass away. Those who have celebrated the frontier have almost always looked backward as they did so, mourning an older, simpler, truer world that is about to disappear forever. That world and all of its attractions, Turner said, depended on free land—on wilderness. Thus, in the myth of the vanishing frontier lay the seeds of wilderness preservation in the United States, for if wild land had been so crucial in the making of the nation, then surely one must save its last remnants as monuments to the American past—and as an insurance policy to protect its future. It is no accident that the movement to set aside national parks and wilderness areas began to gain real momentum at precisely the time that laments about the passing frontier reached their peak. To protect wilderness was in a very real sense to protect the nation's most sacred myth of origin.

18   Among the core elements of the frontier myth was the powerful sense among certain groups of Americans that wilderness was the last bastion of rugged individualism. Turner tended to stress communitarian themes when writing frontier history, asserting that Americans in primitive conditions had been forced to band together with their neighbors to form communities and democratic institutions. For other writers, however, frontier democracy for communities was less compelling than frontier freedom for individuals. By fleeing to the outer margins of settled land and society—so the story ran—an individual could escape the confining strictures of civilized life. The mood among writers who celebrated frontier individualism was almost always nostalgic; they lamented not just a lost way of life but the passing of the heroic men who had embodied that life. Thus Owen Wister in the introduction to his classic 1902 novel *The Virginian* could write of "a vanished world" in which "the horseman, the cow-puncher, the last romantic figure upon our soil" rode only "in his historic yesterday" and would "never come again." For Wister, the cowboy was a man who gave his word and kept it ("Wall Street would have found him behind the times"), who did not talk lewdly to women ("Newport would have thought him old-fashioned"), who worked and played hard, and whose "ungoverned hours did not unman him." Theodore Roosevelt wrote with much the same nostalgic fervor about the "fine, manly qualities" of the "wild rough-rider of the plains." No one

could be more heroically masculine, thought Roosevelt, or more at home in the western wilderness:

> There he passes his days, there he does his life-work, there, when he meets death, he faces it as he has faced many other evils, with quiet, uncomplaining fortitude. Brave, hospitable, hardy, and adventurous, he is the grim pioneer of our race; he prepares the way for the civilization from before whose face he must himself disappear. Hard and dangerous though his existence is, it has yet a wild attraction that strongly draws to it his bold, free spirit.

This nostalgia for a passing frontier way of life inevitably implied ambivalence, if not downright hostility, toward modernity and all that it represented. If one saw the wild lands of the frontier as freer, truer, and more natural than other, more modern places, then one was also inclined to see the cities and factories of urban-industrial civilization as confining, false, and artificial. Owen Wister looked at the post-frontier "transition" that had followed "the horseman of the plains," and did not like what he saw: "a shapeless state, a condition of men and manners as unlovely as is that moment in the year when winter is gone and spring not come, and the face of Nature is ugly." In the eyes of writers who shared Wister's distaste for modernity, civilization contaminated its inhabitants and absorbed them into the faceless, collective, contemptible life of the crowd. For all of its troubles and dangers, and despite the fact that it must pass away, the frontier had been a better place. If civilization was to be redeemed, it would be by men like the Virginian who could retain their frontier virtues even as they made the transition to post-frontier life.

20   The mythic frontier individualist was almost always masculine in gender: here, in the wilderness, a man could be a real man, the rugged individual he was meant to be before civilization sapped his energy and threatened his masculinity. Wister's contemptuous remarks about Wall Street and Newport suggest what he and many others of his generation believed—that the comforts and seductions of civilized life were especially insidious for men, who all too easily became emasculated by the femininizing tendencies of civilization. More often than not, men who felt this way came, like Wister and Roosevelt, from elite class backgrounds. The curious result was that frontier nostalgia became an important vehicle for expressing a peculiarly bourgeois form of antimodernism. The very men who most benefited from urban-industrial capitalism were among those who believed they must escape its debilitating effects. If the frontier was passing, then men who had the means to do so should preserve for themselves some remnant of its wild landscape so that they might enjoy the regeneration and renewal that came from sleeping under the stars, participating in blood sports, and living off the land. The frontier might be gone, but the frontier experience could still be had if only wilderness were preserved.

Thus the decades following the Civil War saw more and more of the nation's wealthiest citizens seeking out wilderness for themselves. The elite passion for wild land took many forms: enormous estates in the Adirondacks and elsewhere (disingenuously called "camps" despite their many servants and amenities), cattle ranches for would-be rough riders on the Great Plains, guided big-game hunting trips in the Rockies, and luxurious resort hotels wherever railroads pushed their way into sublime landscapes. Wilderness suddenly emerged as the landscape of choice for elite tourists, who brought with them strikingly urban ideas of the countryside through which they traveled. For them, wild land was not a site for productive labor and not a permanent home; rather, it was a place of recreation. One went to the wilderness not as a producer but as a consumer, hiring guides and other backcountry residents who could serve as romantic surrogates for the rough riders and hunters of the frontier if one was willing to overlook their new status as employees and servants of the rich.

22   In just this way, wilderness came to embody the national frontier myth, standing for the wild freedom of America's past and seeming to represent a highly attractive natural alternative to the ugly artificiality of modern civilization. The irony, of course, was that in the process wilderness came to reflect the very civilization its devotees sought to escape. Ever since the nineteenth century, celebrating wilderness has been an activity mainly for well-to-do city folks. Country people generally know far too much about working the land to regard *un*worked land as their ideal. In contrast, elite urban tourists and wealthy sportsmen projected their leisure-time frontier fantasies onto the American landscape and so created wilderness in their own image.

There were other ironies as well. The movement to set aside national parks and wilderness areas followed hard on the heels of the final Indian wars, in which the prior human inhabitants of these areas were rounded up and moved onto reservations. The myth of the wilderness as "virgin," uninhabited land had always been especially cruel when seen from the perspective of the Indians who had once called that land home. Now they were forced to move elsewhere, with the result that tourists could safely enjoy the illusion that they were seeing their nation in its pristine, original state, in the new morning of God's own creation. Among the things that most marked the new national parks as reflecting a post-frontier consciousness was the relative absence of human violence within their boundaries. The actual frontier had often been a place of conflict, in which invaders and invaded fought for control of land and resources. Once set aside within the fixed and carefully policed boundaries of the modern bureaucratic state, the wilderness lost its savage image and became safe: a place more of reverie than of revulsion or fear. Meanwhile, its original inhabitants were kept out by dint of force, their earlier uses of the land redefined as inappropriate or even illegal. To this day, for instance, the Blackfeet continue to be accused of "poaching" on the lands of Glacier National Park that originally belonged to them and that were ceded by treaty only with the proviso that they be permitted to hunt there.

24   The removal of Indians to create an "uninhabited wilderness"—uninhabited as never before in the human history of the place—reminds us just

how invented, just how constructed, the American wilderness really is. To return to my opening argument: there is nothing natural about the concept of wilderness. It is entirely a creation of the culture that holds it dear, a product of the very history it seeks to deny. Indeed, one of the most striking proofs of the cultural invention of wilderness is its thoroughgoing erasure of the history from which it sprang. In virtually all of its manifestations, wilderness represents a flight from history. Seen as the original garden, it is a place outside of time, from which human beings had to be ejected before the fallen world of history could properly begin. Seen as the frontier, it is a savage world at the dawn of civilization, whose transformation represents the very beginning of the national historical epic. Seen as the bold landscape of frontier heroism, it is the place of youth and childhood, into which men escape by abandoning their pasts and entering a world of freedom where the constraints of civilization fade into memory. Seen as the sacred sublime, it is the home of a God who transcends history by standing as the One who remains untouched and unchanged by time's arrow. No matter what the angle from which we regard it, wilderness offers us the illusion that we can escape the cares and troubles of the world in which our past has ensnared us.

This escape from history is one reason why the language we use to talk about wilderness is often permeated with spiritual and religious values that reflect human ideals far more than the material world of physical nature. Wilderness fulfills the old romantic project of secularizing Judeo-Christian values so as to make a new cathedral not in some petty human building but in God's own creation, Nature itself. Many environmentalists who reject traditional notions of the Godhead and who regard themselves as agnostics or even atheists nonetheless express feelings tantamount to religious awe when in the presence of wilderness—a fact that testifies to the success of the romantic project. Those who have no difficulty seeing God as the expression of our human dreams and desires nonetheless have trouble recognizing that in a secular age Nature can offer precisely the same sort of mirror.

26   Thus it is that wilderness serves as the unexamined foundation on which so many of the quasi-religious values of modern environmentalism rest. The critique of modernity that is one of environmentalism's most important contributions to the moral and political discourse of our time more often than not appeals, explicitly or implicitly, to wilderness as the standard against which to measure the failings of our human world. Wilderness is the natural, unfallen antithesis of an unnatural civilization that has lost its soul. It is a place of freedom in which we can recover the true selves we have lost to the corrupting influences of our artificial lives. Most of all, it is the ultimate landscape of authenticity. Combining the sacred grandeur of the sublime with the primitive simplicity of the frontier, it is the place where we can see the world as it really is, and so know ourselves as we really are—or ought to be.

But the trouble with wilderness is that it quietly expresses and reproduces the very values its devotees seek to reject. The flight from history that is very nearly the core of wilderness represents the false hope of an escape from responsibility, the illusion that we can somehow wipe clean the slate of our past and return to the tabula rasa that supposedly existed before we began to leave our marks on the world. The dream of an unworked natural landscape is very much the fantasy of people who have never themselves had to work the land to make a living—urban folk for whom food comes from a supermarket or a restaurant instead of a field, and for whom the wooden houses in which they live and work apparently have no meaningful connection to the forests in which trees grow and die. Only people whose relation to the land was already alienated could hold up wilderness as a model for human life in nature, for the romantic ideology of wilderness leaves precisely nowhere for human beings actually to make their living from the land.

28   This, then, is the central paradox: wilderness embodies a dualistic vision in which the human is entirely outside the natural. If we allow ourselves to believe that nature, to be true, must also be wild, then our very presence in nature represents its fall. The place where we are is the place where nature is not. If this is so—if by definition wilderness leaves no place for human beings, save perhaps as contemplative sojourners enjoying their leisurely reverie in God's natural cathedral—then also by definition it can offer no solution to the environmental and other problems that confront us. To the extent that we celebrate wilderness as the measure with which we judge civilization, we reproduce the dualism that sets humanity and nature at opposite poles. We thereby leave ourselves little hope of discovering what an ethical, sustainable, *honorable* human place in nature might actually look like.

Worse: to the extent that we live in an urban-industrial civilization but at the same time pretend to ourselves that our *real* home is in the wilderness, to just that extent we give ourselves permission to evade responsibility for the lives we actually lead. We inhabit civilization while holding some part of ourselves—what we imagine to be the most precious part—aloof from its entanglements. We work our nine-to-five jobs in its institutions, we eat its food, we drive its cars (not least to reach the wilderness), we benefit from the intricate and all too invisible networks with which it shelters us, all the while pretending that these things are not an essential part of who we are. By imagining that our true home is in the wilderness, we forgive ourselves the homes we actually inhabit. In its flight from history, in its siren song of escape, in its reproduction of the dangerous dualism that sets human beings outside of nature—in all of these ways, wilderness poses a serious threat to responsible environmentalism at the end of the twentieth century.

30   By now I hope it is clear that my criticism in this essay is not directed at wild nature per se, or even at efforts to set aside large tracts of wild land, but rather at the specific habits of thinking that flow from this complex cultural construction called wilderness. It is not the things we label as wilderness that are the problem—for nonhuman nature and large tracts of the natural world *do* deserve protection—but rather what we ourselves mean when we use that label. Lest one doubt how pervasive these habits of thought actually are in contemporary environmentalism, let me list some of

the places where wilderness serves as the ideological underpinning for environmental concerns that might otherwise seem quite remote from it. Defenders of biological diversity, for instance, although sometimes appealing to more utilitarian concerns, often point to "untouched" ecosystems as the best and richest repositories of the undiscovered species we must certainly try to protect. Although at first blush an apparently more "scientific" concept than wilderness, biological diversity in fact invokes many of the same sacred values, which is why organizations like the Nature Conservancy have been so quick to employ it as an alternative to the seemingly fuzzier and more problematic concept of wilderness. There is a paradox here, of course. To the extent that biological diversity (indeed, even wilderness itself) is likely to survive in the future only by the most vigilant and self-conscious management of the ecosystems that sustain it, the ideology of wilderness is potentially in direct conflict with the very thing it encourages us to protect.

The most striking instances of this have revolved around "endangered species," which serve as vulnerable symbols of biological diversity while at the same time standing as surrogates for wilderness itself. The terms of the Endangered Species Act in the United States have often meant that those hoping to defend pristine wilderness have had to rely on a single endangered species like the spotted owl to gain legal standing for their case—thereby making the full power of sacred land inhere in a single numinous organism whose habitat then becomes the object of intense debate about appropriate management and use. The ease with which anti-environmental forces like the wise-use movement have attacked such single-species preservation efforts suggests the vulnerability of strategies like these.

32   Perhaps partly because our own conflicts over such places and organisms have become so messy, the convergence of wilderness values with concerns about biological diversity and endangered species has helped produce a deep fascination for remote ecosystems, where it is easier to imagine that nature might somehow be "left alone" to flourish by its own pristine devices. The classic example is the tropical rain forest, which since the 1970s has become the most powerful modern icon of unfallen, sacred land—a veritable Garden of Eden—for many Americans and Europeans. And yet protecting the rain forest in the eyes of First World environmentalists all too often means protecting it from the people who live there. Those who seek to preserve such "wilderness" from the activities of native peoples run the risk of reproducing the same tragedy—being forcibly removed from an ancient home—that befell American Indians. Third World countries face massive environmental problems and deep social conflicts, but these are not likely to be solved by a cultural myth that encourages us to "preserve" peopleless landscapes that have not existed in such places for millennia. At its worst, as environmentalists are beginning to realize, exporting American notions of wilderness in this way can become an unthinking and self-defeating form of cultural imperialism.

Perhaps the most suggestive example of the way that wilderness thinking can underpin other environmental concerns has emerged in the recent debate about "global change." In 1989 the journalist Bill McKibben published a book entitled *The End of Nature,* in which he argued that the prospect of global climate change as a result of unintentional human manipulation of the atmosphere means that nature as we once knew it no longer exists. Whereas earlier generations inhabited a natural world that remained more or less unaffected by their actions, our own generation is uniquely different. We and our children will henceforth live in a biosphere completely altered by our own activity, a planet in which the human and the natural can no longer be distinguished, because the one has overwhelmed the other. In McKibben's view, nature has died, and we are responsible for killing it. "The planet," he declares, "is utterly different now."

34   But such a perspective is possible only if we accept the wilderness premise that nature, to be natural, must also be pristine—remote from humanity and untouched by our common past. In fact, everything we know about environmental history suggests that people have been manipulating the natural world on various scales for as long as we have a record of their passing. Moreover, we have unassailable evidence that many of the environmental changes we now face also occurred quite apart from human intervention at one time or another in the earth's past. The point is not that our current problems are trivial, or that our devastating effects on the earth's ecosystems should be accepted as inevitable or "natural." It is rather that we seem unlikely to make much progress in solving these problems if we hold up to ourselves as the mirror of nature a wilderness we ourselves cannot inhabit.

        To do so is merely to take to a logical extreme the paradox that was built into wilderness from the beginning: if nature dies because we enter it, then the only way to save nature is to kill ourselves. The absurdity of this proposition flows from the underlying dualism it expresses. Not only does it ascribe greater power to humanity than we in fact possess—physical and biological nature will surely survive in some form or another long after we ourselves have gone the way of all flesh—but in the end it offers us little more than a self-defeating counsel of despair. The tautology gives us no way out: if wild nature is the only thing worth saving, and if our mere presence destroys it, then the sole solution to our own unnaturalness, the only way to protect sacred wilderness from profane humanity, would seem to be suicide. It is not a proposition that seems likely to produce very positive or practical results.

36   And yet radical environmentalists and deep ecologists all too frequently come close to accepting this premise as a first principle. When they express, for instance, the popular notion that our environmental problems began with the invention of agriculture, they push the human fall from natural grace so far back into the past that all of civilized history becomes a tale of ecological declension. Earth First! founder Dave Foreman captures the familiar parable succinctly when he writes,

        Before agriculture was midwifed in the Middle East, humans were in the wilderness. We had no concept of "wilderness" because everything was wilderness and *we were a part of it*. But with irrigation ditches, crop surpluses, and permanent villages, we became *apart from* the natural world. . . . Between the wilderness that created us and the civilization created by us grew an ever-widening rift.

In this view the farm becomes the first and most important battlefield in the long war against wild nature, and all else follows in its wake. From such a starting place, it is hard not to reach the conclusion that the only way human beings can hope to live naturally on earth is to follow the hunter-gatherers back into a wilderness Eden and abandon virtually everything that civilization has given us. It may indeed turn out that civilization will end in ecological collapse or nuclear disaster, whereupon one might expect to find any human survivors returning to a way of life closer to that cele-brated by Foreman and his followers. For most of us, though, such a debacle would be cause for regret, a sign that humanity had failed to fulfill its own promise and failed to honor its own highest values—including those of the deep ecologists.

In offering wilderness as the ultimate hunter-gatherer alternative to civilization, Foreman reproduces an extreme but still easily recognizable version of the myth of frontier primitivism.* When he writes of his fellow Earth Firsters that "we believe we must return to being animal, to glorying in our sweat, hormones, tears, and blood" and that "we struggle against the modern compulsion to become dull, passionless androids," he is following in the footsteps of Owen Wister. Although his arguments give primacy to defending biodiversity and the autonomy of wild nature, his prose becomes most passionate when he speaks of preserving "the wilderness experience." His own ideal "Big Outside" bears an uncanny resemblance to that of the frontier myth: wide open spaces and virgin land with no trails, no signs, no facilities, no maps, no guides, no rescues, no modern equipment. Tellingly, it is a land where hardy travelers can support themselves by hunting with "primitive weapons (bow and arrow, atlatl, knife, sharp rock)." Foreman claims that "the primary value of wilderness is not as a proving ground for young Huck Finns and Annie Oakleys," but his heart is with Huck and Annie all the same. He admits that "preserving a quality wilderness experi-ence for the human visitor, letting her or him flex Paleolithic muscles or seek visions, remains a tremendously important secondary purpose." Just so does Teddy Roosevelt's rough rider live on in the greener garb of a new age.

38   However much one may be attracted to such a vision, it entails prob-lematic consequences. For one, it makes wilderness the locus for an epic struggle between malign civilization and benign nature, compared with which all other social, political, and moral concerns seem trivial. Foreman writes, "The preservation of wildness and native diversity is *the* most im-portant issue. Issues directly affecting only humans pale in comparison." Presumably so do any environmental problems whose victims are mainly people, for such problems usually surface in landscapes that have already

* For an argument by Dave Foreman, see pp. 562–570.

"fallen" and are no longer wild. This would seem to exclude from the radical environmentalist agenda problems of occupational health and safety in industrial settings, problems of toxic waste exposure on "unnatural" urban and agricultural sites, problems of poor children poisoned by lead exposure in the inner city, problems of famine and poverty and human suffering in the "overpopulated" places of the earth—problems, in short, of environmental justice. If we set too high a stock on wilderness, too many other corners of the earth become less than natural and too many other people become less than human, thereby giving us permission not to care much about their suffering or their fate.

It is no accident that these supposedly inconsequential environmental problems affect mainly poor people, for the long affiliation between wilderness and wealth means that the only poor people who count when wilderness is *the* issue are hunter-gatherers, who presumably do not consider themselves to be poor in the first place. The dualism at the heart of wilderness encourages its advocates to conceive of its protection as a crude conflict between the "human" and the "nonhuman"—or, more often, between those who value the nonhuman and those who do not. This in turn tempts one to ignore crucial differences *among* humans and the complex cultural and historical reasons why different peoples may feel very differently about the meaning of wilderness.

40   Why, for instance, is the "wilderness experience" so often conceived as a form of recreation best enjoyed by those whose class privileges give them the time and resources to leave their jobs behind and "get away from it all"? Why does the protection of wilderness so often seem to pit urban recreationists against rural people who actually earn their living from the land (excepting those who sell goods and services to the tourists themselves)? Why in the debates about pristine natural areas are "primitive" peoples idealized, even sentimentalized, until the moment they do something unprimitive, modern, and unnatural, and thereby fall from environmental grace? What are the consequences of a wilderness ideology that devalues productive labor and the very concrete knowledge that comes from working the land with one's own hands? All of these questions imply conflicts among different groups of people, conflicts that are obscured behind the deceptive clarity of "human" vs. "nonhuman." If in answering these knotty questions we resort to so simplistic an opposition, we are almost certain to ignore the very subtleties and complexities we need to understand.

But the most troubling cultural baggage that accompanies the celebration of wilderness has less to do with remote rain forests and peoples than with the ways we think about ourselves—we American environmentalists who quite rightly worry about the future of the earth and the threats we pose to the natural world. Idealizing a distant wilderness too often means not idealizing the environment in which we actually live, the landscape that for better or worse we call home. Most of our most serious environmental problems start right here, at home, and if we are to solve those problems, we need an environmental ethic that will tell us as much about *using* nature as about *not* using it. The wilderness dualism tends to cast any use as *abuse*, and thereby denies us a middle ground in which responsible use and non-use might attain some kind of balanced, sustainable relationship. My own belief is that only by exploring this middle ground will we learn ways of imagining a better world for all of us: humans and nonhumans, rich people and poor, women and men, First Worlders and Third Worlders, white folks and people of color, consumers and producers—a world better for humanity in all of its diversity and for all the rest of nature too. The middle ground is where we actually live. It is where we—all of us, in our different places and ways—make our homes.

42   That is why when I think of the times I myself have come closest to experiencing what I might call the sacred in nature, I often find myself remembering wild places much closer to home. I think, for instance, of a small pond near my house where water bubbles up from limestone springs to feed a series of pools that rarely freeze in winter and so play home to waterfowl that stay here for the protective warmth even on the coldest of winter days, gliding silently through steaming mists as the snow falls from gray February skies. I think of a November evening long ago when I found myself on a Wisconsin hilltop in rain and dense fog, only to have the setting sun break through the clouds to cast an otherwordly golden light on the misty farms and woodlands below, a scene so unexpected and joyous that I lingered past dusk so as not to miss any part of the gift that had come my way. And I think perhaps most especially of the blown-out, bankrupt farm in the sand country of central Wisconsin where Aldo Leopold and his family tried one of the first American experiments in ecological restoration, turning ravaged and infertile soil into carefully tended ground where the human and the nonhuman could exist side by side in relative harmony. What I celebrate about such places is not *just* their wildness, though that certainly is among their most important qualities; what I celebrate even more is that they remind us of the wildness in our own backyards, of the nature that is all around us if only we have eyes to see it.

Indeed, my principal objection to wilderness is that it may teach us to be dismissive or even contemptuous of such humble places and experiences. Without our quite realizing it, wilderness tends to privilege some parts of nature at the expense of others. Most of us, I suspect, still follow the conventions of the romantic sublime in finding the mountaintop more glorious than the plains, the ancient forest nobler than the grasslands, the mighty canyon more inspiring than the humble marsh. Even John Muir, in arguing against those who sought to dam his beloved Hetch Hetchy valley in the Sierra Nevada, argued for alternative dam sites in the gentler valleys of the foothills—a preference that had nothing to do with nature and everything with the cultural traditions of the sublime. Just as problematically, our frontier traditions have encouraged Americans to define "true" wilderness as requiring very large tracts of roadless land—what Dave Foreman calls "The Big Outside." Leaving aside the legitimate empirical question in conservation biology of how large a tract of land must be before a given species can reproduce on it, the emphasis on big wilderness reflects a romantic frontier belief that one hasn't really gotten away from civilization unless one can go for days at a time without encountering another human being. By teaching us to fetishize sublime places and wide open country, these peculiarly American ways of thinking about wilderness encourage us to adopt too high a standard for what counts as "natural." If it isn't hundreds of square miles big, if it doesn't give us God's-eye views or grand vistas, if it doesn't permit us the illusion that we are alone on the planet, then it really isn't natural. It's too small, too plain, or too crowded to be *authentically* wild.

44   In critiquing wilderness as I have done in this essay, I'm forced to confront my own deep ambivalence about its meaning for modern environmentalism. On the one hand, one of my own most important environmental ethics is that people should always to be conscious that they are part of the natural world, inextricably tied to the ecological systems that sustain their lives. Any way of looking at nature that encourages us to believe we are separate from nature—as wilderness tends to do—is likely to reinforce environmentally irresponsible behavior. On the other hand, I also think it no less crucial for us to recognize and honor nonhuman nature as a world we did not create, a world with its own independent, nonhuman reasons for being as it is. The autonomy of nonhuman nature seems to me an indispensable corrective to human arrogance. Any way of looking at nature that helps us remember—as wilderness also tends to do—that the interests of people are not necessarily identical to those of every other creature or of the earth itself is likely to foster *responsible* behavior. To the extent that wilderness has served as an important vehicle for articulating deep moral values regarding our obligations and responsibilities to the nonhuman world, I would not want to jettison the contributions it has made to our culture's way of thinking about nature.

If the core problem of wilderness is that it distances us too much from the very things it teaches us to value, then the question we must ask is what it can tell us about *home,* the place where we actually live. How can we take the positive values we associate with wilderness and bring them closer to home? I think the answer to this question will come by broadening our sense of the otherness that wilderness seeks to define and protect. In reminding us of the world we did not make, wilderness can teach profound feelings of humility and respect as we confront our fellow beings and the earth itself. Feelings like these argue for the importance of self-awareness and self-criticism as we exercise our own ability to transform the world around us, helping us set responsible limits to human mastery—which without such limits too easily becomes human hubris. Wilderness is the place where, symbolically at least, we try to withhold our power to dominate.

46   Wallace Stegner once wrote of

the special human mark, the special record of human passage, that distinguishes man from all other species. It is rare enough among men, impossible to any other form of life. *It is simply the deliberate and chosen refusal to make any marks at all. . . .* We are the most dangerous species of life on the planet, and every other species, even the earth itself, has cause to fear our power to exterminate. But we are also the only species which, when it chooses to do so, will go to great effort to save what it might destroy.

The myth of wilderness, which Stegner knowingly reproduces in these remarks, is that we can somehow leave nature untouched by our passage. By now it should be clear that this for the most part is an illusion. But Stegner's deeper message then becomes all the more compelling. If living in history means that we cannot help leaving marks on a fallen world, then the dilemma we face is to decide what kinds of marks we wish to leave. It is just here that our cultural traditions of wilderness remain so important. In the broadest sense, wilderness teaches us to ask whether the Other must always bend to our will, and, if not, under what circumstances it should be allowed to flourish without our intervention. This is surely a question worth asking about everything we do, and not just about the natural world.

When we visit a wilderness area, we find ourselves surrounded by plants and animals and physical landscapes whose otherness compels our attention. In forcing us to acknowledge that they are not of our making, that they have little or no need of our continued existence, they recall for us a creation far greater than our own. In the wilderness, we need no reminder that a tree has its own reasons for being, quite apart from us. The same is less true in the gardens we plant and tend ourselves: there it is far easier to forget the otherness of the tree. Indeed, one could almost measure wilderness by the extent to which our recognition of its otherness requires a conscious, willed act on our part. The romantic legacy means that wilderness is more a state of mind than a fact of nature, and the state of mind that today most defines wilderness is *wonder*. The striking power of the wild is that wonder in the face of it requires no act of will, but forces itself upon us—as an expression of the nonhuman world experienced through the lens of our cultural history—as proof that ours is not the only presence in the universe.

48   Wilderness gets us into trouble only if we imagine that this experience of wonder and otherness is limited to the remote corners of the planet, or that it somehow depends on pristine landscapes we ourselves do not inhabit. Nothing could be more misleading. The tree in the garden is in reality no less other, no less worthy of our wonder and respect, than the tree in an ancient forest that has never known an ax or a saw—even though the tree in the forest reflects a more intricate web of ecological relationships. The tree in the garden could easily have sprung from the same seed as the tree in the forest, and we can claim only its location and perhaps its form as our own. Both trees stand apart from us; both share our common world. The special power of the tree in the wilderness is to remind us of this fact. It can teach us to recognize the wildness we did not see in the tree we planted in our own backyard. By seeing the otherness in that which is most unfamiliar, we can learn to see it too in that which at first seemed merely ordinary. If wilderness can do this—if it can help us perceive and respect a nature we had

forgotten to recognize as natural—then it will become part of the solution to our environmental dilemmas rather than part of the problem.

This will only happen, however, if we abandon the dualism that sees the tree in the garden as artificial—completely fallen and unnatural—and the tree in the wilderness as natural—completely pristine and wild. Both trees in some ultimate sense are wild; both in a practical sense now depend on our management and care. We are responsible for both, even though we can claim credit for neither. Our challenge is to stop thinking of such things according to a set of bipolar moral scales in which the human and the non-human, the unnatural and the natural, the fallen and the unfallen, serve as our conceptual map for understanding and valuing the world. Instead, we need to embrace the full continuum of a natural landscape that is also cultural, in which the city, the suburb, the pastoral, and the wild each has its proper place, which we permit ourselves to celebrate without needlessly denigrating the others. We need to honor the Other within and the Other next door as much as we do the exotic Other that lives far away—a lesson that applies as much to people as it does to (other) natural things. In particular, we need to discover a common middle ground in which all of these things, from the city to the wilderness, can somehow be encompassed in the word "home." Home, after all, is the place where finally we make our living. It is the place for which we take responsibility, the place we try to sustain so we can pass on what is best in it (and in ourselves) to our children.

50   The task of making a home in nature is what Wendell Berry has called "the forever unfinished lifework of our species." "The only thing we have to preserve nature with," he writes, "is culture; the only thing we have to preserve wildness with is domesticity." Calling a place home inevitably means that we will *use* the nature we find in it, for there can be no escape from manipulating and working and even killing some parts of nature to make our home. But if we acknowledge the autonomy and otherness of the things and creatures around us—an autonomy our culture has taught us to label with the word "wild"—then we will at least think carefully about the uses to which we put them, and even ask if we should use them at all. Just so can we still join Thoreau in declaring that "in Wildness is the preservation of the World," for *wild*ness (as opposed to wilderness) can be found anywhere: in the seemingly tame fields and woodlots of Massachusetts, in the cracks of a Manhattan sidewalk, even in the cells of our own bodies. As Gary Snyder has wisely said, "A person with a clear heart and open mind can experience the wilderness anywhere on earth. It is a quality of one's own consciousness. The planet is a wild place and always will be." To think ourselves capable of causing "the end of nature" is an act of great hubris, for it means forgetting the wildness that dwells everywhere within and around us.

Learning to honor the wild—learning to remember and acknowledge the autonomy of the other—means striving for critical self-consciousness in all of our actions. It means that deep reflection and respect must accompany each act of use, and means too that we must always consider the possibility of non-use. It means looking at the part of nature we intend to turn toward our own ends and asking whether we can use it again and again and again—sustainably—without its being diminished in the process. It means never imagining that we can flee into a mythical wilderness to escape history and the obligation to take responsibility for our own actions that history inescapably entails. Most of all, it means practicing remembrance and gratitude, for thanksgiving is the simplest and most basic of ways for us to recollect the nature, the culture, and the history that have come together to make the world as we know it. If wildness can stop being (just) out there and start being (also) in here, if it can start being as humane as it is natural, then perhaps we can get on with the unending task of struggling to live rightly in the world—not just in the garden, not just in the wilderness, but in the home that encompasses them both. ❖

Questions for Meaning

1. Why does Cronon believe that "wilderness" is "a product of civilization"? How has the perception of "wilderness" changed in recent centuries?
2. What is the doctrine of the sublime, and how did it influence the thinking that led to the creation of our first national parks?
3. What kind of values are implicit in our myth of the American frontier?
4. How have race and social class been factors in the creation of national park and wilderness areas?
5. What does Cronon mean in paragraphs 23–29 when he claims that wilderness represents "a flight from history"?
6. How does Cronon think we should respond to nature?
7. Vocabulary: pristine (3), transcendent (3), sojourn (10), icon (13), surrogates (21), tantamount (25), tabula rasa (27), tautology (35), fetishize (43).

Questions about Strategy

1. Consider the memories Cronon tries to invoke in paragraph 4. Who is most likely to have such memories? Is he wise to direct his argument to an audience of this sort?
2. Why does Cronon devote so much space to discussing cultural values that prevailed in the eighteenth and nineteenth centuries?
3. In paragraphs 13–15, Cronon contrasts the experiences of Henry David Thoreau and John Muir. What is the purpose of this contrast?
4. How does Cronon establish that he values wilderness even though he is challenging conventional thinking about it?
5. In his conclusion, Cronon calls for discovering "a common middle ground." Does he give readers any help envisioning what that common ground could be?

DAVE FOREMAN

MISSING LINKS

Although we frequently think of our national parks and wilderness areas in terms of how well they serve our own needs, environmentalists urge us to consider how this land can be used to preserve wildlife. Dave Foreman, Director of the Sierra Club and Chairman of the Wildlands Project, is also the author of *Confessions of an Eco-Warrior* (1991) and coauthor of *The Big Outside* (1992). He first published this argument in a 1995 issue of *Sierra*. As you read, note how he points to positive achievements and emphasizes a proposal for positive change instead of dwelling on the failures of the past.

Field biologists, with their stubbornly insistent focus on the minutiae of the living world, are unlikely people to be scaring the bejesus out of us.

2   But they were the first to see, beginning back in the 1970s, that populations of myriad species were declining and ecosystems were collapsing around the world. Tropical rainforests were falling to saw and torch. Ocean fish stocks were crashing. Coral reefs were dying. Elephants, rhinos, gorillas, tigers, and other "charismatic megafauna" were being slaughtered. Frogs everywhere were vanishing. The losses were occurring in oceans and on the highest peaks, in deserts and in rivers, in tropical rainforests and arctic tundra.

Michael Soulé, a population biologist who founded the Society for Conservation Biology, and Harvard's famed entomologist E. O. Wilson pieced together these disturbing anecdotes and bits of data. By studying the fossil record, they knew that during 500 million years of terrestrial evolution there had been five great extinctions. The last occurred 65 million years ago when the dinosaurs disappeared.

4   Wilson, Soulé, and company calculated that the current rate of extinction is as much as 10,000 times the normal background rate documented in the fossil record. That discovery hit with the subtlety of a comet striking Earth: we are presiding over the sixth great extinction in the planet's history.

Wilson warns that one-third of all species on Earth could die out in the next 40 years. Soulé says that the only large mammals remaining after the year 2000 will be those that humans consciously choose to protect. "For all practical purposes," he says, "the evolution of new species of large vertebrates has come to a screeching halt."

6   Alas, this biological meltdown can't be blamed on something as simple as stray cosmic detritus. Instead, responsibility sits squarely on the shoulders of 5.5 billion eating, manufacturing, warring, breeding, and real-estate-developing humans.

The damage done in the United States is particularly well documented. According to a National Biological Service study released early this year, ecosystems covering half the area of the 48 contiguous states are endangered or threatened. The longleaf-pine ecosystem, for example, once the dominant vegetation of the coastal plain from Virginia to Texas and covering more than 60 million acres, remains only in tiny remnants. Ninety-nine percent of the native grassland of California has been lost. There has been a 90 percent loss of riparian ecosystems in Arizona and New Mexico. Of the 261 types of ecosystems in the United States, 58 have declined by 85 percent or more and 38 by 70 to 84 percent.

8   If the United States had completely ignored its public lands, it might simply be getting what it deserved. But that's not the case. National parks and designated wilderness areas in this country make up the world's finest nature-reserve system. When President Clinton signed into law the California Desert Protection Act in 1994, the acreage of federally designated wilderness carved out of our public lands soared to more than 100 million acres, nearly half of which are outside Alaska. The acreage of the national park system jumped to almost 90 million, more than one-third in the Lower 48. That is much more than I thought we would ever protect when I enlisted in the wilderness wars a quarter-century ago.

     But that's still not enough for Reed Noss, editor of the widely cited scientific journal *Conservation Biology* and one of the National Biological Service report's authors, who claims "we're not just losing single species here and there, we're losing entire assemblages of species and their habitats."

10   How is it that we have lost so many species while we have protected so much?

     The answer, environmental historians tell us, lies in the goals, arguments, and processes used to establish wilderness areas and national parks over the last century. In his epochal study, *National Parks: The American Experience* (University of Nebraska, 1979), Alfred Runte discusses the arguments crafted to support establishment of the early national parks. Foremost was what Runte terms "monumentalism," the preservation of inspirational scenic grandeur like the Grand Canyon or Yosemite Valley, and the protection of curiosities of nature like Yellowstone's hot pots and geysers. Later proposals for national parks had to measure up to the scenic quality of a Mt. Rainier or a Crater Lake. Even the spectacular Olympic Mountains were initially denied national park status because they weren't deemed up to snuff.

12   A second argument for new national parks was based on what Runte calls "worthless lands." Areas proposed for protection, conservationists argued, were unsuitable for agriculture, mining, grazing, logging, and other productive uses. Yellowstone could be set aside because no one in his right mind would try to grow corn there; no one wanted to mine the glaciers of Mt. Rainier or log the sheer cliffs of the Grand Canyon. The worthless-lands argument often led park advocates to agree to boundaries gerrymandered around economically valuable forests eyed by timber interests, or simply to leave out such lands in the first place. Where parks were designated over the objections of extractive industries (such as at Kings Canyon, which was

coveted as a reservoir site by California's Central Valley farmers), protection prevailed only because of the dogged efforts of the Sierra Club and allied groups.

When the great conservationist Aldo Leopold and others suggested that wilderness areas be protected in the national forests in the 1920s and '30s, they adapted the monumentalism and worthless-lands arguments with great success. The Forest Service's enthusiasm for Leopold's wilderness idea was, in fact, partly an attempt to head off the Park Service's raid on the more scenic chunks of the national forests. Wilderness advocates also used utilitarian arguments in their campaigns: the Adirondack Preserve in New York was set aside to protect the watershed for booming New York City, and the first forest reserves in the West were established to protect watersheds near towns and agricultural regions.

14   The most common argument for designating wilderness areas, though, touted their recreational values. Leopold, who railed against "Ford dust" in the backcountry, wanted to preserve scenic areas suitable for roadless pack trips of two weeks' duration. Bob Marshall expanded the recreational theme, defending wild areas as "reservoirs of freedom and in-spiration" for those willing to hike the trails and climb the peaks.

In the final analysis, though, most national parks and wilderness areas were (and are) decreed because they had friends. Conservationists know that the way to protect an area is to develop a constituency for it. We rally support for wilderness designation by giving people slide shows, tak-ing them into the area, and urging them to write letters, lobby, or even put their bodies on the line in protest. If we're lucky, and not too many conces-sions are made to resource industries, we end up with wilderness that we can be proud of. The result is that wilderness areas tend to be spectacularly scenic, rugged enough to thwart resource exploitation (or simply lacking valuable timber and minerals altogether), and popular for non-motorized recreation.

16   But there's one problem: that's not necessarily what wildlife needs.

It's important to note that ecological integrity has always been at least a minor goal and argument in wilderness and national-park advocacy. In the 1920s and '30s, the Ecological Society of America and the American So-ciety of Mammalogists developed proposals for ecological reserves on the public lands. Aldo Leopold was a pioneer in the sciences of wildlife manage-ment and ecology, and argued for wilderness areas as ecological baselines. Even the Forest Service applied ecosystem thinking when it recommended areas for wilderness in its second Roadless Area Review and Evaluation (RARE II) in the late 1970s. Somehow, though, professional biologists and advocates for wilderness preservation drifted apart—far enough so that the Forest Service now lumps its wilderness program under its division of recreation.

18   It took news of a global biological meltdown to shake up both biology and conservation. Biology could no longer be removed from activism.

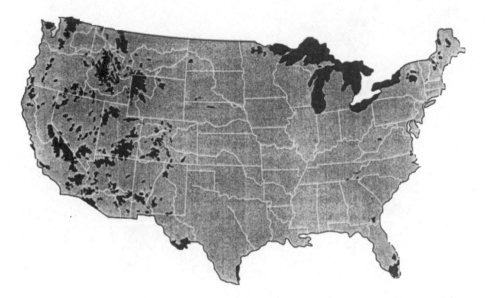

Largest remaining roadless areas in the contiguous United States. The map above shows roadless areas of more than 100,000 acres in the west and 50,000 acres in the East. There are more than 385 such areas in the continental United States, ranging from Idaho's 3.3-million-acre "River of No Return" area to Vermont's 50,000-acre Meachum Swamp. But the 10 percent of the Lower 48 that remains wild is shrinking by 2 million acres a year.

Conservation could no longer be just about outdoor museums and backpacking parks. Biologists and conservationists all began to understand that species can't be brought back from the brink of extinction one by one. Nature reserves had to protect entire ecosystems, guarding the flow and dance of evolution.

For insight, conservation biologists drew on an obscure corner of population biology called "island biogeography." In the 1960s, E. O. Wilson and Robert MacArthur studied colonization and extinction rates in oceanic islands like the Hawaiian chain. They hoped to devise a mathematical formula for the number of species that an island can hold, based on factors such as the island's size and its distance from the mainland.

20   They also looked at islands, places like Borneo or Vancouver, that were once part of nearby continents. When the glaciers melted 10,000 years ago and the sea level rose, these high spots were cut off from the mainland. Over the years, continental islands invariably lose species of plants and animals that remain on their parent continents, a process called "relaxation."

Certain generalities jumped out at the researchers. The first species to vanish from continental islands are the big ones—the tigers and elephants. The larger the island, the slower the rate at which species disappear. The

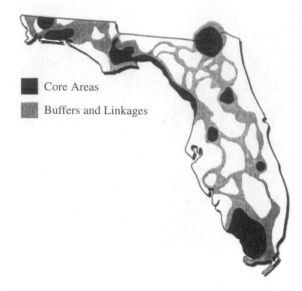

Core Areas

Buffers and Linkages

Panther paths. To protect wildlife in the nation's fastest-growing state, Florida agencies adopted and refined Reed Noss' core-and-buffer nature-reserve scheme. Using computer mapping, they identified biodiversity hot spots on nearly 5 million acres. If these are added to the state's 7 million acres of protected lands, the black bear and the panther may have a fighting chance. Florida is now working with landowners to protect strategic areas and has appropriated $3.2 billion to purchase key lands by the year 2000.

farther an island is from the mainland, the more species it loses; the closer, the fewer. If an island is isolated, it loses more species than one in an archipelago.

22   In 1985, ecologist William Newmark looked at a map of the western United States and realized that its national parks were also islands. The smaller the park and the more isolated it was from other wildlands, the more species it had lost. The first to go had been the large wide-ranging creatures: gray wolf, grizzly bear, wolverine. Relaxation had occurred, and was still occurring. Newmark predicted that all national parks would continue to lose species. Even a big protected area like Yellowstone isn't large enough to maintain viable populations of the largest wide-ranging mammals. Only the complex of national parks in the Canadian Rockies is substantial enough to ensure their survival.

While Newmark was applying island biogeography to national parks, Reed Noss and Larry Harris at the University of Florida were studying the state's endangered panther and its threatened black bear, hoping to design nature reserves for these species that were more than outdoor museums. A small, isolated group of bears or panthers faces two threats. Because it has few members, inbreeding can lead to genetic defects. And a small population is more vulnerable to extinction ("winking out" in eco-logical jargon) than a larger one. If the animals are isolated, their habitat can't be recolonized by nearby members of the species. But if habitats are connected so that animals can move between them—even as little as one horny adolescent every ten years—then inbreeding is thwarted and a habi-tat can be recolonized.

24   Noss and Harris designed a nature-reserve system for Florida consist-ing of core reserves surrounded by buffer zones and linked by habitat corri-dors. Over the past decade this visionary application of conservation biology has been refined by the state of Florida, and now state agencies and The Nature Conservancy are using it to set priorities for land acquisition and protection of key areas. Once a pie-in-the-sky proposal, a conservation-biology-based reserve system is now the master plan for land protection in Florida.

Ecosystem theory has caused biologists to rethink the way they viewed large carnivores, too. Scientists had always considered the biggest animals perched atop the food chain to be sovereign species whose condition had lit-tle effect on the well-being of the flora and fauna down below. Until the 1930s, in fact, the National Park Service used guns, traps, and poison to ex-terminate wolves and mountain lions from Yellowstone and other parks. Early in his career, even Aldo Leopold beat the drum for killing predators.

26   Today, biologists know that lions and bears and wolves are ecologically essential to entire systems. For example, the eastern United States is overrun with white-tailed deer, which devastate trees with their excess foraging. If allowed to return, wolves and mountain lions would move deer from their concentrated wintering yards and reduce their numbers, thereby allowing the forest to return to more natural patterns of succession and species composition.

Even songbirds suffer when wolves and cougars disappear. The decline in populations of migrant neotropical songbirds such as warblers, thrushes, and flycatchers as a result of forest fragmentation in Central and North America is well documented. But the collapse is also partly attributable to the absence of large carnivores. Cougars and gray wolves don't eat warblers or their eggs, but raccoons, foxes, and possums do, and the cougars and wolves eat these midsize predators. When the big guys were hunted out, the populations of the middling guys exploded—with dire results for the birds.

28   In addition to being critical players in various eat-or-be-eaten schemes, large carnivores are valuable as "umbrella" species. Simply put, if enough habitat is protected to maintain viable populations of large mam-mals like wolverines or jaguars, then most of the other species in the region will also be protected.

A final piece in conservation biology's big-picture puzzle is the impor-tance of natural disturbances to various ecosystems. To be viable, habitats must be large enough to absorb major natural disturbances (known as "sto-chastic events" in ecologist lingo). When Yellowstone burned in 1988, there was a great hue and cry over the imagined destruction. But ecologists tell us that the fire was natural and beneficial. Because Yellowstone covers 2 million acres and is surrounded by several million acres more of national-forest wilderness, the extensive fires affected only a portion of the total reserve area.

30   Things didn't turn out so well when The Nature Conservancy's Cathedral Pines Preserve in Connecticut was hammered by tornadoes in 1989. In this tiny patch of remnant old-growth white-pine forest, 70 percent of the trees were knocked flat, devastating the entire ecosystem. Had the tornadoes ripped through a forest of hundreds of thousands of acres, they instead would have played a positive role by opening up small sections of the forest to new growth.

Conservation biology's central tenets are not hard to grasp. For a natural habitat to be viable (and for a conservation strategy to succeed) there is a handful of general rules: bigger is better; a single large habitat is usually better than several small, isolated ones; large native carnivores are better than none; intact habitat is preferable to artificially disturbed habitat; and connected habitats are usually better than fragmented ones.

32   Too often, wilderness areas and national parks in the United States fail to qualify as viable habitat. They are pretty, yet unproductive. For the most part, the richer deep forests, rolling grasslands, and fertile river valleys on which a disproportionate number of rare and endangered species depend have passed into private ownership or been released for development. To make matters worse, the elimination of large carnivores, control of natural fire, and livestock grazing have degraded even our largest and most remote parks and wilderness areas.

          Conservation biologists tell us we must go beyond our current national park, wildlife refuge, and wilderness area systems. What's needed are large wilderness cores, buffer zones, and biological corridors. The cores would be managed to protect and, where necessary, restore native biological diversity and natural processes. Wilderness recreation is compatible with these areas, as long as ecological considerations come first. Surrounding the cores would be buffer zones where increasing levels of compatible human activity would be allowed as one moved away from the center. Corridors would provide secure routes between cores, enabling wide-ranging plant and animal species to disperse and facilitating genetic exchange between populations.

34   Existing wilderness areas, national parks, and other federal and state reserves are the building blocks for this ecologically based network. While rarely extensive enough to protect habitat in and of themselves, these fragmented wildland chunks preserve imperiled and sensitive species. Had today's parks and wilderness areas not been protected through the tireless efforts of wilderness conservationists over the years, these species would be much more in danger than they are today, if they existed at all.

          In the northern Rockies, groups such as the Alliance for the Wild Rockies and the Greater Yellowstone Coalition have been working to turn fragmented wildlands into viable habitat. They reckon that if Yellowstone isn't large enough to maintain healthy populations of grizzlies and wolverines, then we need to link the park with larger areas.

36   At a minimum that means treating the national forests around the park as integral to the park itself. Even grander ideas would link Yellowstone with the vast wilderness areas of central Idaho, the Glacier National Park/Bob Marshall Wilderness complex in northern Montana, and on into Canada.

These efforts produced the most expansive ecosystem-based legislation ever proposed in the United States. The Northern Rockies Ecosystem Protection Act (NREPA) would designate 20 million acres of new wilderness areas and identify essential corridors between them. The bill, endorsed by the Sierra Club, currently has 35 cosponsors.

38   Through its Critical Ecoregions Program, the Sierra Club is applying ecosystem principles to other large landscapes across North America. . . . But conservation biology's tenets can also be applied on a traditional scale. Across the country, activists are helping shape the next generation of national-forest management plans. They are identifying habitat for sensitive species, remnants of national forest, and travel corridors for wide-ranging species. They can then champion the creation of wildlife linkages and expansion of existing wilderness areas into ecologically rich habitats. In many places, they'll be able to make the case that roads be closed to protect sensitive ecosystems, that once-present species like wolves and mountain lions be reintroduced, and that damaged watersheds be restored.

But it gets even wilder.

40   In late 1991 a small group of scientists and activists married conservation biology and conservation activism on the grandest and most visionary scale yet. The Wildlands Project has set itself the all-encompassing goal of designing science-based reserve networks that will protect and restore the ecological richness and native biodiversity of North America from Alaska to Panama.

At a time when legislators are handing out private rights to public lands like candy, such visions may seem like delusions. Congress is dominated by zealots who would tear down decades of conservation policy and open public lands to the exploiters Teddy Roosevelt fought almost a century ago. Senator Slade Gorton (R-Wash.) does the bidding of the timber industry in trying to gut the Endangered Species Act; just across the hall Representative Billy Tauzin (D-La.) unleashes lies and demagoguery against wetlands protection and the Clean Water Act. Lurching through the Contract With America checklist, Congress threatens wilderness in the Arctic National Wildlife Refuge, in the Northern Rockies, and in the slickrock canyons of Utah. Even the national parks aren't safe from legislators who know the price of everything and the value of nothing.

42   An understanding of conservation biology and a vision of ecologically designed wilderness cores, corridors, and buffer zones can help stop the war being waged on the environment. First, conservation policies and arguments are strengthened by a grounding in sound science. Second, a big-picture

view allows activists to see that they are not isolated, that their campaigns to protect local wildlands fit into a national, even continental plan.

And it is no small benefit that a vision of wilderness recovery allows us to show what conservationists are *for*. Too often, activists are dismissed as negative, whining doomsayers. By developing long-term proposals for wilderness, we say, "Here is our vision for what North America should look like. Civilization and wilderness can coexist. By acting responsibly with respect for the land, we can become a better people."

44   A management plan that treats Florida as an ecological whole, a federal bill that crosses borders to protect wildlands throughout the northern Rockies, and a continent-wide proposal like The Wildlands Project's wrest the fundamental debate from those who would gladly plunder our natural heritage. Do we have the generosity of spirit, the greatness of heart to share the land with other species? I think we do. ❖

Questions for Meaning

1. What is the significance of the research by Michael Soulé and E. O. Wilson? What are the implications of this research for policies determining the management of national parks and other public lands?
2. What types of land were originally set aside as wilderness areas and national parks? What values support this kind of thinking?
3. What does Foreman mean by "ecological integrity"?
4. How can national parks be defined as "islands"? What does "island biogeography" indicate will happen to animals living in these "islands"?
5. What are the basic principles of conservation biology? What kind of changes would be necessary to honor these principles in resource management?
6. Vocabulary: myriad (2), entomologist (3), detritus (6), contiguous (7), riparian (7), epochal (11), extractive (12), utilitarian (13), archipelago (21), viable (22), carnivores (25), tenets (31), integral (36), wrest (44).

Questions about Strategy

1. Although his argument is focused on the future of publicly held land in the United States, Foreman begins by referring to tropical rainforests, elephants, and gorillas. What does this strategy accomplish?
2. How credible is the evidence presented in this argument?
3. Why does Foreman believe conservationists must argue for projects they support instead of simply arguing against what they oppose? How successfully does his own argument illustrate this approach?
4. What values does Foreman appeal to in his conclusion? What does he accomplish by appealing specifically to these values at the end of his argument?

James Duffus

A REPORT FROM THE GENERAL ACCOUNTING OFFICE

When members of Congress and other influential members of the federal government need information, they can turn not only to their staffs but to the General Accounting Office, a nonpartisan branch of the federal bureaucracy charged with responsibility for keeping track of expenditures and evaluating how dollars are spent. This 1995 report was requested by the Senate Committee on Energy and Natural Resources and the House Subcommittee on National Parks, Forests, and Lands. At that time, James Duffus was Director of National Resources Management at the General Accounting Office and was responsible for the report issued in his name. As you read, note how the report includes information that can be useful to policymakers but does not specifically recommend how that information should be used.

Purpose

In recent years, concern has grown over the health of America's national parks, which now serve more than 270 million visitors a year. These parks contain many of the country's most significant natural areas and historic sites. In response to several congressional requesters, GAO reviewed the National Park Service's efforts at meeting its dual missions of serving visitors and protecting the natural and cultural resources entrusted to it. The review focused on determining (1) what, if any, deterioration in visitor services or park resources is occurring at the 12 park units that GAO visited; (2) what factors contribute to any degradation of visitor services and parks' natural and cultural resources; and (3) what choices are available to help deal with identified problems.

Background

2 The Department of the Interior's National Park Service manages 368 park units that together cover more than 80 million acres. Thirty-one of those units have been added in the last 10 years. The units are diverse in size and purpose, ranging from large natural areas to battlefields and monuments. Balancing the dual objectives of providing for the public's enjoyment and preserving the resources for future generations has long shaped the debate about how best to manage the system.

      GAO's review focused on 12 park units: 4 national parks, 2 historic parks and 1 historic site, 2 monuments, 1 battlefield, 1 recreation area, and 1 seashore. Chosen for the diversity they present in size, type, and geographic location, these units represent a cross section of units in the system.

Results in Brief

4   There is cause for concern about the health of national parks for both visitor services and resource management. The overall level of visitor services was deteriorating at most of the park units that GAO reviewed. Services were being cut back, and the condition of many trails, campgrounds, and other facilities was declining. Trends in resource management were less clear because most park managers lacked sufficient data to determine the overall condition of their parks' natural and cultural resources. In some cases, parks lacked an inventory of the resources under their protection.

   Two factors particularly affected the level of visitor services and the management of park resources. These were (1) additional operating requirements placed on parks by laws and administrative requirements and (2) increased visitation, which drives up the parks' operating costs. These two factors seriously eroded funding increases since the mid-1980s.

6   The national park system is at a crossroads. While the system continues to grow, conditions at the parks have been declining, and the dollar amount of the maintenance backlog has jumped from $1.9 billion in 1988 to over $4 billion today. Dealing with this situation involves making difficult choices about how parks are funded and managed. These choices call for efforts on the part of the Park Service, the administration, and the Congress and center on one or more of the following: (1) increasing the amount of financial resources going to the parks, (2) limiting or reducing the number of units in the park system, and (3) reducing the level of visitor services. Additionally, the Park Service should be able to stretch available resources by operating more efficiently and continuing to improve its financial management and performance measurement systems.

Principal Findings

Eleven of the 12 parks in GAO's review had cut visitor services. For example, at Shenandoah National Park in Virginia, programs to help visitors understand the park's natural and scenic aspects were cut by more than 80 percent from 1987 to 1993. At Padre Island National Seashore in Texas, no lifeguards were on duty along the beach during the summer of 1994 for the first time in 20 years. Such cutbacks can affect the visitors' safety and health as well as their enjoyment of and access to a park's amenities.

8   In addition, at those parks with significant cultural resources, the condition of these resources was generally declining. For example, at Ellis Island in New York, the nation's only museum devoted exclusively to immigration, 32 of 36 historic buildings have seriously deteriorated, and according to park officials, about two-thirds of these buildings could be lost within 5 years if not stabilized. In some parks, the location and the status of cultural resources—primarily archeological—were largely unknown. For example, at Hopewell Furnace National Historic Site—an 850-acre park in Pennsylvania

that depicts part of the nation's early industrial development—the Park Service has never performed a complete archeological survey of the park to identify and inventory all its cultural resources.

Likewise, officials at large natural parks, such as Yosemite and Glacier, knew little about the condition of many natural resources. At Yosemite, for example, officials knew little about the condition of birds, fish, and such mammals as badgers, river otters, and wolverines. The Park Service has not systematically collected scientific data to inventory its natural resources or monitor changes in their condition over time. As a result, the agency cannot now determine whether the overall condition of many key natural resources is improving, deteriorating, or remaining constant.

10   Park Service policy directs that park management be based on knowledge of the parks' cultural and natural resources and their condition. The Park Service's lack of progress in addressing this decades-old concern is threatening its ability to preserve and protect the resources entrusted to it.

Two Main Factors Contribute to the Current Situation

Although many parks have received operating budget increases since 1985, laws, administrative rules, and other policy changes have given parks many additional operating requirements. While not disagreeing with the merits of these requirements, park managers said that the requirements affected the availability of funds for visitor services and resource management activities because parks often had not received enough funds to cover the entire cost of compliance and managers therefore had to use funds from existing operating budgets. For example, in fiscal year 1994, Yosemite spent $42,000 to meet several Occupational Safety and Health Act requirements and $80,000 to identify and remove hazardous waste. The park did not receive additional funds to cover this $122,000 expense. Officials also cited required cost-of-living increases and employer retirement contributions that were not accompanied by sufficient additional funds to pay for them. Because salaries and benefits constitute such a large percentage of a park's budget—in most cases, over 75 percent for the parks in GAO's review—nearly any such increase can have a major impact.

12   Increased visitation was the second main factor eroding the parks' ability to keep up with visitor and resource needs. Eight of the 12 parks that GAO reviewed experienced increased visitation since 1985; the average increase was 26 percent. At some parks, the substantial increase in visitation has driven up costs for such activities as waste disposal, general maintenance and supplies, utilities, and employee overtime. Moreover, the expanded length of the tourist season at many parks requires providing at least minimal visitor services for longer periods. To address this need, some parks have cut back on the scope and amount of services available during the peak season.

Choices for Addressing Park Conditions Center on Three Alternatives

If current circumstances continue, further deterioration in park conditions is likely. Choices to deal with this situation center on three alternatives: (1) increasing the amount of financial resources going to the parks, (2) limiting or reducing the number of units in the park system, and (3) reducing the level of visitor services.

14   One alternative to address the deteriorating conditions is to increase the amount of financial resources available to the parks. While increased appropriations are one source of dollars, they are unlikely in today's tight fiscal climate. Other revenue sources are potentially available, including increased park entrance and other user fees, higher returns from in-park concessioners, and funds from partnership agreements with nonfederal entities. Less than 8 percent of the system's annual operating budget is currently generated through such means. However, for parks to benefit from such changes, the increased revenues would need to stay within the park system and not be returned to the U.S. Treasury, as now occurs. Imposing or increasing fees may also affect park visitation and use, a consequence that would need to be considered.

A second alternative would limit or perhaps even cut back the number of units in the national park system. As the system keeps growing, associated infrastructure and development needs will also increase, putting more park units in competition for the limited federal funding available. While not an answer to all the current problems, limiting or cutting back park units until conditions could be adequately addressed would help ease the Park Service's financial pressures.

16   A third alternative would reduce the visitor services provided by the parks to more closely match the level of services that can be realistically accomplished with available resources. This could include, for example, limiting operations of fewer hours per day and fewer days per year, limiting the number of visitors, or perhaps temporarily closing some facilities to public use.

The Park Service Can Better Focus Resources

Previous work by GAO and the Department of the Interior's Inspector General has shown that the Park Service lacks (1) necessary financial and program data on its operations, (2) adequate internal controls on how its funds are spent, and (3) performance measures on what is being accomplished with the money being spent. Currently, the Park Service is taking corrective actions to resolve its problems with financial data and internal controls and is in the process of developing performance measurement systems. While these actions alone will probably not be sufficient to meet all of the Park Service's funding needs, they should increase efficiency so that the Park Service can do more under current funding levels.

Recommendations

18 GAO is making no recommendations in this report.

Agency Comments and GAO's Evaluation

GAO provided a draft of this report to National Park Service officials for their review and comment. On July 13, 1995, GAO met with Park Service officials—including the Park Service's Director and Associate Directors of Administration and Professional Services—to obtain their comments. Overall, the officials agreed with the factual content and conclusions of the report. They suggested several technical clarifications throughout the report and provided updated information. Changes to the report were made as appropriate. The officials also offered several comments relating to the alternatives to deal with the problems identified in the report. Park Service officials said that increased appropriations was an alternative that was not delineated in the report. GAO agrees that it is an alternative, but an unlikely one in today's tight fiscal climate. The report was revised to reflect this comment. Park Service officials also commented that private capital is another alternative. GAO agrees and believes that this point is included in the report's discussion of more entrepreneurial management by park managers.

20   Park Service officials further commented that increasing fees at national parks would not make the system self-sufficient, although they support the need for increased fees. They also said that there may be some units for which fees should not be charged because of their national significance. GAO agrees that increasing fees will not solve all of the parks' financial problems. GAO also recognizes that charging fees may be undesirable or infeasible for some units. The report has been revised to reflect both points. Park Service officials also commented on the alternative of limiting or reducing the number of park units. They said that there is no evidence that the addition of new units has affected the amount of resources for existing units. GAO believes that given the current tight fiscal climate, future growth in appropriations is unlikely; accordingly, new units would be competing for available funds.   ❖

Questions for Meaning

1. What is the dual mission of the National Park Service? What potential conflict is there between these two elements of its mission?
2. What sites did the GAO investigate for this report, and why were these sites selected?
3. What factors have been affecting the quality of services and management in our national parks? What evidence is there that the park system is under strain?
4. According to its own policy, how should the Park Service determine the way parks are managed? Is the Service honoring its policy?

5. If the federal government decides to halt further deterioration in park conditions, what options does it have, according to this report? In your opinion, which of these options is most feasible?

Questions about Strategy

1. How does Duffus establish the focus of this report? Is this focus appropriate for a report from the General Accounting Office? Are any management issues excluded by this focus?
2. How would you describe the tone of this report? Is it appropriate for its original audience and purpose?
3. Although this report finds problems within the administration of the National Park Service, it makes no specific recommendations. What does this decision reveal? Can any recommendations be inferred from this report?
4. This report concludes with a statement describing a meeting between representatives of the General Accounting Service and the National Park Service. What did this meeting accomplish? What does Duffus accomplish by putting this information in his report?

ONE STUDENT'S ASSIGNMENT

Drawing on the material in *The Informed Argument* and at least two sources that you have discovered on your own, evaluate the current condition of our national parks and recommend how they should be managed in the future. Use the numbered system for documentation recommended by the Council of Biology Editors. (Arrange your reference list in alphabetical order; then number your sources according to this order. When you refer to a source within your paper, cite the corresponding number from the reference list.)

Preserving Our Parks

Amy Karlen

As a girl, I remember traveling many miles cramped between my two brothers in the backseat of our parents' powder-blue Crown Victoria wagon. This trusty old Ford, stocked with enough crackers, chips, pop, and Mad-Libs to last for months, carried our family to a number of national parks around the country. Once, while driving through Yellowstone, my dad had to stop the car to avoid colliding with a half dozen buffalo making their way across the road. When we started driving again, I turned to watch the buffalo through the back window. It amazed me how fearlessly these animals stepped out in front of us as if to say, "Hey! Get out of the way! This is *our* area. We were here first!"

2   Years later, I came to realize how many of our national parks, which Americans assume to reflect the finest and best in our country's values, often reflect the worst. To most Americans, myself included, the definition of a "park" seems obvious. However, the *concept* of a park has changed over the years. While the early meaning of "park" meant "an enclosed preserve for beasts of the chase," it was later extended to include "a large, 'ornamental' piece of ground, used for recreation"[5]. Today, it seems the mission of many national parks no longer emphasizes a preservation of animals and conservation of natural resources, so much as it focuses on pleasing the public.

      I am all for promoting community interaction at the national park level, for without such establishments, many suburban and metropolitan visitors may otherwise not have an opportunity to experience nature. Yet, I still find it disturbing that the mission of species and resource conservation has taken a backseat to keeping Americans self-satisfied. If truly concerned about the environment, Americans should recognize that the preservation of natural habitats is more important than whether their recreational needs are met.

4   To encourage easy access by vacationers, many parks were designed with easy access for motorized vehicles, enabling the Forest Service to lump its wilderness program under the division of recreation. As a result, not only is traffic congestion commonplace during some seasons, but campgrounds fill up early in the morning and muddy trails erode from heavy use. Today, park visitors find that more than "one-third of all roads in the parks need repair"[4]. A 1980 proposal by the Department of Interior, calling for the reduction of accommodations at Yosemite National Park, the elimination of its parking lots, the relocation of some campsites, and a new limit on the number of visitors, collapsed from lack of funding. As a result, by the late 1990s, "the park has made scant headway on the most challenging problem, the flood of cars, trucks and recreational vehicles that make a mile-long trip through Yosemite Village seem like a Manhattan Rush Hour"[3]. What this demonstrates is that the original function of a park becomes blurred when it tries to equally satisfy the preservation of nature and the recreational needs of the public.

      Overuse and underfunding have caused park wildlife to suffer. In fact, the current rate of extinction is as much as "10,000 times the normal background rate documented in the fossil record"[2]. Biologists warn that one-third of our species could die out within 40 years. According to Dave Foreman, director of the Sierra Club, American national park and wilderness areas make up the world's finest nature-reserve service. Why then are we losing so many species? The answer is poor management. As of last year, "officials at many large national parks knew little about the condition of their natural resources"[1]. At Yosemite, for example, the bird, fish, and mammal condition was unknown, and as of 1995, the Park Service had no systematic way to collect data in order to inventory natural resources or monitor their changes over time. As a result, "it is unknown whether the overall condition of many key natural resources is improving, deteriorating, or remaining constant"[1].

6   Although overcrowding threatens our habitats, and although it seems unlikely that Congress could substantially increase the amount of financial resources going to our parks, it is not too late to restore what should be their main mission—"a preserve for beasts of the chase."

Park officials must restrict more tightly which areas are open to the general public—and, in particular, which are open for motorized recreation. Scheduling particular recreations on particular days in particular places would allow visitors to exercise their preferred activity without the interference of other recreational users, and more importantly, without wearing down the same areas of land day after day. While some forms of recreation, such as hiking and mountain climbing, do little harm to the natural resources of the park, motorized recreation threatens to disrupt natural habitats. I do not intend to judge any form of recreation as better than another, but we need to realize that certain activities are more likely to harm our parks than others—and at a much quicker rate. Reserving specific days for specific users will ensure that all visitors have an opportunity to fully experience all the park has to offer—yet not necessarily whenever they choose.

8   Although a proposal of this sort seems unlikely to be implemented soon, Congress has at least taken a step forward, when, in 1996, it approved and President Clinton signed into law a measure to raise entrance fees to our nation's most popular national parks, or in some cases, begin charging for the first time. 1997 introduced the most significant increases under this program when the cost of an annual pass per carload at Yellowstone, Yosemite, Grand Canyon and Grand Tetons parks rose from $15 to $40. The seven-day pass rose from $10–$20 per car. "These new fees will be a down payment on the resource protection, restoration and general maintenance that the parks desperately need," said Paul Pritchard, president of the National Parks and Conservation Association[6].

Whether by recreation or exploration, parks allow visitors to escape the constraints of everyday life. However, while guests may pack up and leave as they wish, our animals *live* in these parks. Isolating animals within a single habitat terminates recolonization by nearby specie members. As a result, species often inbreed, causing severe genetic defects. According to Foreman, America needs to treat the national forests around the parks as integral to the park itself. Connecting habitats by corridors would allow animals to move more freely between the two regions, ceasing inbreeding and recolonizing habitats. As truly concerned Americans, we must allow our animals, as we do ourselves, the freedom to escape from constraint.

10   We need to remember that while national parks may offer sport and recreation for visitors, their primary purpose should be to preserve America's natural resources. I too, admit falling prey to national park misconception. However, we all need to remember that nature is not a toy. We cannot just play with it one day and ignore it the next. And while we must take care not to play with it any way we choose, this does not mean we cannot play with it at all. By working together and appropriating divisions for both recreation and habitat, all species can share the land.

I only wish that someday, I too will buckle my children in our backseat, cramped between bags of low-fat tortilla chips, no-fat cookies, and 100 percent fresh-squeezed, organic orange juice, and show them the beauty, wonder—yet more importantly, the *life*—preserved in our national parks. This time, however, *I'll* be driving with my husband in something more rugged than a powder-blue Crown Victoria wagon.

References

1. Duffus, J. A report from the General Accounting Office. In: Miller R. The informed argument. Forth Worth: Harcourt; 1998. 571–575.
2. Foreman, D. Missing links. In: Miller R. The informed argument. Fort Worth: Harcourt; 1998. 562–570.
3. Golden, T. In Yosemite, nature may have its way yet. The New York Times 1997 Feb 2; Sect 1: 1+ (column 1).
4. Lowry, W. Promises, promises. In: Miller R. The informed argument. Fort Worth: Harcourt; 1998. 517–522.
5. Olwig, K. Reinventing nature. In: Miller R. The informed argument. Fort Worth: Harcourt; 1998. 523–539.
6. Sonner, S. Entrance fees to national parks will rise to fund improvements. St. Paul Pioneer Press 1996 Nov 27; Sect 1: 1+ (column 1).

SUGGESTIONS FOR WRITING

1. Drawing on the argument by Terry Anderson and on additional research, write a plan for making national parks profitable.
2. Synthesize the articles by Lowry, Foreman, and Duffus by writing an essay focused on reporting problems in our national park system.
3. Write an essay defining "park," "wilderness," or "nature."
4. Drawing on Olwig or Cronon, write an essay explaining the values that led to the creation of our first national parks.

5. Read the full text of *The Deserted Village;* then write an essay evaluating how effectively Olwig has used that poem in "Reinventing Nature."
6. Write an argument on behalf of preserving natural resources.
7. If you have ever been to a national park or wilderness area, write an essay describing where you went and evaluating what you experienced there.
8. Write an essay about how to enjoy nature in a city or suburb.
9. Find a color reproduction of one of the paintings featured in this section (pages 537 and 543) and then write an essay analyzing how this work encourages viewers to see nature.
10. Research how publicly held lands are managed in another country and write a report comparing that system with our own.

COLLABORATIVE PROJECT

Looking at photographs or videos of someone else's vacation can sometimes feel like an endurance test, but material of this sort can also be considered historical documents. Ask friends, colleagues, and family members for any pictures they have showing what they consider "nature." Gather a large sample, keeping track of who owns what material so that you can return the contributions at the end of your project. Look for patterns in what people choose to photograph and how they present themselves and others when being photographed in a natural setting. If you have any questions about the material you have gathered, interview the people who contributed it. Then write an essay in which you analyze what this sample group seems to value about nature.

PART 6

SOME CLASSIC ARGUMENTS

PLATO

THE ALLEGORY OF THE CAVE

One of the most important thinkers in the history of Western civilization, Plato (c. 428–348 B.C.) grew up in Athens during the difficult years of the Peloponnesian War. He was the student of Socrates, and it is through Plato that Socratic thought has been passed down to us. Socrates is the principal figure in Plato's early dialogues—discussing with the young such questions as "What should men live for?" and "What is the nature of virtue?" Plato devoted his life to answering questions of this sort and teaching others to understand them. In 387 B.C., he founded his Academy, where he taught the future rulers of numerous Greek city-states. The Academy survived for almost a thousand years, before closing in A.D. 529.

Plato's major works include *Gorgias, Meno, Phaedo, Symposium, The Republic,* and *Phaedrus.* In each of these works, Plato insists on two ideas that are fundamental to his philosophy. He believed that man has an immortal soul existing separately from the body both before birth and after death. Also, he believed that the physical world consists only of appearances; truth consists of ideas that can be discovered and understood only through systematic thought.

"The Allegory of the Cave" is from *The Republic,* which is widely considered Plato's greatest work. It is written in the form of a dialogue. The speaker is Socrates, and his "audience" is Glaucon, Plato's brother. But the dialogue should be regarded as a literary device, rather than an actual conversation. Its ultimate audience consists of everyone who wants to think seriously about the nature of truth, justice, and wisdom.

Next, said I, here is a parable to illustrate the degrees in which our nature may be enlightened or unenlightened. Imagine the condition of men living in a sort of cavernous chamber underground, with an entrance open to the light and a long passage all down the cave. Here they have been from childhood, chained by the leg and also by the neck, so that they cannot move and can see only what is in front of them, because the chains will not let them turn their heads. At some distance higher up is the light of a fire burning behind them; and between the prisoners and the fire is a track with a parapet built along it, like the screen at a puppet-show, which hides the performers while they show their puppets over the top.

2   I see, said he.

Now behind this parapet imagine persons carrying along various artificial objects, including figures of men and animals in wood or stone or other materials, which project above the parapet. Naturally, some of these persons will be talking, others silent.

4   It is a strange picture, he said, and a strange sort of prisoners.

Like ourselves, I replied; for in the first place prisoners so confined would have seen nothing of themselves or of one another, except the shadows thrown by the fire-light on the wall of the Cave facing them, would they?

6   Not if all their lives they have been prevented from moving their heads.

And they would have seen as little of the objects carried past.

8   Of course.

Now, if they could talk to one another, would they not suppose that their words referred only to those passing shadows which they saw?

10   Necessarily.

And suppose their prison had an echo from the wall facing them? When one of the people crossing behind them spoke, they could only suppose that the sound came from the shadow passing before their eyes.

12   No doubt.

In every way, then, such prisoners would recognize as reality nothing but the shadows of those artificial objects.

14   Inevitably.

Now consider what would happen if their release from the chains and the healing of their unwisdom should come about in this way. Suppose one of them were set free and forced suddenly to stand up, turn his head, and walk with eyes lifted to the light; all these movements would be painful, and he would be too dazzled to make out the objects whose shadows he had been used to see. What do you think he would say, if someone told him that what he had formerly seen was meaningless illusion, but now, being somewhat nearer to reality and turned towards more real objects, he was getting a truer view? Suppose further that he were shown the various objects being carried by and were made to say, in reply to questions, what each of them was. Would he not be perplexed and believe the objects now shown him to be not so real as what he formerly saw?

16   Yes, not nearly so real.

And if he were forced to look at the fire-light itself, would not his eyes ache, so that he would try to escape and turn back to the things which he could see distinctly, convinced that they really were clearer than these other objects now being shown to him?

18   Yes.

And suppose someone were to drag him away forcibly up the steep and rugged ascent and not let him go until he had hauled him out into the sunlight, would he not suffer pain and vexation at such treatment, and, when he had come out into the light, find his eyes so full of its radiance that he could not see a single one of the things that he was now told were real?

20   Certainly he would not see them all at once.

He would need, then, to grow accustomed before he could see things in that upper world. At first it would be easiest to make out shadows, and then the images of men and things reflected in water, and later on the things themselves. After that, it would be easier to watch the heavenly bodies and the sky itself by night, looking at the light of the moon and stars rather than the Sun and the Sun's light in the day-time.

22   Yes, surely.

Last of all, he would be able to look at the Sun and contemplate its nature, not as it appears when reflected in water or any alien medium, but as it is in itself in its own domain.

24   No doubt.

And now he would begin to draw the conclusion that it is the Sun that produces the seasons and the course of the year and controls everything in the visible world, and moreover is in a way the cause of all that he and his companions used to see.

26   Clearly he would come at last to that conclusion.

Then if he called to mind his fellow prisoners and what passed for wisdom in his former dwelling-place, he would surely think himself happy in the change and be sorry for them. They may have had a practice of honouring and commending one another, with prizes for the man who had the keenest eye for the passing shadows and the best memory for the order in which they followed or accompanied one another, so that he could make a good guess as to which was going to come next. Would our released prisoner be likely to covet those prizes or to envy the men exalted to honour and power in the Cave? Would he not feel like Homer's Achilles, that he would far sooner 'be on earth as a hired servant in the house of a landless man' or endure anything rather than go back to his old beliefs and live in the old way?

28   Yes, he would prefer any fate to such a life.

Now imagine what would happen if he went down again to take his former seat in the Cave. Coming suddenly out of the sunlight, his eyes would be filled with darkness. He might be required once more to deliver his opinion on those shadows, in competition with the prisoners who had never been released, while his eyesight was still dim and unsteady; and it might take some time to become used to the darkness. They would laugh at him and say that he had gone up only to come back with his sight ruined; it was worth no one's while even to attempt the ascent. If they could lay hands on the man who was trying to set them free and lead them up, they would kill him.

30   Yes, they would.

Every feature in this parable, my dear Glaucon, is meant to fit our earlier analysis. The prison dwelling corresponds to the region revealed to us through the sense of sight, and the fire-light within it to the power of the Sun. The ascent to see the things in the upper world you may take as standing for the upward journey of the soul into the region of the intelligible; then you will be in possession of what I surmise, since that is what you wish to be told. Heaven knows whether it is true; but this, at any rate, is how it appears to me. In the world of knowledge, the last thing to be perceived and only with great difficulty is the essential Form of Goodness. Once it is perceived, the conclusion must follow that, for all things, this is the cause of whatever is right and good; in the visible world it gives birth to light and to the lord of light, while it is itself sovereign in the intelligible world and the parent of intelligence and truth. Without having had a vision of this Form no one can act with wisdom, either in his own life or in matters of state.

32   So far as I can understand, I share your belief.

Then you may also agree that it is no wonder if those who have reached this height are reluctant to manage the affairs of men. Their souls long to spend all their time in that upper world—naturally enough, if here once more our parable holds true. Nor, again, is it at all strange that one who comes from the contemplation of divine things to the miseries of human life should appear awkward and ridiculous when, with eyes still dazed and not yet accustomed to the darkness, he is compelled, in a law-court or elsewhere, to dispute about the shadows of justice or the images that cast those shadows, and to wrangle over the notions of what is right in the minds of men who have never beheld Justice itself.

34   It is not at all strange.

No; a sensible man will remember that the eyes may be confused in two ways—by a change from light to darkness or from darkness to light; and he will recognize that the same thing happens to the soul. When he sees it troubled and unable to discern anything clearly, instead of laughing thoughtlessly, he will ask whether, coming from a brighter existence, its unaccustomed vision is obscured by the darkness, in which case he will think its condition enviable and its life a happy one; or whether, emerging from the depths of ignorance, it is dazzled by excess of light. If so, he will rather feel sorry for it; or, if he were inclined to laugh, that would be less ridiculous than to laugh at the soul which has come down from the light.

36   That is a fair statement.

If this is true, then, we must conclude that education is not what it is said to be by some, who profess to put knowledge into a soul which does not possess it, as if they could put sight into blind eyes. On the contrary, our own account signifies that the soul of every man does possess the power of learning the truth and the organ to see it with; and that, just as one might have to turn the whole body round in order that the eye should see light instead of darkness, so the entire soul must be turned away from this changing world, until its eye can bear to contemplate reality and that supreme splendour which we have called the Good. Hence there may well be an art whose aim would be to effect this very thing, the conversion of the soul, in the readiest way; not to put the power of sight into the soul's eye, which already has it, but to ensure that, instead of looking in the wrong direction, it is turned the way it ought to be.

38   Yes, it may well be so.

It looks, then, as though wisdom were different from those ordinary virtues, as they are called, which are not far removed from bodily qualities, in that they can be produced by habituation and exercise in a soul which has not possessed them from the first. Wisdom, it seems, is certainly the virtue of some diviner faculty, which never loses its power, though its use for good or harm depends on the direction towards which it is turned. You must have noticed in dishonest men with a reputation for sagacity the shrewd glance of a narrow intelligence piercing the objects to which it is directed. There is nothing wrong with their power of vision, but it has been forced into the service of evil, so that the keener its sight, the more harm it works.

40   Quite true.

And yet if the growth of a nature like this had been pruned from earliest childhood, cleared of those clinging overgrowths which come of gluttony and all luxurious pleasure and, like leaden weights charged with affinity to this mortal world, hang upon the soul, bending its vision downwards; if, freed from these, the soul were turned round towards true reality, then this same power in these very men would see the truth as keenly as the objects it is turned to now.

42   Yes, very likely.

Is it not also likely, or indeed certain after what has been said, that a state can never be properly governed either by the uneducated who know nothing of truth or by men who are allowed to spend all their days in the pursuit of culture? The ignorant have no single mark before their eyes at which they must aim in all the conduct of their own lives and of affairs of state; and the others will not engage in action if they can help it, dreaming that, while still alive, they have been translated to the Islands of the Blest.

44   Quite true.

It is for us, then, as founders of a commonwealth, to bring compulsion to bear on the noblest natures. They must be made to climb the ascent to the vision of Goodness, which we called the highest object of knowledge; and, when they have looked upon it long enough, they must not be allowed, as they now are, to remain on the heights, refusing to come down again to the prisoners or to take any part in their labours and rewards, however much or little these may be worth.

46   Shall we not be doing them an injustice, if we force on them a worse life than they might have?

You have forgotten again, my friend, that the law is not concerned to make any one class specially happy, but to ensure the welfare of the commonwealth as a whole. By persuasion or constraint it will unite the citizens in harmony, making them share whatever benefits each class can contribute to the common good; and its purpose in forming men of that spirit was not that each should be left to go his own way, but that they should be instrumental in binding the community into one.

48   True, I had forgotten.

You will see, then, Glaucon, that there will be no real injustice in compelling our philosophers to watch over and care for the other citizens. We can fairly tell them that their compeers in other states may quite reasonably refuse to collaborate: there they have sprung up, like a self-sown plant, in despite of their country's institutions; no one has fostered their growth, and they cannot be expected to show gratitude for a care they have never received. 'But,' we shall say, 'it is not so with you. We have brought you into existence for your country's sake as well as for your own, to be like leaders and king-bees in a hive; you have been better and more thoroughly educated than those others and hence you are more capable of playing your part both as men of thought and as men of action. You must go down, then, each in his turn, to live with the rest and let your eyes grow accustomed to the darkness. You will then see a thousand times better than those who live there always; you will recognize every image for what it is and know what it represents, because you have seen justice, beauty, and goodness in their reality; and so you and we shall find life in our commonwealth no mere dream, as it is in most existing states, where men live fighting one another about shadows and quarreling for power, as if that were a great prize; whereas in truth government can be at its best and free from dissension only where the destined rulers are least desirous of holding office.'

50   Quite true.

Then will our pupils refuse to listen and to take their turns at sharing in the work of the community, though they may live together for most of their time in a purer air?

52   No; it is a fair demand, and they are fair-minded men. No doubt, unlike any ruler of the present day, they will think of holding power as an unavoidable necessity.

Yes my friend; for the truth is that you can have a well-governed society only if you can discover for your future rulers a better way of life than being in office; then only will power be in the hands of men who are rich, not in gold, but in the wealth that brings happiness, a good and wise life. All goes wrong when, starved for lack of anything good in their own lives, men turn to public affairs hoping to snatch from thence the happiness they hunger for. They set about fighting for power, and this internecine conflict ruins them and their country. The life of true philosophy is the only one that looks down upon offices of state; and access to power must be confined to men who are not in love with it; otherwise rivals will start fighting. So

whom else can you compel to undertake the guardianship of the commonwealth, if not those who, besides understanding best the principles of government, enjoy a nobler life than the politician's and look for rewards of a
different kind?

54   There is indeed no other choice.   ❖

Questions for Meaning

1. Describe the cave and the situation of the men who live within it.
   What must be done before anyone can leave the cave?
2. According to Plato, the men in the cave see only the moving shadows
   of artificial objects that are paraded before them. What activities do
   people pursue today that involve watching artificial images move
   across a screen? If you spent a lifetime watching such images, would
   you mistake the artificial for the real?
3. Having escaped from the cave, why would anyone want to return to it?
4. In paragraph 29, Plato claims that the men in the cave would kill
   someone who returned from the upper world to teach them the truth.
   What reason did Plato have for making this claim?
5. What does "The Allegory of the Cave" reveal about the importance of
   education? Why is education necessary before one can leave the cave?
   How does Plato perceive the nature of education?
6. What types of people should be excluded from government in an
   ideal republic? Why would it be necessary to force philosophers to
   rule, and why does Plato believe that making such men rule against
   their will is ethically defensible?
7. If philosophers are attuned to a higher "reality" than the men and
   women they govern, how can they understand the problems of the
   people they rule?
8. What would Plato think of American politics?
9. Vocabulary: parapet (1), perplexed (15), vexation (19), surmise (31),
   affinity (41), collaborate (49).

Questions about Strategy

1. What assumptions about human nature underlie Plato's allegory?
   What assumptions does he make about the nature of government? If
   you were to summarize Plato's argument and put it into deductive
   form, what would be your premise?
2. How effective is the use of dialogue as a method for developing an argument? Is it hard to follow?
3. What role does Glaucon serve? Why does he usually agree rather than
   ask difficult questions?
4. What is the function of paragraph 31?

Niccolò Machiavelli

SHOULD PRINCES TELL THE TRUTH?

Historian, playwright, poet, and political philosopher, Niccolò Machiavelli (1469–1527) lived in Florence during the turbulence of the Italian Renaissance. From 1498 to 1512, he served in the Chancellery of the Florentine Republic and held the position of secretary for the committee in charge of diplomatic relations and military operations. In fulfilling his responsibilities, Machiavelli traveled to France, Germany, and elsewhere in Italy—giving him the opportunity to observe numerous rulers and the strategies they used to maintain and extend their power. When the Florentine Republic collapsed in 1512 and the Medici returned to power, Machiavelli was dismissed from office, tortured, and temporarily exiled. He retired to an estate not far from Florence and devoted himself to writing the books for which he is now remembered: *The Prince* (1513), *The Discourses* (1519), *The Art of War* (1519–1520), and the *Florentine History* (1525). Of these works the most famous is *The Prince.*

In writing *The Prince,* Machiavelli set out to define the rules of politics as he understood them. His work became a handbook on how to acquire and maintain power. Machiavelli's experience taught him that successful rulers are not troubled by questions of ethics. He observed that it is better to be feared than to be loved. As the following excerpt reveals, he believed that virtues such as honesty are irrelevant to the successful pursuit of power. The amorality of Machiavelli's book continues to disturb many readers, and its shrewd observations on the nature of politics have made the author's name synonymous with craftiness and intrigue.

How laudable it is for a prince to keep good faith and live with integrity, and not with astuteness, every one knows. Still the experience of our times shows those princes to have done great things who have had little regard for good faith, and have been able by astuteness to confuse men's brains, and who have ultimately overcome those who have made loyalty their foundation.

2   You must know, then, that there are two methods of fighting, the one by law, the other by force: the first method is that of men, the second of beasts; but as the first method is often insufficient, one must have recourse to the second. It is therefore necessary for a prince to know well how to use both the beast and the man. This was covertly taught to rulers by ancient writers, who relate how Achilles and many others of those ancient princes were given to Chiron the centaur to be brought up and educated under his discipline. The parable of this semi-animal, semi-human teacher is meant to indicate that a prince must know how to use both natures, and that the one without the other is not durable.

A prince being thus obliged to know well how to act as a beast must imitate the fox and the lion, for the lion cannot protect himself from traps, and the fox cannot defend himself from wolves. One must therefore be a fox to recognise traps, and a lion to frighten wolves. Those that wish to be only lions do not understand this. Therefore, a prudent ruler ought not to keep faith when by so doing it would be against his interest, and when the reasons which made him bind himself no longer exist. If men were all good, this precept would not be a good one; but as they are bad, and would not observe their faith with you, so you are not bound to keep faith with them. Nor have legitimate grounds ever failed a prince who wished to show colourable excuse for the non-fulfillment of his promise. Of this one could furnish an infinite number of modern examples, and show how many times peace has been broken, and how many promises rendered worthless by the faithlessness of princes, and those that have been best able to imitate the fox have succeeded best. But it is necessary to be able to disguise this character well, and to be a great feigner and dissembler; and men are so simple and so ready to obey present necessities, that one who deceives will always find those who allow themselves to be deceived.

4   I will only mention one modern instance. Alexander VI did nothing else but deceive men, he thought of nothing else, and found the occasion for it; no man was ever more able to give assurances, or affirmed things with stronger oaths, and no man observed them less; however, he always succeeded in his deceptions, as he well knew this aspect of things.

It is not, therefore, necessary for a prince to have all the above-named qualities, but it is very necessary to seem to have them. I would even be bold to say that to possess them and always to observe them is dangerous, but to appear to possess them is useful. Thus it is well to seem merciful, faithful, humane, sincere, religious, and also to be so; but you must have the mind so disposed that when it is needful to be otherwise you may be able to change to the opposite qualities. And it must be understood that a prince, and especially a new prince, cannot observe all those things which are considered good in men, being often obliged, in order to maintain the state, to act against faith, against charity, against humanity, and against religion. And, therefore, he must have a mind disposed to adapt itself according to the wind, and as the variations of fortune dictate, and, as I said before, not deviate from what is good, if possible, but be able to do evil if constrained.

6   A prince must take great care that nothing goes out of his mouth which is not full of the above-named five qualities, and, to see and hear him, he should seem to be all mercy, faith, integrity, humanity, and religion. And nothing is more necessary than to seem to have this last quality, for men in general judge more by the eyes than by the hands, for every one can see, but very few have to feel. Everybody sees what you appear to be, few feel what you are, and those few will not dare to oppose themselves to the many, who have the majesty of the state to defend them; and in the actions of men, and especially of princes, from which there is no appeal, the end justifies the means. Let a prince therefore aim at conquering and maintaining the state, and the means will always be judged honourable and praised by every one, for the vulgar is always taken by appearances and the issue of the event; and

the world consists only of the vulgar, and the few who are not vulgar are isolated when the many have a rallying point in the prince. A certain prince of the present time, whom it is well not to name, never does anything but preach peace and good faith, but he is really a great enemy to both, and either of them, had he observed them, would have lost him state or reputation on many occasions. ❖

Questions for Meaning

1. What are the two methods of fighting cited by Machiavelli? Why is it important for princes to master both?
2. Machiavelli insists that princes must be both "lions" and "foxes." Explain what he means by this.
3. Under what circumstances should princes break their word?
4. Why is it useful for princes "to seem merciful, faithful, humane, sincere, religious, and also to be so"?
5. In paragraph 6, Machiavelli observes, "men in general judge more by the eyes than by the hands, for every one can see, but very few have to feel." What does this mean? Describe Machiavelli's opinion of the average man.

Questions about Strategy

1. What premise underlies Machiavelli's argument, and where does he first state it?
2. Consider the tone of this work. What sort of assumptions has Machiavelli made about his audience?
3. Machiavelli mentions Alexander VI by name in paragraph 4, but refuses to identify the prince he alludes to in paragraph 6. What does this reveal?
4. How would you characterize Machiavelli's point of view? Is it cynical or realistic?

ANDREW MARVELL

TO HIS COY MISTRESS

Andrew Marvell (1621–1678) was a Puritan patriot and political writer who is now remembered for writing a book of poetry that was published after his death. He graduated from Trinity College, Cambridge, in 1639, and after the death of his father in 1641, he spent several years traveling in Europe, presumably as a tutor. Upon his return to England, he became tutor to a ward of Oliver Cromwell, the man who ruled England during the period between the execution of Charles I in 1649 and the restoration of the monarchy in 1660. Through his connection with Cromwell, Marvell became assistant Latin Secretary for the Council of State, but he was not seriously involved in government until 1658, when he was elected to Parliament. He served in Parliament for the next twenty years, and his political experience led him to write a number of prose satires on government and religion. Claiming that Marvell owed her money at the time of his death in 1678, his housekeeper went through his private papers, gathered together the miscellaneous poems that Marvell had written for his own pleasure, and arranged for their publication in 1681.

The seventeenth century was a great age for English poetry, and although Marvell cannot be said to rank with Shakespeare, Milton, or Donne, a few of his poems are so very fine that they have won for him an honored place in the history of literature. Of these poems, the most famous is "To His Coy Mistress," an argument in the form of a poem.

To His Coy Mistress

Had we but world enough, and time,
This coyness, lady, were no crime.
We would sit down, and think which way
To walk, and pass our long love's day.
Thou by the Indian Ganges' side
Should'st rubies find: I by the tide
Of Humber would complain. I would
Love you ten years before the Flood,
And you should, if you please, refuse
Till the conversion of the Jews.
My vegetable love should grow
Vaster than empires, and more slow.
An hundred years should go to praise
Thine eyes, and on thy forehead gaze.
Two hundred to adore each breast:
But thirty thousand to the rest.

An age at least to every part,
And the last age should show your heart.
For, lady, you deserve this state,
20   Nor would I love at lower rate.
          But at my back I always hear
Time's wingèd chariot hurrying near;
And yonder all before us lie
Deserts of vast eternity.
25   Thy beauty shall no more be found,
Nor in thy marble vault shall sound
My echoing song; then worms shall try
That long preserved virginity,
And your quaint honor turn to dust,
30   And into ashes all my lust.
The grave's a fine and private place,
But none, I think, do there embrace.
          Now therefore, while the youthful hue
Sits on thy skin like morning dew,
35   And while thy willing soul transpires
At every pore with instant fires,
Now let us sport us while we may;
And now, like am'rous birds of prey,
Rather at once our time devour,
40   Than languish in his slow-chapt power,
Let us roll all our strength, and all
Our sweetness, up into one ball;
And tear our pleasures with rough strife
Thorough the iron gates of life.
45   Thus, though we cannot make our sun
Stand still, yet we will make him run. ❖

Questions for Meaning

1. What do we learn from the title of this poem? In the seventeenth century, "mistress" was a synonym for "sweetheart." But what does Marvell mean by "coy"?
2. What kind of woman inspired this poem? Identify the lines that reveal her character as it is presented in the poem.
3. How does the poet feel about this woman? Does he love her? Is this a love poem?
4. What is the poet urging this woman to do? Under what circumstances would he be willing to spend more time pleading with her? Why is this not possible?
5. Why does the poet describe his feelings as a "vegetable love"? What are the implications of this phrase?
6. What is the "marble vault" referred to in line 26?

7. Identify the references to "Ganges" (line 5), "Humber" (line 7), and "the Flood" (line 8). What does Marvell mean by "Time's wingèd chariot" (line 22) and "the iron gates of life" (line 44)?

8. Explain the last two lines of the poem. Is the sun a figure of speech? How is it possible to make it "run" when we lack the power to make it stand still?

Questions about Strategy

1. This poem is divided into three sections. Consider separately the tone of each. How do they differ?

2. Summarize the argument of this poem in three sentences, one for each section. Is the conclusion valid, or does it rest on a questionable premise?

3. What role does humor play in the poem? What serious emotions does the poet invoke in order to make his argument more persuasive?

4. How does Marvell use rhyme as a device for advancing his argument?

JONATHAN SWIFT

A MODEST PROPOSAL

For preventing the Children of Poor People in Ireland from Being a Burden to Their Parents or Country, and for Making Them Beneficial to the Public

Jonathan Swift (1667–1745) was a clergyman, poet, wit, and satirist. Born in Ireland as a member of the Protestant ruling class, Swift attended Trinity College in Dublin before settling in England in 1689. For the next ten years, he was a member of the household of Sir William Temple at Moor Park, Surrey. It was there that Swift met Esther Johnson, the "Stella" to whom he later wrote a famous series of letters known as *Journal to Stella* (1710–1713). Although he was ordained a priest in the Church of Ireland in 1695, and made frequent trips to Ireland, Swift's ambition always brought him back to England. His reputation as a writer grew rapidly after the publication of his first major work, *A Tale of a Tub*, in 1704. He became a writer on behalf of the ruling Tory party, and was appointed Dean of St. Patrick's Cathedral in Dublin as a reward for his services. When the Tories fell from power in 1714, Swift retired to Ireland, where he remained for the rest of his life, except for brief visits to England in 1726 and 1727. It was in Ireland that he wrote *Gulliver's Travels* (1726), which is widely recognized as one of the masterpieces of English literature, and "A Modest Proposal" (1729), one of the most memorable of all essays.

Ruled as an English colony and subject to numerous repressive laws, Ireland in Swift's time was a desperately poor country. Swift wrote "A Modest Proposal" in order to expose the plight of Ireland and the unfair policies under which it suffered. As you read it, you will find that Swift's proposal for solving the problem of poverty is anything but "modest." Even when we know that we are reading satire, this brilliant and bitter essay retains the power to shock all but the most careless of readers.

It is a melancholy object to those who walk through this great town or travel in the country, when they see the streets, the roads, and cabin doors, crowded with beggars of the female sex, followed by three, four, or six children, all in rags and importuning every passenger for an alms. These mothers, instead of being able to work for their honest livelihood, are forced to employ all their time in strolling to beg sustenance for their helpless infants, who, as they grow up, either turn thieves for want of work, or leave their dear native country to fight for the Pretender in Spain, or sell themselves to the Barbados.*

2   I think it is agreed by all parties that this prodigious number of children in the arms, or on the backs, or at the heels of their mothers, and frequently of their fathers, is in the present deplorable state of the kingdom a very great additional grievance; and therefore whoever could find out a fair, cheap, and easy method of making these children sound, useful members of the commonwealth would deserve so well of the public as to have his statue set up for a preserver of the nation.

But my intention is very far from being confined to provide only for the children of professed beggars; it is of a much greater extent, and shall take in the whole number of infants at a certain age who are born of parents in effect as little able to support them as those who demand our charity in the streets.

4   As to my own part, having turned my thoughts for many years upon this important subject, and maturely weighed the several schemes of other projectors, I have always found them grossly mistaken in their computation. It is true, a child just dropped from its dam may be supported by her milk for a solar year, with little other nourishment; at most not above the value of two shillings, which the mother may certainly get, or the value in scraps, by her lawful occupation of begging; and it is exactly at one year that I propose to provide for them in such a manner as instead of being a charge upon their parents or the parish, or wanting food and raiment for the rest of their lives, they shall on the contrary contribute to the feeding, and partly to the clothing, of many thousands.

There is likewise another great advantage in my scheme, that it will prevent those voluntary abortions, and that horrid practice of women

---

* The Pretender was James Stuart, the Catholic son of James II. Exiled in Spain, he sought to gain the throne his father had lost to the Protestant rulers William and Mary in 1688. Attempting to escape from destitution, many Irish people went to Barbados and other colonies as indentured servants.

murdering their bastard children, alas, too frequent among us, sacrificing the poor innocent babes, I doubt, more to avoid the expense than the shame, which would move tears and pity in the most savage and inhuman breast.

6   The number of souls in this kingdom being usually reckoned one million and a half, of these I calculate there may be about two hundred thousand couples whose wives are breeders; from which number I subtract thirty thousand couples who are able to maintain their own children, although I apprehend there cannot be so many under the present distress of the kingdom; but this being granted, there will remain an hundred and seventy thousand breeders. I again subtract fifty thousand for those women who miscarry, or whose children die by accident or disease within the year. There only remain an hundred and twenty thousand children of poor parents annually born. The question therefore is, how this number shall be reared and provided for, which, as I have already said, under the present situation of affairs, is utterly impossible by all the methods hitherto proposed. For we can neither employ them in handicraft or agriculture; we neither build houses (I mean in the country) nor cultivate land. They can very seldom pick up a livelihood by stealing till they arrive at six years old, except where they are of towardly parts; although I confess they learn the rudiments much earlier, during which time they can however be looked upon only as probationers, as I have been informed by a principal gentleman in the county of Cavan, who protested to me that he never knew above one or two instances under the age of six, even in a part of the kingdom so renowned for the quickest proficiency in that art.

I am assured by our merchants that a boy or a girl before twelve years old is no salable commodity; and even when they come to this age they will not yield above three pounds, or three pounds and half a crown at most on the Exchange; which cannot turn to account either to the parents or the kingdom, the charge of nutriment and rags having been at least four times that value.

8   I shall now therefore humbly propose my own thoughts, which I hope will not be liable to the least objection.

I have been assured by a very knowing American of my acquaintance in London, that a young healthy child well nursed is at a year old a most delicious, nourishing, and wholesome food, whether stewed, roasted, baked, or boiled; and I make no doubt that it will equally serve in a fricassee or a ragout.

10   I do therefore humbly offer it to public consideration that of the hundred and twenty thousand children, already computed, twenty thousand may be reserved for breed, whereof only one fourth part to be males, which is more than we allow to sheep, black cattle, or swine; and my reason is that these children are seldom the fruits of marriage, a circumstance not much regarded by our savages, therefore one male will be sufficient to serve four females. That the remaining hundred thousand may at a year old be offered in sale to the persons of quality and fortune through the kingdom, always advising the mother to let them suck plentifully in the last month, so as to

render them plump and fat for a good table. A child will make two dishes at an entertainment for friends; and when the family dines alone, the fore or hind quarter will make a reasonable dish, and seasoned with a little pepper or salt will be very good boiled on the fourth day, especially in winter.

I have reckoned upon a medium that a child just born will weigh twelve pounds, and in a solar year if tolerably nursed increaseth to twenty-eight pounds.

12   I grant this food will be somewhat dear, and therefore very proper for landlords, who, as they have already devoured most of the parents, seem to have the best title to the children.

Infant's flesh will be in season throughout the year, but more plentiful in March, and a little before and after. For we are told by a grave author, an eminent French physician,* that fish being a prolific diet, there are more children born in Roman Catholic countries about nine months after Lent than at any other season; therefore, reckoning a year after Lent, the markets will be more glutted than usual, because the number of popish infants is at least three to one in this kingdom; and therefore it will have one other collateral advantage, by lessening the number of Papists among us.

14   I have already computed the charge of nursing a beggar's child (in which list I reckon all cottagers, laborers, and four-fifths of the farmers) to be about two shillings per annum, rags included; and I believe no gentleman would repine to give ten shillings for the carcass of a good fat child, which, as I have said, will make four dishes of excellent nutritive meat, when he hath only some particular friend or his own family to dine with him. Thus the squire will learn to be a good landlord, and grow popular among the tenants; the mother will have eight shillings net profit, and be fit for work till she produces another child.

Those who are more thrifty (as I must confess the times require) may flay the carcass; the skin of which artificially dressed will make admirable gloves for ladies, and summer boots for fine gentlemen.

16   As to our city of Dublin, shambles may be appointed for this purpose in the most convenient parts of it, and butchers we may be assured will not be wanting; although I rather recommend buying the children alive, and dressing them hot from the knife as we do roasting pigs.

A very worthy person, a true lover of his country, and whose virtues I highly esteem, was lately pleased in discoursing on this matter to offer a refinement upon my scheme. He said that many gentlemen of his kingdom, having of late destroyed their deer, he conceived that the want of venison might be well supplied by the bodies of young lads and maidens, not exceeding fourteen years of age nor under twelve, so great a number of both sexes in every country being now ready to starve for want of work and service; and these to be disposed of by their parents, if alive, or otherwise by their nearest relations. But with due deference to so excellent a friend and so

---

* François Rabelais (1494?–1533) was the author of *Gargantua and Pantagruel*, a five-volume satire much admired by Swift.

deserving a patriot, I cannot be altogether in his sentiments; for as to the males, my American acquaintance assured me from frequent experience that their flesh was generally tough and lean, like that of our schoolboys, by continual exercise, and their taste disagreeable; and to fatten them would not answer the charge. Then as to the females, it would, I think with humble submission, be a loss to the public, because they soon would become breeders themselves; and besides, it is not improbable that some scrupulous people might be apt to censure such a practice (although indeed very unjustly) as a little bordering upon cruelty; which, I confess, hath always been with me the strongest objection against any project, how well soever intended.

18   But in order to justify my friend, he confessed that this expedient was put into his head by the famous Psalmanazar,* a native of the island of Formosa, who came from thence to London about twenty years ago, and in conversation told my friend that in his country when any young person happened to be put to death, the executioner sold the carcass to persons of quality as a prime dainty; and that in his time the body of a plump girl of fifteen, who was crucified for an attempt to poison the emperor, was sold to his Imperial Majesty's prime minister of state, and other great mandarins of the court, in joints from the gibbet, at four hundred crowns. Neither indeed can I deny that if the same use were made of several plump young girls in this town, who without one single groat to their fortunes cannot stir abroad without a chair, and appear at the playhouse and assemblies in foreign fineries which they never will pay for, the kingdom would not be the worse.

    Some persons of a desponding spirit are in great concern about that vast number of poor people who are aged, diseased, or maimed, and I have been desired to employ my thoughts what course may be taken to ease the nation of so grievous an encumbrance. But I am not in the least pain upon that matter, because it is very well known that they are every day dying and rotting by cold and famine, and filth and vermin, as fast as can be reasonably expected. And as to the younger laborers, they are now in almost as hopeful a condition. They cannot get work, and consequently pine away for want of nourishment to a degree that if any time they are accidentally hired to common labor, they have not strength to perform it; and thus the country and themselves are happily delivered from the evils to come.

20   I have too long digressed, and therefore shall return to my subject. I think the advantages by the proposal which I have made are obvious and many, as well as of the highest importance.

    For first, as I have already observed, it would greatly lessen the number of Papists, with whom we are yearly overrun, being the principal breeders of the nation as well as our most dangerous enemies; and who stay at home on purpose to deliver the kingdom to the Pretender, hoping to take their advantage by the absence of so many good Protestants, who have chosen

* George Psalmanazar (1679?–1763) published an imaginary description of Formosa (Taiwan) and became well known in English society.

rather to leave their country than to stay at home and pay tithes against their conscience to an Episcopal curate.

22   Secondly, the poorer tenants will have something valuable of their own, which by law may be made liable to distress, and help to pay their landlord's rent, their corn and cattle being already seized and money a thing unknown.

Thirdly, whereas the maintenance of an hundred thousand children, from two years old and upwards, cannot be computed at less than ten shillings a piece per annum, the nation's stock will be thereby increased fifty thousand pounds per annum, besides the profit of a new dish introduced to the tables of all gentlemen of fortune in the kingdom who have any refinement in taste. And the money will circulate among ourselves, the goods being entirely of our own growth and manufacture.

24   Fourthly, the constant breeders, besides the gain of eight shillings sterling per annum by the sale of their children, will be rid of the charge of maintaining them after the first year.

Fifthly, this food would likewise bring great custom to taverns, where the vintners will certainly be so prudent as to procure the best receipts for dressing it to perfection, and consequently have their houses frequented by all the fine gentlemen, who justly value themselves upon their knowledge in good eating; and a skillful cook, who understands how to oblige his guests, will contrive to make it as expensive as they please.

26   Sixthly, this would be a great inducement to marriage, which all wise nations have either encouraged by rewards or enforced by laws and penalties. It would increase the care and tenderness of mothers toward their children, when they were sure of a settlement for life to the poor babes, provided in some sort by the public, to their annual profit instead of expense. We should see an honest emulation among the married women, which of them could bring the fattest child to the market. Men would become as fond of their wives during the time of their pregnancy as they are now of their mares in foal, their cows in calf, or sows when they are ready to farrow; nor offer to beat or kick them (as is too frequent a practice) for fear of a miscarriage.

Many other advantages might be enumerated. For instance, the addition of some thousand carcasses in our exportation of barreled beef, the propagation of swine's flesh, and improvements in the art of making good bacon, so much wanted among us by the great destruction of pigs, too frequent at our tables, which are no way comparable in taste or magnificence to a well-grown, fat, yearling child, which roasted whole will make a considerable figure at a lord mayor's feast or any other public entertainment. But this and many others I omit, being studious of brevity.

28   Supposing that one thousand families in this city would be constant customers for infants' flesh, besides others who might have it at merry meetings, particularly weddings and christenings, I compute that Dublin would take off annually about twenty thousand carcasses, and the rest of the kingdom (where probably they will be sold somewhat cheaper) the remaining eighty thousand.

I can think of no one objection that will possibly be raised against this proposal, unless it should be urged that the number of people will be thereby much lessened in the kingdom. This I freely own, and it was indeed one principal design in offering it to the world. I desire the reader will observe, that I calculate my remedy for this one individual kingdom of Ireland and for no other that ever was, is, or I think ever can be upon earth. Therefore let no man talk to me of other expedients: of taxing our absentees at five shillings a pound: of using neither clothes nor household furniture except what is of our own growth and manufacture: of utterly rejecting the materials and instruments that promote foreign luxury: of curing the expensiveness of pride, vanity, idleness, and gaming in our women: of introducing a vein of parsimony, prudence, and temperance: of learning to love our country, in the want of which we differ even from Laplanders and the inhabitants of Topinamboo: of quitting our animosities and factions, nor acting any longer like the Jews, who were murdering one another at the very moment their city was taken: of being a little cautious not to sell our country and conscience for nothing: of teaching landlords to have at least one degree of mercy toward their tenants: lastly, of putting a spirit of honesty, industry, and skill into our shopkeepers; who, if a resolution could now be taken to buy only our native goods, would immediately unite to cheat and exact upon us in the price, the measure, and the goodness, nor could ever yet be brought to make one fair proposal of just dealing, though often and earnestly invited to it.

30   Therefore I repeat, let no man talk to me of these and the like expedients, till he hath at least some glimpse of hope that there will ever be some hearty and sincere attempt to put them in practice.

But as to myself, having been wearied out for many years with offering vain, idle, visionary thoughts, and at length utterly despairing of success, I fortunately fell upon this proposal, which, as it is wholly new, so it hath something solid and real, of no expense and little trouble, full in our own power, and whereby we can incur no danger in disobliging England. For this kind of commodity will not bear exportation, the flesh being of too tender a consistence to admit a long continuance in salt, although perhaps I could name a country which would be glad to eat up our whole nation without it.

32   After all, I am not so violently bent upon my own opinion as to reject any offer proposed by wise men, which shall be found equally innocent, cheap, easy, and effectual. But before something of that kind shall be advanced in contradiction to my scheme, and offering a better, I desire the author or authors will be pleased maturely to consider two points. First, as things now stand, how they will be able to find food and raiment for an hundred thousand useless mouths and backs. And secondly, there being a round million of creatures in human figure throughout this kingdom, whose sole subsistence put into a common stock would leave them in debt two millions of pounds sterling, adding those who are beggars by profession to the bulk of farmers, cottagers, and laborers, with their wives and children who are beggars in effect; I desire those politicians who dislike my overture, and may perhaps be so bold to attempt an answer, that they will first ask the

parents of these mortals whether they would not at this day think it a great happiness to have been sold for food at a year old in this manner I prescribe, and thereby have avoided such a perpetual scene of misfortunes as they have since gone through by the oppression of landlords, the impossibility of paying rent without money or trade, the want of common sustenance, with neither house nor clothes to cover them from the inclemencies of the weather, and the most inevitable prospect of entailing the like or greater miseries upon their breed forever.

I profess, in the sincerity of my heart, that I have not the least personal interest in endeavoring to promote this necessary work, having no other motive than the public good of my country, by advancing our trade, providing for infants, relieving the poor, and giving some pleasure to the rich. I have no children by which I can propose to get a single penny; the youngest being nine years old, and my wife past childbearing. ❖

Questions for Meaning

1. What do we learn in this essay about the condition of Ireland in Swift's time, and how Ireland was viewed by England? Does Swift provide any clues about what has caused the poverty he describes?
2. What specific "advantages" does Swift cite on behalf of his proposal?
3. Why does Swift limit his proposal to infants? On what grounds does he exclude older children from consideration as marketable commodities? Why does he claim that we need not worry about the elderly?
4. What does this essay reveal about the relations between Catholics and Protestants in the eighteenth century?
5. Where in the essay does Swift tell us what he really wants? What serious reforms does he propose to improve conditions in Ireland?
6. Vocabulary: importuning (1), sustenance (1), prodigious (2), rudiments (6), ragout (9), collateral (13), desponding (19), inducement (26), emulation (26), propagation (27), parsimony (29), incur (31).

Questions about Strategy

1. How does Swift present himself in this essay? Many readers have taken this essay seriously and come away convinced that Swift was heartless and cruel. Why is it possible for some readers to be deceived in this way? What devices does Swift employ to create the illusion that he is serious? How does this strategy benefit the essay?
2. Does the language of the first few paragraphs contain any hint of irony? At what point in the essay did it first become clear to you that Swift is writing tongue-in-cheek?
3. Where in the essay does Swift pretend to anticipate objections that might be raised against his proposal? How does he dispose of these objections?

4. How does the style of this essay contrast with its subject matter? How does this contrast contribute to the force of the essay as a whole?
5. What is the function of the concluding paragraph?
6. What is the premise of this essay if we take its argument at face value? When we realize that Swift is writing ironically, what underlying premise begins to emerge?
7. What advantage is there in writing ironically? Why do you think Swift chose to treat his subject in this manner?

THOMAS JEFFERSON

THE DECLARATION OF INDEPENDENCE

Thomas Jefferson (1743–1826) was the third president of the United States and one of the most talented men ever to hold that office. A farmer, architect, writer, and scientist, Jefferson entered politics in 1769 as a member of the Virginia House of Burgesses. In 1775, he was a member of Virginia's delegation to the Second Continental Congress. He was governor of Virginia from 1779 to 1781, represented the United States in Europe from 1784 to 1789, and was elected to the first of two terms as president in 1801. Of all his many accomplishments, Jefferson himself was most proud of having founded the University of Virginia in 1819.

Although the Continental Congress had delegated the responsibility for writing a declaration of independence to a committee that included Benjamin Franklin and John Adams as well as Jefferson, it was Jefferson who undertook the actual composition. His colleagues respected him as the best writer among them. Jefferson wrote at least two, and possibly three, drafts during the seventeen days allowed for the assignment. His work was reviewed by the other members of the committee, but they made only minor revisions—mainly in the first two paragraphs. When it came to adopting the declaration, Congress was harder to please. After lengthy and spirited debate, Congress made twenty-four changes and deleted over three hundred words. Nevertheless, "The Declaration of Independence," as approved by Congress on July 4, 1776, is almost entirely the work of Jefferson. In addition to being an eloquent example of eighteenth-century prose, it is a clear example of deductive reasoning.

When in the Course of human events, it becomes necessary for one people to dissolve the political bands which have connected them with another, and to assume among the powers of the earth, the separate and equal station to which the Laws of Nature and of Nature's God entitle them, a decent respect to the opinions of mankind requires that they should declare the causes which impel them to the separation.

2   We hold these truths to be self-evident, that all men are created equal, that they are endowed by their Creator with certain unalienable Rights, that among these are Life, Liberty and the pursuit of Happiness. That to secure these rights, Governments are instituted among Men, deriving their just powers from the consent of the governed. That whenever any Form of Government becomes destructive of these ends it is the Right of the People to alter or to abolish it, and to institute new Government, laying its foundation on such principles and organizing its powers in such form, as to them shall seem most likely to effect their Safety and Happiness. Prudence, indeed, will dictate that Governments long established should not be changed for light and transient causes; and accordingly all experience has shewn, that mankind are more disposed to suffer, while evils are sufferable, than to right themselves by abolishing the forms to which they are accustomed. But when a long train of abuses and usurpations, pursuing invariably the same Object evinces a design to reduce them under absolute Despotism, it is their right, it is their duty, to throw off such Government, and to provide new Guards for their future security. Such has been the patient sufferance of these Colonies; and such is now the necessity which constrains them to alter their former Systems of Government. The history of the present King of Great Britain is a history of repeated injuries and usurpations, all having in direct object the establishment of an absolute Tyranny over these States. To prove this, let Facts be submitted to a candid world.

He has refused his Assent to Laws, the most wholesome and necessary for the public good.

4   He has forbidden his Governors to pass Laws of immediate and pressing importance, unless suspended in their operation till his Assent should be obtained; and when so suspended, he has utterly neglected to attend to them. He has refused to pass other Laws for the accommodation of large districts of people, unless those people would relinquish the right of Representation in the Legislature, a right inestimable to them and formidable to tyrants only.

He has called together legislative bodies at places unusual, uncomfortable, and distant from the depository of their public Records, for the sole purpose of fatiguing them into compliance with his measures.

6   He has dissolved Representative Houses repeatedly, for opposing with manly firmness his invasions on the rights of the people.

He has refused for a long time, after such dissolutions, to cause others to be elected; whereby the Legislative powers, incapable of Annihilation, have returned to the People at large for their exercise; the State remaining in the mean time exposed to all the dangers of invasion from without, and convulsions within.

8   He has endeavoured to prevent the population of these States; for that purpose obstructing the Laws for Naturalization of Foreigners; refusing to pass others to encourage their migrations hither, and raising the conditions of new Appropriations of Lands.

He has obstructed the Administration of Justice, by refusing his assent to Laws for establishing Judiciary powers.

10   He has made Judges dependent on his Will alone, for the tenure of their offices, and the amount and payment of their salaries.

     He has erected a multitude of New Offices, and sent hither swarms of Officers to harass our People, and eat out their substance.

12   He has kept among us, in times of peace, standing Armies without the Consent of our legislatures.

     He has affected to render the Military independent of and superior to the Civil power.

14   He has combined with others to subject us to a jurisdiction foreign to our constitution, and unacknowledged by our laws; giving his Assent to their Acts of pretended Legislation:

     For Quartering large bodies of armed troops among us:

16   For protecting them, by a mock Trial, from punishment for any Murders which they should commit on the Inhabitants of these States:

     For cutting off our Trade with all parts of the world:

18   For imposing Taxes on us without our Consent:

     For depriving us in many cases of the benefits of Trial by Jury:

20   For transporting us beyond Seas to be tried for pretended offences:

     For abolishing the free System of English Laws in a neighbouring Province, establishing therein an Arbitrary government, and enlarging its Boundaries so as to render it at once an example and fit instrument for introducing the same absolute rule into these Colonies:

22   For taking away our Charters, abolishing our most valuable Laws, and altering fundamentally the Forms of our Governments:

     For suspending our own Legislatures, and declaring themselves invested with power to legislate for us in all cases whatsoever.

24   He has abdicated Government here, by declaring us out of his Protection and waging War against us.

     He has plundered our seas, ravaged our Coasts, burnt our towns, and destroyed the Lives of our people.

26   He is at this time transporting large Armies of foreign Mercenaries to compleat the works of death, desolation and tyranny, already begun with circumstances of Cruelty & perfidy scarcely paralleled in the most barbarous ages, and totally unworthy the Head of a civilized nation.

     He has constrained our fellow Citizens taken Captive on the high Seas to bear Arms against their Country, to become the executioners of their friends and Brethren, or to fall themselves by their Hands.

28   He has excited domestic insurrections amongst us, and has endeavoured to bring on the inhabitants of our frontiers, the merciless Indian Savages, whose known rule of warfare, is an undistinguished destruction of all ages, sexes and conditions.

     In every stage of these Oppressions We have Petitioned for Redress in the most humble terms: Our repeated Petitions have been answered only by repeated injury. A Prince, whose character is thus marked by every act which may define a Tyrant, is unfit to be the ruler of a free people.

30   Nor have We been wanting in attentions to our British brethren. We have warned them from time to time of attempts by their legislature to

extend an unwarrantable jurisdiction over us. We have reminded them of the circumstances of our emigration and settlement here. We have appealed to their native justice and magnanimity, and we have conjured them by the ties of our common kindred to disavow these usurpations, which, would inevitably interrupt our connections and correspondence. They too have been deaf to the voice of Justice and of consanguinity. We must, therefore, acquiesce in the necessity, which denounces our Separation, and hold them, as we hold the rest of mankind, Enemies in War, in Peace Friends.

We, therefore, the Representatives of the United States of America, in General Congress, Assembled, appealing to the Supreme Judge of the world for the rectitude of our intentions, do, in the Name, and by Authority of the good People of these Colonies, solemnly publish and declare, That these United Colonies are, and of Right ought to be Free and Independent States; that they are Absolved from all Allegiance to the British Crown, and that all political connection between them and the State of Great Britain, is and ought to be totally dissolved; and that as Free and Independent States, they have full Power to levy War, conclude Peace, contract Alliances, establish Commerce, and to do all other Acts and Things which Independent States may of right do. And for the support of this Declaration, with a firm reliance on the protection of divine Providence, we mutually pledge to each other our Lives, our Fortunes and our sacred Honor.

John Hancock	Thomas Lynch Junr.	Thos. Jefferson
Button Gwinnett	Arthur Middleton	Benja. Harrison
Lyman Hall	Samuel Chase	Thos. Nelson jr.
Geo. Walton	Wm. Paca	Francis Lightfoot Lee
Wm. Hooper	Thos. Stone	Carter Braxton
Joseph Hewes	Charles Carroll	Robt. Morris
John Penn	of Carrollton	Benjamin Rush
Edward Rutledge	George Wythe	Benja. Franklin
Thos. Heyward Junr.	Richard Henry Lee	John Morton
Geo. Clymer	Frans. Lewis	John Adams
Jas. Smith	Lewis Morris	Robt. Treat Paine
Geo. Taylor	Richd. Stockton	Elbridge Gerry
James Wilson	Jno. Witherspoon	Step. Hopkins
Geo. Ross	Fras. Hopkinson	William Ellery
Caesar Rodney	John Hart	Roger Sherman
Geo. Read	Abra. Clark	Saml. Huntington
Tho. McKean	Josiah Bartlett	Wm. Williams
Wm. Floyd	Wm. Whipple	Oliver Wolcott
Phil. Livingston	Saml. Adams	Matthew Thornton ❖

Questions for Meaning

1. What was the purpose of "The Declaration of Independence"? What reason does Jefferson himself give for writing it?

2. In paragraph 1, what does Jefferson mean by "the Laws of Nature and of Nature's God"?
3. Paragraphs 3 through 28 are devoted to enumerating a list of grievances against King George III. Which of these are the most important? Are any of them relatively trivial? Taken together do they justify Jefferson's description of George III as "A Prince, whose character is thus marked by every act which may define a Tyrant"?
4. How would you summarize Jefferson's conception of the relationship between people and government?
5. How does Jefferson characterize his fellow Americans? At what points does he put the colonists in a favorable light?
6. What does Jefferson mean by "the Supreme Judge of the world"? Why does he express "a firm reliance on the protection of a divine Providence"?
7. Vocabulary: transient (2), evinces (2), usurpations (2), candid (2), annihilation (7), render (13), perfidy (26), unwarrantable (30), consanguinity (30), acquiesce (30), rectitude (31).

Questions about Strategy

1. In paragraph 2, why does Jefferson declare certain truths to be "self-evident"? Paraphrase this paragraph and explain the purpose it serves in Jefferson's argument.
2. In evaluating "The Declaration of Independence" as an argument, what do you think is more important: the general "truths" outlined in the second paragraph, or the specific accusations listed in the paragraphs that follow? If you were to write a counterargument to "The Declaration of Independence," on what points would you concentrate? Where is it most vulnerable?
3. Jefferson is often cited as a man of great culture and liberal values. Are there any points of "The Declaration of Independence" that now seem illiberal?
4. Does Jefferson use any loaded terms? He was forced to delete exaggerated language from his first two drafts of "The Declaration." Do you see any exaggerations that Congress failed to catch?
5. For what sort of audience did Jefferson write "The Declaration of Independence"? Is it directed primarily to the American people, the British government, or the world in general?

MARY WOLLSTONECRAFT

THE PLAYTHINGS OF TYRANTS

An English writer of Irish extraction, Mary Wollstonecraft (1759–1797) was an early advocate of women's rights. After working as a governess and a publisher's assistant, she went to France in 1792 in order to witness the French Revolution. She lived there with an American, Captain Gilbert Imlay, and had a child by him in 1794. Her relationship with Imlay broke down soon afterward, and, in 1795, Wollstonecraft tried to commit suicide by drowning herself. She was rescued, however, and returned to London, where she became a member of a group of radical writers that included Thomas Paine, William Blake, and William Godwin. Wollstonecraft became pregnant by Godwin in 1796, and they were married the following year. Their child, Mary (1797–1851), would eventually win fame as the author of *Frankenstein.* Wollstonecraft died only eleven days after Mary's birth.

Wollstonecraft's fame rests on one work, *A Vindication of the Rights of Women* (1792). Although she had written about the need for educated women several years earlier in *Thoughts on the Education of Daughters* (1787), she makes a stronger and better-reasoned argument in her *Vindication.* "The Playthings of Tyrants" is an editor's title for an excerpt from the second chapter, "The Prevailing Opinion of a Sexual Character Discussed." As the excerpt suggests, Wollstonecraft was not especially interested in securing political rights for women. Her object was to emancipate women from the roles imposed upon them by men and to urge women to think for themselves.

To account for, and excuse the tyranny of man, many ingenious arguments have been brought forward to prove, that the two sexes, in the acquirement of virtue, ought to aim at attaining a very different character: or, to speak explicitly, women are not allowed to have sufficient strength of mind to acquire what really deserves the name of virtue. Yet it should seem, allowing them to have souls, that there is but one way appointed by Providence to lead *mankind* to either virtue or happiness.

2   If then women are not a swarm of ephemeron triflers, why should they be kept in ignorance under the specious name of innocence? Men complain, and with reason, of the follies and caprices of our sex, when they do not keenly satirize our headstrong passions and groveling vices.—Behold, I should answer, the natural effect of ignorance! The mind will ever be unstable that has only prejudices to rest on, and the current will run with destructive fury when there are no barriers to break its force. Women are told from their infancy, and taught by the example of their mothers, that a little knowledge of human weakness, justly termed cunning, softness of temper, *outward* obedience, and a scrupulous attention to a puerile kind

of propriety, will obtain for them the protection of man; and should they be beautiful, every thing else is needless, for, at least, twenty years of their lives.

Thus Milton* describes our first frail mother; though when he tells us that women are formed for softness and sweet attractive grace, I cannot comprehend his meaning, unless, in the true Mahometan strain, he meant to deprive us of souls, and insinuate that we were beings only designed by sweet attractive grace, and docile blind obedience, to gratify the senses of man when he can no longer soar on the wing of contemplation.

4   How grossly do they insult us who thus advise us only to render ourselves gentle, domestic brutes! For instance, the winning softness so warmly, and frequently, recommended, that governs by obeying. What childish expressions, and how insignificant is the being—can it be an immortal one? who will condescend to govern by such sinister methods! 'Certainly,' says Lord Bacon,† 'man is of kin to the beasts by his body; and if he be not of kin to God by his spirit, he is a base and ignoble creature!' Men, indeed, appear to me to act in a very unphilosophical manner when they try to secure the good conduct of women by attempting to keep them always in a state of childhood. Rousseau‡ was more consistent when he wished to stop the progress of reason in both sexes, for if men eat of the tree of knowledge, women will come in for a taste; but, from the imperfect cultivation which their understandings now receive, they only attain a knowledge of evil.

Children, I grant, should be innocent; but when the epithet is applied to men, or women, it is but a civil term for weakness. For if it be allowed that women were destined by Providence to acquire human virtues, and by the exercise of their understandings, that stability of character which is the firmest ground to rest our future hopes upon, they must be permitted to turn to the fountain of light, and not forced to shape their course by the twinkling of a mere satellite. Milton, I grant, was of a very different opinion; for he only bends to the indefeasible right of beauty, though it would be difficult to render two passages which I now mean to contrast, consistent. But into similar inconsistencies are great men often led by their senses.

> 'To whom thus Eve with *perfect beauty* adorn'd.
> 'My Author and Disposer, what thou bidst
> '*Unargued* I obey; So God ordains;
> 'God is *thy law; thou mine:* to know no more
> 'Is Woman's *happiest* knowledge and her *praise.*'

6   These are exactly the arguments that I have used to children; but I have added, your reason is now gaining strength, and, till it arrives at some

---

* John Milton (1608–1674) was an important English poet best known for *Paradise Lost.*

† Francis Bacon (1561–1626) was an English statesman, philosopher, and essayist.

‡ Jean Jacques Rousseau (1712–1778) was an influential philosopher and political theorist best known for *Discourse on the Inequalities of Men* (1754) and *The Social Contract* (1762).

degree of maturity, you must look up to me for advice—then you ought to *think,* and only rely on God.

Yet in the following lines Milton seems to coincide with me; when he makes Adam thus expostulate with his Maker.

> 'Hast thou not made me here thy substitute,
> 'And these inferior far beneath me set?
> 'Among *unequals* what society
> 'Can sort, what harmony or true delight?
> 'Which must be mutual, in proportion due
> 'Giv'n and receiv'd; but in *disparity*
> 'The one intense, the other still remiss
> 'Cannot well suit with either, but soon prove
> 'Tedious alike: of *fellowship* I speak
> 'Such as I seek, fit to participate
> 'All rational delight—'

8   In treating, therefore, of the manners of women, let us, disregarding sensual arguments, trace what we should endeavour to make them in order to cooperate, if the expression be not too bold, with the supreme Being.

By individual education, I mean, for the sense of the word is not precisely defined, such an attention to a child as will slowly sharpen the senses, form the temper, regulate the passions as they begin to ferment, and set the understanding to work before the body arrives at maturity; so that the man may only have to proceed, not to begin, the important task of learning to think and reason.

10   To prevent any misconstruction, I must add, that I do not believe that a private education can work the wonders which some sanguine writers have attributed to it. Men and women must be educated, in a great degree, by the opinions and manners of the society they live in. In every age there has been a stream of popular opinion that has carried all before it, and given a family character, as it were, to the century. It may then fairly be inferred, that, till society be differently constituted, much cannot be expected from education. It is, however, sufficient for my present purpose to assert, that, whatever effect circumstances have on the abilities, every being may become virtuous by the exercise of its own reason; for if but one being was created with vicious inclinations, that is positively bad, what can save us from atheism? or if we worship a God, is not that God a devil?

Consequently, the most perfect education, in my opinion, is such an exercise of the understanding as is best calculated to strengthen the body and form the heart. Or, in other words, to enable the individual to attain such habits of virtue as will render it independent. In fact, it is a farce to call any being virtuous whose virtues do not result from the exercise of its own reason. This was Rousseau's opinion respecting men: I extend it to women, and confidently assert that they have been drawn out of their sphere by false refinement, and not by an endeavour to acquire masculine qualities. Still the regal homage which they receive is so intoxicating, that till the manners of the times are changed, and formed on more reasonable principles, it may be impossible to convince them that the illegitimate power, which they obtain, by degrading themselves, is a curse, and that they must return to nature and equality, if they wish to secure the placid satisfaction that unsophisticated affections impart. But for this epoch we must wait—wait, perhaps, till kings and nobles, enlightened by reason, and, preferring the real dignity of man to childish state, throw off their gaudy hereditary trappings: and if then women do not resign the arbitrary power of beauty—they will prove that they have *less* mind than man. . . .

12   Many are the causes that, in the present corrupt state of society, contribute to enslave women by cramping their understandings and sharpening their senses. One, perhaps, that silently does more mischief than all the rest, is their disregard of order.

To do every thing in an orderly manner, is a most important precept, which women, who, generally speaking, receive only a disorderly kind of education, seldom attend to with that degree of exactness that men, who from their infancy are broken into method, observe. This negligent kind of guesswork, for what other epithet can be used to point out the random exertions of a sort of instinctive common sense, never brought to the test of reason? prevents their generalizing matters of fact—so they do to-day, what they did yesterday, merely because they did it yesterday.

14   This contempt of the understanding in early life has more baneful consequences than is commonly supposed; for the little knowledge which women of strong minds attain, is, from various circumstances, of a more desultory kind than the knowledge of men, and it is acquired more by sheer observations on real life, than from comparing what has been individually observed with the results of experience generalized by speculation. Led by their dependent situation and domestic employments more into society, what they learn is rather by snatches; and as learning is with them, in general, only a secondary thing, they do not pursue any one branch with that persevering ardour necessary to give vigour to the faculties, and clearness of the judgment. In the present state of society, a little learning is required to support the character of a gentleman; and boys are obliged to submit to a few years of discipline. But in the education of women, the cultivation of the understanding is always subordinate to the acquirement of some corporeal accomplishment; even while enervated by confinement and false notions of modesty, the body is prevented from attaining that grace and beauty which relaxed half-formed limbs never exhibit. Besides, in youth their faculties are not brought forward by emulation; and having no serious scientific study, if they have natural sagacity it is turned too soon on life and manners. They dwell on effects, and modifications, without tracing them back to causes; and complicated rules to adjust behaviour are a weak substitute for simple principles.

As a proof that education gives this appearance of weakness to females, we may instance the example of military men, who are, like them, sent into the world before their minds have been stored with knowledge or fortified by principles. The consequences are similar; soldiers acquire a little superficial knowledge, snatched from the muddy current of conversation, and, from continually mixing with society, they gain, what is termed a knowledge of the world; and this acquaintance with manners and customs has frequently been confounded with a knowledge of the human heart. But can the crude fruit of casual observation, never brought to the test of judgment, formed by comparing speculation and experience, deserve such a distinction? Soldiers, as well as women, practice the minor virtues with punctilious politeness. Where is then the sexual difference, when the education has been the same? All the difference that I can discern, arises from the superior advantage of liberty, which enables the former to see more of life.

16   It is wandering from my present subject, perhaps, to make a political remark; but, as it was produced naturally by the train of my reflections, I shall not pass it silently over.

Standing armies can never consist of resolute, robust men; they may be well disciplined machines, but they will seldom contain men under the influence of strong passions, or with very vigorous faculties. And as for any depth of understanding, I will venture to affirm, that it is as rarely to be found in the army as amongst women; and the cause, I maintain, is the same. It may be further observed, that officers are also particularly attentive to their persons, fond of dancing, crowded rooms, adventures, and ridicule. Like the *fair* sex, the business of their lives is gallantry.—They were taught to please, and they only live to please. Yet they do not lose their rank in the distinction of sexes, for they are still reckoned superior to women, though in what their superiority consists, beyond what I have just mentioned, it is difficult to discover.

18   The great misfortune is this, that they both acquire manners before morals, and a knowledge of life before they have, from reflections, any acquaintance with the grand ideal outline of human nature. The consequence is natural; satisfied with common nature, they become a prey to prejudices, and taking all their opinions on credit, they blindly submit to authority. So that, if they have any sense, it is a kind of instinctive glance, that catches proportions, and decides with respect to manners; but fails when arguments are to be pursued below the surface, or opinions analyzed.

May not the same remark be applied to women? Nay, the argument may be carried still further, for they are both thrown out of a useful station by the unnatural distinctions established in civilized life. Riches and hereditary honours have made cyphers of women to give consequence to the numerical figures; and idleness has produced a mixture of gallantry and despotism into society, which leads the very men who are the slaves of their mistresses to tyrannize over their sisters, wives, and daughters. This is only keeping them in rank and file, it is true. Strengthen the female mind by enlarging it, and there will be an end to blind obedience; but, as blind obedience is ever sought for by power, tyrants and sensualists are in the right when they endeavor to keep women in the dark, because the former only wants slaves, and the latter a play-thing. The sensualist, indeed, has been the most dangerous of tyrants, and women have been duped by their lovers, as princes by their ministers, whilst dreaming that they reigned over them. ❖

Questions for Meaning

1. What is wrong with treating women as children and expecting "blind obedience"?
2. What causes does Wollstonecraft cite for the degradation of women? On what grounds does she defend their "follies" and "vices"?
3. What does Wollstonecraft mean by "false refinement" in paragraph 11? Explain why she believes it is dangerous to acquire "manners before morals."
4. Where in her essay does Wollstonecraft define the sort of education she believes women should receive? Why does she object to educating women privately in their homes?
5. Wollstonecraft was perceived as a radical by her contemporaries, and relatively few people took her ideas seriously. Looking back on her work after two hundred years, can you find any traditional values that Wollstonecraft accepted without question? Could you argue that she was conservative in some ways?
6. Explain why "the sensualist" has been "the most dangerous of tyrants."
7. Vocabulary: ephemeron (2), specious (2), caprices (2), puerile (2), propriety (2), insinuate (3), docile (3), sanguine (10), desultory (14), corporeal (14), enervated (14), sagacity (14), punctilious (15), cyphers (19).

Questions about Strategy

1. What is the premise of this argument? Where does Wollstonecraft first state it, and where is it restated?
2. What is the function of the last sentence in the second paragraph?
3. Why does Wollstonecraft quote Francis Bacon and John Milton? What do these quotations contribute to her argument?
4. Comment on the analogy Wollstonecraft makes between women and soldiers. What type of soldiers did she have in mind? Is her analogy valid?
5. Do you think Wollstonecraft wrote this argument primarily for men or for women? What kind of an audience could she have expected in the eighteenth century?

KARL MARX AND FRIEDRICH ENGELS

THE COMMUNIST MANIFESTO

Karl Marx (1818–1883) was a German social scientist and political philosopher who believed that history is determined by economics. Originally intending to teach, Marx studied at the University of Berlin, receiving his PhD in 1841. But, in 1842, he abandoned academics to become editor of the *Rheinische Zeitung,* an influential newspaper published in Cologne. His editorials led the government to close the paper within a year, and Marx went into exile—first in France and Belgium, and eventually in England, where he spent the last thirty-three years of his life.

In 1843, Marx met Friedrich Engels (1820–1895), the son of a wealthy German industrialist with business interests in England. The two men discovered that they shared the same political beliefs, and they worked together closely for the next forty years. Not until 1867 was Marx able to publish the first volume of *Das Kapital,* his most important work. The second and third volumes, published after Marx's death, were completed by Engels, who worked from Marx's extensive notes. *Das Kapital,* or *Capital,* provided the theoretical basis for what is variously known as "Marxism" or "Communism." It is an indictment of nineteenth-century capitalism that predicts a proletarian revolution in which the workers would take over the means of production and distribute goods according to needs, creating an ideal society in which the state would wither away.

Marx and Engels had outlined their views long before the publication of *Das Kapital.* In 1848, they published a pamphlet called *The Communist Manifesto.* It was written during a period of great political unrest. Within months of its publication, revolutions broke out in several European countries. Most of the revolutions of 1848 were quickly aborted, but "the specter of Communism" continued to haunt the world. Here are the first few pages of this classic argument.

A specter is haunting Europe—the specter of Communism. All the Powers of old Europe have entered into a holy alliance to exorcise this specter; Pope and Czar, Metternich and Guizot,* French Radicals and German police-spies.

2   Where is the party in opposition that has not been decried as communistic by its opponents in power? Where the Opposition that has not hurled

---

* Clemens Metternich (1773–1859) was an Austrian statesman who gained great political influence in early nineteenth-century Europe. He was widely associated with the use of censorship and espionage to suppress revolutionary movements. François Guizot (1787–1874) was a French statesman associated with preserving the status quo.

back the branding reproach of Communism against the more advanced opposition parties, as well as against its reactionary adversaries?

Two things result from this fact.

I. Communism is already acknowledged by all European Powers to be itself a Power.

II. It is high time that Communists should openly, in the face of the whole world, publish their views, their aims, their tendencies, and meet this nursery tale of the specter of Communism with a Manifesto of the party itself.

4 To this end, Communists of various nationalities have assembled in London and sketched the following Manifesto, to be published in the English, French, German, Italian, Flemish and Danish languages.

Bourgeoisie and Proletarians[1]

The history of all hitherto existing society is the history of class struggles.

6 Freeman and slave, patrician and plebian, lord and serf, guild-master and journeyman, in a word, oppressor and oppressed, stood in constant opposition to one another, carried on uninterrupted, now hidden, now open fight, a fight that each time ended, either in a revolutionary re-constitution of society at large, or in the common ruin of the contending classes.

In the earlier epochs of history we find almost everywhere a complicated arrangement of society into various orders, a manifold gradation of social rank. In ancient Rome we have patricians, knights, plebians, slaves; in the Middle Ages, feudal lords, vassals, guild-masters, journeymen, apprentices, serfs; in almost all of these classes, again, subordinate gradations.

8 The modern bourgeois society that has sprouted from the ruins of feudal society, has not done away with class antagonisms. It has but established new classes, new conditions of oppression, new forms of struggle in place of the old ones.

Our epoch, the epoch of the bourgeoisie, possesses, however, this distinctive feature; it has simplified the class antagonisms. Society as a whole is more and more splitting up into two great hostile camps, into two great classes directly facing each other: Bourgeoisie and Proletariat.

10 From the serfs of the Middle Ages sprang the chartered burghers of the earliest towns. From these burgesses the first elements of the bourgeoisie were developed.

The discovery of America, the rounding of the Cape, opened up fresh ground for the rising bourgeoisie. The East Indian and Chinese markets, the

---

[1] By bourgeoisie is meant the class of modern Capitalists, owners of the means of social production and employers of wage labor. By proletariat, the class of modern wage laborers who, having no means of production of their own, are reduced to selling their labor-power in order to live. [Marx's note]

colonization of America, trade with the colonies, the increase in the means of exchange and in commodities generally, gave to commerce, to navigation, to industry, an impulse never before known, and thereby, to the revolutionary element in the tottering feudal society, a rapid development.

12 The feudal system of industry, under which industrial production was monopolized by closed guilds, now no longer sufficed for the growing wants of the new market. The manufacturing system took its place. The guild-masters were pushed on one side by the manufacturing middle-class: division of labor between the different corporate guilds vanished in the face of division of labor in each single workshop.

Meantime the markets kept ever growing, the demand ever rising. Even manufacture no longer sufficed. Thereupon, steam and machinery revolutionized industrial production. The place of manufacture was taken by the giant, Modern Industry, the place of the industrial middle-class, by industrial millionaires, the leaders of whole industrial armies, the modern bourgeois.

14 Modern industry has established the world market, for which the discovery of America paved the way. This market has given an immense development to commerce, to navigation, to communication by land. This development has, in its turn, reacted on the extension of industry; and in proportion as industry, commerce, navigation, railways extended, in the same proportion the bourgeoisie developed, increased its capital, and pushed into the background every class handed down from the Middle Ages.

We see, therefore, how the modern bourgeoisie is itself the product of a long course of development, a series of revolutions in the modes of production and of exchange.

16 Each step in the development of the bourgeoisie was accompanied by a corresponding political advance of that class. An oppressed class under the sway of the feudal nobility, an armed and self-governing association in the medieval commune, here independent urban republic (as in Italy and Germany), there taxable "third estate" of the monarchy (as in France), afterwards, in the period of manufacture proper, serving either the semi-feudal or the absolute monarchy as a counterpoise against nobility, and, in fact, cornerstone of the great monarchies in general, the bourgeoisie has at last, since the establishment of Modern Industry and of the world-market, conquered for itself, in the modern representative State, exclusive political sway. The executive of the modern State is but a committee for managing the common affairs of the whole bourgeoisie.

The bourgeoisie, historically, has played a most revolutionary part.

18 The bourgeoisie, wherever it has got the upper hand, has put an end to all feudal, patriarchal, idyllic relations. It has pitilessly torn asunder the motley feudal ties that bound man to his "natural superiors," and has left no other nexus between man and man than naked self-interest, than callous "cash payment." It has drowned the most heavenly ecstasies of religious fervor, of chivalrous enthusiasm, of Philistine sentimentalism, in the icy water

of egotistical calculation. It has resolved personal worth into exchange value, and in place of the numberless indefeasible chartered freedoms, has set up that single, unconscionable freedom—Free Trade. In one word, for exploitation, veiled by religious and political illusions, it has submitted naked, shameless, direct, brutal exploitation.

The bourgeoisie has stripped of its halo every occupation hitherto honored and looked up to with reverent awe. It has converted the physician, the lawyer, the priest, the poet, the man of science, into its paid wage laborers.

20   The bourgeoisie has torn away from the family its sentimental veil, and has reduced the family relation to a mere money relation.

The bourgeoisie has disclosed how it came to pass that the brutal display of vigor in the Middle Ages, which reactionists so much admire, found its fitting complement in the most slothful indolence. It has been the first to show what man's activity can bring about. It has accomplished wonders far surpassing Egyptian pyramids, Roman aqueducts and Gothic cathedrals; it has conducted expeditions that put in the shade all former Exoduses of nations and crusades.

22   The bourgeoisie cannot exist without constantly revolutionizing the instrument of production, and thereby the relations of production, and with them the whole relations of society. Conservation of the old modes of production in unaltered form was, on the contrary, the first condition of existence for all earlier industrial classes. Constant revolutionizing of production, uninterrupted disturbance of all social conditions, everlasting uncertainty and agitation distinguish the bourgeois epoch from all earlier ones. All fixed, fast frozen relations, with their train of ancient and venerable prejudices and opinions, are swept away, all new formed ones become antiquated before they can ossify. All that is solid melts into the air, all that is holy is profaned, and man is at last compelled to face with sober senses, his real conditions of life, and his relations with his kind.

The need of a constantly expanding market for its products chases the bourgeoisie over the whole surface of the globe. It must nestle everywhere, settle everywhere, establish connections everywhere.

24   The bourgeoisie has through its exploitation of the world-market given a cosmopolitan character to production and consumption in every country. To the great chagrin of reactionists, it has drawn from under the feet of industry the national ground on which it stood. All old-established national industries have been destroyed or are daily being destroyed. They are dislodged by new industries, whose introduction becomes a life and death question for all civilized nations, by industries that no longer work up indigenous raw material, but raw material drawn from the remotest zones; industries whose products are consumed, not only at home, but in every quarter of the globe. In place of the old wants, satisfied by the productions of the country, we find new wants, requiring for their satisfaction the products of distant lands and climes. In place of the old local and national seclusion and self-sufficiency, we have intercourse in every direction, universal

interdependence of nations. And as in material, so also in intellectual production. The intellectual creations of individual nations become common property. National onesidedness and narrowmindedness become more and more possible, and from the numerous national and local literatures there arises a world-literature.

The bourgeoisie, by the rapid improvement of all instruments of production, by the immensely facilitated means of communication, draws all, even the most barbarian nations into civilization. The cheap prices of its commodities are the heavy artillery with which it batters down all Chinese walls, with which it forces the barbarians' intensely obstinate hatred of foreigners to capitulate. It compels all nations, on pain of extinction, to adopt the bourgeois mode of production; it compels them to introduce what it calls civilization into their midst, i.e., to become bourgeois themselves. In a word, it creates a world after its own image.

26   The bourgeoisie has subjected the country to the rule of the towns. It has created enormous cities, has greatly increased the urban population as compared with the rural and has thus rescued a considerable part of the population from the idiocy of rural life. Just as it has made the country dependent on the towns, so it has made barbarian and semi-barbarian countries dependent on civilized ones, nations of peasants on nations of bourgeois, the East on the West.

The bourgeoisie keeps more and more doing away with the scattered state of the population, of the means of production, and of property. It has agglomerated population, centralized means of production, and has concentrated property in a few hands. The necessary consequence of this was political centralization. Independent, or but loosely connected provinces, with separate interests, laws, governments, and systems of taxation, become lumped together in one nation, with one government, one code of laws, one national class interest, one frontier and one customs tariff.

28   The bourgeoisie, during its rule of scarce one hundred years, has created more massive and more colossal productive forces than have all preceding generations together. Subjection of Nature's forces to man, machinery, application of chemistry to industry and agriculture, steam-navigation, railways, electric telegraphs, clearing of whole continents for cultivation, canalization of rivers, whole populations conjured out of the ground—what earlier century had even a presentiment that such productive forces slumbered in the lap of social labor?

We see then: the means of production and of exchange on whose foundation the bourgeoisie built itself up, were generated in feudal society. At a certain stage in the development of these means of production and of exchange, the conditions under which feudal society produced and exchanged, the feudal organization of agriculture and manufacturing industry, in one word, the feudal relations of property became no longer compatible with the already developed productive forces; they became so many fetters. They had to burst asunder; they were burst asunder.

30 Into their places stepped free competition, accompanied by social and political constitution adapted to it, and by economical and political sway of the bourgeois class.

A similar movement is going on before our own eyes. Modern bourgeois society with its relations of production, of exchange and of property, a society that has conjured up such gigantic means of production and of exchange, is like the sorcerer, who is no longer able to control the powers of the nether world whom he has called up by his spells. For many a decade past, the history of industry and commerce is but the history of the revolt of modern productive forces against modern conditions of production, against the property relations that are the conditions for the existence of the bourgeoisie and of its rule. It is enough to mention the commercial crises that by their periodical return put on its trial, each time more threateningly, the existence of the entire bourgeois society. In these crises a great part not only of the existing products, but also of the previously created productive forces, are periodically destroyed. In these crises there breaks out an epidemic that, in all earlier epochs, would have seemed an absurdity—the epidemic of overproduction. Society suddenly finds itself put back into a state of momentary barbarism; it appears as if a famine, a universal war of devastation, had cut off the supply of every means of subsistence; industry and commerce seem to be destroyed; and why? Because there is too much civilization, too much means of subsistence, too much industry, too much commerce. The productive forces at the disposal of society no longer tend to further the development of the conditions of the bourgeois property; on the contrary, they have become too powerful for these conditions by which they are fettered, and as soon as they overcome these fetters they bring disorder into the whole of bourgeois society, endanger the existence of bourgeois property. The conditions of bourgeois society are too narrow to comprise the wealth created by them. And how does the bourgeoisie get over these crises? On the one hand by enforced destruction of a mass of productive forces; on the other, by the conquest of new markets, and by the more thorough exploitation of the old ones. That is to say, by paving the way for more extensive and more destructive crises, and by diminishing the means whereby crises are prevented.

32 The weapons with which the bourgeoisie felled feudalism to the ground are now turned against the bourgeoisie itself.

But not only has the bourgeoisie forged the weapons that bring death to itself; it has also called into existence the men who are to wield those weapons—the modern working class—the proletarians.

34 In proportion as the bourgeoisie, i.e., capital, is developed, in the same proportion is the proletariat, the modern working class, developed, a class of laborers who live only so long as they find work, and who find work only so long as their labor increases capital. These laborers, who must sell themselves piecemeal, are a commodity, like every other article of commerce, and are consequently exposed to all the vicissitudes of competition, to all the fluctuations of the market.

Owing to the extensive use of machinery and to division of labor, the work of the proletarians has lost all individual character, and, consequently, all charm for the workman. He becomes an appendage of the machine, and it is only the most simple, most monotonous and most easily acquired knack that is required of him. Hence, the cost of production of a workman is restricted almost entirely to the means of subsistence that he requires for his maintenance, and for the propagation of his race. But the price of a commodity, and also of labor, is equal to its cost of production. In production, therefore, as the repulsiveness of the work increases the wage decreases. Nay more, in proportion as the use of machinery and division of labor increases, in the same proportion the burden of toil increases, whether by prolongation of the working hours, by increase of the work enacted in a given time, or by increased speed of the machinery, etc.

36   Modern industry has converted the little workshop of the patriarchal master into the great factory of the industrial capitalist. Masses of laborers, crowded into factories, are organized like soldiers. As privates of the industrial army they are placed under the command of a perfect hierarchy of officers and sergeants. Not only are they the slaves of the bourgeois class and of the bourgeois state, they are daily and hourly enslaved by the machine, by the overlooker, and above all, by the individual bourgeois manufacturer himself. The more openly this despotism proclaims gain to be its end and aim, the more petty, the more hateful and the more embittering it is.

    The less the skill and exertion or strength implied in manual labor, in other words, the more modern industry becomes developed, the more is the labor of men superseded by that of women. Differences of age and sex have no longer any distinctive social validity for the working class. All are instruments of labor, more or less expensive to use, according to their age and sex.

38   No sooner is the exploitation of the laborer by the manufacturer, so far at an end, that he receives his wages in cash, than he is set upon by the other portions of the bourgeoisie, the landlord, the shopkeeper, the pawnbroker, etc.

    The lower strata of the middle class—the small trades-people, shopkeepers and retired tradesmen generally, the handicraftsmen and peasants— all these sink gradually into the proletariat, partly because their diminutive capital does not suffice for the scale on which Modern Industry is carried on, and is swamped in the competition with the large capitalists, partly because their specialized skill is rendered worthless by new methods of production. Thus the proletariat is recruited from all classes of the population.

40   The proletariat goes through various stages of development. With its birth begins its struggle with the bourgeoisie. At first the contest is carried on by individual laborers, then by the workpeople of a factory, then by the operatives of one trade, in one locality, against the individual bourgeois who directly exploits them. They direct their attacks not against the bourgeois conditions of production, but against the instruments of production themselves; they destroy imported wares that compete with their labor, they

smash to pieces machinery, they set factories ablaze, they seek to restore by force the vanished status of the workman of the Middle Ages.

At this stage the laborers still form an incoherent mass scattered over the whole country, and broken up by their mutual competition. If anywhere they unite to form more compact bodies, this is not yet the consequence of their own active union, but of the union of the bourgeoisie, which class, in order to attain its own political ends, is compelled to set the whole proletariat in motion, and is moreover yet, for a time, able to do so. At this stage, therefore, the proletarians do not fight their enemies, but the enemies of their enemies, the remnants of absolute monarchy, the landowners, the non-industrial bourgeois, the petty bourgeoisie. Thus the whole historical movement is concentrated in the hands of the bourgeoisie, every victory so obtained is a victory for the bourgeoisie.

42 But with the development of industry the proletariat not only increases in number; it becomes concentrated in greater masses, its strength grows and it feels that strength more. The various interests and conditions of life within the ranks of the proletariat are more and more equalized, in proportion as machinery obliterates all distinctions of labor, and nearly everywhere reduces wages to the same low level. The growing competition among the bourgeois, and the resulting commercial crisis, makes the wages of the workers even more fluctuating. The unceasing improvement of machinery, ever more rapidly developing, makes their livelihood more and more precarious; the collisions between individual workmen and individual bourgeois take more and more the character of collisions between two classes. Thereupon the workers begin to form combinations (Trades' Unions) against the bourgeois; they club together in order to make provision beforehand for these occasional revolts. Here and there the contest breaks out into riots.

Now and then the workers are victorious, but only for a time. The real fruit of their battle lies not in the immediate result but in the ever-expanding union of workers. This union is helped on by the improved means of communication that are created by modern industry, and that places the workers of different localities in contact with one another. It was just this contact that was needed to centralize the numerous local struggles, all of the same character, into one national struggle between classes. But every class struggle is a political struggle. And that union, to attain which the burghers of the Middle Ages with their miserable highways, required centuries, the modern proletarians, thanks to railways, achieve in a few years.

44 This organization of the proletarians into a class, and consequently into a political party, is continually being upset again by the competition between the workers themselves. But it ever rises up again, stronger, firmer, mightier. It compels legislative recognition of particular interests of the workers by taking advantage of the divisions among the bourgeoisie itself. Thus the ten hours' bill in England was carried.

Altogether collisions between the classes of the old society further, in many ways, the course of development of the proletariat. The bourgeoisie finds itself involved in a constant battle. At first with the aristocracy; later on, with those portions of the bourgeoisie itself whose interests have become antagonistic to the progress of industry; at all times, with the bourgeoisie of foreign countries. In all these battles it sees itself compelled to appeal to the proletariat, to ask for its help, and thus, to drag it into the political arena. The bourgeoisie itself, therefore, supplies the proletariat with its own elements of political and general education; in other words, it furnishes the proletariat with weapons for fighting the bourgeoisie.

46   Further, as we have already seen, entire sections of the ruling classes are, by the advance of industry, precipitated into the proletariat, or are at least threatened in their conditions of existence. These also supply the proletariat with fresh elements of enlightenment and progress.

Finally, in times when the class-struggle nears the decisive hour, the process of dissolution going on within the ruling class—in fact, within the whole range of an old society—assumes such a violent, glaring character that a small section of the ruling class cuts itself adrift and joins the revolutionary class, the class that holds the future in its hands. Just as, therefore, at an earlier period, a section of the nobility went over to the bourgeoisie, so now a portion of the bourgeoisie goes over to the proletariat, and in particular, a portion of the bourgeois ideologists, who have raised themselves to the level of comprehending theoretically the historical movements as a whole.

48   Of all the classes that stand face to face with the bourgeoisie today the proletariat alone is a really revolutionary class. The other classes decay and finally disappear in the face of modern industry; the proletariat is its special and essential product.

The lower middle class, the small manufacturer, the shopkeeper, the artisan, the peasant, all these fight against the bourgeoisie, to save from extinction their existence as fractions of the middle class. They are therefore not revolutionary, but conservative. Nay, more; they are reactionary, for they try to roll back the wheel of history. If by chance they are revolutionary, they are so only in view of their impending transfer into the proletariat; they thus defend not their present, but their future interests; they desert their own standpoint to place themselves at that of the proletariat.

50   The "dangerous class," the social scum, that passively rotting mass thrown off by the lowest layers of old society, may, here and there, be swept into the movement by a proletarian revolution; its conditions of life, however, prepare it far more for the part of a bribed tool of reactionary intrigue.

In the conditions of the proletariat, those of the old society at large are already virtually swamped. The proletarian is without property; his relation to his wife and children has no longer anything in common with the bourgeois family relations; modern industrial labor, modern subjection to capital, the same in England as in France, in America as in Germany, has stripped him of every trace of national character. Law, morality, religion, are to him so many bourgeois prejudices, behind which lurk in ambush just as many bourgeois interests.

52   All the preceding classes that got the upper hand sought to fortify their already acquired status by subjecting society at large to their conditions of

appropriation. The proletarians cannot become masters of the productive forces of society, except by abolishing their own previous mode of appropriation, and thereby also every other previous mode of appropriation. They have nothing of their own to secure and to fortify; their mission is to destroy all previous securities for and insurances of individual property.

All previous historical movements were movements of minorities, or in the interest of minorities. The proletarian movement is the self-conscious, independent movement of the immense majority. The proletariat, the lowest stratum of our present society, cannot stir, cannot raise itself up without the whole superincumbent strata of official society being sprung into the air.

54

Though not in substance, yet in form, the struggle of the proletariat with the bourgeoisie is at first a national struggle. The proletariat of each country must, of course, first of all settle matters with its own bourgeoisie.

In depicting the most general phases of the development of the proletariat, we traced the more or less veiled civil war, raging within existing society, up to the point where that war breaks out into open revolution, and where the violent overthrow of the bourgeoisie, lays the foundations for the sway of the proletariat.

56

Hitherto every form of society has been based, as we have already seen, on the antagonism of oppressing and oppressed classes. But in order to oppress a class, certain conditions must be assured to it under which it can, at least, continue its slavish existence. The serf, in the period of serfdom, raised himself to membership in the commune, just as the petty bourgeois, under the yoke of feudal absolutism managed to develop into a bourgeois. The modern laborer, on the contrary, instead of rising with the progress of industry, sinks deeper and deeper below the conditions of existence of his own class. He becomes a pauper, and pauperism develops more rapidly than population and wealth. And here it becomes evident that the bourgeoisie is unfit any longer to be the ruling class in society, and impose its conditions of existence upon society as an over-riding law. It is unfit to rule, because it is incompetent to assure an existence to its slave within his slavery, because it cannot help letting him sink into such a state that it has to feed him, instead of being fed by him. Society can no longer live under this bourgeoisie; in other words, its existence is no longer compatible with society.

The essential condition for the existence, and for the sway of the bourgeois class, is the formation and augmentation of capital; the condition for capital is wage labor. Wage labor rests exclusively on competition between the laborers. The advance of industry, whose involuntary promoter is the bourgeoisie, replaces the isolation of the laborers, due to competition, by their involuntary combination, due to association. The development of Modern Industry, therefore, cuts from under its feet the very foundation on which the bourgeoisie produces and appropriates products. What the bourgeoisie therefore produces, above all, are its own grave diggers. Its fall and the victory of the proletariat are equally inevitable. ❖

Questions for Meaning

1. Comment on the authors' claim in paragraph 5 that the "history of all hitherto existing society is the history of class struggles." What does this mean?
2. In paragraph 9, the authors write: "Society as a whole is more and more splitting up into two great hostile camps, into two great classes directly facing each other: Bourgeoisie and Proletariat." Has history proven them right? How would you describe class relations within the United States? Can American history be seen in Marxist terms?
3. Explain the distinction in paragraph 12 between the feudal and manufacturing systems of industry.
4. Do Marx and Engels concede that modern history has accomplished anything admirable? Do they credit the bourgeoisie with any virtues?
5. Why do Marx and Engels believe that the bourgeoisie is unfit to rule? Why do they believe that the rise of the proletariat is inevitable?
6. What do Marx and Engels mean when they claim "there is too much civilization, too much means of subsistence, too much industry, too much commerce"? Paraphrase paragraph 31.
7. What is "the social scum" that Marx and Engels dismiss in paragraph 50? Why do they believe this class is dangerous?
8. Vocabulary: exorcise (1), patrician (6), plebeian (6), vassals (7), patriarchal (18), nexus (18), slothful (21), indigenous (24), agglomerated (27), presentiment (28), vicissitudes (34), diminutive (39), obliterates (42), precarious (42), augmentation (57).

Questions about Strategy

1. Why do Marx and Engels open their manifesto by describing Communism as "a specter"? Explain what they mean by this and how it serves as an introduction to the political analysis that follows.
2. In interpreting history entirely in economic terms, are there any major conflicts that Marx and Engels overlook?
3. What is the function of paragraphs 29 and 30?
4. Can you point to anything in this work that reveals that Marx and Engels were writing for an international audience?
5. What parts of this essay are the strongest? Where do Marx and Engels make the most sense?
6. Can you identify any exaggerations in *The Communist Manifesto*? If you were to write a rebuttal, are there any claims that you could prove to be oversimplified?
7. Is this "manifesto" an argument or an exhortation? Is it designed to convince readers who have no political opinions, or to rally the men and women who are already committed to revolution? What is its purpose?

CHARLOTTE PERKINS GILMAN

CONCERNING CHILDREN

Best known today for her fiction, especially her story "The Yellow Wall-Paper" (1892), Charlotte Perkins Gilman (1860–1935) was a leading intellectual in the women's movement at the turn of the century. In *Women and Economics* (1898), she offered an extensive analysis of women's role in society and why women have been undervalued. In *Herland* (1915), she described a utopian society of women without men. "Concerning Children" was first published in 1900. As you read, ask yourself whether parents could still profit from Gilman's advice.

The rearing of children is the most important work, and it is here contended that, in this great educational process, obedience, as a main factor, has a bad effect on the growing mind. A child is a human creature. He should be reared with a view to his development and behaviour as an adult, not solely with a view to his behaviour as a child. He is temporarily a child, far more permanently a man; and it is the man we are training. The work of "parenthood" is not only to guard and nourish the young, but to develop the qualities needed in the mature.

2   Obedience is defended, first, as being necessary to the protection of the child, and, second, as developing desirable qualities in the adult. But the child can be far better protected by removing all danger, which our present civilization is quite competent to do; and "the habit of obedience" develops very undesirable qualities. On what characteristics does our human pre-eminence rest? On our breadth and accuracy of judgment and force of will. Because we can see widely and judge wisely, because we have power to do what we see to be right, therefore we are the dominant species in the animal kingdom; therefore we are consciously the children of God.

These qualities are lodged in individuals, and must be exercised by individuals for the best human progress. If our method of advance were that one person alone should be wise and strong, and all other persons prosperous through a strict subservience to his commands, then, indeed, we could do no better for our children than to train them to obey. Judgment would be of no use to them if they had to take another's: will-power would be valueless if they were never to exercise it.

4   But this is by no means the condition of human life. More and more is it being recognized that progress lies in a well-developed average intelligence rather than in a wise despot and his stupid serfs. For every individual to have a good judgment and a strong will is far better for the community than for a few to have these qualities and the rest to follow them.

The "habit of obedience," forced in upon the impressible nature of a child, does not develop judgment and will, but does develop that fatal facility in following other people's judgment and other people's wills which tends to make us a helpless mob, mere sheep, instead of wise, free, strong individuals. The habit of submission to authority, the long deeply impressed conviction that to "be good" is to "give up," that there is virtue in the act of surrender,—this is one of the sources from which we continually replenish human weakness, and fill the world with an inert mass of mind-less, will-less folk, pushed and pulled about by those whom they obey.

6   Moreover, there is the opposite effect,—the injurious reaction from obedience,—almost as common and hurtful as its full achievement; namely, that fierce rebellious desire to do exactly the opposite of what one is told, which is no nearer to calm judgment than the other.

In obeying another will or in resisting another will, nothing is gained in wisdom. A human creature is a self-governing intelligence, and the rich years of childhood should be passed in the guarded and gradual exercise of those powers.

8   Now this will, no doubt, call up to the minds of many a picture of a selfish, domineering youngster, stormily ploughing through a number of experimental adventures, with a group of sacrificial parents and teachers prostrate before him. Again an unwarranted assumption. Consideration of others is one of the first laws of life, one of the first things a child should be taught; but consideration of others is not identical with obedience. Again, it will be imagined that the child is to be left to laboriously work out for himself the accumulated experiments of humanity, and deprived of the profits of all previous experience. By no means. On the contrary, it is the business of those who have the care of the very young to see to it that they do benefit by that previous experience far more fully than is now possible.

Our system of obedience cuts the child off from precisely this advantage, and leaves him longing to do the forbidden things, generally doing them, too, when he gets away from his tutelage. The behaviour of the released child, in its riotous reaction against authority as such, as shown glaringly in the action of the average college student, tells how much judgment and self-control have been developing behind the obedience.

10   The brain grows by exercise. The best time to develop it is in youth. To obey does not develop the brain, but checks its growth. It gives to the will a peculiar suicidal power of aborting its own impulse, not controlling it, but giving it up. This leaves a habit of giving up which weakens our power of continued effort.

All this is not saying that obedience is never useful in childhood. There are occasions when it is; and on such occasions, with a child otherwise intelligently trained, it will be forthcoming. We make a wide mistake in assuming that, unless a child is made to obey at every step, it will never obey. A grown person will obey under sharp instant pressure.

12   If there is a sudden danger, and you shriek at your friend, "Get up—quick!" or hiss a terrified, "Sh! Sh! Be Still!" your friend promptly obeys. Of course, if you had been endeavouring to "boss" that friend with a thousand pointless caprices, he might distrust you in the hour of peril; but if he knew

you to be a reasonable person, he would respond promptly to a sudden command.

Much more will a child so respond where he has full reason to respect the judgment of the commander. Children have the same automatic habit of obedience by the same animal inheritance that gives the mother the habit of command; but we so abuse that faculty that it becomes lost in righteous rebellion or crushed submission. The animal mother never misuses her precious authority. She does not cry, "Wolf! Wolf!" We talk glibly about "the best good of the child," but there are few children who are not clearly aware that they are "minding" for the convenience of "the grown-ups" the greater part of the time. Therefore, they suspect self-interest in even the necessary commands, and might very readily refuse to obey in the hour of danger.

14   It is a commonplace observation that the best children—i.e., the most submissive and obedient—do not make the best men. If they are utterly subdued, "too good to live," they swell the Sunday-school list of infant saints, die young, and go to heaven: whereas the rebellious and unruly boy often makes the best citizen.

The too obedient child has learned only to do what he is told. If not told, he has no initiative; and, if told wrong, he does wrong. Life to him is not a series of problems to be solved, but a mere book of orders; and, instead of understanding the true imperious "force" of natural law, which a wise man follows because he sees the wisdom of the course, he takes every "must" in life to be like a personal command,—a thing probably unreasonable, and to be evaded, if possible.

16   The escaped child, long suppressed under obedience, is in no mood for a cheerful acceptance of real laws, but imagines that there is more "fun" in "having his own way." The foolish parent claims to be obeyed as a god; and the grown-up child seeks to evade God, to treat the law of Nature as if she, too, were a foolish parent.

Suppose you are teaching a child arithmetic. You tell him to put down such and such figures in such a position. He inquires, "Why?" You explain the reason. If you do not explain the reason, he does not understand the problem. You might continue to give orders as to what figures to set down in what place; and the child, obeying, could be trotted through the arithmetic in a month's time. But the arithmetic would not have gone through him. He would be not better versed in the science of numbers than a typesetter is in the learned books he "sets up." We recognize this in the teaching of arithmetic, and go to great lengths in inventing test problems and arranging easy stages by which the child may gradually master his task. But we do not recognize it in teaching the child life. The small acts of infancy are the child's first problems in living. He naturally wishes to understand them. He says, "Why?" To which we reply inanely, "Because I tell you to!" That is no reason. It is a force, no doubt, a pressure, to which the child may be compelled to yield. But he is no wiser than he was before. He has learned nothing except the lesson we imagine so valuable,—to obey. At the very best, he may remember always, in like case, that "mamma would wish me to do so," and do it. But, when cases differ, he has no guide. With the best intentions in life, he can but cast about in his mind to try to imagine what some one else might tell him to do if present: the circumstances themselves mean nothing to him. Docility, subservience, a quick surrender of purpose, a wavering, untrained, easily shaken judgment,—these are the qualities developed by much obedience.

18   Are they the qualities we wish to develop in American citizens? ❖

Questions for Meaning

1. What should be one's goal when raising children?
2. On what grounds does Gilman challenge the value of obedience?
3. What does Gilman mean in paragraph 13 when she writes, "Children have the same automatic habit of obedience by the same animal inheritance that gives the mother the habit of command"? Do you agree with her?
4. Why does Gilman recommend providing children with explanations?
5. Vocabulary: subservience (3), serfs (4), prostrate (8), unwarranted (8), forthcoming (11), caprices (12), glibly (13), docility (17).

Questions about Strategy

1. Where does Gilman anticipate and respond to opposition?
2. Does Gilman make any concessions about the value of obedience?
3. Consider the generalization about college students in paragraph 9. Does it help or injure Gilman's argument?
4. How effective is Gilman's analogy between teaching arithmetic and raising children?
5. Gilman concludes with a rhetorical question. What answer does she expect, and how has she prepared for it?

MARGARET SANGER

THE CAUSE OF WAR

A pioneering advocate of birth control, Margaret Sanger (1883–1966) was one of eleven children. She studied nursing and worked as an obstetrical nurse in the tenements of Manhattan's Lower East Side. She became convinced of the importance of birth control in 1912 when a young woman died in her arms after a self-induced abortion. Sanger went to Europe in 1913 to study contraception, and she is credited with having coined the phrase "birth control." Upon her return to the United States, she founded a magazine, *Woman Rebel,* in which she could publish her views. In 1916, she was jailed for opening a birth control clinic in New York, the first of many times she would be imprisoned for her work. She founded the National Birth Control League in 1917, an organization that eventually became the Planned Parenthood Federation of America. By the time Sanger was elected the first president of the International Planned Parenthood Federation in 1952, her views had come to be widely accepted.

A lecturer and a writer, Sanger published several books. The following essay is drawn from *Woman and the New Race* (1920). Writing at a time when Europe had not yet recovered from the horrors of World War I, Sanger argued that the underlying cause of the war was excessive population growth. Although most historians would argue that the war had multiple causes, you should consider whether Sanger makes a persuasive case.

In every nation of militaristic tendencies we find the reactionaries demanding a higher and still higher birth rate. Their plea is, first, that great armies are needed to *defend* the country from its possible enemies; second, that a huge population is required to assure the country its proper place among the powers of the world. At bottom the two pleas are the same.

2   As soon as the country becomes overpopulated, these reactionaries proclaim loudly its moral right to expand. They point to the huge population, which is the name of patriotism they have previously demanded should be brought into being. Again pleading patriotism, they declare that it is the moral right of the nation to take by force such room as it needs. Then comes war—usually against some nation supposed to be less well prepared than the aggressor.

Diplomats make it their business to conceal the facts, and politicians violently denounce the politicians of other countries. There is a long beating of tom-toms by the press and all other agencies for influencing public opinion. Facts are distorted and lies invented until the common people cannot get at the truth. Yet, when the war is over, if not before, we always find that "a place in the sun," "a path to the sea," "a route to India" or something of the sort is at the bottom of the trouble. These are merely other names for expansion.

4   The "need of expansion" is only another name for overpopulation. One supreme example is sufficient to drive home this truth. That the Great War, from the horror of which we are just beginning to emerge, had its source in overpopulation is too evident to be denied by any serious student of current history.

For the past one hundred years most of the nations of Europe have been piling up terrific debts to humanity by the encouragement of unlimited numbers. The rulers of these nations and their militarists have constantly called upon the people to breed, breed, breed! Large populations meant more people to produce wealth, more people to pay taxes, more trade for the merchants, more soldiers to protect the wealth. But more people also meant need of greater food supplies, an urgent and natural need for expansion.

6   As shown by C. V. Drysdale's famous "War Map of Europe," the great conflict began among the high birth rate countries—Germany, with its rate of 31.7, Austria-Hungary with 33.7 and 36.7, respectively, Russia with 45.4, Serbia with 38.6. Italy with her 38.7 came in, as the world is now well informed through the publication of secret treaties by the Soviet government of Russia, upon the promise of territory held by Austria. England, owing to her small home area, is cramped with her comparatively low birth rate of 26.3. France, among the belligerents, is conspicuous for her low birth rate of 19.9, but stood in the way of expansion of high birth rate Germany. Nearly all of the persistently neutral countries—Holland, Denmark, Norway, Sweden and Switzerland have low birth rates, the average being a little over 26.

Owing to the part Germany played in the war, a survey of her birth statistics is decidedly illuminating. The increase in the German birth rate up to 1876 was great. Though it began to decline then, the decline was not sufficient to offset the tremendous increase of the previous years. There were more millions to produce children, so while the average number of births per thousand was somewhat smaller, the net increase in population was still huge. From 41,000,000 in 1871, the year the Empire was founded, the German population grew to approximately 67,000,000 in 1918. Meanwhile her food supply increased only a very small percent. In 1910, Russia had a birth rate even higher than Germany's had ever been—a little less than 48 per thousand. When czarist Russia wanted an outlet to the Mediterranean by way of Constantinople, she was thinking of her increasing population. Germany was thinking of her increasing population when she spoke as with one voice of a "place in the sun." . . .

8   The militaristic claim for Germany's right to new territory was simply a claim to the right of life and food for the German babies—the same right that a chick claims to burst its shell. If there had not been other millions of people claiming the same right, there would have been no war. But there *were* other millions.

The German rulers and leaders pointed out the fact that expansion meant more business for German merchants, more work for German workmen at better wages, and more opportunities for Germans abroad. They also pointed out that lack of expansion meant crowding and crushing at home, hard times, heavy burdens, lack of opportunity for Germans, and what not. In this way, they gave the people of the Empire a startling and true picture of what would happen from overcrowding. Once they realized the facts, the majority of Germans naturally welcomed the so-called war of defense.

10   The argument was sound. Once the German mothers had submitted to the plea for overbreeding, it was inevitable that imperialistic Germany should make war. Once the battalions of unwanted babies came into existence—babies whom the mothers did not want but which they bore as a "patriotic duty"—it was too late to avoid international conflict. The great crime of imperialistic Germany was its high birth rate.

It has always been so. Behind all war has been the pressure of population. "Historians," says Huxley,* "point to the greed and ambition of rulers, the reckless turbulence of the ruled, to the debasing effects of wealth and luxury, and to the devastating wars which have formed a great part of the occupation of mankind, as the causes of the decay of states and the foundering of old civilizations, and thereby point their story with a moral. But beneath all this superficial turmoil lay the deep-seated impulse given by unlimited multiplication."

12   Robert Thomas Malthus,† formulator of the doctrine which bears his name, pointed out, in the closing years of the eighteenth century, the relation of overpopulation to war. He showed that mankind tends to increase faster than the food supply. He demonstrated that were it not for the more common diseases, for plague, famine, floods and wars, human beings would crowd each other to such an extent that the misery would be even greater than it now is. These he described as "natural checks," pointing out that as long as no other checks are employed, such disasters are unavoidable. If we do not exercise sufficient judgment to regulate the birth rate, we encounter disease, starvation and war.

Both Darwin and John Stuart Mill recognized, by inference at least, the fact that so-called "natural checks"—and among them war—will operate if some sort of limitation is not employed. In his *Origin of Species*, Darwin says: "There is no exception to the rule that every organic being naturally increases at so high a rate, if not destroyed, that the earth would soon be covered by the progeny of a single pair." Elsewhere he observes that we do not permit helpless human beings to die off, but we create philanthropies and charities, build asylums and hospitals and keep the medical profession busy preserving those who could not otherwise survive. John Stuart Mill, supporting the views of Malthus, speaks to exactly the same effect in regard to the multiplying power of organic beings, among them humanity. In other

---

* Thomas Huxley (1825–1895) was an influential English biologist who supported Darwin's theory of evolution but argued that progress could be achieved through scientific control of evolution.

† Best known for *An Essay on the Principles of Population* (1798).

words, let countries become overpopulated and war is inevitable. It follows as daylight follows the sunrise.

14   When Charles Bradlaugh and Mrs. Annie Besant were on trial in England in 1877 for publishing information concerning contraceptives, Mrs. Besant put the case bluntly to the court and the jury:

"I have no doubt that if natural checks were allowed to operate right through the human as they do in the animal world, a better result would follow. Among the brutes, the weaker are driven to the wall, the diseased fall out in the race of life. The old brutes, when feeble or sickly, are killed. If men insisted that those who were sickly should be allowed to die without help of medicine or science, if those who are weak were put upon one side and crushed, if those who were old and useless were killed, if those who were not capable of providing food for themselves were allowed to starve, if all this were done, the struggle for existence among men would be as real as it is among brutes and would doubtless result in the production of a higher race of men.

16   "But are you willing to do that or to allow it to be done?"

We are not willing to let it be done. Mother hearts cling to children, no matter how diseased, misshapen and miserable. Sons and daughters hold fast to parents, no matter how helpless. We do not allow the weak to depart; neither do we cease to bring more weak and helpless beings into the world. Among the dire results is war, which kills off, not the weak and the helpless, but the strong and the fit.

18   What shall be done? We have our choice of one of three policies. We may abandon our science and leave the weak and diseased to die, or kill them, as the brutes do. Or we may go on overpopulating the earth and have our famines and our wars while the earth exists. Or we can accept the third, sane, sensible, moral and practicable plan of birth control. We can refuse to bring the weak, the helpless and the unwanted children into the world. We can refuse to overcrowd families, nations and the earth. There are these ways to meet the situation, and only these three ways.

The world will never abandon its preventive and curative science; it may be expected to elevate and extend it beyond our present imagination. The efforts to do away with famine and the opposition to war are growing by leaps and bounds. Upon these efforts are largely based our modern social revolutions.

20   There remains only the third expedient—birth control, the real cure for war. This fact was called to the attention of the Peace Conference in Paris, in 1919, by the Malthusian League, which adopted the following resolution at its annual general meeting in London in June of that year:

"The Malthusian League desires to point out that the proposed scheme for the League of Nations has neglected to take account of the important questions of *the pressure of population,* which *causes the great international economic competition* and rivalry, and of the *increase of population,* which is put forward as a justification for *claiming increase of territory.* It, therefore, wishes to put on record its belief that the League of Nations will only be able to fulfill its aim *when it adds a clause* to the following effect:

22   "'That each Nation desiring to enter into the League of Nations shall pledge itself *so to restrict its birth rate* that its people shall be able to live in comfort *in their own dominions without need* for territorial expansion, and that it shall recognize that *increase of population shall not justify* a demand either for increase of territory or for the compulsion of other Nations to admit its emigrants; so that when all Nations in the League have shown their ability to live on their own resources without international rivalry, they will be in a position to fuse into an international federation, and territorial boundaries will then have little significance.' "

     As a matter of course, the Peace Conference paid no attention to the resolution, for, as pointed out by Frank A. Vanderlip, the American financier, that conference not only ignored the economic factors of the world situation, but seemed unaware that Europe had produced more people than its fields could feed. So the resolution amounted to so much propaganda and nothing more.

24   This remedy can be applied only by woman and she will apply it. She must and will see past the call of pretended patriotism and of glory of empire and perceive what is true and what is false in these things. She will discover what base uses the militarist and the exploiter made of the idealism of peoples. Under the clamor of the press, permeating the ravings of the jingoes, she will hear the voice of Napoleon, the archetype of the militarists of all nations, calling for "fodder for cannon."

     "Woman is given to us that she may bear children," said he. "Woman is our property, we are not hers, because she produced children for us—we do not yield any to her. She is, therefore, our possession as the fruit tree is that of the gardener."

26   That is what the imperialist is *thinking* when he speaks of the glory of the empire and the prestige of the nation. Every country has its appeal—its shibboleth—ready for the lips of the imperialist. German rulers pointed to the comfort of the workers, to old-age pensions, maternal benefits and minimum wage regulations, and other material benefits, when they wished to inspire soldiers for the Fatherland. England's strongest argument, perhaps, was a certain phase of liberty which she guarantees her subjects, and the protection afforded them wherever they may go. France and the United States, too, have their appeals to the idealism of democracy—appeals which the politicians of both countries know well how to use, though the peoples of both lands are beginning to awake to the fact that their countries have been living on the glories of their revolutions and traditions, rather than the substance of freedom. Behind the boast of old-age pensions, material benefits and wage regulations, behind the bombast concerning liberty in this country and tyranny in that, behind all the slogans and shibboleths coined out of the ideals of the peoples for the uses of imperialism, woman must and will see the iron hand of that same imperialism, condemning women to breed and men to die for the will of the rulers.

     Upon woman the burden and the horrors of war are heaviest. Her heart is the hardest wrung when the husband or the son comes home to be buried or to live a shattered wreck. Upon her devolve the extra tasks of filling out the ranks of workers in the war industries, in addition to caring for the children and replenishing the war-diminished population. Hers is the crushing weight and the sickening of soul. And it is out of her womb that those things proceed. When she sees what lies behind the glory and the horror, the boasting and the burden, and gets the vision, the human perspective, she will end war. She will kill war by the simple process of starving it to death. For she will refuse longer to produce the human food upon which the monster feeds.   ❖

Questions for Meaning

1. According to Sanger, what motives have led governments to encourage population growth?
2. From an evolutionary point of view, why is war unacceptable as a "natural check" on population growth?
3. What are the three policies that Sanger believes nations must inevitably choose among? Are there any alternatives that she overlooks?
4. World War II began less than twenty years after the publication of this essay. Do you know anything about the conditions under which that war began that could be used as evidence to support Sanger's thesis that "militarists" and "reactionaries" favor high birth rates?
5. Vocabulary: belligerents (6), conspicuous (6), turbulence (11), debasing (11), foundering (11), inference (13), base (24), jingoes (24), bombast (26), shibboleths (26).

Questions about Strategy

1. Is Sanger ever guilty of oversimplification? Can you think of any causes of war that have nothing to do with population?
2. How useful are the statistics cited in paragraphs 6 and 7?
3. Of the various quotations that Sanger includes in her essay, which is the most effective?
4. How would you describe the tone of this essay? Is it suitable for the subject?
5. Do you detect any bias in this essay? Does Sanger ever seem to suggest that World War I was caused by one country in particular? Is such an implication historically valid?

ADOLF HITLER

THE PURPOSE OF PROPAGANDA

A frustrated artist, Adolf Hitler (1889–1945) served in the German Army during World War I, and became the leader of the National Socialist Party in 1920, during the turbulent period that followed the German defeat. In 1923, Hitler led a revolt in Munich, for which he subsequently served nine months in prison, using this time to write *Mein Kampf (My Struggle)*. Under his direction, the Nazis gained political influence throughout the 1920s, and, in 1933, Hitler became Chancellor of Germany. Upon the death of President Paul von Hindenburg in 1934, Hitler assumed dictatorial powers and ruled Germany as Der Führer (The Leader). More than any other individual, he is responsible for World War II and the deliberate murder of millions of people during that war.

Many factors contributed to Hitler's rise to power; one of them was the skill with which the Nazis used propaganda. The 1925 publication of *Mein Kampf*, from which the following excerpt is taken, outlined Hitler's views. But at the time, many people did not take them seriously.

Ever since I have been scrutinizing political events, I have taken a tremendous interest in propagandist activity. I saw that the Socialist-Marxist organizations mastered and applied this instrument with astounding skill. And I soon realized that the correct use of propaganda is a true art which has remained practically unknown to the bourgeois parties. Only the Christian-Social movement, especially in Lueger's time, achieved a certain virtuosity on this instrument, to which it owed many of its successes.

2   But it was not until the War that it became evident what immense results could be obtained by a correct application of propaganda. Here again, unfortunately, all our studying had to be done on the enemy side, for the activity on our side was modest, to say the least. The total miscarriage of the German "enlightenment" service stared every soldier in the face, and this spurred me to take up the question of propaganda even more deeply than before.

There was often more than enough time for thinking, and the enemy offered practical instruction which, to our sorrow, was only too good.

4   For what we failed to do, the enemy did, with amazing skill and really brilliant calculation. [See illustration on page 679.] I, myself, learned enormously from this enemy war propaganda. But time passed and left no trace in the minds of all those who should have benefited; partly because they considered themselves too clever to learn from the enemy, partly owing to lack of good will.

Did we have anything you could call propaganda?

6   I regret that I must answer in the negative. Everything that actually was done in this field was so inadequate and wrong from the very start that it certainly did no good and sometimes did actual harm.

The form was inadequate, the substance was psychologically wrong: a careful examination of German war propaganda can lead to no other diagnosis.

8   There seems to have been no clarity on the very first question: Is propaganda a means or an end?

It is a means and must therefore be judged with regard to its end. It must consequently take a form calculated to support the aim which it serves. It is also obvious that its aim can vary in importance from the standpoint of general need, and that the inner value of the propaganda will vary accordingly. The aim for which we were fighting the War was the loftiest, the most overpowering, that man can conceive: it was the freedom and independence of our nation, the security of our future food supply, and—our national honor; a thing which, despite all contrary opinions prevailing today, nevertheless exists, or rather should exist, since peoples without honor have sooner or later lost their freedom and independence, which in turn is only the result of a higher justice, since generations of rabble without honor deserve no freedom. Any man who wants to be a cowardly slave can have no honor, or honor itself would soon fall into general contempt.

10   The German nation was engaged in a struggle for a human existence, and the purpose of war propaganda should have been to support this struggle; its aim to help bring about victory.

When the nations on this planet fight for existence—when the question of destiny, "to be or not to be," cries out for a solution—then all considerations of humanitarianism or aesthetics crumble into nothingness; for all these concepts do not float about in the ether, they arise from man's imagination and are bound up with man. When he departs from this world, these concepts are again dissolved into nothingness, for Nature does not know them. And even among mankind, they belong only to a few nations or rather races, and this in proportion as they emanate from the feeling of the nation or race in question. Humanitarianism and aesthetics would vanish even from a world inhabited by man if this world were to lose the races that have created and upheld these concepts.

12   But all such concepts become secondary when a nation is fighting for its existence; in fact, they become totally irrelevant to the forms of the struggle as soon as a situation arises where they might paralyze a struggling nation's power of self-preservation. And that has always been their only visible result.

As for humanitarianism, Moltke* said years ago that in war it lies in the brevity of the operation, and that means that the most aggressive fighting technique is the most humane.

14   But when people try to approach these questions with drivel about aesthetics, etc., really only one answer is possible: where the destiny and existence of a people are at stake, all obligation toward beauty ceases. The

---

* Count Helmuth von Moltke (1848–1916) was a German general who served as chief of staff during World War I.

most unbeautiful thing there can be in human life is and remains the yoke of slavery. Or do these Schwabing* decadents view the present lot of the German people as "aesthetic"? Certainly we don't have to discuss these matters with the Jews, the most modern inventors of this cultural perfume. Their whole existence is an embodied protest against the aesthetics of the Lord's image.

And since these criteria of humanitarianism and beauty must be eliminated from the struggle, they are also inapplicable to propaganda.

16   Propaganda in the War was a means to an end, and the end was the struggle for the existence of the German people; consequently, propaganda could only be considered in accordance with the principles that were valid for this struggle. In this case the most cruel weapons were humane if they brought about a quicker victory; and only those methods were beautiful which helped the nation to safeguard the dignity of its freedom.

This was the only possible attitude toward war propaganda in a life-and-death struggle like ours.

18   If the so-called responsible authorities had been clear on this point, they would never have fallen into such uncertainty over the form and application of this weapon: for even propaganda is no more than a weapon, though a frightful one in the hand of an expert.

The second really decisive question was this: To whom should propaganda be addressed? To the scientifically trained intelligentsia or to the less educated masses?

20   It must be addressed always and exclusively to the masses.

What the intelligentsia—or those who today unfortunately often go by that name—what they need is not propaganda but scientific instruction. The content of propaganda is not science any more than the object represented in a poster in art. The art of the poster lies in the designer's ability to attract the attention of the crowd by form and color. A poster advertising an art exhibit must direct the attention of the public to the art being exhibited; the better it succeeds in this, the greater is the art of the poster itself. The poster should give the masses an idea of the significance of the exhibition, it should not be a substitute for the art on display. Anyone who wants to concern himself with the art itself must do more than study the poster; and it will not be enough for him just to saunter through the exhibition. We may expect him to examine and immerse himself in the individual works, and thus little by little form a fair opinion.

22   A similar situation prevails with what we today call propaganda.

The function of propaganda does not lie in the scientific training of the individual, but in calling the masses' attention to certain facts, processes, necessities, etc., whose significance is thus for the first time placed within their field of vision.

24   The whole art consists in doing this so skillfully that everyone will be convinced that the fact is real, the process necessary, the necessity correct,

* A district in Munich favored by students, writers, and artists.

etc. But since propaganda is not and cannot be the necessity in itself, since its function, like the poster, consists in attracting the attention of the crowd, and not in educating those who are already educated or who are striving after education and knowledge, its effect for the most part must be aimed at the emotions and only to a very limited degree at the so-called intellect.

All propaganda must be popular and its intellectual level must be adjusted to the most limited intelligence among those it is addressed to. Consequently, the greater the mass it is intended to reach, the lower its purely intellectual level will have to be. But if, as in propaganda for sticking out a war, the aim is to influence a whole people, we must avoid excessive intellectual demands on our public, and too much caution cannot be exerted in this direction.

26   The more modest its intellectual ballast, the more exclusively it takes into consideration the emotions of the masses, the more effective it will be. And this is the best proof of the soundness or unsoundness of a propaganda campaign, and not success in pleasing a few scholars or young aesthetes.

The art of propaganda lies in understanding the emotional ideas of the great masses and finding, through a psychologically correct form, the way to the attention and thence to the heart of the broad masses. The fact that our bright boys do not understand this merely shows how mentally lazy and conceited they are.

28   Once we understand how necessary it is for propaganda to be adjusted to the broad mass, the following rule results:

It is a mistake to make propaganda many-sided, like scientific instruction, for instance.

30   The receptivity of the great masses is very limited, their intelligence is small, but their power of forgetting is enormous. In consequence of these facts, all effective propaganda must be limited to a very few points and must harp on these in slogans until the last member of the public understands what you want him to understand by your slogan. As soon as you sacrifice this slogan and try to be many-sided, the effect will piddle away, for the crowd can neither digest nor retain the material offered. In this way the result is weakened and in the end entirely cancelled out.

Thus we see that propaganda must follow a simple line and correspondingly the basic tactics must be psychologically sound.

32   For instance, it was absolutely wrong to make the enemy ridiculous, as the Austrian and German comic papers did. It was absolutely wrong because actual contact with an enemy soldier was bound to arouse an entirely different conviction, and the results were devastating; for now the German soldier, under the direct impression of the enemy's resistance, felt himself swindled by his propaganda service. His desire to fight, or even to stand firm, was not strengthened, but the opposite occurred. His courage flagged.

By contrast, the war propaganda of the English and Americans was psychologically sound. By representing the Germans to their own people as barbarians and Huns, they prepared the individual soldier for the terrors of war, and thus helped to preserve him from disappointments. After this, the most terrible weapon that was used against him seemed only to confirm what his propagandists had told him; it likewise reinforced his faith in the truth of his government's assertions, while on the other hand it increased his rage and hatred against the vile enemy. For the cruel effects of the weapon, whose use by the enemy he now came to know, gradually came to confirm for him the "Hunnish" brutality of the barbarous enemy, which he had heard all about; and it never dawned on him for a moment that his own weapons possibly, if not probably, might be even more terrible in their effects.

34   And so the English soldier could never feel that he had been misinformed by his own countrymen, as unhappily was so much the case with the German soldier that in the end he rejected everything coming from this source as "swindles" and "bunk." All this resulted from the idea that any old simpleton (or even somebody who was intelligent "in other things") could be assigned to propaganda work, and the failure to realize that the most brilliant psychologists would have been none too good.

          And so the German war propaganda offered an unparalleled example of an "enlightenment" service working in reverse, since any correct psychology was totally lacking.

36   There was no end to what could be learned from the enemy by a man who kept his eyes open, refused to let his perceptions be classified, and for four and a half years privately turned the storm-flood of enemy propaganda over in his brain.

          What our authorities least of all understood was the very first axiom of all propagandist activity: to wit, the basically subjective and one-sided attitude it must take toward every question it deals with. In this connection, from the very beginning of the War and from top to bottom, such sins were committed that we were entitled to doubt whether so much absurdity could really be attributed to pure stupidity alone.

38   What, for example, would we say about a poster that was supposed to advertise a new soap and that described other soaps as "good"?

          We would only shake our heads.

40   Exactly the same applies to political advertising.

          The function of propaganda is, for example, not to weigh and ponder the rights of different people, but exclusively to emphasize the one right which it has set out to argue for. Its task is not to make an objective study of the truth, in so far as it favors the enemy, and then set it before the masses with academic fairness; its task is to serve our own right, always and unflinchingly.

42   It was absolutely wrong to discuss war-guilt from the standpoint that Germany alone could not be held responsible for the outbreak of the catastrophe; it would have been correct to load every bit of the blame on the shoulders of the enemy, even if this had not really corresponded to the true facts, as it actually did.

          And what was the consequence of this half-heartedness?

44   The broad mass of a nation does not consist of diplomats, or even professors of political law, or even individuals capable of forming a rational

opinion; it consists of plain mortals, wavering and inclined to doubt and uncertainty. As soon as our own propaganda admits so much as a glimmer of right on the other side, the foundation for doubt in our own right has been laid. The masses are then in no position to distinguish where foreign injustice ends and our own begins. In such a case they become uncertain and suspicious, especially if the enemy refrains from going in for the same nonsense, but unloads every bit of blame on his adversary. Isn't it perfectly understandable that the whole country ends up by lending more credence to enemy propaganda, which is more unified and coherent, than to its own? And particularly a people that suffers from the mania of objectivity as much as the Germans. For, after all this, everyone will take the greatest pains to avoid doing the enemy any injustice, even at the peril of seriously besmirching and even destroying his own people and country.

Of course, this was not the intent of the responsible authorities, but the people never realize that.

46   The people in their overwhelming majority are so feminine by nature and attitude that sober reasoning determines their thoughts and actions far less than emotion and feeling.

And this sentiment is not complicated, but very simple and all of a piece. It does not have multiple shadings; it has a positive and a negative; love or hate, right or wrong, truth or lie, never half this way and half that way, never partially, or that kind of thing.

48   English propagandists understood all this most brilliantly—and acted accordingly. They made no half statements that might have given rise to doubts.

Their brilliant knowledge of the primitive sentiments of the broad masses is shown by their atrocity propaganda, which was adapted to this condition. As ruthless as it was brilliant, it created the preconditions for moral steadfastness at the front, even in the face of the greatest actual defeats, and just as strikingly it pilloried the German enemy as the sole guilty party for the outbreak of the War: the rabid, impudent bias and persistence with which this lie was expressed took into account the emotional, always extreme, attitude of the great masses and for this reason was believed.

50   How effective this type of propaganda was is most strikingly shown by the fact that after four years of war it not only enabled the enemy to stick to its guns, but even began to nibble at our own people.

It need not surprise us that our propaganda did not enjoy this success. In its inner ambiguity alone, it bore the germ of ineffectualness. And finally its content was such that it was very unlikely to make the necessary impression on the masses. Only our feather-brained "statesmen" could have dared to hope that this insipid pacifistic bilge could fire men's spirits till they were willing to die.

52   As a result, their miserable stuff was useless, even harmful in fact.

But the most brilliant propagandist technique will yield no success unless one fundamental principle is borne in mind constantly and with unflagging attention. It must confine itself to a few points and repeat them over and over. Here, as so often in this world, persistence is the first and most important requirement for success.

54   Particularly in the field of propaganda, we must never let ourselves be led by aesthetes or people who have grown blasé: not by the former, because the form and expression of our propaganda would soon, instead of being suitable for the masses, have drawing power only for literary teas; and of the second we must beware, because, lacking in any fresh emotion of their own, they are always on the lookout for new stimulation. These people are quick to weary of everything; they want variety, and they are never able to feel or understand the needs of their fellow men who are not yet so callous. They are always the first to criticize a propaganda campaign, or rather its content, which seems to them too old-fashioned, too hackneyed, too out-of-date, etc. They are always after novelty, in search of a change, and this makes them mortal enemies of any effective political propaganda. For as soon as the organization and the content of propaganda begin to suit their tastes, it loses all cohesion and evaporates completely.

The purpose of propaganda is not to provide interesting distraction for blasé young gentlemen, but to convince, and what I mean is to convince the masses. But the masses are slow-moving, and they always require a certain time before they are ready even to notice a thing, and only after the simplest ideas are repeated thousands of times will the masses finally remember them.

56   When there is a change, it must not alter the content of what the propaganda is driving at, but in the end must always say the same thing. For instance, a slogan must be presented from different angles, but the end of all remarks must always and immutably be the slogan itself. Only in this way can the propaganda have a unified and complete effect.

This broadness of outline from which we must never depart, in combination with steady, consistent emphasis, allows our final success to mature. And then, to our amazement, we shall see what tremendous results such perseverance leads to—to results that are almost beyond our understanding.

58   All advertising, whether in the field of business or politics, achieves success through the continuity and sustained uniformity of its application.

Here, too, the example of enemy war propaganda was typical; limited to a few points, devised exclusively for the masses, carried on with indefatigable persistence. Once the basic ideas and methods of execution were recognized as correct, they were applied throughout the whole War without the slightest change. At first the claims of the propaganda were so impudent that people thought it insane; later, it got on people's nerves; and in the end, it was believed. After four and a half years, a revolution broke out in Germany; and its slogans originated in the enemy's war propaganda.

60   And in England they understood one more thing: that this spiritual weapon can succeed only if it is applied on a tremendous scale, but that success amply covers all costs.

There, propaganda was regarded as a weapon of the first order, while in our country it was the last resort of unemployed politicians and a comfortable haven for slackers.

62   And, as was to be expected, its results all in all were zero.   ❖

Questions for Meaning

1. Why did Hitler's interest in propaganda increase after World War I? How important is propaganda in his view?
2. According to Hitler, how did English and American propaganda differ from German propaganda in World War I?
3. Why did Hitler believe that some people do not deserve freedom?
4. How important are truth and aesthetics in propaganda?
5. According to Hitler, what is the key to success in propaganda?
6. How does Hitler characterize the average person?

Questions about Strategy

1. Throughout this argument, Hitler emphasizes that Germany's opponents in World War I used propaganda "with amazing skill and really brilliant calculation." What advantage does he gain from making this point?
2. This argument was first published twenty years before the Allied liberation of Nazi concentration camps. Can you detect any signs of racism within it? Judging from this excerpt, how honest was Hitler in revealing his values before he came to power?
3. In paragraphs 38–40 and 58, Hitler compares propaganda to advertising. Is this a fair comparison? Why is it worth making?
4. Would this argument appeal to the average person? Would it appeal to intellectuals? What sort of audience was most likely to respond favorably to Hitler?

MAHATMA GANDHI

BRAHMACHARYA

The single most important figure in the struggle for Indian independence from British rule, Mohandas Karamchand Gandhi (1869–1948) earned the title "Mahatma," or "Great-Souled" by virtue of an almost saintlike commitment to nonviolence, coupled with a deep belief in the sanctity of all life and an almost complete disregard for his own physical comfort.

Raised in a strict, religious environment, Gandhi traveled to England in 1888 to study law. While there, he met George Bernard Shaw and other British intellectuals concerned with the need for social change. From 1893 to 1914, he lived and worked in South Africa—an experience that had a profound effect on his political development. Shortly after his arrival in South Africa, Gandhi experienced humiliations such as being thrown off a train because of the color of his skin. After leading the campaign for improving the conditions under which the large Indian population in South Africa lived, Gandhi entered Indian politics in 1919. Throughout the 1920s and 1930s he used nonviolent methods to protest British rule. Gandhi's greatest disappointment was that when independence from Britain was finally secured in 1947, India was partitioned into the separate countries of India and Pakistan (now India, Pakistan, and Bangladesh). When riots broke out that year between Hindus and Moslems, he traveled around the country to bring an end to violence. By fasting in Calcutta in 1947, he managed to end a period of prolonged violence in that city; a subsequent fast in Delhi was also successful. But within a few days of ending the riots in Delhi, Gandhi was shot and killed while on his way to prayer.

Before you read the following selection from 1947, you might note that Gandhi was married at the age of thirteen.

If it is contended that birth control is necessary for the nation because of over-population, I dispute the proposition. It has never been proved. In my opinion by a proper land system, better agriculture and a supplementary industry, this country is capable of supporting twice as many people as there are in it to-day.

2   What, then, is Brahmacharya? It means that men and women should refrain from carnal knowledge of each other. That is to say, they should not touch each other with a carnal thought, they should not think of it even in their dreams. Their mutual glances should be free from all suggestion of carnality. The hidden strength that God has given us should be conserved by rigid self-discipline, and transmitted into energy and power—not merely of body, but also of mind and soul.

But what is the spectacle that we actually see around us? Men and women, old and young, without exception, are caught in the meshes of sensuality. Blinded for the most part by lust, they lose all sense of right and wrong. I have myself seen even boys and girls behaving as if they were mad under its fatal influence. I too have behaved likewise under similar influences, and it could not well be otherwise. For the sake of a momentary pleasure, we sacrifice in an instant all the stock of vital energy that we have laboriously accumulated. The infatuation over, we find ourselves in a miserable condition. The next morning we feel hopelessly weak and tired, and the mind refuses to do its work. Then in order to remedy the mischief, we consume large quantities of milk, bhasmas, yakutis and what not. We take all sorts of "hervine tonics" and place ourselves at the doctor's mercy for repairing the waste, and for recovering the capacity for enjoyment. So the days pass and years, until at length old age comes upon us, and finds us utterly emasculated in body and in mind.

4   But the law of Nature is just the reverse of this. The older we grow the keener should our intellect be; the longer we live the greater should be our capacity to communicate the benefit of our accumulated experience to our fellow men. And such is indeed the case with those who have been true Brahmacharis. They know no fear of death, and they do not forget God even in the hour of death; nor do they indulge in vain desires. They die with a smile on their lips, and boldly face the day of judgment. They are true men and women; and of them alone can it be said that they have conserved their health.

We hardly realize the fact that incontinence is the root cause of most vanity, anger, fear and jealousy in the world. If our mind is not under our control, if we behave once or oftener every day more foolishly than even little children, what sins may we not commit consciously or unconsciously? How can we pause to think of the consequences of our actions, however vile or sinful they may be?

6   But you may ask, 'Who has ever seen a true Brahmachari in this sense? If all men should turn Brahmacharis, would not humanity be extinct and the whole world go to rack and ruin?' We will leave aside the religious aspect of this question and discuss it simply from the secular point of view. To my mind, these questions only betray our timidity and worse. We have not the strength of will to observe Brahmacharya and therefore set about finding pretexts for evading our duty. The race of true Brahmacharis is by no means extinct; but if they were commonly to be met with, of what value would Brahmacharya be? Thousands of hardy labourers have to go and dig deep into the bowels of the earth in search for diamonds, and at length they get perhaps merely a handful of them out of heaps and heaps of rock. How much greater, then, should be the labour involved in the discovery of the infinitely more precious diamond of a Brahmachari? If the observance of Brahmacharya should mean the end of the world, this is none of our business. Are we God that we should be so anxious about its future? He who created it will surely see to its preservation. We need not trouble to inquire whether other people practise Brahmacharya or not. When we enter a trade or profession, do we ever pause to consider what the fate of the world would

be if all men were to do likewise? The true Brahmachari will, in the long run, discover for himself answers to such questions.

But how can men engrossed in the cares of the material world put these ideas into practice? What about those who are married? What shall they do who have children? And what shall be done by those people who cannot control themselves? We have already seen what is the highest state for us to attain. We should keep this ideal constantly before us, and try to approach it to the utmost of our capacity. When little children are taught to write the letters of the alphabet, we show them the perfect shapes of the letters, and they try to reproduce them as best they can. In the same way, if we steadily work up to the ideal of Brahmacharya we may ultimately succeed in realizing it. What if we have married already? The law of Nature is that Brahmacharya may be broken only when the husband and wife feel a desire for progeny. Those, who, remembering this law, violate Brahmacharya once in four or five years, will not becomes slaves to lust, nor lose much of their stock of vital energy. But, alas! How rare are those men and women who yield to the sexual craving merely for the sake of offspring! The vast majority turn to sexual enjoyment merely to satisfy their carnal passion, with the result that children are born to them quite against their will. In the madness of sexual passion, they give no thought to the consequences of their acts. In this respect, men are even more to blame than women. The man is blinded so much by his lust that he never cares to remember that his wife is weak and unable to bear or rear up a child. In the West, indeed, people have transgressed all bounds. They indulge in sexual pleasures and devise measures in order to evade the responsibilities of parenthood. Many books have been written on this subject and a regular trade is being carried on in contraceptives. We are as yet free from this sin, but we do not shrink from imposing heavy burden of maternity on our women, and we are not concerned even to find that our children are weak, impotent and imbecile.

8 We are, in this respect, far worse than even the lower animals; for in their case the male and the female are brought together solely with the object of breeding from them. Men and women should regard it a sacred duty to keep apart from the moment of conception up to the time when the child is weaned. But we go on with our fatal merry-making blissfully forgetful of that sacred obligation. This almost incurable disease enfeebles our mind and leads us to an early grave, after making us drag a miserable existence for a short while. Married people should understand the true function of marriage, and should not violate Brahmacharya except with a view to progeny.

But this is so difficult under present conditions of life. Our diet, our ways of life, our common talk, and our environments are all equally calculated to rouse animal passions; and sensuality is like a poison eating into our vitals. Some people may doubt the possibility of our being able to free ourselves from this bondage. This book is written not for those who go about with such doubting of heart, but only for those who are really in earnest, and who have the courage to take active steps for self-improvement. Those who are quite content with their present abject condition will find this tedious even to read; but I hope it will be of some service to those who have realized and are disgusted with their own miserable plight.

10   From all that has been said it follows that those who are still unmarried should try to remain so; but if they cannot help marrying, they should defer it as long as possible. Young men, for instance, should take a vow to remain unmarried till the age of twenty-five or thirty. We cannot consider here all the advantages other than physical which they will reap and which are as it were added unto the rest.

My request to those parents who read this chapter is that they should not tie a millstone round the necks of their children by marrying them young. They should look to the welfare of the rising generation, and not merely seek to pamper their own vanity. They should cast aside all silly notions of family pride or respectability, and cease to indulge in such heartless practices. Let them rather, if they are true well-wishers of their children, look to their physical, mental and moral improvement. What greater disservice can they do to their progeny than compel them to enter upon married life, with all its tremendous responsibilities and cares, while they are mere children?

12   Then again the true laws of health demand that the man who loses his wife, as well as the woman that loses her husband, should remain single ever after. There is a difference of opinion among medical men as to whether young men and women need ever let their vital energy escape, some answering the question in the affirmative, others in the negative. But while doctors thus disagree we must not give way to over-indulgence from an idea that we are supported by medical authority. I can affirm, without the slightest hesitation, from my own experience as well as that of others, that sexual enjoyment is not only not necessary for, but is positively injurious to health. All the strength of body and mind that has taken long to acquire is lost all at once by a single dissipation of the vital energy. It takes a long time to regain this lost vitality, and even then there is no saying that it can be thoroughly recovered. A broken mirror may be mended and made to do its work, but it can never be anything but a broken mirror.

As has already been pointed out, the preservation of our vitality is impossible without pure air, pure water, pure and wholesome food, as well as pure thoughts. So vital indeed is the relation between health and morals that we can never be perfectly healthy unless we lead a clean life. The earnest man, who, forgetting the errors of the past, begins to live a life of purity, will be able to reap the fruit of it straightaway. Those who practise true Brahmacharya even for a short period will see how their body and mind improve steadily in strength and power, and they will not at any cost be willing to part with this treasure. I have myself been guilty of lapses even after having fully understood the value of Brahmacharya, and have of course paid dearly for it. I am filled with shame and remorse when I think of the terrible contrast between my condition before and after these lapses. But from the errors of the past I have now learnt to preserve this treasure intact, and I fully hope, with God's grace to continue to preserve it in the future; for I have, in my own person, experienced the inestimable benefits of Brahmacharya. I was married early, and had become the father of children as a mere youth. When at length, I awoke to the reality of my situation, I found that I was steeped in ignorance about the fundamental laws of our being. I shall consider myself amply rewarded for writing this chapter if at least a single reader takes a warning from my failings and experiences, and profits thereby. Many people have told—and I also believe it—that I am full of energy and enthusiasm, and that I am by no means weak in mind; some even accuse me of strength bordering on obstinacy. Nevertheless there is still bodily and mental ill-health as a legacy of the past. And yet when compared with my friends, I may call myself healthy and strong. If even after twenty years of sensual enjoyment, I have been able to reach this state, how much better off should I have been if I had kept myself pure during those twenty years as well? It is my full conviction, that if only I had lived a life of unbroken Brahmacharya all through, my energy and enthusiasm would have been a thousandfold greater and I should have been able to devote them all to the furtherance of my country's cause as my own. If an imperfect Brahmachari like myself can reap such benefit, how much more wonderful must be the gain in power—physical, mental, as well as moral—that unbroken Brahmacharya can bring to us.

14   When so strict is the law of Brahmacharya what shall we say of those guilty of the unpardonable sin of illegitimate sexual enjoyment? The evil arising from adultery and prostitution is a vital question of religion and morality and cannot be fully dealt with in a treatise on health. Here we are only concerned to point out how thousands who are guilty of these sins are afflicted by venereal diseases. God is merciful in this that the punishment swiftly overtakes sinners. Their short span of life is spent in object bondage to quacks in a futile quest after a remedy for their ills. If adultery and prostitution disappeared, at least half the present number of doctors would find their occupation gone. So inextricably indeed has venereal disease caught mankind in its clutches that thoughtful medical men have been forced to admit, that so long as adultery and prostitution continue, there is no hope for the human race, all the discoveries of curative medicine notwithstanding. The medicines for these diseases are so poisonous that although they may appear to have done some good for the time being, they give rise to other and still more terrible diseases which are transmitted from generation to generation.

No one need therefore despair. My Mahatmaship* is worthless. It is due to my outward activities, due to my politics which is the least part of me and is therefore evanescent. What is of abiding worth is my insistence on truth, non-violence and Brahmacharya, which is the real part of me. That

---

* Mahatma is a Hindu term of respect for a man known for being high-minded and spiritual.

permanent part of me, however small, is not to be despised. It is my all. I prize even the failures and disillusionments which are but steps towards success. ❖

Questions for Meaning

1. How does Gandhi define *Brahmacharya?*
2. According to Gandhi, what are the advantages of abstaining from sex?
3. What advice does Gandhi offer on the subject of marriage?
4. Does Gandhi believe that men and women experience sexual desire to the same degree?
5. In his conclusion, Gandhi predicts the rise of "other and still more terrible diseases" unless prostitution and adultery are eliminated. Has history proved him right?
6. Vocabulary: carnal (2), emasculated (3), incontinence (5), impotent (7), progeny (8), evanescent (15).

Questions about Strategy

1. Why do you think Gandhi begins his case by dismissing an argument that he could have used when arguing on behalf of celibacy?
2. Where does Gandhi admit to having experienced sexual activity? What does he gain from making this admission?
3. How does Gandhi respond to opponents who might argue that there would be no future for humanity if everyone practiced Brahmacharya?
4. Does Gandhi make any claims that leave him open to counterargument?
5. In paragraph 7, Gandhi contrasts behavior in his own culture with behavior in Western culture. Is his point useful for the purpose of this argument?
6. Why does Gandhi direct part of his argument to parents?

Carl Rogers

DEALING WITH BREAKDOWNS IN COMMUNICATION

Carl Rogers (1902–1987) was a psychotherapist who developed an innovative approach that emphasized the importance of positive reinforcement during therapy. He delivered the following argument at Northwestern University in 1951, when the United States and what was then the Soviet Union were at the height of the Cold War and Senator Joseph McCarthy was questioning the loyalty of many Americans. As you read, note how Rogers refers to these events in order to illustrate his point that understanding begins with careful listening. In recent years, Rogers's views have become influential in rhetoric as scholars have reexamined long-standing ideas about the nature of persuasion. (If you are interested in Rogerian argument, see pages 19–21 and 284–286 of this book.)

It may seem curious that a person whose whole professional effort is devoted to psychotherapy should be interested in problems of communication. What relationship is there between providing therapeutic help to individuals with emotional maladjustments and the concern of this conference with obstacles to communication? Actually the relationship is very close indeed. The whole task of psychotherapy is the task of dealing with a failure in communication. The emotionally maladjusted person, the "neurotic," is in difficulty first because communication within himself has broken down, and second because as a result of this his communication with others has been damaged. If this sounds somewhat strange, then let me put it in other terms. In the "neurotic" individual, parts of himself which have been termed unconscious, or repressed, or denied to awareness, become blocked off so that they no longer communicate themselves to the conscious or managing part of himself. As long as this is true, there are distortions in the way he communicates himself to others, and so he suffers both within himself, and in his interpersonal relations. The task of psychotherapy is to help the person achieve, through a special relationship with a therapist, good communication within himself. Once this is achieved he can communicate more freely and more effectively with others. We may say then that psychotherapy is good communication, within and between men. We may also turn that statement around and it will still be true. Good communication, free communication, within or between men, is always therapeutic.

2   It is, then, from a background of experience with communication in counseling and psychotherapy that I want to present here two ideas. I wish to state what I believe is one of the major factors in blocking or impeding communication, and then I wish to present what in our experience has proven to be a very important way of improving or facilitating communication.

I would like to propose, as an hypothesis for consideration, that the major barrier to mutual interpersonal communication is our very natural tendency to judge, to evaluate, to approve or disapprove, the statement of the other person, or the other group. Let me illustrate my meaning with some very simple examples. As you leave the meeting tonight, one of the statements you are likely to hear is, "I didn't like that man's talk." Now what do you respond? Almost invariably your reply will be either approval or disapproval of the attitude expressed. Either you respond, "I didn't either. I thought it was terrible," or else you tend to reply, "Oh, I thought it was really good." In other words, your primary reaction is to evaluate what has just been said to you, to evaluate it from *your* point of view, your own frame of reference.

4   Or take another example. Suppose I say with some feeling, "I think the Republicans are behaving in ways that show a lot of good sound sense these days," what is the response that arises in your mind as you listen? The overwhelming likelihood is that it will be evaluative. You will find yourself agreeing, or disagreeing, or making some judgment about me such as "He must be a conservative," or "He seems solid in his thinking." Or let us take an illustration from the international scene. Russia says vehemently, "The treaty with Japan is a war plot on the part of the United States." We rise as one person to say "That's a lie!"

This last illustration brings in another element connected with my hypothesis. Although the tendency to make evaluations is common in almost all interchange of language, it is very much heightened in those situations where feelings and emotions are deeply involved. So the stronger our feelings, the more likely it is that there will be no mutual element in the communication. There will be just two ideas, two feelings, two judgments, missing each other in psychological space. I'm sure you recognize this from your own experience. When you have not been emotionally involved yourself, and have listened to a heated discussion, you often go away thinking, "Well, they actually weren't talking about the same thing." And they were not. Each was making a judgment, an evaluation, from his own frame of reference. There was really nothing which could be called communication in any genuine sense. This tendency to react to any emotionally meaningful statement by forming an evaluation of it from our own point of view, is, I repeat, the major barrier to interpersonal communication.

6   But is there any way of solving this problem, of avoiding this barrier? I feel that we are making exciting progress toward this goal and I would like to present it as simply as I can. Real communication occurs, and this evaluative tendency is avoided, when we listen with understanding. What does that mean? It means *to see the expressed idea and attitude from the other person's point of view, to sense how it feels to him, to achieve his frame of reference in regard to the thing he is talking about.*

Stated so briefly, this may sound absurdly simple, but it is not. It is an approach which we have found extremely potent in the field of psychotherapy. It is the most effective agent we know for altering the basic personality structure of an individual, and improving his relationships and his communications with others. If I can listen to what he can tell me, if I can understand how it seems to him, if I can see its personal meaning for him, if I can sense the emotional flavor which it has for him, then I will be releasing potent forces of change in him. If I can really understand how he hates his father, or hates the university, or hates communists—if I can catch the flavor of his fear of insanity, or his fear of atom bombs, or of Russia—it will be of the greatest help to him in altering those very hatreds and fears, and in establishing realistic and harmonious relationships with the very people and situations toward which he has felt hatred and fear. We know from our research that such empathic understanding—understanding *with* a person, not *about* him—is such an effective approach that it can bring about major changes in personality.

8   Some of you may be feeling that you listen well to people, and that you have never seen such results. The chances are very great indeed that your listening has not been of the type I have described. Fortunately I can suggest a little laboratory experiment which you can try to test the quality of your understanding. The next time you get into an argument with your wife, or your friend, or with a small group of friends, just stop the discussion for a moment and for an experiment, institute this rule. "Each person can speak up for himself only *after* he has first restated the ideas and feelings of the previous speaker accurately, and to that speaker's satisfaction." You see what this would mean. It would simply mean that before presenting your own point of view, it would be necessary for you to really achieve the other speaker's frame of reference—to understand his thoughts and feelings so well that you could summarize them for him. Sounds simple doesn't it? But if you try it you will discover it one of the most difficult things you have ever tried to do. However, once you have been able to see the other's point of view, your own comments will have to be drastically revised. You will also find the emotion going out of the discussion, the differences being reduced, and those differences which remain being of a rational and understandable sort.

Can you imagine what this kind of an approach would mean if it were projected into larger areas? What would happen to a labor-management dispute if it was conducted in such a way that labor, without necessarily agreeing, could accurately state management's point of view in a way that management could accept; and management, without approving labor's stand, could state labor's case in a way that labor agreed was accurate? It would mean that real communication was established, and one could practically guarantee that some reasonable solution would be reached.

10   If then this way of approach is an effective avenue to good communication and good relationships, as I am quite sure you will agree if you try the experiment I have mentioned, why is it not more widely tried and used? I will try to list the difficulties which keep it from being utilized.

In the first place it takes courage, a quality which is not too widespread. I am indebted to Dr. S. I. Hayakawa, the semanticist, for pointing out that to carry on psychotherapy in this fashion is to take a very real risk, and that courage is required. If you really understand another person in this way, if you are willing to enter his private world and see the way life appears to him, without any attempt to make evaluative judgments, you run the risk of being changed yourself. You might see it his way, you might find yourself influenced in your attitudes of your personality. The risk of being changed is one of the most frightening prospects most of us can face. If I enter, as fully as I am able, into the private world of a neurotic or psychotic individual, isn't there a risk that I might become lost in that world? Most of us are afraid to take that risk. Or if we had a Russian communist speaker here tonight, or Senator Joe McCarthy, how many of us would dare to try to see the world from each of these points of view? The great majority of us could not *listen:* we would find ourselves compelled to *evaluate,* because listening would seem too dangerous. So the first requirement is courage, and we do not always have it.

12   But there is a second obstacle. It is just when emotions are strongest that it is most difficult to achieve the frame of reference of the other person or group. Yet it is the time the attitude is most needed, if communication is to be established. We have not found this to be an insuperable obstacle in our experience in psychotherapy. A third party, who is able to lay aside his own feelings and evaluations, can assist greatly by listening with understanding to each person or group and clarifying the views and attitudes each holds. We have found this very effective in small groups in which contradictory or antagonistic attitudes exist. When the parties to a dispute realize that they are being understood, that someone sees how the situation seems to them, the statements grow less exaggerated and less defensive, and it is no longer necessary to maintain the attitude, "I am 100% right and you are 100% wrong." The influence of such an understanding catalyst in the group permits the members to come closer and closer to the objective truth involved in the relationship. In this way mutual communication is established and some type of agreement becomes much more possible. So we may say that though heightened emotions make it much more difficult to understand *with* an opponent, our experience makes it clear that a neutral, understanding, catalyst type of leader or therapist can overcome this obstacle in a small group.

    This last phrase, however, suggests another obstacle to utilizing the approach I have described. Thus far all our experience has been with small face-to-face groups—groups exhibiting industrial tensions, religious tensions, racial tensions, and therapy groups in which many personal tensions are present. In these small groups our experience, confirmed by a limited amount of research, shows that this basic approach leads to improved communication, to greater acceptance of others and by others, and to attitudes which are more positive and more problem-solving in nature. There is a decrease in defensiveness, in exaggerated statements, in evaluative and critical behavior. But these findings are from small groups. What about trying to achieve understanding between larger groups that are geographically remote? Or between face-to-face groups who are not speaking for themselves, but simply as representatives of others, like the delegates at Kaesong*? Frankly we do not know the answers to these questions. I believe the situation might be put this way. As social scientists we have a tentative test-tube solution of the problem of breakdown in communication. But to confirm the validity of this test-tube solution, and to adapt it to the enormous problems of communication-breakdown between classes, groups, and nations, would involve additional funds, much more research, and creative thinking of a high order.

14   Even with our present limited knowledge we can see some steps which might be taken, even in large groups, to increase the amount of listening *with,* and to decrease the amount of evaluation *about.* To be imaginative for a moment, let us suppose that a therapeutically oriented international group went to the Russian leaders and said, "We want to achieve a genuine understanding of your views and even more important, of your attitudes and feelings, toward the United States. We will summarize and resummarize these views and feelings if necessary, until you agree that our description represents the situation as it seems to you." Then suppose they did the same thing with the leaders in our own country. If they then gave the widest possible distribution to these two views, with feelings clearly described but not expressed in name-calling, might not the effect be very great? It would not guarantee the type of understanding I have been describing, but it would make it much more possible. We can understand the feelings of a person who hates us much more readily when his attitudes are accurately described to us by a neutral third party, than we can when he is shaking his fist at us.

But even to describe such a first step is to suggest another obstacle to this approach of understanding. Our civilization does not yet have enough faith in the social sciences to utilize their findings. The opposite is true of the physical sciences. During the war when a test-tube solution was found to the problem of synthetic rubber, millions of dollars and an army of talent was turned loose on the problem of using that finding. If synthetic rubber could be made in milligrams, it could and would be made in the thousands of tons. And it was. But in the social science realm, if a way is found of facilitating communication and mutual understanding in small groups, there is no guarantee that the finding will be utilized. It may be a generation or more before the money and the brains will be turned loose to exploit that finding.

16   In closing, I would like to summarize this small-scale solution to the problem of barriers in communication, and to point out certain of its characteristics.

I have said that our research and experience to date would make it appear that breakdowns in communication, and the evaluative tendency which is the major barrier to communication, can be avoided. The solution is provided by creating a situation in which each of the different parties comes to understand the other from the *other's* point of view. This has been achieved, in practice, even when feelings run high, by the influence of a

---

* Kaesong is a city near the border between North and South Korea; the Korean War (1950–1953) was being fought at the time Rogers presented this argument.

person who is willing to understand each point of view empathically, and who thus acts as a catalyst to precipitate further understanding.

18   This procedure has important characteristics. It can be initiated by one party, without waiting for the other to be ready. It can even be initiated by a neutral third person, providing he can gain a minimum of cooperation from one of the parties.

This procedure can deal with the insincerities, the defensive exaggerations, the lies, the "false fronts" which characterize almost every failure in communication. These defensive distortions drop away with astonishing speed as people find that the only intent is to understand, not judge.

20   This approach leads steadily and rapidly toward the discovery of the truth, toward a realistic appraisal of the objective barriers to communication. The dropping of some defensiveness by one party leads to further dropping of defensiveness by the other party, and truth is thus approached.

This procedure gradually achieves mutual communication. Mutual communication tends to be pointed toward solving a problem rather than toward attacking a person or group. It leads to a situation in which I see how the problem appears to you, as well as to me, and you see how it appears to me, as well as to you. Thus accurately and realistically defined, the problem is almost certain to yield to intelligent attack, or if it is in part insoluble, it will be comfortably accepted as such.

22   This then appears to be a test-tube solution to the breakdown of communication as it occurs in small groups. Can we take this small scale answer, investigate it further, refine it, develop it and apply it to the tragic and well-nigh fatal failures of communication which threaten the very existence of our modern world? It seems to me that this is a possibility and a challenge which we should explore.   ❖

Questions for Meaning

1. According to Rogers, why do people become "neurotic"?
2. What is the purpose of psychotherapy?
3. What keeps people from communicating effectively with one another?
4. What does it mean to "listen with understanding"? Why does this take courage?
5. Does Rogers offer any practical advice for learning how to listen with understanding?
6. How could listening with understanding lead to conflict resolution?

Questions about Strategy

1. How does Rogers establish his authority to speak on the subject of communication?
2. What is the effect of presenting this argument in the second person?

3. What steps does Rogers take to help his audience grasp the key points of this argument?
4. Rogers made this argument in 1951. What assumptions does he make about gender? Could a writer today safely make the same assumptions?

RACHEL CARSON

THE OBLIGATION TO ENDURE

If the environmental movement during the past quarter century can be traced to any single work, it is probably *Silent Spring* (1962), Rachel Carson's widely read analysis of how pesticides and other chemicals were polluting the earth and endangering wildlife. An aquatic biologist for the U.S. Bureau of Fisheries, Carson (1907–1966) became editor in chief of the publications of the U.S. Fish and Wildlife Service. "The Obligation to Endure" is the second chapter of *Silent Spring.* Carson's other works include *The Sea Around Us* (1951) and *The Edge of the Sea* (1955).

The history of life on earth has been a history of interaction between living things and their surroundings. To a large extent, the physical form and the habits of the earth's vegetation and its animal life have been molded by the environment. Considering the whole span of earthly time, the opposite effect, in which life actually modifies its surroundings, has been relatively slight. Only within the moment of time represented by the present century has one species—man—acquired significant power to alter the nature of his world.

2   During the past quarter century this power has not only increased to one of disturbing magnitude but it has changed in character. The most alarming of all man's assaults upon the environment is the contamination of air, earth, rivers, and sea with dangerous and even lethal materials. This pollution is for the most part irrecoverable; the chain of evil it initiates not only in the world that must support life but in living tissues is for the most part irreversible. In this now universal contamination of the environment, chemicals are the sinister and little-recognized partners of radiation in changing the very nature of the world—the very nature of its life. Strontium 90, released through nuclear explosions into the air, comes to earth in rain or drifts down as fallout, lodges in soil, enters into the grass or corn or wheat grown there, and in time takes up its abode in the bones of a human being, there to remain until his death. Similarly, chemicals sprayed on croplands or forests or gardens lie long in soil, entering into living organisms, passing from one to another in a chain of poisoning and death. Or they pass mysteriously by underground streams until they emerge and, through the

alchemy of air and sunlight, combine into new forms that kill vegetation, sicken cattle, and work unknown harm on those who drink from once pure wells. As Albert Schweitzer* has said, "Man can hardly even recognize the devils of his own creation."

It took hundreds of millions of years to produce the life that now inhabits the earth—eons of time in which that developing and evolving and diversifying life reached a state of adjustment and balance with its surroundings. The environment, rigorously shaping and directing the life it supported, contained elements that were hostile as well as supporting. Certain rocks gave out dangerous radiation; even within the light of the sun, from which all life draws its energy, there were short-wave radiations with power to injure. Given time—time not in years but in millennia—life adjusts, and a balance has been reached. For time is the essential ingredient; but in the modern world there is no time.

4   The rapidity of change and the speed with which new situations are created follow the impetuous and heedless pace of man rather than the deliberate pace of nature. Radiation is no longer merely the background radiation of rocks, the bombardment of cosmic rays, the ultraviolet of the sun that have existed before there was any life on earth; radiation is now the unnatural creation of man's tampering with the atom. The chemicals to which life is asked to make its adjustment are no longer merely the calcium and silica and copper and all the rest of the minerals washed out of the rocks and carried in rivers to the sea; they are the synthetic creations of man's inventive mind, brewed in his laboratories, and having no counterparts in nature.

To adjust to these chemicals would require time on the scale that is nature's; it would require not merely the years of a man's life but the life of generations. And even this, were it by some miracle possible, would be futile, for the new chemicals come from our laboratories in an endless stream; almost five hundred annually find their way into actual use in the United States alone. The figure is staggering and its implications are not easily grasped—500 new chemicals to which the bodies of men and animals are required somehow to adapt each year, chemicals totally outside the limits of biologic experience.

6   Among them are many that are used in man's war against nature. Since the mid-1940s over 200 basic chemicals have been created for use in killing insects, weeds, rodents, and other organisms described in the modern vernacular as "pests"; and they are sold under several thousand different brand names.

These sprays, dusts, and aerosols are now applied almost universally to farms, gardens, forests, and homes—nonselective chemicals that have the power to kill every insect, the "good" and the "bad," to still the song of birds and the leaping of fish in the streams, to coat the leaves with a deadly film, and to linger on in soil—all this though the intended target may be only

---

* A theologian, musician, and physician best known for his missionary work in Africa, Albert Schweitzer (1875–1965) was awarded the Nobel Peace Prize in 1952.

a few weeds or insects. Can anyone believe it is possible to lay down such a barrage of poisons on the surface of the earth without making it unfit for all life? They should not be called "insecticides," but "biocides."

8   The whole process of spraying seems caught up in an endless spiral. Since DDT was released for civilian use, a process of escalation has been going on in which ever more toxic materials must be found. This has happened because insects, in a triumphant vindication of Darwin's principle of the survival of the fittest, have evolved super races immune to the particular insecticide used, hence a deadlier one has always to be developed—and then a deadlier one than that. It has happened also because, for reasons to be described later, destructive insects often undergo a "flareback," or resurgence, after spraying, in numbers greater than before. Thus the chemical war is never won, and all life is caught in its violent crossfire.

Along with the possibility of the extinction of mankind by nuclear war, the central problem of our age has therefore become the contamination of man's total environment with such substances of incredible potential for harm—substances that accumulate in the tissues of plants and animals and even penetrate the germ cells to shatter or alter the very material of heredity upon which the shape of the future depends.

10   Some would-be architects of our future look toward a time when it will be possible to alter the human germ plasm by design. But we may easily be doing so now by inadvertence, for many chemicals, like radiation, bring about gene mutations. It is ironic to think that man might determine his own future by something so seemingly trivial as the choice of an insect spray.

All this has been risked—for what? Future historians may well be amazed by our distorted sense of proportion. How could intelligent beings seek to control a few unwanted species by a method that contaminated the entire environment and brought the threat of disease and death even to their own kind? Yet this is precisely what we have done. We have done it, moreover, for reasons that collapse the moment we examine them. We are told that the enormous and expanding use of pesticides is necessary to maintain farm production. Yet is our real problem not one of *overproduction*? Our farms, despite measures to remove acreages from production and to pay farmers *not* to produce, have yielded such a staggering excess of crops that the American taxpayer in 1962 is paying out more than one billion dollars a year as the total carrying cost of the surplus-food storage program. And is the situation helped when one branch of the Agriculture Department tries to reduce production while another states, as it did in 1958, "It is believed generally that reduction of crop acreages under provisions of the Soil Bank will stimulate interest in use of chemicals to obtain maximum production on the land retained in crops."

12   All this is not to say there is no insect problem and no need of control. I am saying, rather, that control must be geared to realities, not to mythical situations, and that the methods employed must be such that they do not destroy us along with the insects.

The problem whose attempted solution has brought such a train of disaster in its wake is an accompaniment of our modern way of life. Long before the age of man, insects inhabited the earth—a group of extraordinarily varied and adaptable beings. Over the course of time since man's advent, a small percentage of the more than half a million species of insects have come into conflict with human welfare in two principal ways: as competitors for the food supply and as carriers of human disease.

14   Disease-carrying insects become important where human beings are crowded together, especially under conditions where sanitation is poor, as in time of natural disaster or war or in situations of extreme poverty and deprivation. Then control of some sort becomes necessary. It is a sobering fact, however, as we shall presently see, that the method of massive chemical control has had only limited success, and also threatens to worsen the very conditions it is intended to curb.

Under primitive agricultural conditions the farmer had few insect problems. These arose with the intensification of agriculture—the devotion of immense acreages to a single crop. Such a system set the stage for explosive increases in specific insect populations. Single-crop farming does not take advantage of the principles by which nature works; it is agriculture as an engineer might conceive it to be. Nature has introduced great variety into the landscape, but man has displayed a passion for simplifying it. Thus he undoes the built-in checks and balances by which nature holds the species within bounds. One important natural check is a limit on the amount of suitable habitat for each species. Obviously then, an insect that lives on wheat can build up its population to much higher levels on a farm devoted to wheat than on one in which wheat is intermingled with other crops to which the insect is not adapted.

16   The same thing happens in other situations. A generation or more ago, the towns of large areas of the United States lined their streets with the noble elm tree. Now the beauty they hopefully created is threatened with complete destruction as disease sweeps through the elms, carried by a beetle that would have only limited chance to build up large populations and to spread from tree to tree if the elms were only occasional trees in a richly diversified planting.

Another factor in the modern insect problem is one that must be viewed against a background of geologic and human history: the spreading of thousands of different kinds of organisms from their native homes to invade new territories. This worldwide migration has been studied and graphically described by the British ecologist Charles Elton in his recent book *The Ecology of Invasions.* During the Cretaceous Period, some hundred million years ago, flooding seas cut many land bridges between continents and living things found themselves confined in what Elton calls "colossal separate nature reserves." There, isolated from others of their kind, they developed many new species. When some of the land masses were joined again, about 15 million years ago, these species began to move out into new territories— a movement that is not only still in progress but is now receiving considerable assistance from man.

18   The importation of plants is the primary agent in the modern spread of species, for animals have almost invariably gone along with the plants,

quarantine being a comparatively recent and not completely effective innovation. The United States Office of Plant Introduction alone has introduced almost 200,000 species and varieties of plants from all over the world. Nearly half of the 180 or so major insect enemies of plants in the United States are accidental imports from abroad, and most of them have come as hitchhikers on plants.

In new territory, out of reach of the restraining hand of the natural enemies that kept down its numbers in its native land, an invading plant or animal is able to become enormously abundant. Thus it is no accident that our most troublesome insects are introduced species.

20   These invasions, both the naturally occurring and those dependent on human assistance, are likely to continue indefinitely. Quarantine and massive chemical campaigns are only extremely expensive ways of buying time. We are faced, according to Dr. Elton, "with a life-and-death need not just to find new technological means of suppressing this plant or that animal"; instead we need the basic knowledge of animal populations and their relations to their surroundings that will "promote an even balance and damp down the explosive power of outbreaks and new invasions."

Much of the necessary knowledge is now available but we do not use it. We train ecologists in our universities and even employ them in our governmental agencies but we seldom take their advice. We allow the chemical death rain to fall as though there were no alternative, whereas in fact there are many, and our ingenuity could soon discover many more if given opportunity.

22   Have we fallen into a mesmerized state that makes us accept as inevitable that which is inferior or detrimental, as though having lost the will or the vision to demand that which is good? Such thinking, in the words of the ecologist Paul Shepard, "idealizes life with only its head out of water, inches above the limits of toleration of the corruption of its own environment. . . . Why should we tolerate a diet of weak poisons, a home in insipid surroundings, a circle of acquaintances who are not quite our enemies, the noise of motors with just enough relief to prevent insanity? Who would want to live in a world which is just not quite fatal?"

Yet such a world is pressed upon us. The crusade to create a chemically sterile, insect-free world seems to have engendered a fanatic zeal on the part of many specialists and most of the so-called control agencies. On every hand there is evidence that those engaged in spraying operations exercise a ruthless power. "The regulatory entomologists . . . function as prosecutor, judge and jury, tax assessor and collector and sheriff to enforce their own orders," said Connecticut entomologist Neely Turner. The most flagrant abuses go unchecked in both state and federal agencies.

24   It is not my contention that chemical insecticides must never be used. I do contend that we have put poisonous and biologically potent chemicals indiscriminately into the hands of persons largely or wholly ignorant of their potentials for harm. We have subjected enormous numbers of people to contact with these poisons, without their consent and often without their

knowledge. If the Bill of Rights contains no guarantee that a citizen shall be secure against lethal poisons distributed either by private individuals or by public officials, it is surely only because our forefathers, despite their considerable wisdom and foresight, could conceive of no such problem.

I contend, furthermore, that we have allowed these chemicals to be used with little or no advance investigation of their effect on soil, water, wildlife, and man himself. Future generations are unlikely to condone our lack of prudent concern for the integrity of the natural world that supports all life.

26   There is still very limited awareness of the nature of the threat. This is an era of specialists, each of whom sees his own problem and is unaware of or intolerant of the larger frame into which it fits. It is also an era dominated by industry, in which the right to make a dollar at whatever cost is seldom challenged. When the public protests, confronted with some obvious evidence of damaging results of pesticide applications, it is fed little tranquilizing pills of half truth. We urgently need an end to these false assurances, to the sugar coating of unpalatable facts. It is the public that is being asked to assume the risks that the insect controllers calculate. The public must decide whether it wishes to continue on the present road, and it can do so only when in full possession of the facts. In the words of Jean Rostand, "The obligation to endure gives us the right to know." ❖

Questions for Meaning

1. What is the relationship between living things and their surroundings?
2. Why is Carson concerned about time? What does she mean when she writes, "time is the essential ingredient; but in the modern world there is no time"?
3. Consider the distinction in paragraph 7 between "insecticides" and "biocides." What is the difference?
4. Why does Carson believe that the widespread use of insecticides has become "an endless spiral"?
5. According to Carson, how have different species of insect spread in modern times?
6. Vocabulary: magnitude (2), eons (3), millennia (3), futile (5), vernacular (6), advent (13), mesmerized (22), insipid (22), entomologists (23), unpalatable (26).

Questions about Strategy

1. In paragraph 2, Carson writes that the contamination of our environment "is for the most part irrecoverable." Does this statement encourage you to read further or does it make you lose interest?
2. Why does Carson call attention to the Department of Agriculture?

3. Does Carson ever recognize a need for insect control?
4. Does Carson offer any alternative to insecticides?
5. Consider paragraph 25. What does Carson accomplish by directing attention to the future?

MARTIN LUTHER KING, JR.

LETTER FROM BIRMINGHAM JAIL

Martin Luther King, Jr. (1929–1968) was the most important leader of the movement to secure civil rights for black Americans during the mid-twentieth century. Ordained a Baptist minister in his father's church in Atlanta, King went on to receive a PhD from Boston University in 1955. Two years later, he became the founder and director of the Southern Christian Leadership Conference, an organization he continued to lead until his assassination in 1968. He first came to national attention by organizing a boycott of the buses in Montgomery, Alabama (1955–1956)—a campaign that he recounts in *Stride Toward Freedom: The Montgomery Story* (1958). His other books include *The Measure of a Man* (1959), *Why We Can't Wait* (1963), and *Where Do We Go from Here: Chaos or Community?* (1967). An advocate of nonviolence, King was jailed fourteen times in the course of his work for civil rights. His efforts helped secure the passage of the Civil Rights Bill in 1963, and, during the last years of his life, he was the recipient of many awards, most notably the Nobel Peace Prize in 1964.

"Letter from Birmingham Jail" was written in 1963, when King was jailed for eight days as the result of his campaign against segregation in Birmingham, Alabama. In the letter, King responds to white clergymen who had criticized his work and blamed him for breaking the law. But "Letter from Birmingham Jail" is much more than a rebuttal of criticism. It is a well-reasoned and carefully argued defense of civil disobedience as a means of securing civil liberties.

April 16, 1963

My Dear Fellow Clergymen:

While confined here in the Birmingham city jail, I came across your recent statement calling my present activities "unwise and untimely." Seldom do I pause to answer criticism of my work and ideas. If I sought to answer all the criticisms that cross my desk, my secretaries would have little time for anything other than such correspondence in the course of the day, and I would have no time for constructive work. But since I feel that you are men of genuine good will and that your criticisms are sincerely put forth, I want to try to answer your statement in what I hope will be patient and reasonable terms.

2   I think I should indicate why I am here in Birmingham, since you have been influenced by the view which argues against "outsiders coming in." I have the honor of serving as president of the Southern Christian Leadership Conference, an organization operating in every southern state, with headquarters in Atlanta, Georgia. We have some eighty-five affiliated organizations across the South, and one of them is the Alabama Christian Movement for Human Rights. Frequently we share staff, educational, and financial resources with our affiliates. Several months ago the affiliate here in Birmingham asked us to be on call to engage in a nonviolent direct-action program if such were deemed necessary. We readily consented, and when the hour came we lived up to our promise. So I, along with several members of my staff, am here because I was invited here. I am here because I have organizational ties here.

          But more basically, I am in Birmingham because injustice is here. Just as the prophets of the eighth century B.C. left their villages and carried their "thus saith the Lord" far beyond the boundaries of their home towns, and just as the Apostle Paul left his village of Tarsus and carried the gospel of Jesus Christ to the far corners of the Greco-Roman world, so am I compelled to carry the gospel of freedom beyond my own home town. Like Paul, I must constantly respond to the Macedonian call for aid.

4   Moreover, I am cognizant of the interrelatedness of all communities and states. I cannot sit idly by in Atlanta and not be concerned about what happens in Birmingham. Injustice anywhere is a threat to justice everywhere. We are caught in an inescapable network of mutuality, tied in a single garment of destiny. Whatever affects one directly, affects all indirectly. Never again can we afford to live with the narrow, provincial, "outside agitator" idea. Anyone who lives inside the United States can never be considered an outsider anywhere within its bounds.

          You deplore the demonstrations taking place in Birmingham. But your statement, I am sorry to say, fails to express a similar concern for the conditions that brought about the demonstrations. I am sure that none of you would want to rest content with the superficial kind of social analysis that deals merely with effects and does not grapple with underlying causes. It is unfortunate that demonstrations are taking place in Birmingham, but it is even more unfortunate that the city's white power structure left the Negro community with no alternative.

6   In any nonviolent campaign there are four basic steps: collection of the facts to determine whether injustices exist; negotiation; self-purification; and direct action. We have gone through all these steps in Birmingham. There can be no gainsaying the fact that racial injustice engulfs this community. Birmingham is probably the most thoroughly segregated city in the United States. Its ugly record of brutality is widely known. Negroes have experienced grossly unjust treatment in courts. There have been more unsolved bombings of Negro homes and churches in Birmingham than in any other city in the nation. These are the hard, brutal facts of the case. On the basis of these conditions, Negro leaders sought to negotiate with the city fathers. But the latter consistently refused to engage in good-faith negotiation.

Then, last September, came the opportunity to talk with leaders of Birmingham's economic community. In the course of the negotiations, certain promises were made by the merchants—for example, to remove the stores' humiliating racial signs. On the basis of these promises, the Reverend Fred Shuttlesworth and the leaders of the Alabama Christian Movement for Human Rights agreed to a moratorium on all demonstrations. As the weeks and months went by, we realized that we were the victims of a broken promise. A few signs, briefly removed, returned; the others remained.

8   As in so many past experiences, our hopes had been blasted, and the shadow of deep disappointment settled upon us. We had no alternative except to prepare for direct action, whereby we would present our very bodies as means of laying our case before the conscience of the local and the national community. Mindful of the difficulties involved, we decided to undertake a process of self-purification. We began a series of workshops on nonviolence, and we repeatedly asked ourselves: "Are you able to accept blows without retaliating?" "Are you able to endure the ordeal of jail?" We decided to schedule our direct-action program for the Easter season, realizing that except for Christmas, this is the main shopping period of the year. Knowing that a strong economic-withdrawal program would be the by-product of direct action, we felt that this would be the best time to bring pressure to bear on the merchants for the needed change.

Then it occurred to us that Birmingham's mayoral election was coming up in March, and we speedily decided to postpone action until after election day. When we discovered that the Commissioner of Public Safety, Eugene "Bull" Connor,* had piled up enough votes to be in the run-off, we decided again to postpone action until the day after the run-off so that the demonstrations could not be used to cloud the issues. Like many others, we waited to see Mr. Connor defeated, and to this end we endured postponement after postponement. Having aided in this community need, we felt that our direct-action program could be delayed no longer.

10   You may well ask, "Why direct action? Why sit-ins, marches, and so forth? Isn't negotiation a better path?" You are quite right in calling for negotiation. Indeed, this is the very purpose of direct action. Nonviolent direct action seeks to create such a crisis and foster such a tension that a community which has constantly refused to negotiate is forced to confront the issue. It seeks so to dramatize the issue that it can no longer be ignored. My citing the creation of tension as part of the work of the nonviolent-resister may sound rather shocking. But I must confess that I am not afraid of the word "tension." I have earnestly opposed violent tension, but there is a type of constructive, nonviolent tension which is necessary for growth. Just as Socrates felt that it was necessary to create a tension in the mind so that individuals could rise from the bondage of myths and half-truths to the unfettered realm of creative analysis and objective appraisal, so must we see the need for nonviolent gadflies to create the kind of tension in society that

---

* A powerful opponent of integration, Connor (1897–1973) used police force against civil rights demonstrators.

will help men rise from the dark depths of prejudice and racism to the majestic heights of understanding and brotherhood.

The purpose of our direct-action program is to create a situation so crisis-packed that it will inevitably open the door to negotiation. I therefore concur with you in your call for negotiation. Too long has our beloved Southland been bogged down in a tragic effort to live in monologue rather than dialogue.

12   One of the basic points in your statement is that the action that I and my associates have taken in Birmingham is untimely. Some have asked: "Why didn't you give the new city administration time to act?" The only answer that I can give to this query is that the new Birmingham administration must be prodded about as much as the outgoing one, before it will act. We are sadly mistaken if we feel that the election of Albert Boutwell as mayor will bring the millennium to Birmingham. While Mr. Boutwell is a much more gentle person than Mr. Connor, they are both segregationists, dedicated to maintenance of the status quo. I have hoped that Mr. Boutwell will be reasonable enough to see the futility of massive resistance to desegregation. But he will not see this without pressure from devotees of civil rights. My friends, I must say to you that we have not made a single gain in civil rights without determined legal and nonviolent pressure. Lamentably, it is an historical fact that privileged groups seldom give up their privileges voluntarily. Individuals may see the moral light and voluntarily give up their unjust posture; but, as Reinhold Niebuhr has reminded us, groups tend to be more immoral than individuals.

We know through painful experience that freedom is never voluntarily given by the oppressor; it must be demanded by the oppressed. Frankly, I have yet to engage in a direct-action campaign that was "well timed" in the view of those who have not suffered unduly from the disease of segregation. For years now I have heard the word "Wait!" It rings in the ear of every Negro with piercing familiarity. This "Wait" has almost always meant "Never." We must come to see, with one of our distinguished jurists, that "justice too long delayed is justice denied."

14   We have waited for more than 340 years for our constitutional and God-given rights. The nations of Asia and Africa are moving with jetlike speed toward gaining political independence, but we still creep at horse-and-buggy pace toward gaining a cup of coffee at a lunch counter. Perhaps it is easy for those who have never felt the stinging darts of segregation to say, "Wait." But when you have seen vicious mobs lynch your mothers and fathers at will and drown your sisters and brothers at whim; when you have seen hate-filled policemen curse, kick, and even kill your black brothers and sisters; when you see the vast majority of your twenty million Negro brothers smothering in an airtight cage of poverty in the midst of an affluent society; when you suddenly find your tongue twisted and your speech stammering as you seek to explain to your six-year-old daughter why she can't go to the public amusement park that has just been advertised on

television, and see tears welling up in her eyes when she is told that Funtown is closed to colored children, and see ominous clouds of inferiority beginning to form in her little mental sky, and see her beginning to distort her personality by developing an unconscious bitterness toward white people; when you have to concoct an answer for a five-year-old son who is asking, "Daddy, why do white people treat colored people so mean?"; when you take a cross-country drive and find it necessary to sleep night after night in the uncomfortable corners of your automobile because no motel will accept you; when you are humiliated day in and day out by nagging signs reading "white" and "colored"; when your first name becomes "nigger," your middle name becomes "boy" (however old you are) and your last name becomes "John," and your wife and mother are never given the respected title "Mrs."; when you are harried by day and haunted by night by the fact that you are a Negro, living constantly at tiptoe stance, never quite knowing what to expect next, and are plagued with inner fears and outer resentments; when you are forever fighting a degenerating sense of "nobodiness"—then you will understand why we find it difficult to wait. There comes a time when the cup of endurance runs over, and men are no longer willing to be plunged into the abyss of despair. I hope, sirs, you can understand our legitimate and unavoidable impatience.

You express a great deal of anxiety over our willingness to break laws. This is certainly a legitimate concern. Since we so diligently urge people to obey the Supreme Court's decision of 1954 outlawing segregation in the public schools, at first glance it may seem rather paradoxical for us consciously to break laws. One may well ask: "How can you advocate breaking some laws and obeying others?" The answer lies in the fact that there are two types of laws; just and unjust. I would be the first to advocate obeying just laws. One has not only a legal but a moral responsibility to obey just laws. Conversely, one has a moral responsibility to disobey unjust laws. I would agree with St. Augustine that "an unjust law is no law at all."

16   Now, what is the difference between the two? How does one determine whether a law is just or unjust? A just law is a man-made code that squares with the moral law or the law of God. An unjust law is a code that is out of harmony with the moral law. To put it in the terms of St. Thomas Aquinas: An unjust law is a human law that is not rooted in eternal law and natural law. Any law that uplifts human personality is just. Any law that degrades human personality is unjust. All segregation statutes are unjust because segregation distorts the soul and damages the personality. It gives the segregator a false sense of superiority and the segregated a false sense of inferiority. Segregation, to use the terminology of the Jewish philosopher Martin Buber, substitutes an "I–it" relationship for an "I–thou" relationship and ends up relegating persons to the status of things. Hence segregation is not only politically, economically, and sociologically unsound, it is morally wrong and sinful. Paul Tillich has said that sin is segregation. Is not segregation an existential expression of man's tragic separation, his awful estrangement, his terrible sinfulness? Thus it is that I can urge men to obey the 1954

decision of the Supreme Court, for it is morally right; and I can urge them to disobey segregation ordinances, for they are morally wrong.

Let us consider a more concrete example of just and unjust laws. An unjust law is a code that a numerical or power majority group compels a minority group to obey but does not make binding on itself. This is *difference* made legal. By the same token, a just law is a code that a majority compels a minority to follow and that it is willing to follow itself. This is *sameness* made legal.

18   Let me give another explanation. A law is unjust if it is inflicted on a minority that, as a result of being denied the right to vote, had no part in enacting or devising the law. Who can say that the legislature of Alabama which set up that state's segregation laws was democratically elected? Throughout Alabama all sorts of devious methods are used to prevent Negroes from becoming registered voters, and there are some counties in which, even though Negroes constitute a majority of the population, not a single Negro is registered. Can any law enacted under such circumstances be considered democratically structured?

Sometimes a law is just on its face and unjust in its application. For instance, I have been arrested on a charge of parading without a permit. Now, there is nothing wrong in having an ordinance which requires a permit for a parade. But such an ordinance becomes unjust when it is used to maintain segregation and to deny citizens the First-Amendment privilege of peaceful assembly and protest.

20   I hope you are able to see the distinction I am trying to point out. In no sense do I advocate evading or defying the law, as would the rabid segregationist. That would lead to anarchy. One who breaks an unjust law must do so openly, lovingly, and with a willingness to accept the penalty. I submit that an individual who breaks a law that conscience tells him is unjust, and who willingly accepts the penalty of imprisonment in order to arouse the conscience of the community over its injustice, is in reality expressing the highest respect for law.

Of course, there is nothing new about this kind of civil disobedience. It was evidenced sublimely in the refusal of Shadrach, Meshach, and Abednego to obey the laws of Nebuchadnezzar,* on the ground that a higher moral law was at stake. It was practiced superbly by the early Christians, who were willing to face hungry lions and the excruciating pain of chopping blocks rather than submit to certain unjust laws of the Roman Empire. To a degree, academic freedom is a reality today because Socrates practiced civil disobedience. In our own nation, the Boston Tea Party represented a massive act of civil disobedience.

---

* Nebuchadnezzar, King of Babylon, destroyed the temple at Jerusalem and brought the Jewish people into captivity. He set up a huge image in gold and commanded all to worship it. Shadrach, Meshach, and Abednego refused and were thrown into a fiery furnace from which they emerged unscathed. (See Daniel:3.)

22   We should never forget that everything Adolf Hitler did in Germany was "legal" and everything the Hungarian freedom fighters did in Hungary was "illegal."* It was "illegal" to aid and comfort a Jew in Hitler's Germany. Even so, I am sure that, had I lived in Germany at the time, I would have aided and comforted my Jewish brothers. If today I lived in a Communist country where certain principles dear to the Christian faith are suppressed, I would openly advocate disobeying that country's anti-religious laws.

I must make two honest confessions to you, my Christian and Jewish brothers. First, I must confess that over the past few years I have been gravely disappointed with the white moderate. I have almost reached the regrettable conclusion that the Negro's great stumbling block in his stride toward freedom is not the White Citizen's Counciler or the Ku Klux Klanner, but the white moderate, who is more devoted to "order" than to justice; who prefers a negative peace which is the absence of tension to a positive peace which is the presence of justice; who constantly says, "I agree with you in the goal you seek, but I cannot agree with your methods of direct action"; who paternalistically believes he can set the timetable for another man's freedom; who lives by a mythical concept of time and who constantly advises the Negro to wait for a "more convenient season." Shallow understanding from people of good will is more frustrating than absolute misunderstanding from people of ill will. Lukewarm acceptance is much more bewildering than outright rejection.

24   I had hoped that the white moderate would understand that law and order exist for the purpose of establishing justice and that when they fail in this purpose they become the dangerously structured dams that block the flow of social progress. I had hoped that the white moderate would understand that the present tension in the South is a necessary phase of the transition from an obnoxious negative peace, in which the Negro passively accepted his unjust plight, to a substantive and positive peace, in which all men will respect the dignity and worth of human personality. Actually, we who engage in nonviolent direct action are not the creators of tension. We merely bring to the surface the hidden tension that is already alive. We bring it out in the open, where it can be seen and dealt with. Like a boil that can never be cured so long as it is covered up but must be opened with all its ugliness to the natural medicines of air and light, injustice must be exposed, with all the tension its exposure creates, to the light of human conscience and the air of national opinion, before it can be cured.

In your statement you assert that our actions, even though peaceful, must be condemned because they precipitate violence. But is this a logical assertion? Isn't this like condemning a robbed man because his possession of money precipitated the evil act of robbery? Isn't this like condemning Socrates because his unswerving commitment to truth and his philosophical

---

* In 1956, Hungarian citizens temporarily overthrew the communist dictatorship in their country. Unwilling to confront the Soviet Union, western democracies stood by when the Red Army suppressed the revolt.

inquiries precipitated the act by the misguided populace in which they made him drink hemlock? Isn't this like condemning Jesus because his unique God-consciousness and never-ceasing devotion to God's will precipitated the evil act of crucifixion? We must come to see that, as the federal courts have consistently affirmed, it is wrong to urge an individual to cease his efforts to gain his basic constitutional rights because the quest may precipitate violence. Society must protect the robbed and punish the robber.

26   I had also hoped that the white moderate would reject the myth concerning time in relation to the struggle for freedom. I have just received a letter from a white brother in Texas. He writes: "All Christians know that the colored people will receive equal rights eventually, but it is possible that you are in too great a religious hurry. It has taken Christianity almost two thousand years to accomplish what it has. The teachings of Christ take time to come to earth." Such an attitude stems from a tragic misconception of time, from the strangely irrational notion that there is something in the very flow of time that will inevitably cure all ills. Actually, time itself is neutral; it can be used either destructively or constructively. More and more I feel that the people of ill will have used time much more effectively than have the people of good will. We will have to repent in this generation not merely for the hateful words and actions of the bad people, but for the appalling silence of the good people. Human progress never rolls in on wheels of inevitability; it comes through the tireless efforts of men willing to be coworkers with God, and without this hard work, time itself becomes an ally of the forces of social stagnation. We must use time creatively, in the knowledge that the time is always ripe to do right. Now is the time to make real the promise of democracy and transform our pending national elegy into a creative psalm of brotherhood. Now is the time to lift our national policy from the quicksand of racial injustice to the solid rock of human dignity.

You speak of our activity in Birmingham as extreme. At first I was rather disappointed that fellow clergymen would see my nonviolent efforts as those of an extremist. I began thinking about the fact that I stand in the middle of two opposing forces in the Negro community. One is a force of complacency, made up in part of Negroes who, as a result of long years of oppression, are so drained of self-respect and a sense of "somebodiness" that they have adjusted to segregation; and in part of a few middle-class Negroes who, because of a degree of academic and economic security and because in some ways they profit by segregation, have become insensitive to the problems of the masses. The other force is one of bitterness and hatred, and it comes perilously close to advocating violence. It is expressed in the various black nationalist groups that are springing up across the nation, the largest and best-known being Elijah Muhammad's Muslim movement. Nourished by the Negro's frustration over the continued existence of racial discrimination, this movement is made up of people who have lost faith in America, who have absolutely repudiated Christianity, and who have concluded that the white man is an incorrigible "devil."

28   I have tried to stand between these two forces, saying that we need emulate neither the "do-nothingism" of the complacent nor the hatred and

despair of the black nationalist. For there is the more excellent way of love and nonviolent protest. I am grateful to God that, through the influence of the Negro church, the way of nonviolence became an integral part of our struggle.

If this philosophy had not emerged, by now many streets of the South would, I am convinced, be flowing with blood. And I am further convinced that if our white brothers dismiss as "rabble-rousers" and "outside agitators" those of us who employ nonviolent direct action, and if they refuse to support our nonviolent efforts, millions of Negroes will, out of frustration and despair, seek solace and security in black-nationalist ideologies—a development that would inevitably lead to a frightening racial nightmare.

30   Oppressed people cannot remain oppressed forever. The yearning for freedom eventually manifests itself, and that is what has happened to the American Negro. Something within has reminded him of his birthright of freedom, and something without has reminded him that it can be gained. Consciously or unconsciously, he has been caught up by the *Zeitgeist*,* and with his black brothers of Africa and his brown and yellow brothers of Asia, South America, and the Caribbean, the United States Negro is moving with a sense of great urgency toward the promised land of racial justice. If one recognizes this vital urge that has engulfed the Negro community, one should readily understand why public demonstrations are taking place. The Negro has many pent-up resentments and latent frustrations, and he must release them. So let him march; let him make prayer pilgrimages to the city hall; let him go on freedom rides—and try to understand why he must do so. If his repressed emotions are not released in nonviolent ways, they will seek expression through violence; this is not a threat but a fact of history. So I have not said to my people, "Get rid of your discontent." Rather, I have tried to say that this normal and healthy discontent can be channeled into the creative outlet of nonviolent direct action. And now this approach is being termed extremist.

But though I was initially disappointed at being categorized as an extremist, as I continued to think about the matter I gradually gained a measure of satisfaction from the label. Was not Jesus an extremist for love: "Love your enemies, bless them that curse you, do good to them that hate you, and pray for them which despitefully use you, and persecute you." Was not Amos an extremist for justice: "Let justice roll down like waters and righteousness like an everflowing stream." Was not Paul an extremist for the Christian gospel: "I bear in my body the marks of the Lord Jesus." Was not Martin Luther an extremist: "Here I stand; I cannot do otherwise, so help me God." And John Bunyan:† "I will stay in jail to the end of my days before I make a butchery of my conscience." And Abraham Lincoln: "This nation cannot survive half slave and half free." And Thomas Jefferson: "We hold these truths to be self-evident, that all men are created equal. . . . " So

---

* German for "the spirit of the times."

† An important English writer of the seventeenth century, John Bunyan (1628–1688) is best known for his Christian allegory *Pilgrim's Progress from This World to That Which Is to Come.*

the question is not whether we will be extremists, but what kind of extremists we will be. Will we be extremists for hate or for love? Will we be extremists for the preservation of injustice or for the extension of justice? In that dramatic scene on Calvary's hill three men were crucified. We must never forget that all three were crucified for the same crime—the crime of extremism. Two were extremists for immorality, and thus fell below their environment. The other, Jesus Christ, was an extremist for love, truth, and goodness, and thereby rose above his environment. Perhaps the South, the nation, and the world are in dire need of creative extremists.

32   I had hoped that the white moderate would see this need. Perhaps I was too optimistic; perhaps I expected too much. I suppose I should have realized that few members of the oppressor race can understand the deep groans and passionate yearnings of the oppressed race, and still fewer have the vision to see that injustice must be rooted out by strong, persistent, and determined action. I am thankful, however, that some of our white brothers in the South have grasped the meaning of this social revolution and committed themselves to it. They are still all too few in quantity, but they are big in quality. Some—such as Ralph McGill, Lillian Smith, Harry Golden, James McBride Dabbs, Ann Braden, and Sarah Patton Boyle—have written about our struggle in eloquent and prophetic terms. Others have marched with us down nameless streets of the South. They have languished in filthy, roach-infested jails, suffering the abuse and brutality of policemen who view them as "dirty nigger-lovers." Unlike so many of their moderate brothers and sisters, they have recognized the urgency of the moment and sensed the need for powerful "action" antidotes to combat the disease of segregation.

Let me take note of my other major disappointment. I have been so greatly disappointed with the white church and its leadership. Of course, there are some notable exceptions. I am not unmindful of the fact that each of you has taken some significant stands on this issue. I commend you, Reverend Stallings, for your Christian stand on this past Sunday, in welcoming Negroes to your worship service on a nonsegregated basis. I commend the Catholic leaders of this state for integrating Spring Hill College several years ago.

34   But despite these notable exceptions, I must honestly reiterate that I have been disappointed with the church. I do not say this as one of those negative critics who can always find something wrong with the church. I say this as a minister of the gospel, who loves the church; who was nurtured in its bosom; who has been sustained by its spiritual blessings and who will remain true to it as long as the cord of life shall lengthen.

When I was suddenly catapulted into the leadership of the bus protest in Montgomery, Alabama, a few years ago, I felt we would be supported by the white church. I felt that the white ministers, priests, and rabbis of the South would be among our strongest allies. Instead, some have been outright opponents, refusing to understand the freedom movement and misrepresenting its leaders; all too many others have been more cautious than courageous and have remained silent behind the anesthetizing security of stained-glass windows.

36   In spite of my shattered dreams, I came to Birmingham with the hope that the white religious leadership of this community would see the justice of our cause and, with deep moral concern, would serve as the channel through which our just grievances could reach the power structure. I had hoped that each of you would understand. But again I have been disappointed.

There was a time when the church was very powerful—in the time when the early Christians rejoiced at being deemed worthy to suffer for what they believed. In those days the church was not merely a thermometer that recorded the ideas and principles of popular opinion; it was a thermostat that transformed the mores of society. Whenever the early Christians entered a town, the people in power became disturbed and immediately sought to convict the Christians for being "disturbers of the peace" and "outside agitators." But the Christians pressed on, in the conviction that they were "a colony of heaven," called to obey God rather than man. Small in number, they were big in commitment. They were too God-intoxicated to be "astronomically intimidated." By their effort and example they brought an end to such ancient evils as infanticide and gladiatorial contests.

38   Things are different now. So often the contemporary church is a weak, ineffectual voice with an uncertain sound. So often it is an archdefender of the status quo. Far from being disturbed by the presence of the church, the power structure of the average community is consoled by the church's silent—and often even vocal— sanction of things as they are.

But the judgment of God is upon the church as never before. If today's church does not recapture the sacrificial spirit of the early church, it will lose its authenticity, forfeit the loyalty of millions, and be dismissed as an irrelevant social club with no meaning for the twentieth century. Every day I meet young people whose disappointment with the church has turned into outright disgust.

40   Perhaps I have once again been too optimistic. Is organized religion too inextricably bound to the status quo to save our nation and the world? Perhaps I must turn my faith to the inner spiritual church, the church within the church, as the true *ekklesia* and the hope of the world. But again I am thankful to God that some noble souls from the ranks of organized religion have broken loose from the paralyzing chains of conformity and joined us as active partners in the struggle for freedom. They have left their secure congregations and walked the streets of Albany, Georgia, with us. They have gone down the highways of the South on torturous rides for freedom. Yes, they have gone to jail with us. Some have been dismissed from their churches, have lost the support of their bishops and fellow ministers. But they have acted in the faith that right defeated is stronger than evil triumphant. Their witness has been the spiritual salt that has preserved the true meaning of the gospel in these troubled times. They have carved a tunnel of hope through the dark mountain of disappointment.

I hope the church as a whole will meet the challenge of this decisive hour. But even if the church does not come to the aid of justice, I have no despair about the future. I have no fear about the outcome of our struggle in Birmingham, even if our motives are at present misunderstood. We will reach the goal of freedom in Birmingham and all over the nation, because the goal of America is freedom. Abused and scorned though we may be, our destiny is tied up with America's destiny. Before the pilgrims landed at Plymouth, we were here. Before the pen of Jefferson etched the majestic words of the Declaration of Independence across the pages of history, we were here. For more than two centuries our forebears labored in this country without wages; they made cotton king; they built the homes of their masters while suffering gross injustice and shameful humiliation—and yet out of a bottomless vitality they continued to thrive and develop. If the inexpressible cruelties of slavery could not stop us, the opposition we now face will surely fail. We will win our freedom because the sacred heritage of our nation and the eternal will of God are embodied in our echoing demands.

42   Before closing I feel impelled to mention one other point in your statement that has troubled me profoundly. You warmly commended the Birmingham police force for keeping "order" and "preventing violence." I doubt that you would have so warmly commended the police force if you had seen its dogs sinking their teeth into unarmed, nonviolent Negroes. I doubt that you would so quickly commend the policemen if you were to observe their ugly and inhumane treatment of Negroes here in the city jail; if you were to watch them push and curse old Negro women and young Negro girls; if you were to see them slap and kick old Negro men and young boys; if you were to observe them, as they did on two occasions, refuse to give us food because we wanted to sing our grace together. I cannot join you in your praise of the Birmingham police department.

It is true that the police have exercised a degree of discipline in handling the demonstrators. In this sense they have conducted themselves rather "nonviolently" in public. But for what purpose? To preserve the evil system of segregation. Over the past few years I have consistently preached that nonviolence demands that the means we use must be as pure as the ends we seek. I have tried to make clear that it is wrong to use immoral means to attain moral ends. But now I must affirm that it is just as wrong, or perhaps even more so, to use moral means to preserve immoral ends. Perhaps Mr. Connor and his policemen have been rather nonviolent in public, as was Chief Pritchett in Albany, Georgia, but they have used the moral means of nonviolence to maintain the immoral end of racial injustice. As T. S. Eliot has said, "The last temptation is the greatest treason: To do the right deed for the wrong reason."

44   I wish you had commended the Negro sit-inners and demonstrators of Birmingham for their sublime courage, their willingness to suffer, and their amazing discipline in the midst of great provocation. One day the South will recognize its real heroes. They will be the James Merediths, with the noble sense of purpose that enables them to face jeering and hostile mobs, and with the agonizing loneliness that characterizes the life of the pioneer. They will be old, oppressed, battered Negro women, symbolized in a seventy-two-year-old woman in Montgomery, Alabama, who rose up with a sense of dignity and with her people decided not to ride segregated buses,

and who responded with ungrammatical profundity to one who inquired about her weariness: "My feets is tired, but my soul is at rest." They will be the young high school and college students, the young ministers of the gospel and a host of their elders, courageously and nonviolently sitting in at lunch counters and willingly going to jail for conscience's sake. One day the South will know that when these disinherited children of God sat down at lunch counters, they were in reality standing up for what is best in the American dream and for the most sacred values in our Judeo-Christian heritage, thereby bringing our nation back to those great wells of democracy which were dug deep by the founding fathers in their formulation of the Constitution and the Declaration of Independence.

Never before have I written so long a letter. I'm afraid it is much too long to take your precious time. I can assure you that it would have been much shorter if I had been writing from a comfortable desk, but what else can one do when he is alone in a narrow jail cell, other than write long letters, think long thoughts, and pray long prayers?

46   If I have said anything in this letter that overstates the truth and indicates an unreasonable impatience, I beg you to forgive me. If I have said anything that understates the truth and indicates my having a patience that allows me to settle for anything less than brotherhood, I beg God to forgive me.

I hope this letter finds you strong in the faith. I also hope that circumstances will soon make it possible for me to meet each of you, not as an integrationist or a civil-rights leader but as a fellow clergyman and a Christian brother. Let us all hope that the dark clouds of racial prejudice will soon pass away and the deep fog of misunderstanding will be lifted from our fear-drenched communities, and in some not too distant tomorrow the radiant stars of love and brotherhood will shine over our great nation with all their scintillating beauty.

Yours for the cause of Peace and Brotherhood,
Martin Luther King, Jr.   ❖

Questions for Meaning

1. What reason does King give for writing this letter? What justification does he provide for its length? How do these explanations work to his advantage?
2. One of the many charges brought against King at the time of his arrest was that he was an "outsider" who had no business in Birmingham. How does King defend himself? What three reasons does he cite to justify his presence in Birmingham?
3. King also responds to the criticism that his campaign for civil rights was "untimely." What is his defense against this charge?

4. What does King mean by nonviolent "direct action"? What sort of activities did he lead people to pursue? Identify the four basic steps to a direct-action campaign and explain what such campaigns were meant to accomplish.
5. Why did King believe that a direct-action campaign was necessary in Birmingham? Why did the black community in Birmingham turn to King? What problems were they facing, and what methods had they already tried before deciding on direct action?
6. What was the 1954 Supreme Court decision that King refers to in paragraph 16? Why was King able to charge that the "rabid segregationist" breaks the law?
7. King's critics charged that he obeyed the law selectively. He answers by arguing there is a difference between just and unjust laws, and that moral law requires men and women to break unjust laws that are imposed on them. How can you tell the difference between laws that you should honor and laws that you should break? What is King's definition of an unjust law, and what historical examples does he give to illustrate situations in which unjust laws have to be broken?
8. What does King mean, in paragraph 35, when he complains of the "anesthetizing security of stained-glass windows"? How can churches make men and women feel falsely secure?

Questions about Strategy

1. Why did King address his letter to fellow clergymen? Why was he disappointed in them, and what did he expect his letter to accomplish?
2. Is there anything in the substance of this letter that reveals it was written for an audience familiar with the Bible and modern theology? Do you think King intended this letter to be read only by clergy? Can you point to anything that suggests King may have really written for a larger audience?
3. How does King characterize himself in this letter? What sort of a man does he seem to be, and what role does his presentation of himself play in his argument? How does he establish that he is someone worth listening to—and that it is important to listen to what he has to say?
4. *Ekklesia* is Greek for assembly, congregation, or church. Why does King use this word in paragraph 40 instead of simply saying "the church"?
5. Martin Luther King had much experience as a preacher when he wrote this famous letter. Is there anything about its style that reminds you of oratory? How effective would this letter be if delivered as a speech?

BETTY FRIEDAN

THE IMPORTANCE OF WORK

Betty Friedan was one of the founders of the National Organization for Women, serving as NOW's first president between 1966 and 1970. Born in Peoria, Illinois, and educated at Smith College, the University of California, and the University of Iowa, Friedan has lectured at more than fifty universities and institutes. Her essays have appeared in numerous periodicals, including the *Saturday Review, Harper's, McCall's, Redbook,* and the *Ladies' Home Journal.* Her books include *It Changed My Life* (1976), *The Second Stage* (1981), and *The Fountain of Age* (1993).

"The Importance of Work" is drawn from the book that made her famous, *The Feminine Mystique* (1963). More than a quarter of a century has now passed since Friedan published this book, and the leadership of the women's movement has passed to a younger generation. But if the development of that movement could be traced back to the publication of a single work, it would have to be *The Feminine Mystique.* Friedan believed that women needed to escape from the roles they had assumed as wives and mothers, and if her ideas no longer seem as bold as they once were, it is because she anticipated many of the concerns that would dominate the analysis of male/female relations during the 1970s and 1980s. "The Importance of Work" is an editor's title for the concluding pages of Friedan's book, an excerpt that reveals Friedan's conviction that women need to enter the mainstream of the American workforce—not simply as typists and file clerks, but as the full equals of men.

The question of how a person can most fully realize his own capacities and thus achieve identity has become an important concern of the philosophers and the social and psychological thinkers of our time—and for good reason. Thinkers of other times put forth the idea that people were, to a great extent, defined by the work they did. The work that a man had to do to eat, to stay alive, to meet the physical necessities of his environment, dictated his identity. And in this sense, when work was seen merely as a means of survival, human identity was dictated by biology.

2   But today the problem of human identity has changed. For the work that defined man's place in society and his sense of himself has also changed man's world. Work, and the advance of knowledge, has lessened man's dependence on his environment; his biology and the work he must do for biological survival are no longer sufficient to define his identity. This can be most clearly seen in our own abundant society; men no longer need to work all day to eat. They have an unprecedented freedom to choose the kind of work they will do; they also have an unprecedented amount of time apart from the hours and days that must actually be spent in making a living. And

suddenly one realizes the significance of today's identity crisis—for women, and increasingly, for men. One sees the human significance of work—not merely as the means of biological survival, but as the giver of self and the transcender of self, as the creator of human identity and human evolution.

For "self-realization" or "self-fulfillment" or "identity" does not come from looking into a mirror in rapt contemplation of one's own image. Those who have most fully realized themselves, in a sense that can be recognized by the human mind even though it cannot be clearly defined, have done so in the service of a human purpose larger than themselves. Men from varying disciplines have used different words for this mysterious process from which comes the sense of self. The religious mystics, the philosophers, Marx, Freud—all had different names for it: man finds himself by losing himself; man is defined by his relation to the means of production; the ego, the self, grows through understanding and mastering reality— through work and love.

4   The identity crisis, which has been noted by Erik Erikson* and others in recent years in the American man, seems to occur for lack of, and be cured by finding, the work, or cause, or purpose that evokes his own creativity. Some never find it, for it does not come from busy-work or punching a time clock. It does not come from just making a living, working by formula, finding a secure spot as an organization man. The very argument, by Riesman and others, that man no longer finds identity in the work defined as a paycheck job, assumes that identity for man comes through creative work of his own that contributes to the human community: the core of the self becomes aware, becomes real, and grows through work that carries forward human society.

Work, the shopworn staple of the economists, has become the new frontier of psychology. Psychiatrists have long used "occupational therapy" with patients in mental hospitals; they have recently discovered that to be of real psychological value, it must be not just "therapy," but real work, serving a real purpose in the community. And work can now be seen as the key to the problem that has no name. The identity crisis of American women began a century ago, as more and more of the work important to the world, more and more of the work that used their human abilities and through which they were able to find self-realization, was taken from them.

6   Until, and even into, the last century, strong, capable women were needed to pioneer our new land; with their husbands, they ran the farms and plantations and Western homesteads. These women were respected and self-respecting members of a society whose pioneering purpose centered in the home. Strength and independence, responsibility and self-confidence, self-discipline and courage, freedom and equality were part of the American character for both men and women, in all the first generations. The women who came by steerage from Ireland, Italy, Russia, and Poland worked beside

---

* Trained by Sigmund and Anna Freud, Erik Erikson (1902–1994) was an influencial American psychoanalyst and writer best known for *Childhood and Society* (1950).

their husbands in the sweatshops and the laundries, learned the new language, and saved to send their sons and daughters to college. Women were never quite as "feminine," or held in as much contempt, in America as they were in Europe. American women seemed to European travelers, long before our time, less passive, childlike, and feminine than their own wives in France or Germany or England. By an accident of history, American women shared in the work of society longer, and grew with the men. Grade- and high-school education for boys and girls alike was almost always the rule; and in the West, where women shared the pioneering work the longest, even the universities were coeducational from the beginning.

The identity crisis for women did not begin in America until the fire and strength and ability of the pioneer women were no longer needed, no longer used, in the middle-class homes of the Eastern and Midwestern cities, when the pioneering was done and men began to build the new society in industries and professions outside the home. But the daughters of the pioneer women had grown too used to freedom and work to be content with leisure and passive femininity.

8   It was not an American, but a South African woman, Mrs. Olive Schreiner, who warned at the turn of the century that the quality and quantity of women's functions in the social universe were decreasing as fast as civilization was advancing; that if women did not win back their right to a full share of honored and useful work, woman's mind and muscle would weaken in a parasitic state; her offspring, male and female, would weaken progressively, and civilization itself would deteriorate.

The feminists saw clearly that education and the right to participate in the more advanced work of society were women's greatest needs. They fought for and won the rights to new, fully human identity for women. But how very few of their daughters and granddaughters have chosen to use their education and their abilities for any large creative purpose, for responsible work in society? How many of them have been deceived, or have deceived themselves, into clinging to the outgrown, childlike femininity of "Occupation: housewife"?

10   It was not a minor matter, their mistaken choice. We now know that the same range of potential ability exists for women as for men. Women, as well as men, can only find their identity in work that uses their full capacities. A woman cannot find her identity through others—her husband, her children. She cannot find it in the dull routine of housework. As thinkers of every age have said, it is only when a human being faces squarely the fact that he can forfeit his own life, that he becomes truly aware of himself, and begins to take his existence seriously. Sometimes this awareness comes only at the moment of death. Sometimes it comes from a more subtle facing of death: the death of self in passive conformity, in meaningless work. The feminine mystique prescribes just such a living death for women. Faced with the slow death of self, the American woman must begin to take her life seriously.

"We measure ourselves by many standards," said the great American psychologist William James, nearly a century ago. "Our strength and our intelligence, our wealth and even our good luck, are things which warm our heart and make us feel ourselves a match for life. But deeper than all such things, and able to suffice unto itself without them, is the sense of the amount of effort which we can put forth."

12   If women do not put forth, finally, that effort to become all that they have it in them to become, they will forfeit their own humanity. A woman today who has no goal, no purpose, no ambition patterning her days into the future, making her stretch and grow beyond that small score of years in which her body can fill its biological function, is committing a kind of suicide. For that future half a century after the child-bearing years are over is a fact that an American woman cannot deny. Nor can she deny that as a housewife, the world is indeed rushing past her door while she just sits and watches. The terror she feels is real, if she has no place in that world.

The feminine mystique has succeeded in burying millions of American women alive. There is no way for these women to break out of their comfortable concentration camps except by finally putting forth an effort—that human effort which reaches beyond biology, beyond the narrow walls of home, to help shape the future. Only by such a personal commitment to the future can American women break out of the housewife trap and truly find fulfillment as wives and mothers—by fulfilling their own unique possibilities as separate human beings.   ❖

Questions for Meaning

1. In her opening paragraph, Friedan writes, "when work was seen merely as a means of survival, human identity was dictated by biology." What does this mean?
2. Does Friedan believe that all types of work are equally satisfying? Where does she define the type of work that has "human significance"?
3. According to Friedan, what is the historical explanation for the identity crisis many American women suffered during the twentieth century?
4. What's wrong with "Occupation: housewife"? Why does Friedan believe that women cannot find fulfillment simply by being wives and mothers?
5. Explain Friedan's allusion to "feminists" in paragraph 9. Who were the early feminists, and what did they accomplish?
6. Although you have been given only the last few pages of Friedan's book, can you construct a definition for what she means by "the feminine mystique"?
7. Vocabulary: transcender (2), rapt (3), mystics (3), parasitic (8), deteriorate (8), forfeit (10).

Questions about Strategy

1. What is the premise that underlies Friedan's argument on behalf of meaningful careers for women?
2. Why does Friedan discuss women within the context of psychological "identity"? Why is it important for her to link the needs of women with the needs of men?
3. Comment on Friedan's use of quotation. She refers, for support, to four men (Marx, Freud, Erik Erikson, and William James) and to only one woman, Olive Schreiner. Does her reliance on male authorities help or hurt her argument?
4. When Friedan declares that housewives are "committing a kind of suicide" trapped within homes that are "comfortable concentration camps," is she drawing her work together with a forceful conclusion or weakening it through exaggeration?

SUGGESTIONS FOR WRITING

1. Write a dialogue between Plato and Machiavelli on the question of how society should be governed.
2. Using "A Modest Proposal" as your model, write a satirical essay proposing a "solution" to a contemporary social problem other than poverty.
3. As a counterargument to Thomas Jefferson, write "A Declaration of Continued Dependence" from the point of view of George III.
4. Drawing on the work of Mary Wollstonecraft, Margaret Sanger, and Betty Friedan, write a "Declaration of Independence for Women."
5. Marxism seems to have lost most of the appeal it once enjoyed. Evaluate *The Communist Manifesto* in the light of twentieth-century history. Is it entirely out of date or does it advance principles that can still be of use?
6. Respond to Charlotte Perkins Gilman by arguing for the principle you believe is the most important when raising children.
7. Write a dialogue between Margaret Sanger and Mahatma Gandhi on the subject of birth control.
8. Compare the propaganda posters reprinted on pages 679 and 680. How do they reflect the principles outlined by Adolf Hitler in "The Purpose of Propaganda"? Explain the strategy behind each of these posters and determine their relative effectiveness.
9. Research and report on the conditions in Germany that helped Hitler rise to power.
10. Drawing on the work of Carl Rogers, and other research if necessary, write an essay defining what it takes to be a good listener.
11. Research the influence of Carl Rogers on the teaching of argument, and write a synthesis of what you discover.

12. Investigate the fertilizers and pesticides most frequently used by farmers today, and report on the effect they have on the environment.
13. Compare the current condition of a local river, lake, or forest with how it appeared a generation ago.
14. Write a summary of "Letter from Birmingham Jail."
15. Drawing on "Letter from Birmingham Jail," defend an illegal act that you would be willing to commit in order to advance a cause in which you believe.

COLLABORATIVE PROJECT

Form a writing group and decide what roles members want to play in creating a dialogue among Plato, Thomas Jefferson, Adolf Hitler, Martin Luther King, and Betty Friedan. Focus the dialogue on what it means to be free and how freedom can be achieved.

FIGURE 1

Figure 1 is an example of an English poster from the First World War (1914–1919). Figure 2 is a Nazi election poster from the early 1930s. It reads, "Work and Bread through List One." (List One refers to the position of Nazi candidates on the ballot before Hitler seized power.) Figure 3 is a Nazi propaganda poster used in Poland after the German invasion of that country in 1939. The caption, in Polish, reads: "England! This is your work!" The picture shows a wounded Polish soldier pointing to the ruins of Warsaw and addressing Neville Chamberlain, the British Prime Minister at the beginning of the war.

FIGURE 2

FIGURE 3

APPENDIX

SAMPLE RESEARCHED PAPER USING
MLA-STYLE DOCUMENTATION

The following paper was written by a student using the search strategy illustrated in Part 3, "A Guide to Research" (pages 93–120). As his thesis evolved through successive drafts, the author eliminated several sources he had expected to include and located others which better suited his needs. As you read "Crack, Crime, and Kids," note how research data is used to support an argument on behalf of a specific approach to drug-related crime—which is very different from reporting data as an end in itself. Although John Smith draws upon several sources to support his case, the paper as a whole reflects what he came to think as the result of his research.

1″——

}½″

Smith 1

John T. Smith
Professor Miller
English 252
6 March 1997

Double space

Crack, Crime, and Kids: Therapeutic Communities
Provide Hope for Troubled Adolescents

Marcus, as I will call him, is a fifteen-year-old crack-cocaine dealer growing up in New York City. He learned how to get into cars, how to break into places, how to pick locks. More importantly, he learned who to trust and who would shoot him in the back. Hector is another adolescent who was brought into the world of drugs and crime by his older brothers. His brothers told him they couldn't live without the drugs. Only eleven, he is subjected to pressure not only to experiment with crack, but to act as a lookout for the family business. One year older, Lucy is a child also influenced by drugs and crime. The only person she trusts is her source, and she doesn't even know his name. She admits that they mess people up who get in their way. However, if she doesn't make her sales, the dealers will come after her.[1]

Student opens with examples to engage the attention of readers

Reference to content note providing additional information

Evidence suggests that problems such as these will only magnify for adolescents as they get older. Each is only one of thousands of adolescents who will be put through countless court hearings and probation sentences before eventually being imprisoned (Hawkins 151). Dr. James Inciardi, of the University of Delaware, has studied hundreds of individuals who have committed serious crimes; working together with Ruth Horowitz and Anne Pottieger, he found a direct relationship between adolescent drug use and delinquency.[2] All of the youths interviewed had extensive histories of crime and drug involvement—of the 611 adolescents, 96% engaged in drug involvement and theft, with twelve the average starting age for both offenses. During the year prior to the interviews, they were responsible for some 18,477 major felonies (Inciardi, Horowitz, and Pottieger 173). This number is staggering. Moreover, because such adolescents are unlikely to break this pattern, they may be

Student establishes the problem that needs to be solved

Student summarizes an important study

A source by three authors

1″

Smith 2

responsible for a much greater number of felonies as they age
into adulthood (Greenwood 453).

In a pattern similar to the classic addictive drug cycle,
drug dealing finances use, use encourages more use, and more
use requires more profit, increasing crimes of all sorts to
support an ever-growing, addicting use pattern. Until the
1980s, this cycle was much less common among adolescents for
two reasons: First, they did not commonly use addictive drugs
with potentially high financial obligations; and second,
adults severely limited the involvement of adolescents in
drug-marketing networks. The advent of crack changed both of
these factors.

> Student establishes why the drug problem has gotten worse

Crack is so widely available that twelve-year-olds have
no problem finding it, and so powerful and short-acting that
it is both rapidly addicting and unlimited in its potential
financial requirements. An important feature is its low price,
which brought into the cocaine market many low-income people
who could buy it one "hit" at a time. Crack significantly
increased the number of transactions in drug markets—both by
the number of new buyers and the number of transactions each
buyer engaged in per week. In order to accommodate the
increased demand, the drug sellers had to recruit a large number of new sellers. Juveniles were the natural source of sup
ply for that labor market (Blumstein 30). Crack is not only
used by itself; regular use fosters dependence on other drugs
as well. The more deeply a teenager participates in the crack
business, the more likely he or she regularly uses marijuana,
alcohol, and prescription depressants. The degree of crack-
market participation was also related to earlier and greater
crime involvement including violent crime. The more involved a
youth was in crack distribution, the earlier he or she first
committed a crime and was first arrested, convicted, and
incarcerated; and the more likely his or her current involvement in a range of crimes against persons and property. This
analysis suggests that crack use and consequent crack-market
participation have criminogenic effects not previously
observed among adolescent drug users (Inciardi 178).

> Student establishes the significance of data

Smith 3

Research also reveals some major limitations of traditional delinquency theory. The most obvious of these problems is the inadequate attention given by policymakers to the role of drugs in the development of adolescent criminal involvement. Traditional delinquency theory treats drug use simply as another type of delinquent behavior (Bourgois 19). In contrast, the Inciardi study suggests that adolescent drug/crime involvement is much more than this. In his sample, Inciardi points out that drug-involved crimes were a common first time offense. Thus, use of illicit drugs and other illegal behaviors not only first appear at more or less the same time in the histories of these serious delinquents, but regular drug use tends to precede regular profit-making crime. Further, the consequences of crack market participation, as discussed above, add still further pressure toward a life of crime (Inciardi 179).

Student clarifies his position and identifies the heart of the problem

I do not believe the answer to drug-involved crime is as simple as saying drugs cause crime or vice versa, but we need to realize the effect they have on each other. Problems occur when drug- and crime-involved adolescents are removed from street life for a period of time and then returned to the same environment. This suggests that the single most important factor keeping them in "street life" is a street life itself: drug use, fast money, peers with like interests, and the excitement of crime and other risks. Unfortunately, there are few alternatives for adolescents who live a life on the streets and little hope for an improved way of life.

As a result of the street life Inciardi describes, many individuals find themselves in a revolving court room door, without benefitting in any way. A change in lifestyle is essential not only for the well-being of the individual but also for the well-being of our nation. The average cost of incarcerating a juvenile for one year is between $35,000 and $64,000 (Toy 23). In addition, in fiscal 1990, federal, state, and local governments spent $74 billion for civil and criminal justice, a 22% increase over 1988. According to the office of National Drug Control Policy, expenditures for federal drug

Smith 4

control increased from $1.5 billion in fiscal 1981 to $13.2 billion in fiscal 1995. What is most disturbing is that we seem to be spending more and more on criminal justice and drug control, but juvenile crime continues to increase. For example, homicides by youths tripled between 1984 and 1994 (Toy 23). This fact, in conjunction with the expected increase in adolescent population by 30% through 2010 signals that crime will only increase (Califano C7). Environmental factors as well as drug abuse contribute to delinquency; it is essential that we address solutions to break this pattern. Our best hope for doing so requires that we move beyond conventional thinking about imprisoning adolescent offenders to "rehabilitate" them.

Rehabilitation involves a process of renovation and repair and a returning to a useful and constructive place in society; it implies the restoration of something or someone damaged to a prior good condition. Traditional correctional strategies such as imprisonment are adequate for adolescents who live in economic areas where street life is not constant. But the serious delinquents in the Inciardi study—and for that matter, the majority of chronic offenders who clog the nations courts, jails, and correctional systems—were never in good condition in the first place. Hirokazu Yoshikawa, a researcher in the department of psychology at New York University, believes that "serious" delinquents are not in need of rehabilitation—what they need is *habilitation* (5). This means teaching adolescents the skills necessary to support a life without drugs and crime. Of the many programs discussed to help delinquents become contributing members of our society, therapeutic communities in combination with correction programs seem to be the best option for providing the kind of training Yoshikawa envisions.

A therapeutic community (TC) is a treatment environment isolated from the rest of the institutional population—separated from the drugs, the violence, and the norms and values that prevent treatment and habilitation. Individuals are given drug thearpy, job training, and strict discipline. The primary

Student establishes the credentials of a source

Reference is to page number only because author's name is given in the sentence

Student defines and describes the kind of treatment he recommends

clinical staff of the therapeutic community are typically former substance abusers/offenders who themselves have been
clients in therapeutic communities. The treatment perspective
of the TC is that drug involvement is a disorder of the whole
person; that is, the problem is the person not the drug or
crime, and addiction or action is a symptom and not the
essence of the disorder (Inciardi 196).

Student provides an example

Therapeutic communities have been in existence for
decades and their successes have been well documented. For
example, the Cornerstone Program in Oregon is devoted to creating an environment that provides focus on drug abuse and
criminal involvement. Participants are segregated from the
general institutional population and provided with a transition and aftercare service to assure successful community re-
entry. The program is designed for drug-addicted offenders
with long histories of drug use (the average age of first substance use was twelve). The offenders averaged more than thirteen prior arrests and had spent more than seven years in

Data supporting the success of this program

prison. The results from the Cornerstone Program showed that
the longer the time spent in the program the lower the level
of re-involvement. Of the 200 graduates, 74% avoided subsequent incarceration after averaging a year in the program,
while only 15% of those who left the program in less than
sixty days avoided incarceration (Durham 158).

Despite the success of therapy-based settings such as the
Cornerstone Program, few therapeutic communities exist in
either institutional or community-based settings, and an even
smaller number have been designed for juveniles (Toy 23). The
juvenile therapeutic community is the most appropriate setting
for serious delinquents—in-prison settings for those offenders
who represent a threat, in-community settings for those who do
not. The therapeutic community is an essential forum for drug-
abuse treatment in correctional settings because of the many
aspects of the prison environments that make habilitation difficult. Likewise, the availability of drugs in reformatories,
jails, detention centers, and prisons is a pervasive problem.
As one scholar points out:

Smith 6

> But prison may not only fail to deter; it may make matters worse. The overuse of incarceration may strengthen the links between street and prison and help to cement users' and dealers' identity as members of an oppositional drug culture, while simultaneously shutting them off from the prospect of successfully participating in the economy outside the prison. (Currie 161)

Quotations more than four lines are set off as a block. Indent 1" (or ten spaces) and do not use quotation marks.

In addition, there is the violence associated with inmate gangs, often formed for the purpose of establishing and maintaining status, "turf," and unofficial control over sectors of the institution for distributing contraband and providing "protection" for other inmates (Inciardi 197). However, in the therapeutic community, programs such as California's probation camp could be implemented. In this camp, recidivism rate is a respectably low 25% and provides education, tough discipline, drug treatment, and job training ("Putting" 8).

A shortened version of the title is included for an anonymous editorial

My research has shown that drug involvement and crime have been found to feed off the effects of each other and we need to implement programs that address both of these areas. I am sure no one wants the criminal justice system to fail, but that is what the majority of correctional programs are doing. We continue to increase spending on programs that have failed. Attacking the results of juvenile crime only removes individuals from society with the unrealistic hope that they will somehow return with a different attitude. Habilitation programs provide real hope to troubled adolescents.

Student begins to move toward conclusion

We no longer believe that the best way to combat disease is to build more hospitals. We no longer think that the best way to cope with environmental problems is to wait for a disaster to happen and clean up the damage afterward. But our approach to crime and drug abuse is still reactive, not preventative. Just as unbreathable air and an endless flood of toxic wastes tell us that something is fundamentally wrong in the way we organize our technologies of production; drug abuse and crime tells us something is fundamentally wrong in our social organization (Currie 280). We must determine why

adolescents are involved with drugs and crime and look to
reverse their living patterns.

Student appeals to readers' concerns about safety

   I understand that most people are more concerned with
safety than sociology. To this I say that a safer nation would
be the result if we implement more therapeutic communities for
troubled adolescents. As a concerned citizen, I understand the
importance of removing criminals from the streets, but I also
believe we need to look beyond the immediate future and plan
what is best for the long-term condition of the United States.

Student appeals to readers' concerns with costs

Moreover, the operation of a therapeutic community is on average $23,000/year per client, in comparison with the average
cost of incarcerating a juvenile for one year is between
$35,000 to $64,000. This is extremely cost effective when one
considers the success rate of the Cornerstone Program and California's probation camps. Every 100,000 young people kept out
of prison saves the United States $2.5 billion annually in

Student concludes with a rhetorical question

operating costs alone. Safe streets are nice, but why settle
for so little when there's real hope for helping troubled adolescents become contributing members of society?

Smith 8

Double space

Notes

¹ The characters in the introduction were based on the investigative work by Philippe Bourgois. Bourgois spent part of his life studying the drug and crime lifestyles of adolescents in East Harlem, New York.

² Serious delinquency is defined as committing ten FBI Index offenses including homicide, forcible rape, aggravated assault, and robbery and property crimes such as burglary, motor vehicle theft, arson, and larceny/theft. In addition, the neighborhoods included in the Inciardi study were those with high rates of drug involvement and crime, and others were working and middle class communities.

Content notes
supplement
the paper

Smith 9

Double space

Works Cited

Blumstein, Alfred. "Youth Violence, Guns, and the Illicit-Drug Industry." Journal of Criminal Law and Criminology 86 (1995): 10-36.

Bourgois, Philippe. In Search of Respect: Selling Crack in El Barrio. New York: Cambridge UP, 1996.

Califano, Joseph. "America in Denial." The Washington Post. 14 Nov. 1993: C7.

Currie, Elliot. Reckoning. New York: Hill, 1993.

Durham, Alexis III. Crisis and Reform. Boston: Little, 1994.

Greenwood, Peter. "Substance Abuse Problems Among High-Risk Youth and Potential Interventions." Crime and Delinquency 38 (1992): 445-458.

Hawkins, J. David. Delinquency and Crime. New York: Cambridge UP, 1996.

Inciardi, James, Ruth Horowitz, and Anne Pottieger. Street Kids, Street Drugs, Street Crime: An Examination of Drug Use and Serious Delinquency in Miami. Belmont: Wadsworth, 1993.

An anonymous source is alphabetized under the first key word in the article title

"Putting Delinquents in Their Place; If the State Fails to Find Funding for Juvenile Probation Camps, Society Will Pay the Price." Los Angeles Times 26 Dec. 1995: 8.

Toy, Vivian. "Keeping A Stern and Watchful Eye on Juvenile Offenders Is Paying Off Officials Say." New York Times 13 May 1995: 23.

A source obtained electronically, including the data downloaded

Yoshikawa, Hirokazu. "Long-Term Effects of Early Childhood Programs on Social Outcomes and Delinquency." Netscape. U of St. Thomas Lib. Internet. 30 Jan. 1997. The Future of Children 5 (1995).

GLOSSARY OF USEFUL TERMS

ad hominem argument An argument that makes a personal attack on an opponent instead of addressing the issue that is under dispute.

allusion An unexplained reference that members of an audience are expected to understand because of their education or the culture in which they live.

analogy A comparison that works on more than one level, usually between something familiar and something abstract.

anticipating the opposition The process through which a writer or speaker imagines the most likely counterarguments that might be raised against his or her position.

audience Whoever will read what you write. Your audience may consist of a single individual (such as your history teacher), a particular group of people (such as English majors), or a larger and more general group (such as "the American people"). Good writers have a clear sense of audience, which means that they never lose sight of the readers they are writing for.

authority A reliable source that helps support an argument. It is important to cite authorities who will be recognized as legitimate by your audience. This means turning to people with good credentials in whatever area is under consideration. If you are arguing about the economy, cite a prominent economist as an authority.

begging the question An argument that assumes, as already agreed on, whatever it should be devoted to proving.

bibliography A list of works on a particular subject. One type of bibliography is the list of works cited that appears at the end of a paper, article, or book. Another type of bibliography is a work in itself—a compilation of all known sources on a subject. An annotated bibliography is a bibliography that includes a brief description of each of the sources cited.

bogus claim An unreliable or false statement that is unsupported by reliable evidence or legitimate authority.

claim Any assertion that can or should be supported with evidence. In the model for argument devised by Stephen Toulmin, the "claim" is the conclusion that the arguer must try to prove.

cliché A worn-out expression; any group of words that are frequently and automatically used together. In "the real world" of "today's society," writers should avoid clichés because they are a type of instant language that makes writing seem "as dead as a doornail."

concession   Any point that the opponents in an argument are willing to recognize as valid. In argumentation, concessions demonstrate fair-mindedness and help draw different sides together.

connotation   The associations inspired by a word, in contrast to *denotation* (see below).

data   The evidence that an arguer uses to support a claim. It may take the form of personal experience, expert opinion, statistics, or any other information that is verifiable.

deduction   The type of reasoning through which a generally accepted belief leads to a specific conclusion.

denotation   The literal dictionary definition of a word.

diction   Word choice. Having good diction means more than having a good vocabulary; it means using language appropriately by using the right word in the right place.

documentation   The references that writers supply to reveal the sources of the information they have reported.

equivocation   The deliberate use of vague, ambiguous language to mislead others. In writing, equivocation often takes the form of using abstract words to obscure meaning.

evidence   The experience, examples, or facts that support an argument. Good writers are careful to offer evidence for whatever they are claiming (see *claim*).

focus   The particular aspect of a subject on which a writer decides to concentrate. Many things can be said about most subjects. Having a clear focus means narrowing a subject down so that it can be discussed without loss of direction. If you digress from your subject and begin to ramble, you have probably lost your focus.

generalization   Forming a conclusion that seems generally acceptable because it could be supported by evidence. A generalization becomes a problem only when it is easily disputable. You have overgeneralized if someone can think of exceptions to what you have claimed. Be wary of words such as "all" and "every"; they increase the likelihood of overgeneralization.

hyperbole   A deliberate exaggeration for dramatic effect.

hypothesis   A theory that guides your research; a conditional thesis that is subject to change as evidence accumulates.

induction   The type of reasoning through which specific observations lead to a generally acceptable conclusion.

irony   A manner of speech or writing in which one's meaning is the opposite of what one has said.

jargon A specialized vocabulary that is usually abstract and limited to a particular field; when used in an argument, it should be defined for the benefit of those outside the field.

loaded term A word or phrase that is considered an unfair type of persuasion because it is either slanted or gratuitous within its context.

metaphor A comparison in which two unlike things are declared to be the same; for example, "The Lord is my shepherd."

meter The rhythm of poetry, in which stressed syllables occur in a pattern with regular intervals. In the analysis of poetry, meter is measured by a unit called a "foot," which usually consists of two or three syllables of which at least one is stressed.

non sequitur Latin for "it does not follow"; a logical fallacy in which a writer bases a claim on an unrelated point.

paradox A statement or situation that appears to be contradictory but is nevertheless true; for example, "conspicuous by his absence."

paraphrase Restating someone's words to demonstrate that you have understood them correctly or to make them more easily understandable.

personification Giving human qualities to nonhuman objects; for example, "The sofa smiled at me, inviting me to sit down."

persuasion A rhetorical strategy designed to achieve consent. Although there are many different types of persuasion, most involve an appeal to values, desires, and emotions. A persuasive argument would also demonstrate the ability to think critically and support claims with evidence.

plagiarism Taking someone's words or ideas without giving adequate acknowledgment.

point of view The attitude with which a writer approaches a subject. Good writers maintain a consistent point of view within each individual work.

post hoc, ergo propter hoc Latin for "after this, therefore because of this"; a logical fallacy in which precedence is confused with causation.

premise The underlying value or belief that one assumes as a given truth at the beginning of an argument.

rhetorical question A question that is asked for dramatic effect, with the understanding that readers will silently answer the way the writer wants them to answer.

rime scheme (or "rhyme") A fixed pattern of rimes that occurs throughout a poem.

Rogerian argument   A rhetorical approach to conflict resolution that emphasizes treating others with respect and listening carefully and emphatically to what they have to say.

simile   A direct comparison between two unlike things that includes such words as "like" or "as" —for example, "My love is like a red, red rose."

stereotype   An unthinking generalization, especially of a group of people in which all the members of the group are assumed to share the same traits; for example, the "dumb jock" is a stereotype of high school and college athletes.

style   The combination of diction and sentence structure that characterizes the manner in which a writer writes. Good writers have a distinctive style, which is to say their work can be readily identified as their own.

summary   A brief and unbiased recapitulation of previously stated ideas.

syllogism   A three-stage form of deductive reasoning through which a general truth yields a specific conclusion.

thesis   The central idea of an argument; the point that an argument seeks to prove. In a unified essay, every paragraph helps to advance the thesis.

tone   The way a writer sounds when discussing a particular subject. Whereas point of view establishes a writer's attitude toward his or her subject, tone refers to the voice that is adopted in conveying this point of view to an audience. For example, one can write with an angry, sarcastic, humorous, or dispassionate tone when discussing a subject about which one has a negative point of view.

topic sentence   The sentence that defines the function of a paragraph; the single most important sentence in each paragraph.

transition   A link or bridge between topics that enables a writer to move smoothly from one subtopic to another so that every paragraph is clearly related to the paragraphs that surround it.

warrant   A term used by Stephen Toulmin for an implicit or explicit general statement that underlies an argument and establishes a relationship between the data and the claim.

COPYRIGHTS AND ACKNOWLEDGMENTS

INDEX